Communications
in Computer and Information Science   2836

Series Editors

Gang Li, *School of Information Technology, Deakin University, Burwood, VIC, Australia*
Joaquim Filipe, *Polytechnic Institute of Setúbal, Setúbal, Portugal*
Zhiwei Xu, *Chinese Academy of Sciences, Beijing, China*

Rationale

The CCIS series is devoted to the publication of proceedings of computer science conferences. Its aim is to efficiently disseminate original research results in informatics in printed and electronic form. While the focus is on publication of peer-reviewed full papers presenting mature work, inclusion of reviewed short papers reporting on work in progress is welcome, too. Besides globally relevant meetings with internationally representative program committees guaranteeing a strict peer-reviewing and paper selection process, conferences run by societies or of high regional or national relevance are also considered for publication.

Topics

The topical scope of CCIS spans the entire spectrum of informatics ranging from foundational topics in the theory of computing to information and communications science and technology and a broad variety of interdisciplinary application fields.

Information for Volume Editors and Authors

Publication in CCIS is free of charge. No royalties are paid, however, we offer registered conference participants temporary free access to the online version of the conference proceedings on SpringerLink (http://link.springer.com) by means of an http referrer from the conference website and/or a number of complimentary printed copies, as specified in the official acceptance email of the event.

CCIS proceedings can be published in time for distribution at conferences or as post-proceedings, and delivered in the form of printed books and/or electronically as USBs and/or e-content licenses for accessing proceedings at SpringerLink. Furthermore, CCIS proceedings are included in the CCIS electronic book series hosted in the SpringerLink digital library at http://link.springer.com/bookseries/7899. Conferences publishing in CCIS are allowed to use Online Conference Service (OCS) for managing the whole proceedings lifecycle (from submission and reviewing to preparing for publication) free of charge.

Publication process

The language of publication is exclusively English. Authors publishing in CCIS have to sign the Springer CCIS copyright transfer form, however, they are free to use their material published in CCIS for substantially changed, more elaborate subsequent publications elsewhere. For the preparation of the camera-ready papers/files, authors have to strictly adhere to the Springer CCIS Authors' Instructions and are strongly encouraged to use the CCIS LaTeX style files or templates.

Abstracting/Indexing

CCIS is abstracted/indexed in DBLP, Google Scholar, EI-Compendex, Mathematical Reviews, SCImago, Scopus. CCIS volumes are also submitted for the inclusion in ISI Proceedings.

How to start

To start the evaluation of your proposal for inclusion in the CCIS series, please send an e-mail to ccis@springer.com.

Josef F. Krems · Hugo Plácido da Silva ·
Pietro Cipresso
Editors

Computer-Human Interaction Research and Applications

9th International Conference, CHIRA 2025
Marbella, Spain, October 20–21, 2025
Proceedings, Part III

Springer

Editors
Josef F. Krems
Chemnitz University of Technology
Chemnitz, Germany

Pietro Cipresso
University of Turin
Turin, Italy

Hugo Plácido da Silva
IT- Institute of Telecommunications
Lisboa, Portugal

ISSN 1865-0929   ISSN 1865-0937 (electronic)
Communications in Computer and Information Science
ISBN 978-3-032-16453-7   ISBN 978-3-032-16454-4 (eBook)
https://doi.org/10.1007/978-3-032-16454-4

This Springer imprint is published by the registered company Springer Nature Switzerland AG
The registered company address is: Gewerbestrasse 11, 6330 Cham, Switzerland

If disposing of this product, please recycle the paper.

Preface

These three volumes (CCIS 2834-6) contain the proceedings of the 9th International Conference on Computer-Human Interaction Research and Applications. This year, CHIRA was held in Marbella, Spain, on October 20-21, 2025. It was sponsored by the Institute for Systems and Technologies of Information, Control and Communication (INSTICC). CHIRA 2025 was also organized in cooperation with the ACM Special Interest Group on Management Information Systems (SIGMIS) and the European Society for Socially Embedded Technologies (EUSSET).

The purpose of the International Conference on Computer-Human Interaction Research and Applications (CHIRA) is to bring together professionals, academics and students who are interested in the advancement of research and practical applications in its field of interest, covering different aspects of Computer-Human Interaction, including Human Factors and Information Systems, Interactive Devices, Interaction Design and Adaptive and Intelligent Systems.

CHIRA 2025 received 106 paper submissions from 30 countries, of which 21 (20%) were accepted and published as full papers. A double-blind paper review was performed for each submission by at least 2, but usually 3 or more, members of the International Program Committee, which was composed of established researchers and domain experts.

The high quality of the CHIRA 2025 program was enhanced by the two invited talks delivered by internationally distinguished speakers: Alice Chirico (Catholic University of the Sacred Heart, Italy) with "Road to Awe: Perils, Challenges, Findings, and Open Questions"; and Alexander Mädche (Karlsruhe Institute of Technology, Germany) with "Biosignal-Adaptive Systems for Better Work and Life".

All presented papers will be submitted for indexation by DBLP, Google Scholar, EI-Compendex, INSPEC, Japanese Science and Technology Agency, Norwegian Register for Scientific Journals and Series, Mathematical Reviews, SCImago, Scopus, zbMATH and Web of Science / Conference Proceedings Citation Index.

Several awards, based on the combined marks of paper reviewing, as assessed by the Program Committee, and the quality of the presentation, as assessed by session chairs at the conference venue, were conferred at the conference's closing session to recognise the best contributions.

The program for this conference required the dedicated effort of many people. Firstly, we must thank the authors whose research efforts are reported here. Next, we would like to thank the members of the Program Committee and the auxiliary reviewers for their diligent and professional reviews.

We would also like to deeply thank the invited speakers for their invaluable contribution and for taking the time to prepare their talks. Finally, a word of appreciation for the hard work of the INSTICC team; organising a conference of this level is a task that can only be achieved by the collaborative effort of a dedicated and highly competent team.

We hope you all had an exciting and inspiring conference. We hope to have contributed to the development of our research community, and we look forward to having additional research results presented at the next edition of CHIRA, details of which are available at https://chira.scitevents.org.

October 2025

Josef F. Krems
Hugo Plácido da Silva
Pietro Cipresso

Organization

Conference Chair

Pietro Cipresso .... University of Turin, Italy

Program Co-chairs

Josef F. Krems .... Chemnitz University of Technology, Germany
Hugo Plácido da Silva .... Instituto de Telecomunicações, Portugal

Program Committee

Amal Abdulrahman .... Macquarie University, Australia
Sultan A. Alharthi .... University of Jeddah, Saudi Arabia
Nuno Almeida .... University of Aveiro, Portugal
Josef Altmann .... University of Applied Sciences Upper Austria, Austria
Shamsul Arrieya Ariffin .... Independent Researcher, Malaysia
Tamara Babaian .... Bentley University, USA
Michael Behringer .... Universität Stuttgart, Germany
Alper Bilge .... Akdeniz University, Turkey
Cosimo Birtolo .... Poste Italiane, Italy
Guido Borghi .... Università di Bologna, Italy
Paolo Bottoni .... Sapienza University of Rome, Italy
Chris Bowers .... University of Worcester, UK
André Brandão .... Universidade Federal do ABC, Brazil
Giuseppe Caggianese .... National Research Council of Italy, Italy
Kürşat Çağıltay .... Sabanci University, Turkey
Antonio Camurri .... University of Genoa, Italy
Valentín Cardeñoso Payo .... Universidad de Valladolid, Spain
John W. Castro .... University of Atacama, Chile
Stuart Charters .... Lincoln University, New Zealand
Yang-Wai Chow .... University of Wollongong, Australia
Cesar Collazos .... Universidad del Cauca, Colombia
Daniel Cunliffe .... University of South Wales, UK
Vincenzo Deufemia .... Università di Salerno, Italy
Ralf Dörner .... Hochschule RheinMain, Germany

Thomas Eskridge	Florida Institute of Technology, USA
Micaela Esteves	Independent Researcher, Portugal
Ahmed Farooq	University of Tampere, Finland
Ana Ferreira	University of Porto, Portugal
Silas Formunyuy Verkijika	Sol Plaatje University, South Africa
Kaori Fujinami	Tokyo University of Agriculture and Technology, Japan
Giovanni Fulantelli	National Research Council of Italy, Italy
Rosella Gennari	Free University of Bozen-Bolzano, Italy
Neil Gordon	Independent Researcher, UK
Toni Granollers	University of Lleida, Spain
Maki Habib	American University in Cairo, Egypt
Thorsten Händler	Ferdinand Porsche Mobile University of Applied Sciences (FERNFH), Austria
Christopher Healey	North Carolina State University, USA
Rüdiger Heimgärtner	Intercultural User Interface Consulting, Germany
Martin Hitz	Alpen-Adria-Universität Klagenfurt, Austria
Junko Ichino	Waseda University, Japan
Ivan Ivanov	Technical University of Sofia, Bulgaria
Jaroslaw Jankowski	West Pomeranian University of Technology, Poland
M.-Carmen Juan	Instituto Ai2, Universitat Politècnica de València, Spain
Azrina Kamaruddin	Putra Malaysia University, Malaysia
Adi Katz	Shamoon College of Engineering, Israel
Chutisant Kerdvibulvech	National Institute of Development Administration, Thailand
Josef F. Krems	Chemnitz University of Technology, Germany
Claire Lauer	Arizona State University, USA
Yun Li Lee	Sunway University, Malaysia
Gerhard Leitner	Alpen-Adria-Universität Klagenfurt, Austria
Lenka Lhotska	Czech Technical University in Prague, Czech Republic
Hai-Ning Liang	Hong Kong University of Science and Technology (Guangzhou), China
Wen-Chieh Lin	National Chiao Tung University, Taiwan
Angela Locoro	Università di Brescia, Italy
Huizilopoztli Luna García	Autonomous University of Zacatecas, Mexico
Joaquim Madeira	University of Aveiro, Portugal
Marco Manca	CNR-ISTI, Italy
Milosz Marek	Lublin University of Technology, Poland
Stuart Marshall	Victoria University of Wellington, New Zealand
Ecivaldo Matos	University of São Paulo, Brazil

Frédéric Mérienne	Arts et Métiers ParisTech, France
Ahmed Hosny Saleh Metwally	Helwan University, Egypt
Yehya Mohamad	Fraunhofer FIT, Germany
Ana Molina	University of Castilla-La Mancha, Spain
Giulio Mori	Institute of Information Science Technologies, Italy
Alistair Morrison	University of Glasgow, UK
Ricardo Nakamura	University of São Paulo, Brazil
Pietro Neroni	Institute for High Performance Computing and Networking (ICAR), National Research Council of Italy (CNR), Italy
Ovidiu Noran	Griffith University, Australia
Max North	Kennesaw State University, USA
Stavroula Ntoa	Foundation for Research and Technology Hellas, Greece
Yoosoo Oh	Daegu University, Korea, South Korea
Tal Oron-Gilad	Ben-Gurion University of the Negev, Israel
Samir Otmane	University of Évry, France
Sabrina Panëels	CEA, LIST, Paris-Saclay University, France
Stamatios Papadakis	University of Crete, Greece
Kitti Puritat	Chiang Mai University, Thailand
Dorina Rajanen	University of Oulu, Finland
Francisco Rebelo	ITI/LARSys, University of Lisbon, Portugal
Tânia Rocha	University of Tras-os-Montes and Alto Douro, Portugal
Sandra Sanchez-Gordon	Escuela Politécnica Nacional, Ecuador
Carlos Santos	University of Aveiro, Portugal
Comai Sara	Politecnico di Milano, Italy
Trenton Schulz	Norwegian Computing Center, Norway
Gabriel Serna	Tecnológico Nacional de México/CENIDET, Mexico
Jungpil Shin	University of Aizu, Japan
Boštjan Šumak	University of Maribor, Slovenia
Andrea Vázquez-Ingelmo	University of Salamanca, Spain
Gregg Vesonder	Stevens Institute of Technology, USA
Spyros Vosinakis	University of the Aegean, Greece
Aleksandra Vuckovic	University of Glasgow, UK
Sven Wachsmuth	Bielefeld University, Germany
Marcus Winter	University of Brighton, UK
Fan Zhao	Florida Gulf Coast University, USA
Ying Zhu	Georgia State University, USA
Floriano Zini	Free University of Bozen-Bolzano, Italy

Additional Reviewer

Yi-Jheng Huang   Yuan Ze University, Taiwan

Invited Speakers

Alice Chirico   Catholic University of the Sacred Heart, Italy
Alexander Mädche   Karlsruhe Institute of Technology, Germany

Invited Speakers

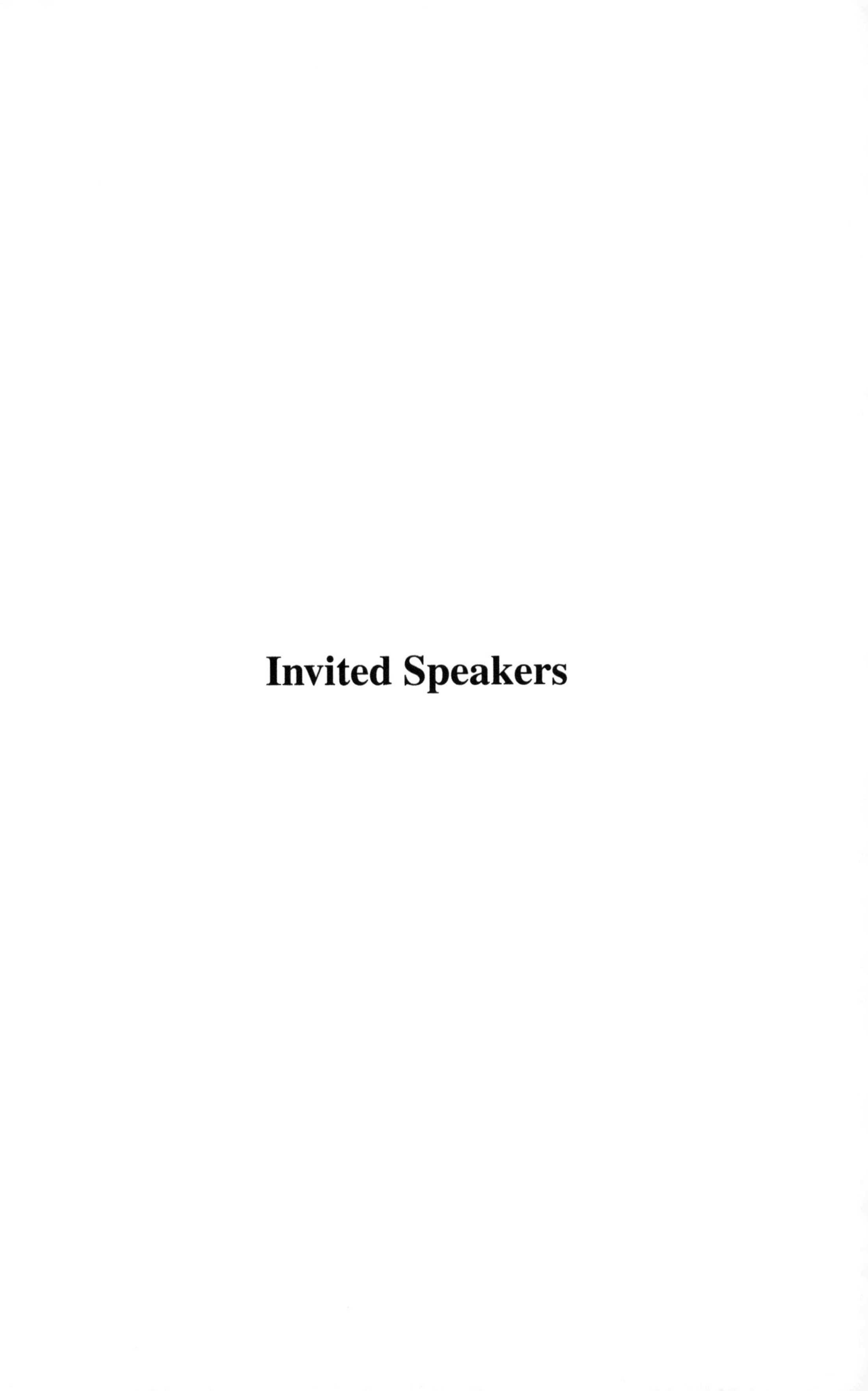

Road to Awe: Perils, Challenges, Findings, and Open Questions

Alice Chirico

Catholic University of the Sacred Heart, Italy

Abstract. Over the past decade, research has increasingly focused on the multifaceted nature of awe, which transcends simple positive and negative valences. Here, I discuss the key findings and theoretical developments that have emerged from this extended investigation, from my research perspective, emphasizing the significance of awe in psychological processes and its potential for practical application. Initially, research focused on defining and measuring awe. It has been conceptualized as an emotion elicited by stimuli perceived as vast—either conceptually or perceptually—triggering a need for cognitive accommodation. Though awe has long been considered a transformative emotion, theoretical evidence suggests that its intensity is often diminished in laboratory settings. In order to address this gap, I refined both the operational definition of awe and the methods used to elicit it by utilizing novel technologies such as virtual reality (VR). Additionally, I began to question the construct validity of existing instruments used to assess awe in experimental settings. The use of immersive videos, which rely on perceptual spatiality, has been demonstrated to be more effective than conventional 2D videos in eliciting intense emotions of awe — but only when they are built on content that has been pre-validated as being capable of eliciting such emotion. By incorporating these insights, we were able to develop novel, interactive, VR-based scenarios to elicit awe both in the lab and in everyday settings. The potential of VR-elicited awe has emerged not only in enhancing short-term creative thinking but also as an epistemic emotion—that is, one capable of motivating learning by bridging knowledge gaps. The PROMETHEUS project, funded by the Cariplo Foundation, capitalized on awe's epistemic properties to design new teaching methodologies and intervention strategies in educational settings marked by high dropout rates. However, awe holds even greater promise for both individual and societal well-being. Through the PONE EU REACT project, we explored the potential of awe-inspiring VR scenarios to foster pro-environmental behaviors—particularly "socially engaging behaviors"—as a result of awe's connection-related appraisals. As evidence for awe's positive impact on psychological and social well-being grows, two further steps are now crucial. First, we must translate lab-based findings on awe and VR into real-world applications. To this end, we have developed and tested a new awe-based training module in social VR aimed at enhancing creativity. Second—and perhaps more challengingly—we must return to the foundational issue of construct validity in awe assessment, especially across cultures. Beyond ongoing cross-cultural validation of dispositional and state scales, there is now an urgent need to revisit and refine the construct itself and the conditions under which it is validly assessed. To this end, I have initiated a novel interdisciplinary research line exploring the relationship between awe and the sublime, with a particular focus on European cultural contexts.

Biosignal-Adaptive Systems for Better Work and Life

Alexander Mädche

Karlsruhe Institute of Technology, Germany

Abstract. Biosignal-adaptive systems represent a new class of human-centered systems that use sensor technology — such as eye-tracking or photoplethysmography (PPG) sensors — to capture both visible and non-visible human activities with biosignals. Biosignals are autonomous signals produced by the living organism, energetically measurable in physical quantities using sensors. Biosignals are interesting because, in addition to self-reported or behavioral data, they provide objective and often unconscious information about physical and psychological user states. The collected biosignals are processed in real-time and used to recognize user states such as attention, flow, mental workload & fatigue by leveraging artificial intelligence (AI) technologies. Being aware of user states in real time lays the foundation for designing personalized interactions advancing human-computer interaction. In my keynote lecture, I will introduce the conceptual foundations of biosignal-adaptive systems and share findings from lab and field studies that we conducted over the past decade. These studies demonstrate how such systems can enhance work and everyday life by improving performance and supporting well-being. In particular, I will showcase the potential of biosignal-adaptive systems in the fields of virtual collaboration as well as personal companions for desktop productivity, learning and emotion regulation. I will conclude my keynote lecture with a number of open research challenges and a call for responsible design of biosignal-adaptive systems.

Contents

Interaction Design

Transforming User Interface Designs for Mixed Reality Using a Meta-UI Tool Prototype

Alecsandru Grigoriu[✉][iD] and Sabin-Corneliu Buraga[iD]

Faculty of Computer Science, Alexandru Ioan Cuza University,
General Berthelot 16, 700483 Iasi, Romania
secretariat@info.uaic.ro
https://www.info.uaic.ro/

Abstract. Designing interfaces for Mixed Reality (MR) applications when transitioning from Web/mobile/desktop platforms presents significant challenges. Transitioning to a 3D Augmented/Virtual Reality environment can complicate the design process. Current practices encompass various approaches, including direct interface translation and creating new versions. We devise a high-fidelity prototype for a multi-purpose Meta-UI tool that assists designers and developers in configuring the applications' UI design for MR. To illustrate the proposal's benefits, we demonstrate how our Meta-UI could transform the design of an educational platform dedicated to increasing sustainable ocean awareness. Furthermore, we recruited over 60 university students enrolled in Human-Computer Interaction classes to envision, sketch, and design UIs for their class projects, with our original prototype serving as a guiding framework while interacting with MR devices. The results revealed a decrease in difficulty when designing by using our prototype.

Keywords: HCI · UI · Distributed User Interface · Meta-UI · Software Tool · Mixed Reality · AR · VR · Design Process · Design Evaluation · Usability Study · Prototype · Educational Platform

1 Introduction

With a continuous diversity in platforms and devices, Mixed Reality (MR) [1] becomes more challenging for designers and developers when building or expanding experiences for Augmented Reality (AR). Without a unified process to offer a common ground regardless of the context (for example, AR through headsets, wearable glasses, and mobile devices), we propose and evaluate a prototype that eases the design of applications for MR targeting wearable devices such as Meta Quest 3[1] or Xreal Air AR Glasses[2].

The constant and fast-paced evolution of MR technologies has changed the way users interact with the digital environments provided. Devices like AR/VR headsets and wearable glasses enable new experiences at the cost of offering new challenges

---

[1] Meta Quest 3 – https://www.meta.com/quest/quest-3/ (accessed on May 6th, 2025).

[2] Xreal Air – https://www.xreal.com/air (accessed on May 6th, 2025).

J. F. Krems et al. (Eds.): CHIRA 2025, CCIS 2836, pp. 3–21, 2026.
https://doi.org/10.1007/978-3-032-16454-4_1

for designers and developers alike [2]. Professionals still face the absence of a unified process that accommodates the wide range of MR platforms and devices [3]. They also encounter technical difficulties, usability challenges, and the urgent need for rapid prototyping [4].

Given the context, the motivation for this research arises from the need to streamline the design process of MR applications while helping the development process. As AR and VR grow in adoption and diversity, stakeholders (designers, developers, and even product managers/owners) require alternatives that support cross-platform adaptability, rapid prototyping, and user-centric evaluation [5]. We aim to fill this tool gap [6] as other studies support the claim of a lack of standards [4] for AR design principles.

Moreover, because MR can provide new layers of engagement and education, we tailor our concepts and prototypes to offer new immersive software tools for a more sustainable world. Therefore, we also directed our design and research efforts to include a perspective on designing a sustainable ocean using AR/VR. This study addresses the challenges by designing and evaluating a prototype of the Meta-UI tool focused on the aspects of ocean sustainability (via a proposed Web platform to increase awareness). This approach simplifies the adaptation of user interface designs for MR. By targeting wearable devices such as headsets and glasses, we offer actionable insights for potential professionals or entry-level practitioners in the field.

Regarding the paper's structure, we first analyze existing research and the progress related to our study (Sect. 2). Then, we present our proposal (Sect. 3), the evaluations performed (Sect. 4), and the results obtained (Sect. 5). Furthermore, Sect. 6 covers various insights we have gathered. Lastly, we end with further work (Sect. 8) and conclusions (Sect. 9).

2 Related Work

2.1 Ocean Sustainability from the Interface Design Perspective

For our case study and prototype, we decided to focus on ocean sustainability mainly because, from an HCI perspective, there are relatively few proposals concerning this domain. A systematic review on VR and AR for environmental sustainability is presented in [7] and concludes with the following "although the results indicate that the volume of literature exploring extended reality (XR) in environmental applications is increasing, empirical evidence of its impact is limited, hindering the possibility of presently drawing significant conclusions on its potential benefits". Several initiatives are focused on various topics such as:

- a sustainable use of the ocean by using metaverses and digital twins [8], including the use of VR/AR technologies to increase the underwater accessibility and to enrich users' experience both for divers and non-divers [9];
- interactions at the intersection of water, humans, and technology, collectively referred to as "WaterHCI" [10];
- using marine, multifunctional, modular, and mobile applications (M4s) [11] from different contexts like designing of playful devices for surfing [12], achieving sustainable diving tourism [13], promoting sustainable user behaviors by designing serious games [14], visualizing cold-water coral reefs and deep-water habitats with the

help of AR and 3D photogrammetry [15], mapping underwater environments [16], mobile crowd sensing in ocean observation [17], or implementing digital marketing and sustainable businesses in tourism [18];
- sustainable exploitation of seabed mineral resources by monitoring in the deep sea all their suitable physical, chemical, geological, and biological characteristics – the TRIDENT project [19].

Other directions of interest are focused on the use of digital technologies in a societal context – for example, several important topics could be mentioned:

- imaging-based ocean conservation by using artificial intelligence [20];
- developing software tools that leverage data to assist human rights investigations at sea [21];
- integration of living microorganisms [22], including explorations of the human microbiome as an intimate material for living interfaces [23];
- phenomenology and post-phenomenology aspects in interaction design [24].

2.2   Interaction Design Processes

Our study centers on aiding the design process by introducing a high-fidelity prototype (effective for identifying usability issues [25]) that guides users to convert or port traditional application designs to MR, while adapting new paradigms to a higher level of immersion, intuition and engagement [1,26].

Current explorations emphasize the design process starting with the ideation phase [27,28] and making their way up through specific and collaborative User Experience (UX) tasks [29] (especially between design and development teams). This way, stakeholders (designers and developers) have the opportunity to iterate and assess different UI decisions very early. Other studies emphasize the lack of a standard and the need for proper AR Design principles [30], confirming the need for balance in the AR design space. To narrow our objectives and for our research purposes, we selected the UI design phase as means of exploration. Moreover, we evaluate the difficulty of sketching and altering the initial look and feel when users adapt the applications' designs to MR. We use custom grading systems and contribute to an already existing group of heuristic evaluations [31], quantitative and qualitative [32], and in the AR field [30].

We tested the prototypes created using on-device Web/mobile AR browsers as alternatives to the traditional Internet exploration [33] which overlay digital information onto the physical world [34], influencing user engagement [35] through various UI layouts and interactive modes specific to MR [36]. Therefore our study contributes to the literature of a *wider Web* [37] with a promising future [38] – especially from the perspective of envisioning augmented reality experiences for social change [39].

Using such devices, allowed us to carefully craft the Meta-UI tool's details taking into account the physical/tangible while pursuing a seamless integration with the real world [40]. Moreover, we used high-fidelity assets [36], in order to minimize the physiological/cognitive effects that using such peripherals can have on the body – for example, disorientation or simulator sickness [41].

On top of all this, the study expands on the notions of user interface plasticity [42,43] and distributed user interfaces [44], proposing a Meta-UI [45] dedicated to extend UI configuration [46,47] for the MR space.

3 Our Proposal

This study currently focuses on individuals with entry level work experience. For that, we voluntarily recruited senior-year University students from a Computer Science Faculty who participated in their Human-Computer Interaction (HCI) class. This way, we ensured that the individuals had the minimum design and interaction knowledge to perform a set of required tasks [48], and based on their curriculum, that they already had previous AR/VR academic knowledge from their other courses.

A total of 69 students participated in the experiments, all between ages 20 and 24 (64% Male, 36% Female). Twenty-two of the participants have or had previous work experience (up to three years) in IT/software companies.

During their HCI class, the students had to complete a project assignment structured into components D (Design) and F (Final Presentation) during a period of 12 weeks. We aligned our study to match the timelines of those two parts. We first included a questionnaire after students finished component D, and then, after finishing component F, participants would test and evaluate our proposed prototypes by using the methods described in [49]. By grouping our prototype testing with the student project evaluation, we managed to extend our research beyond ocean sustainability topic. The projects covered a wide range of diversity in terms of use cases, demonstrating the study's potential for scalability.

The following subsections will detail the requirements for components D and F of the students' projects, followed by descriptions of our questionnaires, prototypes, and their evaluation. Figure 1 summarizes the project requirements, while Fig. 2 highlights the main HCI research methods applied.

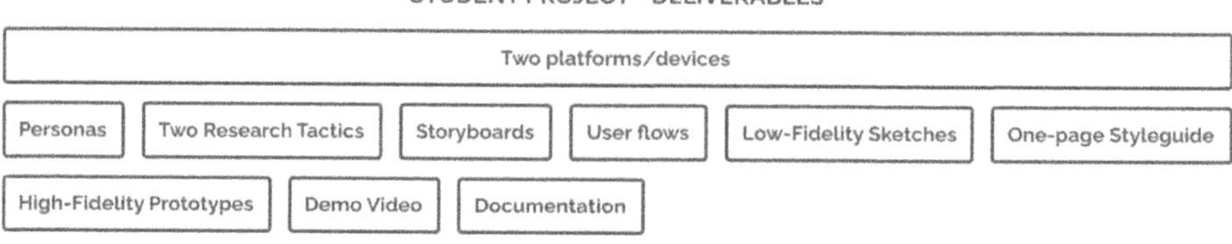

Fig. 1. Student Project Deliverables.

3.1 Student Projects

The students had to work in teams of three or four and either choose a project from a predefined list or (if necessary) propose a new project to match the evaluation requirements. The proposed projects were designed to simulate potential real-world-inspired start-up ideas or research projects.

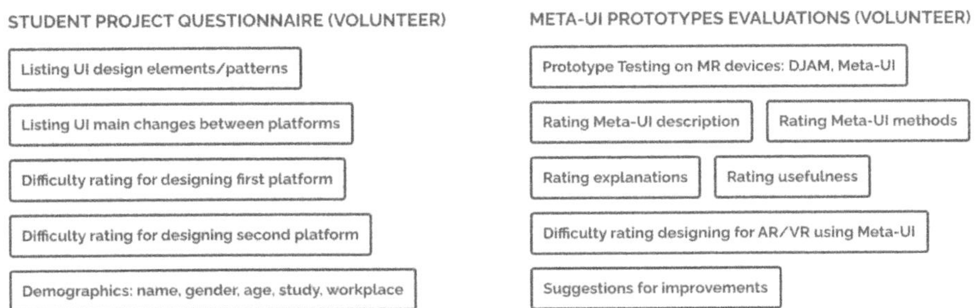

Fig. 2. Study Research Tactics: Questionnaire and Prototype Evaluations.

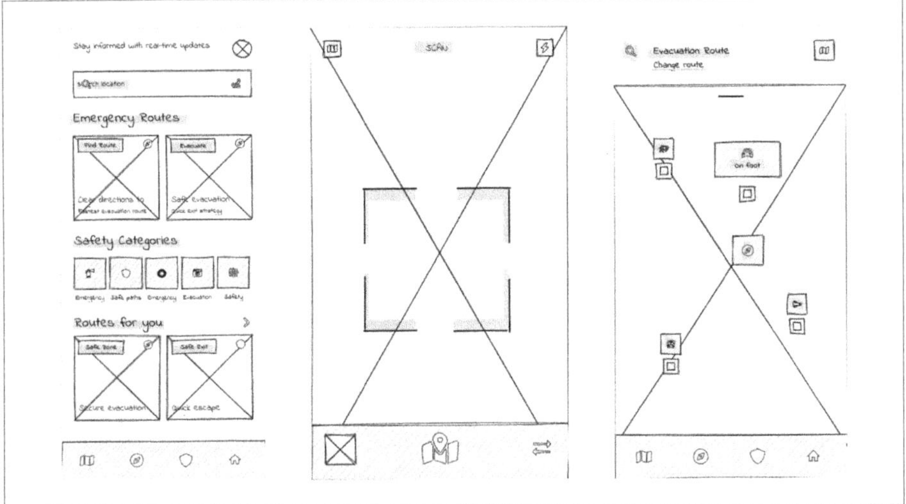

Fig. 3. Sketch deliverable for a custom student project.

3.2 Component D: UI Design

For the first part of their assignment evaluation, students had to create three user personas [50] for their project. The contents of their personas were backed by information collected using two user research tactics [51] of their choice. Then, the students would select two interaction types/platforms for creating their project design deliverables: Desktop/TV, Web, Mobile, Touch, Wear, Conversational, Voice, AR, and VR. The volunteers created storyboards, user flows, and low-fidelity sketches for each of the two selected. Their work would be sent online via a submission Web form. Figure 3 highlights a series of sketches a student has drawn for a custom project as component D deliverables – creating, managing, and using escape routes for hospitals in case of danger.

3.3   Component F: Final Design

Continuing their assignment in the second part of the semester, the students created a one-page style guide highlighting which colors, fonts, and icons they would use in their prototype. For each of the two interaction types/platforms already sketched in the first phase (component D), the students created high-fidelity prototypes using a design tool of their choice (Adobe XD, Canva, Figma, or other). Finally, they updated their documentation and added a video walkthrough of their final prototypes. The assignment ended with the student teams presenting their work on component F before the academic evaluator. Figure 4 lists a series of high-fidelity screens a team has made as deliverables for their *GudBoi* project – a training dog acting as a digital companion for mobile and AR devices.

Fig. 4. High-fidelity prototype for a dog training student project.

3.4   Questionnaire

After the deliverables for component D were sent, we asked volunteer students to fill in a questionnaire in order to understand their design choices and the difficulty level they encountered when sketching their project's UI for the two platforms. The questionnaire had the following questions/requests:

- List the project design elements and patterns for the first and second interaction types/platforms chosen;
- List the main changes from the first platform when sketching for the second;
- Rate the difficulty level when sketching for the first and second platforms (1—lowest rating, 5—highest rating). Also, explain why the volunteers chose the second rating.

- State name, gender, age, field of study for Bachelor of Science Thesis (for instance, interaction design, Web application development, software security, database management, or other), if the volunteers work for a company, the role, and years of experience.

3.5 Prototypes

In order to validate our Meta-UI proposal, we created a series of high-fidelity design prototypes using Figma[3]. First, we designed the concept of a Web educational platform where potential users can listen to various audio lessons (grouped in chapters) and learn about designing solutions for a sustainable ocean [52,53].

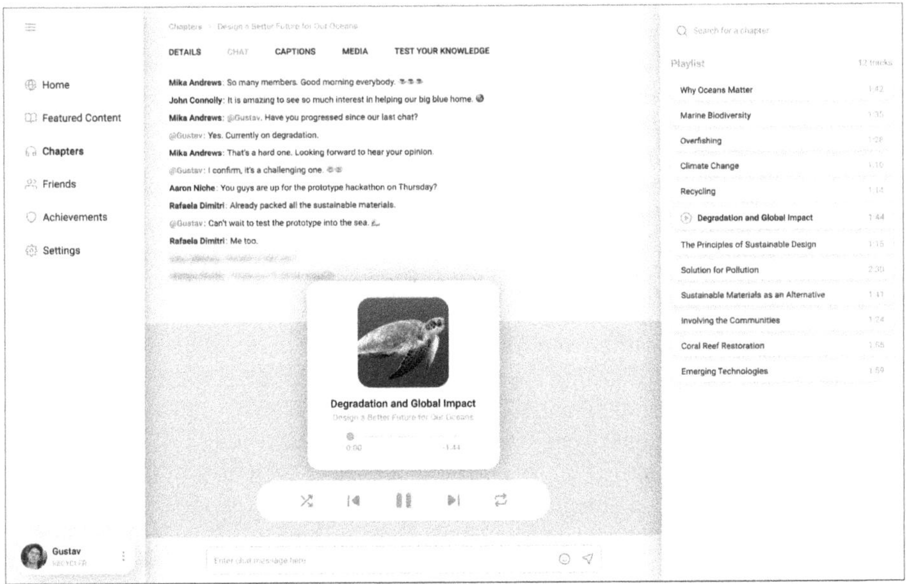

Fig. 5. *DISOCEAN* in Mozilla Firefox Web browser: User chat facility.

After completing a lessons, users test their knowledge and earn achievements. Furthermore, they can interact with other users and organize themselves to complete various challenges (Fig. 5) focused on various ocean sustainability topics such as habitat degradation (e.g., marine pollutants, effects of plastics on aquatic organisms [54]), reducing and preventing overfishing, adapting to climate change, and others. We named the application *DISOCEAN* to ease our validation process – Table 1 lists *DISOCEAN*'s main features.

The second prototype represents a Meta-UI Transformational Tool proposal where users can configure the *DISOCEAN* interface in an AR/VR setting and alter its UI

---

[3] Figma: The Collaborative Interface Design Tool – https://help.figma.com/hc/ (accessed on May 6th, 2025).

Table 1. *DISOCEAN* Web Platform Features.

Feature Name	Feature Description
Featured Content	Users explore content promoted by the platform
Chapters	Users browse all the available chapters within the platform
Friends	Users view and manage their *DISOCEAN* friends
Achievements	Users access all their achievements they received
Profile	Users view and manage their *DISOCEAN* platform
Chat	Users interact with each other via a dedicated chatroom
Captions	Users view captions for the current audio being played
Media	Users view extra content such as videos or image slideshows
Test your knowledge	Users take quizzes to gain points and earn achievements (using Points Badges Leaderboard System)
Audio Player	Users play, pause, shuffle, repeat or move to next/previous audio
Playlist	Users view the entire audio playlist of a chapter

components based on their preferences. More in detail, the Transformation Tool prototype (Fig. 6 and 7) simulates a Meta-UI where users select and manipulate components from their application using the following methods and features:

- **Move** components to different positions;
- **Resize** elements while keeping the aspect ratio;
- **Rotating** components on all axis: X, Y, Z;
- **Duplicate** part of the interface;
- **Change** elements entirely (for example, switching a Web audio player to a voice command interface as a direct alternative/suggestion);
- **Offloading** features to simulate performance optimizations;
- **Hide** UI areas without deleting them;
- **Remove** parts of the UI completely;
- **Attach** or **detach** to/from other groups of UI elements or components;

The prototypes described are designed and tested on Meta Quest 3 (using Meta Browser) and Xreal Air (using Mobile Safari on iOS). To complete the experience, we also designed two more prototypes.

- *DISOCEAN* split into three browser tabs on Meta Browser;
- *DISOCEAN* as a single audio-player component displayed at the top right corner of the user's field of view (accessible via the Xreal Air device);

This way, we provided a complete overview of our proposal: first interacting with the *DISOCEAN* prototype in a single Web browser tab, then accessing the Meta-UI in the same tab, then interacting with the *DISOCEAN* split into multiple tabs, and finally accessing the AR audio player as a single component displayed.

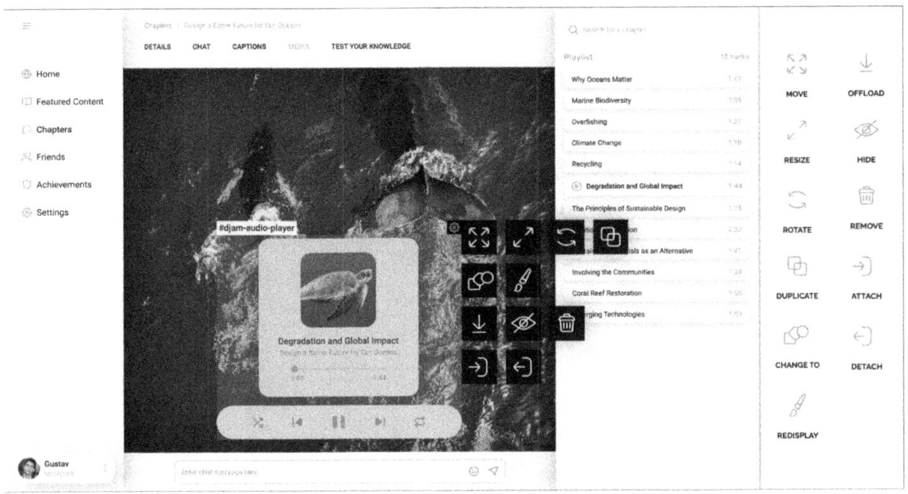

Fig. 6. *DISOCEAN* Meta-UI Transformational Tool.

3.6 Prototype Evaluation

After finishing the final deliverables, we asked volunteers to participate in the second part of the study. We presented our *DISOCEAN* prototype and highlighted how the Meta-UI Transformational Tool prototype works. Then, the volunteers were invited to test the prototypes on our available devices and evaluate our Meta-UI Transformational Tool. The evaluation had the following questions/requests:

- Describe step-by-step how they would use the Meta-UI Transformational Tool to convert the current class project to AR/VR;
- Rate the methods (resize, rotate, attach etc.) for the Transformational Tool (1—lowest rating, 5—highest rating);
- Rate the explanations used to describe the Transformational Tool (1—lowest rating, 5—highest rating);
- Rate the usefulness of the transformational tool (1—lowest rating, 5—highest rating);
- Rate the difficulty sketching/designing for AR/VR using the Transformational Tool; Explain why they chose this specific rating;
- Suggestions or improvements for the Transformational Tool.

4 Evaluation Summary

Practically, after finishing the first part of the assignment (component D), the students completed the questionnaire we submitted to them voluntarily. Then, after presenting the final part of the assignment (Component F), we showcased our original prototypes (initial *DISOCEAN* design, Meta-UI Transformational Tool, *DISOCEAN* design split

Fig. 7. Modifying a component using Meta-UI Transformational Tool.

into three tabs, and *DISOCEAN* converted into a single audio player component for AR) so that the participants could fully understand them.

Moreover, we had actual devices on location, Meta Quest 3 and Xreal Air, to provide a real immersive experience. After they tested the prototypes on Meta Browser and Safari iOS Browser, we invited the participants to evaluate them and detail how their projects would look using a tool like ours.

5   Results

5.1   Component D: Design

Volunteers completed our questionnaire after the students had submitted the component D deliverables for their project. We collected **68 valid responses** and concluded with the following important insights:

- To measure the difficulty of sketching interfaces for the **first platform**, we calculated a mean score of **3.04**. The participants' main reasoning behind this score was that there were too many flows/screens to cover, they had little previous experience, and the learning curve was higher than expected.
- The level of difficulty for sketching on the second platform earned an overall score of **2.67**. Those who chose AR or VR specifically as a second platform had an overall difficulty of **2.92**. As in why they chose their ratings, participants mentioned it was easier because they were reusing components and skipping some features when migrating to AR/VR. On the other hand, it was more challenging, because AR/VR was a new interaction paradigm and was initially unfamiliar to interact with.

– Participants listed the preferred choice of AR/VR design elements and patterns when sketching: UI timers, mini-maps, overlays, on-screen arrows/indicators, floating cards, contextual actions, and commands.

We mainly went for two parts of our study to compare difficulty and usefulness of the Meta-UI when participants sketched and made prototypes of their project with and without using our proposal. The first results represent a good starting point and benchmark to compare with the final results after the participants evaluate our proposal.

5.2 Component F: Final Assessment

The second set of results adds more layers into perspective. After presenting their entire project, volunteers tested the prototypes we prepared and evaluated our proposals using the devices we provided: Meta Quest 3 and Xreal Air Glasses. We obtained **69 valid responses**. Before this study, 27 participants (39.13%) had never interacted with mixed reality devices, 28 (40.58%) had interacted once, and 14 (20.29%) had interacted multiple times. **Gaming** is the top use for mixed reality devices, seconded by entertainment, followed by casual and education.

Regarding ratings, using our prototype as a guideline to design for AR/VR provided diverse results. In terms of the rating for the methods proposed, the mean score was **4.23**. The quality of the explanations scored **4.21**, and the grade for usefulness for the prototype was **4.09**. For the difficulty level sketching interfaces for AR/VR, leveraging our prototype as a guiding framework, the mean score was **2.81**.

Comparing the last score with what we obtained in the first batch of findings (component D results), we see a slight 3.77% decrease in difficulty (reminder: 3.04 for sketching the first interface and 2.92 for sketching the second platform specifically for AR/VR). Table 2 provides a direct comparison of the results.

Table 2. Comparing the difficulty scores/ratings.

Stage	Component D	Component D	Component D	Component F
Criteria	**Sketching platform #1: no guidance**	**Sketching platform #2: no guidance**	**Sketching for AR/VR: no guidance**	**Sketching for AR/VR with guidance**
Difficulty score	3.04 out of 5	2.67 out of 5	2.92 out of 5	2.81 out of 5 (↓ **3.77%**)

To investigate the reason behind the final difficulty scores, we analyzed why the students chose such ratings. We list the top insights when the difficulty was higher:

– It is complex, too many details and use cases to cover in little time;
– It requires a high level of adaptability; the user must know their way around AR/VR;
– It does not provide a proper on-boarding, therefore it is not easy to start;
– The end goal is not clear, and the outcome is hard to envision;

- Configuring without knowing whether it is a good/valid configuration requires a decent amount of effort.

On the other side, the students mentioned the following advantages of using the prototype as guidance:

- Having to manipulate components in many ways;
- The methods provided are considered a plus, offering precise control;
- It is perceived as intuitive, easy to configure, and user friendly, especially for Web application design;

As the last part of analyzing their feedback, the suggestions provided by the participants add a vast area of improvement and exploration. The volunteers recommended the following changes:

1. Aid the users once they start interacting with the prototype by offering templates, predefined designs, or presets and have the changes snap to a virtual grid;
2. Have *move*, *resize*, and *rotate* features grouped into one option – similar to photo/ vector editing applications;
3. Multiple users proposed having Artificial Intelligence (AI) contextual adjustments or ChatGPT-like conversational-oriented recommendations packaged as an "auto-transformer" (to automatize and automatically adjust the layouts for AR/VR);
4. Limit the options for failure safety reasons and yet again get recommendations from a Generative AI assistant;
5. Have this tool not just for AR/VR but also for exploring other platforms and devices;
6. Have multiple states of feedback when altering designs (include animations);
7. Have the tool applied to multiple applications, get diverse states for AR/VR, and group the configured applications into one area in the 3D space.

5.3   Lessons Learned

After analyzing the insights gained from both evaluations (questionnaires and prototypes) conducted by our recruited audience (student volunteers), the following conclusions regarding our proposal can be enumerated:

- Users need guidance from the start of the interface interaction; this guidance can take the form of tutorials, templates, documentation, interface assistance;
- Users prefer shortcuts to speed up the process; the multiple mentions of AI assistance reveal their exposure to and preferences for generative content;
- Users need help with configuring a large number of screens. The process should be as streamlined as possible;
- Users prefer to reuse components as much as possible; at the same time, they propose creative methods – e.g., combining multiple applications and their design components into a single experience.

These conclusions motivate us to enhance the prototypes and proceed to the next phase: performing new evaluations with a more experienced audience.

6   Discussion

6.1   Current MR Consumer Devices

On the commercial side, the MR industry is expanding in multiple areas, enforcing the need for a cohesive and user-centered experience [55]. Devices such as Sony PSVR2 [56] prioritize the gaming sector. On the other hand, devices such as Meta Quest 3/Pro [57] and Apple Vision Pro [58] offer a broader pallette of experiences, from productivity to entertainment. Furthermore, more affordable technologies such as RayNeo[4], Even Realities[5], or VITURE Pro XR Glasses[6] blend AR capabilities with multi-monitor display setups [59]. If required, offering a unified experience native or on the web through all these devices forces us to think modular, expandable, and flexible when designing user interfaces.

6.2   Interface Groupings

As we assumed, volunteers proposed using the Meta-UI tool to configure multiple applications' interfaces, not just a single one. This approach allows the creation of new interface groupings [60] from distinct applications, contributing to new setups and optimizing 3D space and productivity [61,62]. We could also explore enhancing this opportunity via Generative AI. Our plans also include inviting participants to use the Meta-UI Transformation Tool combined with support from AI Generative tools to split and group parts of different interfaces the users are interested in combining into one single section. For example, users can alter the proposed *DISOCEAN* application in AR and combine it with video streaming software to create a new (possibly better) custom experience.

6.3   Prototype Improvements

Based on participants' feedback, we also consider modifying our prototypes to offer a more streamlined evaluation experience. We believe that for our next iteration in future experiments, we first split the target application's UI components into separate browser tabs and then apply transformational methods on each tab: *resize, rotate, attach, change*, and more. This way, we can expand the configuration canvas to multiple windows or screens [63].

We observed ourselves that the participants struggle to manipulate a complex single design in AR/VR inside one Web browser tab. Focusing first on creating and managing tabs is a strong assumption we want to pursue.

On the topic itself, the students showed interest in discovering and testing more features for the *DISOCEAN* application. They expressed the desire to have a projects section where they could work on sustainability initiatives in groups. This feedback motivates us to iterate the prototype and include new collaborative features to simulate and test.

---

[4] RayNeo Air 2 XR – www.rayneo.com/products/rayneo-air-2-xr-glasses (accessed on May 6th, 2025).

[5] Even Realities G1 Glasses – www.evenrealities.com/en-EN/g1 (accessed on May 6th, 2025).

[6] VITURE Pro XR Glasses – www.viture.com/product/viture-pro-xr-glasses (accessed on May 6th, 2025).

7   Limitations

We acknowledge several limitations that we were aware of during the making of this research study.

First, the study focuses on students as the primary audience for our user tests. Although this approach covers the entry-level/beginner audience, it leaves a gap that needs to be filled by more experienced, senior-level participants.

Then, by using Figma, we provide a level of interaction that is limited by the tool's actual capabilities. Exploring other high-fidelity prototyping solutions can help us develop a more advanced proof of concept.

Finally, the number of recommendations we provide for changing/configuring a component is limited and needs to be extended. Future versions of the Meta-UI prototype should include a more diverse set of options to configure parts of the UI for Mixed Reality.

8   Further Work

Our results and insights motivate us to continue the study in multiple directions. First, we plan to improve the prototype, add new *DISOCEAN* features (such as group projects), and incorporate more recommendations for replacing/changing the UI elements for MR.

Secondly, we aim to test the prototypes with professionals from the field (senior UX designers and developers), and investigate the study's validity against more experienced participants. A possible endeavor is to organize a collective set of design jam-like events such as "*hackeanos*" – a combination of the "hacking" and "Okeanos" terms [64].

Thirdly, we intend to thoroughly research the potential of GAI to identify user interface components from single or multiple web/desktop/mobile applications and mix and combine them into new groups of interfaces for AR/VR. Also, inspired by [65], a knowledge model expressing the most important concepts involved into this particular approach could be benefic for further developments.

Lastly, we plan to compare the new results and cross-check them with previous experiments and evaluations we performed. Moreover, we are already investigating the potential of a dedicated framework to challenge current explorations [46,66] for designing MR experiences [67]. *Modalverse UI*, as we named it – by combining the words "modal" and "universe" –, is set to ease interface transformation across a multimodal environment using Meta-UIs.

9   Conclusions

Our study contributes to interface multimodality, plasticity, distribution, design processes, and methodologies in a Mixed Reality setting. Prior research highlights that creating or adapting various types of user interfaces – such as Web, mobile, desktop – in an AR/VR setting can vary in complexity from the early stage of the application design process. Our proposal reduces these levels by improving the difficulty in designing low/high fidelity concepts for AR/VR.

Furthermore, this paper also explores the awareness of sustainable oceans by showcasing an interface design for an educational Web platform as part of our Meta-UI tool demonstration.

References

1. Speicher, M., Hall, B.D., Nebeling, M.: What is mixed reality? In: Proceedings of the 2019 CHI Conference on Human Factors in Computing Systems, pp. 1–15 (2019). https://doi.org/10.1145/3290605.3300767
2. Rokhsaritalemi, S., Sadeghi-Niaraki, A., Choi, S.M.: A review on mixed reality: current trends, challenges and prospects. Appl. Sci. **10**(2), 636 (2020). https://doi.org/10.3390/app10020636
3. Krauß, V., Jasche, F., Saßmannshausen, S.M., Ludwig, T., Boden, A.: Research and practice recommendations for mixed reality design – different perspectives from the community. In: Proceedings of the 27th ACM Symposium on Virtual Reality Software and Technology, Article no. 24, pp. 1–13. Association for Computing Machinery (2021). https://doi.org/10.1145/3489849.3489876
4. Krauß, V., Boden, A., Oppermann, L., Reiners, R.: Current practices, challenges, and design implications for collaborative AR/VR application development. In: Proceedings of the 2021 CHI Conference on Human Factors in Computing Systems, Article no. 454, pp. 1–15. Association for Computing Machinery (2021). https://doi.org/10.1145/3411764.3445335
5. Labrie, A., Cheng, J.: Adapting usability heuristics to the context of mobile augmented reality. In: Adjunct Proceedings of the 33rd Annual ACM Symposium on User Interface Software and Technology, pp. 4–6. Association for Computing Machinery (2020). https://doi.org/10.1145/3379350.3416167
6. Börsting, I., Karabulut, C., Fischer, B., Gruhn, V.: Design patterns for mobile augmented reality user interfaces–an incremental review. Information **13**(4), 159 (2022). https://doi.org/10.3390/info13040159
7. Cosio, L.D., Buruk, O., Fernández Galeote, D., Bosman, I.D.V., Hamari, J.: Virtual and augmented reality for environmental sustainability: a systematic review. In: Proceedings of the 2023 CHI Conference on Human Factors in Computing Systems, pp. 1–23 (2023). https://doi.org/10.1145/3544548.3581147
8. Simões-Marques, M., Água, P., Frias, A., Correia, A.: Metaverse and digital twins: contributions, opportunities and challenges to a sustainable use of the ocean. Hum. Factors Syst. Interact. **84**(84) (2023). https://doi.org/10.54941/ahfe1003608
9. Bruno, F., et al.: Digital technologies for the sustainable development of the accessible underwater cultural heritage sites. J. Mar. Sci. Eng. **8**(11), 955 (2020). https://doi.org/10.3390/jmse8110955
10. Mueller, F.F., et al.: Grand challenges in WaterHCI. In: Proceedings of the CHI Conference on Human Factors in Computing Systems, pp. 1–18 (2024). https://doi.org/10.1145/3613904.3642052
11. Xylia, M., Passos, M.V., Piseddu, T., Barquet, K.: Exploring multi-use platforms: a literature review of marine, multifunctional, modular, and mobile applications (M4s). Heliyon **9**(6) (2023). https://doi.org/10.1016/j.heliyon.2023.e16775
12. Montoya, M.F., Saini, A., Overdevest, N., Randall, B., Pell, S.J., Mueller, F.F.: Exploring the design of playful devices for surfing. In: Companion Proceedings of the 2024 Annual Symposium on Computer-Human Interaction in Play, pp. 200–207 (2024). https://doi.org/10.1145/3665463.3678786

13. Novian, D., Triyono, M.B., Pardjono, P., Wardani, R.: Scuba diving virtual reality media design as underwater tourism preparation. In: 5th Vocational Education International Conference (VEIC-5 2023), pp. 712–719. Atlantis Press (2024). https://doi.org/10.2991/978-2-38476-198-2_97

14. Leitão, R., Maguire, M., Turner, S., Arenas, F., Guimarães, L.: Ocean literacy gamified: a systematic evaluation of the effect of game elements on students' learning experience. Environ. Educ. Res. **28**(2), 276–294 (2022). https://doi.org/10.1080/13504622.2021.2007410

15. de Oliveira, L.M.C., de Oliveira, P.A., Lim, A., Wheeler, A.J., Conti, L.A.: Developing mobile applications with augmented reality and 3D photogrammetry for visualisation of cold-water coral reefs and deep-water habitats. Geosciences **12**(10), 356 (2022). https://doi.org/10.3390/geosciences12100356

16. Menna, F., Battisti, R., Nocerino, E., Remondino, F.: FROG: a portable underwater mobile mapping system. Int. Arch. Photogramm. Remote. Sens. Spat. Inf. Sci. **48**, 295–302 (2023). https://doi.org/10.5194/isprs-archives-XLVIII-2-W3-2023-295-2023

17. Guo, S., Xia, M., Xue, H., Wang, S., Liu, C.: OceanCrowd: vessel trajectory data-based participant selection for mobile crowd sensing in ocean observation. IEEE Trans. Sustain. Comput. (2024). https://doi.org/10.1109/TSUSC.2024.3246791

18. Alghizzawi, M., Habes, M., Al Assuli, A., Ezmigna, A.R.: Digital marketing and sustainable businesses: as mobile apps in tourism. In: Artificial Intelligence and Transforming Digital Marketing, pp. 3–13. Springer, Cham (2023). https://doi.org/10.1007/978-3-031-35828-9_1

19. Silva, E., et al.: TRIDENT–technology-based impact assessment tool for sustainable, transparent deep sea mining exploration and exploitation: a project overview. In: OCEANS 2023-Limerick, pp. 1–7. IEEE (2023). https://doi.org/10.1109/OCEANS47358.2023.10180928

20. Crosby, A., et al.: Designing ocean vision AI: an investigation of community needs for imaging-based ocean conservation. In: Proceedings of the 2023 CHI Conference on Human Factors in Computing Systems, pp. 1–16 (2023). https://doi.org/10.1145/3544548.3580886

21. Hancock, J., Hui, R., Singh, J., Mazumder, A.: Seeing human rights at sea: how to align tech development with the needs of maritime human rights investigators and affected communities. In: Extended Abstracts of the CHI Conference on Human Factors in Computing Systems, pp. 1–13 (2024). https://doi.org/10.1145/3613905.3651081

22. Kim, R., Risseeuw, C., Groutars, E.G., Karana, E.: Surfacing livingness in microbial displays: a design taxonomy for HCI. In: Proceedings of the 2023 CHI Conference on Human Factors in Computing Systems, pp. 1–21 (2023). https://doi.org/10.1145/3544548.3581417

23. Bell, F., Ramsahoye, M., Coffie, J., Tung, J., Alistar, M.: μMe: exploring the human microbiome as an intimate material for living interfaces. In: Proceedings of the 2023 ACM Designing Interactive Systems Conference, pp. 2019–2033 (2023). https://doi.org/10.1145/3563657.3596133

24. Glöss, M.: New perspectives for phenomenology in interaction design. In: Proceedings of the 13th Nordic Conference on Human-Computer Interaction, pp. 1–7 (2024). https://doi.org/10.1145/3679318.3685404

25. Walker, M., Takayama, L., Landay, J.A.: High-fidelity or low-fidelity, paper or computer? Choosing attributes when testing web prototypes. In: Proceedings of the Human Factors and Ergonomics Society Annual Meeting, vol. 46, no. 5, pp. 661–665. Sage Publications (2002). https://doi.org/10.1177/154193120204600513

26. Chandana, H.B., Shaik, N., Chitralingappa, P.: Exploring the frontiers of user experience design: VR, AR, and the future of interaction. In: 2023 International Conference on Computer Science and Emerging Technologies (CSET), pp. 1–6. IEEE (2023). https://doi.org/10.1109/CSET58993.2023.10346724

27. Dorta, T.: Design flow and ideation. Int. J. Archit. Comput. **6**(3), 299–316 (2008). https://doi.org/10.1260/1478-0771.6.3.299

28. Vauchez, J., Bailly, C., Castet, J.: UXR-kit: an ideation method for collaborative and user-centered design about extended reality solutions. In: Adjunct Proceedings of the 34th Conference on l'Interaction Humain-Machine, Article no. 5, pp. 1–7. Association for Computing Machinery (2023). https://doi.org/10.1145/3577590.3589605
29. Delgado, B.: User experience (UX) in metaverse: realities and challenges. Metaverse Basic Appl. Res. **1**(9) (2022). https://doi.org/10.56294/mr20229
30. Liu, Z.: Augmented reality user interface: analysing the design principles and evaluation methods of augmented reality (AR) user interfaces to enhance user interaction and experience. Int. J. Comput. Sci. Inf. Technol. **3**, 22–31 (2024). https://doi.org/10.62051/ijcsit.v3n2.04
31. Murtza, R., Monroe, S., Youmans, R.J.: Heuristic evaluation for virtual reality systems. In: Proceedings of the Human Factors and Ergonomics Society Annual Meeting, vol. 61, no. 1, pp. 2067–2071 (2017). https://doi.org/10.1177/1541931213602000
32. Irshad, S., Awang, D.R.B.: A UX oriented evaluation approach for mobile augmented reality applications. In: Proceedings of the 16th International Conference on Advances in Mobile Computing and Multimedia, pp. 108–112. Association for Computing Machinery (2018). https://doi.org/10.1145/3282353.3282357
33. Cao, J., Lam, K.-Y., Lee, L.-H., Liu, X., Hui, P., Su, X.: Mobile augmented reality: user interfaces, frameworks, and intelligence. ACM Comput. Surv. **55**(9), 1–36 (2023). https://doi.org/10.1145/3549937
34. Srinivasa, R.R., Veluchamy, U.P., Bose, J.: Augmented reality adaptive web content. In: Proceedings of the 13th IEEE Annual Consumer Communications & Networking Conference (CCNC), pp. 107–110. IEEE (2016). https://doi.org/10.1109/CCNC.2016.7444740
35. Yan, Z., Lv, C., Chen, Q., Shang, D.: Impact of user engagement on virtual reality behavioral response from the human-computer interaction perspective toward a service context: a hybrid statistics and machine learning approach. Expert Syst. Appl. **247**, 123243 (2024). https://doi.org/10.1016/j.eswa.2024.123243
36. Xing, Y., Shell, J., Fahy, C., Guan, K., Zhang, Q., Xie, T.: User interface research in web extended reality. In: 2021 IEEE 7th International Conference on Virtual Reality (ICVR), pp. 76–81. IEEE (2021). https://doi.org/10.1109/ICVR51878.2021.9483702
37. MacIntyre, B., Smith, T.F.: Thoughts on the future of WebXR and the immersive web. In: 2018 IEEE International Symposium on Mixed and Augmented Reality Adjunct (ISMAR-Adjunct), pp. 338–342. IEEE (2018). https://doi.org/10.1109/ISMAR-Adjunct.2018.00099
38. Qiao, X., Pei, R., Dustdar, S., Liu, L., Ma, H., Chen, J.: Web AR: a promising future for mobile augmented reality - state of the art, challenges, and insights. Proc. IEEE **107**, 1–16 (2019). https://doi.org/10.1109/JPROC.2019.2895105
39. Silva, R.M.L., Principe Cruz, E., Rosner, D.K., Kelly, D., Monroy-Hernández, A., Liu, F.: Understanding AR activism: an interview study with creators of augmented reality experiences for social change. In: Proceedings of the 2022 CHI Conference on Human Factors in Computing Systems, pp. 1–15 (2022). https://doi.org/10.1145/3491102.3517605
40. Billinghurst, M., Grasset, R., Looser, J.: Designing augmented reality interfaces. ACM SIGGRAPH Comput. Graph. **39**, 17–22 (2005). https://doi.org/10.1145/1057792.1057803
41. Kelling, C., et al.: The hierarchy of needs for user experiences in virtual reality. In: Immersive Journalism as Storytelling (2020). https://doi.org/10.4324/9780429437748-14
42. Miraz, M.H., Ali, M., Excell, P.S.: Adaptive user interfaces and universal usability through plasticity of user interface design. Comput. Sci. Rev. **40**, 100363 (2021). https://doi.org/10.1016/j.cosrev.2021.100363
43. Vanderdonckt, J., Calvary, G., Coutaz, J., Stanciulescu, A.: Multimodality for plastic user interfaces: models, methods, and principles. In: Multimodal User Interfaces: From Signals to Interaction, pp. 61–84. Springer, Heidelberg (2008). https://doi.org/10.1007/978-3-540-78345-9_4

44. Elmqvist, N.: Distributed user interfaces: state of the art. In: Distributed User Interfaces: Designing Interfaces for the Distributed Ecosystem, pp. 1–12. Springer, Cham (2011). https://doi.org/10.1007/978-1-4471-2271-5_1

45. Vanderhulst, G., Schreiber, D., Luyten, K., Muhlhauser, M., Coninx, K.: Edit, inspect and connect your surroundings: a reference framework for meta-UIs. In: Proceedings of the 1st ACM SIGCHI Symposium on Engineering Interactive Computing Systems, pp. 167–176. Association for Computing Machinery (2009). https://doi.org/10.1145/1570433.1570466

46. Lu, Y., Hu, Y., Shen, X., Chen, Z.: An immersive layout framework for web design in virtual reality. In: Extended Abstracts of the 2023 CHI Conference on Human Factors in Computing Systems, Article no. 36, pp. 1–7. Association for Computing Machinery (2023). https://doi.org/10.1145/3544549.3585889

47. Gottschalk, S., Yigitbas, E., Schmidt, E., Engels, G.: ProConAR: a tool support for model-based AR product configuration. In: Bernhaupt, R., Ardito, C., Sauer, S. (eds.) HCSE 2020. LNCS, vol. 12481, pp. 207–215. Springer, Cham (2020). https://doi.org/10.1007/978-3-030-64266-2_14

48. Hunsucker, A.J., McClinton, K., Wang, J., Stolterman, E.: Augmented reality prototyping for interaction design students. In: Proceedings of the 2017 CHI Conference Extended Abstracts on Human Factors in Computing Systems, pp. 1018–1023. Association for Computing Machinery (2017). https://doi.org/10.1145/3027063.3053684

49. Speicher, M., Lewis, K., Nebeling, M.: Designers, the stage is yours! medium-fidelity prototyping of augmented & virtual reality interfaces with 360 theater. Proc. ACM Hum.-Comput. Interact. **5**(EICS), 205 (2021). https://doi.org/10.1145/3461727

50. Nielsen, L.: Personas – User Focused Design, 2nd edn. Springer, Cham (2019). https://doi.org/10.1007/978-1-4471-7427-1

51. Goodman, E., Kuniavsky, M., Moed, A.: Observing the User Experience, 2nd edn. Morgan Kaufmann (2012). https://doi.org/10.1016/C2010-0-64844-9

52. Pearlman, J., et al.: Evolving and sustaining ocean best practices to enable interoperability in the UN Decade of Ocean Science for Sustainable Development. Front. Mar. Sci. **8**, 619685 (2021). https://doi.org/10.3389/fmars.2021.619685

53. Tzachor, A., Hendel, O., Richards, C.E.: Digital twins: a stepping stone to achieve ocean sustainability? NPJ Ocean Sustain. **2**(1), 16 (2023). https://doi.org/10.1038/s41500-023-00069-5

54. Du, S., et al.: Environmental fate and impacts of microplastics in aquatic ecosystems: a review. RSC Adv. **11**(26), 15762–15784 (2021). https://doi.org/10.1039/d1ra02955g

55. Rechy-Ramirez, E.J., Marin-Hernandez, A., Rios-Figueroa, H.V.: Impact of commercial sensors in human computer interaction: a review. J. Ambient. Intell. Humaniz. Comput. **9**(5), 1479–1496 (2017). https://doi.org/10.1007/s12652-017-0568-3

56. Zhang, R.: Research on the progress of VR in game. Highlights Sci. Eng. Technol. **39**, 103–110 (2023). https://doi.org/10.54097/hset.v39i.6507

57. De Quinto, C., et al.: On the impact of VR/AR applications on optical transport networks: first experiments with Meta Quest 3 gaming and conferencing applications. In: 2024 24th International Conference on Transparent Optical Networks (ICTON), pp. 1–6 (2024). https://doi.org/10.1109/ICTON62926.2024.10647326

58. Hu, J.: From a new product: apple Vision Pro Impact of VR technology development on VR gaming. Appl. Comput. Eng. **34**, 20230295 (2024). https://doi.org/10.54254/2755-2721/34/20230295

59. Lee, L.-H., Hui, P.: Interaction methods for smart glasses: a survey. IEEE Access **6**, 28712–28732 (2018). https://doi.org/10.1109/ACCESS.2018.2831081

60. Tao, F.: Multi-view web interfaces in augmented reality. Ph.D. thesis (2022). https://doi.org/10.25911/5FRG-J326

61. Daassi, M., Debbabi, S.: Intention to reuse AR-based apps: the combined role of the sense of immersion, product presence and perceived realism. Inf. Manag. **58**(4), 103453 (2021). https://doi.org/10.1016/j.im.2021.103453
62. Abrahão, S., Insfran, E., Sluÿters, A., Vanderdonckt, J.: Model-based intelligent user interface adaptation: challenges and future directions. Softw. Syst. Model. **20**(5), 1335–1349 (2021). https://doi.org/10.1007/s10270-021-00909-7
63. Ichsan, M.H.H., Sik-Lanyi, C., Guzsvinecz, T.: Multi-browser VE: enhancing internet browsing experience through virtual reality. Softw. Impacts 100733 (2024). https://doi.org/10.1016/j.simpa.2024.100733
64. Demarchi, V., Nisi, V., Nunes, N.J.: Hackeanos: a new collaborative event format for hacking the Ocean-humanity relationship. In: Companion Publication of the 2024 ACM Designing Interactive Systems Conference (2024). https://doi.org/10.1145/3656156.3663722
65. Pan, Y.-J.: A marine knowledge system for ocean affairs: integrating data, evaluating usage, and enabling sustainable marine management. J. Mar. Sci. Technol. **32**(3) (2024). https://doi.org/10.51400/2709-6998.2746
66. Xu, X., et al.: XAIR: a framework of explainable AI in augmented reality. In: Proceedings of the 2023 CHI Conference on Human Factors in Computing Systems. Association for Computing Machinery (2023). https://doi.org/10.1145/3544548.3581500
67. Rauschnabel, P.A., Felix, R., Hinsch, C., Shahab, H., Alt, F.: What is XR? Towards a framework for augmented and virtual reality. Comput. Hum. Behav. **133**, 107289 (2022). https://doi.org/10.1016/j.chb.2022.107289

Designing for Wow: Empowering Women Through a Pelvic Health App

Adi Katz[1,2,4]($\boxtimes$) (iD), Yana Sophia[1,2] (iD), and Hadar Ronen[3,4]

[1] Industrial Engineering and Management Department, SCE, Ashdod, Israel
{adis,yanash}@sce.ac.il
[2] YOUsability Center SCE, College, Ashdod, Israel
[3] Department of Education and Society, Ono Academic College, Kiryat Ono, Israel
hadar.ro@ono.ac.il
[4] User Empowering Design (UED) Institution, Tel Aviv, Israel

Abstract. In the dynamic realm of technology design, the User Empowering Design (UED) emerges as the next frontier, elevating user interfaces from merely functional and engaging to profoundly impactful. UED is a framework that extends beyond usability and user experience (UX) to address users' sense of control, self-perception, and personal growth. Drawing on layered psychological needs and the Kano model of user expectations, UED positions empowerment as the "wow" factor in interaction design, enabling technologies to support not just task completion or emotional satisfaction, but personal development. We present the case of *EZpeeZ,* a mobile application designed to empower women managing pelvic floor challenges. Developed through a value-driven, co-design process that integrates playful physiotherapy exercises, humorous interaction, and empathic microcopy, *EZpeeZ* demonstrates how UED can reshape stigmatized health topics into experiences of control, confidence, and dignity. Finally, we outline plans for evaluating the app's impact on users' quality of life and emotional well-being, including focus groups and eye-tracking studies. This work contributes a concrete example of UED in practice and argues for empowerment as a practical imperative in human-centered design.

Keywords: User Empowering Design (UED) · Human-Computer Interaction (HCI) · Co-Design · Women's Health Technology

1 What is User Empowering Design (UED) and Why Now?

The concept of empowering users through technology has long been a focus within human-computer interaction. In his seminal work on empowerment, Shneiderman (1990) emphasized the importance of enabling users to improve job performance and derive satisfaction through successful interactions [1]. However, his view of empowerment was largely situated within the scope of operational interaction, centered on interface usability, task completion, and system effectiveness.

Since then, several studies have advanced the idea of user empowerment within these boundaries. Research has focused on giving users more control during interaction

J. F. Krems et al. (Eds.): CHIRA 2025, CCIS 2836, pp. 22–33, 2026.
https://doi.org/10.1007/978-3-032-16454-4_2

[2], allowing for interface adaptability [3], and building awareness to help users resist manipulation or dark patterns [4]. Some approaches, such as compassionate design, have highlighted broader principles like dignity and emotional security [5], yet even these generally remain confined to the interactional moment emphasizing how users operate within a system rather than how that system influences users' broader lives and identities [6].

User Empowering Design (UED) builds on and transcends this tradition. First envisioned by Gallula and Frank [7], UED expands the concept of empowerment beyond the interaction itself to support users' confidence, self-perception, and ongoing personal growth. Rather than replacing user-centered design (UCD), UED elevates it. UCD has traditionally focused on two primary pillars: usability and user experience (UX). Usability, as defined by Nielsen [8], emphasizes effectiveness and efficiency in achieving task goals. UX, as elaborated by Norman [9], emphasizes emotional responses dimensions like pleasure, satisfaction, and delight.

However, as interactive technologies become deeply embedded in the routines and contexts of daily life and required in almost every activity, functionality and pleasure are no longer sufficient but are increasingly seen as basic and not differentiating. Users expect technologies to contribute to their autonomy, self-expression, and long-term personal growth. We are now in a post-UX era that demands a design philosophy that supports users in realizing their goals and strengthening their capabilities [10]. UED responds to this shift by targeting users' aspirations, strengths, and life goals, not just their in-the-moment needs, aiming to influence life outside the digital product itself.

A UED-oriented product enhances self-efficacy and builds capacity for change. It deliberately supports psychological resilience, identity development, and long-term flourishing. UED is built upon the premise that technology should not only support users in completing tasks or enjoying the interface, but also help them grow, adapt, and realize their potential. This shift moves the focus from the user within the system to the human beyond it. UED is the third revolution in interactive design, following usability and UX. It is not a replacement of these previous layers but a complementary and higher one. It positions technology not merely as a tool or context for action, but as a potential catalyst for personal development.

2 User Needs in Layers: How Psychological Hierarchies and Interface Expectations Converge in UED

User needs, much like human needs, can be conceptualized as a hierarchy, ranging from basic functional requirements to complex aspirations. Drawing inspiration from Alderfer's ERG theory [11], which condenses Maslow's hierarchy into three core needs - Existence, Relatedness, and Growth - we can trace a similar pattern in interface design. The evolution of user-centered design (UCD) can be conceptualized as progressing through three interrelated layers, each expanding the scope of what it means to support users through technology.

2.1 Usability: Functional and Operational Needs

The foundation is usability, which ensures that users can complete tasks efficiently, effectively, and with minimal errors. This layer focuses on instrumental outcomes and cognitive support, prioritizing clarity, functionality, and task success [8].

2.2 User Experience (UX): Emotional and Experiential Needs

Building upon usability, UX addresses how users feel during interaction. Positive emotional experiences - such as pleasure, surprise, and enjoyment - are central to this layer [9, 12]. UX design acknowledges the affective and experiential dimensions of human-technology relationships. At the same time, UX remains a multifaceted and debated concept, with no single agreed definition. Its interpretations vary across academia and industry, emphasizing different factors such as context, temporality, and user expectations [13]. Regardless of these definitional differences, UX largely concentrates on experiences during interaction. It does not explicitly address long-term aspects that extend beyond the interaction itself, a gap that UED seeks to fill.

2.3 User Empowering Design (UED): Growth and Personal Development

UED adds a third and deeper layer, moving beyond the interaction itself to support users' aspirations, personal development, and evolving sense of self. Rather than replacing usability or UX, UED expands the scope of design, positioning technology as a catalyst for confidence, identity building, and long-term empowerment [10].

This pyramid of users' needs aligns with the Kano model, introduced by Noriaki Kano and collaborators [14, 15] which defines three types of user expectations: must-be, want, and wow. These categories reflect a temporal and motivational evolution that maps well onto the hierarchy of usability, UX, and UED. Must-be needs, those users expect by default, correspond to usability. These include functionality, error prevention, and clarity. Their absence causes frustration, but their presence does not create satisfaction, they are assumed. Want needs align with UX. These are features that users value proportionally to their quality: the more aesthetically pleasing or emotionally engaging the product, the more satisfied the user. Wow needs are where UED plays a transformative role. These features exceed user expectations and offer long-term psychological and aspirational value. They inspire users, reinforce their confidence, and support deeper forms of personal growth and identity formation.

By synthesizing the hierarchical model of user needs with the Kano model's classification of satisfaction, we obtain a more nuanced lens for design. Together, they underscore the importance of not only meeting basic and expected needs but also creating experiences that foster enjoyment during interaction and support user fulfillment, growth, and transformation beyond the screen.

This integrated view not only clarifies the structure of user needs but also illuminates the dynamic evolution of user expectations over time. Today's wows often evolve into tomorrow's wants and ultimately into musts [15]. What was once surprising and empowering becomes, over time, a baseline requirement. This progression makes it critical for designers and organizations to anticipate evolving user expectations and integrate empowerment as a strategic imperative.

3   UED Implementation: The Case of *EZpeeZ*

This section presents the central design case of this paper - *EZpeeZ*, a UED project that exemplifies an expansive view of empowerment: one that goes beyond the moment of interaction and seeks to influence users' lives, aspirations, and sense of agency. This project continues a line of work at the YOUsability Center, where the UED methodology is applied to real-life challenges through value-driven design. A previous project, for example, focused on older adults and designed a contextualization feature in instant messaging apps, helping bridge intergenerational communication gaps by explaining slang and emoji meanings [16]. However, *EZpeeZ* represents the most comprehensive implementation of UED to date, integrating physical, emotional, and psychological empowerment into a single mobile platform. *EZpeeZ* is a mobile application developed to empower women experiencing weakened pelvic floor muscles. It is conceived not only as a physiotherapy tool but as an empowering, stigma-reducing experience grounded in the UED framework.

Pelvic floor disorders, including urinary incontinence, affect a significant proportion of women, particularly after childbirth and during menopause [17]. Beyond the physical symptoms, these conditions often lead to embarrassment, anxiety, and restrictions in social and professional life [18]. Women report avoiding travel, reducing participation in physical activities, and experiencing a diminished sense of control over their bodies. These challenges are not purely functional but deeply tied to identity, dignity, and autonomy.

An increasing number of Pelvic Floor Muscle Training (PFMT) apps have proliferated in recent years. Popular solutions such as *Squeezy* and *Easy Kegel* provide structured exercise plans, visual or auditory cues, reminders, and progress tracking features. Similarly, *Pelvic Floor – Kegel Exercises* emphasizes clear instructional guidance through text, images, and video, often paired with adjustable difficulty levels. Other options, such as *Perifit Care*, integrate game-like elements and real-time feedback, but these depend on proprietary hardware, creating cost and accessibility barriers. Beyond pelvic health, physiotherapy-focused apps like *Pocket Physio* and *PhysiApp* deliver diverse rehabilitation programs and educational resources, typically complemented by reminders and progress monitoring. Although these PFMT and physiotherapy apps offer a range of functionalities aimed at improving physical health and adherence, significant limitations persist in both design and conceptual scope. A recent systematic review of traditional PFMT apps highlights critical gaps in interface design that affect usability and adherence [19]. These gaps include limited visual support for training, unclear icons, and a strict clinical focus that prioritizes functionality over experience. As a result, most solutions overlook features that address the emotional and social dimensions of the condition, such as reducing stigma and supporting a sense of autonomy. This leads to designs that lack warmth or approachability and fail to reduce embarrassment. Motivational strategies that could foster engagement—such as humor or value-driven design—are rarely implemented, even though evidence suggests they can significantly improve long-term adherence.

These challenges make pelvic health a compelling context for UED, where empowerment - through humor, empathy, and value-driven design - can transform a stigmatized medical task into an experience of confidence and control. Unlike existing apps, EZpeeZ combines evidence-based pelvic floor exercises with humor, playful microcopy, and value-driven features designed to reinforce self-efficacy, independence, and control. By reframing a stigmatized medical routine into an experience of confidence and dignity, EZpeeZ advances a design philosophy that moves beyond functional success toward meaningful personal empowerment.

The app's name, *EZpeeZ*, playfully combines the idea of easy ("EZ") with the core function ("pee"), creating a light, approachable tone that helps normalize conversations around pelvic health and embodies the empowerment-through-humor strategy. The final syllable ("Z") reinforces the sound of "easy" and adds a casual, friendly feel that invites users into the experience with comfort rather than clinical formality. The name suggests that addressing pelvic floor challenges can be simple and manageable. The app blends physiotherapy-based exercises with a humorous, light-hearted tone and an engaging interface. It addresses not only the physical symptoms, but also the emotional and psychological challenges associated with these experiences. By normalizing conversations around the pelvic floor, *EZpeeZ* reduces stigma and promotes self-acceptance. It enables users to regain a sense of bodily control and dignity through regular practice. The combination of playfulness, empathy, and discretion encourages adherence to routines that are crucial for improving health outcomes.

3.1 Values and Superpowers: Applying UED to Interviews and Personas

To guide the design of *EZpeeZ* through a User Empowering Design (UED) lens, we conducted six in-depth interviews with women of varying ages - both younger and older - to capture experiences of pelvic floor weakness resulting from childbirth or aging. The interviews focused on participants' aspirations, emotions, and deeper self-perceptions. Qualitative interviews offer a powerful foundation for building personas, as they capture rich, contextual user insights that go beyond demographics and tasks [20, 21].

Although the interviews were primarily open-ended to allow for personal exploration, two structured questions were consistently included to anchor the UED approach. First, participants were asked to select three personal values from a predefined list and explain their choices. This exercise aimed to surface core life directions and motivations beyond the technological context, revealing what truly matters to them. The interviews revealed a set of recurring personal values expressed by participants, including *compassion, self-acceptance, openness to change, adaptability, humor,* and *confidence.* These values offered insight into participants' broader life orientations and informed the design process by highlighting the emotional and psychological dimensions of their experiences. In particular, the emphasis on humor and self-acceptance served as guiding principles in shaping the app's tone and interaction style, supporting the integration of empathy and lightness into the user experience.

Second, participants were invited to imagine which superpower they would most like to possess. This creative, nondirected question allowed participants to express deeper emotional desires and vulnerabilities related to pelvic floor challenges in an empowering and indirect way. Examples of desired superpowers included the ability to *turn back time* - reflecting a longing to undo or revisit physical changes - and *read minds*, reflecting a wish for deeper understanding from others without the need to explain or justify one's condition, particularly in emotionally vulnerable situations. Another notable expression was the desire to be transparent, an aspiration that underscores the profound embarrassment and social distress experienced by the interviewee in certain situations.

The imaginative responses to these two questions offered a unique lens into participants' emotional needs and aspirations and served as a foundation for building enriched personas that goes beyond demographic or task-based profiles, integrating users' values, and aspirational identities into the design process.

These enriched personas, grounded in participants' values and aspirational identities, directly informed the design of *EZpeeZ*'s features. In the next phase, we translated these emotional insights into playful, empowering interactions that embody the UED philosophy.

3.2 *EZpeeZ* Features

The features in *EZpeeZ* were co-designed based on both interview input and consultation with a physiotherapist specializing in pelvic floor health. The interviews revealed core personal values and emotional undercurrents in the women's narratives, guiding us to design not only for physical effectiveness but also for emotional resonance. This led us to integrate humor and playfulness into the app, both to legitimize the experience of pelvic floor challenges and to foster motivation through a lighthearted, empowering approach.

UED theory positions personal empowerment as central to design, structured across four key dimensions: **self-efficacy, independence, meaning,** and **control**. These dimensions guided the design of EZpeeZ's features. While the app includes a broader set of features, due to space limitations, we present four representative examples that illustrate the integration of empowerment dimensions into the user experience:

- *Squeezy Stats* – A visual dashboard that displays daily training completion, breakdown by exercise type, and motivational feedback on performance trends, encouraging consistency and celebrating progress. This feature reinforces **self-efficacy** and **control** by enabling women to monitor achievements, celebrate progress, and take responsibility for managing their pelvic health routine.
- *Easy Peezy Road Squeezy* – A training mode designed to integrate pelvic floor exercises seamlessly into daily commutes. Discreet audio prompts encourage practicing pelvic contractions while driving. This feature enhances **control** by allowing women to optimize otherwise unproductive time, integrating physiotherapy into daily routines without adding extra scheduling pressure. Moreover, current designs often lack interactive feedback and voice guidance [19], which research indicates can boost self-efficacy and motivation by providing empathetic encouragement during exercises (e.g., "Squeeze! Hold! Release! Well done!"). Voice interaction is particularly critical in scenarios such as training during driving, where maintaining attention on the road is essential; audio cues enable safe, hands-free engagement.
- *Peelarious* – Users are challenged to delay urination while watching humorous videos and comedy clips, reframing discomfort through laughter. This playful approach supports **self-efficacy** and **meaning**, turning a clinical task into an empowering, lighthearted challenge aligned with personal values. It helps women feel capable and associate pelvic training with positive, enjoyable experiences rather than clinical obligation.

- *Stopee* – A GPS-enabled feature that helps users find the nearest toilet. Beyond reducing anxiety, this enhances **independence** by allowing women to easily plan restroom stops and confidently move beyond familiar environments, expanding their mobility and social freedom.

These features reframe a delicate health challenge for women as an experience of playfulness, lightness, self-compassion, and a renewed sense of control over their bodies that fosters confidence. By embedding values and empathy into feature design, *EZpeeZ* exemplifies the practical application of UED. The humor embedded in the feature names (microcopy) reflects a deliberate strategy to reduce discomfort and enhance engagement through lightness and wordplay. The name *Squeezy Stats* combines the core action of pelvic floor exercises – squeezing - with the notion of performance statistics, framing bodily training data in a light yet purposeful manner that supports user motivation through playful, self-affirming feedback. *Easy Peezy Road Squeezy* riffs on the familiar phrase "easy peasy lemon squeezy," humorously reframed to support discreet pelvic floor exercises during driving; the cheeky tone makes the activity feel natural, even empowering, in an everyday context. *Peelarious* playfully merges "pee" with "hilarious," accompanying a feature that encourages users to delay urination while watching comedy clips; it turns physical discomfort into laughter, helping reduce embarrassment and promoting a sense of bodily control. *Stopee*, a GPS-based toilet locator, uses a simple pun of "stop" + "pee", to soften urgency and create emotional relief in a potentially stressful situation. Together, these names signal that the app speaks in the user's language - lighthearted, human, and gently irreverent - while reinforcing UED's goal of transforming stigma into confidence through empathetic, playful design.

Figures 1, 2, 3 illustrate the UED approach in practice. Figure 1 displays three representative screens from the *EZpeeZ* application. Shown from left to right are: The *EZpeeZ* splash screen, the *Squeezy Stats* screen, and the *Stopee* map screen. The app opens with a playful splash screen featuring the *EZpeeZ* logo, its cheerful mascot, and a welcoming tagline that sets the tone for the user experience The *Squeezy Stats is a* progress summary screen that offers users a visual and encouraging overview of their daily training. It highlights completion status, type-specific exercise breakdown, and personalized feedback on performance improvements, enhancing motivation and fostering a sense of achievement. The *Stopee* screen displays nearby restroom locations on a map, showing real-time distance and estimated walking time. The familiar interface and simple icons make it easy to quickly identify safe, accessible stops when needed.

Figure 2 displays three representative screens from the *Easy Peezy Road Squeezy* feature, shown from left to right are: The first screen introduces the feature with a friendly prompt, encouraging users to complete short training tasks while driving. The second screen mimics a navigation app interface, providing real-time instructions to squeeze and hold during intervals such as stoplights, transforming idle time into effective muscle training. The third screen celebrates the user's progress with playful, affirming feedback language such as "Queen Squeeze," reinforcing motivation through humor and positivity.

Figure 3 displays three representative screens from the *Peelarious* feature, shown from left to right are: The first screen invites users to select a funny video as part of a training task that requires drinking water and holding during laughter. The second screen reminds users to hydrate before starting the timed squeeze, reinforcing behavior

Fig. 1. Representative screens from the *EZpeeZ* application interface.

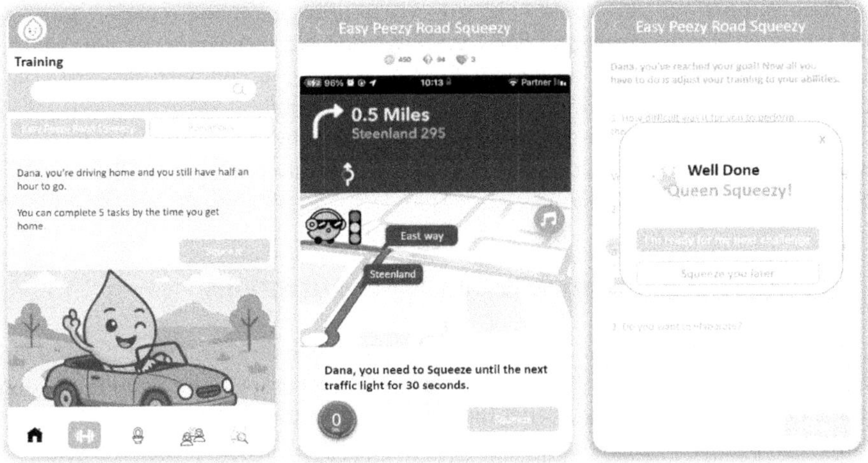

Fig. 2. *Easy Peezy Road Squeezy* screens with playful microcopy.

in a lighthearted way. The third screen uses playful microcopy like "Lady Leakproof!" to celebrate task completion and prompt the next challenge, making training feel enjoyable.

While large-scale user evaluation is planned as the next step, we sought early expert input to validate the conceptual design. A physiotherapist specializing in pelvic floor rehabilitation reviewed the app and provided qualitative feedback on its clinical and motivational aspects. The expert confirmed that the physiotherapy-based exercises integrated into EZpeeZ align with evidence-based practices for pelvic floor strengthening and suggested refinements to ensure clinical accuracy. For example, she provided guidance on recommended water intake in the *Peelarious* feature and offered additional adjustments to optimize exercise parameters and safety. Importantly, she emphasized that the app's

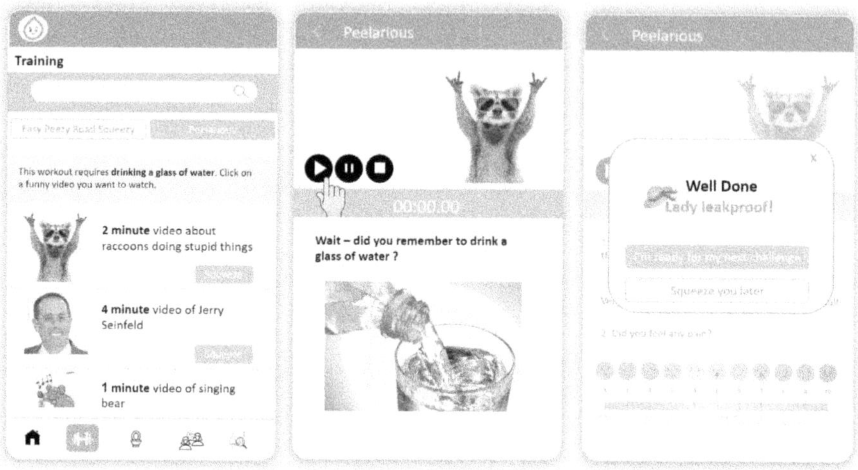

Fig. 3. *Peelarious* screens using humorous microcopy to reframe pelvic floor training.

humorous and playful tone could help reduce embarrassment and increase adherence, if humor remains empathetic and does not downplay the seriousness of the condition. This preliminary input supports the potential of EZpeeZ to combine physical efficacy with emotional resonance, reinforcing its grounding in both medical and user-centered perspectives. Early expert-based evaluations, such as heuristic reviews, are widely recognized as cost-effective methods for identifying usability issues and validating design concepts prior to empirical user testing [22].

4   Conclusions, Limitations and Future Directions

In the dynamic realm of interface design, the emergence of User Empowering Design (UED) signals a critical evolution in the field of human-computer interaction. As digital systems permeate every facet of life, these elements alone no longer suffice to inspire or differentiate. UED emerges as the next frontier and marks a paradigm shift that responds to the evolving expectations of modern users. As usability and UX have become standard design requirements, users increasingly seek technologies that align with their deeper values and aspirations. UED responds to this shift and emphasizes the ability of technology to address higher-order user needs, those related to autonomy, confidence, growth, and a sense of control over one's broader life.

Through the lens of UED, we do not only ask whether users can complete tasks efficiently or enjoyably, but whether the product contributes to their self-efficacy, identity, and long-term well-being. Empowerment becomes the benchmark for meaningful digital innovation. While traditional UCD approaches focus on ensuring functionality, usability, and positive emotional experiences during interaction, UED extends the design process to address empowerment beyond the immediate interface. This expansion introduces both opportunities and challenges in practical development. UED requires a deeper exploration phase, including exercises to identify user values, aspirations, and perceived limitations, as well as additional co-design sessions to translate these insights into empowering features. Creating personas under UED, for instance, involves mapping "main life paths" and strengths/weaknesses, rather than focusing solely on demographics and tasks. These steps often extend early design timelines and require interdisciplinary collaboration (e.g., with domain experts and psychologists). However, they can yield products with greater long-term impact, an outcome that aligns with the growing demand for technologies that improve quality of life.

Our implementation of UED in the '*EZpeeZ*' project demonstrates the practical viability of this approach. By embedding empathy, humor, and user values into the design process, we developed an application that addresses a sensitive medical issue while also enhancing dignity and emotional resilience. The integration of personal 'superpowers' and values into personas exemplifies how UED can transform the traditional design workflow into a deeper and more human-centered process. The activities offered in *EZpeeZ* application create opportunities for women with pelvic floor disorders to take control of their medical condition, while addressing both the practical aspects and emotional well-being.

While humor can reduce stigma and enhance engagement, its integration in health-related applications poses significant design challenges. Since acceptability of humor varies among users, what motivates some may feel trivializing to others. Cultural differences greatly influence how humor is perceived, as highlighted by social media health messaging studies that warn of miscommunication and erosion of trust when humor is misaligned with cultural norms [23]. Experimental work in health media further shows that humor's effectiveness depends on message framing and topic sensitivity, and that it may not uniformly persuade across populations [24]. Even within digital interventions like chatbots, affiliative humor can boost engagement [25], but only when carefully calibrated to user context and expectations. Taken together, these limitations call for inclusive, iterative design and testing with culturally and demographically diverse users, to ensure that humor empowers rather than alienates.

The EZpeeZ app is fully developed and ready for testing; user evaluation studies are the next phase of this research. Building on our completed design process, supported by in-depth interviews and expert feedback, we will conduct individual usability testing sessions within the next 3–4 months to validate and refine EZpeeZ prior to deployment. These sessions will include task-based interaction analysis combined with eye-tracking to identify attention patterns and potential usability barriers in key flows (e.g., exercise initiation, navigation, and progress tracking), providing insights into optimizing design for use while driving or riding as a passenger. We will also examine the impact of our microcopy choices, particularly whether humor is perceived as helpful in reducing embarrassment and legitimizing the medical condition. Following each session, short interviews and standardized questionnaires will assess perceptions of humor, emotional resonance, and perceived empowerment. This mixed-method approach ensures that both functional usability and emotional objectives are achieved before releasing the application to users.

While eye-tracking provides valuable insights into visual attention and interaction patterns, it is limited in capturing real-world, mobile usage contexts. To address this, future work will include field-based evaluations and experience sampling methods to observe interactions in everyday scenarios, as well as longitudinal assessments of empowerment-related outcomes.

In future studies, we plan to examine the app's impact on quality of life across both emotional and physical aspects. Purba [17], for example, used the IIQ-7 quality of life questionnaire for women with urinary incontinence, and found that yoga activities had a greater effect on the emotional aspect of quality of life than physical training. Since our app addresses both the emotional and physical aspects, we aim to explore its influence, as an essential part of empowering women to take control of their condition and improve their overall quality of life.

As designers and researchers, we are called to look beyond usability and delight. UED reminds us that ethical, impactful, and transformative technology is not a luxury, it is a responsibility. By embracing this design paradigm, we can create interfaces that not only serve users but strengthen them.

Acknowledgements. We would like to thank Hadas Vazana and Reut Saban, fourth-year students in the Industrial Engineering and Management Department in SCE, for their significant contributions to the design process and for conducting the in-depth interviews. We also express our gratitude to the UED Institute, and especially to its head, David Gallula, for inspiring us to apply UED principles in our design.

Disclosure of Interests. The authors have no competing interests to declare that are relevant to the content of this article.

References

1. Shneiderman, B.: Human values and the future of technology: a declaration of empowerment. ACM SIGCAS Comput. Soc. **20**(3), 1–6 (1990)
2. Islind, A.S., Rudmark, D., Lind, M.: Proxy design: representing marginalized voices in digital health. arXiv preprint arXiv:2310.18240 (2023)
3. Alt, R., Human, S., Neumann, G.: End-user empowerment in the digital age. In: Bui, T. (ed.) Proceedings of the 53rd Hawaii International Conference on System Sciences, pp. 4099–4101. University of Hawai'i at Mānoa (2020)
4. Lu, X., Kim, Y.H., Rader, E.: Designing Interventions to Empower Users Against Dark Patterns. arXiv preprint arXiv:2310.17846 (2023)
5. Seshadri, P., Joslyn, C., Hynes, M., Reid, T.: Compassionate design: considerations that impact the users' dignity, empowerment and sense of security. Des. Sci. **5**, E21 (2019)
6. Zallio, M., Berry, A., Clarkson, J.: Designing IoT solutions with and for older adults: participatory design and the value of inclusion. arXiv preprint arXiv:2002.06308 (2020)
7. Gallula, D., Frank, A.J.: User empowering design. In: Proceedings of the 2014 European Conference on Cognitive Ergonomics, pp. 1–3 (2014)
8. Nielsen, J.: Usability Engineering. Morgan Kaufmann (1993)
9. Norman, D.A.: Emotional Design: Why We Love (or Hate) Everyday Things. Basic Books (2004)
10. Gallula, D., Ronen, H., Shichel, I., Katz, A.: User empowering design: expanding the users' hierarchy of needs. In: CHIRA, pp. 201–208 (2022)
11. Alderfer, C.P.: An empirical test of a new theory of human needs. Organ. Behav. Hum. Perform. **4**(2), 142–175 (1969)

12. Hancock, P.A., Pepe, A.A., Murphy, L.L.: Hedonomics: The power of positive and pleasurable ergonomics. Ergon. Des. **13**(1), 8–14 (2005)
13. Law, E.L.C., Roto, V., Hassenzahl, M., Vermeeren, A.P., Kort, J.: Understanding, scoping and defining user experience: a survey approach. In: Proceedings of the SIGCHI Conference on Human Factors in Computing Systems, pp. 719–728 (2009)
14. Kano, N.: Attractive quality and must-be quality. J. Japanese Soc. Q. Control **31**(4), 147–156 (1984)
15. Rotar, L.J., Kozar, M.: The use of the Kano model to enhance customer satisfaction. Organizacija **50**(4), 339–349 (2017)
16. Katz, A., Sophia, Y.: A contextualization feature to overcome intergenerational language barriers in communication apps. In: Proceedings of the CHIRA Conference, pp. 166–173 (2021)
17. Purba, J.: Effectiveness of pelvic floor muscle training and yoga on the quality of life in perimenopausal women with urinary incontinence. Nurse Media J. Nurs. **11**(1), 85–93 (2021)
18. Dumoulin, C., Hay-Smith, J., Habée-Séguin, G.: Pelvic floor muscle training versus no treatment, or inactive control treatments, for urinary incontinence in women. Cochrane Database Syst. Rev. **2018**(10), CD005654 (2018)
19. Yi, Z., Romainoor, N.H.: A systematic literature review for interface design of pelvic floor muscle training mobile app based on mHealth (2017–2022). J. Adv. Comput. Technol. Appl. **5**(1), 28–42 (2023)
20. Cooper, A., Reimann, R., Cronin, D.: About Face: The Essentials of Interaction Design, 4th edn. Wiley (2012)
21. Kirmani, N., Rauschenberger, M.: Designing with personas: a case study. J. Usability Stud. **14**(1), 1–14 (2019)
22. Martins, A.I., Queirós, A., Silva, A.G., Rocha, N.P.: Usability evaluation methods: a systematic review. Hum. Factors Softw. Dev. Des. 250–273 (2015)
23. Galea, G., et al.: Funny or risky? Humour in health-related social media. Online J. Commun. Media Technol. **15**(2), e202520 (2025)
24. Suka, M., et al.: Effectiveness of using humor appeal in health promotion materials. Arch Public Health (2023)
25. Sun, X., Teljeur, I., Li, Z., Bosch, J.A.: Can a Funny Chatbot Make a Difference? Infusing Humor into Conversational Agent for Behavioral Intervention. arXiv (2024)

Visual Feature Preferences for Human Vehicle Communication in Mixed Traffic

Lars Gadermann[1]($\boxtimes$) , Julia Schröder[1], Daniel Holder[1] , Miriam Bottesch[2], Cristián Acevedo[2], and Thomas Maier[1]

[1] Institute for Engineering Design and Industrial Design, University of Stuttgart, 70569 Stuttgart, Germany
{lars.gadermann,daniel.holder,
thomas.maier}@iktd.uni-stuttgart.de
[2] studiokurbos GmbH, Königstraße 32, 70173 Stuttgart, Germany
{miriam.bottesch,cristian.acevedo}@kurbos.com

Abstract. With the increasing number of automated vehicles (AV) in future mixed traffic, new challenges arise in the interaction between human road users (HRU) and AVs. External human-machine interfaces (eHMI) are considered a promising approach to bridging the resulting communication gap. Despite numerous investigations and studies, there is still no consensus regarding a satisficing design of eHMI in terms of perceived safety, clarity, and aesthetic appeal. The present paper examines the influence of individual design features on the perception and evaluation of different stakeholders by means of a conjoint analysis. For this purpose, 20 high-quality and professionally created stimulus pattern combinations, based on the features technology, location, colour, and graphic type, were evaluated by 127 participants in an online study. The results show that the feature graphic has the greatest influence of all investigated parameters on the evaluation criteria. Text-based displays particularly enhance clarity and perceived safety, while animations promote aesthetic appeal. A combination of different feature levels could combine positive effects. The study provides specific design indications and highlights the importance of perception- and design-related factors in the development of eHMI.

Keywords: eHMI · Conjoint-Analysis · Vehicle Design Engineering · Mixed Traffic · Human-Machine-Interaction

1 Introduction

Future road traffic will be characterised by the coexistence of automated vehicles (AV) and non-automated or human road users (HRU), such as manual vehicles, pedestrians and cyclists [1–3]. This so-called mixed traffic [4] brings with it new challenges for the interaction of individual road users. As there is no longer a person responsible for controlling the vehicle in automated vehicles, explicit communication is no longer necessary. This previous communication channel has played an important role in existing traffic [5–8].

J. F. Krems et al. (Eds.): CHIRA 2025, CCIS 2836, pp. 34–54, 2026.
https://doi.org/10.1007/978-3-032-16454-4_3

The interaction of vulnerable road users (VRU) such as pedestrians or cyclists with drivers via eye contact or gestures is no longer possible with AVs due to the elimination of the driver. This creates a communication gap between the HRU and the AV, which can lead to comprehension problems, challenges and conflict situations in traffic. As the vehicle's implicit communication via vehicle noise and driving behaviour alone is not sufficient to ensure road safety, a new solution is required at this point. External human-machine interfaces (eHMI) represent a promising and currently frequently investigated option for bridging this communication gap in future road traffic [9, 10].

1.1 Significance

eHMIs represent a technological opportunity to close the communication gap between the AV and the HRU. Various studies already show that the presence of an eHMI increases the efficiency of interaction between the AV and HRU and strengthens the trust of the HRU in the AV [9, 11]. Design studies by vehicle manufacturers and scientific publications show a variety of solution concepts for the design of eHMI on the vehicle [10]. Frequently used methods include a light band, a display or a projection onto the road [10].

In previous research on eHMI, however, there is disagreement about the design of this interface [7, 9, 10, 12]. Questions about the correct positioning, size, colour, technology or even the design of the information content have not yet been clearly clarified and in some cases even show contradictory research results. There are only a few clear and generally valid design recommendations for eHMI [13]. Metaphorically speaking, the eHMI forms a bridge over the communication gap, see Fig. 1. However, there is still no consensus on how this bridge should be built or look so that it is safe to cross, trustworthy and aesthetically pleasing.

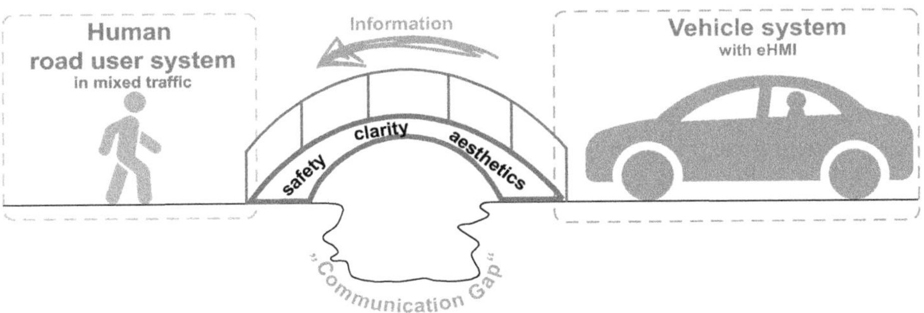

Fig. 1. eHMI as bridge over the communication gap.

1.2 Objective

The aim of this article is to use a conjoint analysis to identify the importance of different design features in terms of perceived safety, clarity and aesthetic appeal. Based on this, design recommendations for eHMI will be developed. For this purpose, visual stimulus patterns from feature combinations of eHMI are created and evaluated by test persons in an online study. The results of the online study and the conjoint analysis will be used to gain insights into the influence of the individual design features on the various requirements of eHMI stakeholders. Based on the conjoint analysis, statements can be made about the relative importance of the features technology, location, colour and graphics for the factors perception of safety, clarity and aesthetic appeal.

2 State of the Art

The selection of features and feature levels in a conjoint analysis can strongly influence the results of the study. For this reason, it is important to make objective and transparently justified assumptions for the selection. For the present study, an extensive review of the state of the art was conducted. A benchmark analysis was used to identify concept vehicles and design studies with a particular focus on identifying key functions and relevant influencing factors that must be considered in the design of an eHMI concept. In addition, a literature review of scientific publications provided insights into the current state of research on eHMI and the effects of different features and variations of eHMI concepts. The following section differentiates between the two areas of benchmark analysis and literature review.

Concept cars are generally used as automotive design studies to present novel approaches [14]. The benchmark analysis shows that many well-known car manufacturers have already dealt with the topic of eHMI. Various communication channels and human sensory perceptions were considered. The eHMI vehicles examined were predominantly presented between 2015 and 2018. In general, the presented eHMI concepts reveal a clear focus on visual representations. Almost all vehicles rely on eHMI concepts with visual stimuli such as displays, light bands, projections, or "digital eyes." These are designed with corresponding text or symbol displays for information transmission.

Regarding the location of eHMI components, a focus on the front of the vehicle (mostly headlights, front bumper, or grille) can be identified. In some cases, extensions at the rear of the vehicle are also visible (e.g., Mercedes-Benz "F015 Concept" or Smart "Vision EQ ForTwo Concept"). Light bands mostly run along the entire side of the body. The main functions of the presented eHMIs include general communication with pedestrians, signaling the possibility of safe road crossing (via text on a display), indicating that the vehicle has noticed the pedestrian, and simulated eye contact.

Most of the concept cars were primarily presented as purely conceptual studies and thus without actual testing or underlying scientific evaluations.

From a scientific perspective, eHMI design is subject to a wide range of influencing factors [15], such as the size and number of observers, light and weather conditions, or the technology used. A frequently studied aspect in this context is the psychological effect of simple eHMI concepts on VRUs interacting with an AV, for instance when they intend to cross the road in front of the AV [10]. However, as the literature review shows, the multitude of existing studies leads in part to contradictory results, making it difficult to derive clear design recommendations [13].

For example, studies by Guo et al. [16] concluded that a pulsing light band or surrounding light strips provide little clarity and thus increase participants' decision times. Oudshoorn et al. [17], Clerq et al. [11], and Wilbrink et al. [18], on the other hand, identified positive effects of pulsing light bands in their studies. Guo et al. [16] also concluded that positioning the eHMI at the front of the vehicle is preferable. Eisma et al. [19] additionally recommended situation-specific displays on the side of the vehicle to convey better-visible information during turning maneuvers. Eisma et al. [18] take a critical view of projecting information onto the road in front of the vehicle, whereas Bazilinskyy et al. [20] and Lui and Rötting [21] support road projections. Contradictions also exist regarding information presentation. For example, Bazilinskyy et al. [20] demonstrated that text is the most clearly understood. However, individual factors such as literacy or language proficiency of VRUs can lead to problems. Rettenmaier et al. [22] also recommend the use of symbols, as these can be perceived from greater distances.

The literature review conducted in this study illustrates the existing discrepancies concerning the effectiveness of various eHMI concepts in the scientific context. Identical or similar concepts led to different results in different studies and experimental setups. This complicates the clear identification of suitable and less suitable concept approaches. Nevertheless, several insights and general recommendations can be derived from the literature.

The evaluation criteria perceived safety and clarity of information can be identified as relevant, as they have been addressed in numerous studies [10, 17, 23, 24]. The location of visual displays, their colour scheme, and content design are also discussed in various studies [10, 23]. As Gadermann et al. [10, 25] show, vehicle design and thus the aesthetic appeal also contribute to the acceptance of eHMIs and consequently of AVs. This is partly due to the fact that different stakeholder groups place different requirements on the vehicle, its design, and its functional components such as eHMIs. In order to consider these different stakeholder interests, the eHMI must be examined from various perspectives [25].

The findings derived from the benchmark analysis and literature review form a meta study which is the basis for the development of the subsequent conjoint analysis.

3 Methods

The method of conjoint analysis originally comes from the field of marketing and is considered one of the most important marketing instruments in that domain. Essentially, this analytical method aims to capture customer preferences in order to improve products or to position them successfully on the market [26]. The term "conjoint" is derived from "considered jointly" [27], which already reflects the core of the method, namely, the joint consideration and evaluation of combinations of individual parameters. Today, conjoint analysis is an established tool in numerous industries [26].

The primary objective of the conjoint method is to determine the utility contributions of individual product attributes. The analysis provides insights into people's preferences regarding products and attributes these to utility values of individual product characteristics. Based on the assumption that overall utility results from the sum of these utility values, a product can be composed of the features with the highest total utility [26, 27]. This multivariate procedure is based on the principle of dependency-analytical methods, where the influence of independent (product) features on dependent variables is estimated [26, 28].

The focus of this paper lies on the rating-based conjoint analysis. In this approach, participants evaluate the stimulus patterns and express a preference; however, they are not required to make an explicit decision for one single variant. The evaluation of the stimulus patterns follows a decompositional approach, meaning that combinations of feature levels are rated and, in a second step, utility contributions of the individual levels and feature relevance are calculated using a top-down method [26, 27, 29]. This holistic evaluation of product alternatives leads to more valid results regarding utility contribution and relevance compared to an isolated assessment of individual features and levels [26].

3.1 Study Design

For the study design of a conjoint analysis, relevant features and characteristics must first be identified and defined. In this case, these resulted from a meta-study of the benchmark analysis and literature research based on design studies and scientific publications. For the further restriction and final selection, a short online survey was also conducted with 133 test subjects (63% male, 37% female, average age 32 years) in order to ascertain preferences and alternatives. The results of the preliminary online survey were incorporated directly into the design of the conjoint study, alongside researched colour effects in the three core markets of Germany, China and the USA as well as symbol effects. Standards and regulations were also considered but were not further taken into account for the present study in order not to further restrict the design freedom for the time being.

The following research question was defined for the conjoint analysis study design:

"What is the utility contribution of different feature levels to the design of eHMIs in terms of perceived safety, clarity, and aesthetic appeal?"

Based on this research question, four features were defined for the analysis on the basis of the literature and benchmark review. The feature *technology* includes the implementation of the individual display concepts of the eHMI. The associated feature levels are *display*, *light band*, and *projection. Location* describes the positioning of the display on the vehicle exterior. The defined levels are *windshield*, *vehicle front*, *roof* or *roof line*, and *vehicle side*. The feature *colour* defines the colour design of the display content and includes the levels *turquoise*, *green*, *pink*, and *orange*. These selected colours were primarily derived from the preliminary online survey. They were associated by participants with automated driving and have so far had little or no usage or meaning in current vehicles. The fourth feature selected was the *graphic* of the display. This includes the levels *text*, *symbol*, and *animation*. Text and symbol are displayed statically, while the abstract animation runs dynamically. Table 1 provides an overview of the defined features and their levels.

The number of feature levels results in $3 \times 4 \times 4 \times 3 = 144$ different combination possibilities. Since this number of stimulus patterns would be far too high for a participant survey, an orthogonal design was applied. This systematically reduced the study design to 16 stimulus patterns, while still allowing for a retrospective calculation of utility values for all possible combinations. In addition to the 16 stimulus pattern combinations, 4 holdout cards were created, resulting in a total of 20 stimulus patterns used in the study.

For conducting the study, the CAWI method (Computer Assisted Web Interviewing) was implemented via the online platform *SoSci Survey* [30]. The desired confidence level of 90% was achieved with a minimum sample size of 68 participants. To motivate participants, an incentive in the form of a prize draw (10 vouchers worth €15 each) was offered. The study design initially included general questions on attitudes toward automated driving. In the main part, the stimulus patterns with the respective feature combinations were evaluated. The order of the 20 stimulus patterns was randomized to avoid sequence effects. At the end, demographic data were collected, and open questions were asked for feedback on the presented stimuli. For those participants who indicated they work professionally in the design field, a design-specific feedback option was provided.

Table 1. Features and feature levels of conjoint analysis.

Features and feature levels of conjoint analysis

Feature	Feature level 1	Feature level 2	Feature level 3	Feature level 4
Technology	Display	Light band	Projection	
Location	Windshield	Front	Roof	Side
Colour	Turquoise	Green	Pink	Orange
Graphics	Text	Symbol	Animation	

To gather multiple perspectives on eHMI design according to Gadermann et al. [25], the following three questions were asked to evaluate the stimulus patterns:

- Perception of safety: *How safe do you feel crossing the road when the following automated vehicle is approaching?*
- Clarity: *How clear is the information from the approaching automated vehicle that you can cross the road?*
- Aesthetic appeal: *How aesthetically appealing do you find the presentation and integration of the eHMI in the shown vehicle design?*

Each question was rated using a 6-point Likert scale (1: very uncertain/very unclear/not at all appealing - 6: very certain/very clear/very appealing) and analysed individually. Three individual conjoint analyses were therefore carried out. The general questions covered attitudes towards automated driving, previous experiences with automated vehicles, demographic questions and open feedback options. In the event that the respondents work in the design sector, there were some design questions and design-specific feedback options. The 20 stimulus patterns with their combinations of characteristics are presented below.

3.2 Stimulus Patterns

The creation of the stimulus patterns for the conjoint analysis was carried out in close collaboration with the Stuttgart-based design studio studiokurbos within the framework of the research project SALSA (Smart, Adaptive, and Learnable Systems for All) [31]. A commonly studied road-crossing scenario was chosen for the online study, in which a pedestrian (from the participant's perspective) intends to cross the road in front of an automated vehicle, see Fig. 2. There were no infrastructural elements such as pedestrian crossings or traffic lights present.

The vehicle shown in the stimulus patterns is a generic vehicle without brand-specific design language or identifying features. A van-like CC design (cf. [32]) was selected as the vehicle class. The scenario is presented as a static image, with the AV approaching from the left side. Apart from the animations, the different displays were also static. All information from the eHMI was presented egocentrically from the vehicle's perspective and always conveyed the message that the vehicle is going to stop.

Fig. 2. Road-Crossing Scenario with perspective of the test persons.

For the *text* level, the static display "I will stop" was selected. The *symbol* level consisted of an image of a vehicle with a walking pedestrian shown in front of it. The *animation* displayed glowing dots moving outward from the center, representing the stopping intention in a highly abstract manner. The stimulus patterns were shown in the colours *turquoise*, *green*, *pink*, and *orange*, and were positioned on the *windshield*, the *front* of the vehicle, the *roof/roof line*, and the *vehicle side*.

For the *display* level, the information content was always placed on a black background, representing the integrated display surface. The *light band* was visualized using a narrow LED strip. The *projection*, in contrast to the commonly studied road projection, was always shown on the vehicle exterior. The difference compared to the *display* lay in the absence of the black background, as illustrated in Fig. 3.

Fig. 3. Comparison between display with text (left) and projection with symbol (right).

All stimulus patterns were developed and discussed iteratively with the designers from studiokurbos. During the creation process, particular attention was paid to the independence of the feature levels, and design integration was also considered. The stimulus patterns stand out from most patterns found in the reviewed studies due to the professional elaboration by the designers. This is based on the fact that many studies mention a desire for a higher degree of realism as one of their limitations [10]. The high-quality exterior designs are intended to also take vehicle design into account, while the overall presentation of the scenario remains at an abstract level in order to maintain the study's focus on the feature levels. Figure 4 shows an overview of the 20 stimulus patterns created and used in the study. The patterns with the animation level (numbers 1, 2, 8, 13, 17) are shown in their full representation in Fig. 4.

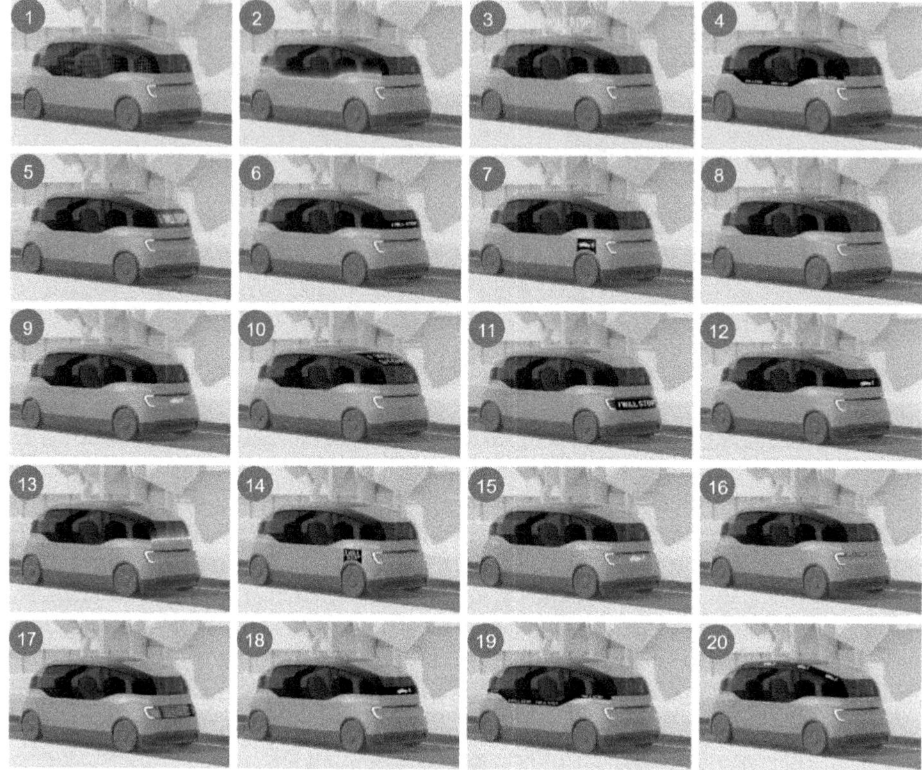

Fig. 4. Overview of the stimulus patterns used in the study.

4 Results

A total of 127 participants took part in the study during a three-week period in March 2025. Of these, 41% were female, 58% male, and 1% diverse. The participants were between 20 and 85 years old, with an average age of 36.21 years and a modal value of 27 years. The sample consisted predominantly of German participants (92%), with a few individuals of other nationalities (Spanish, Egyptian, Bosnian-Herzegovinian, Brazilian, British, Indian, Italian, Pakistani, and Taiwanese - each 1%).

In terms of educational background, 36% of participants reported holding a Master's degree, 35% a Bachelor's degree. Some participants had a high school diploma (9%), vocational training (6%), or a doctoral degree (6%). Professionally, the participants came primarily from the automotive industry (34%), research and development (17%), or were still students (13%). A total of 32% of the participants stated that they work in design, of which 65% are employed in automotive design, 15% in product design, and 13% in UI/UX design. Figure 5 visually presents the most important demographic data.

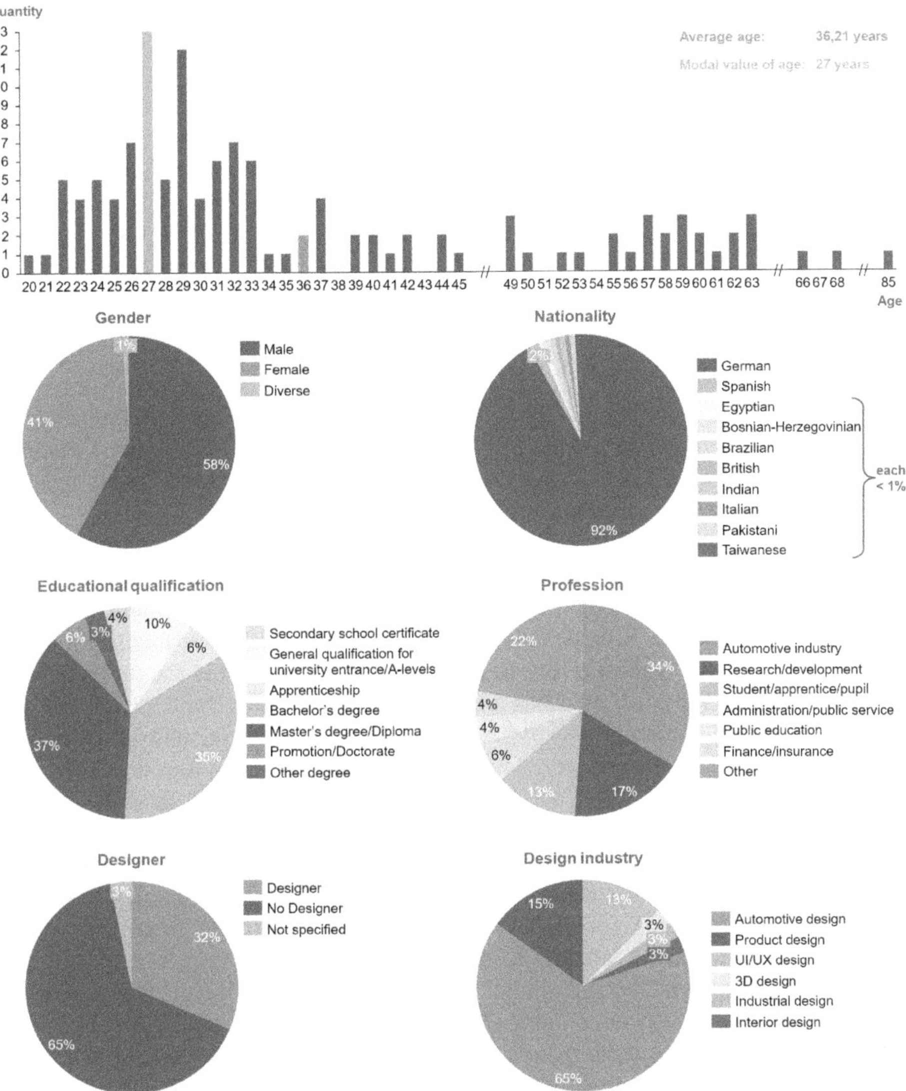

Fig. 5. Demografic data.

The results of the general questions show that 53% of participants completed the study on a computer, 46% on a smartphone, and 1% on a tablet. 98% of participants possessed a driver's license, and only 20% had previously been involved in a traffic accident as a pedestrian or cyclist. 21% had already ridden in an automated vehicle.

Regarding the participants' self-assessment, they indicated a moderate level of risk tolerance, a tendency toward high self-confidence, and low levels of anxiety. Physical activity was mostly rated between medium and very high, while patience was rated between low and high. Figure 6 presents the self-assessment data in bar chart format.

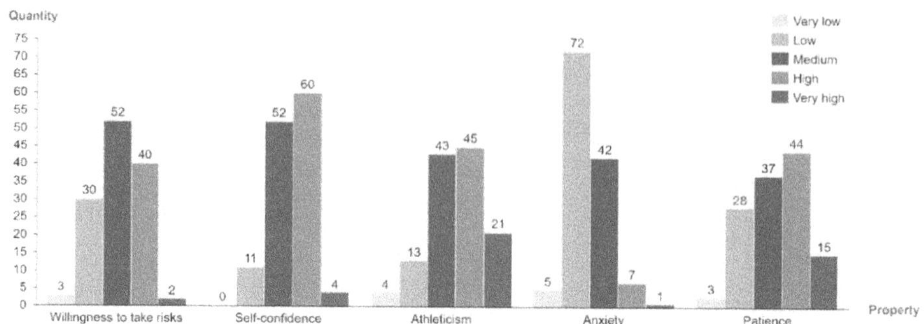

Fig. 6. Bar charts for the self-assessment of the test subjects.

The results of the conjoint analysis for the three questions *perceived safety*, *clarity*, and *aesthetic appeal* are presented in Fig. 7. The figure shows the utility values and standard errors for each feature and its levels for each of the questions. On the right side of the figure, the utility values are also visualized in diagram form.

For perceived safety, the feature *technology* shows that the level *projection* has moderately positive utility values (0.227). The *light band* has moderately negative values (−0.225). For *display*, the standard error is greater than the calculated utility value, so no reliable statement can be made regarding its utility. For the feature *location*, the level *windshield* shows the highest utility value with 0.198. The *front* is also in the positive range with 0.119. The level *roof* has a stronger negative utility value of −0.201. The *side* level lies in the slightly negative range (−0.116). Minor deviations in perceived safety are observed for the feature colour. The utility values for the four levels *turquoise* (−0.064), *green* (0.073), *pink* (0.037), and *orange* (−0.046) are all close to zero, and in all cases the standard error (0.075) is greater than the calculated utility values. The greatest difference between level utility values for perceived safety is found in the feature *graphics*. Here, the level *text* is rated clearly positive (0.883), while the level *symbol* is slightly negative (−0.177), and the level *animation* is rated strongly negative (−0.706). The constant for perceived safety is 3.280.

For the question on clarity, a similar pattern emerges as with perceived safety. The feature *technology* is rated analogously (*light band* −0.248; *projection* 0.254; no reliable statement for *display*), and the feature *location* shows the same tendencies in a similar range as with perceived safety (*windshield* 0.200; *front* 0.125; *roof* −0.194; *side* − 0.131). Again, no reliable statement can be made regarding the feature colour, as the standard error (0.087) is greater than the calculated utility values for *turquoise* (−0.069), *green* (0.034), *pink* (0.065), and *orange* (−0.030). The feature *graphic* also shows similar but even more pronounced utility value variations for clarity. The *text* level has the highest utility contribution with 1.163, while the levels *symbol* (−0.203) and *animation* (−0.959) show slightly to clearly negative contributions. The constant for clarity is 3.144.

For the question on aesthetic appeal, the conjoint analysis reveals similar tendencies, though some differences compared to the other two questions are apparent. The feature *technology* shows a slightly negative utility value for the level *display* (−0.135). For the *light band*, the standard error (0.125) again exceeds the calculated utility value (−0.082). The level *projection* is in the moderately positive range (0.217). The feature *location* shows stronger positive utility values for *windshield* (0.310) and *front* (0.321) for aesthetic appeal compared to the other two questions. *Roof* (−0.346) and *side* (−0.285) are rated more clearly negative. Regarding the feature *colour*, no clear statements can be made (standard error 0.139 > utility value magnitudes for *turquoise* 0.079; *green* 0.002; *pink* 0.091), except for a slightly negative rating of the colour *orange* (−0.173).

The strongest differences in the evaluation of aesthetic appeal compared to the previously mentioned questions appear in the feature *graphic*. While *text* was rated strongly positive for perceived safety and clarity, its utility contribution for aesthetic appeal is slightly negative (−0.114). The *symbol* level is rated more negatively (−0.313). The most significant difference is shown by the *animation* level. While it showed no added value for perceived safety and clarity, *animation* is rated clearly positively for aesthetic appeal (0.427). The constant for aesthetic appeal is 3.449.

Attribute	Characteristics	Perception of safety		Clarity		Aesthetic appeal		Visualization of the utility factors
		Utility factor	Standard error	Utility factor	Standard error	Utility factor	Standard error	
Technology	Display	-0,002	0,057	-0,007	0,067	-0,135	0,107	
	Light band	-0,225	0,067	-0,248	0,078	-0,082	0,125	
	Projection	0,227	0,067	0,254	0,078	0,217	0,125	
Location	Windshield	0,198	0,075	0,200	0,087	0,310	0,139	
	Front	0,119	0,075	0,125	0,087	0,321	0,139	
	Roof	-0,201	0,075	-0,194	0,087	-0,346	0,139	
	Side	-0,116	0,075	-0,131	0,087	-0,285	0,139	
Colour	Turquoise	-0,064	0,075	-0,069	0,087	0,079	0,139	
	Green	0,073	0,075	0,034	0,087	0,002	0,139	
	Pink	0,037	0,075	0,065	0,087	0,091	0,139	
	Orange	-0,046	0,075	-0,030	0,087	-0,173	0,139	
Graphics	Text	0,883	0,057	1,163	0,067	-0,114	0,107	
	Symbol	-0,177	0,067	-0,203	0,078	-0,313	0,125	
	Animation	-0,706	0,067	-0,959	0,078	0,427	0,125	
Constant		3,280	0,048	3,144	0,055	3,449	0,089	

Fig. 7. Results of the conjoint analysis – Utility factors.

Based on the calculated utility values, the relative importance of the features for the three questions can also be determined. These are shown in Fig. 8. The feature *graphic* has the highest relative importance for all three questions, with the most pronounced effects seen for perceived safety and clarity. The feature *location* ranks second in relative importance for each question. Compared to the utility value calculations presented above, it is noticeable that *colour* ranks third and thus shows a higher relative importance than *technology*, which has the lowest relative importance.

Attribute	Perception of safety	Clarity	Aesthetic appeal	Visualization of the relative importance in %
	Relative importance in %	Relative importance in %	Relative importance in %	
Technology	16,400	15,702	19,037	
Location	21,052	19,450	27,141	
Colour	20,139	18,611	23,384	
Graphics	41,616	46,237	30,437	
Total	100	100	100	

Fig. 8. Relative importance of the features for the three questions.

The model quality can be assessed using the four holdout cards implemented in the conjoint analysis. This evaluation is also carried out separately for the assessed criteria perceived safety, clarity, and aesthetic appeal. To validate model quality, the three metrics Pearson's r, Kendall's Tau, and Kendall's Tau for holdout cards are used. Figure 9 summarizes and visualizes the correlation results from the analyses. The bars on the right side of the figure represent the values of the individual metrics.

The Pearson correlation coefficient (Pearson's r) measures the linear relationship between variables and indicates how well the estimated overall utility values from the conjoint analysis correspond to the actual ratings of the holdout cards. Kendall's Tau measures how well the estimated preference model, based on utility values, matches the actual preferences of the participants. The maximum possible value for each correlation is 1.0. The significance value indicates the probability that the results occurred by chance. The smaller the significance value, the more valid the results.

Key figure	Perception of safety		Clarity		Aesthetic appeal		Visualization of the key figure for the model quality
	Value	Significance	Value	Significance	Value	Significance	
Pearson's r	0,991	<0,001	0,993	<0,001	0,931	<0,001	
Kendall's Tau	0,946	<0,001	0,962	<0,001	0,733	<0,001	
Kendall's Tau for test cards	1,000	0,021	1,000	0,021	0,333	0,248	

Fig. 9. Correlations for assessing the quality of the model.

The Pearson's r values are 0.991 for perceived safety, 0.993 for clarity, and 0.931 for aesthetic appeal, all close to the maximum value. The Kendall's Tau values are 0.946 for perceived safety, 0.962 for clarity, and 0.733 for aesthetic appeal. The significance level for these values is < 0.001 and is therefore statistically highly significant. For the holdout cards, the Kendall's Tau values are 1.000 for perceived safety and clarity, and 0.333 for aesthetic appeal. With a significance level of 0.021 for perceived safety and clarity, these results are also significant. For aesthetic appeal, the significance is 0.248.

In addition to model quality, participants' self-assessment of the validity of their stimulus evaluations was collected as part of the study. This included the recognizability of the features (Fig. 10, left), the difficulty in providing a rating (Fig. 10, center), and the confidence that the given ratings reflect their own preferences (Fig. 10, right). The results are shown in Fig. 10 and indicate a medium to very high validity of the stimuli according to participants' self-assessment.

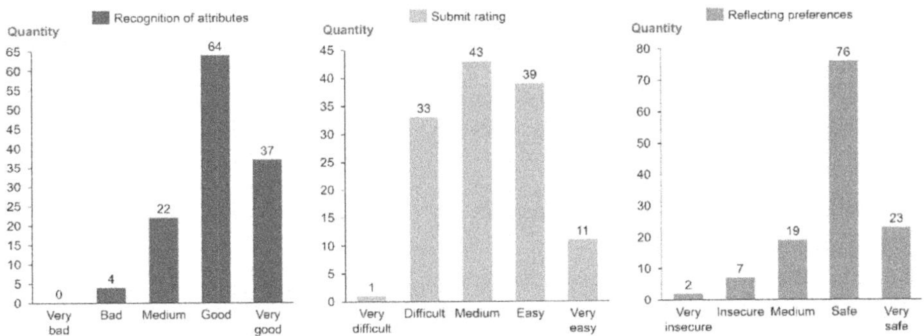

Fig. 10. Evaluation of the supplementary questions on the self-assessment of the respondents' ratings.

The open feedback on positive and negative aspects was categorized and clustered. A frequently mentioned criterion was the positioning. Multiple participants expressed the desire to combine the front and side of the vehicle for the eHMI. The main reason stated was improved visibility and legibility, especially when approaching the vehicle or from oblique angles at close range.

Text-based messages such as "I will stop" were highlighted as particularly clear, while potential limitations for children or individuals with language barriers were also mentioned. It was noted that symbols could be more intuitive and independent of language. Therefore, a combination of text and symbols was suggested to enable more universal use. In addition to the country-specific language, English was recommended as an additional global language. An animated, left-to-right representation with text and symbols was also proposed several times. Furthermore, the idea of using communication strategies depending on the distance to the vehicle was mentioned, such as large, coloured displays on the front for long-range visibility and animated displays on the sides for close-range interaction.

Regarding the design integration of eHMIs into the vehicle body, several designers formulated the goal of creating a unified and harmonious overall appearance. The eHMI components should be seamlessly embedded into the vehicle's design language and materiality. The form-fitting integration of lighting elements into existing body surfaces, such as painted plastic parts on fenders or bumpers, was rated positively. Additional display surfaces mounted on the exterior were rated negatively. From a design perspective, the combination of front and side positioning was also seen as positive. Several designers even recommended "360-degree communication" around the vehicle. Curved surfaces such as windshields were considered less suitable from a technical perspective. Integrated light guidance was emphasized as particularly important, enabling consistent lines without visual breaks.

For the design of the eHMI display, the importance of human perception in stressful situations was emphasized. The detectability of signals within a few seconds, gaze behavior, and fields of view were considered crucial. A combination of text, symbol, and colour was recommended. As a central design principle, the use of internationally comprehensible symbols was proposed, enabling immediate understanding even in the presence of language barriers. Text-based information should not be used alone, but rather in a supporting role to symbols and colour design. Special attention should be given to high-contrast and accessible colour choices, for example, considering red-green colour blindness. Additionally, it was pointed out that a friendly and trust-building design has a positive effect on user acceptance.

5   Discussion and Limitations

The conjoint analysis of the three questions on perceived safety, clarity, and aesthetic appeal shows that the investigated features exhibit clear differences in their influence on participants' perception. The baseline attitude of participants toward the stimulus patterns can be derived from the calculated constants for each question. With values just above 3, the baseline tendency of participants lies in the positive range, when compared to the Likert scale used for the evaluation (1 negative – 6 positive). This baseline attitude, expressed through the constant, is altered to varying degrees by the different features. In general, the greater the range between the part-worth utilities of the feature levels, the stronger the impact on the evaluation of eHMI design.

The feature *graphic* in particular shows a comparatively large range. Accordingly, graphic can be attributed greater importance in design compared to the other features examined. For designers and developers, this means that modifying the graphic element represents the most effective lever among the studied parameters in eHMI design. Thus, the effort invested in developing the graphic is used most efficiently. A well-developed graphic element provides the greatest positive benefit for eHMI design.

Technology, *location*, and *colour* play a rather subordinate role in this context. Nevertheless, some interesting insights can be derived from the results of these features. As the findings show, colour design does not significantly influence perceived safety or clarity. For aesthetic appeal, the effects are also relatively small but already more meaningful. From a design perspective, this may indicate a degree of design flexibility. Since colour design appears to have less impact on safety-relevant functions of eHMI, there is a certain amount of creative freedom here. However, effects of colour and existing meanings in road traffic should still be taken into account.

With regard to *location*, a recommendation can be made for positioning on the front of the vehicle. Depending on the situation, an additional display option on the side or a 360-degree display should also be considered. This is especially evident in the open feedback provided by the design experts. In addition, the experts recommend seamlessly integrating eHMI components into the vehicle's design language and materiality. This interpretation is also supported by the utility values for location and technology. Compared to the stimulus pattern concepts placed on the front of the vehicle, the side-mounted concepts, especially those above the wheel arch, are less integrated into the design language. The side positioning was rated lower overall. Likewise, the display was rated lower than the projection. The only difference between display and projection was the black background of the display. The projection on the vehicle's exterior appears more seamlessly integrated into the overall design. This seems to trigger positive perception effects among participants.

The graphic feature as shown in the presented variants exhibits a goal conflict. While text contributes strongly positively to perceived safety and clarity, and animation strongly negatively, the opposite is observed regarding aesthetic appeal. Combined with the open feedback from participants, this leads to the hypothesis that an optimized solution may lie in combining graphic types. An animated text could create synergy effects, combining the positive, safe, and clear perception of text with the aesthetic of animation. This could potentially be transferred to symbols as well. The slightly negative rating of the symbol may also have been caused by the specific symbol used in the stimulus patterns. A more familiar symbol or an animation of symbols, for instance, using widely recognized pictograms, could alter the perception of this graphic level again. Most importantly, the interpretive ambiguity of the symbol's meaning could be reduced, thus enhancing perceived safety and clarity. In combination with animation, the aesthetic dimension may also be enhanced, since this would broaden the design possibilities. Compared to previous methods used for eHMI studies, see state of the art, conjoint analysis offers the possibility of evaluating the significance of individual features and their relative importance. Due to the variety of design options in eHMI development, it is difficult to find specific good solutions that bring added value. Many adjusting screws that can be changed on the eHMI, such as position, technology, colour, size or even the information content, obscure the effect that the individual changes to the features have. By using conjoint analysis, which originally comes from the marketing sector, precisely these effects can be uncovered in the form of part-worth utility value. This represents a methodological innovation in eHMI development.

The conjoint analysis provides a part-worth utility value for each feature level. Together with the constant, these part-worth utilities can be combined into overall utility values for feature combinations. If, for each feature of this study, the level with the highest part-worth utility is selected, a target configuration can be visualized. This configuration represents the best possible compromise across the three questions on perceived safety, clarity, and aesthetic appeal. The target configuration is therefore a vehicle with a text projection on the windshield in the colour pink. The target configuration is shown in Fig. 11.

Fig. 11. Target configuration with the highest overall utility.

This target configuration represents the theoretically optimal combination of attributes with regard to the three evaluated questions. This theoretical approach of conjoint analysis is commonly used in marketing, as psychological factors influencing purchase decisions can be easily combined in this context. However, in the present case of eHMI product development, the theoretical combination of attributes with their respective best-performing levels must be critically examined.

Despite the high model quality and explanatory power, the conjoint analysis inherently involves limitations due to the definition of features and levels, the stimulus design, and the chosen method itself. The relative importance values only reflect the share of the investigated features in the total utility. It cannot be ruled out that other features not included in the analysis may have a greater influence on utility values. Additionally, due to the strict separation of features and the required independence of levels in conjoint analysis, combinations of levels within a single feature (e.g., symbol and animation, text and animation, symbol and text) cannot be examined. Possible synergy effects that could lead to improved perception can only be assumed and logically derived, but cannot be statistically confirmed using this method.

The target configuration shown above is therefore only of limited significance. The truly relevant contributions to eHMI research can be derived indirectly. As previously mentioned, small variations in the part-worth utilities may indicate a certain degree of design freedom and creative potential, for example in terms of colour or technology. Based on the ratings for projection compared to display, as well as the additive positioning above the wheel arch, conclusions can also be drawn about the level of design integration. The findings of Gadermann et al. [25] are supported by this.

The positive evaluation of text must also be seen in context. Given that the participants, based on the composition of the sample, were most likely all able to read and understand English text, the text level of the *graphic* attribute was likely the most clearly understood. However, since the study involved participants' first contact with the presented concepts and the meanings of symbol and animation were not clearly explained in advance, a distortion may have occurred. A learning effect, similar to that of a traffic light (red = stop, green = go) could also emerge in the case of abstract animations or symbols. These may, in fact, be better suited for inclusion of children or individuals who cannot read or understand the language. In future studies, this hypothesis could be validated by providing prior explanation of animated symbols or similar elements.

Another limitation of the study lies in the design of the stimulus patterns. While great emphasis was placed on professionalism, quality, and realistic integration during the creation of the stimuli, the representation is still a static image, capturing a single moment in time in front of an abstract background. As a result, the level of immersion from the participants' perspective is lower compared to, for example, a VR study or a real-world prototype in traffic. Furthermore, the evaluation was conducted on a screen using a computer or smartphone. In addition to varying display sizes, possibly affecting the visibility of all parameters, distractions such as messenger pop-ups or other people during the evaluation process cannot be excluded.

On the other hand, this is contrasted by the predominantly positive feedback from participants regarding the recognizability of the stimuli, as assessed through self-report.

Moreover, the quality of stimulus visualization, developed by professional designers, stands out clearly in comparison to the visualizations commonly found in the literature.

6 Conclusion and Future Work

As part of this paper, a conjoint analysis was conducted to determine the influence of various design features of eHMIs on the perception and evaluation of participants. The features technology (display, light band, projection), location (windshield, front, roof, side), colour (turquoise, green, pink, orange), and graphic (text, symbol, animation) were combined and visualized in high-quality, professionally created stimulus patterns. In an online survey with 127 participants, the stimulus patterns were evaluated with regard to perceived safety, clarity, and aesthetic appeal. The results were analyzed using a conjoint analysis, and the part-worth utilities of the features as well as their relative importance for eHMI design were determined.

The results of the study show that the effectiveness of eHMIs significantly depends on the design of visual features and their perception by users. In particular, the graphic feature proves to be an effective design lever for eHMIs and a key influencing factor for the three evaluated criteria. Text displays especially promote perceived safety and are clearly understandable, whereas animations are perceived as more aesthetically pleasing. A combination of different feature levels may lead to a balanced and optimized solution.

The preferred placement at the front of the vehicle, as well as the integrative appearance of projection, emphasize the design requirements for integrating eHMI into the vehicle design. The open feedback from participants and design experts also recommends a combination of feature levels integrated into the overall vehicle design. This combination of levels could be examined more closely in future studies. Based on the open feedback from participants, the study design could be further developed, particularly by focusing on the graphic feature, and tested in greater depth using more immersive methods such as VR studies with high-quality, realistic stimuli.

The conjoint results indicate that further development work should be invested in the graphical visualization of eHMI information. In doing so, the integration of the respective technology into the overall vehicle design should always consider various design aspects such as shape or colour. Clear recognizability from different viewing angles is also advantageous. Regarding technology and colour design, there appear to be certain degrees of freedom for designers that allow for harmonious integration into the vehicle design.

Disclosure of Interests.

The authors have no competing interests to declare that are relevant to the content of this article.

Acknowledgments. This research was supported by the German Federal Ministry for Economic Affairs and Climate Action on the basis of a decision by the German Bundestag in the research project "SALSA – Smart, Adaptive and Learnable Systems for All". Special thanks to the Stuttgart design studio studiokurbos for creating and providing the stimulus samples.

References

1. Albrecht, T., Kühne, B., Verse, B.: Digitalisierung und Automatisierung im Verkehr. Ein regulativer Rahmen für eine nachhaltige Entwicklung (2023). https://www.umweltbun desamt.de/sites/default/files/medien/1410/publikationen/2023-07-07_broschuere_digitalisi erung-im-verkehr.pdf. Accessed 28 Apr 2025
2. Kolarova, V., Stark, K., Hedemann, L., Lenz, B., Jung, A., Pützschler, M.: Die Automatisierung des Automobils und ihre Folgen. Chancen und Risiken selbstfahrender Fahrzeuge für nachhaltige Mobilität (2020). https://www.agora-verkehrswende.de/fileadmin/Projekte/2020/Automatisierung_des_Automobils/Agora_Verkehrswende_Automatisierung_des_Automobils_und_ihre_Folgen.pdf
3. Tabone, W., et al.: Vulnerable road users and the coming wave of automated vehicles: expert perspectives. Transp. Res. Interdisc. Perspect. (9) (2021). https://doi.org/10.1016/j.trip.2020.100293
4. Hübner, M., Feierle, A., Rettenmaier, M., Bengler, K.: External communication of automated vehicles in mixed traffic: addressing the right human interaction partner in multi-agent simulation. Transp. Res. Part F Traffic Psychol. Behav. **87**, 365–378 (2022). https://doi.org/10.1016/j.trf.2022.04.017
5. Carmona, J., Guindel, C., Garcia, F., La Escalera, A. de: eHMI: review and guidelines for deployment on autonomous vehicles. Sensors **21**(9) (2021). https://doi.org/10.3390/s21092912
6. Dey, D., Matviienko, A., Berger, M., Pfleging, B., Martens, M., Terken, J.: Communicating the intention of an automated vehicle to pedestrians: the contributions of eHMI and vehicle behavior. Inf. Technol. **63**(2), 123–141 (2021). https://doi.org/10.1515/itit-2020-0025
7. Dey, D., Ackermans, S., Martens, M., Pfleging, B., Terken, J.: Interactions of automated vehicles with road users. In: Riener, A., Jeon, M., Alvarez, I. (Hg.) User Experience Design in the Era of Automated Driving. Studies in Computational Intelligence, Bd. 980, pp. 533–581. Springer, Cham (2022)
8. Lee, Y.M., et al.: Learning to interpret novel eHMI: the effect of vehicle kinematics and eHMI familiarity on pedestrian' crossing behavior. J. Saf. Res. **80**, 270–280 (2022). https://doi.org/10.1016/j.jsr.2021.12.010
9. de Winter, J., Dodou, D.: External human–machine interfaces: gimmick or necessity? Transp. Res. Interdisc. Perspect. **15**, 100643 (2022). https://doi.org/10.1016/j.trip.2022.100643
10. Gadermann, L., Holder, D., Maier, T.: Increasing acceptance through design: review of evaluation methods for interaction design in mixed traffic. NordDESIGN, 12. - 14.08.2024, Reykjavik (2024). https://doi.org/10.35199/NORDDESIGN2024.14
11. de Clercq, K., Dietrich, A., Núñez Velasco, J.P., de Winter, J., Happee, R.: External human-machine interfaces on automated vehicles: effects on pedestrian crossing decisions. Hum. Factors **61**(8), 1353–1370 (2019). https://doi.org/10.1177/0018720819836343
12. Brill, S., Payre, W., Debnath, A., Horan, B., Birrell, S.: External human-machine interfaces for automated vehicles in shared spaces: a review of the human-computer interaction literature. Sensors **23**(9) (2023). https://doi.org/10.3390/s23094454
13. Dey, D., et al.: Taming the eHMI jungle: a classification taxonomy to guide, compare, and assess the design principles of automated vehicles' external human-machine interfaces. Transp. Res. Interdisc. Perspect. **20**(7), 1–24 (2020). https://doi.org/10.1016/j.trip.2020.100174
14. Polestar Performance AB: Die Bedeutung von Konzeptfahrzeugen (2024). https://www.pol estar.com/de/news/the-importance-of-concept-car. Accessed 28 Apr 2025

15. Gadermann, L., Holder, D., Maier, T.: A theoretical approach to design communication in mixed traffic. In: Paetzold-Byhain, K., Augsten, A., Krzywinski, J. (eds.) Entwerfen Entwickeln Erleben 2024. Technical University of Dresden, pp. 183–195 (2024). https://doi.org/10.25368/2024.EEE.016

16. Guo, F., Lyu, W., Ren, Z., Li, M., Liu, Z.: A video-based, eye-tracking study to investigate the effect of eHMI modalities and locations on pedestrian–automated vehicle interaction. Sustainability **14**(9), 5633 (2022). https://doi.org/10.3390/su14095633

17. Oudshoorn, M., de Winter, J., Bazilinskyy, P., Dodou, D.: Bio-inspired intent communication for automated vehicles. Transp. Res. Part F Traffic Psychol. Behav. **80**, 127–140 (2021). https://doi.org/10.1016/j.trf.2021.03.021

18. Wilbrink, M., Lau, M., Illgner, J., Schieben, A., Oehl, M.: Impact of external human–machine interface communication strategies of automated vehicles on pedestrians' crossing decisions and behaviors in an urban environment. Sustainability **13**(15), 8396 (2021). https://doi.org/10.3390/su13158396

19. Eisma, Y.B., van Bergen, S., ter Brake, S.M., Hensen, M.T.T., Tempelaar, W.J., de Winter, J.C.F.: External human–machine interfaces: the effect of display location on crossing intentions and eye movements. Information **11**(1), 13 (2020). https://doi.org/10.3390/info11010013

20. Bazilinskyy, P., Dodou, D., de Winter, J.: Survey on eHMI concepts: the effect of text, colour, and perspective. Transp. Res. Part F Traffic Psychol. Behav. **67**, 175–194 (2019). https://doi.org/10.1016/j.trf.2019.10.013

21. Liu, Y., Rötting, M.: External Human-Machine Interface Designed for Autonomous Vehicle-to-Pedestrian Communication: Effectiveness and User Acceptance, Berlin (2020)

22. Rettenmaier, M., Schulze, J., Bengler, K.: How much space is required? Effect of distance, content, and colour on external human–machine interface size. Information **11**(7), 346 (2020). https://doi.org/10.3390/info11070346

23. Gao, Y., Wang, L., Zhang, Z.: Scalable eHMI: automated vehicles-pedestrian interactions design based on gestalt principles. IASDR 2023: Life-Changing Design, 09/10/2023, Design Research Society (2023)

24. Gadermann, L., Fischer, L., Holder, D., Ihle, N., Schlecht, J., Maier, T.: Design strategies compared: how eHMI are perceived in relation to the exterior design of automated vehicles. In: Ahram, T. (ed.): Ergonomics In Design. 14th International Conference on Applied Human Factors and Ergonomics (AHFE 2023) (2023). https://doi.org/10.54941/ahfe1003417

25. Gadermann, L., Holder, D., Maier, T.: Bridging stakeholder demands: the role of vehicle design in the development of external human-machine interfaces. In: Hölzle, K., Krei-meyer, M., Roth, D., Maier, T., Riedel, O. (eds.): Stuttgarter Symposium für Produkt-entwicklung SSP 2025. Fraunhofer IAO, Stuttgart (2025)

26. Baier, D., Brusch, M.: Conjointanalyse. Springer, Heidelberg (2021). https://doi.org/10.1007/978-3-662-63364-9

27. Backhaus, K., Erichson, B., Gensler, S., Weiber, R., Weiber, T.: Conjoint-analyse. In: Backhaus, K., Erichson, B., Gensler, S., Weiber, R., Weiber, T. (Hg.) Multivariate Analysemethoden. Springer Fachmedien Wiesbaden, Wiesbaden, pp. 577–653 (2021)

28. Homburg, C.: Marketingmanagement. Springer Fachmedien Wiesbaden, Wiesbaden (2020). https://doi.org/10.1007/978-3-658-29636-0

29. Fiedler, H., Kaltenborn, T., Lanwehr, R., Melles, T.: Conjoint-Analyse. Sozialwissenschaftliche Forschungsmethoden, vol. 7, no. 2, Rainer Hampp Verlag, Augsburg, München (2017)

30. SoSci Survey: SoSci Survey – die Lösung für eine professionelle Onlinebefragung (2025). https://www.soscisurvey.de. Accessed 28 Apr 2025

31. SALSA – Smart, Adaptive and Learnable Systems for All. Research Project supported by the German Federal Ministry for Economic Affairs and Climate Action on the basis of a decision by the German Bundestag (2025). https://projekt-salsa.de/
32. Holder, D.: Gefallensurteil und Blickanalyse zum Fahrzeugdesign zukünftiger Aufbaugestalten anhand einer technischen Prognose. Dissertation, Universität Stuttgart, Stuttgart (2016). https://doi.org/10.18419/opus-9045

A Front-End UI Incorporating an Error Detection Function and a Virtual Execution Environment for Setting Rules for IoT Device Behaviors

Masaki Omata[(✉)] and Ayumu Nakano

University of Yamanashi, Kofu, Yamanashi, Japan
`{omata,ayu24na}@hci.media.yamanashi.ac.jp`

Abstract. This paper describes a visual programming interface that enables even inexperienced users to intuitively and easily set automation rules for IoT devices and the usability evaluation. We developed a front-end GUI that allows users to set up rules visually by dragging and dropping blocks with no-code, an "error detection function" that detects and immediately notifies errors, and a "virtual execution function" allows the user to virtually check whether the set rules work as intended. After that, we conducted a usability evaluation experiment to compare the proposed UI with the Node-RED's UI in terms of operation time, accuracy, and subjective satisfaction. The results show that the proposed UI was significantly more effective in reducing operation time and was equivalent to the Node-RED's UI in terms of accuracy of operation, and that the proposed UI was highly evaluated in terms of ease of use and recommendation intention.

Keywords: IoT · Rule Setting · Visual Programming · Front-end UI

1 Introduction

With the spread of smart sensors and IoT (Internet of Things) devices, end users are getting more opportunities to set up automation rules that fit their environment to make their lives more comfortable. For example, a rule to automatically turn on an air conditioner when a temperature sensor reaches a certain temperature, or a rule to automatically turn on a light when a light sensor detects that it has become dark.

However, many current IoT front ends for end users require specialized knowledge and skills from end users who are not experts in programming [1]. For example, they need to code rules using a programming language such as Python, or they need to write trigger-based rules using a system-specific rule syntax. In such a rule-setting environment, it is increasingly difficult for non-expert users to identify and correct causes of rule misconfigurations and runtime errors. Furthermore, in many current IoT programming systems, it is not possible to confirm that a rule works as intended without saving and executing the rule, and it is not possible to set triggers while adjusting environmental values such as temperature.

J. F. Krems et al. (Eds.): CHIRA 2025, CCIS 2836, pp. 55–68, 2026.
https://doi.org/10.1007/978-3-032-16454-4_4

The purpose of our research has been to develop an environment for novice end users to easily and intuitively set up automation rules for IoT devices to solve such problems. As a first step, we developed a front-end GUI (Graphical User Interface) that allows users to set up rules visually by dragging and dropping blocks with no-code, an "error detection function" that detects and immediately notifies an error while the user is setting up the rule, and a "virtual execution function" allows the user to virtually check whether the set rules work as intended, as new additional functions. We believe that the error detection function helps users identify rule configuration errors more easily, and that the virtual execution function helps users confirm how rules execute before any malfunctions occur. After that, we conducted a usability evaluation experiment to compare the proposed UI with the existing Node-RED's UI in terms of operation time, accuracy, and subjective satisfaction. The contributions of this paper are as follows.

- We proposed a GUI design for setting up IoT device operation rules by dragging and dropping blocks.
- We find that the proposed GUI significantly reduces operation time compared to an existing UI, and that it is a simplified UI in terms of subjective satisfaction of the participants.

2 Related Work

Reiss developed a programming model that allows end users to intuitively control IoT devices [1]. Using "smart sign" that operates based on sensor information and time conditions as a case study, four types of interfaces (for programmers, new rule creation, learning, and modularization) were designed, and the advantages and disadvantages of each were analyzed. The results showed that a single interface was not sufficient to meet end-user needs, and that rule conflict resolution and debugging-support functions were important. Furthermore, the results showed that a simple trigger-based model such as IFTTT ("IF This Then That") did not easily accommodate complex conditional settings, and more flexible rule application was needed.

Hoffswell developed a high-level constraint programming language called SetCoLa to reduce burden on end-user programmers by creating an environment that allows them to intuitively understand the state and behavior of programs using visualization techniques [2]. SetCoLa allows end users to create intuitive layouts with one or two orders of magnitude fewer constraints than conventional methods. Furthermore, Hoffswell added real-time program state visualization to the data visualization language Vega, allowing end users to code while checking program behavior in real time without having to switch among multiple views.

Mattioli et al. developed Block Rule Composer, which incorporates Trigger Action Programming (TAP) and allows end users to create rules using visual blocks [3]. The TAP is a rule-based programming method that executes specified behavioral action(s) when specific trigger condition is satisfied. Since it is not easy for end users to select appropriate triggers and actions and combine multiple rules, they introduced a mechanism that suggests optimal rules based on historical rule data. Their experimental results showed that creation of simple rules was intuitive, but creation of complex rules with multiple triggers and actions was time-consuming. They also showed that the recommendation system was effective in facilitating user learning by helping users select appropriate triggers and actions.

Tomlein et al. proposed a visual programming environment called CharIoT that allowed end users to visually construct rules by defining high-level events using virtual sensors and providing an IFTTT-style rule creation interface [4]. It had a graph-based visualization to facilitate intuitive understanding of the rule structure, and a recommendation system that allowed users to refer to rules created by other users.

Corno et al. proposed a high-level representation method called EupONT to solve a problem that programming environments for end users in IoT environments were too dependent on specific technologies and manufacturers [5]. The EupONT enabled abstract rule definition independent of specific technologies by modeling IoT devices and services as abstract functions and capabilities, for example "set the temperature to 20 °C when you enter a room". As a user study, it was shown that the EupONT improved the accuracy of rule creation and reduced the time required to create rules, when compared to existing IFTTT models.

Overall, these studies suggested that an intuitive and visual programming environment was effective for end users. However, few studies have incorporated an error detection function, which is necessary for rule setting operations, and a virtual execution function to check execution of rules after rule setting before actually running the IoT device.

3 Design and Implementation

3.1 Design Policy

Our development objective is primarily to provide a front-end visual programming interface that allows users with little programming experience to intuitively and easily create automation rules for IoT devices. For the intuitive usability, we designed an interface in which visual blocks representing device triggers, actions, and logics are manipulated by drag-and-drops on a smartphone screen. The action blocks are placed below the trigger blocks to facilitate understanding of the flow of processing from the top to the bottom of the screen. In addition, the blocks are color-coded and shaped according to their type to make them easy to identify at a glance. The shape of the blocks is designed to fit together like a jigsaw puzzle, so that the user can visually check whether the blocks can be combined or not.

For the easy operation, we incorporated functions to prevent and compensate for human error. For inexperienced users, operational errors can occur, such as setting values that are outside the range of the device. For the reason, our front-end interface incorporates an "error detection function" and a "virtual execution function." The functions allow the users to visually check and modify correct process and results of set rules in advance. The error detection function immediately determines validity of rules created by the user and displays a message if an error is found. The virtual execution function simulates the created rules on a computer and allows the user to check the behavior of the rules before actually running the IoT device.

3.2 Rule Setting Function

The interface provides the ability to configure rules by visually combining trigger, action, and logic blocks. Figure 1 shows the shape and color of the trigger (a), action (b), and logic (c) blocks on a smartphone screen respectively. In the figure, since the information is presented to a user in Japanese, English notations are added in parentheses as supplements. The trigger blocks are used to set conditions such as "temperature" and "time." The action blocks are used to change an operating status of a device, such as "run," "stop," or "change the temperature setting to 25 °C." The logic blocks are used to set logical operators such as "AND," "OR," and "NOT" to combine multiple trigger blocks.

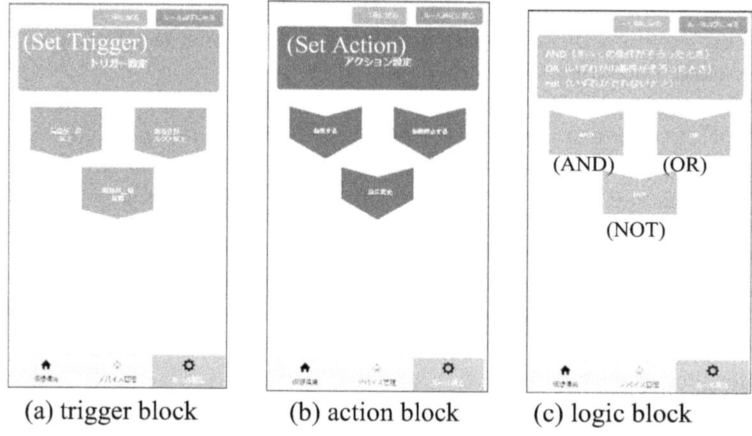

(a) trigger block   (b) action block   (c) logic block

Fig. 1. The shapes and colors of the trigger (a), action (b), and logic (c) blocks.

The blocks are enabled by adding them to the rule setup screen after setting a trigger block in the trigger setup screen and an action block in the action setup screen. Rules are created by connecting the blocks vertically. When connecting the blocks, they have a concave-convex shape, so that they can only be connected from the top of the screen in the order of an action below a trigger. The shape allows for the creation of multiple triggers by connecting two trigger blocks with one logic block, for example, in the order of trigger, logic, trigger, action, from the top.

Figure 2 shows a series of screen transitions for setting a rule to "turn on the light after 14:00". Tapping the "Set Rule" button on the Rule Setting screen at the beginning (Fig. 2 (1)) moves to the screen for selecting the trigger, action, and logic (Fig. 2 (2)). Tapping the "Set Trigger" button on the screen moves to the screen for setting the values of the trigger block (Fig. 2 (3)). After setting the trigger block, tapping the "Decide" button returns to the rule setting screen and displays the trigger block on it. Similarly, after moving to the action-block-setting screen and deciding on an action (Fig. 2 (4)), the action block is displayed on the rule setting screen (Fig. 2 (5)), and connecting the action block to the trigger block completes the rule (Fig. 2 (6)).

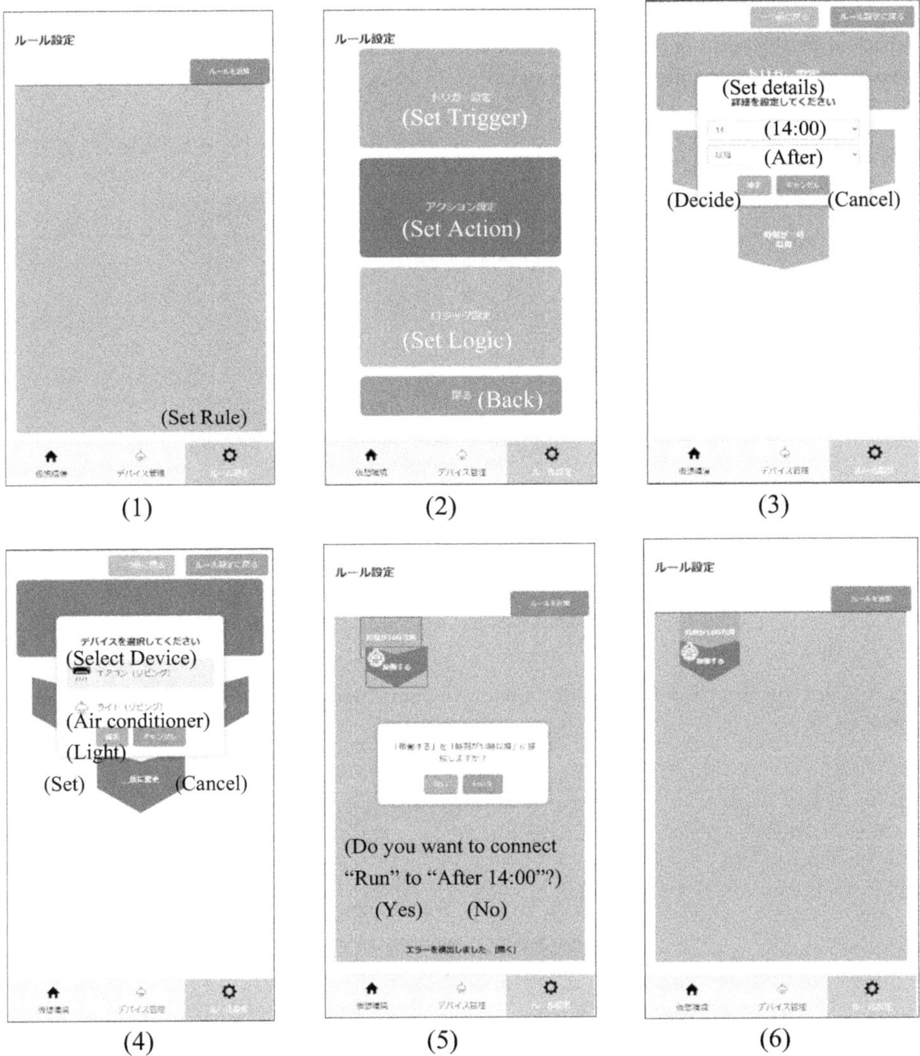

Fig. 2. A series of screen transitions for setting a rule to "turn on the light after 14:00". (1) Rule block placement screen, (2) Block selection screen, (3) Trigger block detail setting popup dialog, (4) Device selection popup dialog for action block, (5) Connection of trigger block and action block on rule-block-placement screen, and (6) Rule-block-placement screen after setting one rule by connecting two blocks.

3.3 Error Detection Function

The error detection function immediately determines validity of settings while the user is creating rules. For example, as shown in Fig. 3, when necessary blocks are not connected to each other, they are surrounded by a red line and an error is displayed at the bottom of the screen (Fig. 3(a)). Tapping on the warning message causes a pop-up window that provides specific details of the error and a suggestion for correction, such as "Please connect the blocks" (Fig. 3(b)). The function streamlines trial-and-error process of conventional programming, in which users code, execute, and then correct, and prevents users from making configuration errors.

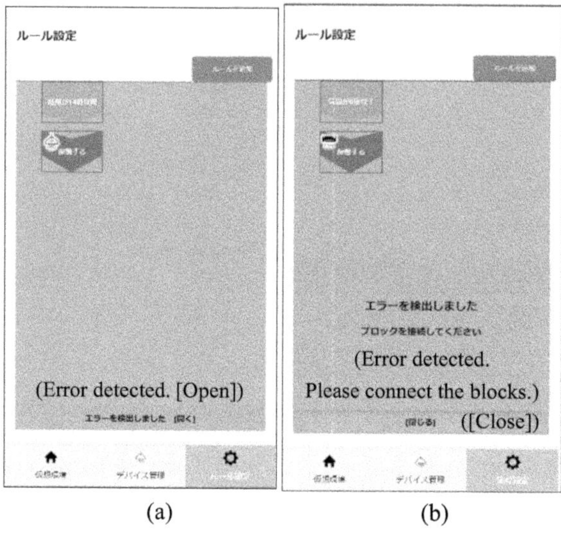

(a)   (b)

Fig. 3. The error detection function. (a) illustrates a small message, and (b) illustrates a detailed message.

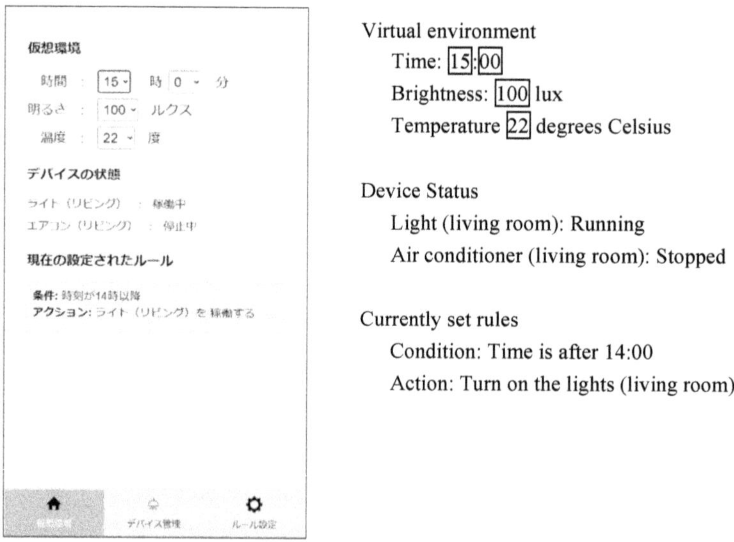

Virtual environment
   Time: 15:00
   Brightness: 100 lux
   Temperature 22 degrees Celsius

Device Status
   Light (living room): Running
   Air conditioner (living room): Stopped

Currently set rules
   Condition: Time is after 14:00
   Action: Turn on the lights (living room)

Fig. 4. The virtual execution function. The actual screen is written in Japanese, so the English translations are added to the right side of the screen rectangle.

3.4 Virtual Execution Function

The virtual execution function is mainly used after the user creates a rule. The user can execute the created rule in a virtual environment and check its behavior before actually running it. As shown in Fig. 4, for example, if the user creates a rule to "run the air conditioner when the room temperature is 25 °C or higher," the user can change the temperature setting of the air conditioner in the virtual environment on the screen to visually check how it switches between 'running' and "stopped" accordingly. Even when multiple rules are set in the virtual environment, changes in the status of each rule are reflected on the screen in conjunction with each other, allowing the user to grasp the sequence of events even in complex settings.

3.5 Architecture

Our proposed GUI is built as a web application using React [6]. Figure 5 shows a UML deployment diagram representing the architecture. The Node-RED are used for our IoT operations [7], which is software for visually creating and managing automation rules for IoT devices. The proposed UI stores the created rules in a list format. The virtual execution function changes the operating state of the device in the virtual environment by referencing the list and retrieving the details of values and actions. The list is categorized into trigger, action, and logic, and when the list is sent to the Node-RED, the Node-RED further subdivides the received rules into action devices and action behaviors and stores the data as global context. MQTT (Message Queuing Telemetry Transport) communication protocol is used to communicate user-created rules and sensor data from IoT devices.

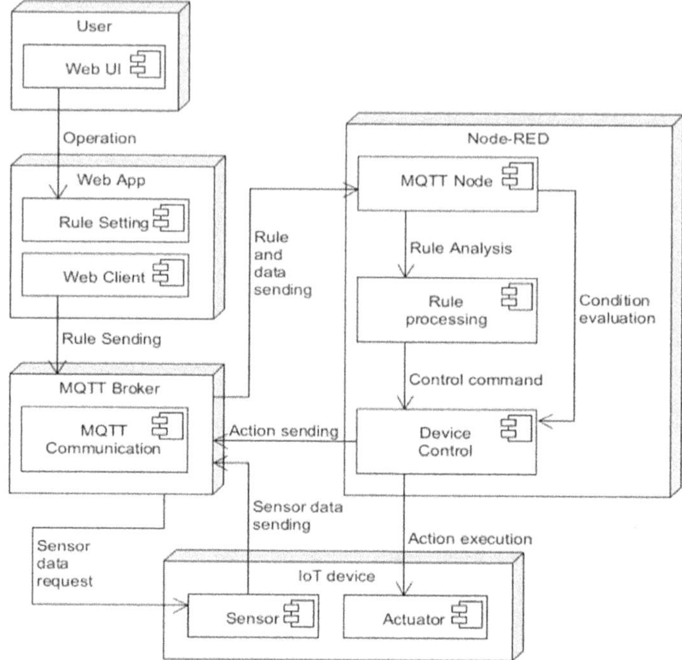

Fig. 5. The UML deployment diagram representing the architecture of our IoT system.

Three Raspberry Pi devices are used as IoT devices for the evaluation experiment of the proposed GUI and are connected to each other via a network. The Node-RED is installed on one of them to control the three devices. A motion sensor (HC-SR501) and a buzzer are connected to it, a temperature sensor (DS18B20) and an LED to another device, and an optical sensor (GL5516) and an LED to another device.

4   Usability Evaluation

We conducted a usability evaluation experiment comparing the proposed UI with the Node-RED's UI to investigate usefulness of the proposed UI. We asked participants to set control rules for IoT devices using the two interfaces, recorded and observed their tasks, and analyzed efficiency and accuracy of the tasks as well as their subjective satisfaction. Task completion time was recorded as the task efficiency. The number of errors was recorded as the task accuracy. The Technology Acceptance Model 3 [8], a dichotomous selection type, was used to select the appropriate UI between the two types of UIs used as the subjective satisfaction.

4.1   Experimental Environment

Figure 6 shows a participant during performance of the experimental task. Our proposed UI assumes use of a smartphone, but to unify the input/output environment with the Node-RED, we used a desktop computer operated with a mouse and keyboard. The three

Raspberry Pi devices and sensors were placed on the desk to the left of the participants. The Node-RED's UI used the entire screen, while the proposed UI was displayed in the center of the screen, resembling a vertical screen area of a smartphone, as shown in Fig. 6. To make the experimental tasks for each of the two UIs similar, when using the Node-RED, the values of the light and temperature sensors were used directly when combining multiple trigger conditions, and the light sensor value was treated as a binary value for "dark" and "light." The AND and OR logic in the Node-RED were set by directly editing code inside a function, rather than using a block.

Fig. 6. A participant during performance of the experimental task.

4.2 Experimental Task

The experimental task was to set operation rules for the IoT devices according to paper instructions provided by an experimenter. The rules are processes that execute actions to activate or deactivate an air conditioner or a light by combining blocks for triggers for room temperature and illuminance, and actions to run or stop the appliances (with logic block if necessary), such as "Run the air conditioner in the living room when the room becomes cold. One of the instructions presented to the participants is shown in Fig. 7. As shown, the time, room temperature, and/or illumination condition(s) is set numerically, and the action of the home appliance(s) is set when the condition(s) is established.

作業 2 （制限時間 5 分）

1．ルール設定画面へ移動する．

2．「温度センサが 25 度以上の場合エアコン（リビング）をオン」を設定する．

3．「光センサが 200 ルクス以下の場合ライト（リビング）をオン」を設定する．

4．仮想環境画面で動作確認を実施する．

5．作業が完了したら声をかけてください．

Task 2 (time limit: 5 minutes)

1. Go to the rule setting screen.
2. Set "Turn on the air conditioner (living room) when the temperature sensor is 25 degrees Celsius or higher.
3. Set "Turn on the light (living room) when the light sensor is less than 200 lux.
4. Check the operation on the virtual environment screen.
5. Tell the experimenter when you have completed this task.

Fig. 7. The task instruction paper. As shown above, the instructions were actually written in Japanese, so an English translation is shown below.

After the rules have been set, the actions were checked in the virtual execution environment in the case of the proposed UI, and the actions were checked using actual sensors in the case of the Node-RED.

4.3 Experimental Procedure

The experiment consisted of the rule-setting phase and the questionnaire response phase. In the rule-setting phase, participants first performed the three tasks to set the rules using either the proposed UI or the Node-RED, according to the instructions given by the experimenter. Then, they performed the three tasks to set the rules by using the other UI. In each UI, the first of the three tasks was the tutorial to learn how to use the UI, and the subsequent two tasks were used for data for usability analysis. The first task was a simple setup, the second was a setup to use the two-sensor data and the two appliances separately, and the third contains a rule that combines the two trigger conditions for two appliances.

The order of use of the two types of UIs was different for each half of all participants, for the counterbalance. For each UI, there was no time limit for the first setup task; the second setup task had a time limit of 5 min; the third task had a time limit of 10 min. The participants were instructed to "perform the setup task as quickly and accurately as possible." The desktop screen of each participant was recorded during the task.

After performing the tasks using both UIs, participants answered questions about the UIs they used in the questionnaire phase. Two questions from each of the three Technology Acceptance Model 3 constructs, "Perceived Usefulness (PU)," "Perceived Ease of Use (PEOU)," and "Behavioral Intentions (BI)," were used as the two-choice options in the questionnaire survey. The text of each question is presented on Table 1 in the next section. The participants answered which of the two UIs was applicable for each question.

4.4 Experimental Result

Eight university students (5 males and 3 females, mean 21.9 years old, standard deviation 1.05 years old) participated in the experiment. The participants were divided into two groups of four according to their programming experience. Participants with no programming experience were those who answered "no" to both questions, which are "I have a rough knowledge of programming" and "I have an understanding of the programming languages I will need after I start working," before starting the experiment.

Task Performance Time
Figure 8 shows the box-and-whisker plot of the total time spent by each participant on the second and third rule-setting tasks for each of the two types of UIs. All participants finished all setup tasks within the time limit. The average time for the two setting tasks was 263.2 s for the proposed UI and 454.1 s for the Node-RED's UI. As shown in Fig. 8, since there was no equal variance in the task performance time for each UI condition, the Welch's t-test shows that there was a significant difference between the two UIs ($p = .009$), indicating that the task performance time of the proposed UI was significantly shorter.

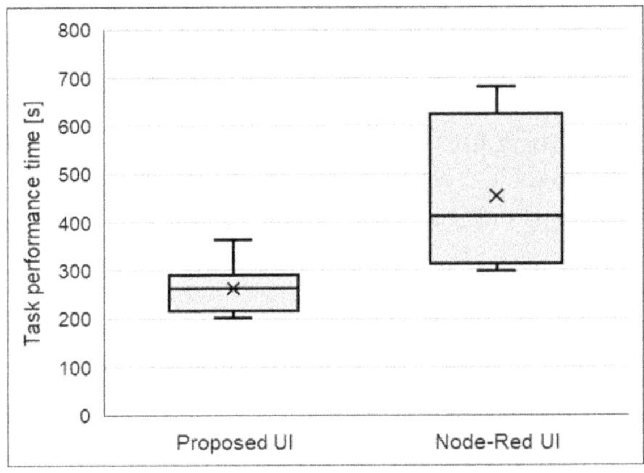

Fig. 8. The box-and-whisker plot of the total task performance time.

Number of Errors
Figure 9 shows a box-and-whisker plot of the total number of errors in the second and third rule-setting tasks for each participant when using each of the two types of UIs. Errors were counted as out-of-range sensor values, misconnected blocks or nodes, execution results that differed from instructions, and UI manipulation errors. Wilcoxon's signed rank test on the number of errors in the two types of UIs shows that there was no significant difference between the proposed UI and the Node-RED ($p = .483$).

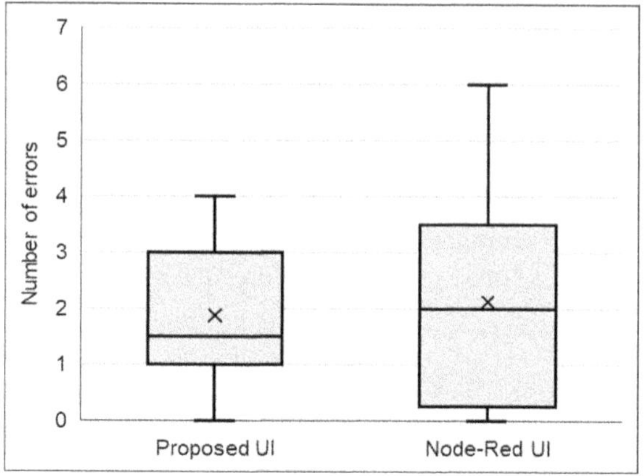

Fig. 9. The box-and-whisker plot of the total number of errors.

Observation of screen recordings shows that in the proposed UI, participants made mistakes in block-to-block connections. Specifically, when moving blocks by drag-and-drop, they connected to blocks that were already connected or tried to connect blocks that could not be connected to each other, and a pop-up window was displayed to inform them of the error. On the other hand, in the Node-RED's UI, mistakes in code descriptions in functions by the participants were noticeable. Specifically, the relationship between the size of comparison operators was written in reverse, and "25 <=" was written for numbers and comparison operators when "<= 25" should have been written. In addition, as observed in the proposed UI, there were errors in which the wrong node was connected, resulting in output that was different from the instructions.

Subjective Satisfaction

Table 1 shows the number of respondents who chose the proposed UI or the Node-RED's UI for each of the six questions. A binomial test was conducted on the number of respondents who chose between the two UIs for each question, and it was found that there was a significant difference ($p = .035$) between the two UIs for the questions "Which system was easier to operate" and "Which system would you recommend to others? We find that our proposed UI is significantly more satisfying than the Node-RED's UI.

Table 1. The results of responses to the questionnaire.

Construct	Question	Number of Participants	
		Proposed UI	Node-RED UI
PU	Which system was more efficient to set up?	6	2
	Which system is more attractive?	6	2
PEOU	Which system was easier to operate?	7	1
	Which system was less stressful to operate?	6	2
BI	Which system would you like to use in the future?	6	2

(continued)

Table 1. (*continued*)

Construct	Question	Number of Participants	
		Proposed UI	Node-RED UI
	Which system would you recommend to others?	7	1

4.5 Discussion

The reasons for the significantly shorter task performance time of our proposed UI compared to the Node-RED's UI include the visual and intuitive block placement operation of the proposed UI and the virtual execution function that allows the user to immediately check the results of rule execution. From the video recordings, it is found that the participants spent more time changing and checking the values of the temperature sensor by warming it with their hands or exposing it to heating air when using the Node-RED's UI, while the participants were able to check the results virtually on the screen in a shorter time when using the proposed UI.

As for the result that there was no significant difference in the number of errors between both UIs, most participants were able to set the rules as instructed without making many errors in either UI, which suggests that both UIs had few problems in terms of accuracy. Although there was no significant difference, based on the video recordings, we consider that the error detection function that pops up when trying to connect blocks that cannot be connected to each other in the proposed UI is useful for novice users.

Regarding the results of subjective satisfaction, we consider that the proposed UI provides an environment that is less stressful for users with little programming experience, because there is no need to write code and the blocks can be manipulated visually and intuitively. However, in the video recording of the proposed UI, some participants seemed to be confused by the placement operation in the task of setting complex rules that combine multiple triggers. This suggests that simple rule settings are intuitive and easy to use, while complex rule settings cause some problems in block placement and manipulation. Additionally, the simple shapes and colors of the blocks may also cause visibility issues. As specific improvement proposals to address the issues, we consider it more effective to incorporate expressions that allow users to intuitively and visually understand a state, such as replacing text indicating time or temperature on a trigger block with clock or thermometer icon to reduce textual information, and making text and an icon in the virtual environment glow or blink depending on an operational status of a device like an air conditioner.

5 Conclusion

In this paper, we proposed a visual programming interface that enables even inexperienced users to intuitively and easily set automation rules for IoT devices and evaluated its usability.

In evaluation experiments, we compared the proposed UI with the Node-RED's UI and found that the proposed UI was significantly more effective in reducing operation time and was equivalent to the Node-RED in terms of accuracy of operation. In the subjective evaluation, the proposed UI was highly evaluated in terms of ease of use and recommendation intention. In particular, the error detection function prevented erroneous operations, and the virtual execution function provided immediate confirmation, which gave novice users a sense of ease, suggesting that the functions led to improved operation efficiency.

The following improvements to the proposed UI are planned as future enhancements.

- To improve visibility, we plan to add icons to blocks so that users can visually obtain more detailed information, and color-code the device status (e.g., running, stopped, etc.) so that users can easily glance at them.
- To improve operability when setting complex rules, we plan to show guidance lines when connecting blocks and highlight connection candidates.

References

1. Reiss, S.P.: IoT end user programming models. In: 2019 IEEE/ACM 1st International Workshop on Software Engineering Research & Practices for the Internet of Things (SERP4IoT), pp. 1–8 (2019)
2. Hoffswell, J.: Languages & visualizations to enable effective end user programming. In: CHI 2019, Proceedings of the 2019 CHI Conference on Human Factors in Computing Systems, pp. 1–5 (2019)
3. Mattioli, A., Paternò, F.: A visual environment for end-user creation of IoT customization rules with recommendation support. In: AVI 2020: Proceedings of the International Conference on Advanced Visual Interfaces, Article No. 24, pp. 1–5 (2020)
4. Tomlein, M., Boovaraghavan, S., Agarwal, Y., Dey, A.K.: CharIoT: an end-user programming environment for the IoT. In: IoT 2017: Proceedings of the Seventh International Conference on the Internet of Things, Article No. 25, pp. 1–2 (2017)
5. Corno, F., De Russis, L., Roffarello, A.M.: A high-level approach towards end user development in the IoT. In: CHI 2017 Extended Abstracts, pp. 1546–1552. ACM (2017)
6. ReactThe library for web and native user interfaces. https://react.dev/. Accessed 14 May 2025
7. Node-RED Low-code programming for event-driven applications.https://nodered.org/. Accessed 14 May 2025
8. Venkatesh, V., Bala, H.: Technology acceptance model 3 and a research agenda on interventions. Decis. Sci. **39**(2), 273–315 (2008)

Exploring Design Alternatives for Automated Web GUI Generation

Hermann Kaindl[1(✉)], Roman Popp[2][iD], and David Raneburger[3]

[1] Institute of Computer Technology, TU Wien, Vienna, Austria
`kaindl@acm.org`
[2] Vienna, Austria
[3] Lienz, Austria

Abstract. For the evaluation of interaction design, usually prototypes are created. For creating high-fidelity prototypes, automated generation may be an option, at least in the case of graphical (Web) user interfaces (GUIs). However, the usability of fully-automatically generated GUIs is considered unsatisfactory. In our opinion, a major reason is that most previous approaches to automated GUI generation do not sufficiently explore *alternatives* in the design space of GUIs, in particular not automatically. Can existing techniques for automated Web GUI generation from high-level representations of interaction design comprehensively support the exploration of design alternatives?

We explain and address this problem and research question, and investigate exploring alternatives (at different stages), both by the designer and the generator tool, which receives high-level representations of interaction design as its input. For the designer, exploring alternatives involves providing alternative high-level models and transformations, selecting from Web GUI interaction strategies (e.g., scrolling vs. using tabs) and defining customizations. Exploring alternatives means for the AI-based generator tool creating alternative widgets and layouts in the course of a heuristic search, and tailoring for different target devices, according to the Web GUI interaction strategy selected by the designer. For making automated GUI generation applicable in the context of general interaction design, we also propose a new iterative and incremental interaction design *process* centered around automated generation.

Keywords: Interaction Design · Design Alternatives · Automated Web GUI Generation

1 Introduction

Any non-trivial graphical user interface (GUI) needs to be designed before it is actually created, whether it is a GUI for the Web or otherwise. Actually, the interaction supposed to be supported by the GUI needs to be designed first. According to [33], *interaction design* typically involves

- requirements,
- *designing alternatives*,
- *prototyping* and

J. F. Krems et al. (Eds.): CHIRA 2025, CCIS 2836, pp. 69–92, 2026.
https://doi.org/10.1007/978-3-032-16454-4_5

– *evaluating,*

and these activities are to be repeated for informing each other. We did not emphasize "requirements" above, since we consider them out of the scope of this paper, in order to focus on the other three key activities shown in italics.

The main focus of this paper is on exploring design alternatives in the context of automated Web GUI generation, which we consider inherently intertwined with their evaluation, both by human and machine. Evaluation, in turn, is inherently related to prototyping. We propose to utilize automated GUI generation for creating high-fidelity prototypes, with a focus on high-level representations of interaction design that the GUI generation takes as input.

Unfortunately, the usability of fully-automatically generated GUIs is considered unsatisfactory [24]. A more general criticism of model-based engineering (MBE) tools in this context was published some time ago [25], and at least some of it is still valid. A key point is the characterization of successful tools, which seem to be low-threshold and low-ceiling, or high-threshold and high-ceiling. According to [25], the "threshold" is how difficult it is to learn how to use the system, and the "ceiling" is how much can be done using the system. It would be desirable to have tools, and in our context specifically tools that automatically generate GUIs, with both a low threshold and a high ceiling at the same time. Achieving that largely remains an important challenge.

Still, there has been progress, and the first author of [25] was also involved in demonstrating the viability of automatically generated user interfaces [27]. Meanwhile, several other approaches to automated generation of user interfaces have been proposed, see, e.g., [6,10,11,13,19,24,26,28,29,32]. We provide an overview of these approaches based on their key features below.

However, there was not much work yet on *alternatives* in the context of GUI generation:

– The work in [8] proposed an "ambiguous mapping model", where platform constraints facilitate disambiguation. Whenever their evaluation leaves ambiguities, the designer has to select one of the remaining alternatives.
– The work in [15] proposed the selection of alternatives based on *quality attributes*, used for calculation of scores and trade-off analysis, based on which the designer selects an alternative.

Neither of these approaches involves any automated search in the space of alternatives and no automated evaluation of the results of (alternative) transformations. Evaluation and selection are to be done by a human designer only.

In contrast, there are two prominent approaches that involve alternatives (and automatic evaluation) in the course of GUI generation by a tool:

– SUPPLE [10,12] introduced an approach that treats GUI generation as an optimization problem (at run-time). For a given functional GUI model, it selects *alternative widgets* and generates *alternative widget layouts*, evaluates them automatically with a parameterized cost function, and selects one of the best (according to this evaluation) found. SUPPLE supports the adaptation of GUIs for users that have not been considered as target users by the original GUI designers (e.g., motor-impaired users).

- UCP[1] [36,42] employs constrained optimization search involving automatic heuristic evaluation (at design-time). For a given Discourse-based Communication Model (on the highest level of abstraction of the Cameleon Reference Framework (CRF) [5], i.e., the "Tasks&Concepts" (T&C) level), this approach automatically generates *alternative GUI models*, and evaluates them automatically with a heuristic cost function for selecting an optimal one according to a *strategy* chosen by a designer before. For Web GUIs, a major concern is to fit different devices with different screen sizes. In contrast to SUPPLE, this approach deals with process-oriented applications usually involving several screens to be optimized together.

Both of these approaches explicitly define search spaces based on design alternatives, which are both generated and evaluated automatically in the course of GUI generation. We elaborate on them in more detail in Sect. 4.

Overall, we propose approaches for exploring alternatives both by human and machine, and on different levels of abstraction in the course of interaction design. Still, this raises the question of how these explorations in the context of automated GUI generation can be utilized for supporting interaction design. For the Hamster system [26], there is a defined process for complementing an existing user interface (manually designed and implemented for operating a command and control system) with GUIs automatically generated at run-time (for a contextual, activity-related user interface) [23]. This process involves automated GUI generation from the T&C level of the CRF through all the other levels down to a "Final" user interface. However, it does not (explicitly) define working with alternatives, evaluation, or iterations.

We propose a defined *iterative and incremental* interaction design process. As a special case, it implements the general idea of iterations according to [33] by including automated GUI generation. It also defines iterations dedicated to adding increments to the source model for automated GUI generation. This process is inspired by iterative and incremental software development (see, e.g., [18]). Still, this defined process only covers the inclusion of automated GUI generation and is, therefore, only a fragment of a comprehensive interaction design process.

Overall, the research question addressed in this paper is as follows:
RQ: Can existing techniques for automated Web GUI generation from high-level representations of interaction design comprehensively support the exploration of design alternatives?

We try to answer this RQ primarily based on the UCP approach. More or less isolated techniques exist for automated GUI generation and we investigate their concerted use for interaction design in general. In this way, our objective in this paper is to contribute a new perspective to the field, by bridging the gap between interaction design and automated (Web) GUI generation. The main contribution of our paper is to show that and to indicate how it can be achieved.

As a running example in this paper, we use simplified travel planning, primarily booking, e.g., flights. These and all the other Web GUIs mentioned in this paper were automatically generated (by UCP) and customized (by ourselves using this tool).

---

[1] UCP stands for Unified Communication Platform, indicating that it covers both Human-Machine and Machine-Machine Communication. In this paper, we simply write UCP as a short-hand for UCP:UI (for creating user interfaces).

The remainder of this paper is organized in the following manner. First, we discuss related work and provide some background material, in order to make this paper self-contained. Then we propose alternatives for the human designer in the context of automated GUI generation, where the generator tool is viewed as a black box. After that, we explain several ways of dealing with alternatives *within* a generator tool. Based on all that, we propose how to explore alternatives supported by automated GUI generation, in the form of an iterative and incremental process. Finally, we discuss our topic more generally, propose future work, and conclude.

2   Related Work and Background

We primarily classify here approaches to automated GUI generation according to run-time or design-time generation, where some of them do both. A run-time approach interprets given models while the application is already running and generates the user interface on demand. In contrast, a design-time approach compiles the code before and only executes it at run-time. This criterion correlates with the highest CRF level for fully-automatic generation, as design-time approaches typically start from a higher level than run-time approaches. As given in Table 1, the run-time approaches start on the "Abstract UI" (AUI), "Concrete UI" (CUI) or "Final UI" (FUI) level, while most of the design-time approaches start at the T&C level. By use of these classifications, Table 1 presents an overview of (G)UI generation approaches together with selected references.

Table 1. Overview of UI Generation Approaches.

	Time of generation		Highest CRF start level for automatic UI generation
	Run-time	Design-time	
Hamster [26]	x		T&C
SUPPLE [10,11]	x		CUI
MML [29]		x	CUI
UCP [6,32]		x	T&C
Useware Engineering [24]		x	T&C
UsiXML [19]		x	T&C
MARIAE [28]	x	x	T&C
UsiComp [13]	x	x	T&C

This table contains also the approach called UCP, which this study on design alternatives is based upon. It is classified as a design-time approach for GUIs only, which starts fully-automatic GUI generation at the T&C level according to CRF. In this way, our own approach is put into context of UI generation in general. While several other approaches are *task*-based, UCP is *discourse*-based as explained below. We found a *duality* of these approaches, see [30].

Since UCP is primarily used in this paper for making our points about exploring alternatives, we also have to provide some background material, in order to make this paper self-contained. UCP uses a device- and modality-independent Discourse-based Communication Model to specify the high-level communicative interaction between two parties. In the context of GUI generation, one party involved in such a discourse is the human user, who interacts with the system (the other party) via a GUI. Such a source model for generation consists of

- a Discourse Model, which specifies all the possible discourses in the sense of dialogues,
- a Domain-of-Discourse (DoD) Model, which specifies the concepts that the two interacting agents can 'talk about', and
- an Action-Notification Model (ANM), which specifies Actions and Notifications to be performed by one of the communicating parties (either the user or the system).

The basic interaction units in such Discourse Models are *Adjacency Pairs* [20] for modeling typical turn-takings in a conversation, like question–answer or offer–accept/reject. Each such Adjacency Pair consists of (one or) two *Communicative Acts* (e.g., a question and an answer), a generalization of so-called Speech Acts [45]. These units are connected (in general recursively) via Discourse Relations, primarily derived from *Rhetorical Structure Theory (RST)* [21] relations. Examples of such Discourse Relations are *Alternative* and *OrderedJoint*. An *Alternative* relation specifies an alternative in the discourse, with procedural semantics that the connected sub-branches can, in principle, be executed concurrently, but that only one sub-branch can be finished. The *OrderedJoint* relation links two or more Adjacency Pairs and specifies that all of them may be executed concurrently, but not in reverse order. If all branches can be executed through the same presentation unit (e.g., a screen), the placement of the related widgets is according to the defined order, from top left to bottom right (as usual in Western cultures). If this is not possible, e.g., the screen is too small, the Ordered-Joint relation defines the sequence of executing the branches, e.g., the sequence of the corresponding screens of a GUI.

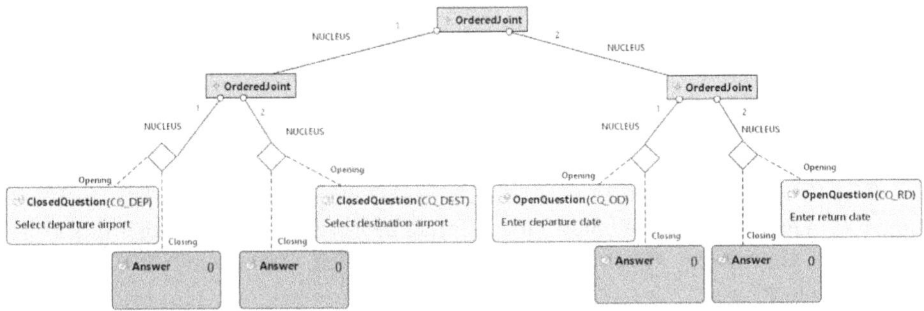

Fig. 1. Discourse Model for flight search derived from the pattern for Concurrent Travel Information Entering as defined in [16].

A very small example of a Discourse Model is shown in Fig. 1, actually an excerpt of the Discourse Model for our running example. It specifies how to find round-trip flights (simplified for this example). Four pieces of information are needed first, the departure airport, the destination airport, the departure date, and the return date. The related questions and answers are modeled as Adjacency Pairs (shown as diamonds), with opening and closing Communicative Acts (shown as yellow and green rounded rectangles, depending on their assignment to one of the two discourse partners). Communicative Acts have *propositional content* (much as Speech Acts do), which in our Discourse Models contains links to DoD and ANM. These Adjacency Pairs are related with each other through OrderedJoint relations (shown as blue rectangles), which specify that all the information can, in principle, be entered concurrently.

UCP supports modeling such Discourse-based Communication Models with a dedicated editor [7]. Most importantly, UCP can fully-automatically generate GUIs from such models [32]. UCP also provides a message-based run-time environment [32], which allows deploying the generated GUIs and application back-ends. This run-time environment uses the Communicative Acts as messages and provides a generic function-based interface for the back-end integration. The functions are implicitly defined in the Discourse-based Communication Model through the propositional content of the Communicative Acts and the interface can be generated automatically. UCP uses a run-time architecture that is based on the Model-View-Controller pattern [31], but does not impose any constraints on the technology to be used to implement the functionality.

In summary, UCP is a fully implemented approach for modeling high-level interaction design in Discourse-based Communication Models and for automatically generating Web GUIs from such models. In this course, it offers many possibilities for exploring alternatives, both by the designer and the machine.

3   Alternatives for the Human Interaction Designer

In general, it is key that a human interaction designer has alternatives available. This aspect has attracted little attention yet in the context of automated generation of user interfaces, however. Of course, the designer can create alternative models, on whatever level of abstraction they reside. Still, what support can she expect in this regard? With regard to model-to-model transformations, are predefined transformation rules, e.g., given, and if so, can alternative rules be defined?

Once models and transformations are defined, a given engine can generate a GUI. However, for which device with its specific properties and, especially screen size, will this GUI fit well? Different devices have different interaction possibilities, such as a mouse vs. a touch-screen, and they have different properties, e.g., with regard to browsing. Which alternatives does a designer have for all that when running an automated GUI generation?

There is consensus that fully-automatically generated GUIs at today's state of the art are, in general, not sufficiently usable. Hence, certain means of *customization* are needed. Which alternatives does the human designer have in this regard?

In this section, we address all these questions and provide some pointers to relevant work in the context of automated GUI generation, with a special focus on our own previous work.

3.1 Alternative Models on Some Level of Abstraction

In principle, any model-driven GUI generation approach allows the interaction designer to create *alternative models* and to generate GUIs for each of them. This would normally happen on the highest level of abstraction that a generation approach supports. Otherwise, when making changes in an already generated model on a lower level, the issue of making such changes persistent arises. We address it below in the context of *customization*, which we implement through *custom rules* and *custom widgets* for making the changes persistent.

However, modeling is intrinsically a challenging task and calls for support. In particular, models specifying interaction designs should not have to be reinvented from scratch. This entails the need for *reusability* of interaction design knowledge in the form of models.

A useful approach to capture knowledge about (generalized) solutions for common problems in a given context are *patterns*. Hence, we propose to employ here *interaction design patterns*, since patterns are a useful means for representing design knowledge to be reused.

Patterns for *task models* have already been proposed some time ago [9]. These pattern approaches for task models typically present a single pattern for a specific problem only, however, e.g., patterns for task models in the context of automated user interface (UI) generation [22], but without providing design alternatives.

How about *alternative patterns* for interaction design models? After all, there are, e.g., alternative patterns representing alternative software architectures [4]. That is why we made a first attempt to define alternative interaction design patterns for automated GUI generation from Discourse-based Communication Models [16]. The three patterns we defined there specify alternative solutions in the form of interaction design models.

Since this particular approach is important for our paper, let us have a closer look. These patterns provide *Context*, *Problem* and *Solution* in the structured way usual for such design patterns, see Tables 2, 3 and 4. They share the same Context, i.e., "Passenger travel applications", which encompasses booking of tickets for, e.g., flights, train or bus rides and ship cruises. That is, these patterns are applicable in different domains in this context. However, the descriptions of the respective Problems vary in the way that the required information is being entered: concurrently, sequentially or incrementally. The corresponding alternative Solutions are given through exemplary models, where the model shown in Fig. 1 is a simple adoption of the solution model in the Concurrent Travel Information Entering Pattern in [16]. While the pattern more generally deals with travel, the model given in Fig. 1 is more specific on travel involving flights. The models given as solutions for the other two patterns are similar, but they use other relations. Actually, they also have a different grouping of the elements for entering the travel information, see [16].

Now let us assume that a designer would like to explore alternatives while modeling a small interaction design for finding round-trip flights. She may want to utilize the

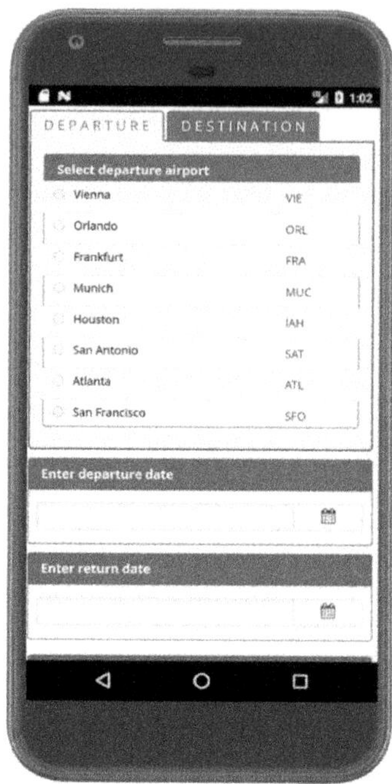

Fig. 2. GUI screen generated from Concurrent Design.

design pattern for Concurrent design above first, for creating a Discourse Model based on this pattern instantiated for flight booking. She can take the model from the pattern (available in the tool) and adapt it through refinement and extensions potentially needed for the specific application at hand. This Discourse Model has to be complemented by a Domain-of-Discourse Model and an Action-Notification Model as explained above. Then the designer can fully-automatically generate a Web GUI for a given device, e.g., a typical smartphone using the generator tool. Figure 2 shows a screen shot of the resulting GUI.

More precisely, this is a GUI generated for a typical smartphone according to an additionally given Device Specification, which may already exist in the tool environment or could be easily adapted for a new smartphone. Since the content does not completely fit into the (small) screen as specified, and since this generation is according to the interaction strategy without scrolling, the concurrent parts are split into the two tabs shown for departure and destination, respectively.

Table 2. Concurrent Approach

Name:	Concurrent Travel Information Entering Pattern
Context:	Passenger travel applications
Problem:	Entering departure/destination locations and outgoing/return dates concurrently
Solution:	More general Discourse Model than the one given in Fig. 1

Table 3. Sequential Approach.

Name:	Sequential Travel Information Entering Pattern
Context:	Passenger travel applications
Problem:	Entering departure/destination locations and outgoing/return dates sequentially
Solution:	Alternative Discourse Model with a Sequence relation

Table 4. Incremental Approach.

Name:	Incremental Travel Information Entering Pattern
Context:	Passenger travel applications
Problem:	Entering departure/destination locations and outgoing/return dates incrementally
Solution:	Yet another alternative Discourse Model with an Elaboration relation

A closer look into this design approach, however, should reveal that it does not exactly serve the need of an airline offering point-to-point flights only, where the selection of a departure airport determines the possible destination airports. Hence, an alternative model should be investigated, which can be built around the pattern for an Incremental approach. Figure 3 shows a screen shot of a GUI resulting through fully-automatic generation from input models including a Discourse Model according to the Incremental design pattern (where the Domain-of-Discourse Model and the Action-Notification Model are the same as for the Concurrent approach). In the Incremental approach, the user has to select a departure airport first, e.g., Frankfurt FRA, since the application back-end needs this piece of information for retrieving the possible connections departing from this selected airport. Actually, also the information on the departure date is needed here upfront. (That is why the grouping of information through the OrderedJoint relations is different in the corresponding pattern.) Only then, the screen can be filled with the list of possible destination airports to select from, as shown in the screen shot depicted in Fig. 4. Actually, this generation is according to the vertical scrolling strategy, as yet another alternative to be explored. Hence, the screen is not split for tabbing as shown above, even though the content to be displayed does not fit the screen size.

When evaluating this prototypical GUI, its scrolling approach may not be assessed as appealing, since still the whole list of departure airports is visible, but not, in general, the selected departure airport. Hence, yet another alternative should be investigated where the information on the selected departure airport is given but not directly on all the other airports, since it clutters the small screen available on the smartphone.

For generating a prototype of such a GUI, an alternative *transformation rule* can be used, see [38], where we presented a related case study for evaluating this approach. It should be an alternative to the transformation rule illustrated in Fig. 5 (through an example sketch of the instantiation of a rule that creates the widget of airports as included in all the GUI screens above). Figure 6 illustrates such an alternative rule. Note, that both rules have the *same* model excerpt to be matched on the left side, but different GUI elements to be created on the right.

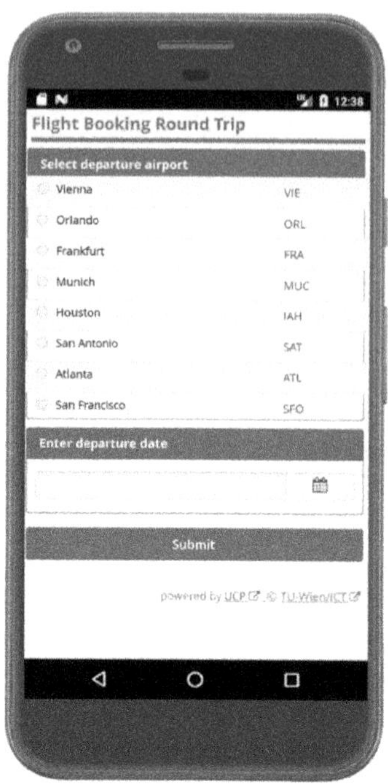

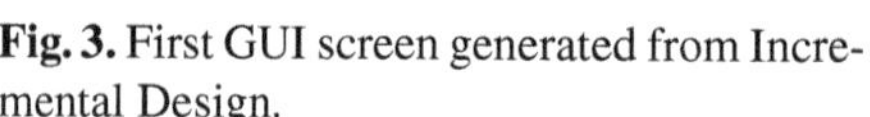

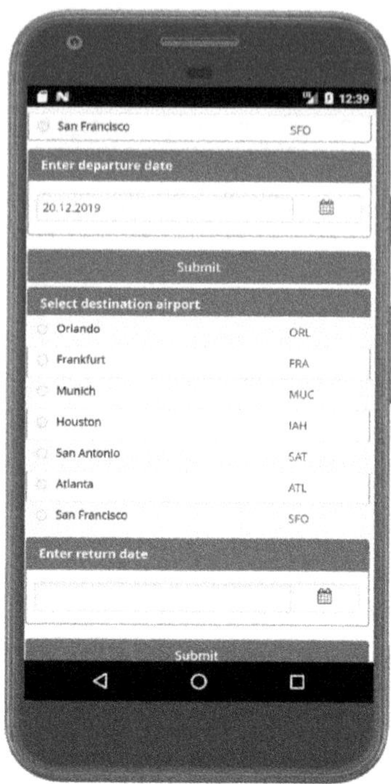

Fig. 3. First GUI screen generated from Incremental Design.

Fig. 4. Subsequent GUI screen generated from Incremental Design.

Using this rule for automatic Web GUI generation instead of the previous one leads to an alternative GUI for the Incremental approach, but obviously with large empty space even for small screens. As explained below, a custom rule overrides the optimization done by the tool (which actually tries to utilize the given space). In order to address this problem, the designer can define yet another rule, see Fig. 7 for an illustration.

The latter rule is different from the ones above, as it matches an Elaboration relation of the model. This relation is derived from RST and has both a NUCLEUS and a SATELLITE branch. The rule in Fig. 7 creates a container each, where the widgets generated for these branches are to be placed in, and an additional picture for filling the space on the screen.

When applying these two rules, the Web GUIs shown in Figs. 8 and 9 are automatically generated. Once a departure airport and a departure date are entered on the first screen and submitted, widgets are added for entering the destination airport and the return date. This results in the subsequent screen of the alternative GUI, while the entered departure information (Frankfurt FRA)is still shown in the upper part of this screen. Whenever the departure airport is changed here, the information on available destination airports is updated. For selecting airports in this GUI, a list of possible airports pops up as shown in Fig. 10.

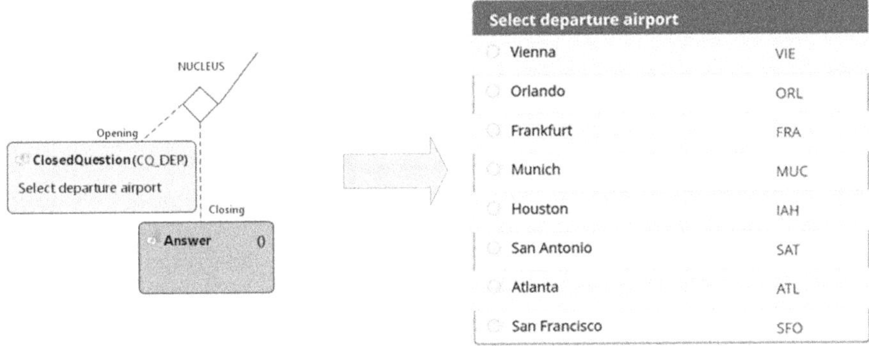

Fig. 5. Sketch of an instantiated transformation rule example – large space.

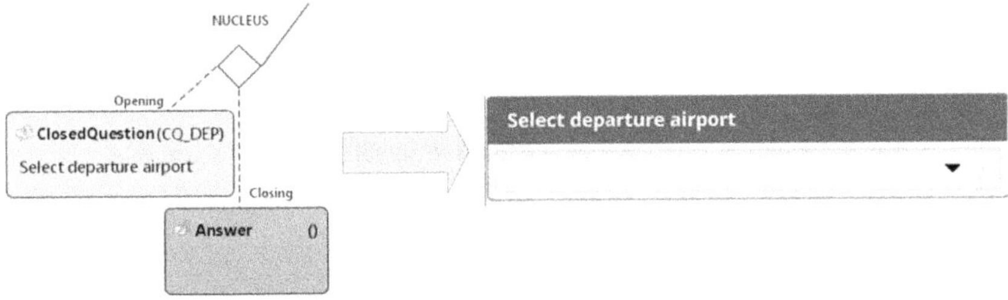

Fig. 6. Sketch of an instantiated alternative transformation rule example – small space.

3.2 Alternatives of Customization

The investigation of these last alternatives can actually be viewed as GUI *customization*, an adaptation of a generated GUI for the case at hand. Since it is done through alternative rules, it is persistent for re-generation (without any extra effort), in contrast to a manual modification on a lower level or even in the GUI code. For this purpose, we provided dedicated *custom rules* for the designer [35]. The technical specialty of such rules is explained in Sect. 4 in the context of alternatives for the generator tool. Note, that the rule illustrated in Fig. 6 actually existed in the rule set and was only labeled as a custom rule for these technical reasons, while the rule illustrated in Fig. 7 is a newly created one.

An evaluation of the results of customization using such custom rules can be found in [39], a user study on whether this kind of customization can actually improve generated GUIs. This study achieved statistically significant results that the adjusted task time of the customized version is less than that of the fully-automatically generated one. The subjective results indicated that attractiveness and wording were improved through customization.

In addition, our approach provides the designer with the possibility of including *custom widgets* as alternatives to the widgets given in the specified toolkit, which was evaluated in a trial application [43]. This is obviously necessary at times for generating usable GUIs, such as for including a usual seat-picker widget for flight booking.

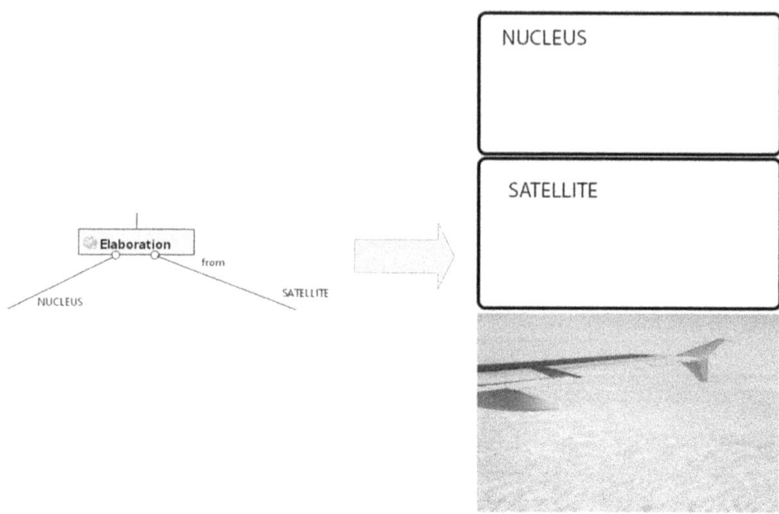

Fig. 7. Sketch of an instantiated custom transformation rule example.

Fig. 8. Alternative first GUI screen generated from Incremental Design.

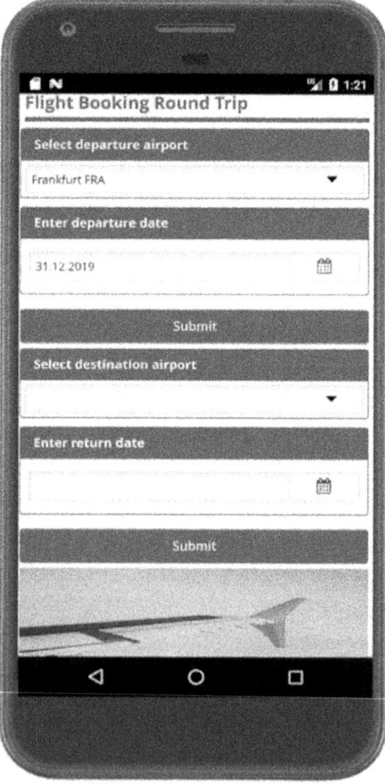

Fig. 9. Alternative subsequent GUI screen generated from Incremental Design.

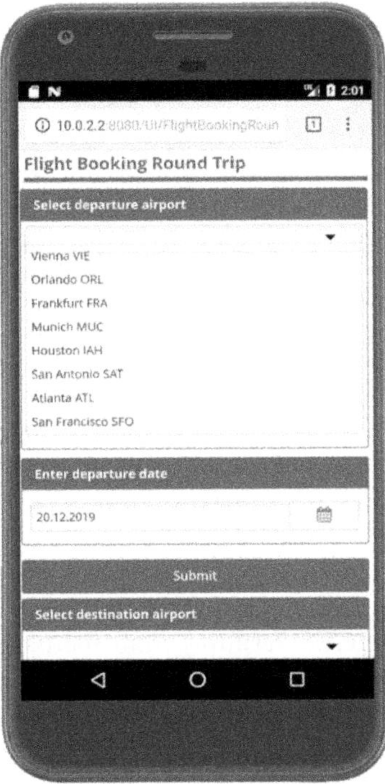

Fig. 10. GUI screen with popped-up list of selectable airports.

3.3   Alternatives for Generation

As indicated above, there are also alternatives for the automated generation. The designer can choose to generate a Web GUI for *different devices* according to Device Specifications. These allow the definition of the screen size and resolution, of course, and the supported widget set. In addition, the designer can specify *pointing granularity* in this way, i.e., whether the user will most likely use fine-grained pointing, e.g., with a mouse, or coarse-grained pointing with her finger [41]. This is actually not only a device-specific alternative but can also be application-specific. For instance, it makes a difference whether a Web GUI will be used on a desk-top computer or on the move, e.g., on a robot trolley, which was evaluated in a user study [3]. Finally, there are alternative *GUI interaction strategies* (e.g., scrolling vs. using tabs) as illustrated above. These are especially important for devices with relatively small screens such as smartphones.

4   Alternatives Within the Generator Tool

For providing alternatives to the designer as illustrated above, a generator tool, in general, needs to transform different source models to different GUIs. This also depends on its transformation rules, i.e., the application of different rules should result in different GUIs as well. In our opinion, it is important to allow for transformation of the same source model to different GUIs. Hence, our tool UCP provides additional means for customization and choices of different interaction strategies. It also investigates alternatives *internally*, for selecting different widgets and for creating different layouts and screens using these widgets. This is the basis for automated optimization, which can be used for tailoring the generated Web GUI to a specific device (and the selected interaction strategy). We also sketch an earlier optimization approach provided by the tool SUPPLE, which was originally motivated for optimization to specific motor impairments of users and evolved to a useful approach addressing accessible GUIs in general.

4.1 Alternatives of GUI Widgets

Hence, alternatives for a GUI generator tool are primarily given by different widgets. Some widgets have the same purpose but different properties (e.g., space requirements). UCP can work with both predefined widgets (of the given tool-kit, for now HTML) and custom widgets to be provided additionally [43].

Alternative widgets are actually generated and instantiated through alternative transformation rules, which create them for defined parts of the given source model. For instance, we showed different GUIs resulting from alternative rules for Adjacency Pairs above. The rule illustrated in Fig. 5 generates radio buttons for the selection of an airport, displaying all of them at the same time. The alternative rule illustrated in Fig. 6 generates a drop-down list instead, which shows only one list entry per default.

There are also alternative rules for *relations between Adjacency Pairs*, which create container widgets. For instance, UCP provides two (predefined) transformation rules for the relation OrderedJoint (such as used in Fig. 1), for large or small screens, respectively. More precisely, one creates a Panel and the other a Tab Control widget, where the first needs more space than the other. However, using the Tab Control will require extra interaction with the user, see also Fig. 2.

Technically, transformation rules in UCP are actually more intricate than suggested by our instantiated examples above as merely used for illustration purposes. Since these transformation rules are implemented in the context of model-driven transformation technology, they are generically defined through *metamodels* (as usual in this technology), so that they can be instantiated for their application in the course of generation. UCP can actually handle alternative rule applications and constrained optimization search. Since this was not widely supported in this technology at the time, we built our own transformation engine for implementing the generator tool, which was also shown in a tool demo [32].

In addition, our model-driven transformation approach runs in interleaved transformation steps [17]:

1. The first step applies rules to Discourse Model elements that generate an overall UI structure by use of pattern matching. These rules generate abstract widgets like labels for headings and placeholders for data of the propositional content. They also associate parts of the propositional content with the generated placeholders.
2. The second step executes content transformation rules within the context of the rules of the first step. This embedding allows the selection of abstract widgets for the

resulting structural UI depending on the content type, the content's referring communicative act type and the current context the communicative act is embedded in, as defined by the enclosing rule.

4.2   Alternatives of GUI Screens/Layouts

Through the application of alternative (instantiated) transformation rules, *alternative GUI screens* with alternative layouts of possibly different widgets are created. Still, which of these GUI screens is "best"? Answering this question calls for an evaluation function that can automatically assess how good a given GUI screen is compared to the others.

UCP actually uses a heuristic evaluation function for sequences of rule applications. In effect, a GUI screen can be evaluated indirectly by this function, since it assigns a heuristic value to a sequence of transformations leading to this particular GUI screen. By generating and evaluating alternatives, an optimization search can be performed. Since (specified) *constraints* are taken into account, this is actually a *constrained optimization search*.

The different interaction strategies to be selected by the designer are also implemented using the constraints. The interaction *strategy without scrolling* obviously tries to keep the limits defined in the Device Specification exactly, while the *vertical scrolling strategy* relaxes the constraint related to the vertical limit. (For completeness, there is also a *horizontal scrolling strategy* relaxing the constraint related to the horizontal limit).

In summary, depending on the chosen strategy and the given device constraints, the constrained optimization search performs a fully-automatic exploration of the space defined by alternative transformation rules. It is actually implemented as a *branch-and-bound search*, which usually allows reducing the computational effort required.

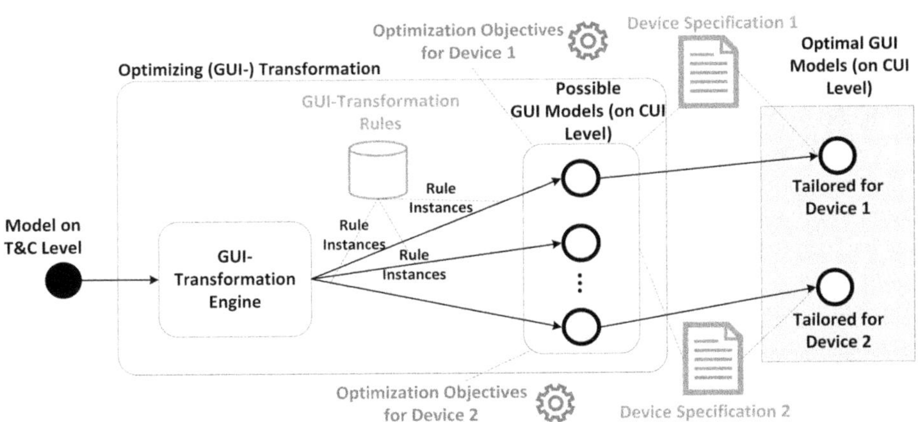

Fig. 11. Model-driven transformation including optimization (adapted from Fig. 3 of [38] according to CRF).

All the details of this approach are available in [36]. Still, let us illustrate it here as an optimization using model-driven transformation technology along the lines of [38] (also abstracting here from the details of interleaved transformation steps as sketched above). Figure 11 illustrates the conceptual approach. Let us focus on the case of a single device first. The Model on the T&C level shown on the left side is the source model transformed into several GUI models to be evaluated through an evaluation function for optimization. This is illustrated inside the rounded box for "Optimizing (GUI-)Transformation" through "Possible GUI Models (on CUI Level)". In addition, also the concrete values of attributes specified in the Device Specification are taken into account. Some of these attributes constrain the space for optimization. One of the generated GUI models highest ranked by the evaluation function that fulfills the constraints is selected as the output of the optimizing transformation and is an optimal GUI model, shown at the right side of Fig. 11. Of course, it is only 'optimal' in the sense of the optimal heuristic value according to the evaluation function.

An evaluation of the results of such optimization searches, i.e., different GUI screens/layouts can be found in [34]. This user study compared tab-based navigation with vertical scrolling on smartphones using automatically generated GUIs optimized according to these different strategies, where vertical scrolling turned out to be more efficient (statistically significant result).

4.3 Alternatives of Target Devices

Also tailoring for different devices as specified by the designer is handled in the course of optimization through taking constraints into account, which are specified in the different device specifications provided by the designer. Hence, our approach covers multi-device optimization. For each device, an optimal GUI model is generated and selected. This actually happens for one device at a time, and one after the other.

Note, that all these optimizations are being performed using a single set of transformation rules, even though happening for one device after the other. In order to make this possible, the rules must not specifically depend on any single device. More precisely, the rules have to be defined independently of the concrete values of the attributes specified in the various Device Specifications, at least for those attributes taken into account for the optimization.

Care must be taken that no 'illegal' GUI models are generated, with characteristics not supported by the corresponding devices (e.g., widgets not supported). Another example for such a restriction is the input method to be used on a given device. On a touchscreen to be used with finger pointing, for instance, widgets too small for that are not to be used. For this reason, the transformation rules are filtered before their execution. Since our approach optimizes for one device at a time, the single rule set for all devices can still be filtered for the device at hand as usual.

In general, UCP receives *process-oriented* models as the source for automatic GUI generation, which specify steps to be performed in defined sequences (possibly conditional and including iterations). Such steps are implemented in different screens in a GUI supporting such a process. Our optimization approach implements specific savings of computational effort for applications with more than one screen, and it tries to make screens of such a process consistent.

Finally, there is a special case defined through the implementation of *custom rules*. They have absolute precedence over the other competing transformation rules in the course of the optimization search, which are not further investigated. In effect, custom rules actually reduce alternatives in the course of optimization according to the explicit choice of the designer. The point is that a designer can 'overrule' possibly different results from an optimization in this way. Note, that any of the rules given in UCP can be simply marked as a custom rule by the designer. Alternatively, new custom rules may be defined by the designer, possibly through copy&edit from already existing transformation rules (see also above).

An evaluation of the results of such optimization searches, i.e., different GUI screens/layouts for different devices can be found, e.g., in [1]. These user studies compared tab-based navigation with scrolling on smartphones and tablet computers using automatically generated GUIs optimized according to these different strategies and device specifications.

Even before the work on UCP started, SUPPLE [10] had already introduced GUI generation as an optimization problem. In particular, it supports the generation of optimal GUIs for specific user abilities or devices, based on functional GUI models. These specify what functionality should be exposed to the user. How this functionality is to be rendered is determined through different types of constraints.

SUPPLE operates at run-time and automatically adapts the GUI through parameterizing the cost function based on so-called user traces or explicit user feedback collected through a tool [12]. This tool lets the user perform several tasks with different GUI renderings initially and configures the cost function automatically, based on the user's performance. Such an automated parameterization mitigates the problem that parameterizing such a cost function is tedious and error prone work, because the effect of a parameter change is hard to anticipate. Nevertheless, it is still hard to achieve a specific customization, because the effect of a specific user trace or performance on the GUI is still hard to anticipate.

Still, SUPPLE offers a very promising approach to providing *accessible* user interfaces [11]. More recently, we adapted our UCP approach for improving low-vision accessibility by combining design-time generation of Web GUIs with *responsive design* [44].[2] While both these approaches intentionally addressed accessibility, the examination of the causes of success and failure in [14] regarding accessibility suggests that improvements may be due, in part, to changes in Website technologies and coding practices rather than a focus on accessibility per se.

In contrast to SUPPLE, our approach focuses on providing GUIs for process-oriented applications (e.g., booking applications), following the gender-inclusive design principle, i.e., we aim at generating GUIs usable for all users. Hence, SUPPLE is a specific *user-centered* GUI generation approach, while UCP is per se *usage-centered* (or *activity-centered*). Still, it may be used in the course of an overall user-centered design approach as discussed below.

Also in contrast to SUPPLE, UCP operates at design-time, which allows starting from a higher CRF level. In particular, compared to SUPPLE's functional GUI models, Discourse-based Communication Models are on a higher level of abstraction. This pro-

---

[2] Technically, responsive design is implemented in the FUI using HTML 5, Bootstrap and vue.js.

vides more flexibility for generating GUIs, especially for process-oriented applications, at the cost of a more elaborate generation approach, however. Design-time generation also allows the designer to keep control over the resulting GUI while performing *customizations* using UCP (see above for this approach to providing alternatives to the designer).

5   How to Explore Alternatives Supported by Automated GUI Generation

Given all those alternatives for the designer and a generator tool, how to systematically explore design alternatives with the support of such a tool? Previously, we studied an iterative [37] as well as an iterative and incremental [40] process for systematically working with UCP on Web GUIs semi-automatically generated from high-level interaction design in the form of Discourse-based Communication Models according to our approach. We synthesize these here and abstract from tool specifics for a simple process fragment as shown in Fig. 12.

Much as informally illustrated above in the context of alternatives for the designer, there are essentially two ways for iterations here, based on evaluation results for the interaction design per se or the generated GUI, respectively. They lead to adaptation of the Discourse-based Communication Model (the source) or Customization of the GUI (the result of generation). In addition, there is an outer loop for adding an increment to the model, which can also be omitted when enacting this process fragment, leading to a pure iterative approach. This process fragment also includes an activity dedicated to a back-end stub, which is needed for running a generated Web GUI.

In more detail, the first activity is *Create/Adapt Communication Model*. Here the designer creates the initial source model, possibly by using a given *pattern* as indicated above, and adapts it in subsequent iterations. Such adaptations can either be modifications due to the results of an evaluation activity, or incremental extensions, or both. Incremental extensions of the interaction design may concern any of the three models that constitute the Discourse-based Communication Model (i.e., the Domain-of-Discourse, the Action-Notification or the Discourse Model). Once a reasonable

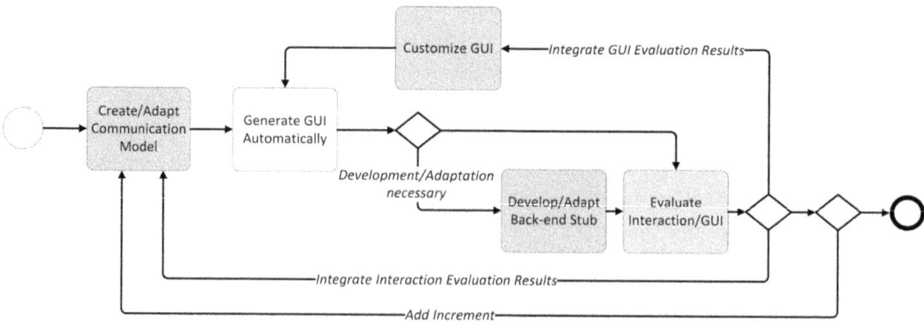

Fig. 12. Iterative and incremental process fragment.

source model is available, the generator tool can transform it in the activity *Generate GUI Automatically* to GUI source code fully automatically.

Unless a fitting back-end stub is available already, the next activity is *Develop/Adapt Back-end Stub*. Developing a back-end stub here means more or less the same work as providing such a stub in more usual prototyping, apart from having to serve specific software interfaces. Adapting the back-end stub can involve modifications due to the results of an evaluation activity, or incremental extensions, or both. Incremental extensions implement the new functionality introduced through an extension of the Discourse-based Communication Model. This activity results in a prototypical application back-end stub, as required to achieve a running application prototype.

A generated GUI together with a fitting back-end stub can be executed and evaluated in the *Evaluate Interaction/GUI* activity, where the focus is on the interaction with a user. Hence, this is primarily an evaluation of the interaction design based on the behavior of this GUI. We do not have any specific restriction on the kind of evaluation to be performed when enacting this process fragment. In principle, it can involve any formative and qualitative or summative and quantitative evaluation, depending on the context and the circumstances. Still, we have anecdotal evidence from a project resulting in an accommodation booking Web GUI, where *heuristic evaluation* was successfully performed by usability experts in the course of an iterative and incremental approach, see [40]. Since there is a running prototype available, also *usability tests* are feasible, but we would suggest to do them with a focus on the interaction rather than the GUI screens per se. As usual, there is a trade-off involved because of the well-known cost of usability tests.

The results of such an evaluation can be used to adapt the Discourse-based Communication Model or to customize the GUI, respectively. In effect, this allows iterating on design alternatives in two different ways, where *Customize GUI* can be through custom rules or custom widgets, or both.

In general, the initial interaction design is *not* supposed to be complete in our proposed process fragment in the sense of covering all the interaction possibilities yet. Especially for relatively large applications, providing an already complete initial model of the interaction design is too difficult to achieve. Hence, like in usual approaches to software development in general, it is preferable to start with an essential part first, to get cyclic feed-back to the current version, to adapt accordingly, and to add an increment in a defined iteration, as defined here through the outer loop in Fig. 12.

6   Discussion and Future Work

In this sense, we propose to utilize automated GUI generation from high-level representations of interaction design that the GUI generation takes as input for creating high-fidelity prototypes. Of course, there is an initial investment before such an approach can be utilized efficiently and effectively, but this applies to any reasonable approach to more conventional high-fidelity prototyping with traditional tools. Our anecdotal experience from projects suggests that especially for multi-device GUIs, this approach can pay off for two or more devices. Hence, whenever low-fidelity prototyping is insufficient for interaction design of GUIs, automated GUI generation is an option.

The range of evaluation options is even wider than sketched for the related activity of our process fragment above. For instance, (constrained) optimization search in the course of automatic generation of GUIs also employs automatic evaluation of alternative GUI models by the machine, both in SUPPLE and in UCP. Of course, such evaluations have to be fast and are certainly not anywhere as good as human evaluations in the course of interaction design. Still, they showed to be useful especially for optimizations regarding accessibility in the case of SUPPLE, and for device-specific tailoring in the case of UCP. Hence, human designers would not necessarily have to deal with such kinds of evaluations any more.

This relates to an interesting observation on UCP's tailoring approach. For smaller screens, e.g., of smartphones, the generated GUIs are relatively better in terms of their usability than GUIs generated automatically for larger screens. This means *relatively* as compared with GUIs created by humans. The reason is that for small screens also humans are usually constrained, so that there is not much opportunity for them to do better than the heuristics involved in a constrained optimization search. For larger screens, however, heuristics employed for layouting cannot match the experience and creativity of human GUI designers in an under-constrained situation.

For future work, we think that humans will need more support for customizations of automatically generated GUIs, especially for GUIs on larger screens. In particular, we envisage letting a human designer explore further alternatives in a screen model (on CUI Level). However, making certain kinds of customizations persistent for round-trip engineering will require more scientific research on *bidirectional* transformations in model-driven development (see, e.g., [2]).

7   Conclusion

In summary, the Conclusion is paper investigates in the context of automated GUI generation

- alternatives for a human interaction designer,
- alternatives within a generator tool, and
- how to explore alternatives supported by a generator tool in an iterative and incremental approach.

Hence, we propose approaches for exploring alternatives both by human and machine, and on different levels of abstraction in the course of interaction design, where such a focus on the exploration of alternatives in the context of automated GUI generation from high-level representations of interaction design is new.

Much as for interaction design in general, exploring alternatives is important for automated GUI generation as well, and high-fidelity prototypes generated automatically are useful for interaction design. Such prototypes can be evaluated by human designers, while automatically generated GUIs are already preselected from design alternatives explored and evaluated by a generator tool, including automated optimization.

Hence, we think that our research question RQ can be answered affirmatively. The techniques for automated Web GUI generation from high-level representations of interaction design for comprehensive support of the exploration of design alternatives already exist. In this paper, we show that and indicate how the support for exploring design alternatives can be achieved.

From the perspective of automated GUI generation, we conjecture that no significant further improvements can be made without taking alternatives into account. This includes both alternatives explored by a tool internally and alternatives suggested by a human designer in the course of customization.

More importantly, advanced approaches to automated GUI generation help human designers explore alternatives in the course of interaction design. Especially when tailored Web GUIs for diverse devices are needed, high-fidelity prototyping becomes more efficient through such tool support.

For systematically utilizing automated GUI generation for interaction design, we propose a defined process fragment for iterative and incremental interaction design. It encompasses a basic iterative approach explained, e.g., in [33] for repeating the key activities. In addition, it includes increments, which is usual for software development. Such an approach may lead towards a better integration of interaction design and software development in the future, and in due course to industrial application.

References

1. Alonso-Ríos, D., Raneburger, D., Popp, R., Kaindl, H., Falb, J.: A user study on tailoring GUIs for smartphones. In: Proceedings of the 29th Annual ACM Symposium on Applied Computing (SAC 2014) (2014)
2. Anjorin, A., Yigitbas, E., Kaindl, H.: Consistent runtime adaptation of user interfaces. In: Proceedings of the Eighth International Workshop on Bidirectional Transformations (Bx 2019), pp. 61–65 (2019). http://ceur-ws.org
3. Bogdan, C., et al.: Evaluation of robot body movements supporting communication: towards HRI on the move. In: New Frontiers in Human Robot Interaction, pp. 185–210. John Benjamins Publishing Company (2011)
4. Buschmann, F., Meunier, R., Rohnert, H., Sommerlad, P., Stal, M.: Pattern-Oriented Software Architecture Volume 1: A System of Patterns. Wiley, Hoboken (1996)
5. Calvary, G., Coutaz, J., Thevenin, D., Limbourg, Q., Bouillon, L., Vanderdonckt, J.: A unifying reference framework for multi-target user interfaces. Interact. Comput. **15**(3), 289–308 (2003). https://doi.org/10.1016/S0953-5438(03)00010-9. http://www.sciencedirect.com/science/article/pii/S0953543803000109
6. Falb, J., Kaindl, H., Horacek, H., Bogdan, C., Popp, R., Arnautovic, E.: A discourse model for interaction design based on theories of human communication. In: Extended Abstracts on Human Factors in Computing Systems (CHI 2006), pp. 754–759. ACM Press: New York (2006). https://doi.org/10.1145/1125451.1125602
7. Falb, J., Kavaldjian, S., Popp, R., Raneburger, D., Arnautovic, E., Kaindl, H.: Fully automatic user interface generation from discourse models. In: Proceedings of the 13th International Conference on Intelligent User Interfaces (IUI 2009), pp. 475–476. ACM Press, New York (2009). https://doi.org/10.1145/1502650.1502722
8. Freund, M., Martin, C., Braune, A.: Platform constraints supporting an ambiguous mapping model. In: Proceedings of 12th IFAC Symposium on Analysis, Design, and Evaluation of Human-Machine Systems, Las Vegas, NV, USA (2013)
9. Gaffar, A., Sinnig, D., Seffah, A., Forbrig, P.: Modeling patterns for task models. In: Proceedings of the 3rd Annual Conference on Task Models and Diagrams, TAMODIA 2004, pp. 99–104. ACM, New York (2004). https://doi.org/10.1145/1045446.1045465

10. Gajos, K., Weld, D.S.: SUPPLE: automatically generating user interfaces. In: Proceedings of the 9th International Conference on Intelligent User Interface (IUI 2004), pp. 93–100. ACM Press, New York (2004). https://doi.org/10.1145/964442.964461

11. Gajos, K.Z., Hurst, A., Findlater, L.: Personalized dynamic accessibility. Interactions **19**(2), 69–73 (2012). https://doi.org/10.1145/2090150.2090167. http://doi.acm.org/10.1145/2090150.2090167

12. Gajos, K.Z., Weld, D.S., Wobbrock, J.O.: Automatically generating personalized user interfaces with supple. Artif. Intell. **174**(12–13), 910–950 (2010). https://doi.org/10.1016/j.artint.2010.05.005. http://www.sciencedirect.com/science/article/pii/S0004370210000822

13. García Frey, A., Céret, E., Dupuy-Chessa, S., Calvary, G., Gabillon, Y.: UsiComp: an extensible model-driven composer. In: Proceedings of the 4th ACM SIGCHI Symposium on Engineering Interactive Computing Systems (EICS 2012), pp. 263–268. ACM, New York (2012). https://doi.org/10.1145/2305484.2305528

14. Hanson, V.L., Richards, J.T.: Progress on website accessibility? ACM Trans. Web **7**(1) (2013). https://doi.org/10.1145/2435215.2435217

15. Insfran, E., Gonzalez-Huerta, J., Abrahão, S.: Design guidelines for the development of quality-driven model transformations. In: Petriu, D.C., Rouquette, N., Haugen, Ø. (eds.) MODELS 2010. LNCS, vol. 6395, pp. 288–302. Springer, Heidelberg (2010). https://doi.org/10.1007/978-3-642-16129-2_21

16. Kaindl, H., Popp, R., Raneburger, D.: Alternative interaction design patterns for automated GUI generation from discourse-based communication models. In: Proceedings of the 2014 IEEE International Conference on Systems, Man and Cybernetics (SMC 2014), San Diego, CA, USA (2014)

17. Kavaldjian, S., Falb, J., Kaindl, H.: Generating content presentation according to purpose. In: Proceedings of the 2009 IEEE International Conference on Systems, Man and Cybernetics (SMC 2009), San Antonio, TX, USA (2009)

18. Larman, C.: Applying UML and Patterns: An Introduction to Object-Oriented Analysis and Design and Iterative Development, 2nd edn. Prentice Hall PTR, Upper Saddle River (2002)

19. Limbourg, Q., Vanderdonckt, J., Michotte, B., Bouillon, L., López-Jaquero, V.: USIXML: a language supporting multi-path development of user interfaces. In: Proceeding of the EHCI-DSVIS 2004, pp. 200–220. IFIP, Hamburg, Germany (2004)

20. Luff, P., Frohlich, D., Gilbert, N.: Computers and Conversation. Academic Press, London (1990)

21. Mann, W.C., Thompson, S.: Rhetorical structure theory: toward a functional theory of text organization. Text **8**(3), 243–281 (1988)

22. Märtin, C., Herdin, C., Engel, J.: Patterns and models for automated user interface construction – in search of the missing links. In: Kurosu, M. (ed.) HCI 2013. LNCS, vol. 8004, pp. 401–410. Springer, Heidelberg (2013). https://doi.org/10.1007/978-3-642-39232-0_44

23. Martinie, C., Navarre, D., Palanque, P.: A multi-formalism approach for model-based dynamic distribution of user interfaces of critical interactive systems. Int. J. Hum.-Comput. Stud. **72**(1), 77–99 (2014). https://doi.org/10.1016/j.ijhcs.2013.08.013. http://www.sciencedirect.com/science/article/pii/S1071581913001110

24. Meixner, G., Paternò, F., Vanderdonckt, J.: Past, present, and future of model-based user interface development. i-com **10**(3), 2–10 (2011)

25. Myers, B., Hudson, S.E., Pausch, R.: Past, present, and future of user interface software tools. ACM Trans. Comput.-Hum. Interact. **7**, 3–28 (2000). https://doi.org/10.1145/344949.344959. http://doi.acm.org/10.1145/344949.344959

26. Navarre, D., Palanque, P., Ladry, J.F., Barboni, E.: Icos: a model-based user interface description technique dedicated to interactive systems addressing usability, reliability and scalability. ACM Trans. Comput.-Hum. Interact. **16**(4), 18:1–18:56 (2009). https://doi.org/10.1145/1614390.1614393. http://doi.acm.org/10.1145/1614390.1614393

27. Nichols, J., Chau, D.H., Myers, B.A.: Demonstrating the viability of automatically generated user interfaces. In: Proceedings of the SIGCHI Conference on Human Factors in Computing Systems, CHI 2007, pp. 1283–1292. ACM, New York (2007). https://doi.org/10.1145/1240624.1240819. http://doi.acm.org/10.1145/1240624.1240819
28. Paternò, F., Santoro, C., Spano, L.D.: MARIA: a universal, declarative, multiple abstraction-level language for service-oriented applications in ubiquitous environments. ACM Trans. Comput.-Hum. Interact. **16**, 19:1–19:30 (2009). https://doi.org/10.1145/1614390.1614394. http://doi.acm.org/10.1145/1614390.1614394
29. Pleuss, A., Hussmann, H.: Model-driven development of interactive multimedia applications with MML. In: Hussmann, H., Meixner, G., Zuehlke, D. (eds.) Model-Driven Development of Advanced User Interfaces. Studies in Computational Intelligence, vol. 340, pp. 199–218. Springer, Heidelberg (2011). https://doi.org/10.1007/978-3-642-14562-9_10
30. Popp, R., Kaindl, H., Badalians, S., Raneburger, D., Paternò, F.: Duality of task- and discourse-based interaction design for GUI generation. In: 2014 IEEE International Conference on Systems, Man and Cybernetics (SMC), pp. 3316–3321 (2014). https://doi.org/10.1109/SMC.2014.6974439
31. Popp, R., Kaindl, H., Raneburger, D.: Connecting interaction models and application logic for model-driven generation of Web-based graphical user interfaces. In: Proceedings of the 20th Asia-Pacific Software Engineering Conference (APSEC 2013) (2013)
32. Popp, R., Raneburger, D., Kaindl, H.: Tool support for automated multi-device GUI generation from discourse-based communication models. In: Proceedings of the 5th ACM SIGCHI Symposium on Engineering Interactive Computing Systems (EICS 2013). ACM, New York (2013)
33. Preece, J., Rogers, Y., Sharp, H.: Interaction Design: Beyond Human-Computer Interaction, 4th edn. Wiley, Hoboken (2015)
34. Raneburger, D., Alonso-Ríos, D., Popp, R., Kaindl, H., Falb, J.: A user study with GUIs tailored for smartphones. In: Kotzé, P., Marsden, G., Lindgaard, G., Wesson, J., Winckler, M. (eds.) INTERACT 2013. LNCS, vol. 8118, pp. 505–512. Springer, Heidelberg (2013). https://doi.org/10.1007/978-3-642-40480-1_34
35. Raneburger, D., Kaindl, H., Popp, R.: Model transformation rules for customization of multi-device graphical user interfaces. In: Proceedings of the 7th ACM SIGCHI Symposium on Engineering Interactive Computing Systems, EICS 2015, pp. 100–109. ACM, New York (2015). https://doi.org/10.1145/2774225.2774839
36. Raneburger, D., Kaindl, H., Popp, R.: Strategies for automated GUI tailoring for multiple devices. In: Proceedings of the 48th Annual Hawaii International Conference on System Sciences (HICSS-48), pp. 507–516. IEEE Computer Society Press, Piscataway (2015)
37. Raneburger, D., Kaindl, H., Popp, R., Šajatović, V., Armbruster, A.: A process for facilitating interaction design through automated GUI generation. In: Proceedings of the 29th Annual ACM Symposium on Applied Computing (SAC 2014) (2014)
38. Raneburger, D., Popp, R., Kaindl, H.: Model-driven transformation for optimizing PSMs: a case study of rule design for multi-device GUI generation. In: Proceedings of the 8th International Joint Conference on Software Technologies (ICSOFT 2013). SciTePress (2013)
39. Raneburger, D., Popp, R., Kaindl, H.: A user study to evaluate the customization of automatically generated GUIs. In: Black, N.L., Neumann, W.P. (eds.) Proceedings of the 21st Congress of the International Ergonomics Association (IEA 2021). LNNS, pp. 683–690. Springer, Cham (2022). https://doi.org/10.1007/978-3-030-74614-8_85
40. Raneburger, D., Popp, R., Kaindl, H., Armbruster, A., Šajatović, V.: An iterative and incremental process for interaction design through automated GUI generation. In: Proceedings of the 16th International Conference on Human-Computer Interaction (2014)

41. Raneburger, D., Popp, R., Kaindl, H., Falb, J.: Automated WIMP-UI behavior generation: parallelism and granularity of communication units. In: 2011 IEEE International Conference on Systems, Man, and Cybernetics (SMC), pp. 2816–2821 (2011). https://doi.org/10.1109/ICSMC.2011.6084099

42. Raneburger, D., Popp, R., Kaindl, H., Falb, J., Ertl, D.: Automated generation of device-specific WIMP UIs: weaving of structural and behavioral models. In: Proceedings of the 3rd ACM SIGCHI Symposium on Engineering Interactive Computing Systems, EICS 2011, pp. 41–46. ACM, New York (2011). https://doi.org/10.1145/1996461.1996492

43. Rathfux, T., Popp, R., Kaindl, H.: Adding custom widgets to model-driven GUI generation. In: Proceedings of the 8th ACM SIGCHI Symposium on Engineering Interactive Computing Systems, EICS 2016, pp. 16–26. ACM, New York (2016). https://doi.org/10.1145/2933242.2933251

44. Rathfux, T., Thöner, J., Kaindl, H., Popp, R.: Combining design-time generation of webpages with responsive design for improving low-vision accessibility. In: Proceedings of the ACM SIGCHI Symposium on Engineering Interactive Computing Systems, EICS 2018, pp. 10:1–10:7. ACM, New York (2018). https://doi.org/10.1145/3220134.3220141. http://doi.acm.org/10.1145/3220134.3220141

45. Searle, J.R.: Speech Acts: An Essay in the Philosophy of Language. Cambridge University Press, Cambridge (1969)

A Usability and Universal Design Investigation into Scrolljacking for Web Pages

Bianca Marilena Voinea and Pietro Murano[✉]

Oslo Metropolitan University, Postboks 4, St. Olavs Plass, 0130 Oslo, Norway
`bianca.m.voinea@gmail.com, pietro.murano@oslomet.no`

Abstract. Scrolljacking is a feature used in web development to hijack and modify the speed, direction, and overall native behaviour of scrolling on a web page. This research study investigated how scrolljacking can influence the usability and the Universal Design of web pages. Two prototypes were designed and developed as part of this research. One prototype had a non-scrolljacking user interface and the other prototype had the same user interface as the first prototype but with scrolljacking functionality. The two prototypes were evaluated in an experiment with 20 participants', where they had to perform similar task-driven actions in the two user interfaces. Accuracy, user satisfaction, and speed were some of the main aspects investigated in this experiment. To measure these aspects, the total time to complete the tasks and the number of errors made per task were collected, as well as the scrolljacking familiarity and the participant's opinion about the topics of ease-of-use control, frustration, and fun during the experiment. Data was collected during the experiment and was analysed by using paired t-tests and Wilcoxon signed-rank tests. The data analysis revealed that there was no statistically significant difference in speed between the two user interfaces. However, there was a statistically significant difference in the accuracy and user satisfaction between the two user interfaces, as the interface using scrolljacking had lower accuracy and user satisfaction scores than the non-scrolljacking interface. The research study suggests that scrolljacking negatively influences the usability and the Universal Design of a web page.

Keywords: Scrolljacking · Non-Scrolljacking · Scroll Hijacking · Web Page Scrolling · User Interface Scrolling · Usability · User Experience · Universal Design · Design For All · Evaluation

1 Introduction

Scrolling on a web page is a fundamental interaction that can take place between users and any number of web pages. Typically, the most well-known type of scrolling is the vertical kind, where one scrolls a web page upwards or downwards. Over the years researchers and designers have tried different types of scrolling behaviours. One such deviation from the well-known scrolling type is scrolljacking.

Scrolljacking also sometimes known as scroll hijacking, is simply defined by Paul [13] as: '...a design pattern that changes the speed and, sometimes, the direction of scrolling on a web page.'

© The Author(s), under exclusive license to Springer Nature Switzerland AG 2026
J. F. Krems et al. (Eds.): CHIRA 2025, CCIS 2836, pp. 93–107, 2026.
https://doi.org/10.1007/978-3-032-16454-4_6

There are some main types of scrollkjacking which have certain behaviours. One kind of scrolljacking (sometimes referred to as a full jack) uses a technique to take over the entire web page, blocking the user from proceeding further until they scroll through the page. It works similarly to a pop-up, limiting the ease of scrolling back and forth between the content of the page. Another kind of scrolljacking works in a similar manner as described, but is only concerned with the background images used on a web page (sometimes referred to as a slight jack). By scrolling, the background images will be changing their position several times, creating an animation effect. Lastly, a third kind of scrolljacking involves both the background and foreground elements in a web page being affected (sometimes referred to as a fading jack). By scrolling, different elements will fade in or out of the page. This type of scrolling behavior can create white space between the content of the page.

Paul's [13] usability test indicated that scrolljacking can negatively impact usability if certain design principles are ignored.

In our research, as far as we have been able to ascertain, there are no peer reviewed published works directly investigating the usability and universal design of scrolljacking.

Therefore, in this paper, we present the novel results of a preliminary experiment comparing identical web pages where they only differed in having scrolljacking or not as an interaction mode. Our main aims were to investigate if scrolljacking had some effect (positive or negative) on usability and universal design.

The next section will briefly consider some previous works in the area of scrolling for user interfaces. This will be followed by a description of our experiment comparing scrolljacking and non-scrolljacking. Then the results of the statistical analysis will be presented. Finally, a discussion with conclusions will complete the paper.

2 Background

Scrolling is a part of many user interfaces in applications and web sites. Over the years different kinds of scrolling approaches have been used. Some have been extensively investigated, while some approaches have not been well investigated.

One approach that has been investigated is parallax scrolling. In Mahardika et al. [11] the authors investigated parallax scrolling. Their testing environments were storytelling and online shopping. From the data collected they concluded that web pages designed with parallax scrolling fostered faster task times and more user engagement. However, it must be noted that the results are aligned to goal-oriented web pages that contain a lot of text. Also, since their work used a between-users design, it is unclear if any bias resulted from differences in the participant sample. Particularly since full details about the participant sample are not given to the reader [7].

However, Murano and Pandey [12] also conducted a study into parallax scrolling and found no statistically significant differences in terms of tasks times and user preferences in the context of using a restaurant type web site. The overall averages in that study though indicated that task times were faster with the non-parallax web pages. Subjective preferences on average were in favour of the parallax web pages. However, the study had a rather small sample size.

Other scrolling types, such as infinite scrolling, have also been investigated by other researchers. Issues of effectiveness and user satisfaction with infinite scrolling are still unclear. However, Loranger [10] suggested that when user tasks are goal-oriented, infinite scrolling is not the best design option. Further, task-driven actions can negatively affect user experience if one is obliged to use infinite scrolling.

Linked to this, Sharma and Murano [14] carried out a study into infinite scrolling, where an experimental evaluation was conducted. They compared four identical prototype web sites, which varied only by the scrolling method. The scrolling methods were 'normal scrolling with default pagination, infinite scrolling, infinite scrolling with a load more button and infinite scrolling with pagination, [14]'.

The authors did not observe any statistically significant differences in terms of task times and errors across the four scrolling types. User experience aspects did not reveal such a clear picture, where opinions were varied in relation to scrolling types [14].

Other less well-known approaches to scrolling have also been investigated in the recent past. Ishak and Feiner [5] investigated 'content aware scrolling', which depending on the content of a certain document, affected the direction of scrolling, the speed and zooming. The authors reported positive informal experiences with this approach.

Also, Bartlett [2] investigated a mobile device option which allows users to use gestures for achieving scrolling, selections and commands. This development meant that other options, e.g. touch interaction were not required. Although mention is made about some kind of testing/evaluation, the details about this are not included in the paper and therefore it is difficult to ascertain any usability outcomes.

In addition, Aceituno et al. [1] investigated various kinds of edge scrolling techniques. They concluded that edge scrolling is in use by some users and that users tend to know about some of the negative issues with the use of edge scrolling. They also found that different implementations of edge scrolling affected performance and how users felt about the level of work involved.

In considering universal design or design for all, Darzentas and Miesenberger [3] some years ago suggested that those involved with information technology and design need to be more engaged and on-board with design for all issues. These observations of some years ago are still relevant, as more recent studies indicate that universal design failings continue to occur on a large scale [4].

This brief selection of related works indicates that for some years researchers have been investigating and trialing different kinds of scrolling. The previous works' results overall tend to be quite mixed in nature and many require further work to concretise initial results. The previous works also continue to indicate failings in the area of universally designed systems. Furthermore, it is indicated in the previous works that peer reviewed and published results on scrolljacking in terms of usability and universal design are lacking. We therefore present in the subsequent sections an experiment and results that aimed to find out if there were any differences in performance and user experience with scrolljacking compared to non-scrolljacking.

3 Experiment

3.1 Experiment Design

A within-users experimental design was chosen for this evaluation. We wanted participants to experience both types of scrolling and therefore be able to make judgements on the impressions gained for both scrolling types.

Figure 1 shows a condensed screenshot for the home page. Both implemented versions of the web site were identical in all aspects, except for the scrolling functionality (non-scrolljacking or scrolljacking).

Fig. 1. Home page of the prototypes showing the layout used and how books were displayed.

3.2 Hypotheses

We had three hypotheses we wished to examine:

H_1: For errors, there will be a statistically significant difference between the scrolljacking and non-scrolljacking user interfaces.

H_0: For errors, there will be no statistically significant difference between the scrolljacking and non-scrolljacking user interfaces.

H_2: For task execution speed, there will be a statistically significant difference between the scrolljacking and non-scrolljacking user interfaces.

H_0: For task execution speed, there will be no statistically significant difference between the scrolljacking and non-scrolljacking user interfaces.

H_3: In terms of user satisfaction, ratings scores will be statistically significantly different and verbally expressed differences and observations will differ, between the scrolljacking and non-scrolljacking user interfaces.

H_0: In terms of user satisfaction, ratings scores will not be statistically significantly different and there will be no verbally expressed differences and observations, between the scrolljacking and non-scrolljacking user interfaces.

3.3 Users

Twenty participants were chosen for this study who were linked to the Information and Communication Technology area. The participants were familiar with using a computer and the internet. Most participants (18) had never heard of scrolljacking, while one participant knew about scrolljacking and one other participant expressed a neutral opinion concerning knowledge of scrolljacking.

The sample of participants consisted of individuals from varied age groups. Six participants were in the 18–30 age group, 12 participants were in the 31–40 age group and two participants were in the 41–50 age group.

3.4 Variables

The independent variables in this study were the two different user interfaces featuring non-scrolljacking and scrolljacking interaction and the tasks.

The dependent variables were accuracy and user satisfaction.

The dependent measures were the total number of errors, the total time to complete the tasks and users' subjective opinions on their feelings of satisfaction and enjoyment.

Errors were defined as any kind of action that was done by the user without their acknowledgment, such as miss-clicking, clicking on a wrongly chosen item, scrolling when the user intended to do a different action, or not scrolling when the user intended to scroll. The total number of errors encountered per task and in the overall experiment were recorded.

Total task time involved the time to complete a single task, as well as the total time to complete the set of tasks. Each user was timed by starting a timer at the start of a task and stopping it at the end of the same task. The total time to complete a set of tasks was simply determined by adding all the times of the tasks in the set.

User satisfaction and enjoyment were measured by means of a post-experiment questionnaire which covered user-experience type topics. Further, verbal comments and informal observations were also included within the experiment and results.

3.5 Apparatus, Materials and Tasks

The apparatus and materials used were:

- An Apple MacBook M1 Pro 2021 16 GB.
- An Apple iPhone XR 2018 64 GB, with its native Calculator application for participants to optionally use in relation to Task 1, where some addition had to be carried out as part of the task (see Pilot Testing section for more details on this aspect).
- A Huawei Watch Fit A96, used by the experimenter as a stopwatch for task timing.
- Google Chrome browser to render the two website prototypes.
- A pre-experiment questionnaire. It contained the ethical aspects of the experiment and was used to register the consent of the participants in the experiment. The questionnaire also elicited age groups and knowledge of scrolljacking from the participants.
- A post-experiment questionnaire containing five questions related to user experience type issues. The first four questions covered aspects of ease of tasks, feelings of control, feelings of frustration, perceived fun and overall preference in terms of the scrolling type. The questionnaire elicited responses to these topics by asking participants to score their opinions on a Likert-type [9] scale. The scale ranged from 1 – strongly disagree to 5 – strongly agree. So that comparisons could be made between the two user interfaces each of the four questions was asked two times. This gave an individual score for each user interface. The fifth question eliciting overall preference for one of the scrolling types contained two options – scrolljacking or non-scrolljacking.

The post-experiment questionnaire was a bespoke questionnaire which was designed to allow participants to give their opinions in a structured manner. The five questions were designed with the main aim of giving us an idea concerning usability and universal design aspects in relation to scrolljacking designs.

The specific tasks designed are shown in Tables 1 and 2.

Table 1. Tasks used in the experiment under the non-scrolljacking condition.

TASK SET 1 USED ON PROTOTYPE 1 NON-SCROLLJACKING	
Task Number	Task Description
1	From the Home Page, find how many genres the store offers
2	From the Home Page, tell me how many pages the book titled *'The Man Without Qualities'* that is under the *'Philosophy'* genre has
3	From the Home Page, add the book *'The Diary of a Madman'* from *'Short Stories'*, *'A Doll's House'* from *'Fiction'* and *'The Tale of Genji'* from *'Romance'* in the cart and then go to checkout

(continued)

Table 1. (*continued*)

TASK SET 1 USED ON PROTOTYPE 1 NON-SCROLLJACKING

Task Number	Task Description
4	From the About Us Page, find information about how you can request a new book

Table 2. Tasks used in the experiment under the scrolljacking condition.

TASK SET 2 USED ON PROTOTYPE 2 WITH SCROLLJACKING

Task Number	Task Description
1	From the Home Page, find how many books the store offers
2	From the Home Page, tell me how many pages the book titled *'Hamlet'* that is under the *'Poetry'* genre has
3	From the Home Page, add the book titled *'Tales'* from *'Short Stories'*, *'The Sound of the Mountain'* from *'Fiction'* and *'Middlemarch'* from *'Romance'* in the cart and then go to checkout
4	From the About Us Page, find information about how you can donate an old book

The tasks were designed to be representative of real-world tasks one might carry out at a bookstore web-shop.

To avoid learning effects, two sets of tasks were designed with approximately equal levels of difficulty.

We aimed to maintain equivalence in difficulty for both sets of tasks by having the actions in each set of tasks of the same difficulty, where the only aspect that was changed was the context of the action (e.g., book A vs book B). Moreover, designing the tasks in such a manner helped to keep the path to task achievement the same in both prototypes. This approach aimed to limit the potential bias for learning while keeping the same level of complexity in both versions of the prototype.

In addition, the tasks, linked to the dependent measures (Sect. 3.4) were designed to allow collection of data that would give indications about usability and universal design aspects for scrolljacking use.

Description of the Scrolljacking Used in the Scrolljack Prototype. In this sub-section we will describe the kinds of scrolljacking that were implemented into the scrolljacking prototype.

As can be seen in Tables 1 and 2, all the tasks were centered around the Home and About Us pages. Therefore the description that follows is in the context of these two specific areas of the scrolljacking prototype. The figures presented are not intended for detailed reading, but merely to give a visual idea of the main design elements.

On the Home page, the full jack effect was implemented. While the visual presentation of the Home page was the same as in the non-scrolljacking version, the content of this page was split up into multiple individual pages. As such, the first page of the Home page was considered the part with the informational banners as seen in Fig. 2. Information points displayed on the Home page. All the subsequent pages were represented by each category of book genres. Thus, in the case of this prototype, the second page was represented by the Adventure category (Fig. 3), and so on. The Home page ended with a Footer (Fig. 4) as its own page.

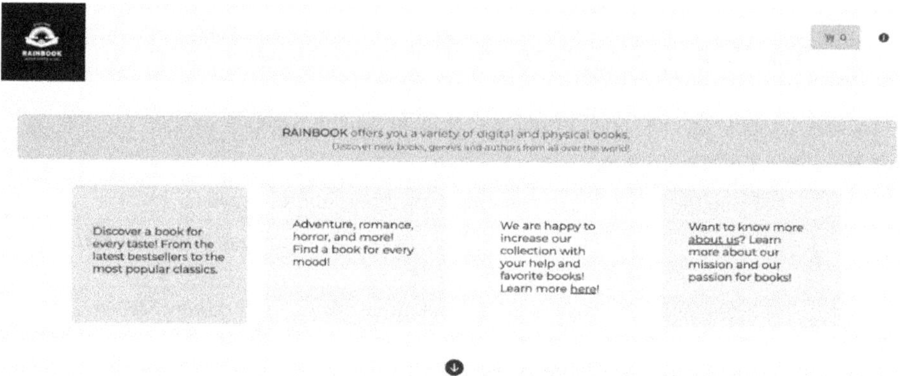

Fig. 2. Information points displayed on the Home page.

Fig. 3. A category with books on the Home page.

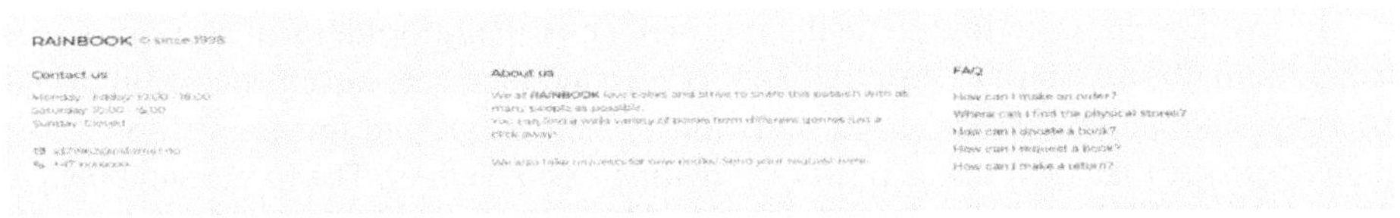

Fig. 4. Page footer.

When the user scrolls to the Home page, they will actually be scrolling between these multiple individual pages. One motion of scrolling down or up will fully load the corresponding page, removing any partial content being cut off as done usually by the native scrolling behavior. This type of scrolling effect will prevent the user from rushing between the content of the Home page, as they need to scroll through the single small pages one by one. Skipping content will also be impossible using the full Jack effect. This means that the user will have to do the action of scrolling as many times as there are categories in the Home page to reach the end of the page.

The About Us page uses two concepts of scrolljacking, the slight Jack and the fading Jack. In contrast to the Home page, where the scrolljacking is applied directly to the page, in the About Us page, scrolljacking is applied to the content inside the page. This means that the text blocks and the images will be influenced by the scrolling motion done by the user.

The About Us page starts with a decorative section as seen in Fig. 5. As the user scrolls down, the circled logo will remain in place while the two borders surrounding it will move up at different speeds, creating an animation effect using slight jack. Scrolling down even more, the user will see more text being scrolljacked by using both slight jack concepts and fading jack concepts. For the text scrolljacked using fading jack, this text will initially be hidden from view until the user scrolls down enough on the page. When this specific point is reached by scrolling, the position of the text will be continuously translated horizontally until it leaves the view again at the opposite end of the page.

Fig. 5. Decorative section in the About us page.

By scrolling more on this page, the user will enter the Informational section as seen in Fig. 6. In this section, background and foreground elements have been scrolljacked, creating multiple animations at the same time. The background images will be scaled higher or lower than their initial position, creating a depth effect. The foreground images will also be scaled in the opposite direction of the background elements. Meanwhile, the foreground text will be continuously translated either from the right, left, up, or down.

Fig. 6. Informational section in the About us page.

3.6 Procedure

Participation in the experiment was voluntary. Each participant was provided with a digital pre-experiment questionnaire dealing with informed consent related to the study and some background questions. The participants were given as much time as they needed to read and sign the consent aspects (Note: the study was conducted in line with ethical requirements for research conducted in Norway). If they agreed to participate in the experiment, a unique identification number was assigned to each individual participant. The number was used to link the experiment results with the user information. No identifying information was collected from the participants.

The experiment was conducted in a private room containing only one participant at a time and the researcher. This allowed for a controlled and quiet space while reducing unnecessary external noise or potential bias. Each individual participant was asked to complete Task set 1 followed by Task set 2 for the experiment. Use of the 'Find in page' browser feature was not allowed. During this process, participants were timed and observed discreetly by the researcher. After the set of tasks was completed by the participant, participants were asked to complete a post-experiment questionnaire with questions related to the overall experiment and their personal experiences.

3.7 Pilot Testing

The described experimental design was the final version used with the participants. An earlier version was pilot tested and a number of small improvements and additional details were achieved for the experiment.

The first aspect was that the pilot testing gave a broad indication of how long the experiment overall might last and so this information was included in the initial information given to participants.

The second issue was that the pilot testing allowed for improvement of the initial information by adding more relevant detail and better formatting.

The third aspect concerned Task 1. After the pilot testing, it was decided to supply participants with a calculator for adding up the number of genres covered and number of books. Use of the calculator was made optional. This allowed the participants to focus more on the tasks than on the actual adding of numbers.

The fourth aspect involved minor changes to the implementation of the prototypes.

The fifth aspect was to design into the procedure the prohibition of using the 'Find in page' browser feature. This was so that the interaction focused on the scrolling aspects under investigation.

3.8 Results

The data collected from the comparisons were statistically analysed for significant differences. In all cases, the data were initially analysed to determine if the data was parametric in nature. The data collected for task times was found to be parametric and was analysed using a t-test. All the other data was found to be non-parametric and was therefore analysed using Wilcoxon Signed Rank Tests. For brevity, the details of the analysis for determining whether the data was parametric in nature, is not included here. All results presented below are in two-tailed format.

Total task times were analysed using a t-test. The mean (M) task time for the non-scrolljacking user interface is $M = 4.39$ (Standard Deviation (SD) $= 1.2$) and $M = 4.56$ (SD $= 1.01$) for the scrolljacking user interface. The paired samples t-test result is not significant: $t(19) = -1.476$, $p = .156$. This is represented by a medium effect, $d = 0.32$.

Total number of errors were analysed using a Wilcoxon Signed Rank Test. The mean errors for the non-scrolljacking user interface are $M = .75$ (SD $= 1.41$) and $M = 4.2$ (SD $= 2.783$) for the scrolljacking user interface. The Wilcoxon Signed Rank Test indicates that the scrolljacking user interface incurred significantly more errors than the non-scrolljacking user interface: $W = .00$; $z = -3.842$, $p < .001$ with a large effect size ($r = .859$).

The next series of results concern the participants' responses to the post-experiment questionnaire.

For the question concerning how easy participants found the tasks under each user interface, the results are the mean score for the non-scrolljacking user interface is $M = 2.85$ (SD $= .988$) and $M = 2.15$ (SD $= 1.226$) for the scrolljacking user interface. The Wilcoxon Signed Rank Test indicates that there is no statistically significant difference between the two scrolling types for ease of the tasks: $W = 42.00$; $z = -1.656$, $p = .098$ with a medium effect size ($r = .370$).

For the question concerning feelings of control whilst using the user interfaces, the results are the mean score for the non-scrolljacking user interface is M = 3.5 (SD = 1.192) and M = 2.3 (SD = 1.302) for the scrolljacking user interface. The Wilcoxon Signed Rank Test indicates that participants felt significantly more control whilst using the user interface with non-scrolljacking: W = 36.00; z = -2.396, p = .017 with a strong effect size (r = .535).

For the question concerning feelings of frustration whilst using the user interfaces, the results are the mean score for the non-scrolljacking user interface is M = 3.45 (SD = 1.276) and M = 4.25 (SD = 1.164) for the scrolljacking user interface. The Wilcoxon Signed Rank Test indicates that there is no statistically significant difference between the two scrolling types for feelings of frustration: W = 36.00; z = -1.682, p = .093 with a medium effect size (r = .376).

For the question concerning fun factor whilst using the user interfaces, the results are the mean score for the non-scrolljacking user interface is M = 2.6 (SD = .821) and M = 2.0 (SD = 1.17) for the scrolljacking user interface. The Wilcoxon Signed Rank Test indicates that there is no statistically significant difference between the two scrolling types for fun factor: W = 47.00; z = -1.730, p = .084 with a medium effect size (r = .386).

The questionnaire also asked participants to make a selection regarding which of the two scrolling types they preferred overall. Thirteen participants chose the non-scrolljacking option as their choice. The remaining seven participants expressed their preference for the scrolljacking user interface.

4 Discussion

Based on the data collected and analyzed from the pre-experiment questionnaires, 90% of the participants had never heard of scrolljacking before the experiment.

For performance, the total time to complete the two sets of tasks was monitored, as well as the total number of errors done in each set of tasks. The data analysis showed that the participants made significantly more errors while using the website with scrolljacking. This could be due to the confusion caused by the unexpected change in scrolling behaviour and by the frustration of having to scroll more than needed.

In view of this result, we accept the positive hypothesis at the beginning of this paper, which stated that for errors, there will be a statistically significant difference between the scrolljacking and non-scrolljacking user interfaces.

When it comes to the total time to complete the tasks, the data analysis revealed that the participants were slightly slower (not statistically significant.) in completing their tasks on the website with scrolljacking. This could be due to the fact that a web page using scrolljacking needs to be scrolled completely from top to bottom, as there are no shortcuts available to skip content.

In view of this result, we accept the null hypothesis at the beginning of this paper, which stated that for task execution speed, there will be no statistically significant difference between the scrolljacking and non-scrolljacking user interfaces.

While undergoing the experiment, some of the participants were vocal about their experience using the two prototypes, and even more about their first-hand experience with scrolljacking.

Many of the participants of the experiment described the experience of using the web page with scrolljacking as 'slow', 'infuriating', 'tiring', and 'frustrating to scroll so much'. It was a noticeable pattern that the users in this experiment were used to scrolling big chunks of content at a time, even scrolling from top to bottom in one single motion. One particular scrolljacking functionality led to exactly the opposite of that behaviour, as it blocks the user from proceeding further until all blocks of content are scrolled. Hence, some of the participants were very frustrated in having to wait to scroll to each part of the page until the bottom.

One comment a participant made during the third task in the second set for the web page with scrolljacking was revealing: 'I would have given up and left the page by now'.

Some of the participants stated that they could see the potential of using scrolljacking in the correct context. They mentioned that they liked how scrolljacking was used for animations, however, it can easily become 'visually weird' if it is overused. Since it could be used for artistic purposes, using it in an online shop where one needs to perform multiple tasks may not represent the best place to use scrolljacking concepts.

During the second set of tasks done on the prototype with scrolljacking, multiple participants tried to scroll the page by grabbing and moving the scrollbar. This capability is not available while using certain kinds of scrolljacking and has been seen as a hindrance by some of the participants, as they were used to the native behaviour of grabbing the scrollbar for scrolling. The fact that the 'Search in Page' browser capability was prohibited during the experiment also represented another hindrance that the participants experienced, as some of them use this capability naturally in their day-to-day tasks.

Multiple users expressed the need to have navigational feedback while they were scrolling on the web page with scrolljacking by mentioning how 'there is no feedback or response from scrolljacking'. Linked to this and aligned to our findings, Ledneva and Kovalev [8] found that a reduction in navigational cues can increase cognitive load.

Many other participants were also looking for navigational components such as 'Go to the top' or 'Go to the bottom', as they were looking for fast ways to jump from one content on the page to another. A web page using scrolljacking does not have these navigational helpers as the implementation forces the user to scroll throughout the entire page. Certain participants appeared to become tired of scrolling more than it was necessary.

In the post-experiment questionnaire, the participants were asked to rate their opinion of four aspects related to the experiment and the use of scrolljacking: ease of use, control, frustration, and fun.

The participants felt the website with scrolljacking to be more difficult for completing their tasks, more frustrating to use and less fun to use. However, the differences are not statistically significant. Further, participants felt that they were a lot less in control whilst using the website with scrolljacking. The differences for feeling of control are statistically significant.

One out four elements on the post-experiment questionnaire is statistically significant (feeling of control). However, taking also into consideration the verbal comments and observations overall, we can accept the positive hypothesis. This stated that in terms of user satisfaction, ratings scores will be statistically significantly different and verbally expressed differences and observations will differ, between the scrolljacking and non-scrolljacking user interfaces. The overall pattern clearly suggests that the non-scrolljacking website was preferred over the scrolljacking version.

In addition, the overall preference question asked in the post-experiment questionnaire shows that 65% of the participants preferred the version of the website without scrolljacking (i.e. native scrolling functionality). Therefore, only 35% of the participants preferred the scrolljacking interaction.

Furthermore, we find our results link with well established principles. During the experiment, the participants were feeling frustrated, confused, and tired while using the web pages with scrolljacking. These results are against the concepts of good usability for a web page, as seen in multiple web guidelines, e.g. [6, 16]. The Web Content Accessibility Guidelines (WCAG) 2.2 has four main principles and two of their principles can be related directly to scrolljacking: Operable and Understandable. These two principles cover guidelines related to the user interface components and navigation, which have been challenged by using scrolljacking:

- The web pages should behave in a predictable way.
- Provide navigational context and help to navigate.
- The content of web pages should not cause seizures.

Concerning universal design, this can be defined as: 'the design of products and environments that can be used and experienced by people of all ages and abilities, to the greatest extent possible, without adaptation [15].' Our experiment has revealed that the users found scrolljacking to be a somewhat tiring and slow user experience. The increased mental effort of using scrolljacking on a web page is directly against the principles of universal design [15], namely the 'Simple and Intuitive Use' and the 'Flexibility in Use' principles. The principle 'Simple and Intuitive to Use' discusses how a design should be easily understood and used by any user, no matter the skill or concentration level. Scrolljacking may violate this principle because our observations suggest that considerably more effort is required on the part of a user when interacting with a web page. The 'Flexibility in Use' is about how the user should have multiple options available in using a certain designed artefact. By imposing scrolljacking concepts on a web page, the user may be forced to scroll through the entire content of a web page with no alternative. Furthermore, although this paper is discussing potential issues in relation to all users, the problems observed in our investigation which can be linked with well-known guidelines, can be even greater for individuals with one or more impairments.

5 Concluding Remarks

As mentioned in the Introduction, our main aims with this study were to investigate if scrolljacking had some effect (positive or negative) on usability and universal design.

As seen in the findings of the experiment, the use of scrolljacking in a web page overall has a negative impact on performance and user experience. In addition, implementing scrolljacking is likely to not meet certain WCAG and universal design principles.

Concerning future work linked to shortcomings in this study, we suggest that this could involve a larger study with a larger sample of participants. Furthermore, it would be good to be able to obtain participants with more diverse backgrounds and having one or more impairments. It might also be useful in terms of results to have more difficult tasks for participants to try in a future study. In addition, sets of tasks that are administered to participants, would ideally be randomized in how they are presented to participants.

References

1. Aceituno, J., Malacria, S., Quinn, P., Roussel, N., Cockburn, A., Casiez, G.: The design, use, and performance of edge-scrolling techniques. Int. J. Hum.-Comput. Stud. **97**, 58–76 (2017). ISSN 1071-5819. https://doi.org/10.1016/j.ijhcs.2016.08.001
2. Bartlett, J.F.: Rock 'n' scroll is here to stay. IEEE Comput. Graph. Appl. **20**(3), 40–45 (2000). https://doi.org/10.1109/38.844371
3. Darzentas, J., Miesenberger, K.: Design for all in information technology: a universal concern. In: Andersen, K.V., Debenham, J., Wagner, R. (eds.) Database and Expert Systems Applications. DEXA 2005. Lecture Notes in Computer Science, vol. 3588. Springer, Heidelberg (2005). https://doi.org/10.1007/11546924_40
4. Ferati, M., Dalipi, F., Kastrati, Z.: Open government data through the lens of universal design. In: Antona, M., Stephanidis, C. (eds.) Universal Access in Human-Computer Interaction. Applications and Practice. HCII 2020. Lecture Notes in Computer Science, vol. 12189. Springer, Cham (2020). https://doi.org/10.1007/978-3-030-49108-6_24
5. Ishak, E.W., Feiner, S.K.: Content-aware scrolling. In: Proceedings of the 19th Annual ACM Symposium on User Interface Software and Technology (UIST 2006), pp. 155–158. Association for Computing Machinery, New York (2006). https://doi.org/10.1145/1166253.1166277
6. Leavitt, M.O., et al.: Research-Based Web Design & Usability Guidelines [2006 edition], U.S. Department of Health and Human Services (2006)
7. Lazar, J., Feng, J., Hochheiser, H.: Research Methods in Human-Computer Interaction, 2nd edn. Morgan Kaufmann, Cambridge (2017)
8. Ledneva, T., Kovalev, A.: Cognitive load measurement during navigation and information retrieval in digital text. Procedia Comput. Sci. **192**, 2720–2730 (2021)
9. Likert, R.: A technique for the measurement of attitudes, Archives of psychology, number 140. Science Press, New York (1932)
10. Loranger, H.: Infinite scrolling is not for every Web site, Nielsen Norman Group (2 February) (2014). http://www.nngroup.com/articles/infinite-scrolling. Accessed Feb 2025
11. Mahardika, W., Wibirama, S., Ferdiana, R., Kusumawardani, S.S.: A novel user experience study of parallax scrolling using eye tracking and user experience questionnaire. Int. J. Adv. Sci. Eng. Inform. Technol. **8**(4) (2018)
12. Murano, P., Pandey, S.: A usability investigation of parallax scrolling for web pages. In: Marcus, A., Rosenzweig, E., Soares, M.M., Rau, PL.P., Moallem, A. (eds.) HCI International 2024 – Late Breaking Papers 26th International Conference on Human-Computer Interaction, HCII 2024 Washington, DC, USA, 29 June – 4 July, 2024 Proceedings, Part VII, Springer, Lecture Notes in Computer Science (LNCS) (2024)
13. Paul, S.: Scrolljacking 101, Retrieved from Nielsen Norman Group April 2025 (2023): https://www.nngroup.com/articles/scrolljacking-101/
14. Sharma, S., Murano, P.: A usability evaluation of web user interface scrolling types. First Monday **25**(3) (2020)
15. Story, M.F.: Maximizing usability: the principles of universal design. Assistive Technol. Official J. RESNA **10**(1), 4–12 (1998)
16. W3C. Web Content Accessibility Guidelines (WCAG) 2.2 (2024). Retrieved from W3C April 2025: https://www.w3.org/TR/WCAG22/

Effect of 360-Degree Video with View Manipulation on Communication and Creative Output in Hybrid Work Environments

Takumi Ishikawa[1(✉)], Ichiro Umata[2], Tsuneo Kato[1], and Sumaru Niida[2]

[1] Doshisha University, Kyotanabe-shi, Kyoto 610-0394, Japan
`ctwk0125@mail4.doshisha.ac.jp`, `tsukato@mail.doshisha.ac.jp`
[2] KDDI Research Inc., Minato-ku, Tokyo 105-0001, Japan
`niida.sumaru@p.chibakoudai.jp`

Abstract. Video conferences, which rapidly became widespread due to the COVID-19 pandemic, have since become established as a hybrid working arrangement. However, significant challenges remain with respect to remote collaboration, particularly the issue that members' performance is not fully utilized in creative collaborative work. This study focuses on the asymmetry in communication in a hybrid work environment where main and remote workplaces coexist, and quantitatively evaluates a system that promotes engagement from the remote workplace using a 360-degree camera. To control the 360-degree video view, two novel interfaces, a hand gesture interface and a touch panel, were proposed in addition to the standard mouse-based operation. The experimental evaluation focused on four metrics: total speaking time, speech overlap rate, and creativity indicators (fluency and originality). The results showed that the touch panel operation maximized total speaking time and speech overlap rate and significantly improved both fluency and originality in creative tasks. The mouse operation increased the amount of speech but did not significantly impact creativity, while the hand gesture operation produced no substantial benefits. These findings suggest that providing remote participants with intuitive touch panel operation of 360-degree video views effectively enhances social presence and collaborative creativity in hybrid working environments. The main contribution of this paper is that it quantitatively demonstrates the effectiveness of intuitively operable 360-degree video information in hybrid work environments.

Keywords: Hybrid Working Environment · 360-degree Camera · Controller

1 Introduction

In 2020, video conferences prevailed in business during the global COVID-19 pandemic, and remote work became popular [1]. Remote work has become one of the standard working styles for office workers, and communication through video conferences is a common practice [2, 11]. As a result of replacing face-to-face meetings with remote ones, social interactions have become less frequent [3], and various new meeting formats and collaborative practices are being explored to compensate for the lack of

J. F. Krems et al. (Eds.): CHIRA 2025, CCIS 2836, pp. 108–128, 2026.
https://doi.org/10.1007/978-3-032-16454-4_7

social relationships [4]. A typical example is a hybrid meeting, in which participants are located in the same physical space, such as an office, and those participating remotely are mixed [5]. However, hybrid meetings have been reported to make creative work and decision-making collaboration particularly difficult and reduce overall productivity [6]. In particular, performance is reduced in tasks that require new ideas [7], and the production of creative ideas is reported to decrease in remote meetings such as brainstorming sessions and workshops, where social interaction is essential [8]. It is also noted that it remains difficult to adequately recreate face-to-face discussions around a whiteboard in an online environment [9]. One of the main factors is that conference participants are connected to different physical spaces, leading to a loss of contextual coherence [10] and the lack of non-verbal cues stifles productive discussion [9]. Nonverbal information in dialogue, such as facial expressions, eye contact, and body language, plays the role of cues to predict utterance and promote empathy and opinion exchange with others, thus not only complementing speech but also activating the dialogue itself [12]. However, traditional online meetings with standard webcams provide only a limited view of the other party. Speakers who tend to step out of the frame miss important physical contexts [13,22]. As a result, remote participants cannot grasp the situation of all members, and this issue reduces the social presence of remote participants. Remote participants have been reported to feel less involved in the meeting due to the small size of the content on the whiteboard at a distance or the insufficient sharing of information from the office workplace [14]. It makes it difficult for them to understand the flow of the dialogue and the intentions of the other participants [15]. Furthermore, the social presence in a hybrid meeting is lower than in a face-to-face meeting, so self-disclosure becomes shallower [16], making it difficult to build trust among participants [17]. Remote participants have also been observed to be intentionally or unintentionally excluded when the office workplace leads the discussion [18].

To address these issues, a remote communication system that installed a 360-degree camera in a main workplace was developed to allow remote participants to manipulate their viewpoints freely [19]. Several hybrid meeting sessions were conducted to examine whether the system promotes collaborative discussions. Through these sessions, it was reported that "the freedom of viewpoint helped remote participants to understand the flow of the conversation and aided their collaboration", and also that "taking speech turn was easier compared to conventional video conference systems with a fixed viewpoint". However, it was also noted that using a mouse to control the viewpoint was inconvenient because it blocked the dominant hand and interfered with participants' work, such as note-taking. Based on these findings, different view angle control interfaces were proposed for remote workers to set their viewpoints on a 360-degree camera and to grasp non-verbal information and content displayed at the main workplace. A preliminary evaluation session was conducted, and the results indicated a promising direction for interaction support systems with viewpoint control using quantitative indices, suggesting the effectiveness of such design and evaluation processes.

In this paper, building on the prior study [19], we conducted quantitative and detailed evaluation experiments using a 360-degree camera system with three types of viewpoint controllers; a mouse-based controller, a touch panel controller, and a hand gesture recognition controller. We addressed the following two research questions: (1)

to measure the effects of the viewpoint controllers for the 360-degree camera on remote participants' involvement in collaborative work and the quality of creative outcomes, and (2) to identify the most effective viewpoint controller.

To assess the impact of viewpoint control on creativity in collaborative work, we used the Picture Completion task from the Torrance Tests of Creative Thinking (TTCT). In this task, participants were asked to create as many completed figures as possible based on an incomplete figure through group discussion. The experiment was conducted in a hybrid working environment with two participants in the main workplace and one in the remote workplace. We measured the total speaking time of the remote participant and the overlap rate between participants as two indices of the remote participant's engagement in communication with those in the main workplace. For the evaluation of creativity, we measured fluency—the number of ideas generated during the meeting— and originality, which indicates the novelty and rarity of those ideas.

The remainder of this paper is organized as follows. Section 2 describes the system and interfaces. Section 3 outlines the experimental design. Section 4 presents the results. Section 5 discusses the findings, and Sect. 6 concludes the paper.

2   Hybrid Work Environment Connected with Viewpoint-Controllable 360-Degree Camera

This section outlines the experimental system configuration and details the three types of viewpoint control interfaces utilized in the experiment.

2.1   Hybrid Work Environment Connected with 360-Degree Camera

In conventional hybrid meetings, the limited viewing angle of a webcam has been reported as a problem, preventing remote participants from fully understanding the in-room situation and visual materials such as memos and whiteboards used for the generation of ideas [9]. This constraint has also been associated with a shift toward report-style meetings, limiting the potential for cooperative interaction [13].

To address this, a 360-degree camera was installed in the main workplace to transmit immersive video to remote participants, allowing them to control their viewpoints interactively (see Fig. 1). This system is expected to improve communication quality and enhance the outcomes of creative collaborative work. The TTCT was used to evaluate these effects [21].

2.2   Controllers for 360-Degree Camera

A webcam with a fixed viewpoint does not allow remote participants to actively explore the situation at the main workplace. On the other hand, when a 360-degree camera is used, it is essential to provide an interface for users to control their viewpoints arbitrarily. Three types of controllers were prepared to support remote participants in engaging more effectively in cooperative work in a hybrid work environment. Specifically, we prepared controllers with (1) mouse operation, which is a standard interface for 360-degree camera operation, (2) hand gesture operation using the Leap Motion Controller 2 (LMC2), and (3) touch panel operation using a tablet.

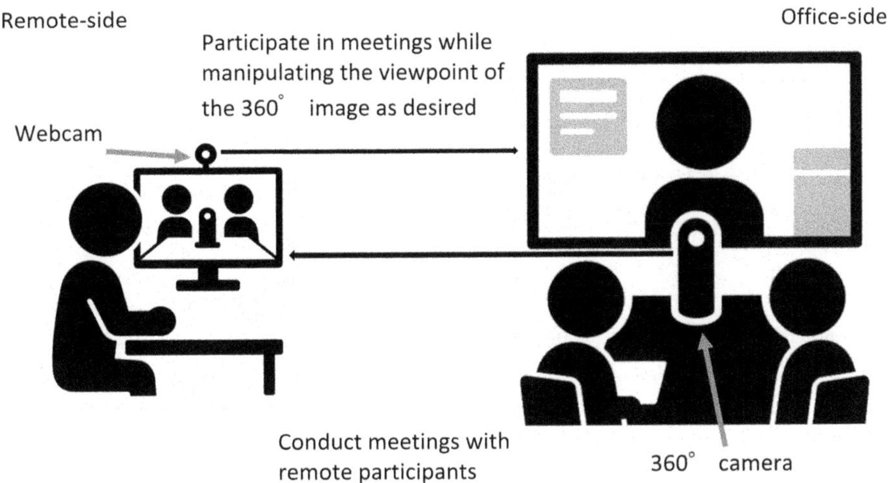

Fig. 1. Overview of proposed hybrid working environment.

The mouse-based controller operates by combining cursor movement and button presses: the left button is used to move the viewpoint, while the right button is used to zoom. To zoom in or out, the user moves the cursor upward by pressing the right mouse button to magnify the image or downward to minimize it.

With the controller with a touch panel, the 360-degree video view on the display is manipulated directly by the touch of a finger on a tablet. Specifically, the 360-degree video view can be shifted by sliding the tablet with a single finger on the screen. For zooming in or out, the user pinches two fingers outward to magnify the image or pinches inward to minify it.

With the hand gesture controller, the Leap Motion Controller 2 (LMC2) recognizes specific hand postures to manipulate the 360-degree video view on the display. Specifically, the position of the user's hand over the LMC2 corresponds to the cursor on the display. The movement of the user's hand while clenching the fist is used for viewpoint control and zooms in and out. Two modes of viewpoint control and zoom-in/out switches with a hand gesture rotating the palm of the hand more than 90° from a posture directing the palm downward. Implementing mode-switching reduced the overall recognition errors in hand gesture operation (see Fig. 2).

Table 1 lists the controllers with their operation.

Table 1. Viewpoint controllers and their operation.

Controller	Function	Operation
Mouse	Viewpoint pan	Press left button and move cursor
	Zoom in	Press right button and move upward
	Zoom out	Press right button and move downward
Hand gesture (LMC2)	Cursor move	Move hand over LMC sensor
	Pan/Zoom	Move clenched fist
	Toggle pan and zoom	Rotate palm downward
Touch panel	Viewpoint pan	Slide with one finger (pan)
	Zoom in	Pinch-out with two fingers
	Zoom out	Pinch-in with two fingers

Grip-and-drag interaction for visual manipulation (viewpoint control or scaling).
Tilting the palm switches between the viewpoint-control and scaling modes.

Fig. 2. Viewpoint control with hand gesture.

3 Experimental Method

This section describes the experimental design, including the task selection, participant arrangement, and procedure used to evaluate the effectiveness of the viewpoint control interfaces.

3.1   Participants

We conducted collaborative work with three participants per group, two in the main workplace and one in a remote workplace, with a total of 12 groups of 36 university students aged 21–24 years. All participants were acquainted with each other prior to the experiment. The participants consisted of 31 males and 5 females. There were 9 male-only groups, 2 mixed-sex groups, and 1 female-only group.

3.2   Settings of Hybrid Work Environment

Figures 3 and 4 show elevation views of the main and remote workplaces in the conventional and proposed hybrid work environments, respectively. Figure 3 shows a conventional hybrid work environment in which the main and remote workplaces are connected by a webcam. Figure 4 shows the proposed hybrid work environment in which a 360-degree camera is installed at the center of a circular table in the main workplace and the video images are transmitted to the remote workplace. Remote participants can participate in collaborative work in the main workplace using a viewpoint controller. The remote workplace is equipped with a mouse, the LMC2, a touch panel to be used according to the experimental conditions, and a webcam above the display to transmit images to the main workplace. In all conditions, a whiteboard was placed in the main workplace behind the participants to share their ideas with a remote participant. In addition, an iPad for an online whiteboard is installed in both workplaces for the remote participant to share ideas.

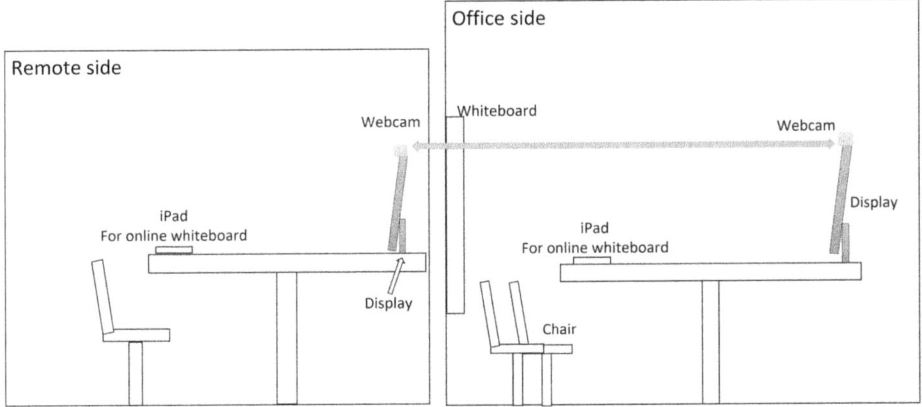

Fig. 3. Elevation views of conventional main and remote workplaces connected with fixed-viewpoint webcams.

Figures 5, 6, and 7 show contents of images in displays at the main workplace, the remote workplace (webcam), and the remote workplace (360-degree camera), respectively. Participants in the main workplace undertake collaborative work with remote participants by communicating with the webcam image at the remote workplace.

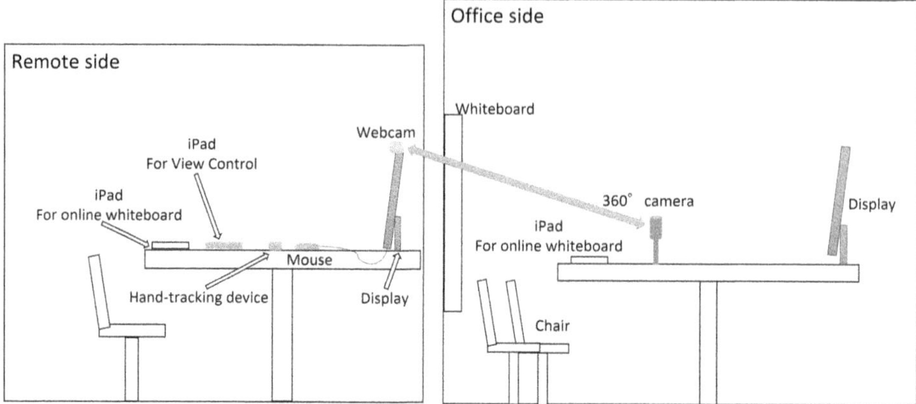

Fig. 4. Elevation views of proposed main and remote workplaces equipped with 360-degree camera in main workplace and its viewpoint controller in remote workplace.

Remote participants participate in the collaborative work by communicating with the fixed-viewpoint webcam image in the conventional system (Fig. 6) or the viewpoint-controllable 360-degree camera image in the proposed system (Fig. 7). Since the field of view of the standard webcam image is limited, only a specific part of the main workplace is shown in the image. On the other hand, the remote participants can manipulate the 360-degree camera video view so that they can communicate with any participant in the main workplace while collecting the necessary information for communication, such as on the desktop or the whiteboard.

3.3   Experimental Subject

We employed the "Picture Completion" task, one of the subsets of the TTCT, as the experimental task that allows us to examine participation in collaborative work and creativity of the outcome in the hybrid work environment. This is a type of creativity test developed by E. P. Torrance in 1962, in which participants are asked to complete a picture by adding lines freely to an incomplete figure and to evaluate their performance by giving a title to it. The test is not intended to assess drawing or painting skills, but is assessed based on the originality and fluency of the completed pictures within a certain period of time.

3.4   Experimental Conditions

We conducted comparative experiments with four conditions. In all conditions, the collaborative work was carried out by three participants: two in the main workplace and one in the remote workplace. Table 2 summarizes the experimental conditions with short descriptions. Figure 8 shows snapshots of a remote participant communicating while viewing the main workplace and controlling his/her viewpoint with three types

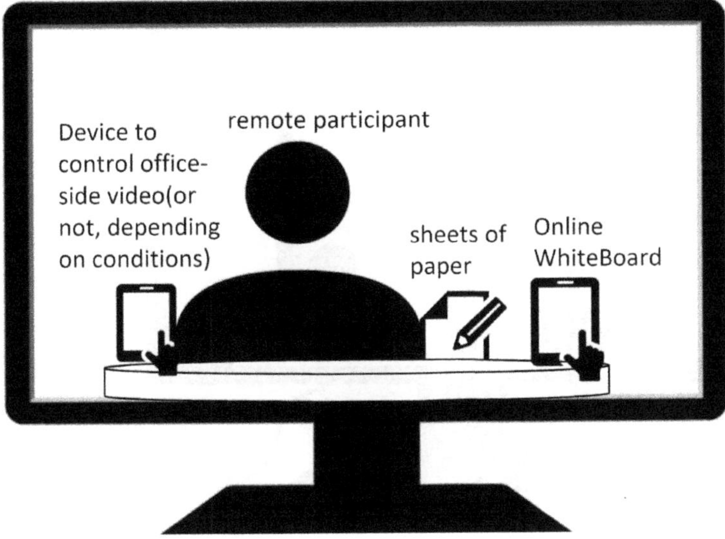

Fig. 5. Contents of image in display at main workplace.

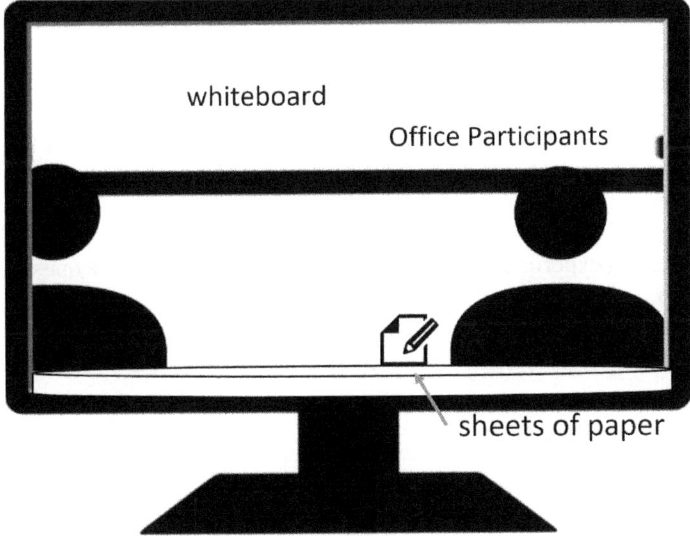

Fig. 6. Contents of image in display at remote workplace (webcam).

of controllers. To avoid learning and order effects, the order in which the conditions were performed and the incomplete figure presented in each condition were randomized between groups.

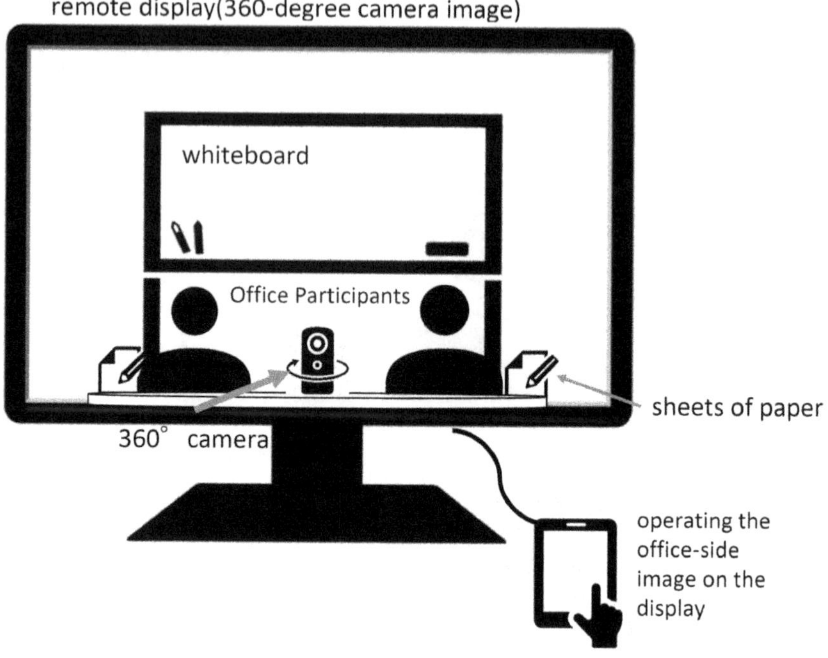

Fig. 7. Contents of image in display at remote workplace (360-degree camera).

3.5 Procedure

The experiments consisted of the following four steps: (1) a 5-minute practice session for the Picture Completion task using a sample figure, (2) a 10-minute training session for the remote participant to practice operating the three types of controllers (mouse, hand gestures, and touch panel), (3) four 10-minute trials of the Picture Completion task under different experimental conditions, and (4) completion of a questionnaire after each condition.

In addition, all sessions were video-recorded so that participants' body gestures, timing of speech, and interactions with others could be analyzed at a later date.

3.6 Evaluation Method

We quantitatively evaluate the degree of involvement of a remote participant in the communication with the main workplace and the influence on the creative outcome. For this purpose, the total speaking time and overlap rate of the remote participants' utterances are employed as indices of their participation in multi-user communication. The total speaking time demonstrates the temporal occupancy that the participants spoke during the collaborative work and is an indicator of their involvement [24]. Since the overlap rate of utterances includes not only the overlap of utterances in conflictive interactions such as intense negotiation but also the overlap of utterances in active and cooperative

Table 2. Experimental conditions.

Condition	Description
Fixed Viewpoint	A fixed-viewpoint webcam is used so that both parties can see what the other is doing.
Mouse	A remote participant can communicate with the main workplace by viewing a 360-degree image of the main workplace with mouse operation, and participants in the main workplace can view the webcam image of the remote workplace.
Hand Gesture	A remote participant can gesture-control the 360-degree video of the main workplace, and participants in the main workplace can check the webcam video of the remote workplace.
Touch Panel	A remote participant can join the 360-degree video of the main workplace with touch panel operation, and participants in the main workplace can view the remote participant through webcam video.

Condition 1: Fixed Viewpoint   **Condition 2: Mouse**

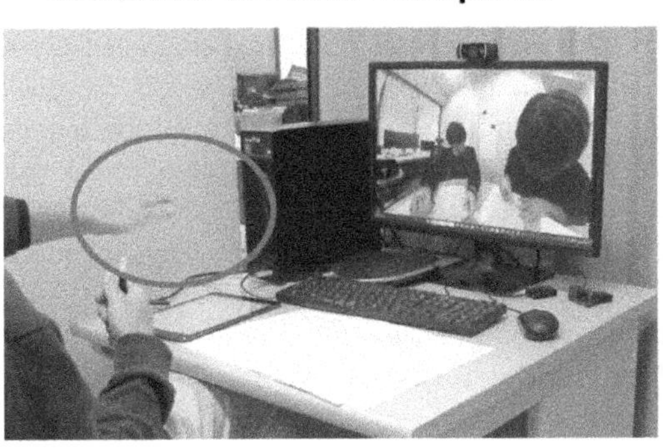

Condition 3: Hand Gesture   **Condition 4: Touch panel**

Fig. 8. Snapshots of remote participant controlling viewpoint in four conditions.

interactions such as back-channeling and consent responses [23], it is an indicator of the degree of involvement and social presence of the remote participants.

To evaluate the outcomes of the collaborative work in the whole group, we adopted the indicators proposed by TTCT: fluency and originality [25]. Fluency measures the total number of appropriate responses (ideas) generated to the incomplete figures. Originality is an index that evaluates the degree of novelty and rarity by extracting appropriate statistically rare (infrequent) responses among those generated [25].

Indices for Involvement of Remote Participants. The total speaking time is the total time that the remote participant speaks during the meeting. The total speaking time, T_{total}, is obtained by summing up the duration from the start $t_{i,\text{start}}$ to the end $t_{i,\text{end}}$ of each speech segment i ($i = 1, \ldots, N$) as shown in Eq. (1).

$$T_{\text{total}} = \sum_{i=1}^{N} \left(t_{i,\text{end}} - t_{i,\text{start}} \right), \tag{1}$$

where N is the number of speech segments of a remote participant.

The overlap rate of utterances R_{overlap} is a ratio of the total time that a participant's speech overlapped with other speakers T_{overlap} to the participants' total speaking time T_{total}.

$$R_{\text{overlap}} = \frac{T_{\text{overlap}}}{T_{\text{total}}}. \tag{2}$$

The overlap rate includes not only collisions of utterances in a collisional exchange such as a heated discussion but also agreement responses in cooperative communication.

Indices of Creativity. Fluency is a measure of the total number of appropriate responses that participants produced based on a randomly presented incomplete figure during a limited time of the meeting for each experimental condition. Three evaluators (the first author and two students) check and score all the responses produced under each condition. Firstly, the evaluators check whether each response meets the basic scoring criteria of TTCT, 'the incomplete figure must be discernible' and 'the incomplete figure must actually be incorporated into the work' [25]. Next, they check two additional requirements specific to Picture Completion tasks: whether the contents of the completed picture and the title of the work match and whether it is possible to clearly grasp what is being expressed from the completed picture alone.

Appropriate responses are those that go beyond the mere addition of lines, utilize the unfinished figure as a component of the work, make it clear what the finished figure represents, and maintain consistency with the title of the work. Figure 9 shows examples of appropriate and inappropriate responses. In the appropriate response shown in the upper left, the diagonally placed rectangles are regarded as a part of the crane arm, and the storyline of 'grabbing an article in a crane game' can be read by depicting a scene of grabbing an article. The inappropriate response in the lower left does not meet the criteria because it is difficult to identify what the completed picture represents only by itself and there is no correspondence with the title. Fluency functions as a filter for scoring originality, another TTCT index, and responses that do not satisfy this criterion are excluded from the originality evaluation.

Originality is an index based on rarity in which the less frequently an idea appears, the more highly it is evaluated, and measures the quality of the responses. The scoring method is based on the occurrence frequency of each idea in all responses that meet the fluency criterion. Then, a score is assigned according to the frequency. Ideas with an occurrence frequency less than 1% are assigned a score of 2, those with an occurrence frequency between 1% and 5% are assigned a score of 1, and those with an occurrence frequency greater than 5% are assigned a score of 0 [26]. The final originality is obtained by summing the scores for all responses.

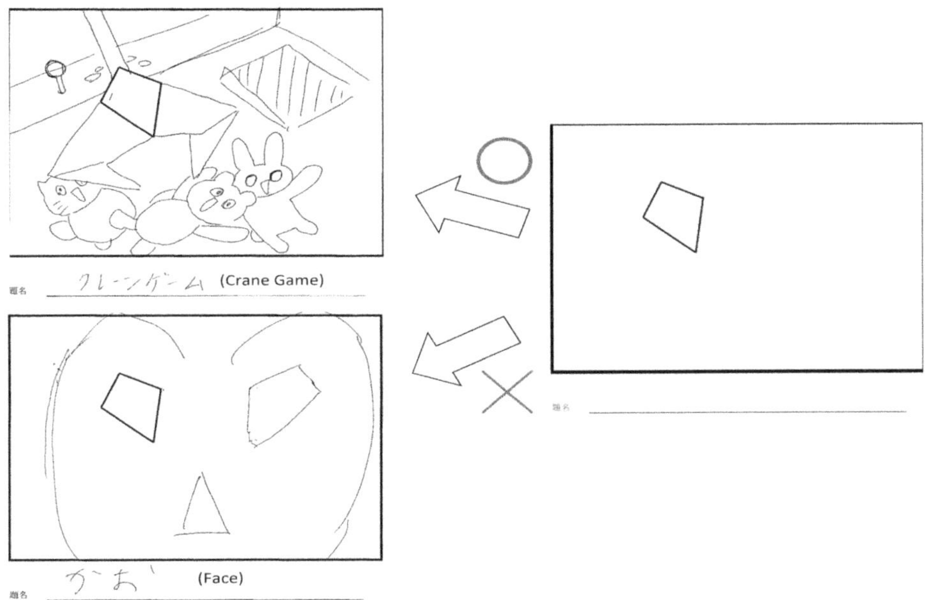

Fig. 9. Examples of responses in picture completion task.

Questionnaire. To subjectively evaluate the usability of the controllers and the effectiveness of the 360-degree video view, a questionnaire was conducted to remote participants after experimenting with each controller. The questionnaire consisted of seven items designed to evaluate the usability and convenience of each controller. The responses were collected on a 5-point Likert scale. In addition, open-ended questions were included to collect subjective evaluations of the controller that could not be captured by the Likert scale items alone, such as impressions, advantages and disadvantages, and suggestions for improvement. Table 3 lists the queries.

4   Experimental Results

This section explains the evaluation metrics used in the experiment, focusing on quantitative measures of communication activity and creativity.

Table 3. Queries in questionnaire.

	Query
1.	How much did you feel excluded from the group?
2.	How much were you able to contribute to the group?
3.	How much were you able to take the lead in the discussion?
4.	How easy was the camera to operate?
5.	How much were you able to understand the other participants' opinions?
6.	How much were you able to express your own opinions?
7.	How much do you feel the meeting was successful?

Table 4. Results of Wilcoxon rank sum tests for total speaking time.

Pair of Conditions	p-value
Touch Panel & Mouse	0.7471
Touch Panel & Fixed Viewpoint	0.0088
Touch Panel & Hand Gesture	0.0293
Mouse & Fixed Viewpoint	0.0088
Mouse & Hand Gesture	0.0059
Fixed Viewpoint & Hand Gesture	0.3193

4.1 Involvement of Remote Participants

Total Speaking Time. Figure 10 shows the average total speaking time (in seconds) for the four conditions. The average total speaking time was 131 s for the fixed viewpoint, 170 s for the mouse operation, 120 s for the hand gesture operation, and 211 s for the touch panel operation. To examine the statistical significance of the difference among the conditions, we conducted the Friedman rank sum test at a significance level of 5%. The results confirmed significant difference ($\chi^2 = 23.77, p < .05$). We then performed post hoc comparisons using the Wilcoxon signed rank test with p values adjusted by the Bonferroni correction. Table 4 lists the results of the post hoc comparisons. The results showed that the total speaking time was significantly longer for the touch panel operation than for the fixed viewpoint and the hand gesture operation, and significantly longer for the mouse operation than for the fixed viewpoint and the hand gesture operation. There was no significant difference between the touch panel operation and the mouse operation.

Overlap Rate of Remote Participants. Figure 11 shows the average overlap rate (%) for the four conditions. The average overlap rates were 14.3% for the fixed viewpoint, 17.4% for the mouse operation, 11.2% for the hand gesture operation, and 26.4% for the touch panel operation. We performed the Friedman rank sum test at a significance level of 5% among the conditions. The results confirmed a significant condition effect

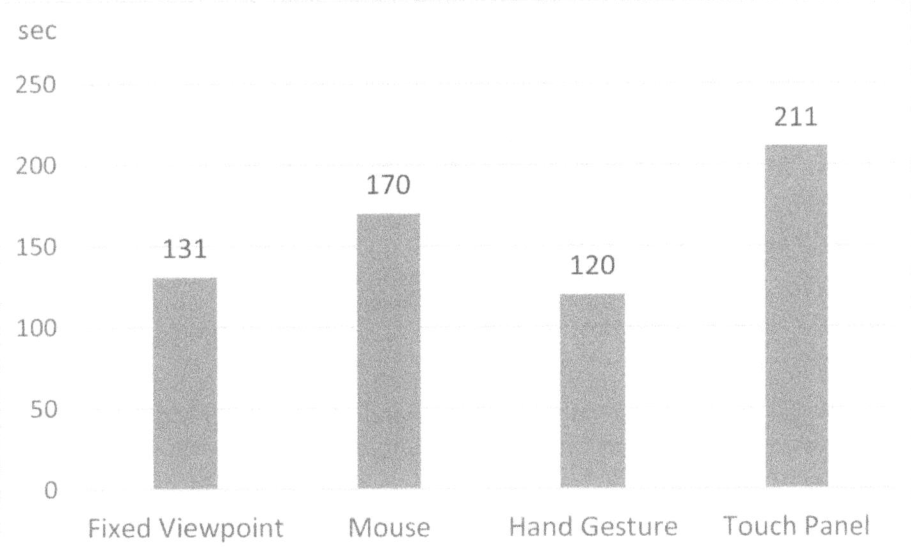

Fig. 10. Average total speaking time in four conditions.

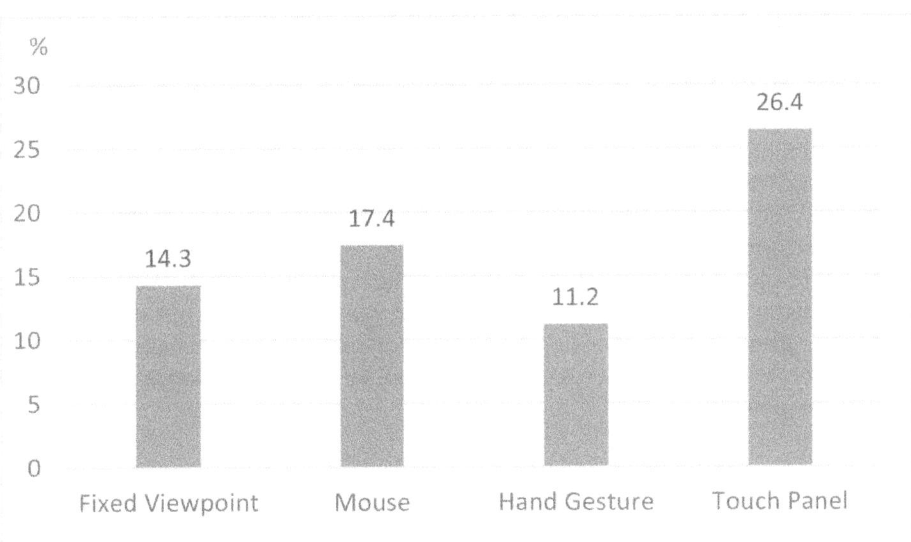

Fig. 11. Average overlap rate for four conditions.

($\chi^2 = 18.7$, $p < .05$). We then performed post hoc comparisons using the Wilcoxon signed rank test with p values adjusted by the Bonferroni correction. Table 5 shows the results of the post hoc comparisons. The results showed that the touch panel operation had a significantly higher overlap rate than the fixed viewpoint and the hand gesture

Table 5. Results of Wilcoxon rank sum tests for overlap rate.

Pair of conditions	p-value
Touch Panel & Mouse	0.1260
Touch Panel & Fixed Viewpoint	0.0088
Touch Panel & Hand Gesture	0.0029
Mouse & Fixed Viewpoint	2.0361
Mouse & Hand Gesture	0.0205
Fixed Viewpoint & Hand Gesture	0.9082

operation, and the mouse operation also had a significantly higher overlap rate than the hand gesture operation. There was no significant difference between the touch panel and the mouse operations.

4.2   Results of Creativity Assessment

Fluency.   Three evaluators counted the responses generated in all the experiments, and the number of responses (ideas) generated in all the experiments was 437. The evaluators checked the appropriateness of the responses, and the number of appropriate responses was 382. The agreement among the evaluations was moderate, with a Kappa coefficient of 0.52. Figure 12 shows the average numbers of responses for the four conditions. The average number of responses was 7.81 for the fixed viewpoint, 8.56 for the mouse operation, 6.57 for the hand gesture operation, and 8.94 for the touch panel operation. We performed the Friedman rank sum test at a significance level of 5% among the conditions. The results confirmed a significant condition effect ($\chi^2 = 7.92$, $p < .05$). We then performed post hoc comparisons using the Wilcoxon signed rank test. Table 6 shows the results of the post hoc comparisons. The results showed that the touch panel operation had a significantly higher number of responses than the fixed viewpoint, and the mouse operation also had a significantly higher number of responses than the hand gesture operation. There was no significant difference between the touch panel and the mouse operations.

Table 6. Results of Wilcoxon rank sum tests for fluency.

Pair of conditions	p-value
Touch Panel & Mouse	0.6211
Touch Panel & Fixed Viewpoint	0.0303
Touch Panel & Hand Gesture	0.0684
Mouse & Fixed Viewpoint	0.2871
Mouse & Hand Gesture	0.0322
Fixed Viewpoint & Hand Gesture	0.1455

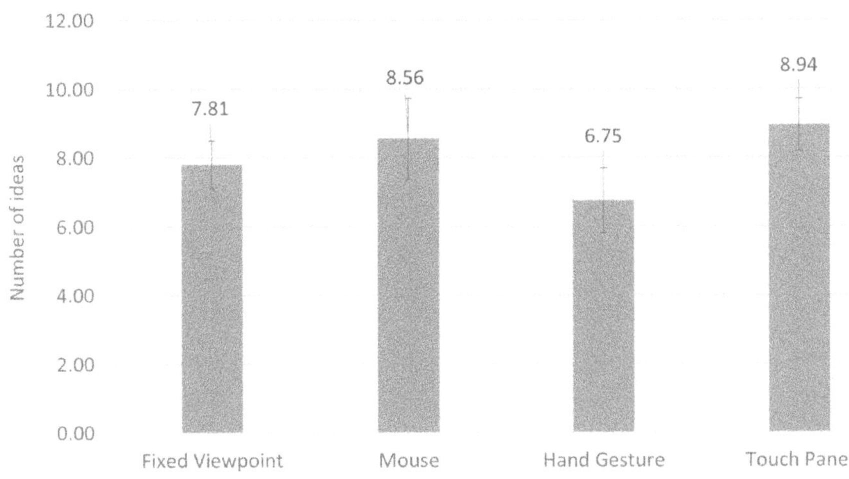

Fig. 12. Average numbers of ideas (fluency) in four conditions.

Originality. The responses that met the fluency criterion consisted of 207 types of ideas. Figure 13 shows the mean originality scores for the four conditions. The average scores were 10.9 for the fixed viewpoint, 12.0 for the mouse operation, 10.6 for the hand gesture operation, and 13.8 for the touch panel operation. We performed the Friedman rank sum test at a significance level of 5% among the conditions. The results confirmed a significant condition effect ($\chi^2 = 9.28$, $p < .05$). We then performed post hoc comparisons using the Wilcoxon signed rank test. Table 7 shows the results of the post hoc comparisons. The results showed that the touch panel operation had significantly higher response originality than the fixed viewpoint and the hand gesture operation. There was no significant difference between the touch panel and the mouse operations.

Pairwise comparisons were conducted using the Wilcoxon rank sum test. As shown in Table 7, the originality score for the touch panel operation was significantly higher than that for the fixed viewpoint.

Table 7. Results of Wilcoxon rank sum tests for originality.

Pair of conditions	p-value
Touch Panel & Mouse	0.2925
Touch Panel & Fixed Viewpoint	0.0254
Touch Panel & Hand Gesture	0.0430
Mouse & Fixed Viewpoint	0.6533
Mouse & Hand Gesture	0.3311
Fixed Viewpoint & Hand Gesture	0.7939

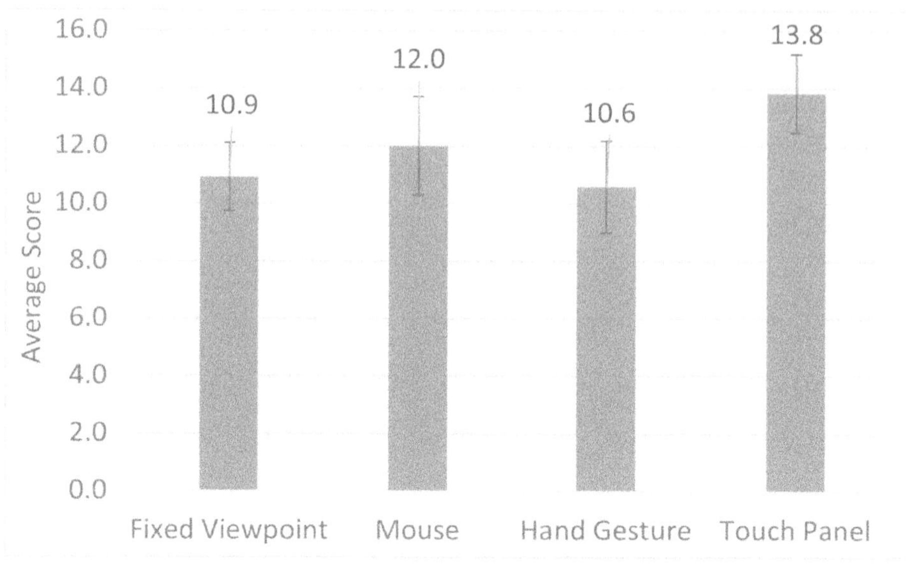

Fig. 13. Average originality scores for four conditions.

4.3   Answers to Questionnaire

Figure 14 shows the results of the questionnaire to the remote participants. The touch panel and mouse operations received high usability scores, whereas the hand gesture operation received consistently lower scores across all items.

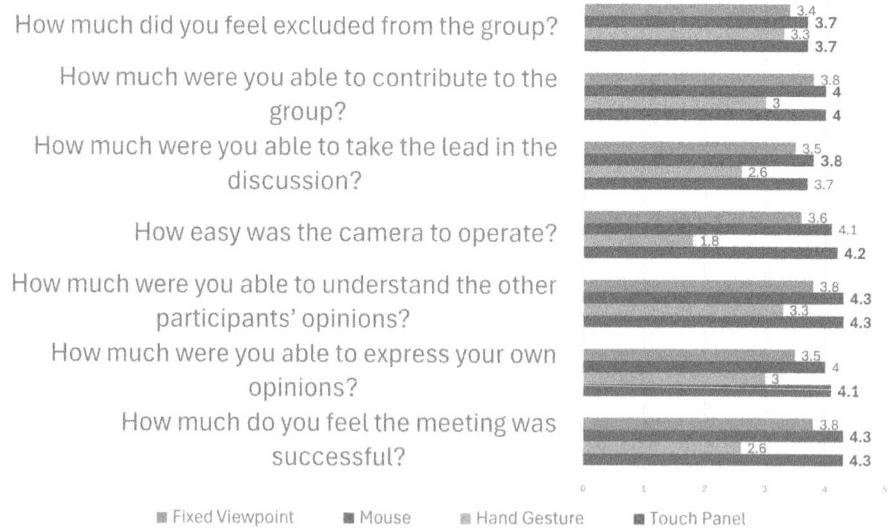

Fig. 14. Results of answers to questionnaire to remote participants.

In the open-ended responses, the touch panel operation received many favorable comments, such as "the touch panel operation was the easiest to operate" and "the controllers with the mouse and the touch panel were easy to operate and to grasp the situation of the whiteboard and other participants". Several participants reported usability issues with the hand gesture operation, such as "It took me some time to get used to the hand gesture operation because it was my first time to use it" and "The sensitivity of the viewpoint movement was high, and it was difficult to adjust it".

5   Discussion

The comparative experiments demonstrated that the communication system equipped with the viewpoint-controllable 360-degree camera is promising for hybrid working environments. In the analysis of total speaking time, significant differences were observed among the four conditions. Pairwise comparisons revealed that both the touch panel and the mouse operations led to significantly longer total speaking time compared to the conventional fixed viewpoint webcam. Although there was no significant difference between the touch panel and the mouse operations, the touch panel operation was found to be the interface that facilitates active interaction. The hand gesture operation had the shortest speaking time, suggesting that it is not an effective interface.

In the analysis of the overlap rate, interesting trends were observed among the controllers. Notably, the overlap rate was significantly higher with the touch panel operation compared to the conventional fixed viewpoint webcam. One of the reasons for this is that the task of this experiment was to generate as many ideas as possible and shape them, and it was a cooperative task that did not include confrontational elements. From the videos recorded in the experiments, cooperative utterances, such as agreeing with each other, were frequently observed, and most of the overlaps in the conversation were friendly and cooperative. Therefore, it is considered that the viewpoint controller with the touch panel worked effectively in activating such friendly and cooperative work.

In terms of fluency, the touch panel operation resulted in a significantly higher number of ideas than the conventional fixed viewpoint webcam. Among the conditions, the touch panel operation generated the highest average number of ideas, followed by the mouse operation.

Originality analysis similarly favored the touch panel operation, which scored significantly higher than the fixed viewpoint webcam. Compared among the conditions, the touch panel operation gained the highest mean originality score, followed by the mouse operation. This indicates that the quality of ideas—measured by their novelty—may be closely tied to the sense of spatial awareness and interaction control afforded by the touch interface.

Based on the analysis of remote participants' performance and creativity outcomes, the touch panel interface appears to enhance collaborative creative work by helping remote participants better understand the situation in the main workplace and engage more actively in interaction. The most favorable factor in touch panel operation was that the participants were used to using it with smartphones and other devices, according to the results of the post-experiment questionnaire. In particular, since the participants in this experiment were university students in their 20 s, it can be estimated that the high affinity for the touch panel operation over the mouse operation led to positive results in all four indices [20]. On the other hand, the reason for the low performance with the hand gesture operation is considered to be the fact that it was the first time the participants used this controller.

6   Conclusion

This study quantitatively examined the effectiveness of viewpoint control interfaces for remote participants in hybrid work environments. Using a 360-degree camera, we compared three types of controllers—mouse, hand gestures, and touch panel—in a creativity-focused collaborative task. Experimental results revealed that the touch panel interface significantly enhanced communication engagement and creativity, as evidenced by longer speaking times, higher overlap rates, and greater fluency and originality in ideas. The mouse interface also increased engagement but had less impact on creativity, while the hand gesture interface showed minimal benefit. These findings highlight the potential of intuitive viewpoint control systems, particularly touch-based ones, to enhance social presence and collaborative performance in hybrid work environments. Future research may explore personalized or adaptive viewpoint interfaces to further support diverse working styles and technological familiarity.

Acknowledgments. This work was supported by Council for Science, Technology and Innovation (CSTI), Cross-ministerial Strategic Innovation Promotion Program (SIP), the 3rd period of SIP "Creation of new ways of learning and working in a post-COVID-19 era" Grant Number JPJ012347 (Funding agency:JST).

References

1. Aksoy, C.G., Barrero, J.M., Bloom, N., Davis, S.J., Dolls, M., Zarate, P.: Working from Home Around the World, Brookings Papers on Economic Activity, Economic Studies Program, The Brookings Institution, vol. 53(2) Fall, pp. 281–360 (2022)
2. Barrero, J.M., Bloom, N., Davis, S.J.: The evolution of working from home. J. Econ. Perspect. **37**(4), 23–50 (2023). https://doi.org/10.1257/jep.37.4.23
3. Takami, T.: Remote work and well-being in the post-COVID-19 era. Ind. Health **61**, 171–172 (2023). https://doi.org/10.2486/indhealth.61_300
4. Domae, H., Nakayama, M., Takemura, K., et al.: Antecedents and consequences of telework during the COVID-19 pandemic: a natural experiment in Japan. Humanit. Soc. Sci. Commun. **11**, 314 (2024). https://doi.org/10.1057/s41599-024-02770-7
5. Saatçi, B., Rädle, R., Rintel, S., O'Hara, K., Nylandsted Klokmose, C.: Hybrid meetings in the modern workplace: stories of success and failure. In: Nakanishi, H., Egi, H., Chounta, I.-A., Takada, H., Ichimura, S., Hoppe, U. (eds.) CRIWG+CollabTech 2019. LNCS, vol. 11677, pp. 45–61. Springer, Cham (2019). https://doi.org/10.1007/978-3-030-28011-6_4
6. Orts-Escolano, S., et al.: Holoportation: virtual 3D teleportation in real-time. In: Proceedings of the 29th Annual Symposium on User Interface Software and Technology, pp. 741–754. Association for Computing Machinery, New York (2016). https://doi.org/10.1145/2984511.2984517

7. Miller, C., Rodeghero, P., Storey, M.-A., Ford, D., Zimmermann, T.: "How was your weekend?" software development teams working from home during COVID-19. In: 2021 IEEE/ACM 43rd International Conference on Software Engineering (ICSE), Madrid, ES, pp. 624–636 (2021). https://doi.org/10.1109/ICSE43902.2021.00064

8. Brucks, M.S., Levav, J.: Virtual communication curbs creative idea generation. Nature **605**, 108–112 (2022). https://doi.org/10.1038/s41586-022-04643-y

9. Baym, N., et al.: Collaboration and meetings. In: Teevan, J., Hecht, B., Jaffe, S. (eds.) The New Future of Work: Research from Microsoft on the Impact of the Pandemic on Work Practices, 1st edn. Microsoft (2021). https://aka.ms/newfutureofwork

10. Tomprou, M., Kim, Y.J., Chikersal, P., Woolley, A.W., Dabbish, L.A.: Speaking out of turn: how video conferencing reduces vocal synchrony and collective intelligence. PLoS One **16**(3), e0247655 (2021). https://doi.org/10.1371/journal.pone.0247655

11. Aksoy, C.G., Barrero, J.M., Bloom, N., Davis, S.J., Dolls, M., Zarate, P.: Working from home around the globe: 2023 report. EconPol Policy Brief **53** (2023)

12. Develotte, C., Guichon, N., Vincent, C.: The use of the webcam for teaching a foreign language in a desktop video-conferencing environment. ReCALL **22**(3), 293–312 (2010). https://hal.archives-ouvertes.fr/hal00806433/

13. Matthews, B., See, Z.S., Day, J.: Crisis and extended realities: remote presence in the time of COVID-19. Media Int. Australia **178**(1), 198–209 (2021). https://doi.org/10.1177/1329878X20967165

14. Rogers, B., Apperley, M., Reyes, E.D., Masoodian, M.: Wedge Video: Supporting Remote Participants in a Mixed-Mode Videoconference Meeting. Interacting with Computers. https://doi.org/10.1093/IWC/IWAD032

15. Heath, C., Luff, P.: Disembodied conduct: communication through video in a multi-media office environment. In: Proceedings of the SIGCHI Conference on Human Factors in Computing Systems (CHI 1991), pp. 99–103. Association for Computing Machinery, New York (1991). https://doi.org/10.1145/108844.108859

16. Ruppel, E., Gross, C., Stoll, A., Peck, B., Allen, M., Kim, S.-Y.: Reflecting on connecting: meta-analysis of differences between computer-mediated and face-to-face self-disclosure: computer-mediated and face-to-face self-disclosure. J. Comput.-Mediated Commun. **22** (2016). https://doi.org/10.1111/jcc4.12179

17. Olson, G.M., Olson, J.S.: Distance matters. Hum.-Comput. Interact. **15**(2–3), 139–178 (2000). https://doi.org/10.1207/S15327051HCI1523_4

18. Bos, N., Sadat Shami, N., Olson, J.S., Cheshin, A., Nan, N.: In-group/out-group effects in distributed teams: an experimental simulation. In: Proceedings of the 2004 ACM Conference on Computer Supported Cooperative Work (CSCW 2004), pp. 429–436. Association for Computing Machinery, New York (2004). https://doi.org/10.1145/1031607.1031679

19. Umata, I., Ishikawa, T., Niida, S., Kato, T.: Supporting hybrid interaction: a design approach for mitigating the "barrier" encountered by remote participants in hybrid working environments. In: Coman, A., Vasilache, S. (eds.) HCII 2024. LNCS, vol. 14705, pp. 49–60. Springer, Cham (2024). https://doi.org/10.1007/978-3-031-61312-8_4

20. Busch, P.A., Hausvik, G.I., Ropstad, O., Pettersen, D.T.M.: Smartphone usage among older adults. Comput. Hum. Behav. **121**, 106783 (2021). https://doi.org/10.1016/j.chb.2021.106783

21. Torrance, E.P.: The Manifest: A Guide to developing a creative career 2002 USA Library of Congress Cataloging-in-Publication Data

22. Standaert, W., Muylle, S., Basu, A.: How shall we meet? Understanding the importance of meeting mode capabilities for different meeting objectives. Inf. Manage. **58**(1), 103393 (2021). https://doi.org/10.1016/j.im.2020.103393

23. Margariti, E., Rintel, S., Murphy, B., Sellen, A.: Automated mapping of competitive and collaborative overlapping talk in video meetings. In: Extended Abstracts of the 2022 CHI Conference on Human Factors in Computing Systems (CHI EA 2022), Article no. 311, pp. 1–8. Association for Computing Machinery, New York (2022). https://doi.org/10.1145/3491101.3519612
24. Kim, T., Chang, A., Holland, L., Pentland, A.: Meeting mediator: enhancing group collaboration with sociometric feedback. In: CHI 2008 Extended Abstracts on Human Factors in Computing Systems (CHI EA 2008), pp. 3183–3188. Association for Computing Machinery, New York (2008). https://doi.org/10.1145/1358628.1358828
25. Alabbasi, A.M.A., Paek, S.H., Kim, D., Cramond, B.: What do educators need to know about the Torrance Tests of Creative Thinking: a comprehensive review. Front. Psychol. **13**, 1000385 (2022)
26. Plucker, J.A., Qian, M., Schmalensee, S.L.: Is what you see what you really get? Comparison of scoring techniques in the assessment of real-world divergent thinking. Creativity Res. J. **26**(2), 135–143 (2014). https://doi.org/10.1080/10400419.2014.901023

Development of the PEDADI Educational Gamification Design Framework

Marisa Venter[✉] [iD]

Central University of Technology Free State, Bloemfontein, South Africa
`marisa@cut.ac.za`

Abstract. Gamification has emerged as a promising approach to enhance student motivation and engagement in various educational settings. Despite its growing adoption, there remains limited guidance on how to design effective and pedagogically sound gamified learning experiences. This paper addresses this gap by presenting the PEDADI educational gamification design framework, which consists of four key phases: Preparation, Engagement Design, Activity Design, and Implementation. Drawing on established gamification models, the framework provides a structured, step-by-step process to support the development of educational gamification systems. Additionally, the paper introduces a motivation and engagement design template aimed at helping educators and instructional designers tailor experiences to diverse student needs. The PEDADI design process is also outlined, highlighting how each phase informs the next. The framework serves as a practical tool for educators and instructional designers to design engaging, learner-centered educational experiences. It lays the foundation for future research focused on its application across disciplines, as well as its integration with emerging educational technologies.

Keywords: Motivational Design · Player Type · Instructional Design · Learning Experience Design

1 Introduction

When motivation lags, learning stalls—but gamification alone is not a magic wand; it needs a blueprint. This idea reflects what Werbach and Hunter [1] caution against: simply adding game-like features doesn't guarantee results. For gamification to be effective, it needs to be thoughtfully designed with the context and learners in mind. While gamification is often praised for its ability to increase motivation in education [2], there is still limited guidance on how to design these experiences [3]—especially in the context of higher education programming courses [4].

Designing and developing a successful gamified learning environment is not an easy task [5], because the enjoyable, captivating and emotionally engaging aspects of games cannot simply be reduced into a checklist of components or procedural guidelines [1]. Mere integration of game mechanics, such as points, badges and leaderboards, into gamified systems or applications does not inherently guarantee an enjoyable or engaging

© The Author(s), under exclusive license to Springer Nature Switzerland AG 2026
J. F. Krems et al. (Eds.): CHIRA 2025, CCIS 2836, pp. 129–148, 2026.
https://doi.org/10.1007/978-3-032-16454-4_8

user experience [6]. Instead, gamified systems should be systematically designed to promote desired behaviors [7].

Although the careful consideration of gamification design is important [8], scholarly investigations pertaining to gamification in educational settings have, thus far, neglected to adequately address the fundamental aspect of gamification design [6]. Specifically, two extensive educational gamification literature reviews, conducted by [9] and [10] investigated the justification of combining certain game elements in gamified learning systems. Through an analysis of the empirical studies included in these systematic literature reviews, these authors found that none of the reviewed works provided detailed information on how instructors and designers integrated different game elements. In all the reviewed papers, the game elements used to gamify learning systems were merely enumerated. Moreover, none of the studies offered any justification for their selection of game elements, nor did they explain how these elements were combined in the gamified learning systems. The authors of these two systematic reviews, conclude that further research is necessary to provide the designers of educational gamified systems with theoretically underpinned design guidelines that provide justification for the way specific game design elements influence the behavioral and motivational outcomes of users. Consequently, to address this research gap, the aim of this paper was to develop an educational gamification design framework with an accompanying gamification design process by making use of design aspects observed in existing gamification design frameworks.

The structure of the paper is as follows. First, a review of existing gamification frameworks is presented. This is followed by the extraction of key design aspects from the reviewed frameworks. Next, the development of the PEDADI educational gamification design framework is discussed, incorporating the identified design elements. Finally, the paper concludes with a summary of key findings, implications and future research.

2 Review of Existing Gamification Frameworks

In order to develop an educational gamification design framework, a comprehensive review of existing gamification design frameworks was undertaken to build on established scholarly foundations and to identify recurring design patterns. The design and development phases of gamification are very important. Therefore, it is necessary to follow a systematic methodology that will guide the gamification design process [8].

Four studies that investigated gamification design frameworks were analyzed. Three of these studies focused on gamification design frameworks that were used by scholars in various educational contexts [8, 11, 12]. In turn, a study by [13] focused on the gamification design frameworks most widely cited in gamification research. Six predominant gamification design frameworks were highlighted by the four review studies, as listed below:

- D6 gamification framework [1];
- DMC pyramid [1];
- Marczewski gamification design framework [14];
- Gamification model canvas [15];
- MDA Framework [16];
- The Simões framework for educational gamification [17].

In Table 1, each framework and its associated review studies are listed.

Table 1. Gamification design frameworks identified in the literature.

Gamification design frameworks	[8]	[12]	[11]	[13]	Tot
D6 gamification framework	✓	✓		✓	3
DMC pyramid				✓	1
Gamification model canvas				✓	1
Marczewski gamification design framework	✓				1
MDA framework		✓	✓		2
The Simões framework for educational gamification		✓	✓		2

It can be seen that the D6 gamification framework of Werbach and Hunter [1] is the predominantly cited framework, followed by the MDA[16] and the Simões framework [17] for educational gamification, which were each cited by two studies. The DMC pyramid and the Marczewski gamification design framework were cited by one study each. The six identified gamification design frameworks will be elaborated upon in the next subsections.

2.1 D6 Gamification Framework

Werbach and Hunter [1] created the D6 gamification framework to assist designers to develop gamified systems. This framework endeavors to integrate creativity and structure and to align the needs of individuals with technical feasibility and business imperatives. The framework consists of six steps, each starting with the letter 'D', as shown in Fig. 1. These six steps will be discussed next.

Define Business Objectives. This stage involves establishing precise performance objectives for a gamified system, such as enhancing customer retention, fostering brand loyalty or boosting employee productivity [1].

Delineate Target Behaviors. Once the justification behind gamification has been identified, attention should be directed towards determining the desired actions of the players and devising appropriate measurement methods. It is advisable to consider behaviours and metrics in combination. The behaviours sought after should align with the overarching business objectives previously outlined. After compiling a comprehensive list of the desired behaviours, designers should proceed to formulate metrics for evaluating success. These metrics serve as means to translate behaviours into measurable outcomes [1].

Describe Your Players. It is important to acknowledge that user characteristics vary. Therefore, segmentation of players is advisable, to ensure that the system caters effectively for multiple subgroups. Game designers utilize various models of player types as foundational frameworks for the segmentation process. Gamification designers must

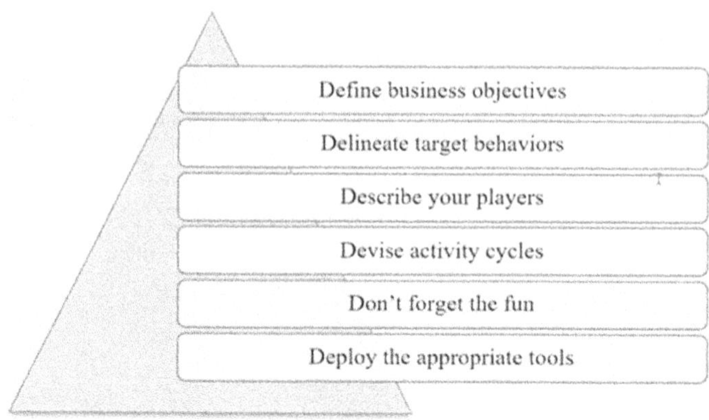

Fig. 1. D6 gamification framework [1].

take the differences between the various player types into consideration by ensuring that their gamified systems have something to offer each player type [1].

Devise Activity Cycles. Gamification maintains user engagement through two key cycles: engagement loops and progression stairs [1]. Engagement loops provide immediate feedback (e.g., points or badges) in response to user actions, reinforcing continued participation. Progression stairs structure the overall user journey with short- and long-term goals that increase in complexity, starting with simple tasks to build confidence and evolving to sustain interest over time [1].

Don't Forget the Fun. Before commencing the implementation of a gamified system, it is imperative to pause and ask, is it enjoyable? Amidst the assembly of game elements and management of the complexities surrounding players, objectives, rules and motivation, the fundamental aspect of fun may, mistakably, be overlooked [1].

Deploy Appropriate Tools. The implementation phase marks the typical starting point of discussions of gamification involving the selection of suitable mechanics and components and integrating them into systems through coding or selecting an appropriate existing platform. Gamification, much like games themselves, does not inherently rely on technology. However, it is particularly well-suited for integration into online systems [1].

2.2 Dynamics Mechanics Components Pyramid

The DMC pyramid was created by Werbach and Hunter with the sole purpose of providing developers of gamified systems with a structured 'toolkit' consisting of common elements prevalent in gamification [1]. The primary aim of the framework is to delineate how diverse elements or components of games can be applied in various ways. A total of 30 different game elements are placed in three different layers in the pyramid: game dynamics (top layer), game mechanics (middle layer) and game components (bottom layer), as shown in Fig. 2.

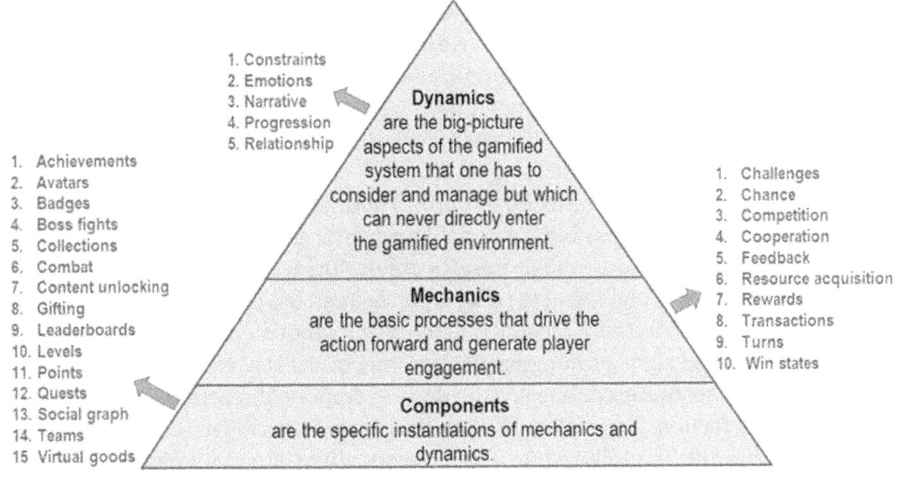

Fig. 2. DMC pyramid [1].

2.3 Gamification Model Canvas

The Gamification Model Canvas was developed with the primary purpose of breaking down game-oriented thinking and mechanics into comprehensible components tailored for professionals working in non-game contexts [18]. It is an adaptable, agile, and methodical tool designed to support the identification and evaluation of solutions based on game design principles, ultimately aiming to foster desired behaviors in non-game environments (see Fig. 3).

The foundation of the gamification model canvas drew inspiration from the conceptualization of a business model [19], complemented by the MDA framework [16]. The gamification model canvas comprises nine segments that delineate essential aspects of gamification project design as illustrated in Fig. 3 [18].

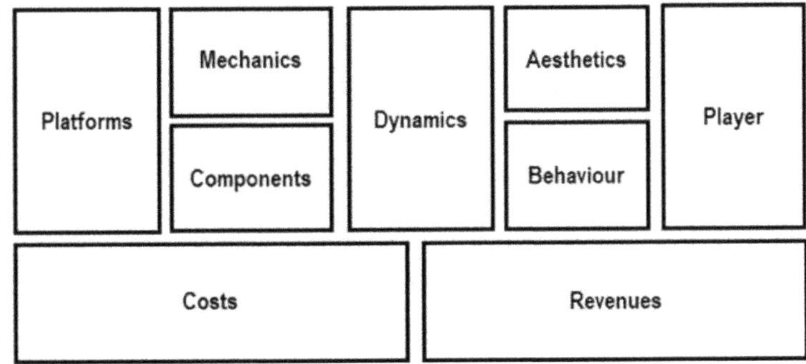

Fig. 3. Gamification model canvas [18].

The canvas is structured into two sections: the left side embodies the designer and efficiency, while the right side signifies the player and value. On the left side, **platforms** delineate the technological infrastructure where game mechanisms will be integrated. **Costs** outline the primary expenses or investments involved in project development, which serve as a foundation for budgeting purposes. **Mechanics** establish the operational rules for the gamified environment, such as rewarding users with extra points for watching a video or progressing to the next level after completing a quiz. **Components** contribute to game dynamics by defining its elements or features, facilitating the creation of mechanics, and providing feedback to users. These components may include points, badges, leaderboards, progress bars, and achievements, among others. In the center of the gamification model canvas, the **dynamics** are outlined, encompassing the real-time interaction of mechanics that affect the player throughout the experience. These dynamics include aspects such as status, scarcity, identity and productivity, which relate closely to motivation. On the right of the gamification model canvas, representing the player and value aspects, **aesthetics** delineates the desired emotional reactions evoked in users during game interaction. Examples of aesthetics include narrative, challenge, discovery, fantasy, sensation and fellowship. This concept aligns closely with fun. **Behaviors** delineate the essential actions that users must undertake to receive benefits from a gamification project, such as watching a video, completing a quiz, reading content, making recommendations or participating in forums. **Players** delineate the identity and characteristics of players, along with their desires and requirements. **Revenues** outline the anticipated economic or social outcomes of implementing gamification, as well as the metrics for assessing success.

2.4 Marczewski Gamification Design Framework

The Marczewski gamification design framework consists of three main stages, namely define, design and refine, as shown in Fig. 4 [14]. These three stages will be discussed next.

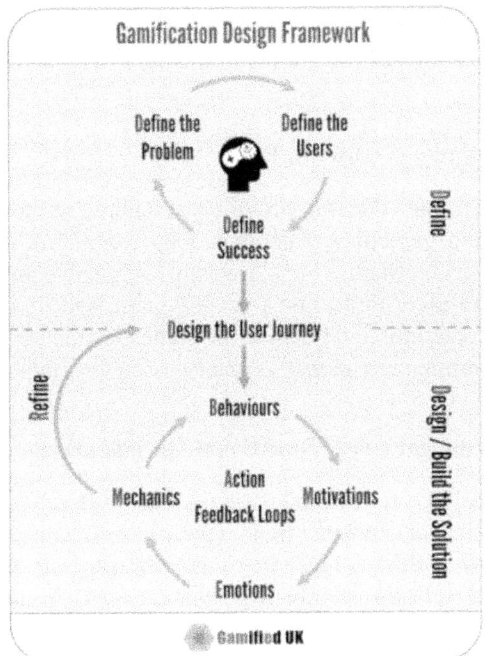

Fig. 4. Gamification design framework [14].

Define Stage. The define stage centers on clarifying the real problem to be solved and understanding the intended users of the solution. It involves three key steps. First, it is crucial to distinguish between what clients want and what they actually need by uncovering the root problem through persistent inquiry [14]. Second, the users must be identified and understood, as their perspectives may differ from the client's. Effective user research—through dialogue and workshops—is essential. Marczewski's HEXAD user typology is recommended for designing gamified systems [14][20]. Lastly, defining success involves establishing clear goals for both the client and users, along with measurable criteria to evaluate outcomes [14].

Design Stage. The design stage consists of two main components: designing the user journey and establishing action/feedback loops. First, the user journey is mapped across five phases—discover, on-board, immerse, master, and replay—focusing on the user's evolving experience with the system. Designers then explore key psychological and design dimensions: desired behaviors, user motivations (guided by the RAMP framework: relatedness, autonomy, mastery, purpose), target emotions (e.g., fun, fear, affection), and mechanics that drive engagement, such as storytelling, strategy, or exploration. The 4Keys 2Fun framework helps identify different types of fun users may experience, including people fun, easy fun, hard fun, and serious fun [14][21].

Second, action/feedback loops integrate all prior elements. Users respond to a call to action, receive feedback from the system, which then adapts, prompting ongoing engagement in a continuous loop [14].

Refine Stage. Ultimately, game designers should engage in iterative refinement of the designs, making adjustments as required until the desired results are attained [14].

2.5 Mechanics Dynamics Aesthetics Framework

The goal of the MDA framework is to provide a structured approach for understanding and designing engaging gameplay experiences, by examining the interplay between mechanics, dynamics and aesthetics [16]. Mechanics are the technical components that, based on the logic and algorithms, construct the game and its environment, whereas dynamics is about the reactions and interactions of the mechanics and the player. Finally, aesthetics describes emotional responses, such as discovery, fantasy or fun [22].

2.6 The Simões Framework for Educational Gamification

The Simões framework [23] offers a model for implementing gamification in social learning environments to enhance students' flow experiences. It identifies three core components for achieving flow and fun: (1) feedback and rewards (e.g., points, badges, leaderboards), (2) social interaction (e.g., sharing achievements, exchanging virtual goods), and (3) game experience elements (e.g., levels, clear goals, progressive rewards). These components operate within a cyclical process rather than a linear sequence.

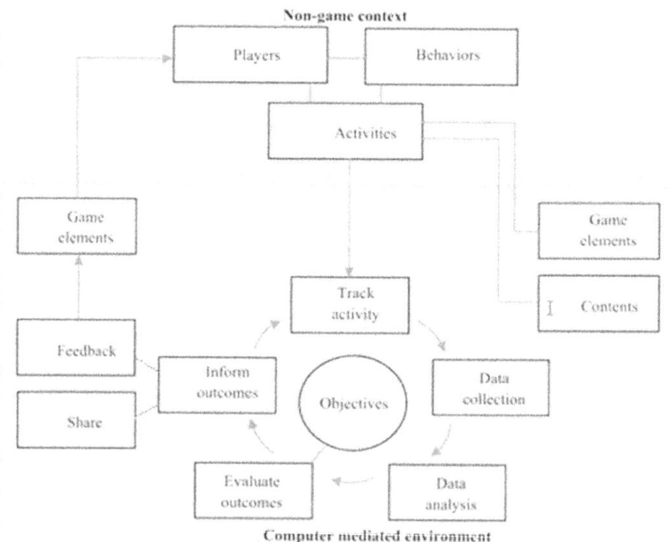

Fig. 5. The Simões framework for educational gamification [23].

In this model, participants—termed players—engage with gamified activities embedded in real or virtual non-game contexts, aiming to develop targeted behaviors through defined objectives integrated with educational content and tailored game elements. The system continuously monitors player activity, collects and analyses data relative to objectives, and provides feedback by sharing results via social or platform channels. This feedback enables players to adjust their actions to better meet the desired goals, supporting ongoing behavioral development [23].

3 Design Aspects Extracted from Gamification Frameworks

In the previous section, the predominant gamification design frameworks used in education settings were reviewed. A total of 10 design aspects that are applicable to educational settings were extracted and are summarized in Table 2.

Table 2. Gamification design frameworks identified in the literature.

Gamification design frameworks*

	Design aspects	1	2	3	4	5	6	Tot
1	Fun/emotions	✓	✓	✓	✓	✓	✓	6
2	Dynamics/mechanics/components/aesthetics		✓	✓	✓	✓	✓	5
3	User type/players	✓		✓	✓		✓	4
4	Target behaviors	✓		✓	✓		✓	4
5	Activity design	✓			✓		✓	3
6	Motivation	✓			✓			2
7	Main objectives/problems	✓			✓			2
8	Platform			✓				1
9	Cost			✓				1
10	Educational content						✓	1

Notes. Total refers to the number of frameworks that referred to a particular design aspect
* Key for design frameworks: 1 = D6 framework, 2 = DMC pyramid, 3 = Gamification model canvas, 4 = Gamification design framework, 5 = MDA framework, 6 = Simões framework for educational gamification

In the next session a discussion of the design aspects extracted from the six reviewed frameworks, will be discussed in the same order they are presented in Table 2.

3.1 Fun/Emotion

The fun/emotion aspect is mentioned by all six frameworks. The fun aspect is the foundation of all gamified systems [24] and is a relevant aspect that has to be considered during the gamification design process [12]. The gamification design framework of Marczewski [14] recommends that designers make use of a framework to identify different kinds of fun that players in gamified environments may experience. As mentioned before, the fun framework endorsed by Marczewski [25] is the 4Keys 2Fun framework [21], which is also the fun framework that was used in the gamification design framework of the current study. The developers of this framework [21], identified the four keys to emotion in games as follows:

People fun (social bonding): Arises from fostering social connections and collaborative efforts. Engaging in activities associated with social enjoyment involves competition, cooperation and communication, which facilitate the development of social bonds and teamwork [21].

Easy fun (curiosity and imagination): Stems from exploration and role-playing activities. Engaging in actions related to easy fun involves exploration, imaginative play and creative endeavors, and evoking emotions such as curiosity, surprise, wonder and awe [21].

Hard fun (mastery): Is derived from overcoming challenges, which leads to mastery and feelings of accomplishment. Hard fun involves setting goals, navigating constraints and employing strategic approaches, and eliciting emotions such as frustration and relief [21].

Serious fun (meaning): Players experience serious fun when they derive meaning from experiences that change how they think, feel or behave, or when they can make a meaningful difference in the real world. Actions that might lead to serious fun include repetition, rhythm and collection [21].

3.2   Dynamics, Mechanics, Components, Aesthetics

Game elements, including dynamics, mechanics, components and aesthetics, are included in five frameworks. It was apparent that different frameworks attach different meanings to these terms. Consequently, in order to ensure consistency in the use of these terms, the conceptualization of the DMC pyramid [1] was used in the gamification design framework of the current study.

3.3   User Type/Players

User type and players are mentioned by four frameworks each. The reviewed frameworks emphasize the importance of understanding the needs and preferences of users that will be using the gamified system. Insight into user types among students offers valuable understanding of their engagement with gamified experiences. This understanding facilitates the customization of design elements, so that they align more closely with student preferences and motivations [26]. Marczewski [14] formulated the HEXAD typology of gamification user types, specifically for the domain of gamification. The HEXAD user type model presents six distinct user profiles that are characterized by their varying receptivity to motivation, which stem from either intrinsic factors (such as self-realization) or extrinsic incentives (such as rewards). The Marczewski gamification design framework recommends using the HEXAD user topology to segment users; this is also the user topology that was used in the gamification design framework of the current study.

Following is a description of the user types of the HEXAD user typology, alongside the game design elements proposed by Marczewski to cater for the motivations of each type [14].

Philanthropists exhibit motivation rooted in purpose, and are characterized by altruism and a willingness to contribute without seeking personal gain. Recommended design features for this user type include mechanisms for collection and trading, gifting, knowledge sharing, and administrative responsibilities [14].

Socializers are driven by a desire for interpersonal connections and social engagement. They seek interactions with others and aim to foster social relationships. Proposed design components for this user type encompass features such as guilds or teams, social networks, social comparison, social competition and social discovery [14].

Free spirits are primarily motivated by autonomy, which entails the freedom to express themselves and operate without external constraints. They enjoy opportunities for creative expression and exploration in a system. Design recommendations for this user type include features such as exploratory tasks, nonlinear gameplay, hidden objects that need to be discovered, unlockable content, creativity tools and customization options [14].

Achievers are driven primarily by a desire for proficiency and mastery. They strive to advance in a system by accomplishing tasks or demonstrating their capabilities through overcoming challenging obstacles. Design recommendations for this user type encompass features such as challenges, certificates, skill acquisition, quests, progression systems such as levels and significant challenges, such as 'boss battles' [14].

Players are incentivized by external reinforcements, such as rewards or recognition. They are inclined to engage in activities in a system with the aim of attaining rewards, regardless of the nature of the task. Proposed design components for this user group include point systems, rewards, leaderboards, achievement badges, virtual economies and elements of chance, such as lotteries or games of luck [14].

Disruptors do not want to participate in a gamified system and want to disrupt the system. Therefore, motivational game design elements are not applicable to this user type [14].

3.4 Target Behaviors

Target behaviors are mentioned in four frameworks and are generally described as the desired actions users must perform to gain benefits from a gamification project. The D6 framework [1] states that users' target behaviors should align with the overarching objectives of the gamified system. It also emphasizes the need for appropriate measurement methods to assess these behaviors in order to evaluate the system's success. In the gamification design framework of the current study, target behaviors are therefore included under instrumental objectives, as this is where designers or instructors should incorporate students' target behaviors.

3.5 Activity Design

The design aspects of activity cycles are included in three frameworks. According to the D6 framework [1], activity design is concerned with the design of actions that users of gamified systems perform. Various activities in a gamified environment trigger additional activities, thereby establishing a continuous cycle. In the design of the gamification framework of the current study, activity design was split into the design of activities not requiring a technological platform and the design of activities that do require a technological platform. Instructors should therefore design learning activities based on the availability of various technological platforms.

3.6 Motivation

While motivation is integrated within other components of the D6 framework, Marczewski's gamification design framework uniquely highlights motivation as a distinct element [14]. He emphasizes four core human motivational needs—relatedness, autonomy, mastery, and purpose—outlined in his intrinsic motivation RAMP model [27], which guides gamification design by addressing both intrinsic and extrinsic rewards [14]. Given its comprehensive explanation of human motivation, the RAMP model [27] has emerged as a highly beneficial framework in the conceptualization and development of gamified systems [28][29], and was therefore selected for use in the current study's gamification design framework. This model, first proposed by Marczewski in 2013 [27], synthesizes self-determination theory [30] and the drive framework of motivation [31]. Self-determination theory identifies autonomy, competency, and relatedness as key motivational needs, while the drive framework adds purpose alongside autonomy and mastery (akin to competency) [31]. Marczewski's RAMP model thus integrates these four fundamental motivational drivers as essential foundations for effective gamified system design [28, 29].

3.7 Main Objectives or Problems

Only two design frameworks included either the main objectives (D6 framework) or the main problems (Marczewski framework) as design aspects of a gamified system. Defining concise and well-defined objectives is widely acknowledged as the cornerstone of gamification design, while vague or ambiguous objectives frequently contribute to the shortcomings observed in gamification endeavors [12]. The design aspect of objectives, therefore, refers to the importance of defining clear objectives at the start of a gamification design process.

Liu et al. [7] assert that all gamified systems should pursue two primary objectives: experiential and instrumental outcomes. In education settings, experiential outcomes refer to the subjective experiences and emotions individuals encounter during a learning process, such as enjoyment, engagement and a sense of achievement. In turn, instrumental outcomes are tangible and measurable results achieved as a direct consequence of learning, such as acquiring new skills, knowledge or competencies that can be applied in practical situations [7]. In the gamification design framework of the current study, the main objective was consequently split into experiential and instrumental objectives.

3.8 Platform and Cost

Only one gamification framework, namely the gamification model canvas, included the gamification platform or technological aspect of gamification and the costs involved in developing a gamified system explicitly. However, in the D6 framework the selection of an appropriate platform is discussed under their 'deploy appropriate tools' step. According to Baikins [32], it is very important for gamification designers to determine which platforms or technologies are available for the development of gamified systems, so that development initiatives can be as time-efficient as possible. Investigating the costs associated with these platforms is also critical [15], so both platform and cost considerations were included in the gamification design framework of the current study.

3.9 Educational Content

The Simões framework for educational gamification [17] is the only gamification framework that includes educational content in their framework. However, Leopold [33], who adapted the gamification model canvas for e-learning projects, includes content as one of the aspects of his canvas. He indicates that the content aspect refers to the educational themes covered in e-learning projects. Therefore, the educational content aspect was also included in the gamification design framework of the current study.

The next section will report on how the gamification design aspects that were extracted from the review of current gamification frameworks were incorporated in a new educational gamification design framework.

4 PEDADI Educational Gamification Design Framework

4.1 Presentation of the Framework

By making use of the 10 design aspects derived from the reviewed frameworks, the PEDADI (**P**reparation, **E**ngagement **D**esign, **A**ctivity **D**esign, **I**mplementation) educational gamification design framework was developed, as shown in Fig. 6. The PEDADI educational gamification design framework is divided into four stages, namely preparation, engagement design, activity design and implementation. The PEDADI educational gamification design process, which was used to apply the PEDADI educational gamification design framework, is shown in Fig. 8.

The preparation stage entails defining the main objectives, which comprise both the instrumental and the experiential objectives of the gamified learning environment. The instrumental objectives include the educational content of the gamified environment and the target behaviors. The target behaviors should include a description of the academic activities that are intended to take place in the gamified learning environment. As mentioned before, experiential outcomes refer to the subjective experiences and emotions that individuals encounter during a learning process, such as enjoyment, engagement and a sense of achievement [7]. To ensure that the experiential objectives of an educational gamification system are achieved, an engagement design procedure should be followed, which comprises the next stage of the framework.

Preparation

Main objectives

- ♦ Instrumental objectives
  - ◊ Educational content
  - ◊ Target behaviours
- ♦ Experiential objectives

Engagement **D**esign

- ♦ Motivation (Intrinsic Motivation RAMP)
- ♦ User type (HEXAD User Topology)
- ♦ Fun/Emotions (4Keys 2Fun)
- ♦ Game elements (DMC pyramid)

Activity **D**esign

- ♦ Activities not requring a gamified platform
- ♦ Activities requring a gamified platform

Implementation

- ♦ Costs
- ♦ Platforms

Fig. 6. The PEDADI educational gamification design framework.

The engagement design stage consists of the intrinsic motivation RAMP model, the HEXAD user typology, the 4Keys 2Fun framework, and game elements based on the DMC pyramid. These components were combined to develop a motivation and gamification design template which will be presented in Sect. 4.2. The next step of the framework comprises the activity design phase, where input from the engagement design should be used to develop activities that require a gamified platform as well as activities that does not require a gamified platform. The final implementation stage addresses the costs and platform(s) that must be considered in the implementation of educational gamification.

To illustrate which components of the framework should be used as input for others in designing an educational gamification environment, the design process shown in Fig. 8 was also developed and will be discussed in Sect. 4.3.

4.2 Motivation and Gamification Design Template

To assist designers and instructors with the engagement design of their gamified educational systems, this study developed a motivation and gamification design template that conceptually combines the intrinsic motivation RAMP model, the HEXAD user typology, the 4Keys 2Fun framework and game elements based on the DMC pyramid, as presented in Fig. 7. To create the engagement design template, several steps were taken:

- In the top row of the template, the type of motivation was split into intrinsic or extrinsic motivation. The intrinsic motivation dimension was split further into the intrinsic motivation dimension RAMP [27].
- In the second row, the key motivators (for each user type) according the HEXAD user topology were specified [14].
- In the third row, the HEXAD user types were indicated and in row four, the recommended design features of each user type were presented [14].
- Thereafter, the 4Keys 2Fun, including the actions linked to these types of fun [21], were placed in the corresponding HEXAD user type column as conceptualized by Marczewski [25].
- Lastly, the game dynamics, mechanics and components of the DMC pyramid [1] were grouped according to the applicable HEXAD user type column [14].

An explanation of how the various game elements of the DMC pyramid were grouped according to the key motivators of the HEXAD topology is necessary. The explanation is provided from left to right, starting with the DMC pyramid game elements that were grouped under the relatedness motivational need. The relationship game dynamic of the DMC pyramid was grouped under the relatedness motivational need linked to the socializer HEXAD user type.

Type of motivation	Intrinsic motivation dimension (RAMP)				Extrinsic motivation
Key motivator	Relatedness	Autonomy	Mastery	Purpose	Rewards
HEXAD user type	Socialisers	Free spirits	Achievers	Philanthropists	Players
Recommended design features	Teams Social comparison Social competition Social discovery	Creative expression Exploratory tasks Unlockable content Customisation	Learning new skills Difficult challenges Levels or progression, certificates	Collection Trading, gifting Knowledge sharing	Points Rewards Leaderboards Badges Virtual currency
4Keys 2Fun	People fun	Easy fun	Hard fun	Serious fun	NA
Actions	Competition Cooperation Communication	Exploration Fantasy Creativity	Goals Obstacles Strategy	Repetition Rhythm Collection	
DMC pyramid					
Dynamics	Relationship		Progression		
Mechanics	Competition Collaboration		Challenges Feedback		
Components	Leaderboards		Levels		Badges Points Leaderboards Virtual currency

Fig. 7. The motivation and gamification design template of the PEDADI framework.

The relationships game dynamic is described as social interactions that evoke camaraderie, status and altruism, which aligns effectively with the relatedness motivational need [1]. The game mechanics of competition and collaboration and the game component leaderboards were also grouped under the relatedness motivational need.

According to the motivational needs of the HEXAD topology [14], no DMC game elements correlated with the autonomy motivational need linked to the free spirit user type.

The progression game dynamic of the DMC pyramid was grouped under the mastery motivational need (linked to the achiever HEXAD user type). The progression game dynamic refers to the advancement and improvement of users in a gamified system and aligns closely with the need for mastery by users [1]. Also, the game mechanic of challenges and feedback and the game component of levels were grouped under the mastery need, as these game elements provide users with a sense of mastery, achievement and progression [1].

According to the motivational needs of the HEXAD topology [14], no DMC game elements correlated with the purpose motivational need linked to the philanthropist user type. The badges, points, leaderboards and virtual currency game components of the DMC pyramid were grouped in the last motivational need column, namely rewards (linked to the player HEXAD user type).

4.3   PEDADI Design Process

To indicate which aspects of the PEDADI educational gamification design framework serve as input for others, the PEDADI design process was also developed, as shown in Fig. 8.

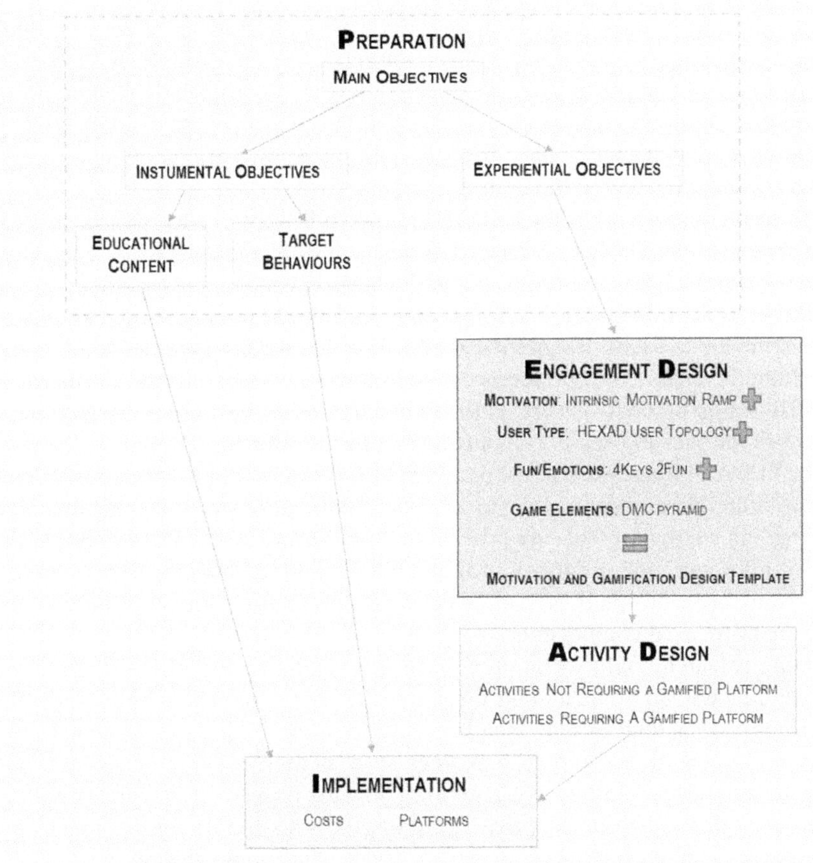

Fig. 8. The PEDADI educational gamification design process.

As mentioned before, the main objectives are divided into instrumental and experiential objectives. On the right side of the design process, the experiential objectives are used in the engagement design phase. As explained in Sect. 4.2, the RAMP model, HEXAD user typology, 4Keys2Fun model, and the DMC pyramid were all used to create a motivation and gamification design template. This template then guides the development of activities requiring a gamified platform and activities that do not require a gamified platform. These designed activities subsequently serve as input for the implementation phase.

On the left side of the design process, the instrumental objectives inform the design of the educational content and the target student behaviors. Both the educational content and the target behaviors also serve as input for the implementation phase of the gamified system.

5 Conclusion

The gamification of education is increasingly recognised as an effective strategy for enhancing student motivation and engagement across various disciplines. However, there remains a lack of comprehensive guidance on how to systematically design meaningful and effective gamified learning experiences [3]. This paper sought to address this gap by developing a novel educational gamification design framework, drawing on key design elements from existing gamification frameworks.

The result of this work is the PEDADI framework—comprising the phases of Preparation, Engagement Design, Activity Design, and Implementation—which provides a structured approach for the design and deployment of educational gamification systems. In addition to the framework itself, the study introduced a motivation and engagement design template to assist designers and educators in creating gamified experiences that cater to the diverse needs, preferences, and motivations of students. Furthermore, the PEDADI design process was presented to illustrate how the various components of the framework interact and serve as inputs to subsequent phases.

The PEDADI framework offers practical value for educators, instructional designers, and curriculum developers seeking to integrate gamification into their teaching practices. By providing a structured design process and supporting tools, it can improve the consistency, relevance, and pedagogical alignment of gamified learning experiences. It also supports inclusive design by accommodating different motivational profiles through its engagement-focused components.

Future research could focus on empirically validating the PEDADI framework in different educational contexts and disciplines to assess its adaptability and effectiveness. Longitudinal studies may also be valuable in examining the sustained impact of using the framework on student outcomes such as motivation, engagement, and academic performance. Additionally, exploring how the framework integrates with emerging technologies—such as adaptive learning platforms, AI-driven personalisation, or virtual reality—could further enhance its relevance and applicability.

Acknowledgements. I would like to acknowledge the financial support provided by the Centre for Innovation in Learning and Teaching, through the Scholarship of Teaching and Learning office, funded by the Department of Higher Education and Training's (DHET) University Capacity Development Grant in South Africa. This support enabled the research and publication of this work. The views expressed are those of the authors and do not necessarily reflect those of the funding bodies.

References

1. Werbach, K., Hunter, D.: For the Win: How Game Thinking Can Revolutionize Your Business. Wharton Digital Press (2012)

2. Hamari, J., Koivisto, J., Sarsa, H.: Does gamification work? A literature review of empirical studies on gamification. In: Proceedings of the Annual Hawaii International Conference on System Sciences, pp. 3025–3034 (2014). https://doi.org/10.1109/HICSS.2014.377
3. Huang, B., Hew, K.F.: Implementing a theory-driven gamification model in higher education flipped courses: effects on out-of-class activity completion and quality of artifacts. Comput. Educ. **125**(May), 254–272 (2018). https://doi.org/10.1016/j.compedu.2018.06.018
4. Venter, M., de Wet, L.: Systematic literature review of gamification design in higher education programming courses: methodological rigor exposed. In: Plácido da Silva, H., Cipresso, P. (eds.) Communications in Computer and Information Science, vol. 2370, pp. 1–8. Springer (2025)
5. Taşkın, N., Kılıç Çakmak, E.: Effects of gamification on behavioral and cognitive engagement of students in the online learning environment. Int. J. Hum. Comput. Interact. **39**(17), 3334–3345 (2023). https://doi.org/10.1080/10447318.2022.2096190
6. An, Y.: Designing effective gamified learning experiences. Int. J. Tech-nol. Educ. **3**(2), 62 (2020). https://doi.org/10.46328/ijte.v3i2.27
7. Liu, D., Santhanam, R., Webster, J.: Toward meaningful engagement: a framework for design and research of gamified information systems. MIS Q. **41**(4), 1011–1034 (2017). https://doi.org/10.1007/s13398-014-0173-7.2
8. Taşkın, N., Kılıç Çakmak, E.: Player/user types for gamification. In: Bernardes, O., Amorim, V., Moreira, A. (eds.) Handbook of Research on Cross-Disciplinary Uses of Gamification in Organizations, pp. 62–85. IGI Global (2022)
9. Dichev, C., Dicheva, D.: Gamifying education: what is known, what is believed and what remains uncertain: a critical review. Int. J. Educ. Technol. High. Educ. **14**(1), 1–36 (2017). https://doi.org/10.1186/s41239-017-0042-5
10. Khaldi, A., Bouzidi, R., Nader, F.: Gamification of e-learning in higher education: a systematic literature review. Smart Learn. Environ. **10**(10), 1–31 (2023). https://doi.org/10.1186/s40561-023-00227-z
11. Garone, P., Nesteriuk, S.: Gamification and learning: a comparative study of design frameworks. LNCS, vol. 11582, pp. 473–487 (2019). https://doi.org/10.1007/978-3-030-22219-2_35
12. Mora, A., Riera, D., González, C., Arnedo-Moreno, J.: Gamification: a systematic review of design frameworks. J. Comput. High. Educ. **29**(3), 516–548 (2017). https://doi.org/10.1007/s12528-017-9150-4
13. Costa, C.J., Aparicio, M., Aparicio, S., Aparicio, J.T.: Gamification usage ecology. In: SIG-DOC 2017 - 35th ACM International Conference on the Design of Communication (2017). https://doi.org/10.1145/3121113.3121205
14. Marczewski, A.: Even Ninja Monkeys Like to Play, Unicorn. Gamified UK (2018)
15. Jimenez, S.: Gamification model canvas (2013). https://www.gamedeveloper.com/business/gamification-model-canvas. Accessed 20 Apr 2024
16. Hunicke, R., LeBlanc, M., Zubek, R.: MDA: a formal approach to game design and game research. In: Proceedings of the AAAI Workshop on Challenges in Game AI, California, USA, pp. 4–9 (2004). 10.1.1.79.4561
17. Simões, J., Redondo, R., Vilas, A., Aguiar, A.: Proposal of a reference model for the application of gamification in social learning environments. In: Proceedings of the VIII International Conference on ICT in Education, pp. 1117–1128 (2013)
18. Escribano, F.: Gamification model canvas evolution. Players profiling and decision support model (2016). https://gecon.es/wp-content/uploads/2017/07/GMC-Evolution_vDef.pdf. Accessed 22 Apr 2024
19. Osterwalder, A., Pigneur, Y., Tucci, C.L.: Clarifying business models: origins, present, and future of the concept. Commun. Assoc. Inf. Syst. **16**, 1–25 (2005). https://doi.org/10.17705/1cais.01601

20. Marczewski, A.: User types. In: Even Ninja Monkeys Like to Play: Gamification, Game Thinking and Motivational Design, CreateSpace Independent Publishing Platform, pp. 65–80 (2015)
21. XEODesign. The 4 keys to fun (2004). https://www.xeodesign.com/research/. Accessed 25 May 2024
22. Schnabel, M.A., Lo, T.T., Aydin, S.: Gamification and rule based de-sign strategies in architecture education. In: DesignED Asia, pp. 1–11 (2014). https://doi.org/10.13140/2.1.5150.3689
23. Simões, J., Redondo, R.D., Vilas, A.F.: A social gamification frame-work for a K-6 learning platform. Comput. Hum. Behav. **29**(2), 345–353 (2013). https://doi.org/10.1016/j.chb.2012.06.007
24. Chou, Y.: Octalysis – complete gamification framework (2015). https://octalysisgroup.com/framework/. Accessed 16 Apr 2024
25. Marczewski, A.: Gamification user types and the 4 keys 2 fun (2013). https://www.gamified.uk/2013/06/05/gamification-user-types-and-the-4-keys-2-fun/. Accessed 25 Apr 2024
26. Rogers, M., Yao, W., Luxton-Reilly, A., Leinonen, J., Lottridge, D., Denny, P.: Exploring personalization of gamification in an introductory programming course. In: 52nd ACM Technical Symposium on Computer Science Education (SIGCSE 2021), pp. 1121–1127 (2021). https://doi.org/10.1145/3408877.3432402
27. Marczewski, A.: The intrinsic motivation RAMP (2013). https://www.gamified.uk/gamification-framework/the-intrinsic-motivation-ramp/. Accessed 25 Apr 2024
28. Bravo, R., Catalán, S., Pina, J.M.: Gamification in tourism and hospitality review platforms: how to R.A.M.P. up users' motivation to create content. Int. J. Hosp. Manag. **99** (2021). https://doi.org/10.1016/j.ijhm.2021.103064
29. López-Ardao, J.C., Rodríguez-Rubio, R.F., Herrería-Alonso, S., Pérez, M.R., Sousa-Vieira, M.-E.: APAR: a structural design and guidance framework for gamification in education. Preprints 2024 (2024). https://www.preprints.org/manuscript/202403.1711/v1
30. Deci, E.L., Ryan, R.M.: The general causality orientations scale: self-determination in personality. J. Res. Pers. **19**(2), 109–134 (1985). https://doi.org/10.1016/0092-6566(85)90023-6
31. Pink, D.H.: Drive: The Surprising Truth About What Motivates Us. Canongate Books, New York (2009)
32. Baikins, P.: Gamification project design framework (2017). https://gamificationplus.uk/gamification-project-design-framework/. Accessed 24 Apr 2024
33. Leopold, E.: Using canvas model for e-learning projects (2016). https://elearningstorm.wordpress.com/2016/09/26/using-canvas-model-for-elearning- projects/. Accessed 20 Apr 2024

Human-Centered Design for a Usable Privacy SCALE in Healthcare

Catarina Silva[1,2], Rita Alves[3], Isaac Nunes[3], Joana Pinto[3], and Ana Ferreira[4(✉)]

[1] Departamento de Electrónica, Telecomunicações e Informática, Universidade de Aveiro, 3810-193 Aveiro, Portugal
`c.alexandracorreia@ua.pt`
[2] Instituto de Telecomunicações, 3810-164 Aveiro, Portugal
[3] Faculty of Fine Arts, University of Porto, Porto, Portugal
[4] RISE-Health, Department of Population Studies, School of Medicine and Biomedical Sciences, University of Porto, Porto, Portugal
`amlaf@med.up.pt`

Abstract. The pervasive adoption of digital technologies in healthcare has resulted in an exponential increase in the volume of sensitive patient data being collected, processed and shared. This necessitates a paradigm shift towards enhanced transparency and user empowerment regarding data handling practices. Privacy quantification can help address such challenges by translating complex policy analyses into easily interpretable, quantifiable metrics that provide users with actionable insights into the privacy risks associated with different healthcare services. In this paper, we propose a prototype of an application, named SCALE, which focuses on providing a user-friendly design interface to represent the results of privacy quantification in an accessible way. SCALE aims to enable users to make informed decisions and exercise greater control over the privacy of their personal health information. We discuss usability tests and metrics used to evaluate our prototype. Most tasks were completed efficiently, and generally, users considered the privacy SCALE adequate for its purpose. After analyzing the results, we also propose a set of recommendations for this type of privacy representation.

Keywords: Healthcare Privacy · Privacy Quantification · User Empowerment · Privacy SCALE · Usability

1 Introduction

In today's digital landscape, user data collection has become widespread. Despite this, individuals often lack the means to understand how online services manage their personal information [7]. This disconnect between data collection practices and user understanding is intensified by the opacity of privacy policies, which, despite being legally mandated, are frequently inaccessible and incomprehensible to the average user [21]. In response to the challenge of making privacy information more accessible, privacy quantification has emerged as a strategy to enhance transparency in data handling by converting complex policy analyses into quantifiable, user-friendly metrics. This empowers

J. F. Krems et al. (Eds.): CHIRA 2025, CCIS 2836, pp. 149–173, 2026.
https://doi.org/10.1007/978-3-032-16454-4_9

individuals with concise insights into privacy risks, enabling informed and privacy-conscious decisions [26].

This paper presents a usability study of SCALE, a prototype application that transforms detailed policy assessments into a standardized, color-coded visual collection, third-party sharing, data retention policies and user control mechanisms. The system aims to bridge the gap between expert privacy evaluations and user comprehension. The study investigates whether this quantified, visual representation of privacy risk effectively communicates key information, thereby fostering trust and enhancing comprehension. It also explores the influence of onboarding processes on privacy evaluation tasks, aiming to identify best practices and guiding users for effective system use. The core goal is to determine whether SCALE can empower users to assess and act on privacy risks confidentially.

To assess the usability and perceived value of the SCALE system, we conducted in-person usability testing with healthcare professionals, a group for whom data privacy is of paramount importance, given the sensitive nature of the information they handle. Prior studies emphasize the importance of usability testing to ensure the effectiveness of interactive visualizations and decision support tools, particularly in fields like healthcare [31]. The healthcare context provides a rigorous test environment for evaluating the effectiveness of privacy quantification tools, as healthcare professionals are accustomed to dealing with complex regulations and sensitive data. The insights gained from this study will inform the design and development of future privacy quantification tools, contributing to the creation of more user-friendly and effective solutions for promoting data privacy.

The evaluation was guided by the following research questions: 1) Is the privacy SCALE intuitive and easy to navigate for users with varying levels of technical expertise? 2) Does the presence of onboarding processes significantly influence user success in completing privacy evaluation tasks within the application? 3) Can users accurately interpret the quantified privacy ratings provided by the system, and can they articulate the implications of these ratings for their own privacy? The answers were highlighted by app users and address how issues can be resolved to improve the app's usability [3]. User satisfaction and experience of the system are also significant, regardless of the product type [1].

The remainder of this paper is organized as follows: Sect. 2 describes the relevant background and related work; Sect. 3 presents the proposed prototype, including its design objectives, interface, core features, and privacy score representation; Sect. 4 details the methodology followed; usability results are presented in Sect. 5, and user study results are in Sect. 6; finally, Sect. 7 discusses the main findings, limitations, and study conclusions.

2   User-Centric Privacy Visualization for Healthcare

The integration of digital health tools into healthcare settings has revolutionized patient care, offering enhanced communication, personalized treatment plans, and improved overall outcomes; however, this digital transformation also introduces complex challenges concerning patient privacy and the management of sensitive health information [6]. As healthcare providers increasingly rely on electronic health records, online platforms, and mobile health applications, it becomes crucial to address the perceptions and experiences of both health professionals and patients regarding the adequacy and usability of digital tools designed to manage and communicate patient privacy preferences [33].

Due to this "need for privacy" [11], strategies such as privacy enhancing-technologies and privacy quantification approaches are being explored across the literature. Privacy quantification, such as Differential Privacy (DP) [22] strategies enable informed decision-making by users, especially when interacting with medical applications that handle sensitive personal data [29]. It represents a multifaceted domain, aiming to measure and express privacy levels in a understandable manner, particularly vital in sensitive sectors like healthcare [15]. This quantification allows for a more transparent understanding of the privacy implications associated with using such applications, empowering both medical professionals and patients to assess and manage their privacy risks effectively [28]. The complexity of privacy in the digital age requires a comprehensive approach that integrates legal, philosophical, and technical perspectives [32]. Several elements, including the type of data, the goal, the context, and the obligations involved, need to be taken into account when evaluating data privacy [23].

To take advantage from the result of the privacy quantification, a properly result representation is essential to consider human-centered endeavor [8]. A visual representation can range from simple privacy scores to more elaborate dashboards that detail the various factors contributing to the overall privacy level. In all cases, to take advantage from this method, it requires user-centric design approaches for ensuring that these displays are not only accurate but also easily interpretable by the intended audience.

However, in the context of medical applications, with higher data sensitivity [18], the challenge lies in translating the mathematical guarantees of privacy quantification into intuitive and actionable information for end-users. Moreover, the exchange of information across multiple distributed entities will lead to better healthcare quality, but such frameworks need to ensure data privacy.

Another approach involves the use of privacy risk assessment models, which evaluate the potential privacy risks associated with different data processing activities. These models often assign scores or ratings to different privacy risks, providing a high-level overview of the overall privacy posture of a system or application. A critical prerequisite for the sustained adoption and effectiveness of healthcare technologies lies in fostering unwavering confidence among patients, clinicians, and the broader public, thereby emphasizing the indispensable role of transparent and responsible data governance frameworks [20].

A critical gap remains in human-centered privacy scales capable of visually representing the privacy level resulting from evaluation and quantification. For example, Öztürk et al. [17] proposed a study focused on the development and validation of a patient privacy scale to assess whether nurses observe or violate patient privacy in the workplace, however, while their proposed approach provides a means of quantifying patient privacy, the paper does not discuss visualizing these results. Focused on usable privacy, Alohaly and Takabi [2] proposed an approach to quantify data collection practices in application privacy policies, however, the authors only discussed usable privacy in the context of how their quantification method could be used to improve privacy notices and make them more understandable to users. They proposed the usage of pie charts as nano-sized notice to deliver the information on data collection practices, however, they did not detail a user-centric design process for creating privacy interfaces. Moreover, Halimi and Ayday [13] focused on real-time privacy risk quantification and intended to provide users with information about their privacy risks while not explicitly mention a specific scale, it considered the probability of a user being vulnerable to profile matching attacks where if the returned probability is higher than a threshold, the user is classified as vulnerable. Finally, other studies only refer to the need for privacy quantification [4, 30].

Visualizing privacy scales presents a complex challenge due mainly to the inherent subjectivity and context dependence of privacy itself. Effectively communicating the varying levels and implications of privacy depends on individuals' perceptions, concerns, and desired levels of control over their personal information, which vary significantly based on individual traits, cultural norms, and specific situations. Consequently, designing visualizations that capture this diverse understanding of privacy is a significant challenge. Adding to this complexity is the multidimensional nature of privacy, encompassing informational, psychological, physical, and social and cultural aspects. Integrating these diverse dimensions into an intuitive and coherent visual representation requires user study and user-centric design approaches to avoid oversimplification or misrepresentation. Moreover, the use of different research designs, combining quantitative surveys with qualitative interviews, can provide a more nuanced understanding of privacy concerns and benefits.

Regarding privacy preferences, users gain experience with a system, encounter new risks, or simply shift their attitudes toward data sharing. Their privacy settings may evolve. Adapting visualizations to reflect these changes in real time or providing mechanisms for users to explore different privacy configurations presents considerable technical and design challenges. Developing effective visualization techniques is crucial not only for representing the current state of privacy settings but also for illustrating the potential consequences of various choices. Another key challenge involves bridging the gap between technical privacy controls and user comprehension. Often expressed in complex technical approaches, privacy settings can be difficult for non-experts to understand, hindering their ability to make informed decisions. For instance, the privacy protections offered by differentially private mechanisms lack contextual awareness, remaining agnostic to the social context of a dataset or analysis. Visualizations should therefore aim to translate these technical details into intuitive visual interfaces, enabling users to intuitively understand the implications of their choices without requiring specialized knowledge [5].

Moreover, when devising scales for privacy perception, it is imperative to account for individual variations in privacy attitudes, and the cognitive biases that affect privacy decision making [10]. One must also consider the cognitive biases and heuristics that influence individuals' privacy decision-making processes, as these biases can significantly impact the accuracy and rationality of privacy choices. An approach called "privacy by architecture" minimizes the collection of identifiable personal data by emphasizing anonymization and client-side data storage and processing [27]. Also, one can integrate privacy into design by developing a framework that offers embodied privacy care with diverse interactions [16]. Another framework focuses on evaluating current privacy by design methods with an emphasis on smart homes. As a result, a more holistic approach is needed when evaluating how users think and act when it comes to privacy. By addressing these biases and incorporating user-centered design principles, it is possible to create privacy levels scale representations that empower individuals to make informed choices and effectively manage their privacy in an increasingly complex digital landscape.

Furthermore, when analyzing levels of privacy representation, the level of users' influence to privacy-related behaviors and decisions should also be considered [14]. This involves understanding the relation between individual's autonomy and collective interests, as well as addressing the ethical implications to shape privacy choices. It is essential to ensure that privacy interventions respect individual's autonomy and promote transparent data handling practices [14]. Moreover, exploring innovative approaches to privacy education and awareness, such as gamification and interactive tutorials, can empower individuals to develop a deeper understanding of privacy risks and mitigation strategies. Drawing upon insights from behavioral economics, psychology, and human-computer interaction, it is possible to design privacy levels scale representations that effectively promote privacy-protective behaviors and empower individuals to navigate the complexities of the digital world with greater confidence and control. Understanding the privacy paradox, where individuals state privacy concerns but behave otherwise, can provide insights into this intricate decision-making process. Exploring methods to enhance privacy awareness can help bridge the gap between intentions and actions [19].

The design of effective privacy scale visualizations must also mitigate the potential for cognitive overload, where users feel overwhelmed by excessive information or overly intricate visual representations. Achieving a balance between providing sufficient detail and maintaining clarity is paramount to ensure users can effectively navigate and interpret the visualization without feeling lost. User interaction is a vital component of privacy scale visualization, empowering users to actively explore and manage their privacy settings. Interactive visualizations should allow users to easily adjust their preferences, examine the ramifications of different choices, and receive feedback on the effectiveness of their privacy configurations. Moreover, these visualizations should be accessible to users with diverse abilities and technical skills, ensuring universal benefits from enhanced privacy awareness and control. Leveraging existing literature on information visualization can contribute significantly to achieving this goal.

Online privacy literacy, which encompasses both factual and procedural knowledge regarding online privacy, is known to be strongly connected to motivational factors [11]. Privacy literacy affects privacy protection behaviors, which are also related to informational and psychological needs for privacy [11]. Offline privacy concerns are strongly influenced by the psychological need for privacy [11]. The privacy paradox highlights the inconsistencies between privacy attitudes and behaviors, underscoring the need for a better understanding of the factors influencing privacy-related decision-making [11, 12]. It is imperative to consider the multifaceted aspects of privacy, including its social, psychological, and cognitive dimensions [34]. The development of scales to measure patient privacy in various settings highlights the ongoing efforts to assess and address privacy concerns in healthcare [34]. Furthermore, the use of alternative regulatory mechanisms, such as privacy nudges, underscores the need for innovative approaches to promote privacy-protective behaviors in online environments. This necessitates a move beyond traditional notions of privacy, to encompass the broader concept of control over one's personal information and experiences [34].

3   The Prototype: SCALE

The SCALE application was developed to address the challenge of translating complex privacy policy information into clear, actionable insights for end users. Based in a privacy quantification framework, it enables users to evaluate and compare the privacy practices of digital services through a standardized, visually intuitive scoring system. By presenting concise, comprehensible privacy metrics, SCALE eliminates the need for users to interpret complex legal or technical documents and supports informed decision-making. Within the healthcare sector, where personal health data is highly sensitive and subject to rigorous confidentiality requirements, SCALE is particularly relevant. Healthcare professionals and patients frequently engage with applications that collect, process, and share confidential information, often lacking transparent communication regarding their privacy practices. Traditional privacy policies, typically presented as complex legal documents, often fail to provide meaningful insights to end users, thereby hindering informed consent and eroding trust. SCALE addresses this critical gap by converting detailed privacy assessments into an accessible, color-coded interface that clearly conveys the privacy implications of healthcare applications. This capability is particularly crucial in medical contexts, where the potential ramifications of data misuse or unauthorized access are significantly amplified due to the inherent risks to patient confidentiality and professional liability. By allowing healthcare professionals to compare privacy practices across digital health tools and highlighting potential non-compliance, SCALE supports responsible, privacy-aware decision-making. The inclusion of multilingual support and user-friendly onboarding further improves accessibility for users with varying levels of digital literacy. Consequently, SCALE not only aids in regulatory compliance and risk awareness but also fosters patient autonomy and trust, which are fundamental values for ethical healthcare delivery in the digital age.

3.1   Design Objectives

SCALE was designed around four key principles: comprehensibility, transparency, comparability, and accessibility.

First, SCALE aims to ensure that privacy risk information is easy to interpret, even for users who lack technical expertise. By using visual metaphors and clear interaction patterns, the interface facilitates quick judgments about an application's data practices.

Second, transparency is achieved by explicitly linking privacy scores to concrete evaluation criteria, enabling users to understand not just the outcome, but the rationale behind it.

Third, the system ensures comparability across digital services by applying a consistent set of dimensions and visual formats to all assessments.

Finally, the interface is designed to be accessible to users with varying levels of digital literacy, ensuring that the tool can be used confidently and effectively across broad user populations, including non-expert and vulnerable groups such as patients or medical doctors in healthcare settings.

3.2 Privacy Quantification and Scoring Framework

At the core of SCALE lies a privacy quantification model that translates complex legal and technical aspects of privacy policies into structured, measurable indicators. This model is organized into several high-level dimensions, such as data collection, third-party sharing, user control, retention practices, and transparency. Each dimension is decomposed into specific categories that represent particular privacy requirements or practices. These are evaluated for each application, and compliance or non-compliance is used to generate a cumulative privacy score. For instance, Data Collection is quantified by assessing aspects such as the volume and sensitivity of personal data gathered, and its necessity for core functionality. Third-Party Sharing considers the number and type of entities data is shared with and the clarity of user consent. User Control is measured by the granularity and accessibility of privacy settings and data deletion options. Retention Practices evaluate data retention periods and anonymization efforts, while Transparency is assessed through the readability of policies and accessibility of information. These granular, quantified aspects contribute to the overall dimension scores and ultimately to the cumulative privacy score, reflecting a comprehensive and detailed privacy posture of the analyzed application.

The DevPrivOps-aligned [24] privacy quantification architecture, which underpins these scores, is based on two main deployment phases: Development Analysis and Risk Analysis. The Development Analysis phase integrates a tool denoted by PrivGuide [9] and the Data Management component to ensure privacy-by-design from the planning stage of the Software Development Lifecycle (SDLC). Data Management employs a proposed categorization model of privacy-related data types, Privacy-sensitive Data Categorization (PsDC) [23], for clustering data into privacy-based categories, considering Personally Identifiable Information (PII) inference and user preferences. PrivGuide assists in implementing privacy-by-design by enforcing continuous Data Protection Impact Assessments (DPIAs), verifying compliance, and assessing use and misuse cases. The integration of PrivGuide with PsDC enhances this analysis by offering a fine-grained categorization of data based on sensitivity and user expectations, enabling the assessment of both structural compliance and contextual data sensitivity. Following this, the Risk Analysis phase estimates the likelihood and impact of security threats with privacy implications. This phase incorporates ASAP [25] to identify applications with dangerous or potentially unwanted permissions. Also, privacy threat analysis includes semantic interpretation of privacy policies and data flows, utilizing machine learning and Natural Language Processing (NLP) to detect discrepancies and identify privacy-sensitive attributes. DP is considered for privacy quantification [22], and its integration with PsDC is crucial to mitigate profiling attacks that DP alone may not address. The cumulative results from these layers of analysis are then compiled into a machine-readable Privacy Manifest File (PMF), to determine the privacy level.

The scores are then presented through a multi-level rating system that uses color and structure to determine the degree of privacy risk. This multi-level rating system visually translates complex privacy policy assessments into an easily interpretable format. For example, dimensions with strong privacy practices are prominently displayed in green, indicating a high level of trustworthiness and compliance. Conversely, dimensions exhibiting shortcomings or non-compliance are highlighted in yellow or red, providing immediate visual cues about potential privacy risks. This approach moves beyond binary compliant/non-compliant outcomes by emphasizing a gradation of privacy, enabling users to discern both the strengths and weaknesses of an application's data handling practices.

The main screen of the SCALE application offers a visual summary of an application's overall privacy score, which is further segmented by dimension and supported by clear explanatory labels and color gradients. Users can interact with this visual summary by expanding each segment to reveal the individual indicators, thereby allowing for a detailed inspection of which specific privacy requirements were met or unmet.

3.3   Interface and Core Features

SCALE user interface has been designed to provide intuitive access to privacy information through a small set of well-integrated components.

The main screen presents users with a visual summary of an application's overall privacy score, segmented by dimension and supported by explanatory labels and color gradients (Fig. 1 - Left). Each segment can be expanded to reveal individual indicators (Fig. 1 - Right), allowing users to see which privacy requirements were met or unmet.

This interactivity supports both high-level and deeper inspections depending on users' goals. A prominent search bar enables quick access to evaluated applications and a comparison feature allows users to view multiple apps side-by-side.

The interface supports multilingual navigation with the option to switch languages through the user profile, enhancing accessibility for non-native speakers.

Two versions of the prototype were tested: one with onboarding screens explaining the structure and use of the SCALE, and one without, allowing the team to assess the importance of guided onboarding in the user experience.

3.4   Task Design

A representative usage scenario informed the task design for usability testing. In this scenario, users, modeled as healthcare professionals, were asked to evaluate and compare the privacy scores of digital health applications (*Libreview, SNS 24*), assist a non-native speaker in navigating the app, and interpret the implications of privacy classifications.

These tasks simulate real-world decision-making contexts where privacy concerns intersect with professional responsibility and user advocacy.

The application used in testing was a high-fidelity prototype with functional interactive flows for evaluation. While some backend functionalities (e.g., real-time policy analysis) were simulated, the visual and navigational components reflected the intended

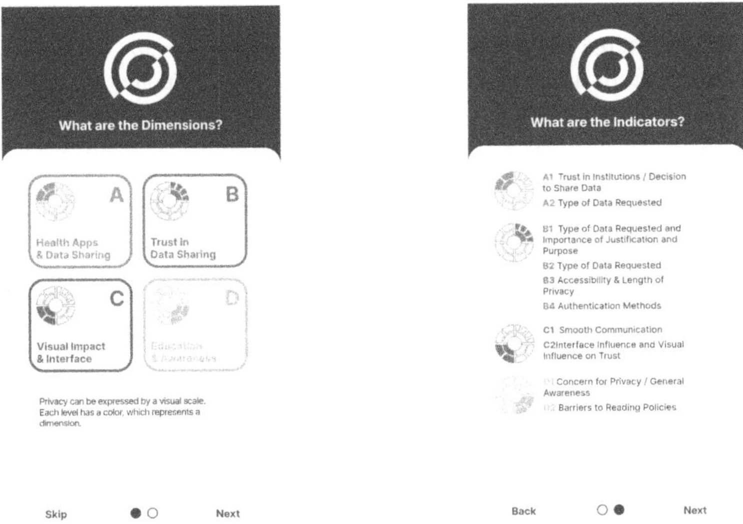

Fig. 1. Explanation of the colors and levels for the privacy score representation.

production design. This approach enabled realistic usability evaluation while preserving flexibility in iteration.

4   Methodology

Usability testing was employed as the primary method to evaluate the effectiveness and clarity of the SCALE application. This approach involved observing participants as they interacted with the system in a controlled setting, with a focus on task performance, user behavior, and subjective feedback. As defined by the Interaction Design Foundation, usability testing is "the practice of testing how easy a design is to use with a group of representative users".

Participants completed three structured tasks while being observed by a moderator, who followed a standardized protocol to ensure consistency across sessions. The moderator facilitated the in-person, individual sessions and employed a think-aloud method, prompting participants to verbalize their thoughts, decisions, and reactions in real time. This approach enabled the capture of both verbal and non-verbal cues, such as facial expressions and body language, providing richer insights into the user experience.

Each session lasted approximately 45 min and comprised three phases: an introductory briefing, task execution, and a concluding interview. At first, participants reviewed and signed informed consent forms (including nondisclosure and recording agreements), and provided demographic and background information, including gender, age, educational background (PhD, Master's, or bachelor's degree), occupation, and experience with mobile interfaces. The study's objectives, the session structure, and the importance of their input were explained.

During the task phase (approximately 30 min), participants used the SCALE application to complete three predefined tasks. The moderator observed silently, taking notes and recording verbalizations and behavioral cues to capture potential usability issues without influencing participants' interaction patterns. The workflow (Fig. 2) illustrates the sequence of screens and actions that participants followed while completing the main tasks during the usability test.

Following task completion, a post-test interview of approximately 10 min invited participants to reflect on their experience, share preferences, and comment on any difficulties encountered. This phase also allowed the moderator to probe observations from the task phase, providing deeper insights into user's understanding and interface design effectiveness. To explore the usability of the SCALE application, a set of predefined tasks guided participants through key features and identified areas for improvement. These tasks were embedded in a realistic scenario, simulating a typical work situation for healthcare professionals, ensuring ecological validity and authentic decision-making.

To assess the role of onboarding in user performance and comprehension, two application versions were tested: Version A included onboarding screens introducing the SCALE system, whereas Version B omitted them. This enabled evaluation of onboarding's effectiveness in facilitating navigation and understanding, helping determine the most promising design for final implementation.

The workflow (Fig. 2) illustrates the sequence of screens and actions that participants followed while completing the main tasks during the usability test.

In this simulated context, the participant assumes the role of a healthcare provider at the end of a workday:

At the end of the day, a patient arrives at your office and mentions using the Libreview app to monitor their glucose levels. Although you've heard of the app, you are concerned about its privacy practices. Recalling the SCALE app, you use it to assess Libreview's privacy score. After reviewing the overall score, you want to understand which dimensions and indicators contributed to it—particularly those that show weak compliance with privacy standards. During this process, the patient—who does not speak Portuguese—asks for your help navigating the app and interpreting its privacy SCALE. You locate the option to switch the app's language. Curious about other healthcare-related applications, you search for the SNS 24 app on SCALE and compare its privacy score with Libreview's, identifying which dimensions are missing indicators or fall short of compliance.

This scenario was intentionally designed to consider common challenges related to privacy comprehension, language accessibility, and comparative decision-making. By embedding the tasks within a realistic context, the study evaluated not only the functional usability of the interface but also its effectiveness in supporting informed, real-world privacy decisions among healthcare professionals.

Participants were asked to complete three structured tasks based on the scenario described above. Tasks were carefully worded to be specific and neutral, avoiding any hints that might guide participants' behavior or responses.

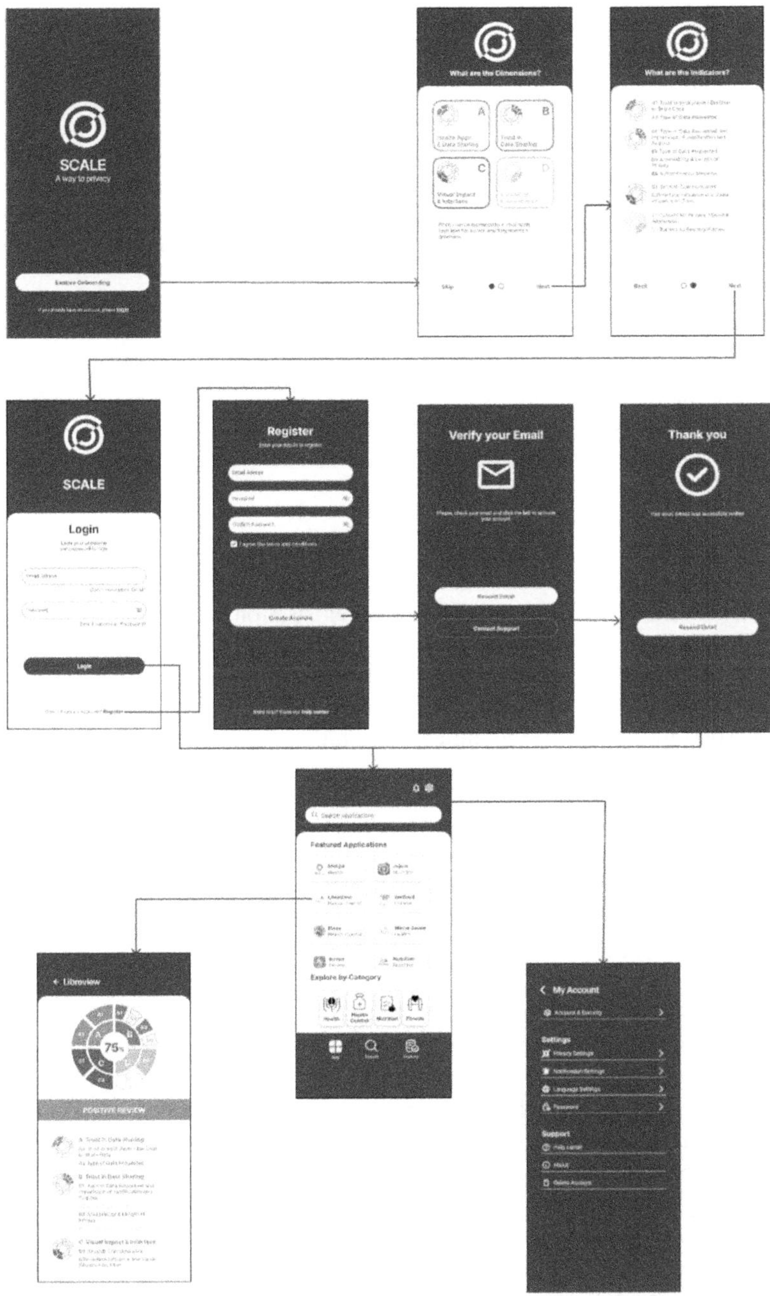

Fig. 2. Workflow of the SCALE application used during the usability test.

- **Task 1**
  1. Open the SCALE application;
  2. Read information about onboarding (only version A);
  3. Click on the "Register" and follow the registration steps;
  4. Fill in the required fields;
  5. Confirm the registration via email verification;
  6. Select the *Libreview* app (Main screen);
  7. Interpret the score and the dimensions/indicators and decide whether to use the *Libreview* application.
- **Task 2**
  1. Open the SCALE application;
  2. Click on the "Register" and follow the registration steps;
  3. Fill in the required fields;
  4. Confirm the registration via email verification;
  5. Go to "Profile" in the application;
  6. Locate "Language Settings" option;
- **Task 3**
  1. Open the SCALE application;
  2. Read information about onboarding (only version A);
  3. Click on the "Register" and follow the registration steps;
  4. Fill in the required fields;
  5. Confirm the registration via email verification;
  6. Select the *SNS 24*(Main screen);
  7. Interpret the score and the dimensions/indicators and decide whether to use the *SNS 24* application.

Throughout the task sessions, moderators guided participants and encouraged them to verbalize their thought processes using the think-aloud protocol. All interactions, including on-screen activity and spoken feedback, were recorded using a smartphone for later analysis.

As testers were guided through the tasks by moderators, their verbal feedback and on-screen interactions were recorded using a smartphone. The task-based segment of our user test was complemented by several additional activities designed to enhance the study by providing deeper insights into the users and their experiences during task completion.

In addition to the task-based evaluations, we conducted complementary assessments to gather comprehensive user feedback. Pre-test questionnaires were administered to collect data on participants' demographics and their prior experience with mobile interfaces, including average daily usage, ease of navigation, and familiarity with health-related applications. Post-task questionnaires captured participants' immediate reflections and experiences following the completion of each task. To gain deeper insights into participants' overall impressions and user experience with the system, we conducted post-test interviews. Finally, System Usability Scale (SUS) assessments were employed to quantitatively evaluate users' perceptions of the prototype's usability.

These tasks and activities enabled to collect data used to assess the interface and provided a comprehensive assessment of the SCALE application's usability, functionality, and perceived value in supporting privacy-aware decision-making.

4.1 Usability Tests

The usability tests were conducted in a controlled, in-person environment that was designed to replicate real-world conditions, ensuring reliable and valid data collection. The testing space was chosen to be quiet and free from distractions, allowing participants to focus fully on the tasks. A moderator was present throughout the sessions to observe participant behavior, take detailed notes, and offer any necessary instructions.

For the execution and analysis of the tests, a smartphone was provided for testing the SCALE application itself, while another smartphone was used to record audio and capture the interactions on-screen. To collect data, pre-test questionnaires were used to gather demographic and background information, while follow-up questions and post-test interviews were conducted to gather qualitative insights into participants' experiences. The SUS was employed to measure overall user satisfaction and impressions of the prototype.

The logistics of participant recruitment and session scheduling were carefully managed to ensure a smooth testing process. Six participants were selected, ensuring that their profiles matched the target user group. Recruitment was carried out through internal contacts to identify suitable candidates. The test sessions were scheduled in 45-min intervals, with time slots allocated based on participant availability. All sessions were conducted at the participants' workplaces to create a familiar and contextually relevant environment. To minimize external influences, individual tests were conducted for each participant.

Performance measures were used to evaluate task efficiency, success rate, and overall user performance. These metrics help quantify how effectively users interact with the application, providing insights into potential areas for improvement. The performance measures include several key metrics such as the error rate, which tracks the number of mistakes users make while completing tasks, such as clicking the wrong button or failing to find a feature. Additionally, navigation efficiency was assessed by counting the number of steps taken to complete a task in comparison to the expected optimal steps. The effectiveness of the application was measured by recording the number of tasks completed successfully, both with and without assistance, and calculating the percentage of users who were able to complete tasks independently.

Qualitative data, on the other hand, provides deeper insights into users' perceptions, frustrations and expectations. Those data was collected through think-aloud observations, where users verbalized their thoughts as they interacted with the application. Additional qualitative feedback was gathered from users' comments on the clarity of the privacy risk scores and explanations provided by the app. The test also identified specific challenges or usability barriers that users encountered, offering valuable insights into areas of confusion or difficulty.

Preference measures were employed to capture user preferences related to usability, design, and functionality. These measures include user satisfaction scores, where participants rated their immediate experience with the application's ease of use, clarity, and usefulness on a SCALE from 1 to 5. Post-task questions were also used to evaluate the ease of use of the application after each task, providing feedback on how users perceived individual features.

By analyzing these performance, qualitative, and preference measures, we identified key pain points in the interface and developed recommendations for improving usability. The goal is to make the privacy SCALE more accessible, consistent, and easy to understand for a diverse range of users, including those with varying backgrounds or literacy levels.

5   Usability Test Results

The usability evaluation of the proposed privacy SCALE generated a comprehensive dataset of both quantitative and qualitative findings, the analysis of which is detailed in this section.

By examining objective metrics such as task completion rates, efficiency (number of attempts, actions, and completion times), and the overall SUS score, in conjunction with the feedback obtained through participant interviews, an understanding of the SCALE's user experience was achieved.

Organized around the central research questions that guided the study, the subsequent subsections explore specific facets of participants' interaction and perception. This approach allows for a detailed assessment of the SCALE's usability and its effectiveness in conveying crucial privacy information to users.

5.1   Participant's Data Summary

The usability tests were conducted with six participants who voluntarily agreed to participate, providing their informed consent. The sample primarily consisted of females (n = 5), all of whom were healthcare professionals, including five nurses and one physiotherapist. The average age of the participants was 44.8 years, and all held at least one higher education degree (Fig. 3).

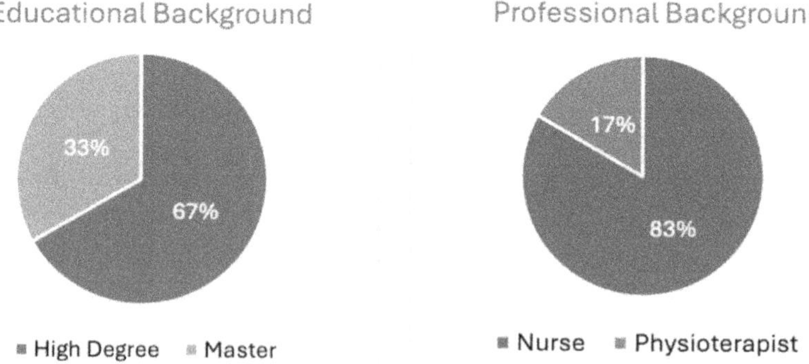

Fig. 3. General data of usability test participants.

In terms of digital literacy, all participants regularly used applications in their daily lives, particularly for leisure, services, social networking, and home banking, spending an average of 1,5 h per day, demonstrating ease in navigating digital platforms. Most participants reported frequent use of health-related applications (Fig. 4).

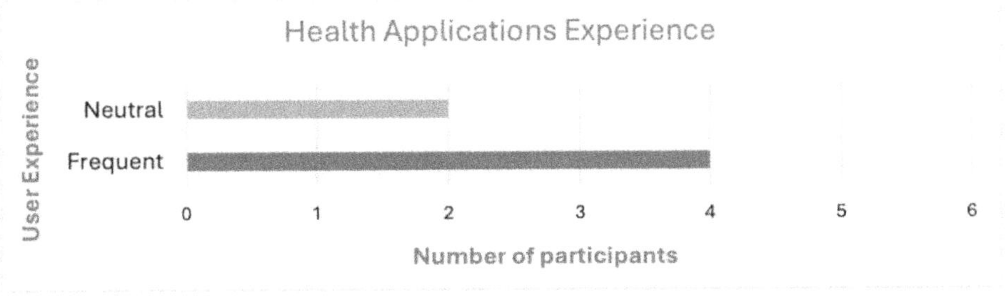

Fig. 4. Data of usability test participant's about health applications digital experience.

To explore the influence of onboarding on the users performance and perception of the privacy scale, participants were randomly assigned to one of two experimental conditions:

- Condition A (with onboarding): The three participants included in this group were exposed to a short interactive onboarding screen before beginning the tasks. The onboarding introduced the structure of the privacy scale, explained the color-coded privacy risk levels and clarified how the scale classifies applications based on privacy risk.
- Condition B (without onboarding): The three participants included in this group, accessed the application directly without any prior explanation or tutorial. They interacted with the privacy scale based solely on the interface, without guidance on how to interpret scores.

This division allowed for a comparative analysis of the role of onboarding in user understanding, confidence and task success. However, due to the limited sample size (n = 6), the conclusions drawn regarding group differences are exploratory in nature and should be interpreted with caution.

5.2   Results of the Privacy SCALE User Study

To clarify the structure of the results and address the three main research questions guiding this evaluation, the ten detailed usability questions presented in this section are thematically grouped under each research question. These sub-questions were operationalized during the usability sessions to elicit specific performance, perception and experience data relevant to each research question. The mapping is as follows:

- **Research question 1**: Is the privacy SCALE intuitive and easy to navigate for users with varying levels of technical expertise?
- **Research question 2**: Does the presence of onboarding processes significantly influence user success in completing privacy evaluation tasks?

– **Research question 3**: Can users accurately interpret the quantified privacy ratings provided by the system and can they articulate the implications of these ratings for their own privacy?

Each of these ten sub-questions and associated findings presented below corresponds to specific dimensions of these research questions and serves to operationalize them into testable usability indicators. More specifically:

– Sub-questions 1,4,6 and 7 relate primarily to research question 1, evaluating ease of navigation, clarity of the structure, sufficiency of information and visual consistency.
– Sub-questions 2 and 4 provide direct evidence to answer research question 2, comparing performance and understanding across onboarding conditions (condition A vs condition B).
– Sub-questions 3,5,6 and 8 address research question 3, assessing ability to interpret scores, understand implications and describe privacy risks.
– Sub-questions 9 and 10, although supportive in nature, offer insights into additional usability variables such as language accessibility, which further inform the general assessment of research question 1.

Thus, while ten sub-questions were used during testing to obtain detailed feedback, each contributes to a deeper exploration of the three central research questions, allowing a more nuanced understanding of how users interact with and comprehend the privacy SCALE. This also facilitates a detailed usability analysis, which can inform future design iterations and improve the application accessibility and interpretability for several user groups. This section delves into user evaluation of the proposed privacy SCALE, to answer key questions regarding its usability and effectiveness in communicating privacy information.

Question 1: Is the Privacy SCALE Easy to Understand and Navigate? From the analysis of task 1, all participants successfully completed the task, with only one requiring assistance from the moderator to complete the initial action. In terms of efficiency, users needed no more than two attempts to complete the task, with an average of three actions per task.

During the post-task interview, all users were able to identify the privacy rating scale, accurately interpret the score, recognize the number of dimensions and categories and determine which of these were not complied with.

In the post-test interview, all users described their experience with the application as "positive", "intuitive", "easy" and "useful". The SUS score was 82,92.

Question 2: Does the Starting Point (onboarding) Make Any Difference in Whether Users Are Successful in Reaching Their Goal? All users who performed test A (with onboarding) rated the ease of accessing information about dimensions and categories as 5 (very easy). In contrast, 66,7% of users who completed test B (without onboarding) gave a score of 1 or 2 (very difficult or difficult) to access the same information.

In the post-test interview, 66.7% of users who tested version A (with onboarding) reported they did not find any information confusing or difficult to understand. All users of version B (without onboarding) reported that information about dimensions and categories was difficult or confusing to understand.

Question 3: Can Users Easily Interpret the Privacy Rating of a Given Application/ Service? All users successfully identified and interpreted the privacy score on their first attempt, completing the task with a single action and taking an average of 28 s. In the post-task interview, they rated ease of access the privacy score in the application between 3 and 5 (neutral to very easy).

Question 4: Can Users Quickly Understand the Meaning of the SCALE Classifications? All users correctly identified the number of dimensions and categories, and which categories did not meet the privacy requirements. Participants who tested version B of the test reported greater difficulty in understanding the meaning of dimensions and categories. On average, users completed this task in 36,7 s, requiring only one attempt and an average of 2,3 actions.

In the post-test interview, 66,7% of users reported that information about dimensions and categories was confusing or was difficult to understand.

Question 5: Does the Color Scheme Help Users to Understand Privacy Risks Effectively? Which Ones Are Problematic? Why? All users were able to identify the colors associated with the dimensions and categories. In the post-test interview, 33,3% of users highlighted colors as the most useful element in how the SCALE conveys privacy risks.

Question 6: Do Users Feel that the SCALE Provides Enough Information for Them to Make an Informed Privacy Decision? All users rated as easy or very easy to understand an application's privacy rating using this SCALE. Additionally, all participants considered themselves able to explain an application's privacy risks using the Privacy SCALE.

Question 7: Does the Format and Structure of the SCALE Facilitate Its Understanding? In the post-test interview, all users mentioned the graph's shape, color, scheme and structure as the most important elements in how the SCALE presents the privacy risks.

Question 8: How Easily and Successfully Can Users Change the Application Language? From the analysis of task 2, all participants successfully completed the task, with only two requiring moderator assistance for the initial action. In terms of efficiency, users required no more than two attempts to complete the task, with an average of 2,6 actions per task. However, 83,3% of users reported difficulty in associating the icon with access to *"My Account"* screen. Those who reported difficulties took an average of 44 s to access *"My Account"* screen, while the overall average completion time was 26,2 s. On *"My Account"* screen, users required just one attempt and a maximum of two actions to change the language, completing this task in an average of 3,5 s.

Question 9: How Easily Can the Users Find the Application that They Want to See Classified? In task 3 all users were able to find the application they wanted to view classified on the main screen without assistance, completing the task in a single attempt and action, with an average completion of 2,5 s. In the post-test interview, 83,3% of users rated accessing other health apps within the SCALE app as easy or very easy. Only one user found the process difficult.

Question 10: Is the Privacy SCALE More Effective in Communicating Risk Than Traditional Privacy Notices or Terms of Service? All users agreed that SCALE was more effective in communicating privacy risks than traditional privacy notices or terms of service. Participants described the SCALE application as "simpler", "clearer", "faster", "more useful" and "more objective".

6   User Study Results and Design Iterations

This section details the user experience and subsequent design iterations across three distinct tasks designed to evaluate the usability and interpretability of the privacy scale within the *Libreview* and *SNS 24* applications. Task 1 focused on initial comprehension and navigation within the *Libreview* application, revealing challenges related to onboarding, understanding the privacy scale, and interpreting the definitions of its dimensions and categories. Task 2 then explored the intuitiveness of language settings within the SCALE application, highlighting issues with icon recognition for accessing account preferences. Finally, Task 3 examined the discoverability of the privacy scale screen within the *SNS 24* application, uncovering difficulties in locating the relevant access point. The findings from each task informed specific design changes to improve user experience, as illustrated in Figs. 5, 6, and 7.

During the first task, users interpreted the privacy score, dimensions, and indicators to make informed decisions about whether to use the *Libreview* application. The main finding indicated that users experienced difficulty navigating from the home screen to the next screen.

On the home screen, 60% of users reported difficulties in navigating to the next screen. They assumed that the descriptive sentences explaining the application's purpose were clickable links. Among those who experienced difficulties, the average time to complete this task was 40.5 s, compared to just 4.5 s for users who encountered no issues. Additionally, 30% of participants required assistance from the moderator to successfully complete the task.

We updated the prototype with a prominent button labeled"Explore Onboarding" to guide users through the initial experience (Fig. 5). We replaced the explanatory sentences with a concise and engaging slogan that effectively conveys the application's purpose.

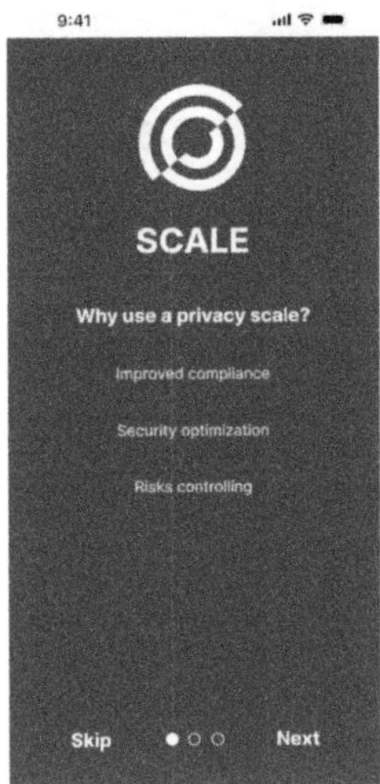

Fig. 5. Homepage screen updated to accomodate the recommendations.

Also during the first task, users indicated that the lack of onboarding made it difficult to interpret the privacy scale.

To evaluate the relevance of onboarding in understanding the privacy scale, an A/B test was conducted. Users in group B (without onboarding) took an average of 35.3 s to complete the task, compared to 20.6 s for users in group A (with onboarding).

Among group B users, 66.7% rated access to information about dimensions and categories as difficult or very difficult. In contrast, all group A users classified access to the same information as easy or very easy.

During the post-test interview, all participants who tested version B reported confusion or difficulty in understanding the dimensions and categories due to a lack of sufficient explanatory information about them. One participant noted, *"...But then I don't really understand the issues of dimension and what each one means"* (T2-version B). We maintained the initial onboarding while making information about the dimensions clearer to the user.

Finally, for Task 1, the users had difficulty understanding the definition of dimensions and categories. Sixty-six percent of users reported that the information about dimensions and categories was confusing or difficult to understand. One user stated, *"Since it didn't have all the parameters, only A and B but not C and D, which also met the criteria, it confused me a bit. Initially, if all the parameters had been present, it would have been easier to understand"* (T3). To improve access to information about dimensions and categories, we added interactivity to the scale (Fig. 6). This could include displaying descriptions of all dimensions and categories in a text box below the scale, with color gradients to distinguish those that comply from those that do not.

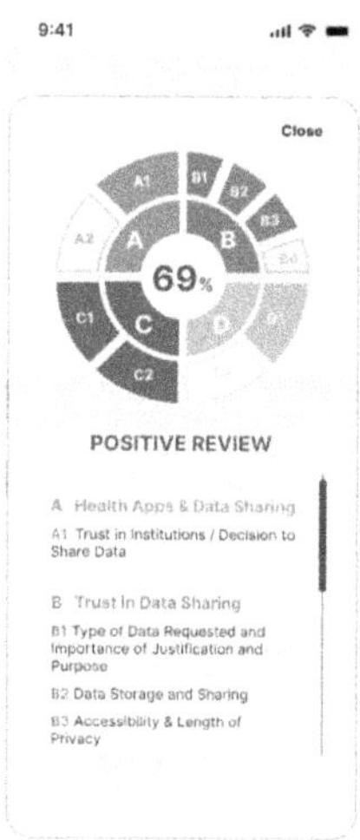
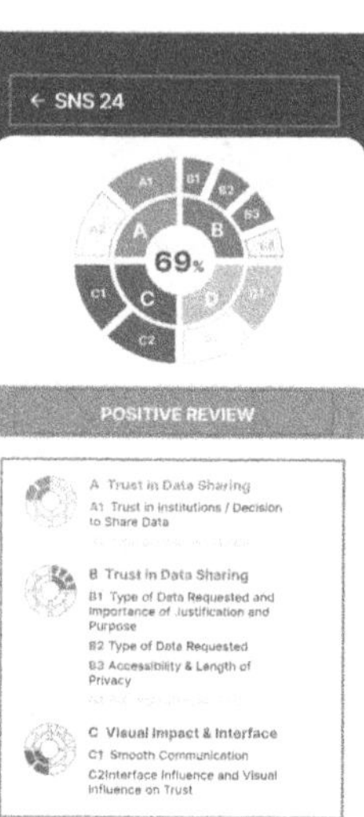

Fig. 6. Updated the interface to display a text based color to quickly identify the compliance/non-compliance privacy level of the evaluated application.

For Task 2, where users had to change the language of SCALE application, they did not associate the profile icon with access to *My Account* screen. For this task, 33.3% of users rated the ease of changing the language as neutral. 66.6% of users performed more than one action (ranging from 2 to 4) to access the *My Profile* screen, hesitating when choosing the icon. One user required assistance from the moderator to complete the task. For users who encountered difficulties, the average time to complete the action was 27.5 s.

The icon intended for changing the language was referred to as something confusing or difficult to understand.

We changed the icon associated with the profile to be more intuitive (Fig. 7) and expanded the range of applications available on the main screen.

Regarding Task 3, users interpreted the score and the dimensions/indicators to decide whether to use the *SNS 24* application.

Users had difficulty identifying the button to access the privacy scale screen.

All users were unable to identify the button to access the privacy scale screen of the *SNS 24* application without assistance. On average, they attempted the task twice before succeeding and performed 5 or 6 actions to complete it.

We deleted the screen with the application image and the button for accessing the privacy scale screen. We created a direct connection between the main menu screen and the privacy scale screen of the selected application.

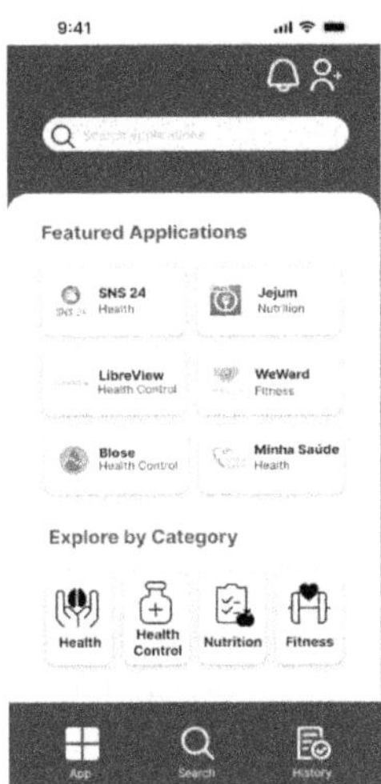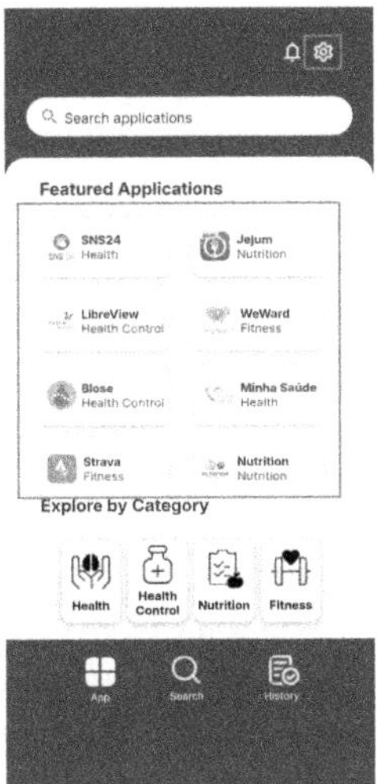

Fig. 7. Updated the interface to change the icon for accessing to account settings and add more applications to the main screen.

7 Discussion and Conclusion

In this paper, we introduced and evaluated SCALE, a prototype application designed to enhance the transparency and usability of privacy information in healthcare settings through a human-centered design approach. Our findings indicate that the visual and interactive representation of privacy metrics in SCALE significantly aids user comprehension, particularly among healthcare professionals who handle sensitive data. The usability testing confirmed that participants found the application intuitive and effective in communicating privacy risks, especially when supported by onboarding elements and clear visual cues.

The usability tests conducted on the SCALE application provided valuable insights into user's experience, revealing both strengths and areas for improvement. Overall, participants found the application intuitive and visually appealing, but certain usability challenges were identified, particularly concerning icon comprehension and feature accessibility. The analysis of task performance, which included completion times, success rates, and user feedback, confirmed that most tasks were completed efficiently. However, some tasks required moderator intervention and additional attempts to end successfully. Post-test interviews indicated that users appreciated the structured design, the SCALE, and the color scheme. But some elements, such as the meaning of icons and menu structure, caused confusion. Based on these findings, several key recommendations emerged, including enhancing the clarity of icons and refining the menu layout to improve usability and ensure a more seamless user experience.

Beyond its internal usability, a key aspect of SCALE's contribution lies in its ability to more effectively communicate privacy issues compared to traditional approaches. Current standards for communicating privacy primarily rely on privacy notices and policies, often presented as lengthy, complex legal documents that lack clarity and accessibility, hindering informed decision-making for the average user. Research indicates that these traditional "notice and choice" mechanisms are frequently ineffective, as users tend to ignore them due to their usability issues and perceived lack of usefulness. While regulations advocate for clear, transparent, and easily accessible information, a critical gap remains in human-centered privacy scales capable of visually representing privacy levels. Existing approaches often focus on quantifying data collection without detailing user-centric design processes for interfaces or provide real-time risk quantification without explicit scales. Furthermore, designing effective visualization faces challenges due to the inherent subjectivity, multidimensionality, and context-dependence of privacy, alongside the risk of cognitive overload.

SCALE directly addresses these limitations by transforming complex policy assessments into a standardized, visual, and multi-level system. The prototype's visual metaphors, clear interaction patterns, and color-coded, multidimensional ratings facilitate quick judgments about an application's data practices. Usability tests confirmed that participants could accurately interpret the privacy ratings and articulate their implications, particularly when supported by onboarding elements and clear visual cues. Unlike generic policies, SCALE provides quantifiable metrics across dimensions like data collection methods, third-party sharing arrangements, data retention policies, and user control mechanisms. Each dimension's score is explicitly linked to concrete evaluation criteria, allowing users to understand not just the outcome but the rationale behind it. The ability to expand segments to reveal individual indicators offers deeper inspection, catering to different user needs for detail. By providing clear, concise, and interpretable information about privacy risks, SCALE aims to empower users to make informed decisions and exercise greater control over their personal health information. The consistent application of dimensions and visual formats ensures comparability across digital services. Multilingual support and user-friendly onboarding further enhance accessibility for diverse user populations, contributing to fostering confidence among patients, clinicians, and the broader public in transparent and responsible data governance frameworks.

While the findings from this study offer valuable insights into the usability and comprehension of the privacy scale prototype, several limitations must be acknowledged. First, the number of participants was limited to six, which constrains the generalizability of the results. Furthermore, the sample was highly homogeneous (participants were of similar age range and shared a common professional background in healthcare), reducing the diversity of perspectives typically present in a broader user population. Second, the evaluation focused on short, task-based interactions conducted within a single session. This approach provided a useful snapshot of initial usability but did not allow for assessment of long-term user experience, learning curves, or sustained engagement with the application. Third, all usability testing sessions were conducted in a controlled environment, either moderated or semi-moderated, which may differ from the app's natural use in real-world contexts. Furthermore, although several interface improvements were identified during testing, a second round of usability testing was not conducted after implementing these changes.

To further enhance the usability and effectiveness of the SCALE application, future work should focus on iterative design improvements, by making the recommended changes and conducting follow-up usability tests to evaluate their impact. Additionally, broader user testing is essential, expanding the test group to include a more diverse range of users with varying levels of digital literacy, ensuring the application is accessible to a wider audience. SCALE represents a promising step toward bridging the gap between complex privacy policies and user understanding. Future work will focus on broader user testing, improved accessibility, and integrating real-time privacy analysis to further refine the tool. Ultimately, this research contributes to the development of privacy solutions that are not only compliant and secure but also transparent, comprehensible, and empowering users in critical domains such as healthcare.

Acknowledgements. Ana Ferreira is supported by Fundação para a Ciência e Tecnologia (FCT), project DRAPE, Ref. 2022.00381.CEECIND/CP1712/CT0001.

References

1. Almasi, S., Bahaadinbeigy, K., Ahmadi, H., Sohrabei, S., Rabiei, R.: Usability evaluation of dashboards: a systematic literature review of tools, January 2023. https://doi.org/10.1155/2023/9990933
2. Alohaly, M., Takabi, H.: If you can't measure it, you can't manage it: towards quantification of privacy policies. In: 2016 IEEE 2nd International Conference on Collaboration and Internet Computing (CIC), pp. 539–545 (2016). https://doi.org/10.1109/CIC.2016.082
3. Alturki, R., Gay, V., Awan, N., Alshehri, M.D., Mohammed, J., Kundi, M.: Analysis of an ehealth app: privacy, security and usability. Int. J. Adv. Comput. Sci. Appl. **11** (2020). https://doi.org/10.14569/ijacsa.2020.0110428
4. Askin, Ö., Kutta, T., Dette, H.: Statistical quantification of differential privacy: a local approach. In: 2022 IEEE Symposium on Security and Privacy (SP), pp. 402–421. IEEE (2022)
5. Barth, S., Ionita, D., de Jong, M.D., Hartel, P., Junger, M.: Privacy rating: a user-centered approach for visualizing data handling practices of online services. IEEE Trans. Prof. Commun. **64**, 354–373 (2021). https://doi.org/10.1109/tpc.2021.3110617
6. Demiris, G., et al.: Patient-centered applications: use of information technology to promote disease management and wellness. A white paper by the AMIA knowledge in motion working group (2007). https://doi.org/10.1197/jamia.m2492
7. Emami-Naeini, P., et al.: Privacy expectations and preferences in an IoT world. In: Symposium on Usable Privacy and Security, July 2017, pp. 399–412 (2017)
8. Ermakova, T., Fabian, B., Kornacka, M., Thiebes, S., Sunyaev, A.: Security and privacy requirements for cloud computing in healthcare. ACM Trans. Manag. Inf. Syst. **11**, 1–29 (2020). https://doi.org/10.1145/3386160
9. Felisberto, J., Silva, C., Barraca, J.P., Salvador, P., Tomás, P.: PrivGuide: a planning tool for proactive privacy integration in the DevPrivOps lifecycle (2025)
10. Fox, G.: "to protect my health or to protect my health privacy?" a mixed-methods investigation of the privacy paradox. J. Assoc. Inf. Sci. Technol. **71**, 1015–1029 (2020). https://doi.org/10.1002/asi.24369
11. Frener, R., Dombrowski, J., Trepte, S.: Development and validation of the need for privacy scale (NFP-S). Commun. Meth. Meas. **18**, 48–71 (2023). https://doi.org/10.1080/19312458.2023.2246014

12. Gerber, N., Gerber, P., Volkamer, M.: Explaining the privacy paradox: a systematic review of literature investigating privacy attitude and behavior (2018). https://doi.org/10.1016/j.cose.2018.04.002
13. Halimi, A., Ayday, E.: Real-time privacy risk quantification in online social networks. In: Proceedings of the 2021 IEEE/ACM International Conference on Advances in Social Networks Analysis and Mining, pp. 74–81 (2021)
14. Ioannou, A., Tussyadiah, I., Miller, G., Li, S., Weick, M.: Privacy nudges for disclosure of personal information: a systematic literature review and meta-analysis (2021). https://doi.org/10.1371/journal.pone.0256822
15. Kroes, S.K.S., Janssen, M.P., Groenwold, R.H.H., van Leeuwen, M.: Evaluating privacy of individuals in medical data. Health Inform. J. 27 (2021). https://doi.org/10.1177/1460458220983398
16. Mehta, V., Gooch, D., Bandara, A.K., Price, B., Nuseibeh, B.: Privacy care 21, 1–32 (2021). https://doi.org/10.1145/3430506
17. Özturk, H., Bahçecik, N., Özçelik, K.S.: The development of the patient privacy scale in nursing. Nurs. Ethics 21(7), 812–828 (2014)
18. Price, W.N., Cohen, I.G.: Privacy in the age of medical big data (2018). https://doi.org/10.1038/s41591-018-0272-7
19. Pötzsch, S.: Privacy awareness: a means to solve the privacy paradox? In: Matyáš, V., Fischer-Hübner, S., Cvrček, D., Švenda, P. (eds.) Privacy and Identity 2008. IAICT, vol. 298, pp. 226–236. Springer, Heidelberg (2009). https://doi.org/10.1007/978-3-642-03315-5_17
20. Reddy, S., Allan, S., Coghlan, S., Cooper, P.: A governance model for the application of AI in health care. J. Am. Med. Inform. Assoc. 27, 491–497 (2019). https://doi.org/10.1093/jamia/ocz192
21. Rossi, A., Lenzini, G.: Transparency by design in data-informed research: a collection of information design patterns. Comput. Law Secur. Rev. 37, 105402–105402 (2020). https://doi.org/10.1016/j.clsr.2020.105402
22. Silva, C., Barraca, J., Salvador, P.: Evaluating the effectiveness of differential privacy against profiling. In: Proceedings of the 2025 The International Conference on Consumer Technology, ICCT-Europe 2025, Algarve, Portugal, pp. 28–30 (2025)
23. Silva, C., Barraca, J.P., Salvador, P.: Proactive data categorization for privacy in DevPrivOps. Information 16(3), 185 (2025)
24. Silva, C., Cunha, V.A., Barraca, J.P., Salvador, P.: Privacy-based deployments: the role of DevPrivOps in 6G mobile networks. IEEE Commun. Mag. 62(6), 66–72 (2024)
25. Silva, C., Felisberto, J., Barraca, J.P., Salvador, P.: ASAP 2.0: autonomous & proactive detection of malicious applications for privacy quantification in 6G network services. Comput. Commun. 237, 108145 (2025)
26. Solove, D.J.: Privacy self-management and the consent dilemma. SSRN Electron. J. (2013)
27. Spiekermann, S., Cranor, L.F.: Engineering privacy. IEEE Trans. Softw. Eng. 35, 67–82 (2008). https://doi.org/10.1109/tse.2008.88
28. Thapa, C., Camtepe, S.: Precision health data: requirements, challenges and existing techniques for data security and privacy (2020). https://doi.org/10.1016/j.compbiomed.2020.104130
29. Torkzadehmahani, R., et al.: Privacy-preserving artificial intelligence techniques in biomedicine. Meth. Inf. Med. 61 (2022). https://doi.org/10.1055/s-0041-1740630
30. Vatsalan, D., Rakotoarivelo, T., Bhaskar, R., Tyler, P., Ladjal, D.: Privacy risk quantification in education data using Markov model. Br. J. Edu. Technol. 53(4), 804–821 (2022)
31. Zakkar, M.A., Sedig, K.: Interactive visualization of public health indicators to support policymaking: an exploratory study. Online J. Public Health Inform. 9 (2017). https://doi.org/10.5210/ojphi.v9i2.8000

32. Zandesh, Z.: Privacy, security, and legal issues in the health cloud: structured review for taxonomy development. JMIR Formative Res. **8** (2024). https://doi.org/10.2196/38372

33. Zhang, S., Song, J.: An empirical investigation into the preferences of the elderly for user interface design in personal electronic health record systems. Front. Digit. Health **5** (2024). https://doi.org/10.3389/fdgth.2023.1289904

34. Öztürk, H., Bahçecik, N., Özçelik, K.S.: Nursing Ethics **21**, 812–828 (2014). https://doi.org/10.1177/0969733013515489

Playing by Ear: Advancements in Sound-Based Game Accessibility

Alexander Espeseth[1(✉)], Ivar Kjellmo[2], and Kjetil Raaen[1]

[1] School of Economy, Innovation and Technology, Kristiania University of Applied Sciences, Oslo, Norway
alexander.espeseth@kristiania.no
[2] School of Arts, Design and Media, Kristiania University of Applied Sciences, Oslo, Norway

Abstract. Video games have cemented their role as an influential cultural force, shaping experiences and communities across the world. However, there is a lack of accessibility features for blind players, denying this group access to an important part of culture. To address this issue, we are developing an accessible framework for the Unreal Engine, designed specifically to streamline the process of creating audio-centric experiences for blind players. This approach seeks to establish a new standard in accessibility, underscoring the idea that games, when designed with inclusion in mind, can change lives for the better. By integrating sound-based navigational mechanics, we found that players could successfully navigate game environments without relying on visual elements. The results suggest that the system successfully enhances navigation and engagement for blind players, providing a solid foundation for further development and refinement, aligning well with the goal of improving accessibility in gaming.

Keywords: Accessibility · Video Games · Sound Design · Plugin Development · Disability inclusion

1 Introduction

In recent years, video games have cemented their role as an influential cultural force, shaping experiences and communities across the world. However, for many, particularly those with visual impairments, video games remain largely inaccessible, excluding them from fully engaging in this cultural medium. This exclusion persists despite advances in technology that could make meaningful inclusion possible. The documentary Ibelin [12] serves as a critical example of the possible life-changing impacts accessible games could have on impaired players. Through exploring the journey of Mats Steen, who longs to experience life on equal footing despite his condition, Ibelin illustrates both the personal and social significance of inclusive game design. It reveals how gaming, beyond just being a form of entertainment, can enhance quality of life, build connections, and offer a vital sense of agency and escapism for all people.

Historically, game accessibility has centred on visual adjustments, such as colourblind modes and scalable icons, which, though helpful, fall short for those who rely on non-visual navigation. More experimental adaptations have emerged, like the NavStick

J. F. Krems et al. (Eds.): CHIRA 2025, CCIS 2836, pp. 174–189, 2026.
https://doi.org/10.1007/978-3-032-16454-4_10

[19] device, which simulates a white cane within game environments, or AudioQuake [3], a mod, short for modification [17] which means that AduioQuake is an altered version of the original game Quake [15], This version provides navigational information via audio feedback. However, while effective in aiding navigation, these tools often lack the immersive quality crucial to the appeal of gaming. For blind players, access must mean more than just navigation; it must provide a rich and engaging experience that captures the essence of the game world.

Although high-budget games like Forza Motorsport 2023 [23] have set a precedent by implementing sophisticated accessibility features such as voiceover menus and nuanced audio cues, most game studios cannot afford such extensive accessibility measures. This creates a gap in the industry, leaving independent and smaller studios in need of practical, budget-friendly solutions. The ambition of this project is to bridge that gap, offering blind players access to the full experience of immersion in gaming.

As there is no unified framework or guidelines for designing accessible games for blind users, especially in 3D environments, we are currently developing an accessible framework for Unreal Engine [1], which includes a step-by-step guide for setting the proposed Solution. The framework will also contain instructional video tutorials and a stand-alone test project that allows developers to explore and evaluate the system without requiring a pre-existing game environment [2]. It is designed specifically to streamline the process of creating audio-centric experiences for blind players for game developers, which is the end goal for this research project. Through an initial maze-like prototype, players use only audio cues to navigate, demonstrating the potential of sound as an immersive tool for accessibility. This test bed serves as a foundation for broader implementation, with the objective of giving game developers a versatile and cost-effective option to make their games accessible without compromising the immersive quality that defines impactful gameplay. By integrating sound cues in a way that enhances, rather than interrupts, the gaming experience, this approach seeks to establish a new standard in accessibility, underscoring the idea that games, when designed with inclusivity in mind, can change lives for the better.

The target audience for this project is people who are blind or have low vision. For the sake of readability throughout this paper, we have chosen to use the collective term *blind players* when referring to this group. This decision is made solely to improve clarity and narrative flow, and not to diminish the diversity of experiences within the community. Following current best practices in inclusive language, we intentionally avoid overly clinical or outdated terminology, instead adopting language that focusses on the individual rather than the disability [11]. This approach not only demonstrates respect for the lived experiences of our users, but also aligns with broader standards of accessibility and inclusion in both research and game development. By focusing on the specific needs of blind and low vision players, the project aims to create meaningful and immersive gameplay experiences that address longstanding gaps in game accessibility.

As the previous version of the system served as a test of the initial model, several improvements have been implemented based on its high success rate [6]. In the current version presented in this paper, the primary participant group has changed from sighted individuals wearing blindfolds to individuals with visual impairments. A control group of blindfolded sighted individuals was tested before the main study to provide a basis for comparison. In addition, several updates and enhancements have been made, which are detailed later in this paper.

2   Background

Games are a unique class of applications. Most applications are designed to enable users to perform a task. This enables a relatively straightforward measure of usability as well as accessibility. How well are users able to perform the task? In games, even the basic definition of accessibility is difficult to pin down. Making it trivial to complete tasks is certainly not ideal. Thus, we need other measures of success [9]. Presence and flow are classic concepts that evaluate the quality of games and can be easily adapted to accessibility. *Presence* is the feeling or illusion of being present in the game world. *Flow* is the feeling of being absorbed in an activity and in a state of deep concentration. These are important design goals for games and can be applied to accessibility. Clearly, traditional goals of being able to perform a task are also relevant in games.

Over the years, various people both in industry and academia have suggested approaches for making games for blind players. A common approach is to develop games specifically for blind players, mainly children [8,9,18]. These use relatively basic tactile and auditive modes for communicating with players. These suffer from the weakness of requiring games to be designed from the ground up for blind people and using special hardware. Although the idea is interesting, the limitations of their approach are many. First of all, it is aimed at children, even very young children. We argue that computer games are a medium for all and an even more important part of culture for adults. Furthermore, this framework only allows uniquely designed games, precluding adaption of games that peers would be talking about. Lastly, it is rather unclear how the development of new content for such specialised systems will be supported in the future.

Some have explored more portable ideas about the sonification of games. Apavou et al. [7] has selected an important interaction used in many games, the aim action, and are working to optimise the sonification of this particular interaction. They are using pitch and tempo to indicate how close to pointing at the target a player is. Unfortunately, at the current date they do not have data on how well this works.

There is a growing body of research examining how blind players can effectively navigate 3D environments using sensory techniques derived from real-world experience. A notable strategy in this field is the use of spatial audio and echolocation-inspired cues, which provide intuitive ways for users to orient themselves in virtual spaces. For instance, studies have shown that spatial audio is commonly employed to convey information about object locations, either by replicating familiar real-world sounds or by mimicking echolocation behaviours [21]. However, despite its potential, there remains a significant gap in the standardization of audio feedback design, limiting broader adoption and consistency across applications.

The effectiveness of such techniques is further illustrated in research by Picinali et al. [21], who demonstrated how blind individuals could explore and construct spatial knowledge of architectural spaces through auditory virtual reality. Their findings indicate that with the right audio cues, users are able to develop accurate mental maps of their surroundings, enabling confident navigation in complex environments. Similarly, Siu et al. explored the combination of haptic and auditory feedback in virtual settings, showcasing a virtual white cane system that allowed blind users to traverse intricate 3D spaces effectively, an approach that mirrors real-world navigation tools used by many people with visual impairments [22].

Adding to this, Andrade et al. investigated how echolocation, both natural and digitally simulated, can support people who are blind or have low vision in acquiring spatial knowledge of virtual environments. Their study emphasizes that echolocation is not only viable but can significantly enhance spatial understanding when integrated thoughtfully into virtual navigation systems [5].

Collectively, these studies underline a recurring challenge: while the technological tools for creating accessible navigation systems are readily available, the cost and complexity of implementation often pose barriers, particularly for indie developers or smaller studios. Although some of this research focuses on virtual reality, the underlying design philosophies are equally applicable to non-virtual reality platforms. By leveraging existing features within modern game engines like Unreal Engine, such as spatialized audio and blueprint scripting, developers can translate these real-world techniques into accessible game design practices. This reinforces the notion that creating inclusive navigation systems is not only achievable but can be implemented efficiently when grounded in practical, real-world sensory methodologies.

We believe that the approach of selecting a mechanic that is frequently used in games and making an accessible system for it is a fruitful approach. Our project, SonicPlay, is focussing on a important interaction used in many games: navigation. In our initial experiments, we tested the system exclusively with blindfolded sighted participants to establish a controlled baseline for navigation using only auditory feedback. By integrating sound-based mechanics, such as directional cues, step-based audio feedback, and collision sounds, we found that players could successfully navigate game environments without relying on visual elements. These findings provided strong support for the viability of a sound-driven navigation system [6]. This makes it the first test we performed with the target demographic.

3   Method

Expanding on this foundation, the gameplay of SonicPlay is designed to test the effectiveness of a purely auditory navigation system. Players must traverse a virtual environment using only sound-based cues, as no visual elements are provided. The game world is structured with a combination of spatial audio, environmental soundscapes, and interactive sonic feedback to convey direction, obstacles, and objectives.

The core objective of SonicPlay is to reach a designated goal within a level by interpreting various auditory signals. Players rely on step-based feedback to gauge movement, collision sounds to identify walls or barriers, and distinct guiding sounds, such as directional beacons or environmental cues, to orient themselves. In addition, interactive elements within the game provide contextual audio feedback to reinforce spatial awareness and ensure that the player remains immersed in the experience.

By refining and evaluating this system, SonicPlay aims to establish a framework that allows game developers to cater their games to blind players to engage with video games on a more equitable level, expanding the possibilities for accessible game design.

3.1 System Design

The prototype was developed using Unreal Engine, employing audio cues to motivate and guide players toward their objectives. In this initial phase, we incorporated a set of audio tools to test their effectiveness in helping participants navigate the environment. The features included are the following.

1. **Narrative Guidance:** At the start of the game, players heard a monologue delivered by a voice actor rather than artificial sound. The dialogue was crafted to fit the narrative tone of the game, offering hints such as "Perhaps there is a sound to follow" and "Avoid walking on the grass." This introduction provided a thematic and functional foundation for the gameplay.
2. **Terrain-Dependent Sounds:** Footstep noises were associated with specific ground surfaces, such as grass and wood. The players learnt to associate wooden floors with the correct path through the monologue presented in the beginning, while the sounds of the grass indicated the need to adjust their route. These audio elements were synchronised with the character's movement animations for a cohesive experience.
3. **Collision Alerts:** The walls emitted an unpleasant auditory signal upon contact, ensuring immediate feedback and encouraging players to change direction. This mechanism reinforced spatial awareness and was implemented via triggers embedded in the level design.
4. **Environmental Reverb:** Reverb zones were placed throughout the level to reflect the acoustic characteristics of different spaces: small, medium, and large rooms, as well as corridors. These zones created distinct auditory environments that allowed players to sense spatial transitions and track their progress.
5. **Sonic Pathways:** Bird chirps served as navigational checkpoints, highlighted during the opening monologue. Spatial audio techniques ensured that these cues were dynamic, scaled in volume and directionality based on the player's movement. Unlike earlier versions where cues disappeared upon being reached, the updated system made the sounds adaptive, maintaining a consistent distance to guide players if they strayed off course.
6. **Player-Activated Sonar:** This feature allowed participants to emit a sound pulse, interacting with the acoustic model of the game to provide an additional layer of spatial feedback. Sonar acted as a backup tool, helping players regain their bearings when they felt disoriented.

By incorporating these elements, the prototype aimed to balance accessibility with immersion, offering an intuitive and rewarding gameplay experience for blind players. The iterative design approach allowed us to refine these features and test their impact on player performance and engagement.

The key advances since the previous paper, Playing Games Without Sight: Sonic Play [6] include an adaptive navigation system that dynamically adjusts to the player's movements. Instead of guiding players through fixed checkpoints, the system now continuously adapts, ensuring that the guiding sound remains close and consistently directs the player toward the goal.

In addition, a second level was introduced to examine whether players used the first level as a learning phase to familiarise themselves with the system and subsequently performed better in the second. Another major improvement is the inclusion of a sonar feature, providing players with an additional layer of auditory feedback for spatial awareness.

The acoustic system has also been significantly upgraded. Previously, it relied on simple reverb cubes, but now features a fully rendered acoustics system that adapts based on the materials and dimensions of different environments, enhancing immersion and realism.

Finally, while not a feature, a crucial shift in this study is the transition from testing with sighted participants using blindfolds to working directly with blind players. This change ensures that the findings and improvements are grounded in the experiences and needs of the target audience.

Participants interacted with the game using conventional gaming controls: The first option was a keyboard and mouse, using WASD keys, which are the keys with the same letter on a computer keyboard for movement, popularized by the Quake [15] player Dennis "Thresh" Fong [24]. A computer mouse for directional control, and a click to activate sonar. The other option was a game controller using analogue sticks for movement and aiming, trigger for sonar. To ensure immersion, participants wore headphones for spatial audio and blindfolds to standardise the experience, as visual impairment varies significantly between individuals. Performance metrics, such as time to complete tasks, were tracked during the game.

In designing the system, our goal was to create an engaging and accessible experience for blind players, drawing inspiration from the iconic level structure of *Doom II*. The level consisted of three rooms of varying sizes connected by corridors, with a focus on gradually teaching players to rely on sound cues for navigation.

Visually as seen in Fig. 1, the environment is designed mainly for the developers themselves, and to allow the experimenter to monitor the progress of the participants. This helps improve the design for future iterations.

3.2   Experiment

For this study, 10 participants were recruited to participate in a 15-min game session. Unlike earlier tests conducted solely with sighted individuals, this iteration was in collaboration with Blindeforbundet (The Norwegian Association of the Blind and Partially Sighted) and Greåker High School, a hub school that have a special focus on adapted education for blind and partially sighted students. However, we did have a control group of 10 individuals with sight, but blindfolded to set their results up against the blind players results. The participants were divided into five pairs, forming small groups based on the equipment and space available at the time. The experimental setup included essential components such as a monitor, keyboard, mouse, USB controller, headphones, and blindfolds. As seen in Fig. 2 Participants received a brief introduction explaining the

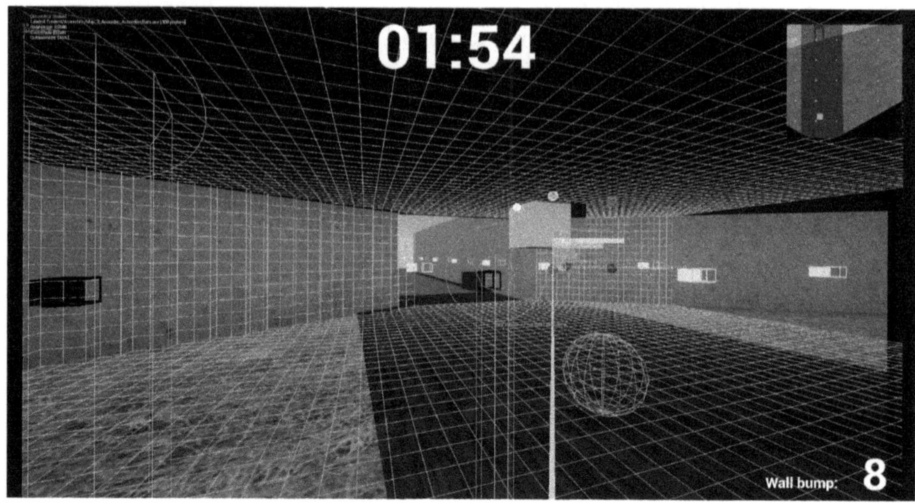

Fig. 1. In game visual with SonicPlay in use. Visuals are included for the use of experimenters to monitor progress and identify problems.

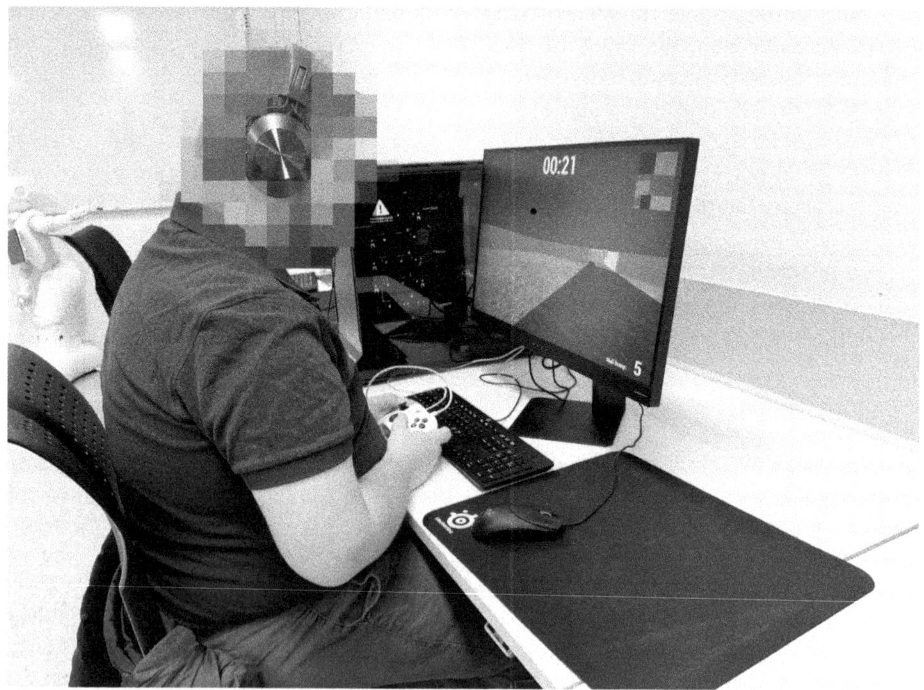

Fig. 2. Blind participant testing SonicPlay.

study objectives, the metrics that would be evaluated, and the assurance that no personal data would be retained.

Blindfolds were used for all participants, even those who were blind players, to ensure consistency in a spectrum of sight impairments. During the test, participants were assigned to navigate a level designed to rely entirely on sound signals, and their performance was assessed through a combination of quantitative and qualitative measures.

Metrics and Feedback Collection. To evaluate player performance, all players played both levels. The system used one key metric: Completion time, with a maximum time limit of five minutes, meaning finishing the levels within that time frame were measured as success. There were also given a short explanation of the task before start and time to answer a questionnaire after finishing the test. The limit of five minutes were chosen because the game is designed to be finished in about one or two minutes if the player has a perfect run. The added three minutes were for those who needed a bit of time to understand the system and lock in. Upon completing the game session, participants responded to a series of targeted questions aimed at gathering subjective feedback about their experience. These questions were designed to assess both the practical and emotional aspects of their participation in the system. The survey was designed using "Nettskjema," the Norwegian academic standard for surveys, ensuring complete anonymity. They were the following:

1. **Controls and Preferences**
    - Do you prefer to use a mouse and keyboard or a controller for gaming?
    - Would you consider yourself familiar with video and computer games?
2. **Player Demographics**
    - How old are you?
    - What gender do you identify as?
3. **Gameplay Feedback**
    - Did you feel any urge to give up?
    - I enjoyed playing the game (scale).
    - The controls were confusing (scale).
    - I felt immersed in the world of the game (scale).
    - The game made me feel frustrated (scale).
    - I felt aware of my surroundings in the game (scale).
    - During the test, I was distracted by outside thoughts (scale).
    - Do you have any suggestions for improving future iterations of this system?

These questions drew inspiration from Jennett's [16] framework for evaluating player experiences in video games, focussing on immersion, frustration, and emotional response. By incorporating established methodologies and open feedback prompts, the study sought to capture a nuanced understanding of participant participation and identify areas for system improvement.

Importance of Participant Feedback. Including a feedback loop for participants was particularly valuable, as blind individuals involved in the study often have first-hand experience with accessibility features in gaming. Their insights provided critical information on which features worked well and what could be improved. Feedback from participants not only guided potential enhancements but also ensured that future iterations of the system aligned closely with the practical needs of blind players.

This dual focus on quantitative performance data and qualitative player impressions allowed for a comprehensive evaluation of the effectiveness of the system and identified opportunities to further refine the design for greater accessibility.

4   Results

The results are categorized into two main sections. The first section focusses on the technical data collected from the experiment, primarily examining players' completion times. The second section explores the qualitative responses gathered through the questionnaire. This structured approach allows for a balanced evaluation of both performance metrics and player perceptions.

4.1   Performance Analysis

As seen in Fig. 3, 80% for level 1 of the participants and 95% for level 2 of the participants successfully completed the level within the designated time limit, demonstrating that they were able to navigate effectively using the auditory cues of the game. The data suggest that the integration of spatial audio and sonic feedback provided meaningful support in guiding the players. Although some participants did not finish within the allocated time, overall completion rates indicate that the system was intuitive and accessible. Group one was the sighted players and group two was the blind players. In particular, both groups achieved relatively short completion times, implying a strong understanding of the mechanics. The differences between the groups were not statistically significant.

These findings reinforce the effectiveness of spatial audio and sonic cues in facilitating navigation, underscoring the potential of this technology to improve accessibility in games.

4.2   Experience Feedback

In the responses to the questionnaire, the responses were overwhelmingly positive. The control question, which assessed the participants' familiarity with video games, showed that the majority of players had prior gaming experience. The responses to subsequent questions further supported the effectiveness of the system.

Ten out of ten of the participants did not experience a strong desire to quit during the gameplay session, suggesting a positive initial engagement with the prototype. Eight described the experience as enjoyable, which is a significant indicator of early success, particularly when considering that enjoyment is often closely tied to player retention and interest in repeated play. In addition, controls were generally perceived as intuitive

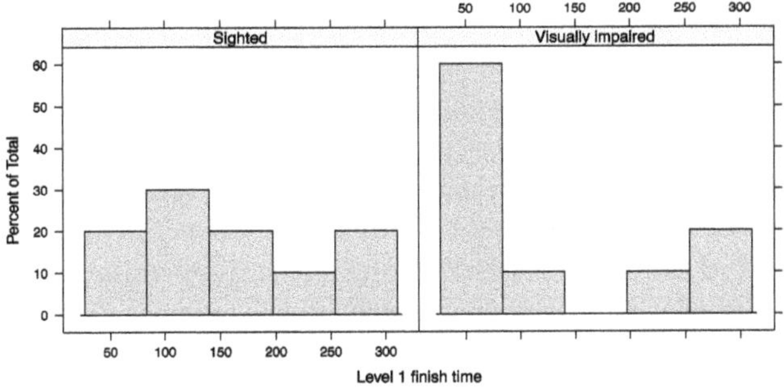

(a) Histogram of players' time in seconds to finish level 1 for sighted and blind players.

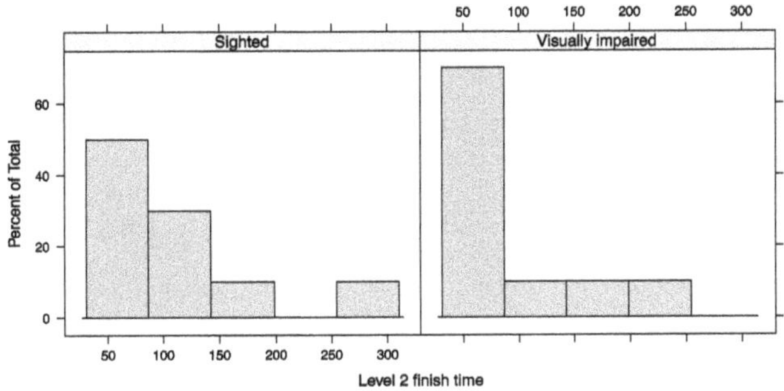

(b) Histogram of players' time in seconds to finish the levels for sighted and blind players.

Fig. 3. Time to finish level 2 for sighted and blind players.

and accessible, and participants reported that they could quickly grasp the mechanics without requiring extensive instruction. This aligns with design goals emphasizing minimal learning curves, especially for systems intended to support accessibility.

Players also reported a strong sense of immersion, indicating that they felt thoroughly absorbed in the game world. This level of engagement is particularly meaningful in the context of accessible design, as it points to the potential for inclusive games to provide experiences comparable in richness and depth to those enjoyed by sighted players in traditional game settings. Only one of the participants noted any frustration, which could be attributed to specific features or environmental challenges that will be considered for refinement in future iterations.

Feedback regarding spatial awareness and environmental perception was more varied. While the majority of participants expressed confidence in their understanding of the in-game space, others described a more neutral or ambiguous sense of orientation. This variation highlights the challenge of designing universally intuitive auditory environments, particularly when simulating complex 3D spaces without visual cues. It also suggests that further iteration may be needed in the design of spatial audio and cue placement to enhance clarity and consistency across different types of players.

Interestingly, external distractions appeared to have minimal impact on participants' concentration levels. This finding is notable because it reinforces the immersive quality of the gameplay, suggesting that the sound design and interaction systems were effective in maintaining attention and engagement. The minimal influence of the external environment may also reflect the strength of the player experience and speaks to the potential of well-designed auditory systems to anchor players in the game world.

Taken together, these observations reinforce the early promise of the prototype and validate many of the design choices made during development. At the same time, the feedback provides clear direction for future enhancements, particularly in refining spatial awareness cues and ensuring that the sense of immersion is preserved across a broader spectrum of players. This iterative process remains essential to achieving the project's overarching goal: to create a framework for game designers to streamline the process to make their games accessible, enjoyable, and immersive gameplay experiences for blind players.

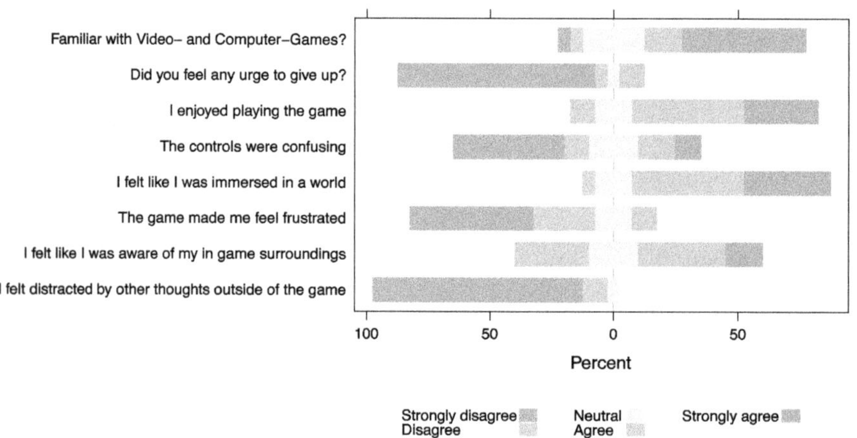

Fig. 4. Results form the user experience questionnaire for blind players. These results are presented as a diverging stacked bar-chart. That means that the neutral value is centred and higher and more extreme values are to either side of the middle. Every second question is worded so that a high number represent either a positive or negative quality alternately.

In general, the results of the questionnaire indicate a favourable reception of the game and its accessibility features as seen in Fig. 4. The combination of positive qualitative feedback and strong performance metrics suggests that the system successfully enhances navigation and engagement among blind players. These results provide a solid foundation for further development and refinement, aligning well with the goal of improving accessibility in gaming.

4.3 Qualitative Feedback

As responses to our open question, we received several targeted suggestions during testing that we plan to implement and further explore in the upcoming iteration of the project. One of the main points of feedback was to make the guiding sound cue more adaptive to the player's movement rather than anchoring it to static locations. This would create a more fluid and intuitive navigational experience, allowing the cue to dynamically follow the player's orientation and progress. In Unreal Engine, this can be achieved by attaching the cue to a target actor or spline that constantly updates its position based on the player's current location and direction, perhaps with a delay or smoothing function to avoid erratic behavior.

Another suggestion focused on enhancing spatial orientation by altering the quality of the cue depending on whether the player is facing it directly. By adjusting the sound's timbre or clarity based on orientation, players would more easily be able to determine directionality, thus improving their ability to stay on course without visual cues. We plan to use dot product calculations in Blueprint to compare the player's forward vector with the direction to the sound cue. Based on this, we can switch between audio assets or apply real-time audio effects such as filtering or volume attenuation to suggest whether the cue is behind, beside or in front of the player.

In addition, the testers expressed the desire for the sonar sound to be replaced by something more realistic and familiar. A more naturalistic echo could strengthen the player's spatial awareness and lend a more immersive, relatable auditory experience. In this case, we plan to experiment with different impulse responses and possibly integrate convolution reverb tools available in Unreal's audio engine, allowing us to craft echoes that respond to material types and spatial dimensions in a believable way.

A further recommendation was to incorporate a sound-based system that communicates progression through the level. By integrating subtle audio indicators that evolve or trigger at key milestones, players can gain a sense of how far they've traveled or how close they are to reaching their goal, fostering motivation and orientation. We are considering a layered sound approach using event triggers along a level timeline. These could play short audio cues or gradually change the intensity or pitch of a looping track, using Blueprint's timeline and trigger volume systems to manage the progression states.

Finally, the introduction of a "fail-safe" mechanism was proposed, such as holding down a button to reorient or redirect the player toward the next objective. We chose not to include this feature in the current version used for testing. This allows us to study unaided navigation, we acknowledge its potential to reduce player frustration. We aim to include this as an optional element in the finalized framework, giving developers the tools to implement such support systems if desired. Technically, this could be implemented by having a temporary override where holding a specific input (such as a key or controller button) adjusts the player's yaw to face the sound cue directly, perhaps accompanied by a confirmation audio cue to reinforce that the action was successful.

5   Discussion and Future Directions

This experiment confirms that the updated system functions effectively for the intended audience. Sixteen of the twenty participants were able to navigate successfully, demonstrating that the sonic cues fulfilled their intended role of guiding players through the game. Key auditory elements, such as introduction monologue, step sounds, and wall collision feedback, were instrumental in keeping players orientated. In addition, the combination of spatial audio and bird chirping signals proved to be an effective means of directing players toward their objective.

As this marks the second iteration of the system, our objective is to investigate further refinements based on feedback gathered during previous testing. This includes evaluating the system across different environments and substituting existing audio cues to determine whether accessibility remains effective under varied acoustic conditions. Key suggestions from testers included making the guidance sound cue more adaptive, adjusting in real-time to the player's movement rather than jumping between predefined locations, introducing a distinct audio change when the cue is positioned behind the player, enhancing the realism of the sonar effect to increase its usability and recognizability, and using audio to communicate progress through the level. Additionally, participants proposed implementing a form of "fail-safe" for players who become disoriented or stuck. While this feature is valid for enhancing user experience and reducing frustration, it will not be included in the version used for testing, but will be incorporated into the finalized framework for developers. The reason for this decision is that we don't want the blind players to be able to rely on a tool that will automatically help them, we want them to rely on the tool developed for them to get an gauge of to what degree it works.

The overarching aim is to develop a structured, cost-effective framework that enables game developers to integrate accessibility features for blind players. Although the primary focus remains on navigation, future iterations will explore how various biomes (which are different areas with different climates, animals, plants etc. [10]) have alternative soundscapes influence the player experience. Given that navigation is a core mechanic in most games, ensuring its accessibility is a critical priority moving forward. A few local game studios have already shown interest in testing out the framework and we are to test it out with select studios in the near future.

This framework is designed to streamline the process of making 3D first-person and third-person games accessible to blind players. Objects to achieve this by providing clear and concise guidelines geared toward developers familiar with Unreal Engine's Blueprint visual scripting system. The framework emphasizes ease of integration, avoiding unnecessary complexity, and ensuring compatibility with pre-existing game systems to facilitate efficient and scalable implementation. By leveraging technologies already integrated into Unreal Engine, alongside resources typically available at most game studios working with Unreal Engine, this approach offers a cost-effective method for developing a navigation system for 3D games in both first- and third-person perspectives. Utilizing Unreal Engine's Blueprint visual scripting system, which many developers are already familiar with, eliminates the need to build fully custom solutions for each game, thereby keeping down cost for the development process while maintaining accessibility goals.

Although the experiment demonstrated the viability of the system, more research is needed to refine the elements necessary to maximise its impact. Insights gained from existing technologies have been valuable, but certain limitations require a deeper examination. Future research will explore impulse responses, surround sound, and how spatial audio can be used to enhance orientation. Additionally, investigating how footsteps or other dedicated sounds can function as a sonar-like system can provide players with enhanced feedback on their surroundings, further improving immersion and accessibility.

Previous research [5] has highlighted several open questions that warrant further investigation. As mentioned in the previous paper of this project [6], we question how to balance realistic acoustic environments with entertainment value. For example, would highly accurate spatial sound interfere with immersive experience in a stylised game like *Super Mario* [20], or would it only be effective in games designed with realistic settings? Our feedback during this test was that most of the players used the main sound cues but did not pay much attention to the acoustics in the navigation. Another critical issue brought up in the previous article, as noted in [4], was the industry's lack of investment in accessibility for blind players. Looking at proposed laws from EU [13], there appear to be improvements on the way. Accessibility features for the blind players are mandated in future technology. It will be quite exciting to follow this and see if the same type of mandate will include the video game industry. If this were the case, our model would be of even more use than we anticipated when we started this project.

Lastly, it is important to address why our project does not utilize virtual reality, despite its apparent suitability for simulating realistic scenarios, such as head-tracking combined with spatial audio to provide an immersive navigational experience, as demonstrated in research like [14]. While virtual reality offers clear advantages in replicating real-world spatial interactions, our decision to avoid it is driven by two key considerations.

First, our primary goal is to develop a framework that is as broadly applicable and accessible as possible for developers working with first- and third-person games in Unreal Engine. Although virtual reality is growing in popularity, it has yet to become a mainstream standard in game development. By focussing on conventional 3D gameplay environments, we increase the likelihood that our framework can be adopted by a wider range of developers, thereby making more games accessible to blind and low vision players.

Second, from a user perspective, virtual reality equipment is not yet a standard household item in the way that headsets or game controllers are. Building our framework around VR would risk excluding users who cannot afford or do not have access to this hardware. This would run counter to one of the core goals of our project: to lower barriers and improve accessibility, not introduce new ones. Thus, while virtual reality presents exciting opportunities for future development, we have chosen to prioritize a more inclusive and widely adoptable approach at this stage.

6   Conclusion

This project has successfully demonstrated that it is possible to design a fully playable game experience using only sound while maintaining the sense of immersion that is essential for player enjoyment. Moving forward, our focus will be on refining this technology by incorporating direct feedback from blind players. Their insights, gathered during the experiment, will be instrumental in shaping a more accessible and intuitive framework for future games.

Based on this feedback, our next step is to simplify the acoustic environment, creating on a more intuitive and easily navigable system. Our testing revealed that participants could traverse the level effectively, not due to complex acoustics, but rather through an immersive soundscape and the sound-based navigation system. This suggests that intricate acoustic details may be unnecessary for successful navigation. Moving forward, we plan to refine and apply this approach across different biomes and soundscapes to evaluate whether players can seamlessly adapt to varied environments while using the same core mechanics.

If these adjustments yield successful results and are well received by our partners at Blindeforbundet (The Norwegian Association of the Blind and Partially Sighted) and Greåker High School, we will move toward developing a standardised framework for game developers. This effort will involve collaboration with Norwegian game studios that have expressed interest in the project, including Snowcastle Games in Oslo. By working directly with industry professionals, we aim to ensure that the framework is both practical and seamlessly integrated into existing development workflows, particularly within Unreal Engine. Gathering input from programmers and designers will be key to refining the framework so that it aligns with industry needs and encourages widespread adoption.

The long-term vision is to establish a universally applicable framework that can be implemented across the gaming industry, benefiting both AAA and indie studios alike. By fostering collaboration between accessibility organisations and game developers, we strive to make this technology an industry standard, improving accessibility in video games and ensuring that blind players have greater opportunities to engage with interactive entertainment.

Acknowledgment. Writefull AI has been used as a proofreading and editing aid throughout the writing process (`writefull.com`). However, no part of the text can be considered "written by AI".

Data collections were handled by questionnaires created with nettskjema.no, survey solution developed and hosted by the University of Oslo (nettskjema@usit.uio.no).

References

1. Unreal engine (1998-present). https://www.unrealengine.com/
2. Agrimi, E., Battaglini, C., Bottari, D., Gnecco, G., Leporini, B.: Game accessibility for visually impaired people: a review. Soft Comput., 1–18 (2024). https://doi.org/10.1007/s00500-024-09827-4. Accessed 29 Jul 2025
3. AGRIP: Audioquake. Video game (2003)
4. Andrade, R., Rogerson, M.J., Waycott, J., Baker, S., Vetere, F.: Playing blind: revealing the world of gamers with visual impairment. In: 2019 CHI Conference on Human Factors in Computing Systems, CHI '19, pp. 1–14. Association for Computing Machinery, New York (2019). https://doi.org/10.1145/3290605.3300346
5. Andrade, R., Waycott, J., Baker, S., Vetere, F.: Echolocation as a means for people with visual impairment (PVI) to acquire spatial knowledge of virtual space. ACM Trans. Access. Comput. **14**(1) (2021). https://doi.org/10.1145/3448273
6. Anonymized: Anonymized. In: Anonymized (Anonymized)

7. Apavou, F., Bouchara, T., Bourdot, P.: AVA: an audio-based virtual aiming system for accessible VR shooting games. In: 2025 IEEE Conference on Virtual Reality and 3D User Interfaces Abstracts and Workshops (VRW), pp. 1172–1173 (2025). https://doi.org/10.1109/VRW66409.2025.00232

8. Archambault, D., Olivier, D.: How to make games for visually impaired children. In: Proceedings of the 2005 ACM SIGCHI International Conference on Advances in Computer Entertainment Technology, ACE '05, pp. 450–453. Association for Computing Machinery, New York (2005). https://doi.org/10.1145/1178477.1178578

9. Archambault, D., Ossmann, R., Gaudy, T., Miesenberger, K.: Computer games and visually impaired people. Upgrade, January 2007

10. BBC: Explore biomes (2025). https://www.bbc.co.uk/bitesize/articles/zvsp92p#zmvsf82. Accessed 28 Jul 2025

11. Be My Eyes: Inclusive language guide (2023). https://www.bemyeyes.com/blog/be-my-eyes-inclusive-language-guide. Accessed 23 May 2025

12. Ree, B.: The remarkable life of Ibelin. Documentary (2024)

13. European Commission: European accessibility act (2021). https://commission.europa.eu/strategy-and-policy/policies/justice-and-fundamental-rights/disability/union-equality-strategy-rights-persons-disabilities-2021-2030/european-accessibility-act_en. Accessed 13 Jan 2024

14. Guerreiro, J., Kim, Y., Nogueira, R., Chung, S.A., Rodrigues, A., Oh, U.: The design space of the auditory representation of objects and their behaviours in virtual reality for blind people. IEEE Trans. Vis. Comput. Graph. **29**(5), 2552–2562 (2023). https://doi.org/10.1109/TVCG.2023.3244443

15. id Software: Quake. Video game (1996)

16. Jennett, C., et al.: Measuring and defining the experience of immersion in games. Int. J. Hum. Comput. Stud. **66**(9), 641–661 (2008). https://doi.org/10.1016/j.ijhcs.2008.04.004, https://www.sciencedirect.com/science/article/pii/S1071581908000499

17. Łącka, K.: What is modding in gaming? (2025). https://www.g2a.com/news/glossary/what-is-modding-in-gaming/. Accessed 28 Jul 2025

18. Matsuo, M., Miura, T., Sakajiri, M., Onishi, J., Ono, T.: ShadowRine: accessible game for blind users, and accessible action RPG for visually impaired gamers. In: 2016 IEEE International Conference on Systems, Man, and Cybernetics (SMC), pp. 002826–002827 (2016). https://doi.org/10.1109/SMC.2016.7844667

19. Nair, V., et al.: NavStick: making video games blind-accessible via the ability to look around. In: The 34th Annual ACM Symposium on User Interface Software and Technology, UIST '21, pp. 538–551. Association for Computing Machinery, New York (2021). https://doi.org/10.1145/3472749.3474768

20. Nintendo EAD and Nintendo EPD: Super Mario series. Video game (1985-present)

21. Picinali, L., Afonso, A., Denis, M., Katz, B.F.: Exploration of architectural spaces by blind people using auditory virtual reality for the construction of spatial knowledge. Int. J. Hum Comput Stud. **72**(4), 393–407 (2014). https://doi.org/10.1016/j.ijhcs.2013.12.008

22. Siu, A.F., Sinclair, M., Kovacs, R., Ofek, E., Holz, C., Cutrell, E.: Virtual reality without vision: a haptic and auditory white cane to navigate complex virtual worlds. In: Proceedings of the 2020 CHI Conference on Human Factors in Computing Systems, pp. 1–13. Association for Computing Machinery (2020). https://doi.org/10.1145/3313831.3376408

23. Turn 10 Studios: Forza Motorsport 2023. Video Game (2023)

24. Wilde, T.: How WASD became the standard PC control scheme (2016)

Exploring Social Robot-Based Games for Enhancing Sustainable Living at Home: A Co-design Study with Families with Children

Nasim Beheshtian, Aino Ahtinen(✉), and Kaisa Väänänen

Computing Sciences, Tampere University, 33100 Tampere, Finland
{nasim.beheshtian,aino.ahtinen,kaisa.vaananen}@tuni.fi

Abstract. Social robots have been utilized in education, healthcare, customer service, and domestic environments. However, there is limited research on their role in promoting sustainable living at home through playful interactions. This study extends the theme of family-robot interaction (FRI) within human-robot interaction (HRI) by integrating social robots and game-based interactions to enhance sustainability at home. We conducted a one-month qualitative study with 32 participants (parents and children) from eight families, using a family-centered design approach and participatory co-design method. Each family hosted a robot at home for one month. Through co-design sessions, they first shared their expectations for how social robots could support eco-friendly living, then ideated robot-based games to promote sustainability. Our findings showed that social robots were perceived as more engaging and appealing to children than adults. Children saw social robots as companions and were eager to learn pro-environmental practices through the robots' interactive and playful features. The study's eco-friendly focus, along with the co-design tasks around the robot, inspired some children to participate in sustainable living practices at home and encouraged their parents to do the same. The ideated robot-based games incorporated competition, collaboration, and reward elements, aiming to enhance interest and eco-friendly living and awareness. Overall, adults were more reserved about social robots, expressing concerns about the robots' ability to maintain long-term engagement once the novelty effect fades. This study suggests that social robots have the potential to raise intergenerational environmental awareness at home, with children acting as the primary interest group who transfer their eco-friendly knowledge to their parents.

Keywords: Social Robots · In-home Social Robots · Family-Centered Design · Co-Design · Environmental Sustainability

1   Introduction

Global warming and the increasing strain on natural resources highlight the urgent need for sustainable living practices [8]. Household activities, maintenance, and indoor environmental quality significantly affect energy use [18]. Households account for 40% of nonrenewable resource consumption and greenhouse gas emissions [14,17], emphasizing the importance of promoting sustainability at home. Among these households,

J. F. Krems et al. (Eds.): CHIRA 2025, CCIS 2836, pp. 190–209, 2026.
https://doi.org/10.1007/978-3-032-16454-4_11

families, especially those with children, play a crucial role in shaping long-term behaviors and daily routines. With 65.5 million families with children (out of 220 million households) in Europe alone [21,22], fostering sustainable practices at home can create ripple effects that support broader societal change and lead to substantial environmental benefit. Employing technological solutions that enhance sustainable living practices at home can have a profound environmental impact. Humanoid social robots offer a promising technological approach by enabling natural, intuitive, and multimodal interaction [5,9,12,19]. As physically embodied agents, social robots engage with users on emotional and social levels [11] and are already used in homes as assistants [35], playmates [36], and socially assistive support for children and older adults [37]. Their role as social motivators makes them well-suited to encourage eco-friendly practices [11,13,15,16,20,34], helping families reassess their resource consumption. However, despite their growing presence in various domains [35–37], their potential to support sustainable living within domestic settings, particularly within family context, remains underexplored and warrants further investigation.

This one-month qualitative and exploratory study employed a family-centered design approach [5,7] to engage families in co-designing scenarios where social robots foster sustainable living at home. We also explored the potential of a game-based approach as a motivating tool, with families ideating robot-based game scenarios to promote eco-friendly awareness [11,27]. Conducted remotely during the COVID-19 pandemic, the study used online co-design sessions developed by the researchers. Each family received an Alpha Mini robot and supporting materials for in-home co-design sessions. It is important to note that the study did not aim to measure behavioral change or assess the social robot's influence but rather to explore the design potential of social robots in fostering sustainable practices at home. Our goal was to answer the following research questions: (1) What expectations do families have on how social robots could enhance family members' sustainable living at home? (2) What kinds of social robot-based games would engage and encourage family members to participate in sustainable activities at home?

Contribution. This study contributes to the emerging theme of family-robot interaction (FRI) [42] within the broader field of human-robot interaction (HRI). Research on the use of in-home humanoid social robots to promote sustainable living, especially among families with children, is still limited, with only a few previous studies focusing on this area [38,42]. Our work extends this area with a long-term home-based study, exploring the potential of social robots to enhance sustainability through their interactive capabilities. We also study families' preferred features and scenarios for social robot-based games, fostering eco-friendly awareness and practices at home.

2   Related Work

The related work is covered in four sections: 1) In-home social robots, 2) Privacy concerns in domestic use of social robots, 3) Social robots enhancing environmental sustainability at home, and 4) Social robots and games.

2.1   In-Home Social Robots

Social robots are physically embodied agents designed to interact with humans on social and emotional levels [11]. Their growing presence in domestic settings stems from their ability to support daily routines, enhance social engagement, and provide educational and emotional benefits [3, 10]. Cagiltay [42] examined families' preferences and design considerations for social robots for long-term home interactions. She found that families favored robots that acted as companions or assistants, especially in shared activities and group settings. Similarly, Chen et al. [1] explored how social robots could foster long-term interaction between parents and children in domestic environments over several weeks. The study revealed that successful engagement requires the robot to adapt to changing parent-child dynamics, offering personalized and flexible support for diverse family needs.

What sets social robots apart from technologies such as smart home systems or virtual interfaces is their ability to convey nonverbal behaviors and gestures and emotional expressions; these features reduce miscommunication and enhance task performance, making interactions feel more natural and intuitive [58, 59]. Emotion-based adaptation further boosts user engagement and perceived likeability, leading to longer and more meaningful interactions [6]. In-home settings, social robots can take on varying social roles such as peer, subordinate, or superior depending on the task and context [60]. These capabilities make them valuable in education [14], healthcare [13, 61], and in promoting environmental and social sustainability.

2.2   Privacy Concerns in Domestic Use of Social Robots

Integrating social robots into home environments raises important privacy concerns due to their capacity to collect and process sensitive data. Almohri et al. [40] identified two key dimensions of privacy in this context. The first dimension relates to personal space, as robots operate within private domestic settings, making sensor-based data collection potentially intrusive. The second dimension is informational privacy, where individuals desire to control how their data is used by manufacturers, institutions, or potential cyber intruders.

To address privacy concerns, transparent design is essential [63]. Social robots should clearly indicate when data is being collected, for example, through visible indicators on cameras or microphones [40]. Additionally, giving users control to adjust the sensors and the option to disable audio or video recording further supports privacy [40]. As social robots continue to become more common in homes, clear privacy guidelines must be established to balance functionality with data protection. Ensuring transparency and offering robust privacy controls will be vital for building trust and encouraging long-term adoption in domestic spaces [63].

2.3   Social Robots Enhancing Environmental Sustainability at Home

Engaging residents, especially families with children, is vital for encouraging sustainable living. Active involvement in resource management has been shown to strengthen a family's commitment to sustainability [24]. Instilling pro-environmental awareness from an early age is crucial, as childhood education fosters values and skills that can carry into adulthood [25,26]. Parents play a key role by shaping their children's environmental attitudes and behaviors [30,50], but this influence can also be reciprocal [50]; children can impact their parents' decisions on purchasing decisions, technology use, and social values [50,52–54]. Environmental education that targets children while promoting intergenerational learning can effectively transfer knowledge, behaviors, and attitudes to adults [50]. Such programs can enable children to influence their parents' energy use [55], environmental knowledge [56], and waste management education [57].

Social robots can assist household members in reflecting on their environmental impact by promoting more mindful resource consumption [8]. For children, interacting with social robots supports social, developmental, and educational growth; similarly, robot-mediated learning at home can increase the motivation, interest, and attention of children [6]. Over time, playful and game-based learning strategies can encourage children to take on household tasks like cleaning and organizing. Due to their interactive and engaging nature, social robots are well-suited to influence behavior change [13,15, 16], making them effective tools for fostering eco-friendly habits through interactive, family-centered experiences.

Several studies have explored how social robots can influence eco-friendly behaviors through persuasive interaction. For instance, Ham and Midden [16], designed a persuasive robot that delivered either positive or negative social feedback to encourage energy-saving behavior in adults. Their study showed that personalized and socially framed robot messages could lead to measurable reductions in energy use, but it was conducted in a short-term lab setting with individual participants. Similarly, Mubin et al. [15] introduced Floffy, an outdoor robot designed to prompt children to engage in environmentally responsible activities. These studies demonstrate that social robots can serve as effective motivators for sustainability; however, they are limited to short-term interventions, focused on specific behaviors, and lack user involvement in the design process. Overall, there remains a gap in research on how social robots can be integrated into everyday family life to support sustainable practices through interactive, participatory, and engaging formats.

2.4 Social Robots and Games

Games are effective tools for enhancing motivation and engagement in learning, supporting both personal development and knowledge acquisition [27]. Research shows that games can deepen understanding across various subjects [11], and games focused on environmental sustainability can positively shape attitudes and promote eco-friendly behaviors [28]. Integrating robots into children's games further enhances this experience. For instance, in the game Tug-of-War, the robot Paleo acts as a pet, boosting engagement for young players. Similarly, Papero, an entertainment robot, enhances gameplay with interactive features like riddles, fortune-telling, mimicry, and dancing [41]. To be effective, game-playing social robots must deliver enjoyable, engaging experiences that sustain players' motivation and interest.

Social robots are particularly effective in educational games, engaging players through gestures, expressions, and feedback. For instance, in the game PepperRecycle [11], the robot Pepper acted as an opponent, helping children learn about recycling by prompting them to choose the correct waste bin. Players received points based on their performance, and Pepper provided positive feedback and gestures, like clapping or adopting a thoughtful pose, further boosting engagement. Players earned points based on their performance, while Pepper enhanced engagement through positive feedback and expressive gestures, such as clapping or striking a thoughtful pose. The findings showed children had high enjoyment and sustained interaction with robots. Studies show that children prefer playing with physically present robots over screen-based games due to the robots' social presence and interactive nature [27,41]. The robot's physical embodiment enhances the experience, making robot-based games more enjoyable and engaging than those involving virtual characters [27].

3   Methodology

To address our research goals and questions, we conducted a one-month field study with eight families in Finland. The study took place in participants' homes, where families engaged in online co-design sessions designed by the researchers. Following prior research [4,6] we adopted the family-centered design approach, which emphasizes the inclusion of all family members, adults and children, in shaping technology that fits their daily lives. Our goal was to focus on engaging families in the ideation and co-design of scenarios where social robots could foster sustainable living at home. This approach ensures that the design process is informed by the needs and perspectives of both adults and children, fostering a holistic view of how technology integrates into daily family life. In addition, we employed the co-design method, involving both parents and children as active collaborators during the ideation phase [2,6]. This allowed participants to express their needs, concerns, and suggestions while generating ideas for robot-based game scenarios aimed at promoting pro-environmental practices at home.

3.1   Study Setup

During the co-design sessions, families explored the potential of social robots for sustainable living through weekly open-ended hands-on tasks designed for families to explore social robots and become familiar with the possible usage of these robots for sustainable living. Each family received an Alpha Mini robot[1], a 24.5 cm portable robot, from UBITECH for one month (Fig. 1). Used as a technology probe [6], Alpha Mini features basic capabilities such as face recognition, voice interaction, and expressive movements like dancing or exercising. The robot's child-friendly design, ease of use, and graphical block programming made it suitable for home use. Delivered without pre-set programs, the robot allowed families to freely explore its functionalities and to imagine new possibilities for its use in promoting sustainable living.

To stimulate creativity, the study leveraged fiction as a source [6,49] within a fictional design space [49] to stimulate family members' thoughts and to help them envision future interactions with a social robot at home. By employing the Alpha Mini robot as a technology probe, we encouraged families to think beyond what the robot could presently do and imagine how it could evolve to support sustainable practices in their daily lives. The humanoid design and physical presence of Alpha Mini played a key role in this process. Its human-like features, such as movements and gestures, made it

---

[1] https://www.ubtrobot.com/.

Fig. 1. The study material was provided to the family member to be used at home for one month of the study for conducting the hands-on tasks.

relatable, especially for children, fostering engagement and sparking discussions about how social robots could be integrated into everyday life. Concretely, we provided participants with fictional scenarios and visuals showing the robot performing eco-friendly tasks such as reminding family members to turn off lights or suggesting ways to reduce water use. These materials were presented as storyboards, illustrative examples, and a short video clip, which helped families picture possible future behaviors and interactions. These, visual tools complemented the process, while the robot's basic but sufficient features allowed families to reflect on its potential role in supporting sustainable practices.

3.2 Study Design

In co-design sessions, family members worked together to conduct weekly hands-on tasks related to social robots for a month. Prior research [64,65] has shown the significance of hands-on tasks in robotic learning and interaction. The weekly tasks were created using Mural Canvas[2], an online platform, and were shared with each family on their private canvas weekly, accessible only to the researchers and the respective family. The researchers checked the Mural Canvas regularly.

The study began with a face-to-face kickoff meeting, where one adult family member visited the university to submit consent forms, receive detailed instructions, and collect the Alpha Mini robot along with a tablet and printed materials (Fig. 1). Family members needed the additional material to complete the weekly tasks, and then they had to take pictures of their answers and put them on their canvas for researchers to check. They also used virtual sticky notes to communicate their thoughts on the canvas. Each weekly task had a clear goal and built upon the previous week's activities.   In

---

[2] https://www.mural.co/.

the first week, family members familiarized themselves with the robot's movements, speech, and dance moves using the tablet interface. They also experimented with simple block programming through pre-installed sample programs. To expand families' understanding, they were encouraged to search online for other social robots, compare their features, and share their preferences and critiques. In the second week, family members were introduced to the study's sustainability focus through a set of images illustrating both sustainable and unsustainable household behaviors, drawing on approaches used in previous research [31]. They had to select three images and answer the questions on A4 paper templates related to their reasoning behind their choice of images (Fig. 2).

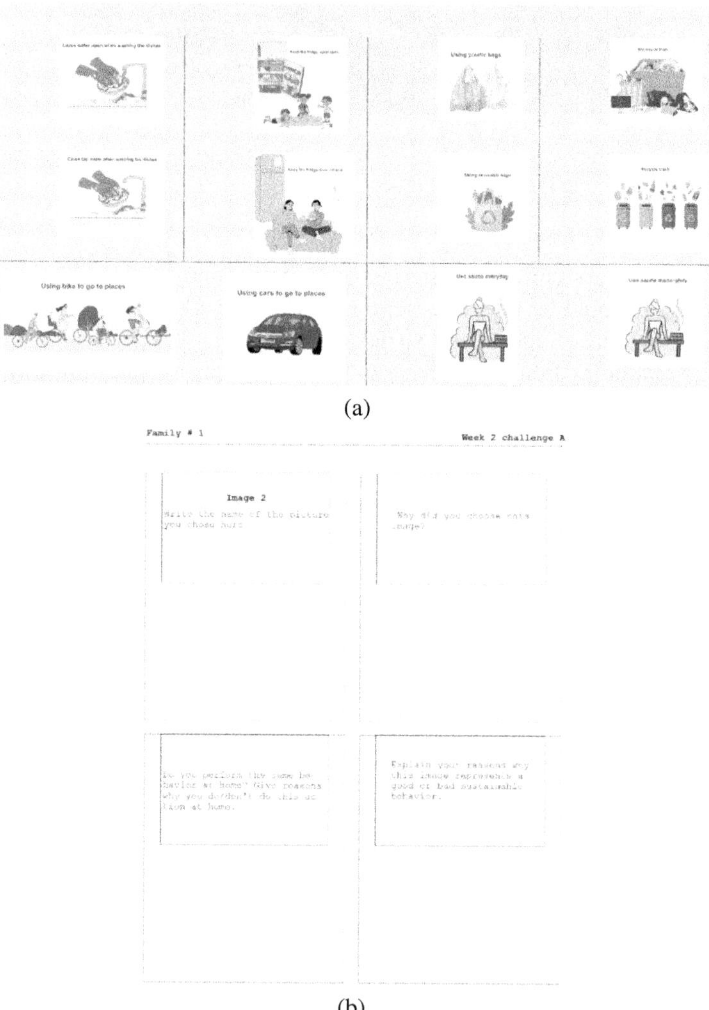

(a)

(b)

Fig. 2. Materials used in Week 2 of the study: (a) Images used by families to identify sustainable and unsustainable behaviors, and (b) Storyboard templates to be completed for reflection on their selected image.

They also explained whether the behavior depicted in each image promoted or hindered eco-friendly behavior. This exercise helped family members reflect on the household's sustainable and unsustainable behaviors at home.

In the third week, the goal was for family members to explore how social robots could support sustainable living at home. To achieve this goal, they first watched a short video created by the first author[3], showing Alpha Mini giving tips on reducing shower water use, shared via Mural Canvas. Afterward, they reflected on the robot's role in promoting sustainability. In the second task, they used storyboard templates to create their own scenarios in which social robots addressed unsustainable household behaviors. To support this ideation, family members were given a written example of Alpha Mini saving a water scenario (Fig. 3), along with images of unsustainable practices and robot visuals to incorporate into their storyboards. In the final week, family members focused on designing robot-based games to promote sustainable living at home. Using A3 paper, they sketched and explained their game concepts, with the option to program elements of the game on the tablet if they wished. This task encouraged creative thinking and allowed family members to explore how playful interactions with the robot could help teach or reinforce eco-friendly behaviors.

Fig. 3. An example scenario was provided by researchers to families to show how Alpha Mini helps family members save water.

---

[3] https://youtu.be/yLXrYRQq4pM?si=A-wzWbL-g4OpJPV.

Each week's task included an open section where families could provide their additional images, screenshots, ideas, and experiences for us. It is worth mentioning that the study was conducted in English, as there were international participants who did not speak Finnish.

3.3 Participants and Ethical Considerations

Eight families (N = 32 family members), including five Finnish and three international households with children, voluntarily participated in the study. Participants included 16 adults (eight males and eight females) and 16 children (11 females and 5 males) living in a metropolitan area in Finland. Most families had two children; one had one child, and another had three. Children were between 6 and 15 years old, with an average age of nine, while the average parental age was 42 for fathers and 40 for mothers. Families with children in this elementary school age were selected based on Piaget's developmental theory [46], which suggests that children aged 6–15 begin to develop logical thinking and abstract reasoning skills essential for understanding sustainability and engaging meaningfully with social robots. Educational initiatives during these years can lead to long-term behavioral change, making this group ideal for the study [45].

Participants were recruited via a university newsletter and personal networks. The study was conducted in three rounds: three families participated in February–March 2021, another three in April–May, and the final two in June. Each family received an Alpha Mini robot during their study period, which was returned afterward. Parental permission was obtained for all child participants, following Finnish guidelines for research involving children under 15 [48]. Ethical approval covered both adults and children through individual consent forms. Before the study, parents and children were provided with their individual consent forms. Parents received detailed forms outlining the study's purpose, procedures, and data privacy measures. Children were given simplified forms with visual aids, and parents were asked to explain the study to them. Parents signed their own forms, while children signed or initialed theirs.

All data was anonymized for analysis, with personal identifiers removed. The study followed strict ethical protocols for data collection, storage, and participant safety, with particular attention to privacy and minimizing potential harm. Children's participation in online interviews was voluntary, always with parental consent and supervision. Parents had control over all the research data collected from their families. The research data was stored on the university's secure drive for five years. Communication with families occurred via email, phone, and Mural Canvas.

3.4 Data Collection and Analysis

In this exploratory study, we collected qualitative data through two online semi-structured interviews with family members during the first and the fourth week. Conducted via Microsoft Teams, each interview lasted about 40 min and was recorded with audio and video. While a structured script with open-ended questions guided the interviews, parents translated for children when needed. Most families participated as a group, though attendance varied. The initial interview focused on family members' views on environmental sustainability, their everyday eco-friendly practices, how children learn sustainable behaviors, and their initial impressions of using social robots for sustainable living. The final interview explored their expectations of social robots in this context, potential robot roles and capabilities, their thoughts on having such technology at home, and reflections on the robot-based games they had designed. Additional qualitative data was collected from families' responses to the weekly tasks submitted on Mural Canvas.

We conducted a thematic analysis following Braun and Clarke's guidelines [23], using semi-structured interviews as the primary data source and the Mural Canvas content, including weekly tasks, as supporting data. The first author began by transcribing the interviews and conducting an inductive analysis, generating initial codes and excluding content unrelated to the study's goals. Descriptive codes were assigned to key segments and grouped by similarity. A similar approach was applied to the weekly tasks, which were first organized by each family and then categorized and coded based on common themes. Next, the first and the second author collaboratively reviewed, discussed, and refined the codes, organizing them into broader categories to identify emerging themes and review the visual map of the data emerging from the data.

The first author defined and reported the themes as findings, which generally included family members' commitment to environmental sustainability, perceptions of social robots in the home, expected features of social robots that foster sustainability both for children and adults, engagement and interest of adults and children in interacting with social robots, the potential roles of these robots within the household environment, the concerns and challenges of using social robots at home, and the families' social robot-based game ideas. To ensure anonymity, families were identified using codes (e.g., Fa3 for Family 3), and individual members were labeled as F (father), M (mother), C1 (oldest child), and C2 (second child); for example, Fa3C2 refers to the second child in Family 3.

4 Findings

The following section reports the findings from the qualitative data of the interviews and the hands-on tasks in co-design sessions (Fig. 4). It is important to note that almost all family members attended the co-design sessions. All parents except the father in Fa8 attended both interview sessions. All children except Fa8 and Fa2C2 were present in the interview sessions. Those children who did not attend were either too young or not available to attend the interviews.

Fig. 4. Children interacting with the Alpha Mini robot and completing the weekly tasks at home.

4.1   Commitment to Sustainable Practices

Families mostly revealed a commitment to eco-friendly habits by recycling, conserving energy, and reducing waste. Most families recognized the long-term benefits of sustainable living for future generations: *"By behaving sustainably, we can save the earth for the next generations, and nature will be saved for us and other forms of organisms"* (Fa4, M). Larger families were especially conscious of their higher impact on resource consumption, acknowledging that more household members could lead to a greater environmental footprint: *"Of course, as a family of four, we consume more resources compared to when it was only two of us"* (Fa1, F). The findings also revealed that children played a role in spreading pro-environmental information within the household. While children primarily learned about sustainability from school, they were active in sharing this knowledge with their families, effectively educating their parents: *"Most of the time, children teach us new information they learn from school and let us know how to behave pro-environmentally"* (Fa3, F).

4.2   Expected Features of Social Robots Enhancing Sustainability

Initially, family members had limited ideas about how social robots could support pro-environmental living. However, through weekly tasks such as exploring Alpha Mini's features, researching other social robots, viewing our sample video on Mural, and brainstorming home scenarios, they developed a clearer understanding of the robots' potential roles and design possibilities. Family members generally perceived social robots as an effective tool for raising eco-friendly awareness at home. They expected the robot to offer feedback and information on the household's resource consumption to increase awareness and support over their environmental impact: *"It would be helpful if the robot could tell how much water or electricity we are using in the house"* (Fa4, M). Immediate feedback was seen as a valuable feature in helping family members adjust their consumption habits: *"It would be helpful if Mini reacts automatically to the sound of water, and it could give feedback that the water is running. It [the robot] could bring some value"* (Fa3, F). Additionally, it was mentioned that by making consumption patterns visible, the robot can help family members adjust their behaviors promptly: *"The robot could show me how much electricity my PlayStation uses every day, then I know my contribution to the electricity usage, and if it is too much, I will reduce it"* (Fa4, C2).

Family members also expected the robot to act as an educator by providing instructions and suggestions: *"It would be nice if it [the robot] could measure and tell us what to do when water and electricity usage is going up."* (Fa2, M). Engaging and fun interactions with the robot were highlighted as valuable features in enhancing sustainable learning. Most parents expected the robot to make sustainability awareness enjoyable specifically for their children, believing that children tend to respond well to playful and interactive learning: *"If it [the robot] can do environmental education through playful and fun games, that will have quite a lot of values at least for children, and some adults like me"* (Fa4, F). Family members also expected personalized interactions with the robot, ensuring it could adapt to the diverse needs of each household member: *"I may like to play a game, and my parents may want to hear about recycling information, so it is good for the robot to give separate information"* (Fa2, C1). Personalized interaction was seen to enhance interest in interacting with the robot and improving eco-friendly habits: "*It would be great if the robot could recognize us by our faces, names, and our history of sustainable habits, then it could help us with personalized tips to improve these habits*" (Fa3, M).

4.3   The Potential of Social Robots in Motivating Family Members

Parents generally believed the robot's ability to deliver sustainability-related feedback and facts as its most encouraging feature. However, parents were more reserved about social robots' long-term appeal, noting that the novelty might fade and questioning its ability to maintain sustained engagement. They also felt that interaction with the robot could become repetitive over time, highlighting the need for continuous updates to sustain engagement: "*The main question is for how long adults can stay interested because for adults it is difficult to change habits. I don't think a robot can change habits, but it can make us think*" (Fa5, M). "*Curiosity towards social robots can attract attention initially, but as the novelty disappears, the interest decreases*" (Fa2, F). Despite some concerns, most parents, except (Fa1, F), (Fa4, F), and (Fa3, F) preferred interacting with a social robot over other devices like screens, tablets, or smart home applications. They felt that, if regularly updated and equipped with accurate data, social robots could provide a more interactive, novel, and natural experience than traditional technologies. Similarly, they believed these robots could foster more engaging interactions and bring family members together, in contrast to the often isolated experience of using tablets.

Children, in contrast to their parents, were more eager to interact with the Alpha Mini robot from the first week and showed greater enthusiasm for completing the weekly tasks on Mural Canvas, even though most family members participated in the co-design sessions. Furthermore, children (<10 years) showed more interest than their parents and older siblings in exploring the robot's features. They actively engaged with its programming functions, creating short programs to make the robot talk and move. Children also demonstrated greater enthusiasm when completing weekly tasks that involved ideating scenarios for robot use at home. It was reported that our sample video of Alpha Mini and the Week 3 tasks, focused on exploring and ideating scenarios for eco-friendly living, increased children's awareness of sustainable habits and prompted them to remind their parents about pro-environmental behaviors: "*My kid told me to close the fridge door or be careful about water consumption*" (Fa5, M). In Fa3, the son started taking shorter showers after watching the video and reminded his parents to do the same: "*My son told us he learned it is not good to use so much water in the shower, and he told us to do the same*" (Fa3, M). Fa8 reported that their older child wanted the robot to talk to her and teach her about ways to save water, as she learned in her school that saving water is important. Additionally, Fa2 noted that their child was eager to watch more sample videos of the robot talking about sustainability. Also, in Fa2, Fa7, and Fa3, children made short programs on the tablet of Alpha Mini to give sustainability information to other family members. In Fa7, children were interested in ideating several social robot-based games that addressed different pro-environmental aspects. Children perceived Alpha Mini as a friend or a companion, while most parents viewed it as an educator. For instance, in Fa2, C2 (<7 years old) took the robot with her everywhere in the house, talked to it, and repeated the robot's movements and talks.

Two children (Fa2, C1 and Fa4, C2) mentioned they preferred to listen to Alpha Mini and learn from it than from their parents, as it was like listening to a friend: *"The kids who do not like to listen to their parents might prefer to listen to their friend"* (Fa2, C1).

4.4   Robot-Based Game Characteristics for Motivating Sustainable Behavior

In Week 4, families ideated several creative social robot-based game ideas designed to promote sustainable living and environmental awareness at home. Some families ideated short games, while others brainstormed brief interactive scenarios. A common feature across most game ideas was the inclusion of collaborative elements, where family members worked together to earn points, fostering a sense of teamwork in achieving eco-friendly goals (Fig. 5). Also, all game ideas incorporated rewards in the form of points, stickers, or robot movements such as dance moves. For instance, Fa4 ideated a monthly shower challenge in which the social robot monitored each household member's shower time, and it awarded points to encourage less water consumption. Some families incorporated competitive elements into their game ideas to boost motivation. Fa2 ideated a game based on Harry Potter's "House Points system", where family members competed to earn more points in the form of stickers for more sustainable behaviors. The robot monitored and provided feedback and suggestions to encourage better pro-environmental practices among family members. By the end of the week, the robot compared everyone's stickers, announced the winner, and showed a few dance moves as a reward to the winner.

Fa3's game awarded points for recycling, which could be redeemed for fun robot movements; for instance, for 50 points, the robot danced, and for 100 points, it played a song. The social comparison element was also ideated in some games. For instance, Fa3 proposed a playful interaction where players collected points for biking or recycling. By the end of the week, the robot announced the overall points for each family member and compared them with other families in the community using the same robot at home. Additionally, all families' ideas included opportunities for robots to provide feedback about water or electricity consumption, as well as suggestions and instructions on ways to reduce resources' consumption levels or recycle. For instance, Fa5's game was called "Peek-a-Boo", in which the robot facilitated a recycling challenge by giving the players encouraging feedback by saying "Great job" as they recycled the garbage in the right waste bin; it could also provide recycling tips. Some game scenarios provided information. For example, in Fa7's recycling board game, the robot gave information about recycling a specific object in the pictures on the board and asked questions. Players had to answer the questions to progress in the games and earn points.

4.5   Concerns and Challenges of In-Home Social Robots

Several families expressed concerns about the cost of owning a social robot for sustainability, with a few families (Fa2, Fa3) hesitant to invest in such a robot unless it was provided for free or through educational programs offered by schools or libraries. Another concern revolved around the environmental contradiction of using a robot to foster eco-friendly living when the robot itself consumes electricity and may not be produced sustainably (Fa2). Families noted that this inconsistency could undermine the

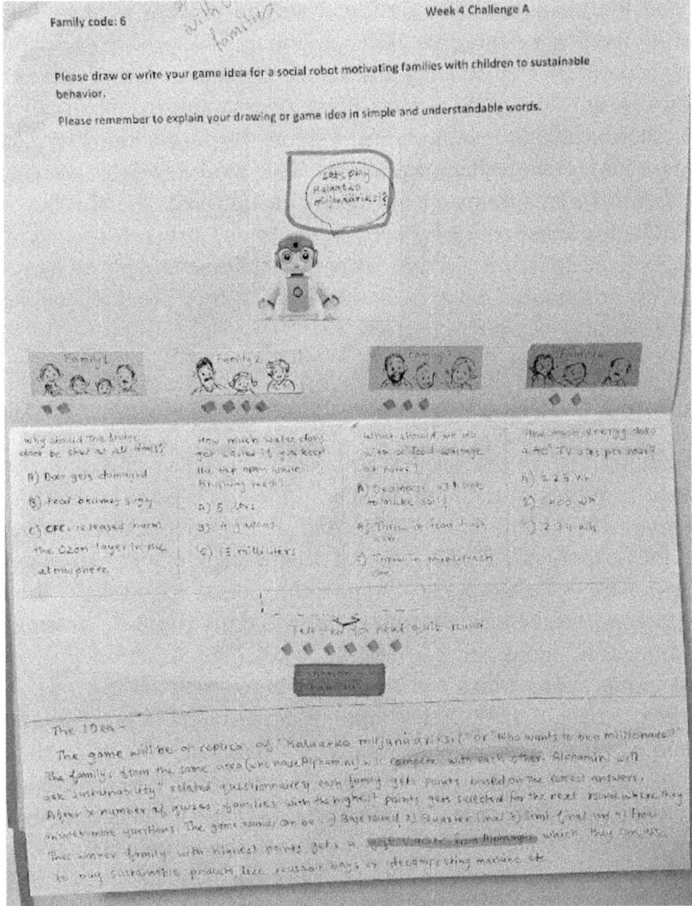

Fig. 5. Game designed by family 6.

message of sustainable living if the robot's energy use and production processes are not aligned with the principles of environmental responsibility. Privacy was another major concern raised by families, as they worried about the robot's ability to collect personal data through sensors and cameras, particularly in private areas of the home, compromising the household's privacy. Some parents also voiced concerns about over-reliance on robots, specifically for children. They worried that increased dependence on social robots could reduce human interaction and hinder the development of critical thinking or independent problem-solving skills in young users.

5 Discussion and Conclusion

This study explored the potential of social robots to support eco-friendly living at home, with the Alpha Mini robot serving as a probe for ideation and engagement. The Alpha

Mini robot and the hands-on tasks designed around it were used to stimulate ideas and gave family members a more tangible experience in co-design sessions. This approach encouraged families to envision and ideate sustainable living in ways they might not have otherwise considered. Some family members preferred using robots over other technologies, such as tablets or smart home systems, for sustainable living at home. This finding aligns with [58,59], which highlights that, unlike tablets, screens, or passive smart home systems that automate tasks in the background, social robots create more natural and engaging interactions by actively involving users. Moreover, the embodiment and interactive capabilities of these robots enable them to play a more meaningful role in enhancing sustainable living and awareness, as they provide feedback and guidance through a socially engaging experience.

5.1 Social Robots Fostering Intergenerational Pro-Environmental Awareness

Younger children (<10 years) showed greater interest and engagement with social robots than adults, making them a promising interest group for promoting sustainable living. Prior research [11] has shown that children tend to view social robots as companions, and they experience greater joy and deeper engagement, which enhances their learning experience. As educational companions, social robots have the potential to embed pro-environmental education into children's daily routines, making sustainability learning more continuous and relevant [11,14,32]. Focusing on children as the primary interest group, these robots can support intergenerational learning. Children can be the "agents of change" [51] by learning about sustainable practices through robot interaction and passing this knowledge on to their parents, influencing the household's sustainable attitudes and awareness [49]. While traditionally parents shape children's environmental attitudes [50], recent research suggests this influence can be a reciprocal dynamic. For instance, when environmental education is targeted at children, they can, in turn, positively influence their parents' behaviors in areas like recycling, energy use, and waste management [55–57].

5.2 Social Robot-Based Games for Sustainable Living

The co-design sessions generated several ideas aimed at promoting sustainability. These games featured motivational elements such as competition, collaboration, rewards, and social comparison, proven strategies for enhancing engagement [33,43]. Integrating feedback, rewards, and educational content reflects the principles of serious games, which leverage game mechanics to support learning and behavioral change [44]. Employing these elements in pro-environmental contexts can foster more eco-friendly practices [28]. While the generated robot-based game ideas had the potential to support sustainable living, the role of the social robot extended beyond facilitating the games. In all the game ideas, the robot was expected to serve not only as the facilitator but also as a guide, fostering family interactions around sustainability. Unlike traditional games, where engagement often stems solely from the content, here the robot was perceived as a novel social dynamic supporting collaboration within families and raising eco-awareness, particularly among children.

To ensure the long-term effectiveness of social robots in supporting sustainable living at home, it is essential to address the challenge of sustaining user engagement beyond the initial novelty phase. Designing robots with adaptive features that respond to user interaction and offer personalized experiences is key to maintaining interest over time [15,29,39,47]. Incorporating adaptive game mechanics such as evolving challenges, dynamic rewards, and tailored feedback can sustain engagement and appeal to all family members.

5.3 Balancing Concerns in Using Social Robots

While social robots can support sustainable living, their use also raises important concerns. For instance, privacy is a key issue in the use of these robots at home, as these robots rely on sensors and cameras to collect data. Building trust within families requires transparent data practices, giving users clear control over what is collected and how it is used [63]. Additionally, over-reliance on robots, especially among children, could weaken human interaction and independent decision-making. To avoid this, robots should be designed to encourage critical thinking and engaging interactions, serving as guides rather than replacements [62]. When thoughtfully designed, social robots can complement human influence by fostering curiosity and problem-solving while supporting pro-environmental learning.

5.4 Limitations and Future Work

This qualitative and exploratory study examined the potential of social robots in supporting sustainable living at home, though several limitations emerged. Due to COVID-19, the study was conducted remotely, restricting direct observation of family-robot interactions. Data were collected via online interviews and weekly tasks, which limited accuracy. The Alpha Mini robot, chosen for its child-friendly design and easy setup, had limited functionalities, reducing the depth of interaction. Language barriers also affected data quality, as the study was in English while most participants were Finnish, posing challenges, especially for children.

Additionally, the environmental footprint of the robots themselves can create concerns; although they may promote sustainability, their production, use, and disposal introduce ecological challenges. Future research should prioritize eco-friendly, durable, and recyclable robot designs. Furthermore, participant selection also posed a challenge, as most families were already interested in participating in the study and were motivated to reduce their environmental footprint, potentially introducing bias. However, this participant selection aligns with the study's purpose of exploring families' perceptions and expectations, rather than measuring behavioral change. Their interest and motivation in participation ensured that the study could capture feedback on the potential impact of these robots, which might be less apparent in less motivated households.

The study was conducted in Finland with a small sample of eight nuclear families, including only three international families, limiting generalizability. Future research should include more diverse and larger samples. We also plan to develop and test the robot-based game ideas generated in this study with additional families.

Acknowledgments. We would like to express our gratitude to all the family members who participated in our study. We also want to thank Tampere University for supporting our research.

References

1. Chen, H., Ostrowski, A.K., Jang, S.J., Breazeal, C., Park, H.W.: Designing long-term parent-child-robot triadic interaction at home through lived technology experiences and interviews. In: Proceedings of the IEEE International Symposium on Robot and Human Interactive Communication (2022)
2. Fails, J.A., Guha, M.L., Druin, A.: Methods and techniques for involving children in the design of new technology for children. Found. Trends Hum.-Comput. Interact. **6**(2), 85–166 (2013)
3. de Graaf, M.M.A., Ben Allouch, S., van Dijk, J.A.G.M.: Long-term acceptance of social robots in domestic environments: insights from a mixed-methods approach. Int. J. Soc. Robot. **7**(3), 421–441 (2015)
4. Arnold, L., Lee, K.J., Yip, J.C.: Co-designing with children: an approach to social robot design. ACM Hum.-Robot Interact. (HRI) (2016)
5. Cagiltay, B., Ho, H.R., Michaelis, J.E., Mutlu, B.: Investigating family perceptions and design preferences for an in-home robot. In: Proceedings of the Interaction Design and Children Conference, pp. 229–242 (2020)
6. Hutchinson, H., et al.: Technology probes: Inspiring design for and with families. In: Proceedings of the SIGCHI Conference on Human Factors in Computing Systems, pp. 17–24 (2003)
7. Trilar, J., Zavratnik, V., Čermelj, V., Hrast, B., Kos, A., Stojmenova Duh, E.: Rethinking family-centred design approach towards creating digital products and services. Sensors **19**(5), 1232 (2019)
8. Horn, M.S., Davis, P., Hubbard, A.K., Keifert, D., Leong, Z.A., Olson, I.C.: Learning sustainability: families, learning, and next-generation eco-feedback technology. In: Proceedings of the 10th International Conference on Interaction Design and Children (IDC), pp. 161–164 (2011)
9. Li, R.Y.M., Li, H., Mak, C., Tang, T.: Sustainable smart home and home automation: big data analytics approach. Int. J. Smart Home **10**(8), 177–187 (2016)
10. Kidd, C.D., Breazeal, C.: Robots at home: understanding long-term human-robot interaction. Int. J. Soc. Robot. **2**(1), 5–19 (2008)
11. Castellano, G., De Carolis, B., D'Errico, F., Macchiarulo, N., Rossano, V.: Pepperecycle: improving children's attitude toward recycling by playing with a social robot. Int. J. Soc. Robot. **13**(1), 97–111 (2021)
12. Borja, R., De La Pinta, J.R., Álvarez, A., Maestre, J.M.: Integration of service robots in the smart home by means of UPNP: a surveillance robot case study. Robot. Auton. Syst. **61**(2), 153–160 (2013)
13. Ribino, P., Bonomolo, M., Lodato, C., Vitale, G.: A humanoid social robot-based approach for indoor environment quality monitoring and well-being improvement. Int. J. Soc. Robot. 1–20 (2020)
14. Shibata, T.: An overview of human interactive robots for psychological enrichment. Proc. IEEE **92**(11), 1749–1758 (2004)
15. Mubin, O., Vink, L., Oosterwijk, P., Mahmud, A.A., Shahid, S.: Floffy: designing an outdoor robot for children. In: Kotzé, P., Marsden, G., Lindgaard, G., Wesson, J., Winckler, M. (eds.) INTERACT 2013. LNCS, vol. 8120, pp. 563–570. Springer, Heidelberg (2013). https://doi.org/10.1007/978-3-642-40498-6_46

16. Ham, J., Midden, C.J.: A persuasive robot to stimulate energy conservation: the influence of positive and negative social feedback and task similarity on energy-consumption behavior. Int. J. Soc. Robot. **6**(2), 163–171 (2014)
17. European Commission. Communication from the commission to the European parliament, the council, the European economic and social committee and the committee of the regions (2020). https://eur-lex.europa.eu/legal-content/EN/TXT/HTML/?uri=CELEX:52020DC0662&rid=5. Accessed 20 July 2025
18. Mlecnik, E., Hilderson, W., Cré, J.: Learning from best practice low energy housing retrofit. DU o. T. OTB Research Institute for the Built Environment, G. Passiefhuis-Platform vzw, B-2600 Berchem, Belgium & t. BBRI a. UAC Passiefhuis-Platform (eds.) (2010)
19. Lohr, C., Tanguy, P., Chen, Y.: Plug and play your robot into your smart home: illustration of a new framework. KI-Künstliche Intelligenz **31**(3), 283–289 (2017)
20. Beheshtian, N., Moradi, S., Ahtinen, A., Väänänen, K., Kähkonen, K., Laine, M.: Greenlife: a persuasive social robot to enhance the sustainable behavior in shared living spaces. In: Proceedings of the 11th Nordic Conference on Human-Computer Interaction: Shaping Experiences, Shaping Society, pp. 1–12 (2020)
21. Eurostat. Families with children in the EU (2017). https://ec.europa.eu/eurostat/web/products-eurostat-news/-/EDN-20170531-1. Accessed 20 July 2025
22. Eurostat. Household composition statistics - statistics explained (2021). https://ec.europa.eu/eurostat/statistics-explained/index.php?title=Household_composition_statistics. Accessed 20 July 2025
23. Braun, V., Clarke, V.: Reflecting on reflexive thematic analysis. Qual. Res. Sport Exercise Health **11**(4), 589–597 (2019)
24. Léger, M.T.: Challenging families to live more sustainably: a multicase study in adopting eco-sustainable habits in the context of family. J. Sustain. Educ. **5**(1), 1–18 (2013)
25. Engdahl, I.: Early childhood education for sustainability: the OMEP world project. Int. J. Early Childhood **47**(3), 347–366 (2015)
26. Ernst, J., McAllister, K., Siklander, P., Storli, R.: Contributions to sustainability through young children's nature play: a systematic review. Sustainability **13**(13), 7443 (2021)
27. Brooks, A.G., Gray, J., Hoffman, G.: Robot's play: interactive games with sociable machines. In: Proceedings of the 2004 ACM SIGCHI International Conference on Advances in Computer Entertainment Technology, pp. 74–83 (2004)
28. Morganti, L., Pallavicini, F., Cadel, E., Candelieri, A., Archetti, F., Mantovani, F.: Gaming for earth: serious games and gamification to engage consumers in pro-environmental behaviours for energy efficiency. Energy Res. Soc. Sci. **29**, 95–102 (2017)
29. Schadenberg, B.R., Neerincx, M.A., Cnossen, F., Looije, R.: Personalizing game difficulty to keep children motivated to play with a social robot: a Bayesian approach. Cogn. Syst. Res. **43**, 222–231 (2017)
30. Iwaniec, J., Curdt-Christiansen, X.L.: Parents as agents: engaging children in environmental literacy in China. Sustainability **12**(16), 6605 (2020)
31. Kahriman-Ozturk, D., Olgan, R., Tuncer, G.: A qualitative study on Turkish preschool children's environmental attitudes through ecocentrism and anthropocentrism. Int. J. Sci. Educ. **34**(4), 629–650 (2012)
32. Han, J., Jo, M., Park, S., Kim, S.: The educational use of home robots for children. In: IEEE International Workshop on Robot and Human Interactive Communication, ROMAN 2005, pp. 378–383. IEEE (2005)
33. Hamari, J., Koivisto, J., Sarsa, H.: Does gamification work? – a literature review of empirical studies on gamification. In: 2014 47th Hawaii International Conference on System Sciences, pp. 3025–3034. IEEE (2016)

34. Beheshtian, N., Kaipainen, K., Kähkönen, K., Ahtinen, A.: Color game: a collaborative social robotic game for icebreaking; towards the design of robotic ambiences as part of smart building services. In: Proceedings of the 23rd International Conference on Academic Mindtrek, pp. 10–19 (2020)
35. Dautenhahn, K., Woods, S., Kaouri, C., Walters, M.L., Koay, K.L., Werry, I.: What is a robot companion – friend, assistant or butler? In: 2005 IEEE/RSJ International Conference on Intelligent Robots and Systems, pp. 1192–1197. IEEE (2005)
36. Abe, K., et al.: Toward playmate robots that can play with children considering personality. In: Proceedings of the Second International Conference on Human-Agent Interaction, pp. 165–168 (2014)
37. Clabaugh, C., Becerra, D., Deng, E., Ragusa, G., Matarić, M.: Month-long, in-home case study of a socially assistive robot for children with autism spectrum disorder. In: Companion of the 2018 ACM/IEEE International Conference on Human-Robot Interaction, pp. 87–88 (2018)
38. Lacey, C., Caudwell, C.: Cuteness as a 'Dark pattern' in home robots. In: 2019 14th ACM/IEEE International Conference on Human-Robot Interaction (HRI), pp. 374–381. IEEE (2019)
39. Leite, I., Martinho, C., Paiva, A.: Social robots for long-term interaction: a survey. Int. J. Soc. Robot. **5**(2), 291–308 (2013)
40. Lutz, C., Tamà-Larrieux, A.: Do privacy concerns about social robots affect use intentions? Evidence from an experimental vignette study. Front. Robot. AI **8**, 63 (2021)
41. Gonzalez-Pacheco, V., Ramey, A., Alonso-Martín, F., Castro-Gonzalez, A., Salichs, M.A.: Maggie: a social robot as a gaming platform. Int. J. Soc. Robot. **3**(4), 371–381 (2011)
42. Cagiltay, B.: Designing for in-home long-term family-robot interactions: family preferences, connection-making, and privacy. In: Extended Abstracts of the 2023 CHI Conference on Human Factors in Computing Systems, pp. 1–6 (2023)
43. Johnson, D., Horton, E., Mulcahy, R., Foth, M.: Gamification and serious games within the domain of domestic energy consumption: a systematic review. Renew. Sustain. Energy Rev. **73**, 249–264 (2017)
44. Deterding, S., Dixon, D., Khaled, R., Nacke, L.: From game design elements to gamefulness: defining "gamification". In: Proceedings of the 15th International Academic MindTrek Conference: Envisioning Future Media Environments, pp. 9–15 (2011)
45. Chawla, L., Cushing, D.F.: Education for strategic environmental behavior. Environ. Educ. Res. **13**(4), 437–452 (2007)
46. Piaget, J., Inhelder, B.: The Psychology of the Child. Basic Books, New York (1969)
47. Davis, F.D.: Perceived usefulness, perceived ease of use, and user acceptance of information technology. MIS Q. 319–340 (1989)
48. Pekkarinen, E.: Who gives consent in research on children and young people? (2018). https://vastuullinentiede.fi/en/planning/who-gives-consent-research-children-and-young-people. Accessed 20 July 2024
49. Knutz, E., Lenskjold, T.U., Markussen, T.: Fiction as a resource in participatory design. In: Proceedings of DRS 2016 International Conference: Future–Focused Thinking, pp. 1830–1844. Design Research Society (2016)
50. Desjardins, A., Wakkary, R.: How children represent sustainability in the home. In: Proceedings of the 10th International Conference on Interaction Design and Children, pp. 37–45 (2011)
51. Lawson, D.F., Stevenson, K.T., Peterson, M.N., Carrier, S.J., Strnad, R., Seekamp, E.: Intergenerational learning: are children key in spurring climate action? Glob. Environ. Chang. **53**, 204–208 (2018)
52. Walker, C.: Tomorrow's leaders and today's agents of change? Children, sustainability education and environmental governance. Children Soc. **31**(1), 72–83 (2017)

53. Baily, C.: Reverse intergenerational learning: a missed opportunity? AI Soc. **23**, 111–115 (2009)
54. Flurry, L.A., Burns, A.C.: Children's influence in purchase decisions: a social power theory approach. J. Bus. Res. **58**, 593–601 (2005)
55. LaSala, M.C.: Lesbians, gay men, and their parents: family therapy for the coming-out crisis. Fam. Process **39**, 67–81 (2000)
56. Boudet, H., Ardoin, N., Flora, J., Armel, K.C., Desai, M., Robinson, T.N.: Effects of a behaviour change intervention for girl scouts on child and parent energy-saving behaviours. Nat. Energy **1**(8) (2016)
57. Leeming, F.C., Porter, B.E., Dwyer, W.O., Cobern, M.K., Oliver, D.P.: Effects of participation in class activities on children's environmental attitudes and knowledge. J. Environ. Educ. **28**, 33–42 (1997)
58. Maddox, P., Doran, C., Williams, I.D., Kus, M.: The role of intergenerational influence in waste education programmes: the thaw project. Waste Manage. (Oxford) **31**(12), 2590–2600 (2011)
59. Luria, M., Hoffman, G., Zuckerman, O.: Comparing social robot, screen and voice interfaces for smart-home control. In: Proceedings of the 2017 CHI Conference on Human Factors in Computing Systems, pp. 580–628 (2017)
60. Deublein, A., Lugrin, B.: (Expressive) social robot or tablet? – on the benefits of embodiment and non-verbal expressivity of the interface for a smart environment. In: Gram-Hansen, S.B., Jonasen, T.S., Midden, C. (eds.) PERSUASIVE 2020. LNCS, vol. 12064, pp. 85–97. Springer, Cham (2020). https://doi.org/10.1007/978-3-030-45712-9_7
61. Deng, E., Mutlu, B., Mataric, M.J., et al.: Embodiment in socially interactive robots. Found. Trends® Robot. **7**(4), 251–356 (2019)
62. Sovacool, B.K., Martiskainen, M., Del Rio, D.D.F.: Knowledge, energy sustainability, and vulnerability in the demographics of smart home technology diffusion. Energy Policy **153**, 112196 (2021)
63. Sharkey, A.J.C.: Should we welcome robot teachers? Ethics Inf. Technol. **18**(4), 283–297 (2016). https://doi.org/10.1007/s10676-016-9387-z
64. Lutz, C., Tamó-Larrieux, A.: The robot privacy paradox: understanding how privacy concerns shape intentions to use social robots. Hum.-Mach. Commun. **104**, 106167 (2020)
65. Ebelt, K.R.: The effects of a robotics program on students skills in STEM, problem solving and teamwork. Ph.D. thesis, Montana State University–Bozeman (2012)

Serious Games for Climate Change Engagement: A User-Centered Design Approach

Anjalee Wanigarathne and Dorina Rajanen$^{(\boxtimes)}$

Interact Research Unit, Faculty of Information Technologies and Electrical Engineering,
University of Oulu, Oulu, Finland
`{anjalee.wanigarathne,dorina.rajanen}@oulu.fi`

Abstract. Climate change is a critical global challenge that requires innovative educational tools to promote awareness and engagement. This paper examines the potential of serious games as an interactive media tool for climate change engagement, offering a framework and recommendations for future serious game design in this context. To validate the framework, we developed a serious game concept and prototype *EcoLand* using the proposed recommendations. *EcoLand* was created utilizing a user-centered design approach, which integrated gamification techniques and user experience principles to enhance engagement and educational impact. The research process follows the design science research process and includes literature review, game review, conceptual framework development, prototype creation, and user testing through structured tasks and a questionnaire. Our findings suggest that user-centered serious games can effectively simulate real-world climate challenges, enhance experiential learning, and support sustainable thinking and action. This study highlights the value of involving users in the design process to improve both user engagement and communication effectiveness. This paper contributes with both a theoretical design framework and recommendations for designing serious games that make climate change more relatable and actionable for diverse users, as well as empirical findings.

Keywords: Climate change · Serious games · User-centered design · User experience · Gamification · Game design · Sustainability

1 Introduction

Climate change is a global socio-environmental challenge [1] that requires innovative communication strategies to promote awareness, engagement, and sustainable behavior. Despite the importance of addressing this issue, significant gaps in knowledge, awareness, and motivation to act persist, leaving many unaware of the causes and consequences of hazardous behaviors and the need for change [2, 3] as well as the solutions available and the urgency of the situation [4, 5]. Traditional educational and communication methods have struggled to effectively engage audiences and inspire meaningful behavioral change regarding climate change [6]. The complexity of the climate change issue, the cognitive and psychological aspects of information processing, and the politicization of the topic make the communication task difficult or unsuccessful [7].

J. F. Krems et al. (Eds.): CHIRA 2025, CCIS 2836, pp. 210–230, 2026.
https://doi.org/10.1007/978-3-032-16454-4_12

Serious games that entertain while focusing on a specific goal [8] offer a promising alternative. A literature review of several game-based interventions indicated that, when designed using a mix of user-centered design (UCD) approach, user experience (UX) principles and game elements, the serious games can facilitate awareness while encouraging reflection, discussion, and informed action [9]. By combining interactive elements, playful and experiential learning [9], they allow players to explore real-world issues through simulated environments, potentially making complex climate topics more understandable and relevant.

This paper presents a conceptual design framework and recommendations for creating effective serious games for climate change engagement, exploring their potential through the design and evaluation of the *EcoLand* prototype game. The design incorporates game design techniques, UCD principles, and UX design to ensure both engagement and educational value. To guide this investigation, this study addresses the following two research questions:

- RQ1: What recommendations for user-centered design of serious games for climate change engagement can be derived from the literature and best game design examples?
- RQ2: When applying these recommendations in game design, what user-centered process is followed, and what are the results in terms of user engagement?

This study provides recommendations for a conceptual framework for serious game design focused on climate change engagement to answer RQ1. It further assesses the feasibility and effectiveness of these recommendations (RQ2) in game design, demonstrating that a UCD approach, grounded in theory and empirical research, can create effective interactive tools for climate communication, providing insights for designers, educators, and researchers.

2 Research Methodology

This study employs a theoretical analysis, game reviews, and design science research (DSR) to answer the RQs. Three primary outcomes result: literature and game review analysis and findings, a conceptual framework (answering RQ1), and a serious game prototype creation and evaluation (answering RQ2). The DSR methodology [10, 11], a problem-solving approach in five stages, is suitable when the problem is complex and the solution is an innovative artifact whose development is iterative and generates knowledge [10]. DSR methodology provides a structured yet flexible model to iteratively design, test, and refine the solution, in this case, the serious game design. Table 1 summarizes the application of the DSR methodology [11] in this study.

The study contributes both to the knowledge base of HCI through developing a design framework and recommendations as well as to the empirical HCI through developing a design process, a serious game prototype, as well as analyzing user tasks, questionnaires and empirical findings related to evaluating the prototype. Table 2 highlights the research relevance, rigor and contributions according to the DSR framework [10].

The literature review builds the theoretical foundation of the study by examining key concepts such as climate change communication and engagement, game-based learning, user experience and interaction design, and games, serious games, and gamification

Table 1. DSR methodology used in this study following the Peffers et al. [11] model.

DSR Stage	Application in Research
Problem Identification	Recognizing climate change communication and engagement as a critical issue requiring innovative solutions
Objective Definition	Designing a serious game to raise awareness and promote sustainable engagement
Design and Development	Creating the *EcoLand* prototype using the conceptual framework and a user-centered design approach
Evaluation	Conducting user testing to assess usability, engagement, and educational impact
Communication	Sharing findings and refining the game based on the feedback received to improve learning outcomes and engagement

Table 2. Mapping the research components on Hevner et al. [10] research framework.

Framework	Rigor and Relevance	Research Contributions
Environment	*Communicate climate change* to people and organizations using interactive, digital media	People: Target users in age group 16+. Organizations: Society, University, Schools, Media. Technology: Serious games, UX design, Figma
Knowledge base	*Conduct literature review* on related concepts (climate change communication, climate change engagement, gamification, game design, and user-centered design) *Conduct game reviews* to synthesize best practices *Analyze and apply* relevant theories, models and frameworks of communication and design *Use established methodologies in evaluation*: usability and user experience evaluation methods	Literature synthesis, Empirical game review, Design recommendations, Conceptual framework on serious game design, Design process model, User evaluation tasks, scenarios, questionnaires
HCI & UX Research	*Build and evaluate a serious game for climate change engagement*	Develop *EcoLand* game prototypes, User testing, and Questionnaires, Empirical findings

design techniques and elements. Game reviews focused on available games addressing climate change or environment topics. Findings from the literature and game reviews were synthesized into a conceptual framework that offers actionable recommendations for designing serious games for climate change engagement. The proposed conceptual design framework was then used to develop the serious game prototype *EcoLand*.

3 Background

In this section, we summarize key concepts, theories and findings from the literature review that constitute the knowledge base of the study.

3.1 Climate Change Education, Communication and Engagement

Environmental education is a vital tool for promoting sustainable behavior and climate action. However, climate education faces challenges such as scientific complexity, public misconception, misinformation, and lack of engagement [12]. Moreover, traditional fact-based teaching often fails to inspire action. Hence, informal education, through communities, media, and social networks, can inform adults about climate issues, fostering involvement and showing that they can make a meaningful impact [13, 14].

Effective communication should be two-way, interactive, and emotionally resonant, enabling citizens to connect with the issue and participate in solutions [15]. Climate change communication should be interdisciplinary, incorporating scientific, social, political, and economic perceptions [16]. It should use local, visual, and interactive methods that promote critical thinking and reflection on alternative lifestyles. Solutions should integrate awareness, knowledge, skills, values, and participation opportunities for meaningful communication [17].

Climate change engagement is a multidimensional concept incorporating cognitive, affective, and behavioral responses at individual and collective levels; individuals and groups understand and think critically about the climate issues and environment, they feel concerned about them or have emotional connections to climate and environment, and they act or are motivated to act towards mitigating or adapting to climate change [7, 18]. Information communication technology (ICT) and digital media can simplify access to complex issues through visualization, simulation, and interactivity, encourage dialogue, and support climate action through a four-stage engagement process comprising communication, education, empowerment, and deliberation [15].

3.2 Serious Games, Game-Based Learning, and Gamification

Serious games can emotionally and cognitively engage players, supporting behavior change through playful learning, social interaction, and feedback mechanisms [15, 19]. Serious game design relies on game-based learning (GBL) that appeals to users through play, motivational elements and psychological theories [20]. Serious games are intentionally designed to achieve primary goals such as education, competence enhancement, or learning a new skill [8, 21] along with playful experiences. Serious games are thus useful in communicating and enhancing the understanding of complex issues like climate change. By simulating real-world scenarios, these games help players to emotionally connect with problems and explore sustainable solutions [22]. These games simplify the complexities of climate change ramifications, making them more visible, tangible, and relatable. Gamification is a process or solution that incorporates the elements of a game such as mechanics and motivational affordances [23, 24] to increase engagement and boost behavioral change or motivation. Features such as leaderboards, rewards, and collaborative goals foster social connections and pressure, form habits, and enhance emotional engagement, encouraging sustainable behaviors [25, 26].

There are several game design frameworks and more specific serious game and gamification design frameworks and guidelines in the literature (see for reviews, [9, 27–29]). Each of these available frameworks focuses on different issues such as evaluation aspects, the whole design process, or they are based on different research materials such as industry practices [30], empirical research findings [9], and thus they are valuable but have specific applicability.

3.3 User-Centered Design and Interaction Design

The UCD approach aims to enhance usability in systems by addressing user needs, resulting in improved accessibility, satisfaction, and effectiveness. Utilizing UCD principles, such as user involvement, iterative development, simple design, prototyping, contextual evaluation, and multidisciplinary collaboration in serious game development, ensures that the game remains relevant, engaging, and aligned with user expectations [31]. Interaction design is a broader approach that focuses on creating engaging user experiences, interfaces, and human-computer dialogues by improving usability and emotional satisfaction [32]. When applied to game design, it employs principles such as game flow, motivation, and user feedback to ensure the users remain engaged and experience high levels of satisfaction while interacting with the game. Involving users in game design includes workshops [33] but also online sessions or surveys as well as observing or researching existing systems [34] for eliciting initial requirements, design solutions, as well as user evaluations. Combining interaction design, UCD, and serious game design will result in immersive and effective learning experiences [9].

3.4 Empirical Game Review

To answer RQ1, alongside the literature review summarized above, we also reviewed ten environmental games selected systematically based on a protocol defined for this purpose. The games had to be freely available in digital format, designed explicitly to address climate change or environmental sustainability (e.g., global warming, recycling, energy conservation, sustainable practices), provide educational content alongside entertainment, and be available in English language.

The review followed an environmental game design framework [35], which includes four categories of analysis and design: Player actions, Learning and knowledge dissemination, Motivation and engagement, and Social interaction. Each game was evaluated against these four categories and corresponding criteria, such as fun and meaningfulness for Motivation and engagement, achievable and challenging for Player actions, experiential learning and simulation for Learning and knowledge dissemination, and presence of social elements for Social influence category.

The games reviewed provided ideas for the practical implementation of the game elements according to [35]. For example, successful games incorporated decision-making simulations, experiential learning, and interactive quizzes to enhance the understanding of climate change issues. They used clear feedback mechanisms and rewards to motivate continued engagement. Among the flaws observed, some games lack consistent or comprehensive narratives and engaging gameplay, which reduces long-term engagement and educational impact.

Similarly, existing literature reviews on similar games highlighted limitations such as lack of long-term evaluations of these games and how specific gameplay mechanics, such as narrative approach, multiplayer features, feedback, and rewards, impact the learning outcomes [9, 36]. Factors like credibility, achievability, meaningfulness, and social aspects were not thoroughly mapped to impact on users [9].

The game review also indicated that design flaws in terms of lacking in narrative or social features, integrating empathy, and challenging and engaging gameplay can reduce user engagement. Hence, investigating ways to integrate more collaborative features together with optimizing UX is essential for achieving better engagement.

4 Design Recommendations and Conceptual Framework for Climate Change Engagement Serious Games

Based on the literature and game reviews, a comprehensive list of ten recommendations (R1–R10) for the development of climate change serious games is presented. These form the basis of the proposed conceptual framework for serious game design, shown in Table 3, which consists of four components: *Context of use, Gameful and learning experiences, Engagement goals, and Game design principles.*

R1. **Narrative and Engagement:** Create engaging, story-driven scenarios that immerse players in climate decision-making. Use narratives to illustrate the impact of actions, promote empathy through role-playing, and add timed challenges to instill urgency for climate action.

R2. **Scientific Accuracy and Relevance to Real-World Facts:** Integrate real-world climate data and collaborate with scientists for credibility. Using updated local scenarios enhances learning and addresses misconceptions through gameplay.

R3. **Social Interaction and Community Engagement:** Use collaborative or competitive modes for peer learning and engagement. Incorporate forums, group challenges, and community dialogues to promote collaboration. Involve players in real-world climate research through activities like data collection and analysis.

R4. **Learning and Behavioral Change:** Incorporate features like goals, challenges, rewards, and simulations to promote experiential learning and encourage sustainable behaviors. Include adjustable difficulty levels for varied engagement and provide explanations on the real-world consequences of decisions made in the game.

R5. **Long-Term Engagement and Evolution:** Incorporate game elements like leaderboards and ongoing challenges to engage players. Add minigames for variety and regularly update climate change content with the latest science. Reward long-term participation to encourage learning and behavior change.

R6. **User-Centered Design:** Design intuitive navigation and accessible visuals for a better user experience. Offer gameplay customization with options for avatars, narrators, and locations. Ensure multilingual support and culturally sensitive content to engage a diverse audience with varying interests and needs.

R7. **Iterative Design and Feedback:** Continuously assess and refine the game based on feedback from users, experts, and stakeholders. Collaborate with various stakeholders, including educators, scientists, and psychologists, for a balanced design.

R8. **Ethical Design:** Avoid misinformation through oversimplifying or overcomplicating the situations. Fairly represent climate science and communities.

R9. **Platforms and Technologies:** Develop mobile-friendly to maximize accessibility. Use simulations to allow exploration of long-term impacts.

R10. **Integration with Existing Systems or Programs:** Develop curriculum-aligned educational games and partner with environmental organizations to boost credibility and impact. Use tools to track learning outcomes and engagement for evaluation.

Table 3. Conceptual framework for climate engagement serious game design.

Gameful and learning experience	Engagement goals	Game design principles	Context of use
Narrative and engagement (R1) Scientific accuracy and relevance to real-world facts (R2) Social interaction and community engagement (R3)	Learning and behavioral change (R4) Long-term engagement and evolution (R5)	User-centered design (R6) Iterative design and feedback (R7) Ethical design (R8)	Platforms and technologies (R9) Integration with existing systems or programs (R10)

5 *EcoLand* Game Design

To answer RQ2, a serious game prototype was designed by incorporating the conceptual framework and recommendations derived from literature and game reviews. Designed as a mobile game, *EcoLand* aims to engage players with climate change through a playful, emotional experience that educates, simulates real-world scenarios and encourages sustainable actions (R1–R5).

The design followed a UCD approach and process (R6–R10) shown in Fig. 1, that was also created for this study based on existing frameworks, models, and concepts related to software development and game design [34, 37–44]. In short, the game design life cycle (GDLC) process model covers all the stages of developing a serious game while promoting iterative development and improvement by integrating feedback from users, stakeholders, and testers at every stage. It addresses the requirements (R1-R10) in the conceptual framework (Table 3) by defining the context, ideating content and mechanics, and enhancing emotional, cognitive, and behavioral engagement with climate change over time.

The core concept of *EcoLand* is to promote individual engagement with climate change through a structured game flow based on the four-stage engagement model [15]: *communication, education through experiential learning, empowerment,* and *deliberation or agency.* The game story is placed in the fictional state of Climore, where players act as government advisors working to transform the area into a sustainable society, navigating the balance of ecological, financial, and social goals through interactions and decision-making. The following section details the game flows, target audience, and how recommendations were translated into game features.

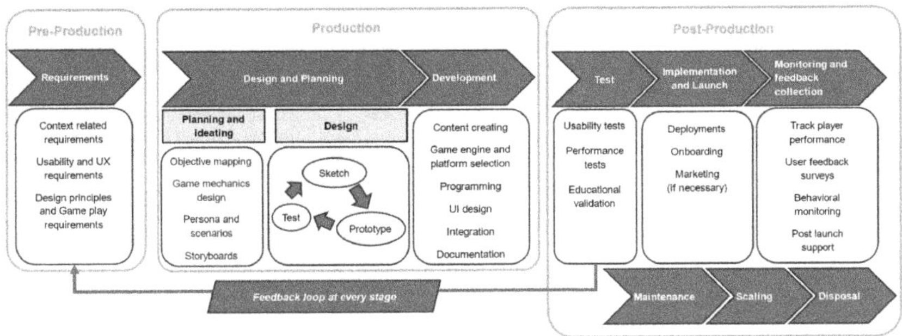

Fig. 1. Game design life cycle (GDLC) for serious games created and applied in this study.

5.1 Game Flows and Game Loops

Game flow is key to player engagement and enjoyment in video games. It refers to a state of immersion where players are fully absorbed in gameplay. Elements like an immersive storyline, clear goals, rewards, and emotional connection to characters maintain the gameplay [45]. *EcoLand* features three main game flows: the **introduction flow** (Fig. 2) for onboarding, story narration and tutorials; the **core game flow** (Fig. 3) for resource management and challenges; and the **endgame flow** (Fig. 4), which summarizes player's choices and concludes the narrative with a cinematic ending.

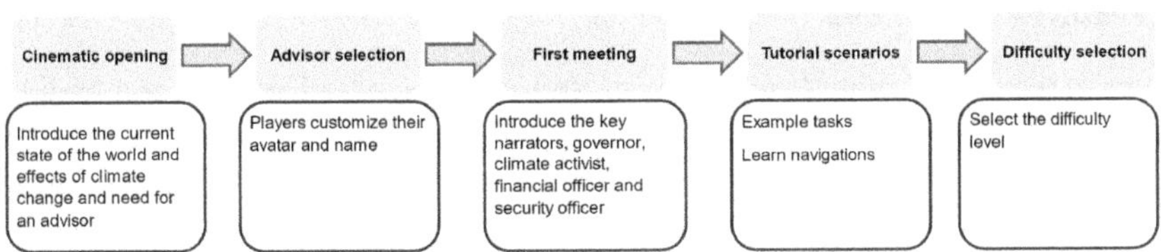

Fig. 2. The introduction game flow (Tutorial and setup).

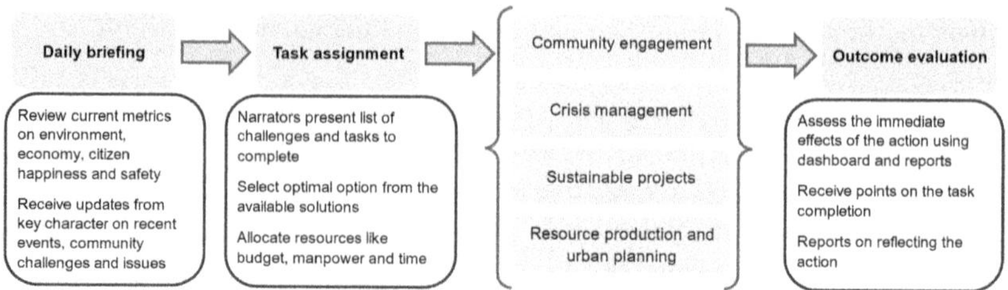

Fig. 3. The core game flow (Decision-making and management).

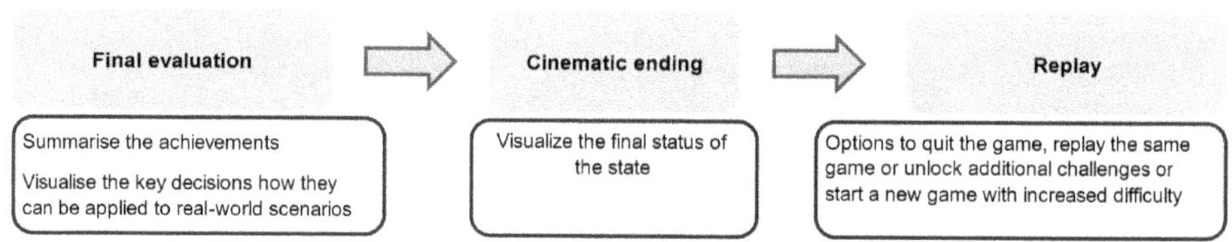

Fig. 4. The endgame flow (Victory or failure).

To maintain the engagement and game flow, EcoLand uses a layered game loop structure [46] that ensures both short-term and long-term commitment. The primary loop includes daily tasks such as decision making, resource allocation, and project execution. The secondary loop introduces dynamic challenges like minigames and disaster events to diversify the gameplay. The tertiary loop supports long-term engagement through fictional media updates, policy reflections, and social sharing features.

5.2 Target Audience

The game targets users aged 16 and above, regardless of their climate change knowledge. Creating user personas representing diverse attitudes and motivations (e.g., high school visionary, gamer, traditionalist, reluctant professional, climate activist) guided the design and understanding of the user interactions [34]. A user scenario and a use case were created to enhance the understanding of user interaction with the game.

5.3 Features of *EcoLand*

Features of the game (Table 4) were chosen and designed based on the recommendations proposed in Sect. 4 and alignment with the goals of the game and user needs as defined by applying the design process in Fig. 1. Key elements like role-playing with important characters, real-world simulations, customizable difficulty levels, and motivational UX elements (rewards and feedback) are employed to encourage meaningful engagement. In *EcoLand*, players face challenges that require balancing environmental, economic, social, and security factors in the state. To enhance engagement, the game includes a 'Minigame Bar' for time-limited minigames that reward players with *eco-points* for use in the main game. Players can also view real-world news or climate research before each minigame, connecting gameplay with current events. Examples include garbage sorting, ocean cleanup, and climate change quizzes.

Table 4. Features used in *EcoLand* according to the proposed list of recommendations.

Recommendation	Features Used in *EcoLand*
1. Narrative and engagement	Starts with a narrative on the climate crisis and the current situation of the state Role-playing with supporting characters like the governor and the environmentalist Include time-based challenges and minigames
2. Scientific accuracy and relevance to real-world facts	Develop with generally correct real climate data and real news Game challenges simulate urban planning, sustainable actions, and real-world scenarios where users can learn by experimenting Challenges present choices that help correct the misassumptions
3. Social interaction and community engagement	Players can add friends, chat, support each other, and share achievements on social media The game includes chat about news, research, and collaborative features Citizen science features are not included in this prototype
4. Learning and behavioral change	Includes motivational features like rewards, reminders, suggestions, praise, trustworthiness, credibility, social support Leveling up increases difficulty and complexity Players visually experience the consequences of their decisions
5. Long-term engagement and evolution	Includes minigames, evolving tasks, and narratives to feel connected Timely news and research data in minigames Rewards like Eco-points, daily login rewards, and achievements to encourage engagement
6. User-centered design	Simple UI focused on enhanced user experience Players can select the difficulty level Accessibility is not addressed fully in the prototype. Development can include multilingual access and future challenges, and news with culturally relevant content

(continued)

Table 4. (continued)

Recommendation	Features Used in *EcoLand*
7. Iterative design and feedback	User evaluation to assess effectiveness and recommendations for future refinement Prototype only includes scientific, environmental, and educational general information. Future development should be done with multi multi-disciplinary team
8. Ethical design	Real-world based, avoids oversimplification
9. Platforms and technologies	Designed as a mobile game Simulates long-term impacts of human actions and decisions through challenges
10. Integration with existing systems or programs	Not included in this prototype, but to be taken into account in the next iteration. The current design was using a scenario and use case where a high school student starts playing the game to learn more about the climate and the environmental behavior

5.4 Design Prototypes

During the initial design stage, paper prototypes were created, followed by digital prototypes (Fig. 5) in Figma (www.figma.com). This iterative process refined the user interface, game flow, and mechanics without fully implementing the software. A limited number of user flows were designed, using images from www.freepik.com under the Free License and Canva Dream Lab (www.canva.com/dream-lab) images under Canva's Content License Agreement.

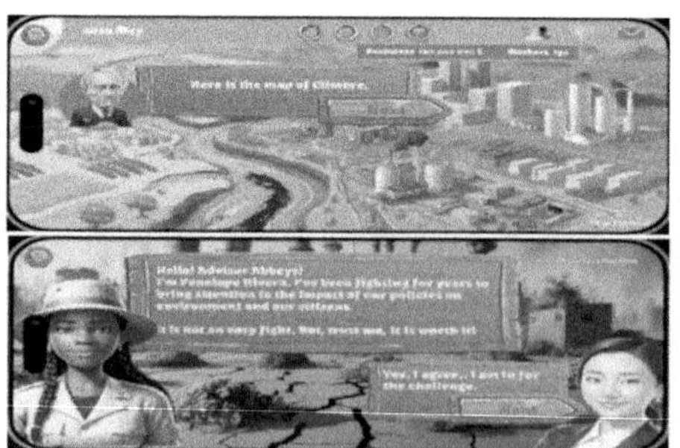
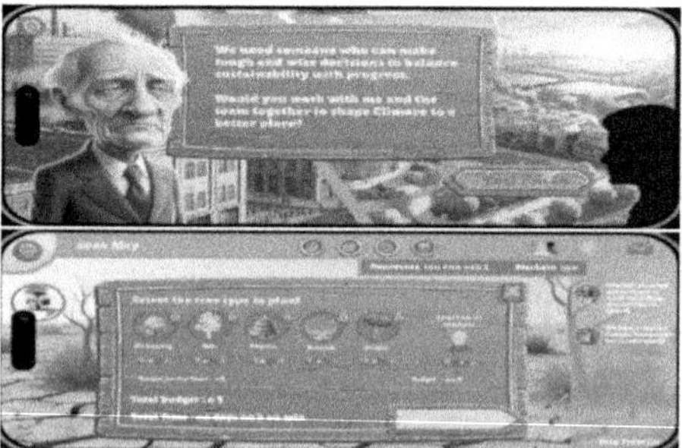

Fig. 5. Some dialogs in EcoLand.

6   User Evaluation and Analysis

To further answer RQ2, a user evaluation of *EcoLand* was conducted online to assess user engagement and its effectiveness in promoting climate change awareness. The focus was to identify usability issues, design flaws, and enhance user experience through feedback [47, 48]. The evaluation included quantitative analyses and qualitative feedback on clarity, functionality, and conceptual effectiveness of the design (player interest, expectations, engagement) rather than gameplay efficiency.

6.1   Test Structure

The test used an online questionnaire divided into three parts. First, a **pre-test** collected demographic data, including age and familiarity with environmental games. Next, participants completed six tasks, each followed by an **in-test questionnaire**. Finally, a **post-test** gathered feedback on overall experience, engagement, usability, and learning.

6.2   Test Participants

An online test invitation was sent to around 100 people aged 18 and older, with 29 responding. Most participants were aged 25–34 (19), followed by 35–44 (7) and 18–24 (3). The gender distribution was 19 females and 10 males, with participants showing varying familiarity with games promoting environmental awareness (see Fig. 6).

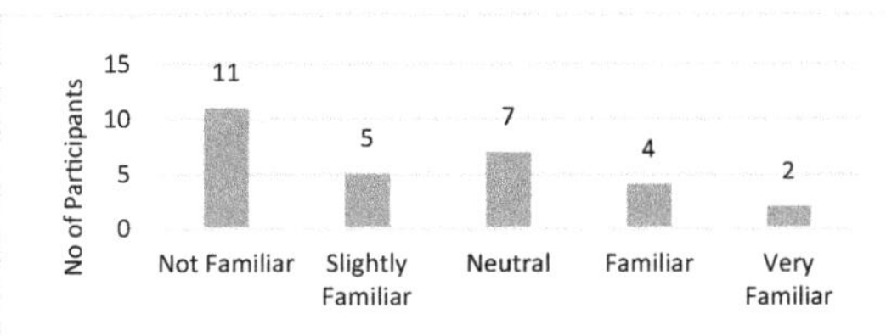

Fig. 6. Participants' familiarity with environmental or climate change awareness games.

6.3   Quantitative Analysis

The quantitative analysis of the evaluation test data focused on three areas:

- Usability assessment and mapping the answers to the system usability scale (SUS).
- User experience of the game.
- Effectiveness and engagement of the game prototype.

Usability Assessment. SUS is a tool that assesses system usability with ten questions focused on user satisfaction and various usability aspects like effectiveness and ease of learning measured on a 5-point Likert scale (1 Strongly Disagree - 5 Strongly Agree) [49]. In this study, questions were mainly based on [22] and adapted to benchmark the game usability. We mapped the questions and the corresponding scales to the SUS scale and obtained an overall estimation of SUS (see Table 5 including the mean and standard deviation SD statistics for the transformed scales).

Table 5. Mapping of user test questions to SUS standard questions [49].

SUS standard question, Likert scale 1–5	Score Type	Mean	SD
1. I think that I would like to use this system frequently	Direct	4.27	0.93
2. I found the system unnecessarily complex	*Reverse*	1.51	0.61
3. I thought the system was easy to use	Direct	4.05	0.91
4. I think that I would need technical support to use this system	*Reverse*	1.18	1.22
5. I found the functions in this system well-integrated	Direct	3.82	1.00
6. I thought there was too much inconsistency in the system	*Reverse*	1.25	1.38
7. I would imagine that most people would learn to use this system very quickly	Direct	4.39	0.67
8. I found the system cumbersome to use	*Reverse*	1.45	0.56
9. I felt very confident using the system	Direct	4.32	0.93
10. I needed to learn a lot before I could use the system	*Reverse*	1.30	0.93

SUS scores for each participant's responses were then calculated using the SUS score calculator [50], obtaining scores in the range 1–100 and categorized into grades A - F (where A signifies the best imaginable usability, and F poor usability). Most participants (59%) rated usability as Grade A+, and 10% as Grade A, indicating the best imaginable usability. Across the sample, the average overall SUS score of 83 highlights exceptional usability (Grade A or best imaginable). Six participants (20%) rated the overall usability as Grade C (good) with scores between 65 and 72.5. Two users indicated poor (42.5) or okay (52.5) usability, finding issues with loaded designs, too small font size, too much text, as well as having problems with profile creation.

User Experience. In this analysis, UX of the game prototype was evaluated based on ten UX features on a scale 1(low UX) -7 (high UX), mapped to six categories: **attractiveness, efficiency, perspicuity, dependability, stimulation,** and **novelty** [51]. Table 6 presents the UX evaluation categories and features, and the evaluation results.

Table 6. UX categories and features evaluated, scale 1 low, 7 high.

UX Category	Description	UX features in the test	Mean	SD
Attractiveness	The overall impression of the product in terms of appeal and enjoyability	Unattractive/Attractive	6.14	0.97
Perspicuity	Easy to learn and understand the system without unnecessary effort	Hard/Easy to learn	6.21	0.89
Efficiency	Product is engaging, exciting and enjoyable to use, enhancing usability	Impractical/Practical	6.28	0.98

(continued)

Table 6. (*continued*)

UX Category	Description	UX features in the test	Mean	SD
Dependability	Users feel confident and predict the system's behavior	Not friendly/User friendly	6.24	1.01
Stimulation	Product is exciting and interesting to use, enhancing motivation	Not interesting/Interesting Demotivating/Motivating Not engaging/Engaging	6.09	1.07
Novelty	Creativity and innovative nature of a system	Useless/Useful Dull/Creative Inferior/Valuable	6.31	0.99

User responses indicate that all six UX categories for the *EcoLand* prototype, attractiveness, efficiency, perspicuity, dependability, stimulation, and novelty, averaged above 6 out of 7, reflecting a strong and consistent UX with low standard deviations.

Effectiveness of Gamification Features. Descriptive statistics were analyzed to assess the effectiveness of gamification features, including narrative, challenge intuitiveness, enjoyment of minigames, inclusion of news articles, and social media sharing (Table 7). Results show relatively high average scores across the sample ranging from 3.45 to 4.59 out of 5, with consistent user feedback (relatively low standard deviation).

Table 7. Statistical summary on the effectiveness of the gamification features (1 low, 5 high).

Feature	Mean	SD
Engagement in the **narrative** introduction	4.14	1.04
Intuitiveness of **challenges**	3.97	0.999
Enjoyability in the **minigame** concept	4.59	0.89
Engagement in the **minigame** concept	4.45	0.97
Interest in **incorporating news and research articles** in the game	3.45	1.40
Opinion on including a feature to **share progress** on social media	4.21	0.92

Climate Change Engagement. The user test evaluated the **player preferences** for the type of engagement (informative, educative, empowering, and agentic [15]) on a 4-point scale (with 1 being the most preferred). The analysis indicated a preference for fact-based, informative (mean rank 1.97) and interactive, educative approach (2.41) in a climate-related game, while empowerment (3.03) and agency (2.59) were valued as secondary preferences among participants.

The evaluation asked also whether participants were interested in the game and whether they believed the game was effective in communicating about climate change.

Interest in Playing the Full Version of the Game. All participants expressed interest in the game, with 69% saying yes and 31% maybe.

Effectiveness of the Game in Educating Climate Change. All participants agreed that the game effectively communicates climate change and sustainability, highlighting its success in delivering educational content in an engaging manner.

6.4 Qualitative Analysis

The qualitative data from the user test provided further insights into the game concept. A thematic analysis was conducted where five codes were identified from 29 responses, yielding 55 coded phrases which were categorized into three main themes, presented with their percentages in Table 8. The key themes from the analysis are:

1. **Effective serious game design for climate change communication and engagement.** It highlights the game's role in enhancing climate change education and promoting real-world impact and behavioral change.
2. **User engagement in gameplay.** It indicates that the game is engaging and interactive, employing gamified features and storytelling.
3. **UCD principles for climate change games.** It emphasizes the importance of user-friendly design elements, focusing on simplicity and accessibility.

Table 8. Thematic analysis of the participant feedback.

Codes	Themes	Coverage
Education and Awareness	Effective Serious Game Design for Climate Change Communication	56%
Real-world Impact and Behavioral Change		
Engagement and Interactivity	User Engagement in Gameplay and Learning	35%
Gamification and Storytelling		
Simplicity and Accessibility	UCD Principles for Climate Change Games	9%
	Total	100%

Feedback from the participants shows that the game prototype effectively engages users and communicates climate change while utilizing UCD principles in game design. Participants (Ps) noted that it provides valuable insights into complex climate topics. One participant stated, *"It will educate people what measures to take in reducing climate effects, what kind of issues will cause climate issues, etc."* (P15), emphasizing the game's potential to inform about practical solutions.

The game offers an engaging way to learn about climate change, simplifying complex topics, as one participant noted: *"This game provides an interactive and engaging way to learn about climate change and sustainability, making complex topics easier to understand and apply in real life"* (P19). Another added, *"I think while playing the game and accomplishing given challenges, users are collecting knowledge and improving their awareness of protecting the environment and sustainability"* (P21).

Related to the second theme, participants found gameful approach to learning more engaging than traditional methods. *"Because it is enjoyable than listening or reading about climate change news or articles. It is interactive, and players can see the effect of their actions immediately"* (P6). *"I believe it's very effective to use gamification to educate people on climate change and sustainability. Because it's difficult to take attention of people for these kinds of topics using traditional methods."* (P7).

Additionally, the engagement is also linked with curiosity and motivation for continued play. One participant reported, *"Because it is engaging and makes users curious about the next steps. So it will eventually teach about climate change and sustainability"* (P25). The ability of the game to maintain interest and motivation to learn is critical to influence behavior and to raise awareness.

Participants valued the storytelling and narrative-driven approach. *"The game has included storytelling related to climate change and sustainability. It is not like reading a report. So users can play the minigames while getting an understanding of it. I think this is an interactive way to get user attention to the main topic"* (P28). *"It teaches you the importance of climate change, and also through the games and the advice by NPCs, we learn different ways to tackle existing issues and also about sustainability"* (P29). *"The narratives give a good understanding of how the problem affects each individual"* (P6). This feedback highlights that user engagement in gameplay directly correlates with interest in climate change and learning, fostering both curiosity and action.

The third theme emphasizes the importance of UCD principles in climate change games, focusing on simplicity, accessibility, and user-friendly features. While direct quotes were not elaborated in this direction, the interaction design and user-centeredness aspects were integrated in their feedback by using words such as "good understanding", "immediate feedback", "interactive", "easier to understand". The positive feedback included also suggestions that design elements like experiential learning, intuitive design, and clear navigation made the game engaging and easy to use, enhancing its effectiveness as an educational tool.

Recommendations for Changes to the Prototype. Participants suggested improving *EcoLand's* user experience by simplifying text, standardizing elements, enhancing button responsiveness, and adding interactivity. Future updates should include animated storytelling, voiceovers, consistent graphics, larger buttons, and reward animations. These insights highlight the importance of engaging storytelling and cohesive design in serious games, as well as the benefits of early user involvement and iterative refinement for effective climate change communication tools.

7 Discussion and Conclusions

We adopted a DSR research methodology to design a climate change engagement serious game. To address RQ1, we conducted a literature review and game analysis to create recommendations and a framework for climate engagement game design, contributing to HCI and UX knowledge. For RQ2, we applied this framework in developing a structured, staged process model for UCD of the serious game. This process, applied in the *EcoLand* prototype, aimed at improving climate change communication and making environmental education engaging. The development process followed iterative UCD practices, including prototyping, user involvement and structured evaluation. User testing involved a sample of participants aged 18 and above and combined both quantitative and qualitative data collection. Employing DSR methodology, incorporating literature review, game analysis, prototype development, and user evaluation, the study makes both theoretical and empirical contributions to HCI and UX research.

7.1 Implications for Game Design

The structured design process and conceptual framework enabled focusing on important aspects in the design, namely *gameful and learning experiences, engagement goals, user-centeredness, and context of use.* The structured evaluation highlighted that elements such as minigames, feedback, rewards, and level progression supported *engagement* and *learning*, while narrative-driven and scenario-based learning made climate issues *relatable* and *actionable.*

Playability was embedded in the design of the game story, game play, mechanics and usability [52] through careful design of the game flow and game loops by following the proposed design recommendations regarding narrative and engagement, social interactions, learning, real-world relevance and scientific accuracy, long-term engagement, ethical design, etc. However, formal evaluation of playability through heuristics or user testing of relevant criteria [53, 54] remains for future work.

Emotion-oriented experiences [55] lead to sustained gameful engagement, while a staged emotional, cognitive and social engagement [15] ensures a more effective and longer-term engagement with the topic. We believe that these elements can or should be integrated through *designing gameful and learning experiences* and *engagement goals.* A design process should also incorporate attention to the *context of use* as well as *user-centered design principles, including iterations with users and ethical design,* as shown in the conceptual framework.

The GDLC model used in this study aligns with structured, feedback-driven cycles for serious game development as described by [40]. It provides a tailored approach for climate education games. Positive feedback and evaluation results affirm the model's effectiveness and practical value in designing engaging climate games.

The positive empirical results confirm that serious games can successfully bridge the gap between awareness and action when designed with engagement and learning goals in mind and following UCD principles and process. The *EcoLand* prototype incorporated narrative-driven gameplay, reward systems, and simulations which are the elements found to be effective in prior works [9]. In *EcoLand*, scenario-based learning helps players understand the impact of their decisions, fostering behavioral change.

Three key themes emerged from the feedback: linking game elements to real-world behaviors, emphasizing interactive storytelling for engagement, and prioritizing simplicity and accessibility through user-centered design. These insights highlight the importance of delivering credible content in an engaging manner and the value of user involvement in the design process.

7.2 Limitations

EcoLand prototype is still in early development and needs refinement for broader use. While the game's content is generally accurate, it relies on publicly available data and would benefit from expert collaboration in climate science and economics. The convenience sample primarily included users aged 18–44, limiting the findings' generalizability to other age groups and demographics. The study also did not assess the long-term effectiveness of the game in maintaining user engagement, nor did it separately assess playability, providing directions for future research.

7.3 Conclusions and Future Work

This study demonstrates the potential of serious games as effective tools for climate change communication. Through the design and evaluation of the *EcoLand* prototype, the research highlights how integrating UCD and game design principles can significantly enhance user engagement, awareness, and motivation for climate action. Positive evaluation results validate the conceptual design framework and the structured GDLC model, confirming their effectiveness and relevance for designing engaging and educational games in this context.

The study contributes with a structured GDLC and ten design recommendations grouped into a conceptual design framework, validated by the positive user reception of *EcoLand* prototype. These tools offer valuable guidance for future developers and researchers aiming to address environmental issues through interactive media.

For future, we aim to develop the game by investigating further and designing the links between the design elements in the conceptual framework and actual gameplay and user experiences, including designing for a specific use context such as high school learners and citizen science. Furthermore, we are interested to examine and understand what triggers players interest in higher level engagement such as empowerment and agency and how playability affects engagement with climate change. Collaboration with climate and financial experts is essential to ensure factual accuracy and credibility. Additionally, longitudinal studies should evaluate the lasting impact of these games on user behavior and climate literacy.

Disclosure of Interests. The authors have no competing interests to declare that are relevant to the content of this article.

References

1. Stevenson, R.B., Nicholls, J., Whitehouse, H.: What is climate change education? Curriculum Perspect. **37**(1), 67–71 (2017)
2. Hoekstra, A.G., Noordzij, K., De Koster, W., Van Der Waal, J.: The educational divide in climate change attitudes: understanding the role of scientific knowledge and subjective social status. Glob. Environ. Chang. **86**, 102851 (2024)
3. Gregersen, T., Doran, R., Storelv, S.: Self-reported reasons for (not) being worried about climate change. Curr. Res. Ecol. Soc. Psychol. **5**, 100154 (2023)
4. Schroth, O., Angel, J., Sheppard, S., Dulic, A.: Visual climate change communication: from iconography to locally framed 3D visualization. Environ. Commun. **8**(4), 413–432 (2014)

5. Wilson, K.M.: Communicating climate change through the media. Environ. Risks Media 201–217 (2000)
6. Rajanen, D., Rajanen, M.: Climate change gamification: a literature review. In: Proceedings of the Gamifin 2019 Conference, pp. 253–264 (2019)
7. Moser, S.C., Dilling, L.: Communicating climate change: closing the science-action gap. In: The Oxford Handbook of Climate Change and Society, pp. 161–174 (2011)
8. Dörner, R., Göbel, S., Effelsberg, W., Wiemeyer, J.: Serious Games: Foundations, Concepts and Practice. Springer, Cham (2016)
9. Galeote, D.F., Rajanen, M., Rajanen, D., Legaki, N., Langley, D.J., Hamari, J.: Gamification for climate change engagement: a user-centered design agenda. In: Proceedings of the 26th International Academic Mindtrek Conference (Mindtrek 2023), pp. 45–56 (2023)
10. Hevner, A.R., March, S.T., Park, J., Ram, S.: Design science in information systems research. MIS Q. 28(1), 75–105 (2004). https://doi.org/10.2307/25148625
11. Peffers, K., Tuunanen, T., Rothenberger, M.A., Chatterjee, S.: A design science research methodology for information systems research. J. Manag. Inf. Syst. 24(3), 45–77 (2007)
12. Monroe, M.C., Plate, R.R., Oxarart, A., Bowers, A., Chaves, W.A.: Identifying effective climate change education strategies: a systematic review of the research. Environ. Educ. Res. 25(6), 791–812 (2017). https://doi.org/10.1080/13504622.2017.1360842
13. Nelson, S., Ira, G., Merenlender, A.M.: Adult climate change education advances learning, self-efficacy, and agency for community-scale stewardship. Sustainability 14(3), 1804 (2022)
14. Wibeck, V.: Enhancing learning, communication and public engagement about climate change – some lessons from recent literature. Environ. Educ. Res. 20(3), 387–411 (2013)
15. Rajanen, D.: Interactive and participatory media for public engagement with climate change: a systematic literature review and an integrative model. INTERACT No. 5, University of Oulu, Finland (2021)
16. Filho, W.L., Mannke, F., Manolas, E., Amin, A.Q.A.: The effectiveness of climate change communication and information dissemination via the internet: experiences from the online climate conference series. Int. J. Glob. Warm. 8(1), 70 (2015)
17. Peralta, T.O., Lobo, M.D.O., Pérez, J.G.: Analysis of online climate change games: exploring opportunities. Rev. Electrón. Investig. Educ. 19(3), 101 (2017)
18. Lorenzoni, I., Nicholson-Cole, S., Whitmarsh, L.: Barriers perceived to engaging with climate change among the UK public and their policy implications. Glob. Environ. Chang. 17(3–4), 445–459 (2007)
19. Galeote, D.F., Hamari, J.: Game-based climate change engagement. Proc. ACM Hum.-Comput. Interact. 5(CHI PLAY), 1–21 (2021)
20. Boyle, E., Connolly, T.M., Hainey, T.: The role of psychology in understanding the impact of computer games. Entertain. Comput. 2(2), 69–74 (2011)
21. Landers, R.N.: Developing a theory of gamified learning: linking serious games and gamification of learning. Simul. Gaming 45(6), 752–768 (2014)
22. Galván-Pérez, L., Ouariachi, T., Pozo-Llorente, M., Gutiérrez-Pérez, J.: Outstanding videogames on water: a quality assessment review based on evidence of narrative, gameplay and educational criteria. Water 10(10), 1404 (2018). https://doi.org/10.3390/w10101404
23. Deterding, S., Dixon, D., Khaled, R., Nacke, L.: From game design elements to gamefulness: defining "gamification". In: Proceedings of the 15th International Academic MindTrek Conference: Envisioning Future Media Environments, pp. 9–15. (2011)
24. Huotari, K., Hamari, J.: Defining gamification: a service marketing perspective. In: Proceeding of the 16th International Academic MindTrek Conference, pp. 17–22 (2012)
25. Douglas, B.D., Brauer, M.: Gamification to prevent climate change: a review of games and apps for sustainability. Curr. Opin. Psychol. 42, 89–94 (2021)
26. White, K., Habib, R., Hardisty, D.J.: How to SHIFT consumer behaviors to be more sustainable: a literature review and guiding framework. J. Mark. 83(3), 22–49 (2019)

27. Mora, A., Riera, D., Gonzalez, C., Arnedo-Moreno, J.: A literature review of gamification design frameworks. In: 2015 7th International Conference on Games and Virtual Worlds for Serious Applications (VS-Games), pp. 1–8. IEEE (2015)
28. Klapztein, S., Guimarães Santos, A.C., Oliveira, W., Harviainen, J.T., Ribeiro de Oliveira, A., Hamari, J.: Game design concepts: a tertiary literature review. In: Companion Proceedings of the 2024 Annual Symposium on Computer-Human Interaction in Play, pp. 139–144 (2024)
29. Tondello, G.F., Kappen, D.L., Mekler, E.D., Ganaba, M., Nacke, L.E.: Heuristic evaluation for gameful design. In: Proceedings of the 2016 Annual Symposium on Computer-Human Interaction in Play Companion Extended Abstracts, pp. 315–323 (2016)
30. Nacke, L.E., Deterding, S.: The maturing of gamification research. Comput. Hum. Behav. **71**, 450–454 (2017)
31. Gulliksen, J., Göransson, B., Boivie, I., Blomkvist, S., Persson, J., Cajander, Å.: Key principles for user-centred systems design. Behav. Inf. Technol. **22**(6), 397–409 (2003)
32. Sharp, H., Preece, J., Rogers, Y.: Interaction Design: Beyond Human-Computer Interaction, 5th edn. Wilcy, Hoboken (2019)
33. Li, Y., Li, Y., Liang, J., Liang, H.-N.: Easy induction: a serious game using participatory design. In: da Silva, H.P., Cipresso, P. (eds.) CHIRA 2023. CCIS, vol. 1997, pp. 192–211. Springer, Cham (2023)
34. Benyon, D.: Designing Interactive Systems: A Comprehensive Guide to HCI, UX and Interaction Design, 4th edn. Pearson, Harlow (2010)
35. Ouariachi, T., Olvera-Lobo, M.D., Gutiérrez-Pérez, J., Maibach, E.: A framework for climate change engagement through video games. Environ. Educ. Res. **25**(5), 701–716 (2018)
36. Flood, S., Cradock-Henry, N.A., Blackett, P., Edwards, P.: Adaptive and interactive climate futures: systematic review of 'serious games' for engagement and decision-making. Environ. Res. Lett. **13**(6), 063005 (2018)
37. Sharma, M.K.: A study of SDLC to develop well engineered software. Int. J. Adv. Res. Comput. Sci. **8**(3), 520–523 (2017)
38. Ragunath, P., Velmourougan, S., Davachelvan, P., Kayalvizhi, S., Ravimohan, R.: Evolving a new model (SDLC Model-2010) for software development life cycle (SDLC). Int. J. Comput. Sci. Netw. Secur. **10**(1), 15–22 (2010)
39. Aydan, U., Yilmaz, M., O'Connor, R.V.: Towards a serious game to teach ISO/IEC 12207 Software Lifecycle Process: an interactive learning approach. In: Auer, M.E., et al. (eds.) CCIS, vol. 492, pp. 217–229. Springer, Cham (2015)
40. Fullerton, T.: Game Design Workshop. CRC Press (2004)
41. Bunt, L., Greeff, J., Taylor, E.: Enhancing serious game design: expert-reviewed, stakeholder-centered framework. JMIR Serious Games **12**, e48099 (2024)
42. Norman, D.: The Design of Everyday Things: Revised and Expanded Edition (2013)
43. Kalmpourtzis, G., Romero, M.: Constructive alignment of learning mechanics and game mechanics in serious game design in higher education. Int. J. Serious Games **7**(4), 75–88 (2020)
44. Alvarez, J., Djaouti, D.: An introduction to serious game definitions and concepts. In: Proceedings of the Serious Games & Simulation for Risks Management Workshop (2011)
45. Nah, F.F.H., Eschenbrenner, B., Zeng, Q., Telaprolu, V.R., Sepehr, S.: Flow in gaming: literature synthesis and framework development. Int. J. Inf. Syst. Manag. **1**(1/2), 83 (2014)
46. Clark, C., Greenberg, I., Ouellette, M.: A model for integrating human computing into commercial video games. In: 2018 IEEE 6th International Conference on Serious Games and Applications for Health (SeGAH), pp. 1–8 (2018)
47. Rubin, J., Chisnell, D.: Handbook of Usability Testing: How to Plan, Design, and Conduct Effective Tests, 2nd edn. Wiley, Hoboken (2008)

48. Yáñez-Gómez, R., Cascado-Caballero, D., Sevillano, J.: Academic methods for usability evaluation of serious games: a systematic review. Multimed. Tools Appl. **76**(4), 5755–5784 (2016)
49. Brooke, J.: SUS: a 'Quick and Dirty' usability scale. In: Jordan, P.W., Thomas, B., Weerdmeester, B.A., McClelland, I.L. (eds.) Usability Evaluation in Industry, pp. 207–212. CRC Press (1996)
50. Bellio, J.: System Usability Scale (SUS) Practical Guide for 2025. Articles on Everything UX: Research, Testing & Design (2024). https://blog.uxtweak.com/system-usability-scale/
51. Schrepp, M., Hinderks, A., Thomaschewski, J.: Design and evaluation of a short version of the User Experience Questionnaire (UEQ-S). Int. J. Interact. Multimed. Artif. Intell. **4**(6), 103 (2017)
52. Desurvire, H., Caplan, M., Toth, J.A.: Using heuristics to evaluate the playability of games. In: CHI 2004 Extended Abstracts on Human Factors in Computing Systems, pp. 1509–1512 (2004)
53. Desurvire, H., Wiberg, C.: Game usability heuristics (PLAY) for evaluating and designing better games: the next iteration. In: International Conference on Online Communities and Social Computing, pp. 557–566. Springer, Heidelberg (2009)
54. Korhonen, H., Koivisto, E.M.: Playability heuristics for mobile multi-player games. In: Proceedings of the 2nd International Conference on Digital Interactive Media in Entertainment and Arts, pp. 28–35 (2007)
55. Mullins, J.K., Sabherwal, R.: Gamification: a cognitive-emotional view. J. Bus. Res. **106**, 304–314 (2020)

An Exploratory Study of Users' Perceptions and Experiences with AI-Based User Interfaces

Gilbert Drzyzga^(✉)

Institute for Interactive Systems, Technische Hochschule Lübeck, Lübeck, Germany
gilbert.drzyzga@th-luebeck.de

Abstract. This study investigates how user perception and recognition of Artificial Intelligence (AI) shape experiences with AI-based User Interfaces (UIs). Addressing critical gaps in understanding user awareness and interaction with AI-driven systems, the research examines the relationship between users' awareness of AI functionality and the problems they encounter. An online survey (n = 386) was conducted in English and German to capture cross-linguistic insights into user experience (UX) with AI-enabled software, applications, and websites. Data were analyzed using a 3×3 matrix framework, mapping perception of AI use against reported interaction problems. Results show that only 25% of users could reliably identify AI usage, 47% were unaware, and 28% were uncertain. A statistically significant positive correlation was found between perceived usefulness and problem frequency (r = 0.299, p < 0.001), suggesting that users who view AI-based UIs as more valuable are more likely to report issues—potentially due to higher engagement, greater expectations, or willingness to tolerate flaws for perceived benefit. As the study is correlational, no causal inferences are warranted. Qualitative feedback from users who encountered problems reveals recurring challenges, including inaccurate or unhelpful responses, slow performance, privacy concerns, and inappropriate outputs. These findings provide actionable insights for UX practitioners, emphasizing the need for transparent, trustworthy, and usable AI-based UIs that prioritize system performance, accuracy, and privacy.

Keywords: Artificial Intelligence · Human-Computer Interaction · User Interface Design · User Perception · User Experience · Interaction Problems

1 Introduction

For decades, Human-Computer Interaction (HCI) has been the focus of research [1]. This field has provided proven guidelines [2], such as heuristics [3], for developing or evaluating User Interfaces (UIs) to improve the usability and User Experience (UX) of systems [4]. The incorporation of Artificial Intelligence (AI) into a variety of software systems is a rapidly expanding phenomenon that offers a wealth of benefits in a wide range of domains [5–7]. The success of these systems depends also on the extent to which users perceive and accept the AI technology embedded in them [8, 9]. Therefore, it is valuable to understand how people interact with AI-based UIs and related technologies,

© The Author(s), under exclusive license to Springer Nature Switzerland AG 2026
J. F. Krems et al. (Eds.): CHIRA 2025, CCIS 2836, pp. 231–249, 2026.
https://doi.org/10.1007/978-3-032-16454-4_13

such as machine learning and deep learning, because this knowledge could help identify potential issues related to interacting with the technology. This can facilitate optimal design decisions and improve the overall experience for users interacting with AI-based UIs. However, AI in UIs can also lead to unforeseen interactions that may obscure their operation for end users [10].

This study centers on *user perception* – a construct in human-centered design [11, 12] – as a critical determinant of the UX with AI-based UIs [13, 14]. *User perception*, in this context, refers to the subjective understanding, awareness, and interpretation that individuals form about the presence, function, and behavior of AI within a software system. It encompasses how users recognize, interpret, and assign meaning to AI-driven actions and outputs, and how these cognitive processes shape their interaction, trust, and satisfaction. A central challenge in AI-enabled systems lies in ensuring that users are not only aware of the AI's role but also able to *recognize* its involvement in decision-making processes – what is here termed *recognizability*. It is defined as the perceived ability of users to identify when AI is actively contributing to the system's behavior, understand its functional role, and assess its impact on outcomes [15]. Recognizing AI is a critical skill for interacting with it in an informed way [16]. This concept extends beyond mere visibility; it includes the user's capacity to interpret how AI influences functionality, supports tasks, or alters interaction dynamics.

Furthermore, the study takes a *high-level*, broad, exploratory investigation that does not focus on a specific application domain, but instead seeks to establish foundational insights into user-AI interactions across contexts. This approach should allow for the identification of recurring patterns, common sources of misunderstanding, and overarching design challenges that may be obscured in application-specific studies. By adopting a high-level lens, this study aims to generate a generalizable framework. Despite the increasing integration of AI into everyday software systems, users often lack awareness of or accurate understanding about the role of AI in shaping system behavior, leading to potential mismatches between user expectations and system capabilities [17, 18]. These mismatches may result in confusion, mistrust, or dissatisfaction, undermining the intended benefits of AI-enhanced UX (e.g., [19, 20]). This gap in understanding could be framed in two interrelated dimensions: (1) users' ability to perceive and recognize the presence and function of AI in a system, and (2) users' ability to identify and report actual or perceived problems during interaction. To address this problem, the study investigates the relationship between user perception of AI and perceived problems in AI-based UIs through a structured, analytical framework.

2   Relationship of Perception and Problems in AI-Based UIs

The relationship between user perception and problems in AI-based UIs is explored by examining how users perceive the impact of AI on system behavior and the challenges they may encounter during interaction.

2.1   The Need to Understand User Perceptions

The well-known *Technology Acceptance Model* (TAM) by [21] and further developments by [22], but also others such as the *Theory of Planned Behavior* or the *Unified Theory of Acceptance and Use of Technology* in [23], to name but a few, provide valuable and proven insights into the perceived usefulness and ease of use of an information system. From a human-centered perspective, it may be beneficial to consider additional factors that could potentially impact understanding. Such factors include transparency as a component of trust, value added through usefulness, intuitive interfaces for ease of use, and satisfaction of needs that ultimately lead to satisfaction with the understanding process [24–27]. When applied to AI-based UIs, such factors could provide insight into user satisfaction, highlight barriers to acceptance, and identify opportunities for improvement to achieve a positive UX (e.g. [13, 28–32]). With regard to the perceptions and problems that users encounter with AI-based UIs, the considerations for this study can be categorized into two main aspects, which as objectives form the essential basis of the investigation.

Category 1: User Perceptions of the Impact of AI on System Behavior. This category is concerned with understanding how users perceive the impact of AI on the functioning or behavior of an AI-based UI. It addresses various aspects related to the influence of AI, including its role in the system, advantages and disadvantages from the user's perspective. The objective is to gain insight into whether and how AI affects the user's experience with the system and to identify potential areas for improvement. Additionally, it aims to assess whether and how AI affects user interactions with the system, and to identify opportunities to enhance user satisfaction and acceptance of AI-based UIs.

Category 2: User Issues When Interacting with AI-Based UIs. The second category focuses on identifying whether and how users face challenges or problems when interacting with an AI-based UI. It aims to analyze user difficulties, frustrations, and pain points in terms of usability, intuitive interface design, ease of use, and overall satisfaction. The goal is to understand the barriers that prevent positive UX and to suggest improvements for better interaction between humans and AI-based UIs.

2.2 Perceptions and Perceived Problems Using AI-Based UIs

"Perception of AI" and *"Perceived Problems with AI"* were derived from the understanding that how users perceive AI technology plays a critical role in how they engage, communicate, and experience when interacting with an AI-based UI, and whether and how problems arise during these interactions (e.g., [8, 9, 33]). By exploring the relationship between these two aspects at a high level, the aim is to determine whether this can improve the way in which such systems are designed and implemented. The criteria evaluate the perception of UX problems when interacting with an AI-based UI and the extent to which these problems are perceived. This is accomplished by considering three underlying states *agree, disagree, no opinion* in relation to two aspects (see the following two sections).

User Perceptions of AI Interaction. This aspect focuses on users' awareness and understanding of AI in a given application or context. It consists of three levels:

1. Users clearly perceive the presence of AI and recognize its role in providing functionality or assistance within the software ("agree", "Yes").

2. Users do not recognize or are unaware that AI is being used to generate results or support their interactions with the interface ("disagree", "No").
3. It is uncertain whether users can tell that AI is being used in the application because there may not be enough information about its role and functionality ("no opinion", "I cannot judge").

The criteria of these levels aim to assess whether or not users are aware that they are interacting with an AI-based UI, and their understanding of its role in the application's functionality. As mentioned earlier, the underlying meaning refers to visibility, and how noticeable the presence of AI elements is within the application, and whether these elements are easy for users to perceive.

Perceived Problems with AI Interaction. This aspect evaluates potential issues that could arise from interacting with an AI-based UI on three levels.

1. Users have encountered problems or challenges while using the software that incorporates AI technology. This could include miscommunication, misunderstanding of AI actions and contributions to functionality, or other usability concerns related to AI elements in the application ("agree", "Yes").
2. Users have no problems interacting with the AI-based UI. They find it easy to understand and engage with the software without encountering problems related to the use of AI technology ("disagree", "No").
3. It is unclear whether users have experienced problems or challenges related to the AI elements in the application, as there may not be sufficient information provided about their experiences or interactions with the interface ("no opinion", "I cannot judge").

The criteria for these levels are designed to assess the extent to which users are aware of the use of AI technology and their (miss-)understanding of the role of AI in the functionality and actions of the system.

Formulating a Decision Matrix to Analyze Interactions Between Users and the AI-Based UI. Based on the previous considerations, the findings regarding users' perceptions of AI interaction and users' perceived problems with AI interaction are transformed into a matrix to assess the extent to which users experience difficulties when interacting with an AI-based UI, based on the criteria. From a technical perspective, the criteria should address issues such as slow response times, incorrect results, or unexpected behavior of the AI-based UI, which have the potential to cause user frustration or dissatisfaction with the application.

The decision matrix (Table 1) integrates the considerations presented in the previous sections and summarizes the two dimensions into nine potential scenarios, each consisting of three factors arranged in a 3×3 matrix. This framework should allow to analyze different scenarios arising from different levels of awareness of the presence and role of AI in UIs.

Research Questions and Study Contribution. These considerations, including *user perception*, *recognizability*, and *perceived problems*, form the basis for three interrelated Research Questions (RQs) that guide this study. The RQs are structured to progress from individual awareness to the interplay between perception and experience, enabling a comprehensive understanding of user-AI interaction dynamics.

Table 1. Decision matrix for judging whether a software is used uses AI to generate results (perception) and experienced problems when interacting with software uses AI helping to identify patterns, trends or correlations

#	Perception of AI	Problems with AI	Description
1	Yes	Yes	AI is being perceived, but problems are being recognized
2	Yes	No	AI is being perceived, but there are no problems are being recognized
3	Yes	I cannot judge	AI is being perceived, but whether there are problems with AI cannot be assessed
4	No	Yes	AI is not being perceived, but problems with AI are being recognized
5	No	No	AI is not being perceived and problems with AI are not being recognized
6	No	I cannot judge	AI is not being perceived and whether there are problems with AI cannot be assessed
7	I cannot judge	Yes	It cannot be assessed whether AI is perceived, but problems are being recognized
8	I cannot judge	No	It cannot be assessed whether AI is perceived, but there are no problems recognized
9	I cannot judge	I cannot judge	It cannot be assessed whether AI is perceived and whether there are problems with it

1. **Can users judge whether they are using AI-based UI, do they perceive AI?**

   This question addresses the baseline condition of user awareness. It investigates whether users are able to recognize the presence of AI in a system and understand its role in delivering functionality. The outcome informs design strategies for increasing visibility and clarity in AI-based UIs.

2. **Can users judge whether they are experiencing problems when interacting with an AI-based UI?**

   This question focuses on users' ability to identify usability issues, inconsistencies, or failures in AI behavior. It assesses whether users can detect anomalies, misinterpretations, or performance problems that may affect trust and task success.

3. **Is there a relationship between users' perceptions of AI and their problems interacting with it, and if so, what is it, and if not, why?**

   This integrative question explores the relationship between awareness and experience. The hypothesis is that there is a statistical relationship between recognizing AI and experiencing problems. For instance, users who fail to recognize AI may be more likely to encounter issues. Conversely, unrecognized issues may exist in systems where AI is clearly present. This relationship could reveal critical flaws in system design, such as the *invisibility of failure modes* or *misperception of control.*

Therefore, this study examines how AI-based UIs could be designed to help users understand the role of AI in shaping their experience. This understanding may help users recognize when AI's influence could lead to errors or inconsistencies, as long as the AI's presence and function are transparent. This approach could also ensure that user feedback is systematically integrated to align perception with performance.

3 Method

To explore user perceptions and experiences with AI-based software, applications, and websites, a pragmatic and scalable online survey was employed to gather high-level insights across diverse user groups. This approach captures initial, raw impressions of AI transparency and UX. It prioritizes broad, exploratory insights over demographic stratification, aligning with the study's goal of identifying emergent patterns in user awareness and perceived challenges with AI systems.

3.1 Questionnaire Design and Implementation

To ensure a diverse sample and the most accurate data, the questionnaire was distributed to three panels: one in the UK (Panel 1, https://www.prolific.com/) and two in Germany (Panels 2, https://www.surveycircle.com/en/ and 3, https://www.surveyswap.io/). These panels offered services in both English and German. The questionnaire was also available in both languages. Participants were given the opportunity to select their preferred language at the beginning of the questionnaire. They were informed that their responses would be treated as strictly confidential in accordance with German data protection laws. Participants were asked to confirm their consent before beginning. A short description of the purpose of the survey was also given, explaining that the intention of the survey was to find out about the use of software applications and apps. The introduction helped by informing them that they would be asked five questions and that it should take them at least two to four minutes to complete the questionnaire.

The questionnaire was divided into two parts. The first section of the questionnaire asked about the most frequently used software, applications, or websites by the participants, with three possible responses as free text fields for each. The first question asked about the most frequently used applications installed on the respondent's personal computer or notebook. The second question asked about the most frequently used applications on the respondent's smartphone or tablet. The third question asked about the most frequently used applications when participants were in transit, such as driving a car or riding a bike.

The second section of the questionnaire addressed the core issues that this study was designed to investigate (user perceptions and perceived problems). The questionnaire in this section asked respondents if they could always judge whether a software, application or website they were using was using AI to generate results. The process is visualized in Fig. 1.

The following section provides a detailed explanation of the construction of the two questions and a thorough analysis of the resulting data.

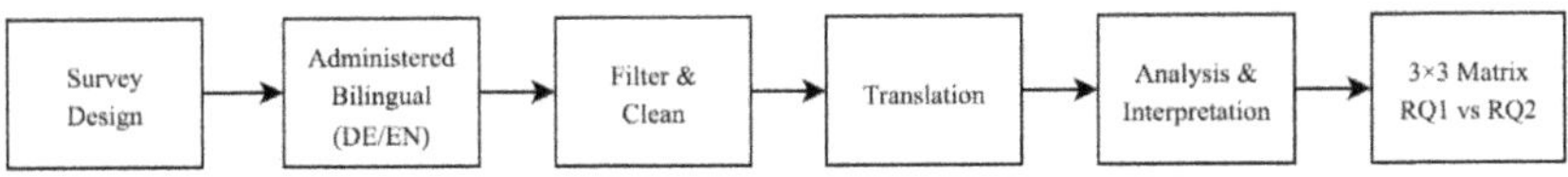

Fig. 1. High-level workflow of the survey-based study. The process includes survey design, bilingual administration, data filtering and cleaning, translation of German responses, and analysis using quantitative and thematic methods. The final interpretation uses a 3×3 matrix (RQ1 vs RQ2). Details on filtering, exclusion, and analysis are provided in the subgraph.

Formulation of the Questions. The aim of this study was to capture users' perspectives on their interactions with AI-based software, applications or websites. While the questions did not directly ask about feelings, they were designed to encourage participants to reflect on their experiences and intuitions when judging whether a given tool uses AI to generate results (Table 2).

Question 1 (Q1): *"Do you feel that you can always judge whether a software/application/website you use uses Artificial Intelligence (AI) to generate results?"*.

The use of "always" emphasizes whether the person can consistently identify when AI is involved. The answers "No" and "I cannot judge" to this question mean that both answers convey that it is difficult or impossible for a person to judge whether a particular software/application/website uses AI all the time. The difference is that answering "No" indicates that a person is confident, based on their knowledge or experience, that it may not be possible to determine whether software, applications, or websites use AI to generate results all the time. This implies that a person should possess the necessary knowledge and skills to make an informed decision about their ability to judge the use of AI. Conversely, if a person answers "I cannot judge", it suggests that they obviously cannot determine whether software, applications, or websites use AI. This may indicate a lack of expertise or uncertainty. They may not have enough knowledge about AI and how it is applied in different contexts.

Question 2 (Q2): *"Have you experienced problems when interacting with software/applications/websites that you know use AI?"*.

This question aims to identify the range of problems users may have experienced when using AI-based UIs, from minor inconveniences to significant barriers. The term "problems" allows for a broad interpretation and encourages participants to reflect on their experiences with these technologies.

In both questions, the inclusion of "applications, websites" in addition to "software" should broaden the scope and allows for a more comprehensive understanding of any issues related to AI-based UIs.

Although the questions posed in this study do not explicitly ask about feelings in the traditional sense, they are designed to encourage users to critically reflect on their interactions with AI-based UIs and to introspectively consider their perceptions and engagement with such technology. While future studies may potentially benefit from more direct questioning of participants' emotions or reflections, this study provides valuable insights into users' perspectives on AI-based UIs based on the given questionnaire design.

Table 2. Items on the questionnaire.

#	Question	Answer options	Goal	Topic
1	Do you feel that you can always judge whether a software/application/website you use uses Artificial Intelligence (AI) to generate results?	"yes", "no", "I cannot judge"	To decide whether the product uses AI	Perception of AI
2	Have you experienced problems when interacting with software/applications/websites that you know use AI?	"yes", "no", "I cannot judge" "yes" opened the option to name the problems in a text box	To decide whether problems have been encountered when interacting with AI	Problems when using AI

Analysis of Responses and Their Potential Combinations. In order to gain a comprehensive understanding of the potential impact of the combinations of answers to Q1 and Q2, a detailed analysis of each answer option for both questions is conducted separately. This approach allows the potential consequences of their combination to be assessed simultaneously (for details, see Table 3 and Table 4, which show the description for each answer option for both questions).

As mentioned above, it should be noted that the analysis is exploratory in nature and broad and high-level. It is not focused on achieving logical consistency between questions and answer options.

In Q2 (see Table 4), respondents are presented with the same three possible responses as in Q1 regarding their experiences with AI-based software, applications, or websites: "yes," "no", and "I cannot judge". These responses are expected to provide valuable insight into whether individuals have encountered difficulties while using such UIs.

In conclusion, while it could be argued that certain combinations may seem less intuitive at first glance (e.g., "I cannot judge" for both questions), all possible response combinations can still provide valuable insights into users' perceptions and experiences with AI-based UIs. In this research, these combinations are intended to help capture a diverse range of responses that may help identify patterns or trends in how people interact with and perceive AI technology.

Technical Design and Relevant Factors. For the two questions there were three possible answers *("yes", "no", "I cannot judge")* and for the second question there was the possibility to give additional information in a text box (Table 2). This option was offered by the survey software if the answer to the second question was *"yes"* (Experienced problems when interacting with software that knowingly uses AI).

Focus on Usability and User Experience. This survey excluded demographic data, as the focus was solely on factors related to usability and UX. The primary objective was to explore users' perceptions of the use of AI and potential problems with AI, rather than

Table 3. Response options for Q1

#	Answer options	Description
1	"yes"	By answering in the affirmative, the respondent expresses confidence in their ability to evaluate the use of AI. Consequently, they are able to provide a definitive answer to Q2 based on their knowledge of the use of AI in a particular application
2	"no"	If the respondent indicates that they do not feel confident in their ability to assess the use of AI, they may still be able to answer Q2 if they have encountered problems with specific software that is known to use AI. However, the certainty of AI involvement may not be based on their own judgment, but rather on information obtained from other sources, such as product descriptions or marketing materials
3	"I cannot judge"	The respondent indicates uncertainty about their ability to determine whether an application uses AI. It is important to note that this response option does not necessarily preclude the respondent from experiencing problems with software that they perceive as using AI based on other cues (as noted above)

Table 4. Response options for Q2

#	Answer options	Description
1	"yes"	An affirmative response to the second question indicates that the respondent has experienced difficulties interacting with known AI applications. This combination is valid regardless of the respondent's answer to Q1, provided that the respondent's perception that certain software uses AI is based on other factors
2	"no"	Indicates that the respondent has not experienced any problems when using known AI applications. This response can be considered valid for all combinations from Q1, as it relates solely to the experience of interacting with AI software and is not dependent on the respondent's ability to discern whether or not an application uses AI
3	"I cannot judge"	The respondent is unsure whether they have experienced problems when using known AI applications. While this response option may seem less straightforward, it still provides valuable information because some users may have experienced problems but are unsure about the role of AI in causing those problems. This combination remains valid because it captures a specific type of UX and perception related to AI-based software, applications, or websites

the specific characteristics of different groups, in order to explore general user opinions across different applications.

Questionnaire Structure. First, an introductory text was given, that provided preliminary information about the purpose of the survey and how the data would be used. There were five items in total. Three of the five were about the use of software in everyday life. Two questions were of interest to the topic of this study, as shown in Table 2. These items were previously administered in a similar form using Particify (https://particify.de/en/) as part of a university-wide lecture on AI and usability. All survey responses were voluntary, and a one-time follow-up was given if a question was not answered.

3.2 Data Preparation, Processing, Analysis and Ongoing Data Quality Control

The data analysis involved the exclusion of specific elements, including content, character sequences, and individual characters such as question marks or hyphens. Moreover, fields containing no or invalid content (e.g., only numbers) and irrelevant entries (e.g., no mention of a specific AI problem) were excluded from the analysis. Furthermore, the following criteria were applied: participants must have knowledge of either English or German; users must have access to software or applications; an acceptable time range for completion of the survey was from a minimum of 25 s to a maximum of 450 s; thus, responses that adhere to these criteria can be considered valid.

The next step was to import the data (CSV file into a Python script). The German opinions were translated into English and analyzed in terms of spelling and grammar. Code functions were then used to analyze the data (statistical reports, quantitative/qualitative). During the analysis process, a sample of the results was continuously checked by hand.

3.3 Structuring the Relationship Between RQ1 and RQ2

The matrix shown in Table 5 is a structuring tool designed to illustrate the relationship between two underlying topics from the survey – *"Perceptions of AI"* and *"Problems with AI"* – and is based on Table 1. Each cell represents a different combination of the two questions. The matrix is intended as an analytical tool to help identify patterns, trends, and correlations. The primary goal of this matrix is to gain insight into users' experiences and attitudes toward AI, which can be achieved by considering a wide range of responses and potential interpretations.

Table 5. 3 × 3-Matrix for the relationship of the two topics.

Perception of AI	Problems with AI		
	Yes	No	I cannot judge
Yes	(Yes, Yes)	(Yes, No)	(Yes, I cannot judge)
No	(No, Yes)	(No, No)	(No, I cannot judge)
I cannot judge	(I cannot judge, Yes)	(I cannot judge, No)	(I cannot judge, I cannot judge)

The first column (*"Perceptions of AI"*) of the matrix represents the three rows below it. The next three columns (*"Problems with AI"*) represent the three columns below. Both define the three categories: *"Yes"*, *"No"* and *"I cannot judge"*. Each cell in the table represents a combination of the three possible responses from each category (nine possible combinations in total). This matrix was designed firstly to provide an understanding of the multifaceted relationship between these two issues. And secondly, to provide a framework for analyzing and interpreting the data from the survey. The survey was conducted using the online questionnaire solution SoSci Survey.

4   Results

The total number of completed questionnaires from the survey was 393. Following the selection criteria (Sect. 3.2), which included excluding directly invalid responses that were removed directly in the survey software, a total of 386 valid completed questionnaires remained.

4.1   Perception of AI

The responses to Q1 *"Do you feel that you can always judge whether a software/application/website you use uses Artificial Intelligence (AI) to generate results"* are shown in Table 6. Of the 386 responses given, 98 (25%) say they can judge whether a software/application/website they use uses AI to generate results, 181 (47%) say they cannot, and 107 (28%) say they cannot judge whether it uses AI.

Table 6. Result if participants can judge whether a software/application/website they use uses AI to generate results.

#	Value	Number of participants
UAI1	yes	98
UAI2	no	181
UAI3	I cannot judge	107

4.2   Problems When Interacting with AI

The responses to Q2 *"Have you experienced problems when interacting with software/applications/websites that you know use AI?"* are shown in Table 7. Here, 55 (14%) said they had experienced a problem when interacting with an AI-based UI, 227 (59%) said they had not experienced a problem, and 104 (27%) said they could not judge it.

Table 7. Result of experienced problems when interacting with software/applications/websites that they know use AI.

#	Value	Number of participants
PAI1	yes	55
PAI2	no	227
PAI3	I cannot judge	104

4.3 The Relationship Between Perception and Issues in AI-Based UIs

The results of the two questions are related according to the methodological approach. Figure 2 shows the values in relation to the submission of all valid questionnaires in the 3×3 matrix as a heatmap. It thus shows the result of the statistical analysis taking into account the votes given per answer.

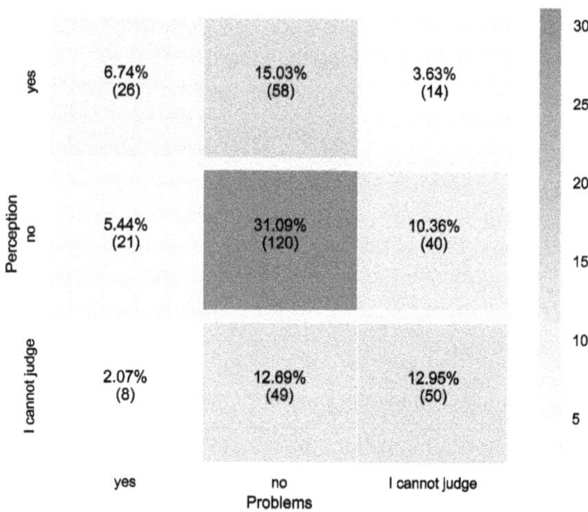

Fig. 2. Heatmap of the relationship between participants' perceptions of AI and problems encountered when interacting with it ($n = 386$)

An analysis of the answers of the three groups of participants (Table 7, #PAI1, #PAI2, #PAI3) in relation to the answers to question 1 is as follows and represent the answers given to the second question for each group. The results and percentages shown below refer to the respective group of participants. The values therefore provide valuable insight into the choices made by respondents between one question and another.

Respondents Who Experienced Problems When Interacting with AI-Based UIs (#PAI1). The group of respondents to question 1 on perceptions of AI who have experienced problems with it (#UAI1) is 98 out of 386 (25%), which is the first row (perception, "yes") in Fig. 2. The results show that 26 (27%) of this group had experienced problems with AI. Conversely, 58 (59%) of these participants had not experienced problems with AI and 14 (14%) of this group could not judge whether there were problems.

Respondents Who Experienced No Problems When Interacting with AI-Based UIs (#PAI2). The group of respondents to question 1 on perceptions of AI who have not identified any problems with it (#UAI2) is 181 out of 386 (47%), which is the second row (perception, "no") in Fig. 2. The results show that 21 (12%) of this group had experienced problems with AI. Conversely, 120 (66%) of these participants had not experienced problems with AI, and 40 (22%) of this group could not judge whether there were problems.

Respondents Who Cannot Judge Whether Problems Have Been Experienced When Interacting with AI-Based UIs (#PAI3). The group of respondents to question 1 on perceptions of AI who cannot judge it (UAI3) is 107 out of 386 (28%), which is the third row (perception, "I cannot judge") in Fig. 2. The results show that 8 (7%) of this group have experienced problems with AI. Conversely, 49 (46%) of these participants had not experienced problems with AI, and 50 (47%) of this group could neither judge that they had problems nor judge whether there were problems.

4.4 Issues with Software that Knowingly Uses AI

The second question of the questionnaire allowed participants to comment on the problems they encountered when they were aware that AI was being used, if they answered *"yes"*. This was done by 55 participants (Table 7, #PAI1). Following Sect. 2.2 (data preparation), the texts were translated and, if necessary, linguistically optimized (spelling and grammar correction) and selected according to the exclusion criteria. This process excluded 12 unusable responses and resulted in 43 valid responses. Of these, 19 said they were aware of AI, 17 said they were not aware of AI and 7 could not judge.

4.5 Categorization of Problems Experienced by Participants Using AI-Based UIs

The comments provided by the 43 participants can be categorized into issues related to "Performance and Accuracy", "Misunderstanding User Intent", "Privacy Breaches" and "Degraded User Experience" (Table 8), as follows:

Table 8. Comments from the respondents who experienced problems in AI-based software systems.

Issue	Summary/Conclusion
Performance and Accuracy	Limited responsiveness, slow responses/crashes, incorrect data/information, incorrect translations indicate that AI-based UIs need to improve their ability to process data efficiently
Misunderstanding User Intent	Misinterpreting user requests or questions, not directly answering the question suggest that AI-based UIs still struggle to understand complex or nuanced user input

(continued)

Table 8. (continued)

Issue	Summary/Conclusion
Privacy Breaches	Data breaches that send ads based on browsing history highlight the need for better privacy mechanisms in AI software, to ensure that users' personal information remains secure and private
Degraded User Experience	Frozen screens, no response, meaningless output, strange grammar or image parts negatively impact the user experience with AI-based UI. In addition, inappropriate responses from chatbots indicate that further development is needed to ensure that these systems can appropriately handle a range of queries and provide helpful solutions or information

4.6 Summarizing the Relationships

Based on the summary of the heatmap table, the relationships between perceptions and problems can be described as follows (diagonal line in the heatmap): There were 26 participants (7% of 386) who could recognize AI but had problems with such systems, 120 (31%) in the group with no recognition of AI but no problems, 50 (13%) who were undecided about their ability to recognize AI and had no problems with these systems. The largest number who had no problems with AI-based UI experienced was in the group that did not perceived AI (120/386 = 31%).

4.7 Testing the Hypothesis

- H_0: There is no relationship between perceived usefulness of an AI UI and the frequency of encountered problems.
- H_1: A positive relationship exists between perceived usefulness of an AI UI and the frequency of problems encountered with it.

The analysis of data from 386 valid questionnaires revealed a statistically significant positive correlation between perceived usefulness and reported problem frequency ($r = 0.299$, $p < 0.001$). This finding supports H_1.

The results indicate that the more useful users perceived the AI UI to be, the more problems they reported (and vice versa). Due to the correlational design of the study, however, no causal direction can be inferred.

5 Conclusion and Discussion

Analyzing the data provided valuable insights into how users perceive AI software systems and their experiences with related issues. The results suggest that many users do not consistently recognize AI in the systems they use. This phenomenon is well-documented in studies of "invisible AI", wherein AI-driven interfaces operate seamlessly in the background, making their underlying intelligence imperceptible to users [34]. Users reported few problems during interaction, which echoes the "trust paradox" identified in recent studies showing that end users often underestimate AI's influence [35–37]. However, variations exist within user groups, revealing nuanced patterns of AI awareness and problem experience.

User-reported problems highlight key challenges. Most systems still fail to provide details about how they make decisions, echoing the known explainability gaps and call for transparency. Reported issues include slow or incorrect responses, difficulty interpreting user intent, data privacy concerns, and frustration with irrelevant or unhelpful outputs. These findings align with previous research on AI usability and explainability (e.g. [38–41]) and underscore the importance of advancing natural language processing, machine learning, privacy safeguards, and conversational AI design (e.g. [42–44]).

Regarding the perception of AI (RQ1), only 25% of participants reported that they could reliably judge whether an interface used AI. This finding is consistent with the TAM, which posits that perceived usefulness and perceived ease of use influence users' awareness of the underlying technology. When AI is hidden or seamlessly integrated, it remains invisible to most users. The remaining 75% either could not judge or explicitly denied recognition, suggesting that many AI-enabled systems are designed as "black boxes" that fail to convey their artificial nature.

When asked about issues with the perception of AI-based UIs (RQ2), 59% of participants reported no problems, while 14% reported yes. The qualitative analysis identified four main categories of issues: performance/accuracy, misunderstanding user intent, privacy breaches, and a degraded user experience. These categories correspond to the key areas of human-AI interaction that have been identified in previous studies: latency, hallucinations, and data security [35, 45, 46].

RQ3 asked whether there is a relationship between perceived usefulness and problem frequency. Together, the heatmap analysis and Pearson correlation confirm a statistically significant positive association ($r = 0.299$, $p < 0.001$) between the perceived usefulness of an AI interface and the frequency of encountered problems. Specifically, users who view the AI interface as more useful tend to report facing problems more often.

This positive relationship can be traced to several potential mechanisms. First, intensive users—those who interact frequently with the system—may recognize its usefulness through extended use while also encountering more problems due to greater exposure to system limitations. Second, users who experience difficulties may develop more nuanced, realistic assessments of the interface's usefulness, rather than relying on overly positive or negative judgments. Third, perceived usefulness may reflect users' willingness to tolerate problems in exchange for valued functionality, suggesting that issues and usefulness can coexist rather than being opposed.

These findings highlight that the relationship between perceived usefulness and problem frequency is more complex than a simple "more useful = fewer problems" inverse link, warranting further investigation into how intensive engagement connects to both higher perceived usefulness and increased problem reporting.

Heatmap analysis further clarifies this relationship. The largest subgroup (31%) neither recognized AI nor reported problems, which suggests that when AI remains invisible, users rarely report issues, either because fewer problems are encountered or because potential faults go unnoticed. In contrast, the subgroup that recognizes AI yet reports no problems (15%) suggests that clear signaling of AI can coexist with a positive user experience when the design aligns with users' expectations.

5.1 Outlook

The findings presented here offer insights that can be integrated into future research and development initiatives with the aim of enhancing the UX and addressing potential issues that may emerge from the utilization of AI technologies. Moreover, this could facilitate the development of more effective, intuitive and reliable AI-based UIs for use in a variety of software, applications or websites. To gain a deeper understanding of how AI is perceived and the problems associated with its use, it would be beneficial to examine in closer detail cases or contexts in which AI has been or is perceived as challenging. Such an approach would facilitate a more comprehensive and detailed investigation of the factors influencing perceptions of AI and the challenges arising from its implementation. Further research could examine specific AI technologies and develop measures to improve users' understanding of and interaction with AI-based UIs. It is important to gain a full and nuanced understanding of the bidirectional influences at play in this relationship. As noted above, future studies may potentially benefit from a more direct approach to asking participants about their emotions or reflections, with the aim of formulating additional related questions for inclusion in the questionnaire. Future work could build on this framework by using validated Likert-type scales or scenario-based items to identify the contextual and demographic factors influencing user perceptions of AI interactions. These designs would enable a comprehensive evaluation of the influence of various factors, such as age, gender, digital literacy, application domain, and specific interaction challenges, on attitudes toward AI. This could provide valuable insights for human-centered design.

5.2 Limitations

This analysis offers valuable insights into user awareness of AI in interfaces, but it has limitations. These include sample size, types of bias (selection and self-selection), the simplicity of the scale, translation issues, the drawbacks of the 3x3 matrix (lack of context and oversimplification), the lack of contextual information, and the rapid evolution of technology. The reliance on self-reported data introduces potential recall bias. Furthermore, the focus on software users who know they are using AI may skew results by missing problems with "invisible" AI. Future research could use qualitative methods and broader application contexts to study the factors that influence people's perceptions of AI, such as sociodemographics, beliefs, and cultural differences. Researchers should also consider interventions to improve public understanding and promote the responsible use of these systems.

References

1. Bai, Y., Fang, X., Wang, Z.: Research on the application of human-computer interaction. In: IEEE 2nd International Conference on Data Science and Computer Application (ICDSCA), pp. 673–678 (2022)
2. Shneiderman, B., Plaisant, C.: Designing the User Interface: Strategies for Effective Human-Computer Interactio. Pearson Education India (2010)
3. Nielsen, J., Molich, R.: Heuristic evaluation of user interfaces. In: Proceedings of the SIGCHI Conference on Human Factors in Computing Systems (1990)
4. Drzyzga, G.: Improving the usability of intelligent interface designs. In: Ahram, T., Falcão, C. (eds.) Usability and User Experience. AHFE (2024) International Conference. AHFE Open Access, AHFE International, USA (2024)
5. Javaid, M., Haleem, A., Singh, R.P., Suman, R.: Artificial intelligence applications for industry 4.0: a literature-based study. J. Ind. Integr. Manage. 7(01), 83–111 (2022)
6. Collins, C., Dennehy, D., Conboy, K., Mikalef, P.: Artificial intelligence in information systems research: a systematic literature review and research agenda. Int. J. Inf. Manage. **60**, 102383 (2021)
7. Ninness, C., Ninness, S.K.: Emergent virtual analytics: artificial intelligence and human-computer interactions. Behav. Soc. Issues **29**(1), 100–118 (2020)
8. Kelly, S., Kaye, S.A., Oviedo-Trespalacios, O.: What factors contribute to the acceptance of artificial intelligence? A systematic review. Telemat. Inform. **77**, 101925 (2023)
9. Choung, H., David, P., Ross, A.: Trust in AI and its role in the acceptance of AI technologies. Int. J. Hum.-Comput. Interact. **39**(9), 1727–1739 (2023)
10. Drzyzga, G.: Incorporating artificial intelligence into design criteria considerations. In: Degen, H., Ntoa, S. (eds.) Artificial Intelligence in HCI (Part II) - Volume 52 of the combined Proceedings of the 26th International Conference on Human-Computer Interaction (HCI International 2024), Washington DC, USA, 29 June–4 July (2024)
11. Moustafa, A.W.: Integrating user experience in practices of human-centered design process in product design. Int. Des. J. **13**(5), 359–375 (2023)
12. Yadav, P.: To empathize or perceive? Towards a 'perceptive design' approach. In: Proceedings of DRS2020: Synergy, vol. 1, pp. 406–422 (2020)
13. Margetis, G., Ntoa, S., Antona, M., Stephanidis, C.: Human-centered design of artificial intelligence. In: Handbook of Human Factors and Ergonomics, pp. 1085–1106 (2021)
14. Bingley, W.J., et al.: Where is the human in human-centered AI? Insights from developer priorities and user experiences. Comput. Hum. Behav. **141**, 107617 (2023)
15. Usmani, U.A., Happonen, A., Watada, J.: Human-centered artificial intelligence: designing for user empowerment and ethical considerations. In: 2023 5th International Congress on Human-Computer Interaction, Optimization and Robotic Applications (HORA) (2023)
16. Long, D., Magerko, B.: What is AI literacy? Competencies and design considerations. In: Proceedings of the 2020 CHI Conference on Human Factors in Computing Systems, pp. 1–16 (2020)
17. Riveiro, M., Thill, S.: "That's (not) the output I expected!" On the role of end user expectations in creating explanations of AI systems. Artif. Intell. (2021)
18. Amershi, S., Kamar, E., Kiciman, E.: People and AI see things different implications of mismatched perception on HCI for AI systems. In: Workshop on Human-Centered Machine Learning Perspectives (2019)
19. Virvou, M.: Artificial intelligence and user experience in reciprocity: contributions and state of the art. Intell. Decis. Technol. (2023)
20. Peters, T.M., Visser, R.W.: The importance of distrust in AI. In: World Conference on Explainable Artificial Intelligence (2023)

21. Davis, F.D.: User acceptance of information technology: system characteristics, user perceptions and behavioral impacts. Int. J. Man Mach. Stud. **38**(3), 475–487 (1993)
22. Gefen, D., Kell, M.: The impact of developer responsiveness on perceptions of usefulness and ease of use: an extension of the technology acceptance model. ACM SIGMIS Database Database Adv. Inf. Syst. **29**(2), 35–49 (1998)
23. Sohn, K., Kwon, O.: Technology acceptance theories and factors influencing artificial Intelligence-based intelligent products. Telemat. Inform. **47**, 101324 (2020)
24. Bach, T.A., Khan, A., Hallock, H., Beltrão, G., Sousa, S.: A systematic literature review of user trust in AI-enabled systems: an HCI perspective. Int. J. Hum. Comput. Interact. **40**(5), 1251–1266 (2022)
25. van Berkel, N., Tag, B., Goncalves, J., Hosio, S.: Human-centred artificial intelligence: a contextual morality perspective. Behav. Inf. Technol. **41**(3), 502–518 (2022)
26. Bernardo, E., Seva, R.: Affective design analysis of explainable artificial intelligence (XAI): a user-centric perspective. Informatics **10**(1), 32 (2023)
27. Wanner, J., Herm, L.V., Heinrich, K., Janiesch, C.: The effect of transparency and trust on intelligent system acceptance: evidence from a user-based study. Electron. Mark. **32**(4), 2079–2102 (2022)
28. Schelenz, L., Segal, A., Gal, K.: Applying transparency in artificial intelligence based personalization systems. In: ECAI 2020 (2020)
29. Rzepka, C., Berger, B.: User interaction with AI-enabled systems: a systematic review of IS research. San Francisco (2018)
30. Wanner, J., Popp, L., Fuchs, K., Heinrich, K., Herm, L.V., Janiesch, C.: Adoption Barriers of AI: a Context-Specific Acceptance Model for Industrial Maintenance (2021)
31. Hartikainen, M., Väänänen, K., Lehtiö, A., Ala-Luopa, S., Olsson, T.: Human-centered AI design in reality: a study of developer companies' practices: a study of developer companies' practices. In: Nordic Human-Computer Interaction Conference (2022)
32. Shin, D.: The effects of explainability and causality on perception, trust, and acceptance: implications for explainable AI. Int. J. Hum. Comput. Stud. **146**, 102551 (2021)
33. Alm, C.O., Alvarez, A., Font, J., Liapis, A., Pederson, T., Salo, J.: Invisible AI-driven HCI systems–when, why and how. In: Proceedings of the 11th Nordic Conference on Human-Computer Interaction: Shaping Experiences, Shaping Society, pp. 1–3 (2020)
34. Glickman, M., Sharot, T.: How human–AI feedback loops alter human perceptual, emotional and social judgements. Nat. Hum. Behav. **9**(2), 345–359 (2025)
35. Kreps, S., George, J., Lushenko, P., Rao, A.: Exploring the artificial intelligence "Trust paradox": evidence from a survey experiment in the United States. PLoS ONE **18**(7), e0288109 (2023)
36. Ding, Y., Herbaut, N., Salinesi, C.: Trust paradoxes in machine learning: an ontological approach. In: International Conference on Advanced Information Systems Engineering, pp. 78–85. Springer, Cham (2025)
37. Cheong, B.: Transparency and accountability in AI systems: safeguarding wellbeing in the age of algorithmic decision-making. Front. Hum. Dyn.
38. Bahja, M.: Natural language processing applications in business. In: E-Business-Higher Education and Intelligence Applications (2020)
39. Saha, G.C., Kumar, S., Kumar, A., Saha, H., Lakshmi, T.K., Bhat, N.: Human-AI collaboration: exploring interfaces for interactive machine learning. uijin Jishu/J. Propulsion Technol. **44**(2) (2023)
40. Pfeuffer, N., et al.: Explanatory interactive machine learning. Bus. Inf. Syst. Eng. 1–25 (2023)
41. Quach, S., Thaichon, P., Martin, K.D., Weaven, S., Palmatier, R.W.: Digital technologies: tensions in privacy and data. J. Acad. Mark. Sci. **50**(6), 1299–1323 (2022)
42. Kunduru, A.R.: Artificial intelligence usage in cloud application performance improvement. Central Asian J. Math. Theory Comput. Sci. **4**(8), 42–47 (2023)

43. Fu, T., Gao, S., Zhao, X., Wen, J.R., Yan, R.: Learning towards conversational AI: a survey. AI Open **3**, 14–28 (2022)
44. Shin, D., Zaid, B., Ibahrine, M.: Algorithm appreciation: algorithmic performance, developmental processes, and user interactions. In: 2020 International Conference on Communications, Computing, Cybersecurity, and Informatics (CCCI), pp. 1–5 (2020)
45. Chen, Z., Schmidt, R.: Exploring a behavioral model of "positive friction" in human-AI interaction. In: International Conference on Human-Computer Interaction, pp. 3–22 (2024)
46. Durango, I., Penichet, V.M.R., Gallud, J.A.: Exploring human-data interaction: an AI-enhanced systematic mapping. Universal Access in the Information Society, pp. 1–18 (2024)

Santa Clara 3D: Digital Reconstruction and Storytelling of a Francoist Concentration Camp

Stinne Zacho, Chris Hall, Jakob Kusnick$^{(\boxtimes)}$ (iD), and Stefan Jänicke (iD)

Department of Mathematics and Computer Science, University of Southern Denmark,
Campusvej 55, 5230 Odense, Denmark
`kusnick@imada.sdu.dk`

Abstract. This paper explores the potential of digital reconstruction and interactive storytelling to preserve historically suppressed sites. The main objective of an interdisciplinary team of data scientists from the MEMORISE project and associates of the memory association Asociación Recuerdo y Dignidad was to preserve the memory of the Francoist Santa Clara concentration camp in Soria, Spain, through the use of digital technology. Combining archival research, 3D modelling, 360° photography, and web development, a prototype digital platform was created to visualise the transformation of the site across three historical phases: its origin as a convent, its use as a Francoist concentration camp, and its present-day condition. The platform allows users to navigate through spatial and temporal layers. Clickable media markers encourage exploration and interaction. Drawing on principles of participatory design, narrative visualisation, and open-ended user engagement, the project demonstrates how digital tools can support memory work, public engagement, and historical reflection. Our low-cost concept is especially adaptable to other physical sites that have been erased or forgotten.

1 Introduction

The use of digital tools is introducing new ways to preserve and share cultural memory, especially in places where the physical signs of the past have been removed or have changed over time. In the growing field of digital heritage, 3D reconstructions and web-based immersive experiences are now being used to engage the public, support learning, and keep memories alive [17,32]. These approaches are useful for remembering places associated with violence or repression, where traditional memorials may be absent and narratives remain suppressed. Developed in collaboration with a local memory association Asociación Recuerdo y Dignidad and as part of the MEMORISE project [18], we explore how digital reconstruction can make hidden or neglected histories more accessible and visible to a broader audience. MEMORISE uses a wide range of digital tools, including interactive storytelling, 3D reconstructions and participatory design, to enhance memory work related to Nazi persecutions.

A main goal of this work is to create a low-cost pipeline for reconstructing former landmarks of persecution, to create at least a virtual space to tell the stories of their

J. F. Krems et al. (Eds.): CHIRA 2025, CCIS 2836, pp. 250–268, 2026.
https://doi.org/10.1007/978-3-032-16454-4_14

victims. Our focus is the Santa Clara Park in Soria, Spain, which functioned as a concentration camp during the early phase of the Spanish Civil War. Today, very few visible traces remain of the camp's structures, and its role in the history of Francoist repression is not widely recognized. We combine historical research with interactive digital design to create a web-based platform, featuring digital 3D reconstructions, 360° photographs and historical context. This allows users to explore the site's transformation across three historical phases: its origin as a convent, its use as a concentration camp and its present-day condition. Our main contributions are:

- A web-based platform for exploring historical information about Santa Clara, from its founding to the present day.
- A virtual 3D reconstruction of the concentration camp at Santa Clara Park, based on historical sources and spatial interpretation.
- A reflection on how digital reconstructions can contribute to memory work in places without physical remains.
- A resource for raising awareness, educating, and informing the public about the historical significance of the site.
- A low-cost reproducible pipeline adaptable to relatable historical sites.

We adopt a hybrid storytelling approach grounded in the research on author-driven and reader-driven data storytelling [35]. Allowing users to follow a structured timeline but also to explore freely based on their interest offers both educational value and emotional impact. To ensure that the final product is meaningful to both experts and the public, we followed a participatory visualisation design approach, which seeks to connect research with public engagement by actively involving users and stakeholders in the design process [19].

Through this work, we contribute to the field of digital heritage by showing how interactive virtual environments can aid in preserving and conveying the stories of neglected historical sites. By combining digital reconstruction with historical context and collaborating with local memory organisations, this thesis seeks to offer innovative approaches to preserving, sharing, and understanding sites of repression. We argue that digital reconstructions, when paired with collaborative storytelling methods, can effectively make suppressed histories more visible, engaging, and educational for diverse audiences.

2 Related Work

Digital technology can support a better understanding and remembrance of traumatic historical events [36] such as the Holocaust or political repression during the Spanish Civil War. The digital reconstruction and storytelling of the Santa Clara Concentration Camp intersects with three main areas of related research. First, related projects concerning digital museums and virtual tours and how they use these platforms to communicate. Secondly, the use of digital reconstruction of historical sites and how they are valuable for reviving lost or transformed historical sites. Finally, the importance of digital storytelling as an asset for educating and conveying historical topics. These areas of research are reflected in the MEMORISE project [18], which combines 3D visualisation and interactive storytelling techniques to support Holocaust memory–approaches that were also used to develop Santa Clara 3D.

2.1 Digital Museums and Virtual Tours

In recent years, digital museums and virtual tours have become a valuable tool for educating and engaging users [13, 15]. In particular, Covid-19 raised awareness on the need to develop solutions that enable remote access to cultural heritage through virtual museums [23, 27, 30]. The creation of guided tours in digital twins of existing memorial sites related to persecution has led to easier access to historical sites, and provided a chance to reach wider audiences. One example is the digital twin of Block 15 of the Haidari concentration camp [14], a building that still exists without being accessible to the public due to its location on a military base. Another example is the Yad Vashem 360° virtual tour [12], which offers an immersive experience of the museum and guides the public through the history of Holocaust. By adding annotations to the 360° images, the viewer is presented with historical videos, survivor testimonies and animated models all contributing to an engaging interactive experience, which can support critical thinking and emotional engagement. Similarly, the Terezín Memorial [9] and Mauthausen [4] virtual tours are examples of digital environments that use annotations to provide the user with information while preserving the memory of these historically significant places. These examples inspire the design of the Santa Clara platform, particularly in using 360° visuals and annotations to create an accessible and emotionally engaging digital environment.

2.2 Digital Reconstruction of Historical Sites

The digital reconstruction of historical sites has been proven to be a very valuable tool for reviving sites that have otherwise been lost or transformed over time. These reconstructions introduce the possibility to visualise buildings, landscapes and architectural details that are no longer visible today [24]. An example of this is the Virtual Reconstruction of Bergen-Belsen Concentration Camp [29]. The model was developed using historical photographs, maps and survivor testimonies. This 3D reconstruction gives visitors the opportunity to learn about its past layout, view areas within the reconstruction and gain insight into the camp's history. Similar projects include the Natzweiler Struthof concentration camp project [21], which used methods like laser scanning, photogrammetry and UAV imagery and the 3D digital reconstruction of Auschwitz-Birkenau [20] that was developed using SketchUp.

The potential of using digital tools such as virtual reality and other technologies for enhancing Holocaust memory and education are emphasized in the article "Virtualising Memoryscapes: Guidelines for the Digital Holocaust Memory Project" [7]. The article argues how the integration of geolocated historical data and storytelling can create immersive educational experiences, a better understanding and deeper engagement. Although Santa Clara is not a Holocaust site, the digital reconstruction draws on similar methods, combining archival materials, historical maps, and digital modelling, to recover a site where physical traces have mostly disappeared.

2.3 Digital Storytelling

Digital storytelling methods have proven to be a valuable asset for engaging audiences with complex historical subjects like the Holocaust. The combination of narrative techniques combined with interactive technologies enhances empathy, understanding and remembrance of these difficult topics. Dimensions in Testimony [11] for example uses natural language processing to interact with pre-recorded interviews of Holocaust survivors. The user can engage in seemingly real-time conversations with the victims, making this an innovative way of preserving and presenting survivors' testimonies. Similarly, the Anne Frank VR Tour [1] shows how interactive storytelling can create a powerful learning tool when combined with personal testimonies and reconstructed environments.

The Spanish Civil War Memory Project [10] is another example of an interactive platform for exploring audiovisual testimonies from survivors of the Francoist regime. By telling their stories, the project aims to create attention about the victims of the Francoist repression, as much of the history and documentation from that time has been destroyed or forgotten.

In a survey conducted by Meffert et al. [26] different ways of using digital storytelling for presenting heritage related to Nazi persecutions are explored. Methods such as linear and non-linear storytelling, interactive timelines and spatial navigation are highlighted as effective ways to make difficult historical topics more engaging and easier to understand. These insights are very relevant to the design of this project, as it emphasizes the importance of interactivity, spatial exploration and contextual information.

Furthermore, the structure of this platform also takes inspiration from the concepts of author-driven and reader-driven storytelling [35]. These concepts offer a balance between narrative control and user flexibility and the article emphasises the benefits of combining these methods to enhance clarity and engagement. In this project, a hybrid storytelling approach is used, allowing the viewer to follow the timeline slider, or explore the 3D models, geo-spatial maps and narratives non-linearly, allowing both guided learning and open-ended interactions with the history, highlighting the involved multimodal entities such as persons, objects and various sets of them with their interconnections [22].

These initiatives reflect the growing importance of digital storytelling in both holocaust education and the broader memorialisation of political violence. The combination of technology with spatial reconstruction and narrative structures, help foster a more personal connection to history, especially important as the generation of eyewitnesses continues to pass away. Like these initiatives, the Santa Clara platform aims to combine spatial reconstruction with interactive storytelling to create a more engaging learning environment.

3 Background

Santa Clara 3D is the result of a close collaboration between the MEMORISE Project [5] and the Asociación Recuerdo y Dignidad [2]. MEMORISE is a Horizon

Europe-funded initiative that aims to preserve the memory of victims of Nazi persecutions and other forms of totalitarian violence through digital tools. As more victims of these persecutions pass away, developing new strategies to tell their stories becomes necessary to keep their memories alive. To achieve this, MEMORISE explores various digital technologies, aiming to make historical testimonies, documents, and sites more accessible and engaging to the public. The Asociación Recuerdo y Dignidad is a volunteer-run association based in Soria, Spain, that is dedicated to recover historical memory of the Spanish Civil War and the Francoist repression. Their work includes archival research, locating and exhuming mass graves, and raising awareness of these histories from a human rights perspective. By providing historical and archival documents, testimonies and expert insights, the collaboration has been essential for the visual and narrative aspects of the reconstruction.

The Santa Clara 3D project focuses on the digital reconstruction and storytelling of the former concentration camp Santa Clara in Soria, Spain. The project demonstrates how lesser known or unavailable sites can be explored digitally, offering educational value and promoting awareness. During and after the Spanish Civil War, the Santa Clara complex served as a concentration camp. The site held mainly political prisoners under harsh conditions, suffering from overcrowding, lack of food and basic hygiene, forced labour and in some cases executions without a trial [33]. Despite the site's historical significance, it has received limited attention and remains relatively unknown to the public. This project seeks to contribute to the recognition of the site by digitally reconstructing the concentration camp and presenting its history through a web-based platform. The target audience includes educators, students, researchers, memory activists and others with an interest in history. The platform aims to make the site's history accessible to a wide audience, encouraging exploration, reflection, and learning across generations.

4   Methodology

The development process reflects an approach inspired by participatory visualization design [19], which highlights the benefits of including stakeholders in the design process, by implementing feedback loops to ensure a satisfying final product. During the design process of Santa Clara 3D, data scientists of the MEMORISE team exchanged frequently with associates of the Asociación Recuerdo y Dignidad. Weekly feedback on prototypes has been essential to assure that the final product aligns with user needs.

A combination of digital reconstruction, interactive media, and storytelling are key methods used to communicate the history of the Santa Clara Concentration Camp. The methodology integrates historical research, architectural reconstruction, and the development of a web-based platform to make a digital experience (see Fig. 1).

4.1   Data Collection

To create a strong foundation and understanding of the project's intentions, it was necessary to collect data to gain deeper insight into the history of Santa Clara. This included historical research not only about the site's time as a concentration camp, but also its origins as a convent and its present-day condition. Since historical information about

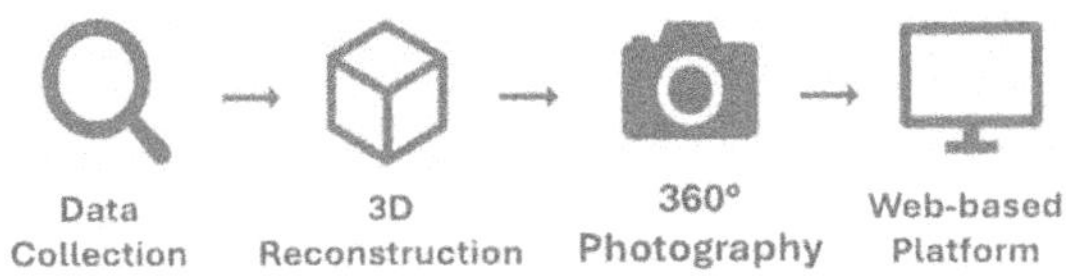

Fig. 1. Methodological overview of the project steps, from collecting and transforming data to integrating it to the digital platform.

the site were limited, most data was gathered from historical articles and a range of archival materials, including old maps, architectural drawings, and testimonies. These documents were used to understand the function, use, and layout of the site over time.

In addition to remote archival research, a field trip to Soria was conducted, aiming to better understand the "domain situation" (in accordance to the nested model for visualization design by Munzner [28]). Our goal was to explore the city and visit historical sites that influenced events during the Spanish Civil War. By participating in guided tours around the city and inside the Santa Clara complex, valuable local insight into the site's historical evolution was gained. Furthermore, expert input was offered by a local archaeologist who has worked on excavations at the Santa Clara site. He provided detailed information about the layout, transformations and historical significance of the complex. Overall, the field trip made a significant contribution to both the digital reconstruction and the storytelling elements integrated into the platform.

4.2 3D Reconstruction

Based on the documentation gathered during the data collection phase, we developed a digital 3D reconstruction of the Santa Clara Concentration Camp. This reconstruction was based primarily on architectural plan drawings from the period when Santa Clara functioned as a concentration camp. The modelling was carried out using SketchUp [8], a tool chosen for its accessibility and suitability for architectural modelling. A free version of SketchUp can be used for reconstruction purposes, however, novice users will face a steep learning curve in translating from historical architectural plans into accurate 3D representations. Santa Clara consisted of sixteen buildings during its time as a concentration camp, and each of these was modelled individually to create a comprehensive visualisation of the camp. The modelling process involved several key steps:

- Loading the architectural plan drawings of each building into SketchUp
- Scaling each drawing to match the real-world dimensions
- Tracing the architectural outlines using vector lines to define walls and floor plans
- Adding architectural elements such as windows, doors and structural features
- Extruding the 2D plans into 3D models
- Applying wall and roof details based on photographic references

Both photographs taken on the site and historical ones from the period when the camp was active were used during the 3D reconstruction phase. The historical photographs were particularly useful for the modelling of stylistic features such as window and door types, with the aim of maintaining architectural consistency with the time.

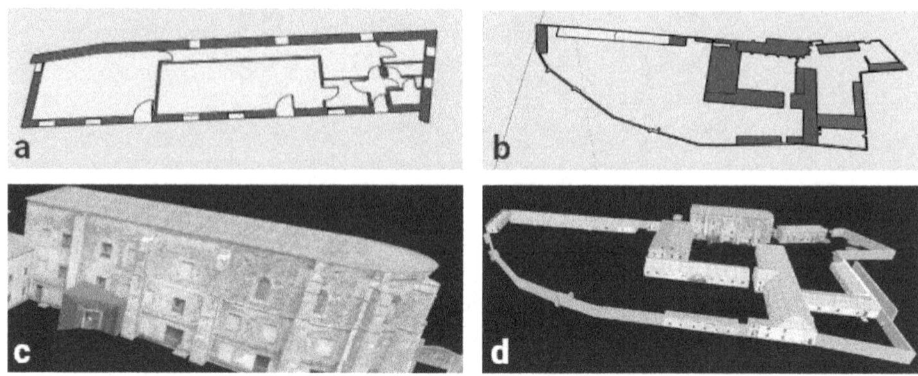

Fig. 2. 3D reconstruction of Santa Clara: (a) 2D floor plan of a single building from the Santa Clara concentration camp, created in SketchUp, (b) 2D overview of the entire camp layout, showing the placement and dimensions of all 16 buildings, (c) 3D model of one reconstructed building, including architectural features and texturing based on historical and photographic references, and (d) 3D overview of the entire camp reconstruction. The image highlights the visual contrast between buildings with and without applied wall textures.

To illustrate parts of the modelling process, Fig. 2 presents both 2D and 3D representations of the reconstruction in SketchUp. Figure 2a shows a 2D floor plan of a single building, while Fig. 2b illustrates an overview of the entire camp layout. Correspondingly, Fig. 2c and d display 3D models of one of the buildings and the complete camp, respectively. In the 3D models, the application of wall and roof textures is visible, with Fig. 2d particularly highlighting the contrast between textured and non-textured surfaces. All modelling decisions were guided by the aim of achieving both spatial and historical accuracy, to make the reconstruction as authentic as possible, based on the available sources.

4.3   360° Photography

In the process of developing the digital twin of the present state of Santa Clara, different methods were considered, including photogrammetry [34] and LiDAR scanning [31]. However, since only three buildings remain, none of which contain original architectural elements from the concentration camp period, a detailed scan of the current structures was deemed less relevant for a project focused on historical reconstruction. As an alternative, the site's present-day state was documented using low-cost 360° photography [25]. This method is quick, easily accessible, and provides sufficient spatial awareness while creating a visual and navigable experience.

During the field trip to Soria, the 360° photographs were captured on site. Polycam [6] was chosen to create the images, as it provides an easy-to-use platform with consistent results. The photographs were taken using an iPad Pro mounted on a tripod to ensure stable movement, making the images more consistent and clearer. Photographs were captured throughout the entire complex, allowing users to explore the site virtually by navigating between images. The 360° photographs were then processed and integrated into the platform using a three.js viewer [16]. This allows users to click and look around freely, providing a realistic impression of how the site appears today. Including these images helps establish a stronger connection between the present-day landscape and the historical events that took place, supporting users in understanding the contrast between past and present.

4.4 Development of Web-Based Platform

To convey the history of Santa Clara and enable public exploration, a web-based platform was created. It was developed using HTML, CSS, and JavaScript, and incorporates libraries such as MapLibre [3] for the interactive map and Three.js [16] for rendering the 3D models. The platform was designed as an immersive way of exploring the history of the Santa Clara site through different technical solutions. By enabling non-linear engagement with Santa Clara's layered history, the project takes inspiration from Mitchell Whitelaw's concept of the Generous Interface [37]. This concept promotes rich, browsable overviews rather than limiting access through search functions or hierarchical menus. Through the integration of an interactive map containing markers with distinguishable icons for different media types (3D model, 360° photographs, video, historical photographs), the platform encourages curiosity and invites exploration.

A timeline slider allows users to switch between three historical layers of the site: (1) its origins as a convent, (2) its use as a concentration camp, and (3) its present-day condition. This multi-layered approach, combined with spatial navigation, helps users develop a deeper understanding of the site's transformation over time. The design avoids predetermined storytelling paths and instead allows users to construct their own narrative journeys through movement, image exploration, and interaction with historical content.

To simplify updates and future changes, the interactive markers were implemented using separate GeoJSON files. These specify where each marker is located and what it contains. Each marker is categorized by their content - such as "3D models," "360° view," "Historical info," or "Video" and represented by custom icons. When a marker is selected, a pop-up window appears displaying a media and a descriptive text. This approach is made to ensure that each piece of content can stand independently, while still contributing to a broader historical narrative. The integration of the 3D reconstruction and the 360° photographs was achieved by exporting the SketchUp models and the Polycam photos into GLB-format and rendering them through use of Three.js library. This allows users to pan, zoom, and explore the virtual content in detail. The interface was developed to offer a meaningful way for users to engage with the memory and legacy of the camp through interaction, spatial awareness, and layered historical context.

5 Results

Santa Clara 3D is an interactive web-based platform that allows users to explore the history and the spatial layout of the former Santa Clara Concentration Camp. By integrating 3D models, 360° photographs, and historical information, the platform creates

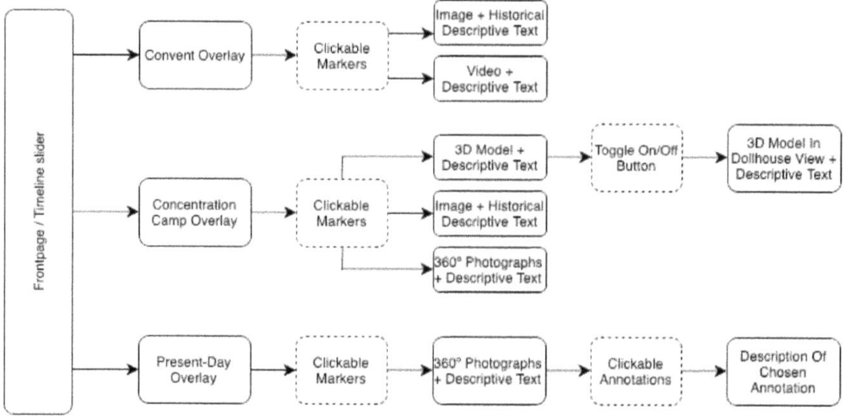

Fig. 3. Flowchart illustration of possible user interactions on the platform.

a layered, explorative digital experience. In the following, the interface is presented through screenshots, and a flowchart illustrates possible user interactions (see Fig. 3).

Upon loading the platform, users see an interactive map centred on the Santa Clara complex. The map allows zooming and panning to navigate the area and includes a timeline slider at the bottom of the interface. This slider allows users to toggle between three historical layers: the site's origin as a convent, its use as a concentration camp, and its present-day condition. In the concentration camp layer, a historical site plan from that period is applied as a map overlay (see Fig. 4), and a hand-drawn map from 1835 serves as the base layer in the convent layer (see Fig. 5). A smooth fade transition between layers helps users visually observe the architectural changes over time.

Each layer contains its own set of markers with custom icons indicating different types of media: 3D models, 360° photographs, historical information, and video. When clicking a marker, a pop-up window appears, displaying the media on the left and a descriptive text on the right. Navigation arrows allow users to move between markers, and an exit button returns them to the main map.

5.1   360° Photograph Annotations

The present-day and the concentration camp layer includes 360° photographs taken on-site using Polycam. These images allow users to virtually "stand" inside the complex and explore the surroundings in a panoramic view. Annotations within the 360° images mark the locations of current buildings and buildings that once existed during the concentration camp period. Clicking an annotation reveals a brief description of that building's former function (see Fig. 6 for an example showing the Small Nave and the former Central Nave).

5.2   3D Model Annotations

Markers labelled with a 3D icon are located on several buildings in the concentration camp overlay and indicate buildings that have been digitally reconstructed. When

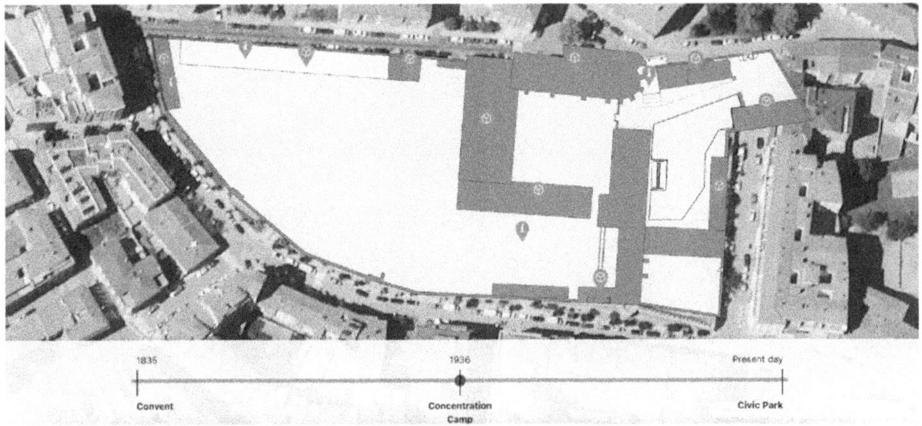

Fig. 4. *Concentration Camp Layer (1936)* – A reconstructed site plan overlays the map, showing the Santa Clara complex during its use as a concentration camp. Markers open 3D models and historical descriptions of the buildings, enabling users to explore the camp's structure and use.

selected, the pop-up displays a 3D model of the Santa Clara complex with the chosen building in focus, along with a descriptive text (see Fig. 7). A toggle button reveals a dollhouse-style view of the building, allowing users to examine the interior layout (see Fig. 8).

To distinguish between buildings that no longer exist and those that still stand today, two different texture styles are applied: photographic textures based on current site visits and historical photos for existing structures, and monochrome textures for non-existing buildings. The models are fully interactive, allowing users to rotate and zoom for better understanding of the site's spatial layout.

5.3   Video Annotations

Markers featuring a "play" icon open embedded videos and a descriptive text when clicked. These short clips, which must be manually started, show a local archaeologist discussing the site's historical significance and providing context primarily about its use prior to becoming a concentration camp.

5.4   Photograph Annotations

Markers with an "i" icon appear in both the convent and concentration camp layers. These provide archival photographs and historical context on key topics such as "Living Conditions", "Types of Prisoners", and "Forced Labour". Figure 9 illustrates a marker presenting a scanned letter from a doctor who evaluated the camp's conditions in 1939. Additionally, the "Forced Labour" marker includes a zoom-out feature that reveals two off-site locations associated with prisoner labour.

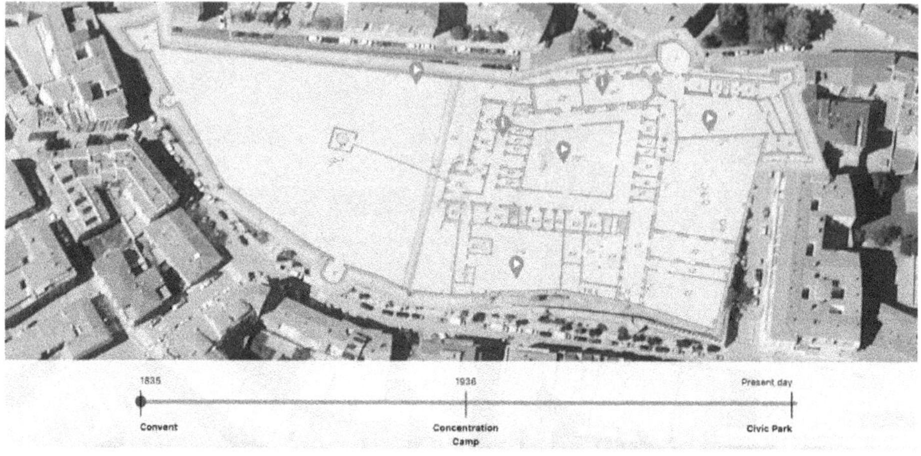

Fig. 5. *Convent Layer (1835)* – A hand-drawn historical map depicts the original layout of the Santa Clara convent. Informational and video markers provide insight into the site's religious function and early architecture.

6 Discussion

In the development of the platform, many design choices were considered to accommodate the implementation of different media types, interactive tools, and historical information.

6.1 Iterative Design Process

As part of the design process, the interface evolved through several sketches (see Fig. 10), aiming to improve user interaction and exploration of the site. In early drafts, a front page focused on the 3D model of Santa Clara with a separate menu for exploring different topics, like the timeline, was imagined (see Fig. 10a). However, this structure lacked the ability to show the historical depth of the site, and the layout felt too separate.

In later sketches (see Fig. 10b), the design shifted toward combining all components into a single main view. The idea of placing the timeline slider directly on the map was implemented, allowing users to move through different historical periods of the site. The platform still included a menu that offered topics such as "Living Conditions" and "Forced Labour". The intention of keeping everything in one view was to make the experience more intuitive and support user-led exploration.

In the final design (see Fig. 10c), the timeline is placed at the bottom of a satellite map, and the menu was replaced by clickable markers that offer an open-ended way of interacting with the site's content. Overall, the design process focused on finding a balance between clarity, engagement, and historical reflection. Each stage helped shape a platform that emphasizes the importance of showing change over time and keeping the memory of these places alive.

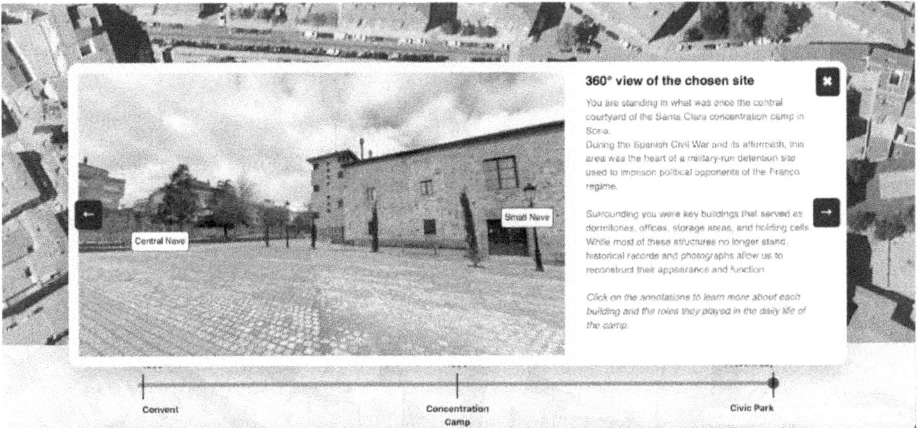

Fig. 6. *360° Photograph with Annotations* – A panoramic image of the Santa Clara site showing the existing Small Nave and the former Central Nave, with clickable annotations that provide historical descriptions of each structure.

6.2 Historical Authenticity

The intention of using digital tools to contribute meaningfully to the remembrance of historical sites associated with difficult pasts, such as the Spanish Civil War and Francoist repression, was a central motivation throughout the creation of this platform. The project aimed to demonstrate how digital technologies can help communicate such complex topics while also encouraging exploration, reflection, and emotional engagement.

A key design strategy was the use of a timeline slider, which allows users to toggle between different historical phases of the Santa Clara complex. Beyond simply visualising change, this feature highlights the site's transformation over time and serves as a narrative device. By allowing users to shift between temporal states, the platform illustrates how historical sites are overwritten and transformed. This intends to invite users to reflect on how histories can be hidden or forgotten, underscoring the importance of remembrance. The monochrome textures applied to the reconstructed 3D buildings reinforce this theme of absence. The use of grayscale signals that these buildings belong to the past and emphasizes that their visualisation is based on interpretation and educated guesses, rather than certainties. The contrast between grayscale and full-colour textures visually conveys the idea of memory and loss, aligning with the idea of the history being partly lost or hidden.

During the development, custom-made markers were implemented to distinguish between different types of media. Options such as numbering the markers to suggest a fixed story order, or using color-coded categories, were considered. However, the design was chosen to allow the users the ability to explore the content in their own way. The open-ended design intends to encourage personal reflection rather than guiding users through a fixed narrative [37].

One central challenge was the limited availability of reliable information and resources about Santa Clara. Much of the history from this period remains undocu-

Fig. 7. 3D reconstruction of the Convent.

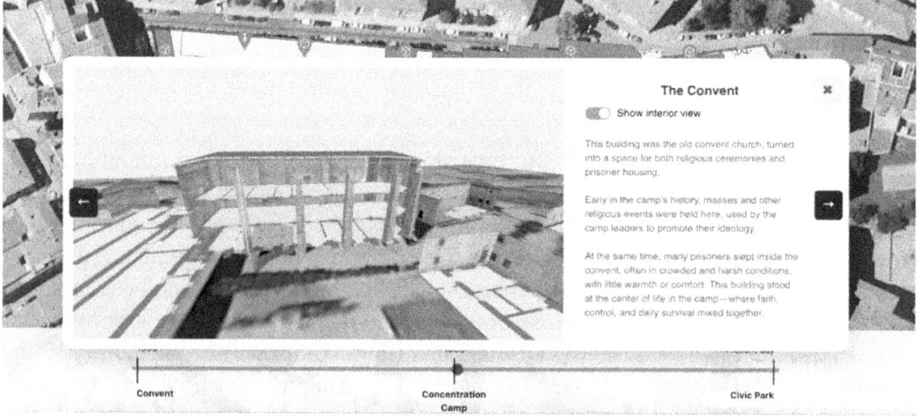

Fig. 8. Dollhouse-view of the 3D reconstruction of the Convent.

mented, or was actively erased, which made it difficult to ensure historical accuracy. As a result, some compromises had to be made, both in the historical content and the design of the platform. This was especially true in the 3D reconstructions, where certain visual details, like building textures or architectural features, had to be based on educated assumptions or comparisons with other structures known to have existed in the camp. These choices inevitably introduce some degree of uncertainty.

Being developed in close collaboration with the MEMORISE project, it was important that the platform aligned with the organization's goals of promoting digital memory activism. Although this platform cannot replace a physical memorial or a historical archive, it offers users the opportunity to explore, interact, and reflect at their own pace. It is the hope that this will provide an intriguing experience especially for younger generations or people unfamiliar with the history. In the end, this platform aims not only

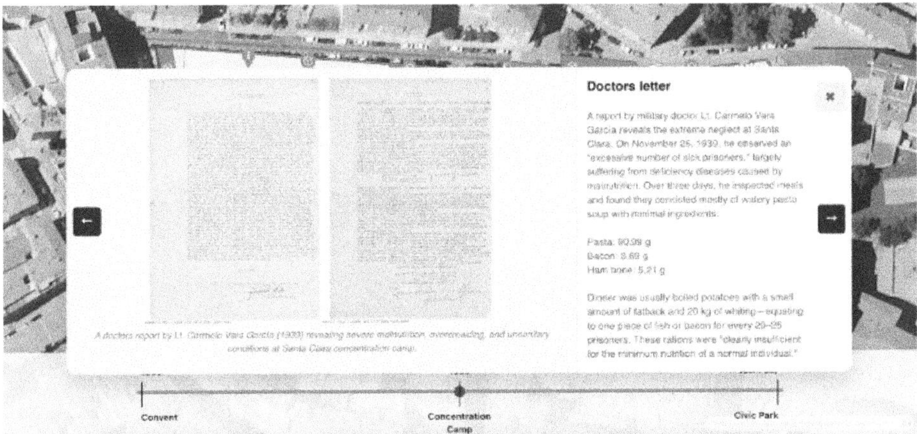

Fig. 9. Pop-up of the concentration camp layer showing a 1939 medical testimony by a doctor who evaluated camp conditions, accompanied by contextual information.

to present the history of Santa Clara, but also to serve as an example of how digital technologies can contribute to memory work, public history, and historical awareness.

6.3   Evaluation

The Asociación Recuerdo y Dignidad played a crucial role in strengthening the platform's historical foundation by supplying archival material and validating historical narratives. Their input on content related to forced labour, types of prisoners, and living conditions helped ensure the platform presents a respectful and accurate portrayal of the site's past.

As part of the final development stage, a meeting was held with three representatives from the Asociación Recuerdo y Dignidad to present and evaluate the final prototype. This expert evaluation confirmed the project's clarity and value, while also proposing improvements such as the addition of an information box on each overlay to introduce and clarify the time period shown.

To further improve the platform, a more comprehensive evaluation should ideally be conducted. By presenting the platform in a controlled setting, such as a physical exhibition, researchers could collect data through direct observations, user interviews, and logging of user behavior across devices. This approach would provide valuable insights into usability and emotional engagement, ultimately enhancing the platform's effectiveness as a tool for historical reflection and education.

This collaborative process ensured that the final platform met its stated objectives, offering a meaningful, research-based, and interactive experience that contributes to the ongoing remembrance of this historical site.

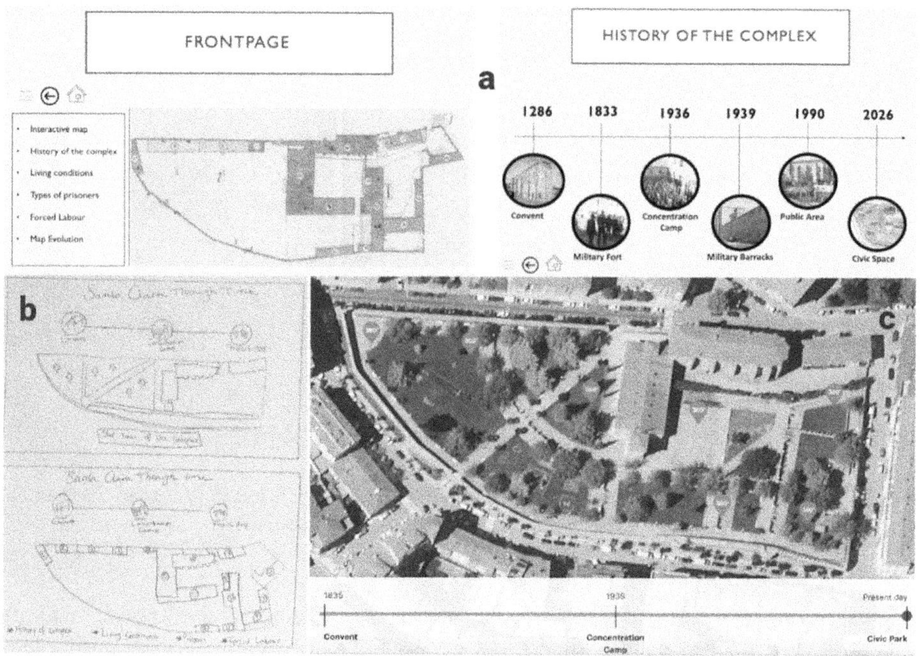

Fig. 10. Sketches from the design process showing the evolution of the platform interface. (a) Early concept with a central 3D model and separate menu. (b) Sketch combining the timeline slider with the main map view, while still including a menu for thematic content. (c) Final design featuring an interactive satellite map with bottom timeline and interactive markers for open-ended exploration.

6.4 Limitations

While the platform successfully meets many of the intended goals, several limitations have influenced the outcome of the project. Working under time constraints inevitably required certain compromises, limiting the final product. The available archival materials, testimonies, and visual references related to the Santa Clara Concentration Camp are very limited. Much of the historical information was retrieved from local articles, and many assumptions about the purpose of specific buildings were based on educated guesses - grounded in historical floor plans and typical uses of similar spaces. Because of the limited material, certain narrative and reconstruction choices relied on interpretation rather than definitive evidence. Although this was acknowledged and addressed throughout the project, it affected the amount of detail that could be included and reduced the level of historical precision in some areas. Additionally, all of the historical documents provided by Asociación Recuerdo y Dignidad were in Spanish, requiring the use of online translation tools to interpret the content. While these translations were handled carefully, they may have introduced slight inaccuracies or misunderstandings that affected the level of detail in some areas.

The collaboration with Asociación Recuerdo y Dignidad was crucial for providing historical context. However, as this organization operates primarily through voluntary work, communication sometimes lagged due to limited availability or resources. This occasionally led to improvised solutions, which may have affected the depth or accuracy of some aspects of the project.

6.5 Future Work

This project contributes to a great first step in using digital tools to engage with the history of Santa Clara Concentration Camp. However, further developments could improve Santa Clara 3D.

- **User Testing:** Throughout the development of the platform, weekly feedback has been essential in shaping the final design choices. However, to reach a broader and more diverse audience, structured user testing could be considered. By observing how different users interact with the platform, improvements in general areas like navigation and overall user-friendliness could be identified. This feedback could lead to the development of a more tailored user experience, enhancing the platform for different user groups.
- **Tutorial:** The implementation of a short introduction or tutorial on how to use the platform could help users understand the platform's structure and tools more easily. This would especially be useful for user groups unfamiliar with digital heritage platforms or 3D interfaces.
- **Expanding Content:** Integrating more archival materials, oral histories, personal testimonies or other resources from families of victims or local residents would greatly enhance the overall user experience. These additions would reinforce the memory of the narratives and add more content to the historical experience.
- **Performance:** Future work could focus on improving the platform's overall technical performance. This might include implementing lower-resolution 3D models to reduce loading times or optimising the code for better cross-device compatibility—especially for mobile devices. Although the platform is currently accessible on smartphones, mobile-specific design adjustments are needed to create a fully usable mobile experience.
- **Extended Reality:** Future development could include incorporating virtual reality (VR) to allow users to explore the reconstructed site in a more immersive and intuitive way. Augmented reality (AR) could also be relevant, enabling users to visualise former buildings digitally while physically present on the site. These technologies could create deeper emotional significance and further strengthen the educational potential of the project.
- **Multi-Language Support:** As this project was developed in collaboration with a Spanish organisation, it would make sense to provide a Spanish translation of the platform. Making the platform multilingual could help attract a more diverse audience and broaden accessibility.

Overall, these suggestions for future improvements could enhance the platform's accessibility, engagement, and educational impact, resulting in a deeper and more immersive exploration of the history of Santa Clara.

7   Conclusion

The main goal of this work was to explore how the implementation of digital tools could enhance the remembrance and interpretation of neglected historical sites. It focused on Santa Clara Park in Soria, Spain, which functioned as a concentration camp during the Spanish Civil War and now shows only minimal traces of its harsh past. Through 3D reconstruction, 360° photography, and historical research, a web-based platform was created to highlight the site's historical significance. The platform demonstrates how digital tools can offer new ways to engage with difficult historical topics. By implementing features such as a timeline slider and layered map overlays, users are invited to explore the site's temporal evolution and reflect on what has been forgotten over time. Design choices, such as the use of custom markers and monochrome textures for non-extant buildings, emphasize historical transformation, spatial change, and emotional engagement. While limitations affected the level of detail and historical precision, the platform offers a strong foundation for future development. Suggestions for further improvement include structured user testing, content expansion, technical optimisation, and the possible integration of VR or AR technologies.

The project highlights the value of digital heritage methods as meaningful tools for memory work. By combining digital reconstruction with an open-ended, exploratory interface and historical narratives, the platform invites a broader reflection on how digital tools can shape the way we remember the past. One of the main contributions of our work is the development of a low-cost pipeline that can easily adapted to reconstruction and storytelling projects for other historical sites.

References

1. Anne Frank House: Anne Frank VR Tour launched (2018). https://www.annefrank.org/en/about-us/news-and-press/news/2018/6/12/anne-frank-house-vr-launched/. Accessed 25 May 2025
2. Asociación Recuerdo y Dignidad. https://recuerdoydignidad.org. Accessed 25 May 2025
3. MapLibre. https://maplibre.org. Accessed 25 May 2025
4. Mauthausen Memorial: Interactive Map. https://mm-tours.org/en/20. Accessed 25 May 2025
5. MEMORISE Project. https://memorise.sdu.dk/about-memorise/. Accessed 25 May 2025
6. Polycam: How to Create 360 Captures. https://learn.poly.cam/hc/en-us/articles/27488059219220-How-to-Create-360-Captures. Accessed 25 May 2025
7. Reframe Project: Virtualising Memoryscapes: Guidelines for the Digital Holocaust Memory Project. University of Sussex (2024). https://reframe.sussex.ac.uk/digitalholocaustmemory/files/2024/07/Virtualising-Memoryscapes-Guidelines-Digital-Holocaust-Memory-Project-1.pdf. Accessed 25 May 2025
8. SketchUp: What is SketchUp?. https://vdci.edu/learn/sketchup/what-is-sketchup. Accessed 25 May 2025
9. Terezin Memorial: Interactive Map. https://www.pamatnik-terezin.cz/map. Accessed 25 May 2025
10. UC San Diego Library: Spanish Civil War Memory Project. https://library.ucsd.edu/dc/collection/bb8602294g. Accessed 25 May 2025
11. USC Shoah Foundation: Dimensions in Testimony. https://sfi.usc.edu/dit. Accessed 25 May 2025

12. Yad Vashem: 360° Virtual Tour. https://www.yadvashem.org/education/educational-materials/learning-environment/virtual-tour.html. Accessed 25 May 2025
13. Antonaci, A., Ott, M., Pozzi, F.: Virtual museums, cultural heritage education and 21st century skills. In: Learning & Teaching with Media & Technology, vol. 185, pp. 1–14 (2013)
14. Benardou, A., Droumpouki, A.M., Papaioannou, G.: First-person interactive experience of a concentration camp: the case of block 15. In: Difficult Heritage and Immersive Experiences, pp. 145–160. Routledge (2022)
15. Chiao, H.M., Chen, Y.L., Huang, W.H.: Examining the usability of an online virtual tour-guiding platform for cultural tourism education. J. Hosp. Leisure Sport Tourism Educ. **23**, 29–38 (2018)
16. Dirksen, J.: Three.js Cookbook. Packt Publishing Ltd. (2015)
17. Gomes, L., Bellon, O.R.P., Silva, L.: 3D reconstruction methods for digital preservation of cultural heritage: a survey. Pattern Recogn. Lett. **50**, 3–14 (2014)
18. Jänicke, S.: Memorise: new digital approaches for Nazi persecution storytelling. Open Access Gov. **44**(1), 255–257 (2024)
19. Jänicke, S., Kaur, P., Kuzmicki, P., Schmidt, J.: Participatory visualization design as an approach to minimize the gap between research and application. In: VisGap@ Eurographics/EuroVis, pp. 35–42 (2020)
20. Jaskot, P.B., Knowles, A.K.: Architecture and maps, databases and archives: an approach to institutional history and the built environment in Nazi Germany. The Iris **15** (2017)
21. Koehl, M., et al.: The memory of a 2nd WW camp: 3D modeling using the combination of hybrid technologies. Int. Arch. Photogramm. Remote. Sens. Spat. Inf. Sci. **43**, 875–882 (2021)
22. Kusnick, J., Mayr, E., Seirafi, K., Beck, S., Liem, J., Windhager, F.: Every thing can be a hero! Narrative visualization of person, object, and other biographies. Informatics **11**, 26 (2024)
23. Li, J., Nie, J.W., Ye, J.: Evaluation of virtual tour in an online museum: exhibition of architecture of the forbidden city. PLoS ONE **17**(1), e0261607 (2022)
24. Liritzis, I., Volonakis, P., Vosinakis, S.: 3d reconstruction of cultural heritage sites as an educational approach. The sanctuary of Delphi. Appl. Sci. **11**(8), 3635 (2021)
25. Matzen, K., Cohen, M.F., Evans, B., Kopf, J., Szeliski, R.: Low-cost 360 stereo photography and video capture. ACM Trans. Graph. (TOG) **36**(4), 1–12 (2017)
26. Meffert, N., Østergaard, C.V., Jänicke, S., Khulusi, R., Rachow, E., Andersen, N.S.: A survey on storytelling techniques for heritage on Nazi persecution. In: VISIGRAPP (1): GRAPP, HUCAPP, IVAPP, pp. 603–615 (2024)
27. Meinecke, C., Hall, C., Jänicke, S.: Towards enhancing virtual museums by contextualizing art through interactive visualizations. ACM J. Comput. Cult. Heritage **15**(4), 1–26 (2022)
28. Munzner, T.: A nested model for visualization design and validation. IEEE Trans. Vis. Comput. Graph. **15**(6), 921–928 (2009)
29. Oliva, L.S., Mura, A., Betella, A., Pacheco, D., Martinez, E., Verschure, P.: Recovering the history of Bergen Belsen using an interactive 3D reconstruction in a mixed reality space the role of pre-knowledge on memory recollection. In: 2015 Digital Heritage, vol. 1, pp. 163–165. IEEE (2015)
30. Pourmoradian, S., Farrokhi, O.S., Hosseini, S.Y.: Museum visitors' interest on virtual tours in COVID-19 situation. J. Environ. Manage. Tourism **12**(4), 877–885 (2021)
31. Raj, T., Hanim Hashim, F., Baseri Huddin, A., Ibrahim, M.F., Hussain, A.: A survey on LiDAR scanning mechanisms. Electronics **9**(5), 741 (2020)
32. Rodríguez-García, B., Guillen-Sanz, H., Checa, D., Bustillo, A.: A systematic review of virtual 3d reconstructions of cultural heritage in immersive virtual reality. Multimedia Tools Appl., 1–51 (2024)

33. Rodríguez González, J., Berzal de la Rosa, E.: Cárceles y campos de concentración en castilla y león. León, Funda-ción **27** (2011)
34. Schenk, T.: Introduction to photogrammetry. The Ohio State University, Columbus **106**(1), 1 (2005)
35. Segel, E., Heer, J.: Narrative visualization: telling stories with data. IEEE Trans. Vis. Comput. Graph. **16**(6), 1139–1148 (2010)
36. Suhardjono, L.A.: The use of digital technologies in the art world to preserve traumatic cultural legacies. In: E3S Web of Conferences, vol. 426, p. 02047. EDP Sciences (2023)
37. Whitelaw, M.: Generous interfaces for digital cultural collections. Digit. Humanit. Q. **9**(1), 1–16 (2015)

Enhancing Industrial Efficiency and Sustainability: A Web-Based Interoperable Solution for Industrial Forms Management

José Cosme[1(✉)] , Armindo Fernandes[2], Vasco Amorim[1,3] , and Vítor Filipe[1,3]

[1] School of Science and Technology, University of Trás-os-Montes e Alto Douro (UTAD), 5000-801 Vila Real, Portugal
a174139@alunos.utad.pt
[2] Continental Advanced Antenna, Sociedade Unipessoal, Lda, Vila Real, Portugal
[3] INESC Technology and Science, 4200-465 Porto, Portugal

Abstract. One of the main challenges in modern industrial environments is managing the large amount of physical documentation obtained during the production process. Companies increasingly seek to adopt paperless alternatives to promote production efficiency and reduce their industrial environmental impact. On the shop floor, each production line relies on standardised forms to verify parameters and conditions before and after production begins; however, the large volume of paper documentation generated from these records led to the need to develop a digital platform capable of streamlining and digitising forms, enhancing process sustainability and efficiency. The proposed interoperable web application provides various features that allow users to create, customise, submit and approve forms digitally. It also integrates automated notifications and alerts for specific situations, enabling more effective responses to the production process's momentary needs. By unifying all processes related to forms management within a digital infrastructure, this solution aligns with the current industrial paradigm, reducing reliance on paper, optimising workflow efficiency, and incorporating innovative and industrial advancements.

Keywords: Digital Transition · Industry 4.0 · Industry 5.0 · Paperless Factory · Industrial Checklists · Ramp-up

1 Introduction

The transition to the factories of the future in the era of the fourth industrial revolution, based on digital transformation, is a significant topic at both academic and industrial levels [1,2]. As a term globally adopted over the past decade, Industry 4.0 is characterised by a paradigm shift in the production environment through the digitalisation and integration of the entire value chain throughout the product lifecycle, leveraging key technological trends such as the Internet of Things (IoT) and Cyber-Physical Production Systems (CPPS) [3,4].

However, despite all the advantages of this revolution and unprecedented innovation and efficiency, new challenges have emerged in modern society, and the importance

J. F. Krems et al. (Eds.): CHIRA 2025, CCIS 2836, pp. 269–281, 2026.
https://doi.org/10.1007/978-3-032-16454-4_15

of social and ecological sustainability is taking on a leading role. Thus, Industry 5.0 appears to combine the technological tools and capabilities developed over the past decade with the need to place the worker at the centre of the production process, aiming to promote a fundamental balance between the efficiency associated with Industry 4.0 and the sustainability related to Industry 5.0 [5].

One of the main challenges in modern industrial environments is managing the large amount of physical documentation produced during the production process. Companies increasingly seek to adopt alternative policies and methodologies for this type of documentation [6].

In this study's industrial context, each production line has an associated paper recording the state/condition of production and equipment [7]. This work, developed as part of the A-MOVER Agenda in partnership with Continental Advanced Antenna (CAA), focuses on creating a digital platform configured as an interoperable web application, unifying and centralising all procedures associated with the production lines [8]. The solution streamlines the creation, customisation, submission and approval of digital forms while incorporating features such as automatic notifications and alerts for specific situations. Despite the challenges that will need to be overcome, such as changing the communication flow on the factory floor, operators' reluctance to transition to a digital solution, and even combining both techniques (manual and digital) during an experimental period in which production cannot stop, the web application represents a promising step in replacing the current paper-based approach, increasing production efficiency, improving the integration and collaboration of different stakeholders, and achieving the goals associated with digital transition and sustainable production [9, 10].

The paper is structured as follows: Sect. 2 covers the technological context and academic work, Sect. 3 details the case study and the proposed solution, Sect. 4 discusses the impact on the factory and establishes a brief conclusion.

2   Background

The digital transformation promoted by Industry 4.0 technologies has highlighted the role of machines in the industry. However, the need presented by Industry 5.0 to combine modern manufacturing efficiency and productivity with sustainability principles and human-centric production promotes solutions capable of reconciling the human-machine connection and the symbiotic relationship between them [11, 12].

Adopting these solutions implies significant changes, particularly in Document Management Systems (DMS) and using technologies capable of promoting their digital transition [13]. Therefore, DMS, a traditional solution to digitise and organise documents, is evolving into electronic Document Management System (eDMS), offering a digital solution capable of improving operational efficiency and data management. These systems align with digital transition strategies, reducing reliance on paper-based documentation and improving operational efficiency and data accessibility. Implementing eDMS allows companies to control the increasing amount of documentation produced. Benefits such as cost and time savings that will enable companies to align with the environmental sustainability goal by reducing reliance on paper [14].

Reducing paper consumption, particularly in industries and scenarios where alternative solutions that don't depend on this resource can be developed and implemented, is essential, given that the paper production industry significantly contributes to deforestation and greenhouse gas emissions. According to recent data from 2022, the pulp and paper industry, being one of the most energy-intensive industries, contributed around 2% of total industrial emissions [15].

The ramp-up checklist, a term used in literature to define the type of forms filled out by the operators on the production lines, is a document commonly used at the beginning of shifts or during changes in production flow [7, 16]. These checklists assist operators and maintenance teams in executing procedures related to equipment, processes, and the production system. While specific items may vary according to operational requirements, an information system that integrates with asset management processes on the factory floor can improve the efficiency of maintenance strategies, reduce costs, enhance equipment reliability, and optimise overall asset use [16].

The existence of case studies related to the design, development, and implementation of information systems based on DMS constitutes a fundamental premise in assessing the feasibility of developing a solution capable of addressing the industrial process described in this study [17, 18]. These approaches demonstrate the ability of different system stakeholders to perform actions, such as updating and modifying documentation, simultaneously and automatically. Additionally, these eDMS can adapt to required demands and overcome intrinsic barriers to physical document management, such as inefficiencies associated with manual processes and record loss.

Integrating the digital checklist with workflow management tools allows the system to have functionalities for task coordination related to completing these records. Situations where anomalies or deviations from the standards for proper production are detected can trigger notification and alert mechanisms for the responsible teams, initiating procedures and actions to address the necessary corrections quickly [16]. This is also related to the system's ability to store previously reviewed and validated documentation, maintaining a record of the activities and changes made. The historical records can be accessed and reviewed at any time for auditing purposes or to conduct performance analysis based on historical data [16, 19].

In summary, all studies and work conducted during the contemporary industrial revolutions, focusing on process digitalisation and the transition to paperless factories, contribute to a solid scientific background, supporting the development of the solution described in the next section.

3   Web Application Proposal

The solution described in this section considers a specific use case at Continental Advanced Antenna. CAA is part of the Continental group, operating at level 1 of the Automotive sector. It primarily collaborates with the premium segment of automotive industry brands and produces approximately 15 million car antennas annually. The need for a document digitisation solution emerged to streamline form creation and management on the production lines.

3.1   Industrial Use Case

At the factory floor level, there is a final stage of production where the Printed Circuit Boards (PCBs) are individualised, and the final assembly is performed. Typically, each type of antenna produced for a specific customer is associated with a dedicated assembly line. At CAA, the startup checklist, Fig. 1, is a document that must be mandatorily and carefully filled out at the beginning of each shift, with every reference change, and after extended maintenance/intervention in the process or quality issue. The purpose of this document is to verify compliance with the defined criteria for all production requirements.

CHECK LIST - PRODUCTION CONTROL

| LINE No. | | | SHIFT: | DATE:___/___/___ | PRODUCT NO.: | | |
| | | | | | HOUR: | h | m |

Responsible for verification:			Verification operation before starting production:	Start of Shift
Op	Sup	VQ		Yes / N/A	No / Fixed
x	x		1 Are the employees able to perform the tasks they will perform (Check Polyvalence matrix and line formation - ILU)?	☐☐	☐☐
x	x		2 Is the electric model OK on the EOL?	☐☐	☐☐
x	x		3 Is the welding program the right one? Check Programs List.	☐☐	☐☐
x	x		4 Is the objective programme the correct one (Antenna reference)?	☐☐	☐☐
x	x		5 Are the status of the FDs correct? (Check status listing)	☐☐	☐☐
x	x		6 Check the date of the fd's (the production date must correspond to the date stated in the fd)	☐☐	☐☐
x	x		7 Do Poka-Yoke detect NOK models?	☐☐	☐☐
x	x		8 Are IFCs visible and placed throughout the process?	☐☐	☐☐
x	x		9 Are the boxes for analysis and scrap empty?	☐☐	☐☐
x	x		10 Do operators comply with ESD protection rules?	☐☐	☐☐
x	x		11 Is the line clean (on the lines with TPM check if the same was performed in the previous shift), tidy and the tools are clean and in good condition?	☐☐	☐☐

Fig. 1. Example of a Paper-based Ramp-up Checklist in CAA.

3.2   Paperless Solution

The operator fills out the checklist on the production line, and despite having access to a computer, this record is manually kept on paper. Introducing digital forms would make their completion more intuitive and less prone to errors. Regarding communication flow, the automatic notification of responsible teams, such as supervision and maintenance, and the creation of alerts would add value to the constant and effective monitoring of production line equipment and communication process efficiency. Retaining a history of completed and validated forms could enable the formulation of analyses and conclusions about potential systematic issues in process and/or equipment, facilitating more appropriate production process planning and preventive maintenance.

The envisioned solution is characterised by its cross-departmental use within the factory, contributing to the efficiency and integrity of operations and workflow. This enhancement in data accuracy empowers teams to make appropriate assessments and conclusions, improving reassurance and confidence.

The main functions of this software would be managing digital forms, allowing their creation, customisation, completion, and validation; generating notifications and alerts; retaining a computerised document history; managing traceability and access; and preserving data associated with backup and recovery plans.

The application architecture (Fig. 2) is based on the client-server paradigm and follows a two-dimensional structure consisting of the presentation layer (Front End) and the logical layer (Back End).

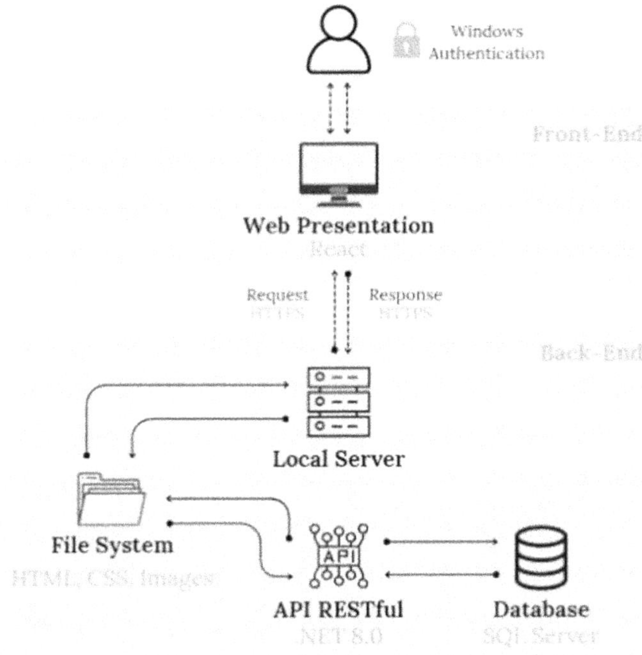

Fig. 2. Application Architecture.

Access to the system would be subject to a login system through defined credentials for all levels of the corporate hierarchy: production operators and versatile operators would have a global account with known credentials, while supervisors, coordinators, and back-office managers would have individual credentials. Thus, different access levels and permissions can be defined based on the hierarchy and the functions assigned to each user. These authentication and permissions policies enable the maintenance of records related to accesses and modifications, ensuring greater traceability and data security. They also generate logs for situations such as accessing documentation history or changes in parameters and document structures.

The user interface is developed in React, one of the most widely used and supported JavaScript libraries. It enables the creation of dynamic, responsive, and interactive user experiences. Communication between the Front-End and Back-End layers is established through HTTPS requests, ensuring the confidentiality and integrity of the data.

The Back-End structure is responsible for defining the application logic and data access. A RESTful API, implemented with .NET 8.0, can manipulate data with endpoints that establish the communication flow between the presentation layer and the database. The local server is responsible for hosting both the API and the file system that supports the application and where all static components are stored, from HTML pages and CSS style sheets to multimedia resources such as images.

The database is built using SQL Server, a relational database management system that allows controlled access to the database and provides optimised query mechanisms. The API interacts with the database through the Entity Framework Core, an object-relational mapping framework for ADO.NET.

Addressing the presentation layer and how the user interacts with the system, initial access to the application is carried out by entering user credentials on a login page. After correct authentication, users are redirected to the respective pages, always in accordance with their hierarchical responsibilities.

Once production operators have successfully authenticated themselves, they are presented with the checklist to complete (Fig. 3). Firstly, the page displays the line, shift, and product numbers associated with the startup checklist. Also, on the horizontal bar where this data is located, there is an icon that, when activated, alerts the supervisors assigned to the line to provide immediate technical assistance.

The main dashboard displays the parameters the operator must verify before, during, and after production starts.

Each parameter has two verification components associated with it to record its status. When the operator verifies that the parameter complies with the standards defined for correct production, he marks it with a check. Still, when this does not happen, he must select the option indicating that the parameter is NOK and write an observation. This information will be associated with the parameter for future analysis and reported directly to the supervisors responsible for the line.

Each parameter also has an option if the operator needs to consult a document related to their verification. The submission of the checklist is only possible when all parameters have a related state selected, thus preventing parameters from being unverified.

In turn, Fig. 4 presents a screenshot of the software for some hierarchical superiors who must actively manage, supervise, and maintain the workflow related to their work and functions. In the presented case, supervisors can maintain control over different val-

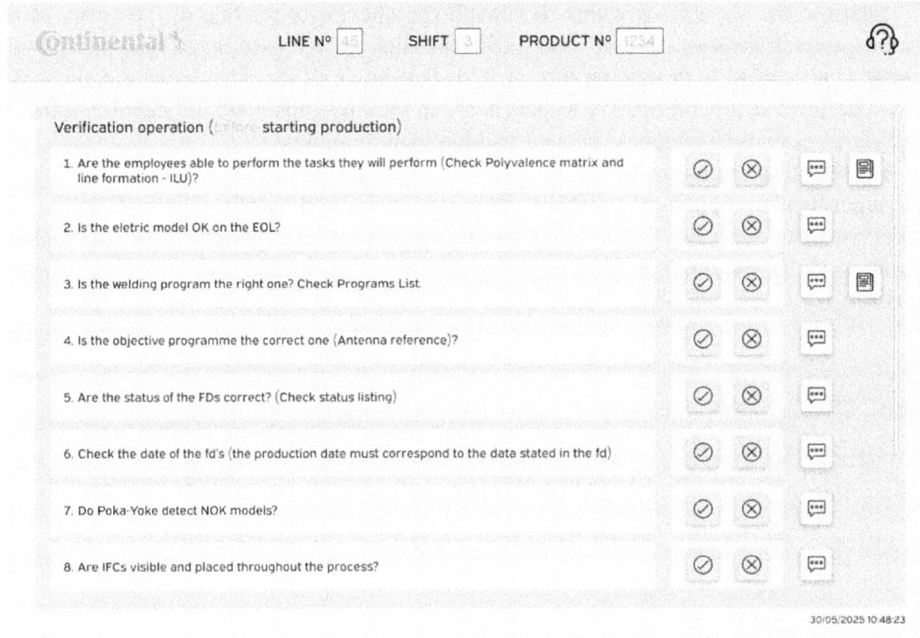

Fig. 3. Ramp-up Checklist Page.

idations and notifications through a single page, with a fixed vertical menu that allows intuitive navigation over different pages dedicated to specific functions.

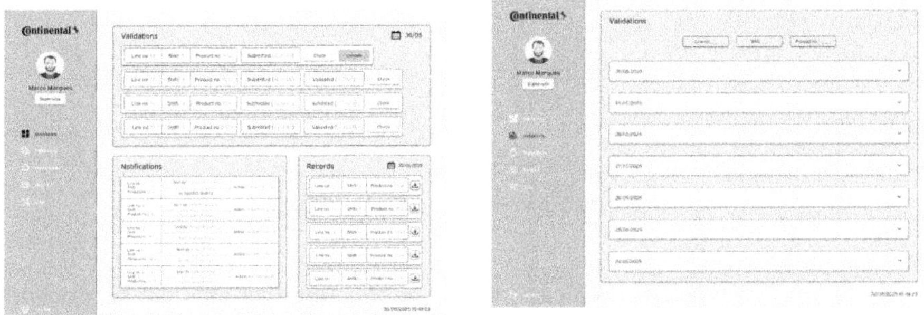

Fig. 4. Supervisor Dashboard Page.

Fig. 5. Supervisor Validations Page.

By selecting the Validations option in the vertical menu, the application redirects the supervisor to a page that presents a list of the last days of activity (Fig. 5). The supervisor can then view all the checklists associated with each day and validate the checklists pending validation. If the checklists the supervisor wishes to consult are not associated with the days shown, he/she can use the search inputs placed at the top of the dashboard to find by line number, shift, or product number.

Suppose the supervisor wants to consult the checklists for one of the seven most recent production days. In that case, they can click on the associated bar, which will reveal a vertical list in dropdown format. This list shows all the already validated checklists and those still pending. The supervisor can then use this page to consult validated and yet-to-be-validated checklists and validate pending ones.

By selecting the Notifications option in the vertical menu, the application redirects the supervisor to a page that displays all notifications addressed to them (Fig. 6). The supervisor can view the notifications from this page in more detail. Each notification displays all the information inherent to the checklist, the sender, time, and type of notification.

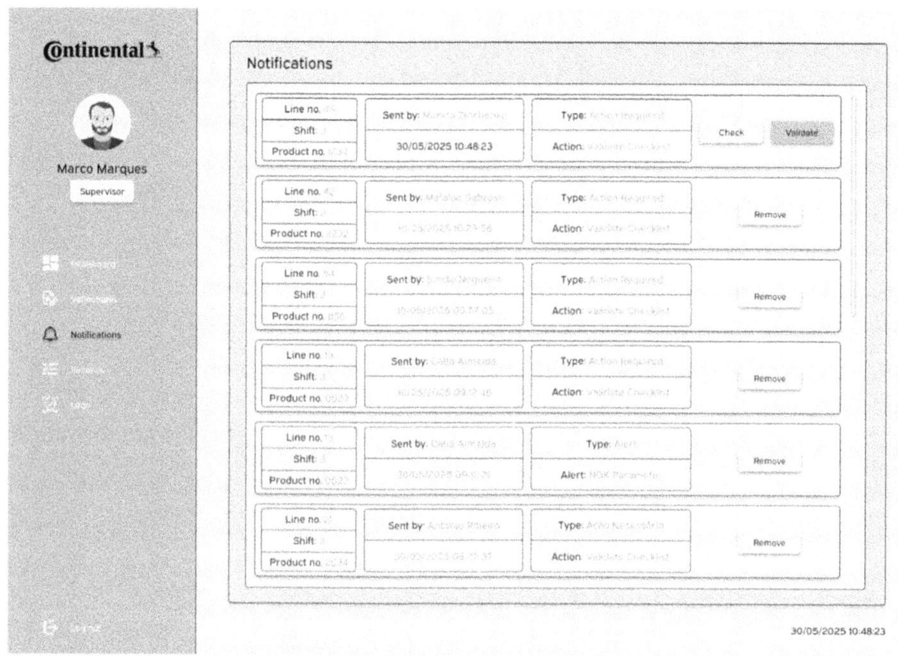

Fig. 6. Supervisor Notifications Page.

There are two types of notifications: the notification that tells the supervisor that an action needs to be taken, and the alert notification. The supervisor's actions can simply be validating a checklist, but an alert notification can indicate the need for a supervisor to go to the line to provide technical assistance. Also, if a notification alerts the supervisor to a pending validation, he can validate it through this page.

By selecting the Records option in the vertical menu, the supervisor is redirected to a page with a list of archived checklists. When initially accessing this page, the checklists displayed relate to the current production day. If the supervisor wants to do a more specific search, he/she can choose the day when the checklist was validated or search by line, shift, or product numbers. This page contains all the information regarding the processing of checklists, and it can be used to view/consult and download it.

Finally, and accessing the last option available to perform any type of productive function, the supervisor can consult the application's access and modification logs by selecting the Logs option. This dashboard displays all the logs registered in the system, including access by any employee and, for example, the change of a parameter of a specific checklist.

Regarding the application's use at the top of the business organisation, we have the coordinators and the back-office managers who, given their hierarchical position, perform the actions related to creating and customising the ramp-up checklists. They are also responsible for managing access and modification permissions.

With this in mind and to maintain a coherent web design, the main dashboard for these stakeholders does not differ substantially from the supervisor's dashboard. The new vertical menu only adds the Documents and Permissions options, removing the Validations option.

By selecting the Documents option in the vertical menu, the coordinator is presented with all existing and active forms in the database. The coordinator can edit, configure, replicate and turn off each form from this list.

Using the editing mechanism (Fig. 7), the coordinator can edit the description of each parameter individually and remove the parameter itself. Adding, updating, and removing documents associated with each parameter is also possible.

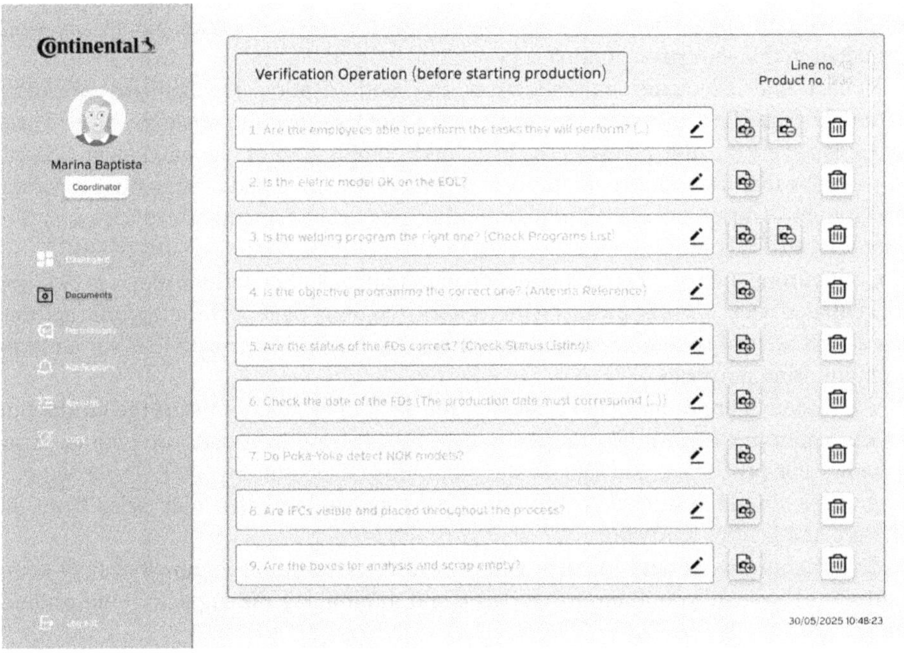

Fig. 7. Forms Edition Page.

In turn, if the user chooses to configure the form, an intuitive menu is displayed where they can directly change the line and product number to which the form corresponds.

One prominent feature of the forms management panel is the replication mechanism. Since many lines and/or products are associated with the same or similar startup checklists, this option allows the assignment of forms to specific lines much faster and more efficiently.

The last functionality made available by the system occurs when the coordinator selects the Permissions option in the vertical menu—a single page where coordinators can control all the access policies and permissions assigned to every application user.

3.3 Limitations

Given that the solution is in the final stages of development, this study's main limitation is the lack of data and testing to support the projected benefits. Therefore, the next step in executing this project will be to plan a testing phase to evaluate impacts, such as reducing errors when completing checklists, increasing communication and operational flow efficiency, and obtaining feedback from all stakeholders involved in the application.

It is necessary to evaluate constraints that may limit or potentially limit the development and implementation of this system, meet users' needs and expectations, and comply with all applicable norms and regulations for software development and work conducted in this industrial context.

Robust and adequate authentication and authorisation mechanisms are non-negotiable regarding the data produced and stored during the system's use. These mechanisms ensure the privacy, security, and compliance of personal data according to applicable laws and regulations and protect sensitive and confidential information through security and encryption methodologies against unauthorised access and/or cyber-attacks.

Configuring controlled access based on hierarchical authorisations requires defining differentiated access levels, ensuring that authorised users only perform specific actions. This access control is complemented by the need to log and trace activities for auditing and monitoring purposes.

The system's importance and criticality for the proper functioning of the production process imply that it must be efficient to avoid processing overloads, operate in parallel with other processes, and ensure the continuity of operations 24/7. These suggest designing a simple system that minimises risks and failures that may arise from the software and factory hardware.

This monitoring should identify and/or resolve potential problems that may arise, ensuring the system's continuous operation and minimising the impact on the production process.

4   Discussion

From the outset, the transition to a digital solution from the paper format promises financial and environmental sustainability benefits, with a direct reduction in paper consumption during the production process.

In quantitative terms, Continental Advanced Antenna production operators fill out an average of 140 daily checklists. Considering an operating year of 358 days, this represents an annual consumption of 50120 A4 sheets.

Avoiding such a substantial amount of paper constitutes an essential contribution to promoting sustainability goals and production aligned with the principles of Industry 5.0, which emphasise the industry's social and ecological responsibility.

As a result of the transition promoted, and with the reduced paper consumption, there is also a significant financial impact. If we consider a symbolic value of 0.06€, associated with the cost of each sheet, excluding the costs of printing equipment and its maintenance and expenses of ink cartridges, a proper digital document management system can generate a minimum saving of over 3000€ per year.

Regarding the impacts directly related to production, premises like ensuring that operators can only submit the ramp-up checklists when every parameter has a selected state will undeniably improve the efficiency of data collection, reducing the likelihood of human errors. Aspects such as automatic notifications and alerts will significantly impact decision-making and interoperability, ensuring interconnectivity and interconnection between stakeholders and systems.

Information traceability, ensured by permanent digital records, enables the adoption of processing and analysis tools capable of real-time monitoring. Traceability enhances the system with extremely valuable predictive and analytical capabilities, guiding present and future decision-making.

All the advantages described, resulting from empirical knowledge but based mainly on literature, will be critical to convincing the collaborators and teams involved in adopting this tool in a demanding and complex transitional process.

This transition will undoubtedly be resisted by those who, over the years, have developed the skills and abilities needed to understand the terms and methodologies required to complete the paper checklists. Therefore, introducing such a disruptive tool requires adequate and gradual adaptation and integration with existing production flows.

Even so, the projected benefits allow us to face the challenge optimistically, believing this is another safe and determined step towards meeting new social and industrial demands.

5   Conclusions

Implementing digitalisation and electronic document management systems in an industrial environment represents a structural shift in how adopting systems capable of simplifying document processes can maximise operational efficiency.

The proposed solution will provide more intuitive document verification and completion, automate notification methodologies, and communicate critical events to the appropriate individuals and teams. Monitoring the production process in real-time will be possible in maintenance and supervision by analysing production conditions and necessary interventions, creating or customising forms from existing templates, and consulting completion histories.

The web application interoperability and interconnection of processes will enable the integration with existing systems and workflows, enhancing communication efficiency. The digital records of information will promote better coordination and internal communication, with more proactive and responsive management of production processes. Regarding sustainability, the significant reduction in the amount of paper used will also be a notable benefit. Another advantage of adopting the application is the improved quality and accuracy of the data collected, reducing errors associated with the manual completion of paper forms.

All these advancements converge on the need to balance productive efficiency and sustainability in the context of Industry 5.0. Given the significant restructuring that the implementation of such a solution entails, it is crucial to plan it adequately. This planning will ensure seamless integration with existing systems, processes and workflows, enabling the transition to a new industrial paradigm. It will also ensure that all stakeholders benefit significantly, justifying all efforts and investments.

Acknowledgments. The study was developed under the Mobilising Agenda "A-MOVER – Development of Products & Systems towards an Intelligent and Green Mobility", operation n.o 02/C05-i01.01/2022.PC646908627-00000069, approved under the terms of the call n.o 02/C05-i01/2022 – Mobilizing Agendas for Business Innovation, financed by European funds provided to Portugal by the Recovery and Resilience Plan (RRP), in the scope of the European Recovery and Resilience Facility (RRF), framed in the Next Generation UE, for the period from 2021–2026.

References

1. Masood, T., Sonntag, P.: Industry 4.0: adoption challenges and benefits for SMEs. Comput. Ind. **121**, 103261 (2020)
2. Bajic, B., Rikalovic, A., Suzic, N., Piuri, V.: Industry 4.0 implementation challenges and opportunities: a managerial perspective. IEEE Syst. J. **15**(1), 546–559 (2021)
3. Ghobakhloo, M.: Industry 4.0, digitization, and opportunities for sustainability. J. Cleaner Prod. **252**, 119869 (2020)
4. Golovianko, M., Terziyan, V., Branytskyi, V., Malyk, D.: Industry 4.0 vs Industry 5.0: co-existence, transition, or a hybrid. Procedia Comput. Sci. **217**, 102–113 (2023)
5. Javaid, M., Haleem, A., Singh, R.P., Suman, R., Gonzalez, E.S.: Understanding the adoption of Industry 4.0 technologies in improving environmental sustainability. Sustain. Oper. Comput. **3**, 203–217 (2022)
6. Prasetyo, S., Damaraji, G., Kusumawardani, S.: A review of the challenges of paperless concept in the Society 5.0. Int. J. Ind. Eng. Eng. Manage. **2**(1), 15–24 (2020)
7. Cosme, J., Pinto, T., Ribeiro, A., Filipe, V., Amorim, E.V.: Paperless checklist for process validation and production readiness: an industrial use case. In: WEBIST 2023, pp. 95–103. Springer, Rome (2023)
8. Cosme, J., Ribeiro, A., Amorim, E.V., Filipe, V.: Digital transition on the factory floor: an interoperable application for web forms management. In: ARCI 2025, pp. 42–46. Springer, Granada (2025)

9. Errida, A., Lotfi, B.: The determinants of organizational change management success: literature review and case study. Int. J. Eng. Bus. Manage. **13**, 18479790211016270 (2021)
10. Ghobakhloo, M., Iranmanesh, M., Morales, M.E., Nilashi, M., Amran, A.: Actions and approaches for enabling Industry 5.0-driven sustainable industrial transformation: a strategy roadmap. Corp. Soc. Responsib. Environ. Manage. **30**(3), 1473–1494 (2023)
11. Xu, X., Lu, Y., Vogel-Heuser, B., Wang, L.: Industry 4.0 and Industry 5.0-inception, conception, and perception. J. Manuf. Syst. **61**, 530–535 (2021)
12. Johri, P., Singh, J.N., Sharma, A., Rastogi, D.: Sustainability of coexistence of humans and machines: an evolution of Industry 5.0 from Industry 4.0. In: 10th International Conference on System Modeling & Advancement in Research Trends (SMART'2021), Moradabad, pp. 410–414. IEEE (2021)
13. Ranjan, P., Chaudhari, S., Singh, S.: Challenges in digital transformation of business processes towards creating a paperless environment: case of an aircraft manufacturing firm. In: IEEE European Technology and Engineering Management Summit (E-TEMS'2023), Kaunas, pp. 85–90. IEEE (2023)
14. Jordan, S., Zabukovšek, S.S., Klančnik, I.Š: Document management system – a way to digital transformation. Naše gospodarstvo/Our Econ. **68**(2), 43–54 (2022)
15. Dai, M., et al.: Country-specific net-zero strategies of the pulp and paper industry. Nature **626**(7998), 327–334 (2024)
16. Biffl, S., Kropatschek, S., Kiesling, E., Meixner, K., Lüder, A.: Risk-driven derivation of operation checklists from multi-disciplinary engineering knowledge. In: IEEE 20th International Conference on Industrial Informatics, INDIN'2022, Perth, pp. 7–14. IEEE (2022)
17. Sihombing, D.J.C.: Implementing an agile document management system to improve efficiency and compliance in the cargo industry. Jurnal Ekonomi **13**(1), 2374–2384 (2024)
18. Nurpandi, F., Koswara, R.A.F.A.: Analysis and design of electronic document management system (case study of faculty of engineering, Suryakancana University). AIP Conf. Proc. **2865**(1), 050001 (2023)
19. Saqlain, M., Piao, M., Shim, Y., Lee, J.Y.: Framework of an IoT-based industrial data management for smart manufacturing. J. Sens. Actuator Netw. **8**(2), 25 (2019)

Designing Interactive Technology Roadmaps: A Visual Analytics Approach

Pawandeep Kaur Betz[1]([✉]) [iD], Karen Kuribayashi[2] [iD], Christian Ulrich[2] [iD], Stephan Schmid[2] [iD], and Andreas Gerndt[1,3] [iD]

[1] German Aerospace Center, Institute for Software Technologies, Braunschweig, Germany
`pawandeep.kaur-betz@dlr.de`
[2] German Aerospace Center, Institute of Vehicle Concepts, Stuttgart, Germany
[3] University of Bremen, Bremen, Germany

Abstract. Technology Roadmaps (TRMs) are valuable tools for aligning research and development efforts with strategic objectives. Highly graphical in nature, TRMs often receive criticism for their static nature and designs. In this study, we propose the integration of visual analytics (VA) techniques to enhance the usability, insights, and interactivity of TRM applications. Following a user-centered design approach, we collected requirements from seven stakeholders and developed two interactive prototypes: a flat-style Dashboard design and a nested-style Drill-down design. Comparative user evaluations revealed differing strengths, favoring Dashboard design particularly for its simplicity and ease of access. Based on our findings, we present a set of generalized design guidelines and introduce a Three-Stage Design Model that guides developers from structuring data to enabling user sensemaking in TRMs.

Keywords: Technology Roadmaps · Visual Analytics · Design Study

1 Introduction

In an era of rapid technological advancement and increasing uncertainty, technology forecasting tools have become indispensable for helping organizations and industries navigate future challenges. One widely used instrument for technology forecasting is the technology roadmaps (TRMs), which visually represents the path of technology development and adoption over time. Technology roadmapping is defined as a process that combines structured systems thinking, visual methodologies, and participatory approaches to address organizational challenges, support strategic planning, and foster innovation management at different levels [26].

Highly visual in nature, roadmaps facilitate communication across diverse stakeholder groups to enhance decision-making and strategic alignment [13]. However, studies [4,15,16] have repeatedly criticized the graphical designs of TRMs, highlighting their poor development and lack of intuitive design principles. Some of the design challenges addressed are information overload, off-putting color schemes, and distracting visual clutter [13]. Further due to its largely static nature, it includes the difficulty of conveying complex, multi-layered information [34] in an intuitive format. This has

J. F. Krems et al. (Eds.): CHIRA 2025, CCIS 2836, pp. 282–299, 2026.
https://doi.org/10.1007/978-3-032-16454-4_16

resulted in roadmaps often being ignored due to limited reliance [34] by practitioners and researchers alike. Kerr and Phal [15] emphasized that roadmapping should be approached as a visualization process for communication rather than a static product, requiring thoughtful integration of design principles, human perception, and visual metaphors. Addressing these shortcomings is especially crucial for the fast-evolving automotive industry, which is experiencing a shift due to current developments in electrification, connectivity, and automation. Companies are therefore faced with the question of which technologies and products will be relevant in the future.

For project *"Technologiekalender Strukturwandel Automobil Baden-Württemberg (TKBW)"*, a Technology Roadmap[1] is created as a website to visualize the expected technological developments of passenger cars until 2035 on the basis of more than 40 modules, with around 150 technologies in the areas of propulsion, connectivity, and automation. This roadmap outlines four parallel development paths: battery-electric drives, hydrogen-based drives, automated driving, and synthetically generated fuels. Although, this roadmap provides foundational guidance to their main stakeholders: small and medium-sized enterprises (SMEs) and research institutes, its static nature presents limitations in user engagement, data exploration, and decision-making support. Further, it fails to capture deviations from planned trajectories or visualize the interdependence of emerging technologies which is also shown in a Technology Roadmap in Appendix 1[2].

Incorporating Visual Analytics (VA) dashboards and storytelling visualizations can significantly improve the platform by intuitively presenting the complex information and making the platform interactive, insightful, and user-friendly. To attain this, we followed a participatory design approach [10], starting with the identification of user needs, followed by the development of functional prototypes, and then iterative evaluation sessions with domain experts. The insights gained from this process informed the derivation of a set of design guidelines and the formulation of a *Three-Stage Design Model* tailored to TRM development. While the guidelines emerged organically through our design, evaluation process and our literature analysis, the resulting framework addresses a critical gap between the fields of TRM and Visual Analytics.

Contribution – Our work represents one of the few VA-driven, user-centered design studies focused specifically on TRMs. The results are grounded in both empirical evidence from users in the vehicle technology sector and broader design knowledge from the VA and Human Computer Interaction (HCI) literature. The derived design guidelines are intended to be domain-agnostic, supporting the development of TRM systems across diverse fields. Additionally, we propose a Three-Stage Design Model that outlines a structured and practical pathway for developers seeking to build interactive, stakeholder-friendly TRMs.

Paper Structure – In this paper, we first present the insights from our literature study in Sect. 2. Then we present the insights gathered from our requirement analysis study (Sect. 3), to identify user needs and expectations for a TRM based VA application for vehicle technologies. Next, we incorporate these insights into the development of two

---

[1] https://tkbw.transformationswissen-bw.de/.
[2] https://doi.org/10.5281/zenodo.17053200.

design prototypes, presented in Sect. 4. In Sect. 5, we then present the results of evaluation conducted on the developed prototypes, focusing on their usability and effectiveness. In Sect. 6 and Sect. 7, we further contribute by proposing derived guidelines and a Three-Stage Design Model for VA-based technology roadmapping tool. Finally, we conclude paper with some discussion in Sect. 8.

2   Related Work

Over the years, scholars have examined the design processes of TRMs and proposed different visual formats and metaphors to guide their construction [13,27,34]. For instance, Phaal et al. [27], identified eight types of TRMs depending on their role in business processes, such as product planning or service planning. Yet, these recommendations largely concern static infographic-style formats with little to no interactive functionality. Their static nature and diversity of formats mean that each new type of roadmap must be tailor made. Phaal's survey [27] highlight this as a drawback, which limits their sustained use within companies and makes them difficult to keep "alive and ongoing". Moreover, TRMs have traditionally been conceived as representational artifacts rather than exploratory tools [23], offering limited functional integration with underlying databases. By contrast, the visualization community has developed a broad repertoire of methods that actively support exploration and sensemaking in complex data environments [31,32]. Dashboards, storytelling interfaces, and multiple linked views have been widely applied in different data domains (e.g., public health dashboards [3], transportation [22]). Despite that the application of VA techniques for TRMs are limited and is largely scenario and static infographic based, offering little support for interactive exploration or user-centered sensemaking. As Spaltini et al. [34] observed, visualization methods for TRMs are still underexplored and lack empirical validation. Thus addressing this gap is the central contribution of our work. To our knowledge, no prior study has systematically contrasted alternative VA interface strategies for TRMs within a user-centered design study.

3   Requirement Analysis Study

The goal of our requirement analysis study was to gather requirements from different user groups about their current understanding, usage, needs, and expectations from the visualization tool representing TRMs. Participants were first shown an introductory presentation on TRMs. Then questions were asked about their familiarity with TRMs, their reasons for using them, and their specific information and visual preferences. The questionnaire is available in the Appendix 2[3]. It was developed by taking assistance from the professionals in vehicle technology management, HCI designer, and a visualization scientist. The requirement analysis study was conducted with three main stakeholder groups, who either provide the data or use the result of this roadmap. There were 3 academics, 3 industry experts, and 1 participant from state administration. The study was conducted online via a face to face interview and a questionnaire to gather their feedback. It lasts for an average of 20 to 30 min for each participant.

---

[3] https://doi.org/10.5281/zenodo.17053200.

3.1   Result

In the following, we have summarized the result of our requirement analysis study:

- **Familiarity with TRMs:** On the 7-point Likert score, participants were asked about: their familiarity with TRMs, how often they use them, reasons for using them, and their specific information preferences. We found out a high level of awareness and familiarity about TRM tools among users with a mean average score of 5.14 out of 7. However, results also show that participants were not frequently using them (3.14 out of 7). This discrepancy among awareness and usage indicate a critical usability gap. Thus, it becomes more significant that TRM tools need to be both informative and accessible, with a limited learning curve.
- **TRM Objectives:** We derived three key motivations for using the technology roadmap tools: 1) gaining insights into technological evolution and interdependencies; 2) facilitating communication and collaboration among stakeholders and 3) identifying trends to guide strategic decisions and product development.
- **Age-Based User Preferences:** We see differences in user preferences across different age groups. Users within age group 25–34 prefer complex, dynamic, and advanced visualizations (e.g., sunburst and network diagrams). They have particular interest in knowing the temporal trends and spans, relationships and different types of technology fields. Those within age group 35–44 value structured, focused visuals like gantt charts and narrations with filtering options. User within age group 55–64 prefer known and straightforward visualizations such as tree diagrams, reflecting their need for clarity and minimal complexity.
- **Sector Based Preferences:** Academics primarily utilize TRMs to gain insight into current developmental progress and to assess project milestones and technological readiness level (TRL). Industries leverage TRMs to stay updated on evolving technological trends, driving innovation and maintaining competitiveness. State Authorities utilize TRMs for comprehensive market research and analysis in technology-related decision-making processes.
- **Other Prolific Insights:** Timelines and timespan are the most important artifacts that are needed to be shown in these roadmaps. However, most participants were less interested in mega trends but were more interested to know the small trends in the evolution that can guide them to timely opt for corrective and transformative measures. As temporal trends were the important insight for them, thus gantt chart was selected as a prominent visualization type, followed by sunburst diagram and other network diagrams. Furthermore, one of the important information to show on the TRMs for vehicle technologies is, 'Market Share' followed by 'Patents' and 'Key Companies'. The most needed option for the tool is to have interactive features, automatic updates, and variant filtering options. Participants are further interested in detailed information with external links to data or information sources, translation, or narration options. These features thus needs to be highly customizable, so that it can be easily adopted to diverse demands and can be easily configurable.

Initial findings from this study, underscore the importance of tailoring the TRM application to meet the diverse needs of users. Table 1 shows the key derived requirements from this study. These requirements, strengthen our claims of using interactive narrative-based visual analytics techniques like storytelling visualizations to present the technology roadmap for its effective and broad usage. Lessons learned from these interviews were applied to the design and development phases, to ensure that the tool seamlessly aligns with user expectations and enhances their overall experience.

Table 1. Design Requirements for Technology Roadmapping Tool.

Components	Requirements
Data and information artifacts	Timelines and timespans, relation between different technology modules and fields, market shares and patents
Visualization artifacts	Gantt Chart, Sunburst and Network Diagrams
Interactive Features	Filtering options, on-demand narrations, hovering, popups
Other features	Automatic updates and detailed information (documentation)

4   Technology Roadmap Designs

For the representation of complex information, VA techniques: narrative and storytelling, could play a critical role. Storytelling in visual analytics goes beyond aesthetics or layout. It provides structure, context, and a cognitive path through the data [32]. In the context of TRMs, by guiding users through sequential, contextual, or thematic progressions, storytelling along with narrative designs help bridge the gap between raw technical data and actionable insight [9, 17]. In our study, we operationalize two distinct narrative strategies from the findings of [32]: a *Dashboard-based design*, which offers a flattened overview with structured entry points, and a nested style *Drill-down design*, which allows users to progressively unfold information through guided transitions. Further, based on the Table 1, we decided which visualizations would be used for representing what relationship types and what information was mapped. These prototypes were developed with Oracle APEX environment[4] using our database [36] on the evolution of technologies over time. Oracle APEX enables rapid creation of scalable and secure data-driven applications through a powerful low-code development platform. The database use TRL and Manufacturing Readiness Level (MRL) for modules from 2019 to 2035 with data based on expert responses to the technology profiles. Both of our prototypes are based on the concept of Multiple Linked Views (MLV), a technique from information visualization that relies on interaction design principles. In this approach, user interaction with one view updates the data and results shown in other coordinated views on the canvas.

Dashboard Design: The Dashboard design prototype (Fig. 1) first provides an overview of the essential components, connected and comprised on the same page. Then through interactions, user delve deeper into specific aspects of each components. There are three primary visualizations through which one can explore data and dive deeper into other

---

[4] https://apex.oracle.com/de/.

options: 1) Sunburst Diagram (Fig. 1a) shows hierarchical data structure based on vehicle types $\longrightarrow$ modules $\longrightarrow$ technologies. In Fig. 1a, Sunburst Diagram shows different vehicle types. When user clicks on any vehicle type (Fig. 1f), related modules open up. 2) The Network Diagram (Fig. 1b) focuses on highlighting connected elements - competing technologies, keywords and competencies. Based on the selected information on the Sunburst Diagram, related data elements and nodes get highlighted as shown in Fig. 1e. 3) The Gantt Chart (Fig. 1d) emphasizes the chronological representation of project timelines and time spans. The Gantt Chart is combined with box plots to provide better view of the time span. Checklist and search option (Fig. 1c) is provided for the user to further add or remove the needed technologies, modules, and competency types. As this tool was developed for German users thus the main language is German, however, on clicking on button "Sprache auswählen", user can change the language to English. The flowchart, full scale images of the design and video of this prototype is provided in Appendix 3[5].

Drill-Down Design: The Drill-down design prototype (Fig. 2) first presents general broad themes and then allows the user to select specific themes to reveal additional details and backstories. It provides a high level view of the data through one Network Diagram (Fig. 2a) which is nested into four levels. This layout unfolds the option based on the semantic layering of different vehicle types $\longrightarrow$ Modules $\longrightarrow$ Technologies associated with it. Each version of this diagram comes with its own interactive components and insights. The upper most level shows the vehicle types which are further connected to modules on the nodes. Clicking on the nodes on this diagram opens up module network associated to the clicked vehicle types as shown in (Fig. 2b). Further clicking on these nodes, opens up the technologies, timelines and timespan associated with that module in the form of Circular Gantt Chart as shown in (Fig. 2c). Each circular bars are technologies and each diamonds are its MRL and TRLs. On the right of the Gantt Chart, user can read the relevant information about selected technology. By clicking on the button 'Gantt Chart', user can transform the Gantt Chart from Circular to Rectangular form in a full screen (Fig. 2d). The flowchart, full scale images of the design and video of this prototype is provided in Appendix 4[6].

5   Evaluation

Further we conducted a usability evaluation of our two developed prototype designs. Participants were asked to perform real-world scenario-based tasks to assess the effectiveness of each design. The objective of this study was twofold: first, to introduce users to our TRM designs tailored to their requirements, and second, to systematically compare the two interface designs to determine which one better aligns with the needs of our stakeholders. The feedback was collected via a questionnaire which was developed by taking assistance of QUIS [5] and NASA TLX [8] survey templates. The study involved 10 participants. The questionnaire is available in the Appendix 5[7]. The results are summarized below:

---

[5] https://doi.org/10.5281/zenodo.17053200.
[6] https://doi.org/10.5281/zenodo.17053200.
[7] https://doi.org/10.5281/zenodo.17053200.

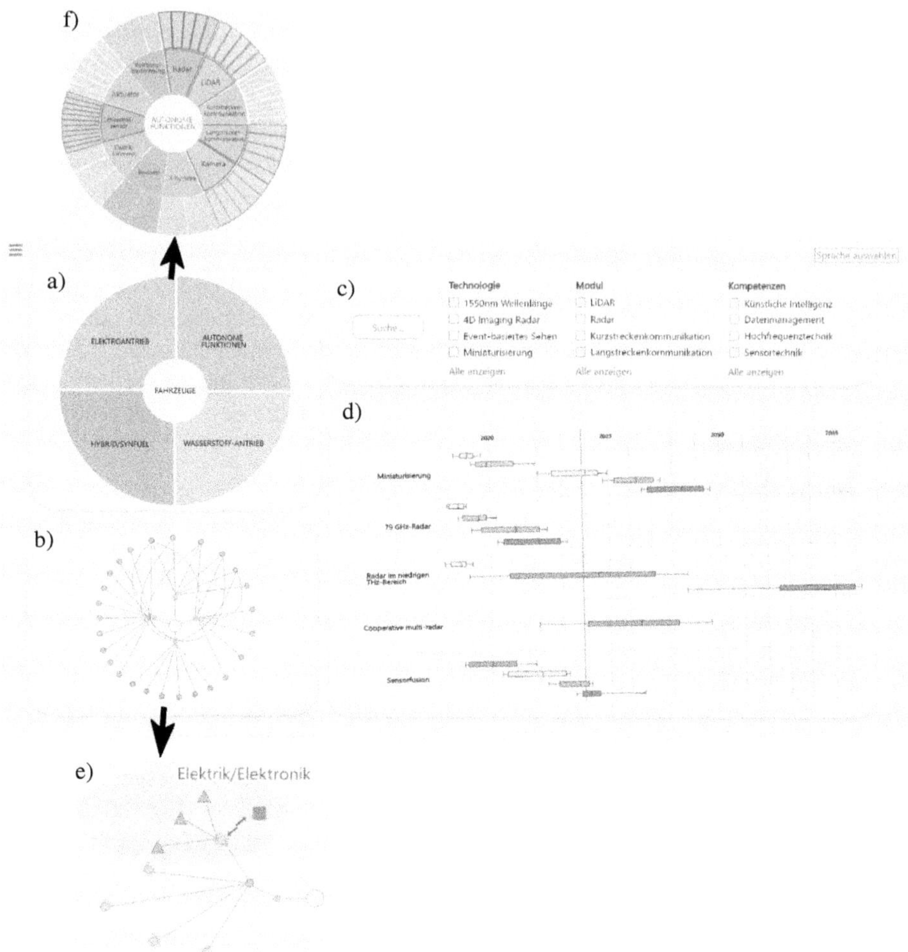

Fig. 1. This is our Dashboard design prototype. Screenshots of clicks are embedded for better understandability of the prototype.

1. **Task Performance:** Participants were asked to perform tasks which were then evaluated to measure performance. Performance is measured in two ways - errors and response time. Errors refer to the incorrect answers of the participant's responses from the performed tasks [29]. Response time is the time it took a participant to complete one task. The performance with Dashboard design is better with an average error score of 7.3% and response time of 56.43 s. The average error score for the Drill-down is 12.9% with the response time of 78.36 s.
2. **Design Choices:** Participants were asked questions about their design choices related to three different pair of alternatives. First comparison was related to the layout of the prototypes. Between Dashboard design and Drill-down design, majority votes (60%) were gone to the Dashboard design. The reason provided by participants

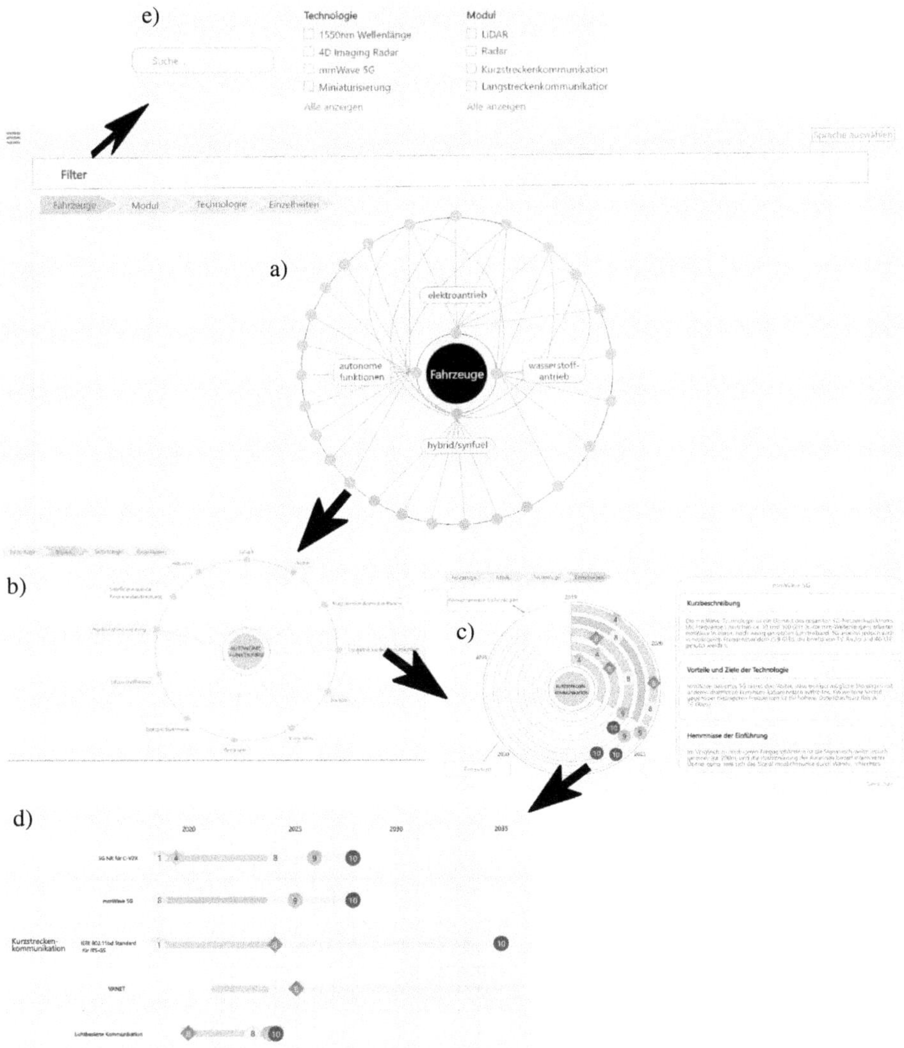

Fig. 2. This is our Drill-down design prototype. Screenshots of clicks are embedded for better understandability of the prototype.

were that they are simple and straightforward. Second comparison was between One Liner Gantt Chart (see Fig. 2d) and Gantt Chart with Boxplot (see Fig. 1d). Here, participants preferred One Liner Gantt Chart (70% votes) primarily because they were already familiar to them. Third comparison was between Sunburst Diagram connected with Network Diagram (see Fig. 1a, b) and Network Diagram (see Fig. 2a) alone. Here, 80% of our participants opted for the connected Sunburst Diagram, owning to the clear overview of the data and insights thereof from this diagram.

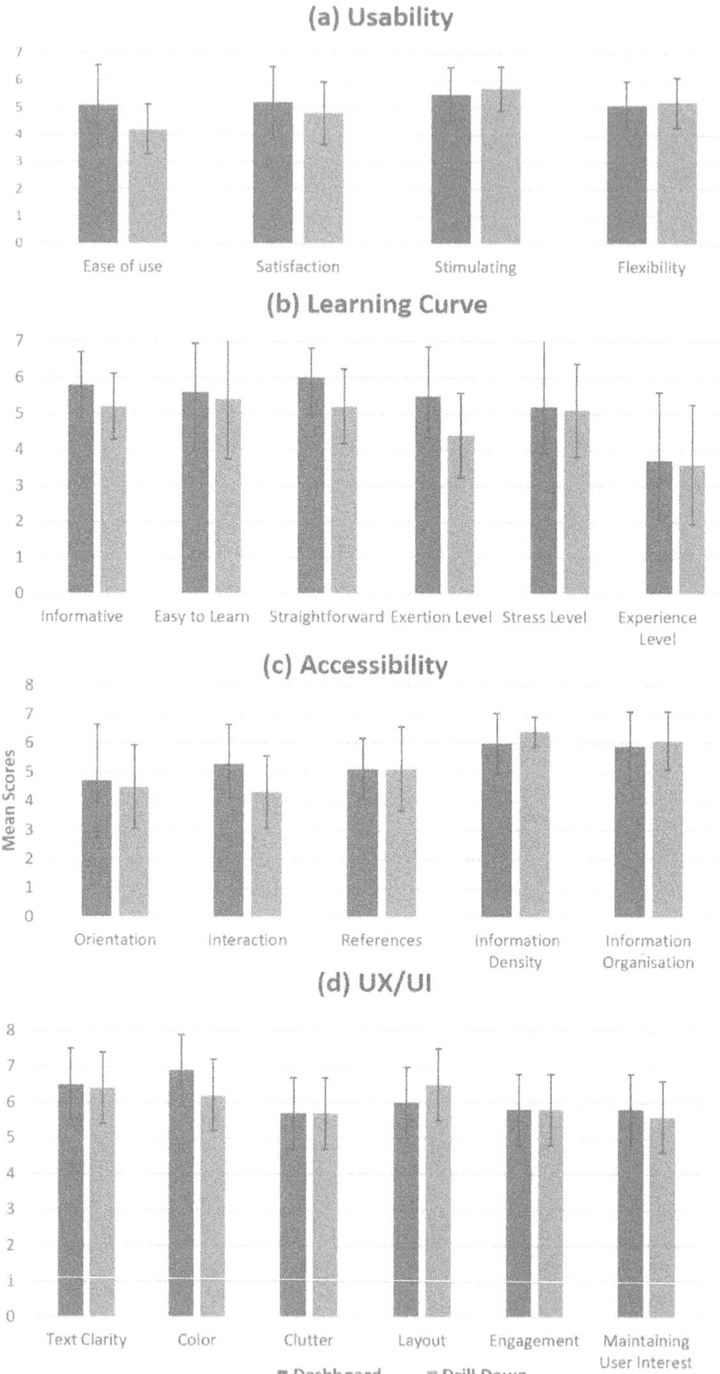

Fig. 3. This figure shows the user evaluation results comparing the Dashboard and Drill-down design prototypes. The bar chart presents mean scores with error bars showing deviation across four key categories: Usability, Learning Curve, Accessibility, and UX/UI.

3. **User Experience:** We measured user experience across four main categories: Usability, Learning Curve, Accessibility and UX/UI elements. Each category included specific subcategories to capture detailed user feedback and assess different aspects of the experience. These were then rated using a 7-point Likert scale. The results are presented in Fig. 3.

   (a) Usability: We analyzed overall usability of these designs based on four metrics: *Ease of use, Satisfaction level, Stimulating and Flexibility.* The results are shown in Fig. 3a. Dashboard scored higher than Drill-down for *Ease of use* and *Satisfaction.* Whereas in *Stimulating* and *Flexibility,* scores of Drill-down are slightly better.

   (b) Learning curve: The parameters on which Learning Curve was scored were: *Informative, Easy to Learn, Straightforward, Exertion Level, Stress Level and Experience Level.* As shown in Fig. 3b, Dashboard design scored higher in all categories. Dashboard design has a slight advantage in performing task straightforward due to its flat layout. Due to the nested layout of Drill-down, the amount of effort needed to perform the task is more and thus the Learning Curve for Drill-down is higher.

   (c) Accessibility: We evaluated different accessibility parameters of our designs: orientation on the screen (*Orientation*), *Interaction,* use of *References, Information Density* and *Information Organization.* Shown in Fig. 3c, Dashboard design is rated higher across *Orientation, Interaction,* and *References.* Drill-down strongly outperformed dashboard in *Information Density* and is also better in *Information Organization.*

   (d) UX/UI: We evaluated User Experience and User Interface (UX/UI) via following parameters: *Text Clarity,* colorscheme used (*Color*), cluttered interface (*Clutter*), attractive layout (*Layout*), user engagement (*Engagement*) and *Maintaining User Interest.* As shown in Fig. 3d, Dashboard design scored higher in *Text Clarity, Color* and *Maintaining User Interest.* Both prototypes have been equally or closely scored for *Clutter* and *Engagement.* Drill-down is scored better for its *Layout* design.

Across all evaluation dimensions (22), participants (n = 10) rated the Dashboard design higher in terms of overall usability, learnability, and accessibility. The Drill-down design was rated more stimulating, but better in information density and organization. Results shows a direct preference towards Dashboard type flat designs.

Further we tried to understand the dependencies and correlation among individual design factors from Fig. 3. Here our goal is to explore which factors are consistent, and which are design-dependent. For that, we used Spearman Correlation Test [35] for our datasets. The results are presented in Fig. 4 and labeled results are provided in Appendix 6[8].

As per the guidelines for interpreting the absolute value of correlation coefficients proposed by [6], above 80% is very strong, above 60% is strong and then below zero is negative. Figure 4a shows that Dashboard design has most positive correlation. Users who rated this design prototype as easy to use (*Ease of use*) has also rated it high

---

[8] https://doi.org/10.5281/zenodo.17053200.

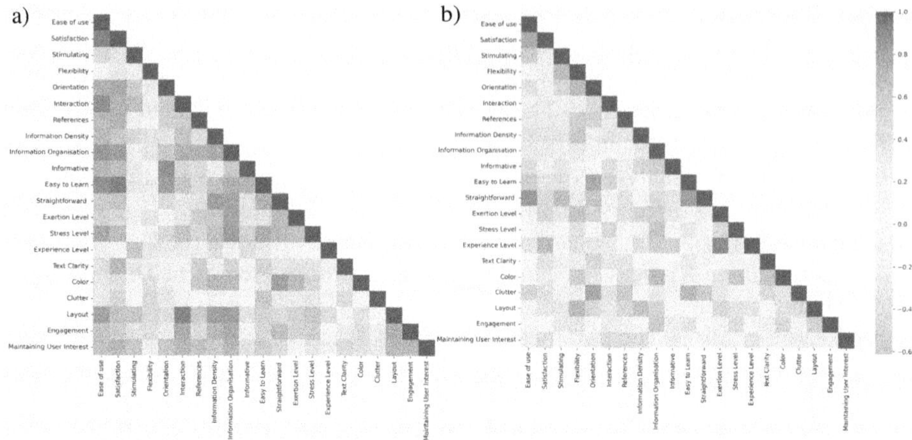

Fig. 4. This figure shows the lower triangle of spearmen's correlation matrix for correlation among different design factors for (a) Dashboard design and (b) Drill-down design. Red color shows the level of positive correlation and blue color shows the negative correlation.

in *Satisfaction, Interaction, Information Organization, Easy to Learn* and low *Stress level* and good *Layout*. There are very few none and negative correlations. However Fig. 4b shows many negative correlation specially with *Experience Level, Information Organization, Stress*. It further suggest that for Drill-down design, the design factors didn't always support each other—improvements in one area often made another area worse. This caused users to experience the interface in different ways.

By analyzing the overall results, we identified both stable and volatile design factors. While core links like *Easy to Learn ∼ Satisfaction* remained strong across designs, other relationships such as *Layout ∼ Engagement* and *Information Organization ∼ Ease to Learn* proved sensitive to design context. Our results highlights the importance of validating interface patterns across multiple conditions rather than assuming universal user behavior.

6   Design Guidelines

Based on our experience from this study and literature analysis, we have derived design guidelines for constructing an effective visual analytics application for technology roadmaps.

1. **Follow Design Principles:** General design principles laid down by scholars [24,25] and researchers are critical and should be followed in the construction of either static infographics or interactive applications. These principles guide users in the creation of clear, uncomplicated, clutter free designs. For example, as per the principle of Alignment, grouping similar items together – visually makes scanning quicker and supports comprehension. Findings from our study as well as previous studies [1] have highlighted the role of creating clear, simple, and straightforward designs with user friendly layout which ultimately reduce unnecessary cognitive load.

2. **User-centric Design Process:** Studies have emphasized on rapidly involving stakeholders in the design and development process [14,33]. Construction of TRMs have been considered as a collective task [34] and thus it is essential that different kinds of stakeholder (data providers, decision makers, users getting influenced from those decisions etc.) should be in a loop during and after the development process.

3. **Scalability and Flexibility:** Scalable and flexible designs [12,38] ensure that roadmaps can be tailored to future datasets and user requirements. They are adaptable to new updates both in data and requirements. Views should be easily customizable that can cater the need of diverse stakeholders' needs [1,7]. Further, scalable and modular design could be a solution to keep TRMs alive and ongoing, a challenge identified by [27]. Modular components and tailored workflows can meet specific user demands effectively. Some of the ways to achieve scalability and flexibility— choosing scalable databases like Graph or NoSQL types, use modular data pipelines, use more hybrid and hierarchical visualizations that are scalable and can show multiple dimensions, compatibility with different devices, allow user to hide and show views based on their requirements, provide role based access and provide more interactivity, filters and nested options.

4. **Collaboration and Knowledge Sharing:** Features allowing collaborative input and document sharing were noted as valuable additions to roadmapping tools as shown in our and also previous studies [1,14]. Collaborative visual features to allow cross-departmental input and sharing views with external stakeholders is seen as successful implementations in large organizations [1].

5. **Guidance and Assistance:** To decrease the learning curve [34] and for better insight generation, it is important to include different guiding and assistive features in the TRM applications. Here, guidance means to allow all those features that provides knowledge about the proper functioning of the tool. Such as, providing proper onboarding, tutorials and contextual tooltips. Whereas assistive features are those which help to cater the need of different types of stakeholders irrespective of their age and other differences. As also showed in our study, that differences in age groups leads to different requirements for the TRMs.

6. **Data Security:** Addressing security concerns related to proprietary data ensures user confidence in the tool. Moreover, user login to a secure system and providing role based views and privileges on the system could further assist in better management of data exposure to different types of interested parties.

Further options could be related to domain specific requirements, for example if data demands comparison among geographical regions then provide both local and global perspectives in technology trends, adoptions, and regulations. These guidelines help developers to decide on various features and the scale of work needed in the development of TRMs .

7 Design Model for Visual Analytics in Technology Roadmapping

In Fig. 5, we propose our Three-Stage Design Model for Visual Analytics in TRM development. This framework is derived based on our own work, as well as, by taking inspiration from established cognitive and interaction frameworks in information

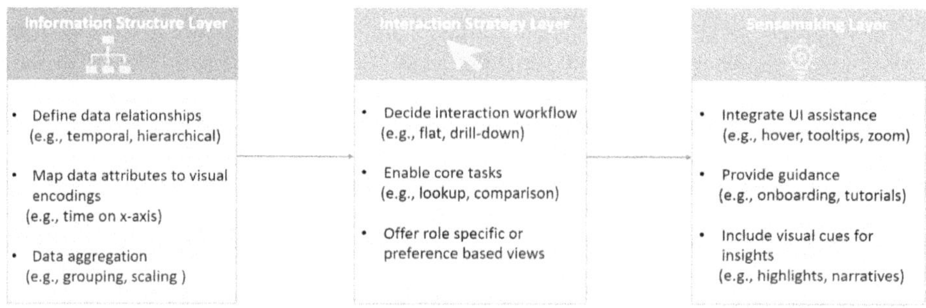

Fig. 5. Three-Stage Design Model for Visual Analytics in Technology Roadmapping. It guides TRM developers from data structuring to user interaction and then to insight generation.

visualization and human-centered design. This model builds up from data structure to user interaction and ultimately to communicative and interpretive visualizations. However before starting to implement this model, a developer has to understand the domain and data well by involving stakeholders and reviewing relevant literature.

1. **Information Structure** - *What has to be visualized?*
   In this foundational stage, developers model and understand the gathered data as a beginning of a design process. It corresponds to the data abstraction and encoding phase of the visualization pipeline, as conceptualized in classic models by [20]. The result of this stage would produce a table similar to the one presented in Table 1 but with more details. This stage can be divided into three layers:
   (a) Define data relationships: Knowing the data well, first developer has to decide the relationship that are depicted from the data elements. These relationships further corresponds to the user goals that can further derived corresponding visualizations [11]. For example: if elements of the dataset shows series of date and time, then it shows temporal relationship and thus can be visualized by temporal visualization (gantt charts, timelines, or bar charts). Knowing such relationships within data elements at the earlier stage assists developer in searching for suitable visualizations and also other alternatives of similar visualizations. Some suitable questions at this stage could be:
   * *What kind of data is involved? (timeline, dependencies, modules, metrics, actors)?*
   * *Is there any apparent data relationship or structure exist? If so, then what are they? (Is it temporal, hierarchical, networked?).*
   * *How can this relationship be visualized (e.g., hierarchical $\longrightarrow$ sunburst, treemap)*
   (b) Map data attributes to visual attributes: Once a developer knows which visualizations to use, the next step is to map different data attributes to visual attributes. The developer then tries to answer the questions *What data elements will be mapped to which visual elements of the chart?* For example in Fig. 1b, nodes in the circular network diagram represent vehicle types. For this process, it is important that developer has a good understanding of types of data

attributes. *Is it categorical, nominal, temporal (Date/Time) etc.?* For example in temporal line chart, 'x' axis could be time line, and 'y' axis could be market shares.

(c) Data aggregation or categorization: Visualization relies on structured aggregation for clarity. As TRMs usually spans from long time horizons (e.g., 2025 → 2050), there are multiple scales of technologies (system → subsystem → module → component) and has diverse stakeholders (policy, R&D, SME, industry). To structure this data, aggregation and categorization is an important step. Aggregation provides a semantic anchoring, without which user could get overwhelmed in multiple level of details. Here, the user has to decide *What levels of aggregation will be shown? (e.g., years → months etc. for temporal and, different nesting levels for sunburst diagrams.)*

2. **Interaction Strategy Layer:** *How will it be explored?*
Once the visual content is defined, the next step is to design the exploratory workflow of the application. This layer addresses exploratory behavior, aligning with the interaction taxonomy defined by [37], cognitive models of exploratory search [21] and narrative flow by [32]. It encapsulates user-driven strategies for interaction flow on the interfaces such as overview-first ⟶ navigation ⟶ progressive filtering ⟶ detail-on-demand ⟶ comparison. These strategies reflect how users cognitively approach roadmap data. This stage is further divided into three sub layers:

(a) Deciding interaction workflow: Whether it is a VA based or any other UI based application, interactive workflow is highly dependent on the layout of the application. For example in our prototypes, we used two types of layouts i.e., flat type Dashboard and nested type Drill-down layout. Even in static infographics, a layout defines the organization of all the elements on the canvas which further intuitively guides the user focus.

(b) Enable core tasks: Next is to decide the core tasks performed by the user in the information seeking process. For example to look up on specific elements, selecting the date range from timeline, clicking and showing the nested hierarchies in sunburst diagram, dragging elements, entering the information, performing comparisons etc. Here the integral question that needs to be answered is *What tasks should the system support?*

(c) User specific views: It is common in data sensitive applications that not all information is relevant for all stakeholders. On the other hand, based on the specific age group or interests, some users prefer alternative views (see our findings from Sect. 3) or have different requirements. Further, some features are only for decision makers, while others are intended for specific role types. To fulfill many of these goals, TRMs architecture should facilitate providing different views, access levels, alternative options, etc., to the users.

3. **Sensemaking Layer:** *How do insights emerge?*
This layer focuses on supporting users in interpreting complex data and generating insights – not just by showing results, but by actively guiding exploration. Rooted in sensemaking theory from visual analytics and exploratory data analysis [28, 30, 31], it aims to help users construct mental models, identify patterns, and reason about underlying phenomena. We observed that successful insight generation requires support at three levels:

(a) Interface-Level Assistance: The first level of support is to enhance the basic understanding of the application by providing different assistive features at the frontend. Foundational support includes tooltips, hover effects, axis labels, and captions that clarify the visual elements and reduce ambiguity.

(b) Guidance and Orientation: Onboarding flows, embedded documentation, and inbuilt tutorials facilitate understanding of both data and visual design. These elements lower the learning curve and support users –especially first-time users – in navigating the roadmaps effectively.

(c) Insight-focused visual cues: Cues such as highlights, annotations, hotspots, or time indicators serve as signifiers (based on principles from interaction design theory by [25]), helping users focus on relevant data regions or patterns. While optional, these cues enhance analytical reasoning by guiding user attention toward potential anomalies, correlations, or critical areas of interest. Their design should be informed by domain-specific knowledge to avoid misdirections.

8 Discussion and Conclusion

In this study, we propose the use of Visual Analytics based narrative and storytelling applications to overcome the limitations of static technology roadmapping tools. Following a user centric design approach, we first gathered requirements from seven different types of stakeholders. Results from the requirement analysis has emerged as a crucial factor, revealing diverse preferences across demographics and professional needs. Based on the gathered requirements, we developed two prototypes: a Drill-down design and a Dashboard design prototypes. A comparative user evaluation, indicated a general preference for Dashboard design, which was praised for its simplicity and accessibility, making them ideal for quick insights. Drill-down design was rated as detail oriented and better in information organization. To further understand the relationship between different design factors, we conducted a Spearman's correlation analysis. Results for the Dashboard design showed mostly positive and harmonious relationships among design factors, whereas, Drill-down design revealed a higher number of negative correlations. We further derived a set of design guidelines for the development of effective TRM applications. We emphasize the importance of user-centered design, flexibility, scalability, collaboration, guidance, and following established design principles for the creation of these applications. To address the gap of limited theoretical frameworks for designing VA-based TRMs, we presented a Three-Stage Design Model for Visual Analytics in TRMs development. This model guides a developer from the stage of data and information structuring to the facilitation of user sensemaking in the development of TRM applications. This model poses reflective questions at each stage and supports decision-making based on the data, user needs, and system context. Together, our design guidelines and framework provide a structured pathway for developing Visual Analytics-based TRM tools that are both functional and insightful.

By taking technology roadmaps (TRMs) in vehicle technologies as an application domain, we demonstrate that the choice of interface structure—flat dashboards versus hierarchical drill-down—significantly influences usability, accessibility, and sensemaking. While existing TRM literature primarily focuses on what to visualize [23], our study provides empirical evidence highlighting the importance of how to visualize. In particular, we contribute to understanding how interaction design impacts the overall user experience in roadmap exploration and decision-making. During the course of our study, we saw a limited research directly comparing flat Dashboard-style interfaces and hierarchical Drill-down interface designs directly in visualization studies. Although both styles are widely used in interface and web application development [19], their relative advantages for different types of data, users, and context remain largely underexplored. Our literature review revealed that most comparative studies focus on different visualization types (bar chart, scatterplot), or on evaluating usability of interactive visualizations [39]. Other studies concentrated on perfecting either of these designs in isolation [2]. Our findings extend prior roadmap visualization studies [4, 13] by empirically comparing interactive layouts. Despite a limited sample size (7 participants for first and 10 participants for second study) our results though not statistically significant but suggestive, indicate that interface layout choices has a measurable influence on user engagement, usability perception, and insight generation. This highlights the need of future research to systematically evaluate the usability, effectiveness, and decision making impact of different VA-based applications across different application domains. Future research can build on our comparative design model to evaluate interactive roadmap applications across additional domains and larger stakeholder groups.

Acknowledgment. The research was carried out when Karen Kuribayashi and Christian Ulrich were employed at the German Aerospace Center. The presented user study of TRM for vehicle technology, was a part of Karen's master thesis available at [18].

References

1. Abdelfattah, M.: A comparison of several performance dashboards architectures. Intell. Inf. Manag. **5**(2), 25–41 (2013). https://doi.org/10.1016/j.techfore.2020.119965
2. Bach, B., et al.: Dashboard design patterns. IEEE Trans. Visual Comput. Graph. **29**(1), 421–431 (2023). https://doi.org/10.1109/TVCG.2022.3209429
3. Betz, P.K., et al.: ESID: exploring the design and development of a visual analytics tool for epidemiological emergencies. In: 2023 IEEE VIS Workshop on Visualization for Pandemic and Emergency Responses (Vis4PandEmRes), pp. 8–14. IEEE (2023). https://doi.org/10.1109/Vis4PandEmRes60343.2023.00007
4. Blackwell, A.F., Phaal, R., Eppler, M., Crilly, N.: Strategy roadmaps: new forms, new practices. In: Stapleton, G., Howse, J., Lee, J. (eds.) Diagrams 2008. LNCS (LNAI), vol. 5223, pp. 127–140. Springer, Heidelberg (2008). https://doi.org/10.1007/978-3-540-87730-1_14
5. Chin, J.P., Diehl, V.A., Norman, K.L.: Development of an instrument measuring user satisfaction of the human-computer interface. In: Proceedings of the SIGCHI Conference on Human Factors in Computing Systems, pp. 213–218 (1988). https://doi.org/10.1145/57167.5720
6. Evans, J.D.: Straightforward Statistics for the Behavioral Sciences. Thomson Brooks/Cole Publishing Co. (1996)

7. Hansen, C., Daim, T., Ernst, H., Herstatt, C.: The future of rail automation: a scenario-based technology roadmap for the rail automation market. Technol. Forecast. Soc. Chang. **110**, 196–212 (2016). https://doi.org/10.1016/j.techfore.2015.12.017

8. Hart, S.: Development of NASA-TLX (task load index): results of empirical and theoretical research. Hum. Mental Workload (1988). https://doi.org/10.1016/S0166-4115(08)62386-9

9. Hullman, J., Diakopoulos, N.: Visualization rhetoric: framing effects in narrative visualization. IEEE Trans. Visual Comput. Graph. **17**(12), 2231–2240 (2011). https://doi.org/10.1109/TVCG.2011.255

10. Jänicke, S., Kaur, P., Kuzmicki, P., Schmidt, J.: Participatory visualization design as an approach to minimize the gap between research and application. In: VisGap@ Eurographics/EuroVis, pp. 35–42 (2020). https://doi.org/10.2312/visgap.20201108

11. Kaur, P., König-Ries, B.: Visualization taxonomy based on the specification of user's goal and data dimensions. In: EuroVis (Posters), pp. 29–31 (2017). https://doi.org/10.2312/eurp.20171161

12. Kerr, C., Farrukh, C., Phaal, R., Probert, D.: Key principles for developing industrially relevant strategic technology management toolkits. Technol. Forecast. Soc. Chang. **80**(6), 1050–1070 (2013). https://doi.org/10.1016/j.techfore.2012.09.006

13. Kerr, C., Phaal, R.: Visualizing roadmaps: a design-driven approach. Res. Technol. Manag. **58**(4), 45–54 (2015). https://doi.org/10.5437/08956308X5804253

14. Kerr, C., Phaal, R.: Defining the scope of a roadmapping initiative: a checklist-based template for organizational stakeholders. In: 2019 Portland International Conference on Management of Engineering and Technology (PICMET), pp. 1–10. IEEE (2019). https://doi.org/10.23919/PICMET.2019.8893851

15. Kerr, C., Phaal, R.: Roadmapping and roadmaps: definition and underpinning concepts. IEEE Trans. Eng. Manage. **69**(1), 6–16 (2021). https://doi.org/10.1109/TEM.2021.3096012

16. Kerr, C., Phaal, R., Probert, D.: Depicting options and investment appraisal information in roadmaps. Int. J. Innov. Technol. Manag. **9**(03), 1250022 (2012). https://doi.org/10.5437/10.1142/S0219877012500228

17. Kosara, R., Mackinlay, J.: Storytelling: the next step for visualization. Computer **46**(5), 44–50 (2013). https://doi.org/10.1109/MC.2013.36

18. Kuribayashi, K.: Storytelling data visualization for technology forecasting: developing an efficient technology roadmap application with database integration (2024). https://elib.dlr.de/203460/

19. Loranger, H., Moran, K.: Flat vs. deep website hierarchies (2020). https://www.nngroup.com/articles/flat-vs-deep-hierarchy/. Accessed 27 Aug 2025

20. Mackinlay, J., Hanrahan, P., Stolte, C.: Show me: automatic presentation for visual analysis. IEEE Trans. Visual Comput. Graph. **13**(6), 1137–1144 (2007). https://doi.org/10.1109/TVCG.2007.70594

21. Marchionini, G.: Exploratory search: from finding to understanding. Commun. ACM **49**(4), 41–46 (2006). https://doi.org/10.1145/1121949.1121979

22. Nazemi, K., Burkhardt, D., Kaupp, L., Dannewald, T., Kowald, M., Ginters, E.: Visual analytics in mobility, transportation and logistics. In: Ginters, E., Ruiz Estrada, M.A., Piera Eroles, M.A. (eds.) ICTE ToL 2019. LNITI, pp. 82–89. Springer, Cham (2020). https://doi.org/10.1007/978-3-030-39688-6_12

23. Nazemi, K., Burkhardt, D., Kock, A.: Visual analytics for technology and innovation management: an interaction approach for strategic decision making. Multimed. Tools Appl. **81**(11), 14803–14830 (2022). https://doi.org/10.1007/s11042-021-10972-3

24. Nielsen, J., Molich, R.: Heuristic evaluation of user interfaces. In: Proceedings of the SIGCHI Conference on Human Factors in Computing Systems, pp. 249–256 (1990). https://doi.org/10.1145/97243.97281

25. Norman Donald, A.: The Design of Everyday Things. MIT Press, Cambridge (2013)
26. Park, H., Phaal, R., Ho, J.Y., O'Sullivan, E.: Twenty years of technology and strategic roadmapping research: a school of thought perspective. Technol. Forecast. Soc. Chang. **154**, 119965 (2020). https://doi.org/10.1016/j.techfore.2020.119965
27. Phaal, R., Farrukh, C.J., Probert, D.R.: Technology roadmapping – a planning framework for evolution and revolution. Technol. Forecast. Soc. Chang. **71**(1), 5–26 (2004). https://doi.org/10.1016/S0040-1625(03)00072-6. Roadmapping: From Sustainable to Disruptive Technologies
28. Pirolli, P., Card, S.: The sensemaking process and leverage points for analyst technology as identified through cognitive task analysis. In: Proceedings of International Conference on Intelligence Analysis, vol. 5, pp. 2–4 (2005). https://doi.org/10.1145/169059.16920
29. Purchase, H.C.: Experimental Human-Computer Interaction: A Practical Guide with Visual Examples. Cambridge University Press (2012). https://doi.org/10.1017/CBO9780511844522
30. Russell, D.M., Stefik, M.J., Pirolli, P., Card, S.K.: The cost structure of sensemaking. In: Proceedings of INTERCHI 1993, pp. 269–276 (1993). https://doi.org/10.1145/169059.1692
31. Sacha, D., et al.: Knowledge generation model for visual analytics. IEEE Trans. Visual Comput. Graph. **20**(12), 1604–1613 (2014)
32. Segel, E., Heer, J.: Narrative visualization: telling stories with data. IEEE Trans. Visual Comput. Graph. **16**(6), 1139–1148 (2010). https://doi.org/10.1109/TVCG.2010.179
33. Spaltini, M., Acerbi, F., Pinzone, M., Gusmeroli, S., Taisch, M.: Defining the roadmap towards industry 4.0: the 6ps maturity model for manufacturing SMEs. Procedia CIRP **105**, 631–636 (2022). https://doi.org/10.1016/j.procir.2022.02.105
34. Spaltini, M., Terzi, S., Taisch, M.: A literature review on technology roadmapping: requisites, dimensions, steps and visualisation methods. Dimensions, Steps and Visualisation Methods (2023). https://doi.org/10.2139/ssrn.4653302
35. Spearman, C.: The proof and measurement of association between two things. Am. J. Psychol. **100**(3/4), 441–471 (1987)
36. Ulrich, C., et al.: Analysis and presentation of the development status of vehicle technologies for electrification and automation by creating a technology calendar. In: Bargende, M., Reuss, H.-C., Wagner, A. (eds.) 21. Internationales Stuttgarter Symposium. P, pp. 321–332. Springer, Wiesbaden (2021). https://doi.org/10.1007/978-3-658-33466-6_22
37. Yi, J.S., ah Kang, Y., Stasko, J., Jacko, J.A.: Toward a deeper understanding of the role of interaction in information visualization. IEEE Trans. Visualization Comput. Graph. **13**(6), 1224–1231 (2007). https://doi.org/10.1109/TVCG.2007.70515
38. Yu, C.J., Daim, T.: Benchmarking of technology roadmapping process in energy sector: a literature review. In: 2017 Portland International Conference on Management of Engineering and Technology (PICMET), pp. 1–10. IEEE (2017). https://doi.org/10.23919/PICMET.2017.8125438
39. Zhuang, M., Concannon, D., Manley, E.: A framework for evaluating dashboards in healthcare. IEEE Trans. Visual Comput. Graph. **28**(4), 1715–1731 (2022). https://doi.org/10.1109/TVCG.2022.3147154

Impact of Multimodal Emotional Input on User Experience in Chatbots

Yifei Li[1]([✉])(iD), Hunter Fong[2](iD), Maurizio Mancini[1](iD),
and Radoslaw Niewiadomski[2](iD)

[1] Department of Computer Science, Sapienza University of Rome, Rome, Italy
{li,m.mancini}@di.uniroma1.it
[2] Department of Informatics, Bioengineering, Robotics and Systems Engineering,
University of Genoa, Genoa, Italy
{hunter.fong,radoslaw.niewiadomski}@unige.it

Abstract. This study investigates whether incorporating multimodal emotional input (self-reported emotion and facial emotion) can enhance users' emotional experiences in interactions with LLM-based chatbots. Twenty-eight participants engaged with four chatbot conditions: (A) text-only, (B) self-reported emotion, (C) facial emotion, and (D) combined input. Despite the hypothesis, perceived empathy was slightly higher in conditions without facial emotion input. However, participants with lower trait emotional expressivity reported more positive affect when facial emotion cues were included. Qualitative interviews further revealed varying perceptions of chatbot sensitivity to emotional needs. Participants with prior chatbot experience also felt a stronger social connection when conversations began with emotional topics. Additionally, older adults, women, and experienced users rated their interactions more positively. These findings suggest that emotional input may not universally enhance affective experiences but could benefit specific user profiles. The study advocates for a personalized, trait-sensitive approach to emotion-aware chatbot design rather than a one-size-fits-all multimodal strategy.

Keywords: Chatbot · LLM · Emotion-Aware · Multimodal

1 Introduction

Advances in Machine Learning and Natural Language Processing have propelled AI-driven chatbots into increasingly important roles across daily life, work, and education. Recent studies demonstrate that personalization and anthropomorphic design can enhance users' perceptions of warmth and empathy in chatbot [23]. However, a critical challenge remains: while several works have addressed the detection and generation of emotional responses in chatbots [9,14,35,38], few have examined whether merely incorporating additional modalities of emotional input can truly enhance user's affective experience.

Developing chatbots with genuine emotional intelligence, which could defined as the ability to understand and share users' positive and negative affective states, is fun-

J. F. Krems et al. (Eds.): CHIRA 2025, CCIS 2836, pp. 300–317, 2026.
https://doi.org/10.1007/978-3-032-16454-4_17

damental to effective human–computer communication and is known to drive user satisfaction and perceived empathy [27,30]. Hence, the emerging trend in chatbot development is the creation of emotionally intelligent agents that can detect user sentiment and generate contextually appropriate responses. Although Large Language Models (LLMs) such as GPT offer new possibilities for more nuanced emotional interaction [5,8,16,45], they often struggle with subtle emotional understanding and tend to produce repetitive or emotionally flat responses [3,17,44,49]. Moreover, current evaluations of LLMs' emotional capabilities are largely focused on domain-specific applications (e.g., healthcare support) [1,4,12], leaving social-oriented conversational contexts lessly explored.

Moreover, recent work has demonstrated that priming ChatGPT-4 with positive, negative, or neutral emotional cues yields markedly different response patterns in tasks involving risk-taking and prosocial decisions [50], underscoring the potential to sway AI behavior via emotional indicators. Consequently, when assessing chatbots that receive multimodal emotional inputs, it is crucial to account for the valence of those inputs. Yet, empirical studies remain scarce on whether chatbots perform more effectively—or are perceived more favorably by users—when responding to strongly emotional user inputs (e.g., anger, sadness, happiness) versus neutral inputs, or when distinguishing among emotions of different valence (e.g., positive vs. negative).

To address these gaps, we examine whether integrating multimodal emotional information into chatbot inputs improves users' affective experience. Specifically, we ask whether (1) self-reported emotion, (2) automatically detected facial emotion, or (3) both modalities together enhance user-perceived empathy, mood, engagement, and social connection, relative to a text-only baseline. We also examine whether initiating conversations with emotional rather than neutral topics improves affective outcomes.

1. **H1 (Multimodal Input Hypothesis):** Providing multimodal emotional information (self-report emotion, automatically-detected facial emotion, or both) will improve users' affective experience compared to a text-only baseline.
2. **H2 (Emotional Topic Hypothesis):** Conversations initiated with emotional topics will elicit more positive affective responses than neutral topics.

Our study used a within-subjects design in which 28 participants interacted with four chatbot variants and completed both neutral and emotional topic tasks. Additionally, we explored whether individual differences—such as age, gender, prior chatbot experience, or emotional expressivity—moderate users' responses to these design choices.

This work contributes to ongoing efforts to personalize chatbot interaction by testing the conditions under which multimodal emotional input enhances or detracts from user experience. Rather than assume that more input is always better, we examine how trait-level factors may influence which users benefit most from different emotional input strategies.

2   Literature Review

2.1   Multimodal Input in Chatbot

Recent advances in Large Language Models (LLMs) demonstrate strong contextual understanding, adaptation, and consistency in processing multimodal inputs [11,22]. These discoveries prove the potential of LLMs to analyze emotional content and generate responses effectively [47]. GPT outperformed the general population on all scales of the Levels of Emotional Awareness Scale (LEAS) when identifying and describing emotions [16], and its responses to emotional scenarios received higher empathy ratings than those written by humans [45]. Additionally, prompt engineering combined with external emotion classifiers has been shown to improve chatbots' ability to discern emotional states and produce natural replies [8]. Despite these successes, LLMs without emotion-specific fine-tuning still perform poorly on many sentiment recognition tasks [17,44,49], and users often perceive machine responses as less understanding than human ones [3,38]. This gap highlights that current LLMs lack the multimodal sensitivity and adaptive emotional reasoning necessary for empathetic intelligence [41].

The integration of multimodal emotional input in chatbots has gained significant attention, with research showing that emotional content can enhance users' emotional experiences. EmoBot [14] can generate appropriate emotions and respond accordingly by analyzing continuous audio and text data, outperforming non-emotional chatbots in user satisfaction. The Sequential Multimodal Emotional Support framework [12] applies therapeutic-skill principles by sequentially incorporating text, voice, and visual cues to simulate therapist empathy. Similarly, an emotional chatbot [35], which uses short, positively valenced emotional expressions and emojis, outperformed a neutral chatbot in terms of trust and user satisfaction. These recent studies illustrate the potential of multimodal, emotion-aware architectures to enhance empathetic AI. However, existing work typically focuses on either discrete emotion expression and mimicry or domain-specific support, rather than examining the combined effects of different emotional input modalities—an area that our research aims to explore.

2.2   Emotional Abilities in Computer

Conversational agents have become increasingly popular in recent years, with applications ranging from customer service to mental health therapy [1,28,30]. Embodied conversational agents with emotion-aware capabilities have demonstrated improved perceived humanness, facilitating more natural and satisfying dialogues [18,42,43]. Yet achieving genuinely empathetic dialogue remains challenging: empathy entails nuanced, context-dependent recognition of another's internal state and an appropriate affective response—skills that demand not only linguistic competence but also a deep understanding of human psychology and social context [20].

Empathy, the ability to understand and share the feelings of another person, is a fundamental aspect of human interaction. It involves a range of cognitive, affective, and compassionate counterparts [15,21,36]. Empathy plays an important role in the success of human-bot interactions [10], and empathetic responses could significantly enhance users' affective feeling [27,30]. Building on this foundation, recent advancements in

Human–Computer Interaction (HCI) have focused on developing systems that harness the power of empathy, since emotion-aware design can enhance user experience by tailoring responses to individual emotional states [31,46].

Empathy research indicates that robust empathic behavior requires real-time perception, recognition, and expression of affective cues across modalities [13,34]. Surveys of empathetic dialogue systems emphasize integrating personal preferences and knowledge with continuous text, audio, and visual emotion signals [29]. Similarly, frameworks for embodied agents call for real-time multimodal emotion perception to enable accurate emotion recognition and response generation [47]. Building on these findings, our study advances LLM-based chatbots by combining conversational context with continuous visual emotion cues, aiming to enhance emotional awareness and deliver genuinely empathetic responses.

3   Methodology

Having introduced our research questions and hypotheses, we now describe the experimental setup used to evaluate users' affective experiences across four chatbot conditions and two topic types. This section outlines the participant sample, chatbot design, procedure, and emotion induction method.

3.1   Participants

Twenty-eight participants (15 male, 13 female) were recruited through the RedBook social platform. All provided informed consent prior to participation. Eligibility was limited to adults (18+ years) without known psychological, psychiatric, or neurodivergent conditions (e.g., depression, autism), and not currently using psychoactive medication. The age distribution was: 9 participants aged 18–24, 7 aged 25–34, 1 aged 35–44, 7 aged 45–54, and 4 aged 55–64. Informed consent included permission for audiovisual recordings during the study.

3.2   Emotion-Aware Chatbot Design

We developed four chatbot variants (Fig. 1). Participants were not informed about the differences between conditions to ensure consistent expectations across sessions.

- **Baseline (Condition A):** Emotion was inferred from the user's text input alone.
- **Self-Reported Emotion (Condition B):** Participants selected their emotional state (happy, sad, neutral, angry, afraid, disgust, surprise) via on-screen buttons; this selection was sent to the chatbot along with the message.
- **Automatically Detected Facial-Emotion (Condition C):** Automatically detected facial emotion data is processed to generate a concise emotional summary, then the summary is sent to the GPT together with the text message.
- **Combined-Emotion (Condition D):** Both self-reported and facially detected emotion were sent with the user's message.

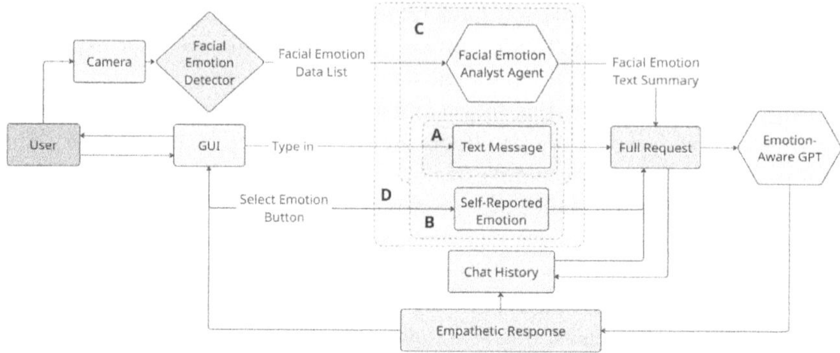

Fig. 1. Overview of the four chatbot conditions: (A) Baseline—emotion inferred only from text; (B) Self-Reported—user selects emotion via buttons; (C) Facial Emotion—emotion automatically detected from facial expressions; (D) Combined—both self-reported and facial inputs used.

Facial emotion was processed using a pre-trained TensorFlow model available via GitHub.[1], which was trained based on Tensorflow and has 62% reported accuracy in classifying seven different emotions (angry, fear, disgust, happy, neutral, sad, surprise). The system sampled frames at 6 fps over a 5-s window (downsampled from 30 fps), generating a list of frame-wise emotion predictions (e.g., *[{'angry': 0, 'disgust': 0, 'fear': 0, 'happy': 4, 'neutral': 4, 'sad': 0, 'surprise': 0}]*). Upon message submission, these chronological lists are forwarded to a specialized Facial Emotion Analyst Agent module—implemented via ChatGPT-4o-mini, which aggregates the frame-wise data to determine the dominant emotion and any temporal shifts, then returns a concise natural-language summary for use by the chatbot. The prompt is as follows: *You are able to analyze the user's sentiment and attitude during a conversation based on real-time facial emotion detection data. You will receive data in chronological order, formatted as a series of dictionaries. Each dictionary represents the detected emotion data collected from the user's facial expressions over a 5-s interval. Your task is to analyze the user's sentiment based on this data and provide a concise summary of their overall emotional state during this time. Your summary should capture the dominant sentiment and attitude of the user. Respond only with your summary of the sentiment in 6–14 words.*

All chatbot responses are generated by the Emotion-Aware GPT(based on Chat-GPT4o), which uses a pre-defined prompt informed by previous research [8,45]. The prompt is as follows: *Empathy is the ability to understand and share the feelings of another person. Empathy is a complex skill that involves cognitive, emotional, and compassionate components. Cognitive empathy is the ability to understand another person's thoughts, beliefs, and intentions. Affective empathy is the ability to experience the emotions of another person. It is feeling what they are feeling, both positive and negative. Compassionate empathy is the ability to not only understand and share another person's feelings but also to be moved to help if needed. It involves a deeper level of*

---

[1] https://github.com/kumarvivek9088/Face_Emotion_Recognition_Machine_Learning.

emotional engagement than cognitive empathy, prompting action to alleviate another's distress or suffering.

3.3   Experiment Procedure

Before the main tasks, participants completed the Emotional Expressivity Scale [25] to assess individual differences in emotional expressivity. The full experiment lasted 50–60 min. Each participant interacted with the chatbot under all four conditions (A–D), presented in randomized order.

For each condition, participants completed two conversation tasks: one with a neutral topic and one with an emotional topic (described below). Each task lasted 2–4 min, during which participants exchanged at least three messages with the chatbot. After each task, participants filled out Chinese translations of the following self-report questionnaires: mood (SIMS) [2], user engagement (UES) [33], perceived empathy (PETS) [39], and social connection (SC) [32], ensuring that no advanced English proficiency was required for participation.

In total, participants completed eight tasks (4 conditions × 2 topic types). Although all interactions were conducted in English, the user interface was automatically translated and presented in Chinese. Figure 2 provides an example of the experiment procedure. Throughout the experiment, we recorded facial video, chatbot logs, timestamped user text, and emotion metadata.

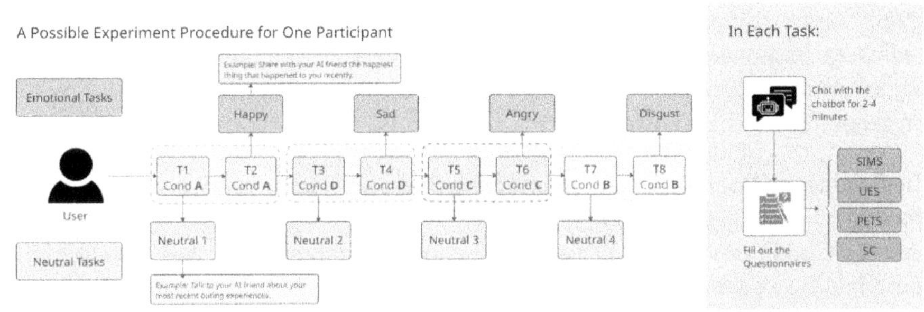

Fig. 2. Diagram showing a possible experiment procedure for one participant.

3.4   Emotion Induction Design

To elicit emotion in a standardized way, we used the Autobiographical Recall method [37,40], which prompts participants to retrieve and describe past emotional experiences. This method has been shown to effectively induce basic emotions such as happiness, sadness, anger, and disgust.

We designed four emotional topics and twelve neutral ones. Emotional prompts took the form: "Share with your AI friend the [happiest/saddest/most frustrating/most disgusting] thing that happened to you recently." Neutral prompts included: "Talk to your AI friend about your most recent outing experience." Before each emotional task, participants were given 30–60 s to recall a relevant experience.

To control for order effects and emotional carryover, each emotional task was preceded by a neutral one. Thus, participants alternated between neutral and emotional tasks throughout the study. This structure ensured both topic types were experienced under each chatbot condition.

4 Results

4.1 Different Chat Conditions

We hypothesized (H1) that integrating multimodal emotional input—via self-report emotion, automatically detected facial emotion, or both—would enhance users' affective experience relative to a text-only baseline (Condition A). Contrary to expectations, no significant main effects were observed: none of the multimodal conditions (B, C, D) resulted in a significant improvement in user outcomes relative to Condition A. The p-values for all variables (Mood, SC, UES, PETS) exceeded 0.1.

We then grouped conditions based on the presence or absence of facial emotion input to test whether facial cues influenced affective outcomes. Surprisingly, Conditions A and B (no facial input) yielded marginally higher perceived empathy scores (mean PETS = 71.71) than Conditions C and D (facial input; mean PETS = 66.54), although this difference approached but did not reach statistical significance ($F(1,222) = 3.31$, $p = .0704$).

Next, we examined whether individual differences in emotional expressivity moderated users' responses. P-values for all comparisons were adjusted using the Bonferroni correction to account for multiple testing. Correlation analyses with the Emotional Expressivity Scale (EES) revealed:

- In Condition D, self-assessed emotional expressivity was negatively correlated with mood ($r = -0.354$, $p = .03$);
- Across Conditions C and D (with facial input), expressivity was also negatively correlated with mood ($r = -0.226$, $p = .033$);
- In contrast, in Conditions A and B (without facial input), expressivity was marginally positively correlated with perceived empathy ($r = 0.204$, $p = .063$) (Figs. 3 and 4).

These results suggest that users' emotional expressivity shaped their experience in opposite ways depending on the condition. More expressive users reported better outcomes in conditions without facial emotion input (A & B), while less expressive users experienced higher mood in conditions with facial input (C & D).

We also examined the effects of self-reported emotion input. Comparing Conditions B and D (with self-report) to Conditions A and C (without), no main effects emerged. However, exploratory analysis revealed an interaction with prior chatbot experience. Among participants with no prior chatbot experience, those in Conditions A and C (no self-report) reported higher engagement and social connection.

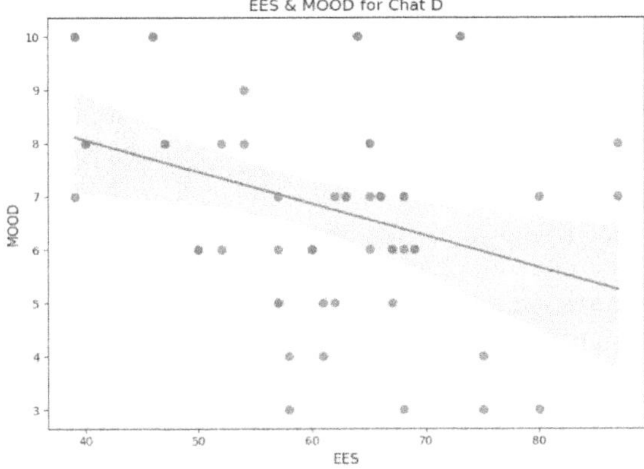

Fig. 3. Correlation between emotional expressivity (EES) and mood in Condition D.

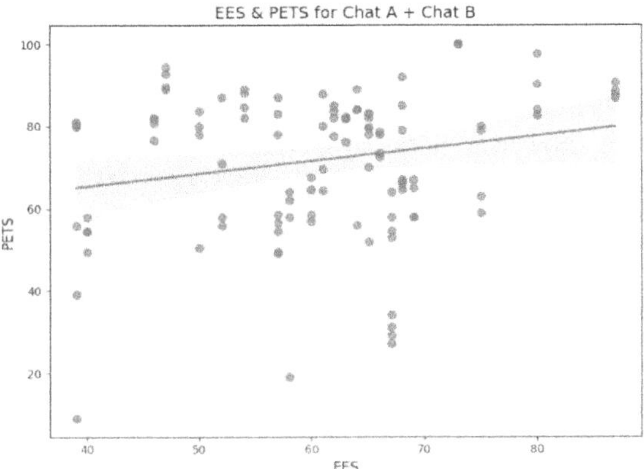

Fig. 4. Correlation between emotional expressivity (EES) and perceived empathy (PETS) in Conditions A & B.

Simple effects analyses showed the following differences:

- **Focused Attention (FA):** A & C = 2.67; B & D = 2.57 ($p = .044$)
- **Partner Responsiveness (PRS):** A & C = 4.87; B & D = 4.63 ($p = .071$)
- **Partner Interest (PIS):** A & C = 5.23; B & D = 4.96 ($p = .065$)

These findings suggest that for inexperienced users, requiring self-reported emotion input may have added interface complexity or cognitive load, reducing engagement and social connection. In contrast, experienced users showed no such effects, implying that self-report features may be more suitable once users are familiar with chatbot interaction.

4.2   Emotional and Neutral Tasks

We hypothesized (H2) that initiating conversations with emotional topics would enhance users' affective experiences compared to neutral topics. However, no significant main effects of topic valence were observed across the full sample. That is, tasks involving emotional prompts (happiness, sadness, anger, or disgust) did not elicit significantly higher mood, engagement, empathy, or social connection than neutral prompts.

Nonetheless, moderation analyses revealed important differences based on individual factors. Among participants with prior chatbot experience (n = 11), a mixed-design ANOVA revealed a significant interaction between topic type and affective experience, specifically on the Affective Experience (AES) subscale of the Social Connection Scale: $F(1,26) = 6.81$, $p = .015$, $\eta^2 = 0.21$. For these participants, emotional topics yielded higher social connection (mean = 6.04) than neutral ones (mean = 5.70), though this effect was only marginally significant at the simple effects level ($r = .284$, $p = .091$).

Post hoc comparisons confirmed that experienced participants reported significantly higher social connection than inexperienced participants in emotional-topic tasks ($r = -0.56$, $p = .023$), suggesting that emotional prompts enhanced perceived connection for those already familiar with chatbot interactions.

A parallel analysis of the Social Responsiveness (SRS) subscale by gender revealed that male participants showed a marginal increase in responsiveness during emotional topics compared to neutral ones ($r = 0.201$, $p = 0.067$; $BF_{10} = 1.26$, Hedges' $g = 0.20$).

Taken together, while emotional topics did not improve affective experience overall, they may enhance perceived connection for certain user groups—specifically, experienced users and possibly male participants.

4.3   Exploratory Analyses

Gender Differences.   Gender appeared to moderate users' affective responses across conditions. Female participants (n = 13) reported significantly higher engagement and social connection than male participants (n = 15). Specifically:

- **Focused Attention (FA, UESSF):** $F(1,27) = 6.94$, $p = .012$; $M_F = 3.08$ vs. $M_M = 2.72$
- **Social Connection (SC):** $F(1,27) = 5.19$, $p = .030$; $M_F = 5.10$ vs. $M_M = 4.73$

These differences suggest that female users found the chatbot interactions more socially rewarding and engaging across all conditions.

Age Differences.   We also examined whether affective responses differed by age. Participants were grouped into younger (18–44 years, n = 16) and older (45–64 years, n = 12) cohorts. Older participants consistently reported higher positive affective responses, while younger participants reported slightly higher attentiveness.

- **Mood (MOOD):** $F(1,207) = 9.80$, $p = .002$; $M_{Old} = 7.45$ vs. $M_{Young} = 6.56$
- **Reward (RW, UESSF):** $F(1,207) = 4.67$, $p = .032$; $M_{Old} = 3.81$ vs. $M_{Young} = 3.51$

- **Empathy (ER, PETS)**: $F(1,207) = 4.40$, $p = .037$; $M_{Old} = 71.60$ vs. $M_{Young} = 65.20$
- **Social Responsiveness (SRS, SC)**: $F(1,207) = 10.27$, $p = .002$; $M_{Old} = 4.70$ vs. $M_{Young} = 3.95$
- **Focused Attention (FA)**: $F(1,207) = 2.74$, $p = .100$ (marginal); $M_{Young} = 3.02$ vs. $M_{Old} = 2.77$
- **Social Connection (SC)**: $F(1,207) = 3.83$, $p = .052$ (marginal); $M_{Old} = 5.12$ vs. $M_{Young} = 4.76$

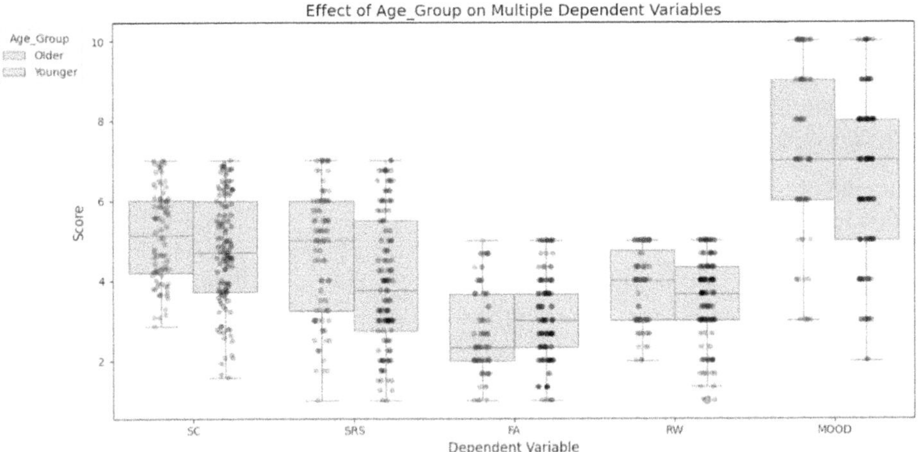

Fig. 5. Age differences in mood, user engagement (UESSF), and social connection (SC).

These findings suggest that older users may experience greater emotional and social benefits from chatbot interactions, while younger users may engage more cognitively (e.g., focused attention) (Fig. 5).

Prior Chatbot Experience. Prior experience may also moderate affective outcomes. Participants who had previously interacted with chatbots (n = 11) reported significantly higher engagement and social connection than those without prior experience (n = 17). Notable differences included:

- **Overall Engagement (UESSF):** $F(1,222) = 12.65$, $p = .0005$; $M_{Experienced} = 3.54$ vs. $M_{Inexperienced} = 3.09$
- **Partner Interest (PIS, SC):** $F(1,222) = 8.88$, $p = .003$; $M_{Experienced} = 5.61$ vs. $M_{Inexperienced} = 5.09$
- **Affective Experience (AES, SC):** $F(1,222) = 7.10$, $p = .008$; $M_{Experienced} = 5.87$ vs. $M_{Inexperienced} = 5.38$

These results suggest that experienced users were more engaged overall and felt more emotionally connected to the chatbot, demonstrating that prior familiarity may enhance receptivity to emotionally intelligent systems.

4.4 Interview Insights

To complement the quantitative findings, we conducted semi-structured interviews to explore participants' subjective impressions of the chatbot conditions and topic types.

Topic Preferences. When asked which types of conversations they preferred, most participants favored emotionally positive or neutral topics. Nineteen participants preferred "happy" topics, 14 preferred neutral ones, while only one participant each preferred "angry" or "disgust" topics. A chi-square test confirmed a significant preference for happy/neutral content over negative themes ($\chi^2(1) = 28.89$, $p < .001$).

Perceived Emotional Sensitivity. Participants also identified which condition they felt was most emotionally responsive. Although results were only marginally significant ($\chi^2(1) = 7.52$, $p = .0571$), Condition C (Facial Emotion) was most frequently rated as emotionally sensitive (12 votes), followed by Condition A (Baseline, 8 votes), Condition D (Combined, 4 votes), and Condition B (Self-Report, 3 votes).

Thematic Impressions. Participants shared rich qualitative feedback on how each condition felt:

- **Conditions C & D (Facial Input):** Users often described these chatbots as "humane," "less official," and "more appropriate." Some noted that they "found topics by themselves" and made the conversation feel "more natural and empathetic." One participant said, "C understands what I mean and reflects my true feelings," while another praised D for follow-up questions that made it feel "less rigid."
- **Condition A (Baseline):** Some users preferred the baseline chatbot for its clarity and relevance. It was perceived as "comprehensive and humane," with participants stating it "understood my difficulties" and "addressed my pain points."
- **Condition B (Self-Report):** This condition received the least feedback, though a few participants found it helpful for clarifying their own emotional state.

Overall Condition Preference. When asked to choose a favorite, 11 participants selected Condition C, 11 chose Condition A, 7 preferred Condition D, and 4 selected Condition B. These preferences closely mirrored the perception of emotional sensitivity and echoed the moderation findings: users responded differently to each input modality depending on their own traits and preferences.

Taken together, the qualitative insights verify that users' emotional experiences with chatbots are not uniformly improved by multimodal input. Instead, preferences and perceived effectiveness vary by input modality and user characteristics, underscoring the importance of personalization in affective chatbot design.

5 Discussion

5.1 Facial Emotional Input

Our findings suggest that integrating multimodal emotional inputs—such as facial expressions and self-reported emotion—does not uniformly enhance user experience. Instead, their effectiveness depends on individual differences, particularly emotional expressivity: the extent to which users outwardly display emotion [25]. This trait shaped how users responded to different input conditions.

Participants high in emotional expressivity reported better mood when interacting with chatbots that relied solely on text. Prior research shows that expressive individuals naturally convey emotional content through verbal and nonverbal textual cues (e.g., affective language, punctuation, emojis) [19]. As such, additional emotional input from facial or self-reported channels may be unnecessary—or even disruptive—when their text already carries strong emotional signals.

Conversely, participants lower in emotional expressivity benefited from the inclusion of facial or self-reported emotion inputs, particularly in Condition D. These users may struggle to convey affect through text, making multimodal input especially useful for signaling emotional state. Interview comments supported this pattern: less expressive users described facial-input conditions as "really understanding my true feelings," even if the system itself was not objectively more accurate. This highlights the potential of multimodal design not as a universal improvement, but as a targeted enhancement for specific user profiles.

However, as noted earlier, Conditions A and B (no facial input) yielded slightly higher perceived empathy scores than Conditions C and D. This pattern may reflect a limitation of the emotion detection model rather than a genuine difference in empathic engagement. Inaccurate facial emotion recognition can produce mismatched or unsuitable responses, leading to user dissatisfaction. Notably, participants with higher Emotional Expressivity Scale (EES) scores may be particularly sensitive to such mismatches: when the system "reads" their face incorrectly, the resulting response violates expectations more saliently, dampening empathy judgments. The potential influence of facial detection inaccuracies on the main outcomes should not be overlooked.

5.2 Self-report Emotional Input

No significant effects were found for self-reported emotion inputs overall. However, subgroup analysis revealed that users without prior chatbot experience reported higher engagement and social connection when self-report emotion was not included. For these users, the additional interface complexity may have added friction. In contrast, experienced users showed no such effect, suggesting that familiarity reduces the cognitive load associated with selecting emotions.

These findings imply that self-report input features should be adapted to users' prior experience levels, potentially introduced gradually or made optional in early interactions.

5.3 Emotion Induction Tasks

Although we observed no significant main effects of topic valence (emotional vs. neutral) or polarity (positive vs. negative) across the full sample, participants with prior chatbot experience and male participants reported greater social connection when conversations began with emotional topics. This finding lends partial support to the notion that initiating chat sessions with emotionally charged content can enhance users' affective engagement with the system. It is consistent with Zhao *et al.*'s demonstration that priming LLMs with emotional cues can sway AI responses in decision-making tasks [50].

We attribute these effects to deeper emotional engagement: the memory-recall induction likely amplified participants' affective states—particularly for those with prior chatbot experience—thereby validating our use of targeted topic prompts to elicit strong emotions at the outset of interaction. In contrast, emotion-induction tasks may pose greater challenges for users without prior experience with chatbot; their lower familiarity with conversational agents may make it harder to openly share more emotions and may heighten perceived social pressure.

Moreover, the results hint that LLM-based chatbots may perform more effectively when they receive richer emotional inputs, suggesting a promising avenue for enhancing the emotional intelligence of conversational agents. Overall, these insights represent a progressive step toward understanding how AI systems can learn from and adapt to human emotional contexts, informing the design of more empathetic and engaging chatbots.

5.4 Gender, Age and Prior Experience Effects

Female participants consistently reported higher engagement and social connection than male participants across conditions, aligning with established findings that women often display greater empathy and emotional sensitivity [6,24]. Interestingly, male participants showed marginally greater responsiveness during emotional-topic tasks, suggesting a potential interaction between gender and content type that merits further study.

Older adults (45+) reported higher mood, empathy, reward, and social connection than younger participants, even though they were less attentive overall and had less prior chatbot experience. These findings are consistent with research showing increased emotional empathy and prosocial orientation in older populations [7,26,48]. This suggests that emotion-aware chatbots may serve as valuable tools for promoting social connectedness in aging populations, especially those at risk of isolation.

Participants with prior chatbot experience reported greater engagement, partner interest, and emotional connection in all conditions. They also responded more positively to emotional-topic tasks, possibly due to greater comfort with self-disclosure in digital contexts. This finding suggests that experience moderates not just usability but also emotional openness. Emotion-aware chatbots may be most effective when calibrated to users' familiarity with the medium—adapting their emotional interface strategies over time as users grow more comfortable.

6 Conclusion

Instead of generalization, the results suggest that personalization is key to improving affective experiences with emotionally intelligent chatbots. Multimodal input did not produce uniform benefits across users; in fact, for expressive users, it sometimes interfered with the affective experience. However, less expressive participants and those with limited prior chatbot exposure gained more from systems that incorporated additional emotional cues. Rather than adding more emotional input, user traits like expressivity, age, gender, and experience should be considered in shaping the effectiveness of different input modalities. Emotion-aware design must move beyond uniform input strategies to tailor chatbot responses based on users' emotional traits and experience levels.

6.1 Limitations

Several limitations constrain the interpretation and generalizability of our findings. First, the sample size (N = 28) and unbalanced distributions across demographic subgroups limited statistical power for interaction effects. Second, data were collected in naturalistic home environments, introducing variability in lighting, camera position, and user behavior. Third, the emotion induction procedure was relatively short (30–60 s), possibly insufficient for sustained emotional engagement. Each task lasted only 2–4 min, while sufficient for a controlled experiment, but measuring complex states like empathy and social connection after such a short interaction by non-professionals, with a non-embodied chatbot is challenging. The results may reflect initial impressions or politeness biases rather than a genuine affective experience, making it questionable if deep affective constructs like perceived empathy and social connection were reliably established.

Moreover, our hypothesis about expressivity and input channel effectiveness remains tentative, as we did not perform in-depth sentiment or behavioral analysis of the chat content itself. The facial emotion model used had limited accuracy (62%), increasing the likelihood of misclassifying expressions and generating mismatched responses, which could in turn lower users' empathy ratings. The summaries produced by the Facial Emotion Analyst Agent—derived from raw and noisy facial emotion data—may have oversimplified participants' dynamic emotional states, as the effectiveness of this summarization in extracting meaningful information remains uncertain. The language processing limitations in GPT for Chinese may have introduced inconsistencies. Recruitment from the RedBook social platform suggests a specific demographic (likely young, tech-savvy, and culturally Chinese), which limits the generalizability of the findings to a broader population. The significant gender and age effects from this study, are still highly exploratory and require replication with a larger, more diverse sample. Future work will address these limitations by extending emotion-induction protocols, deploying higher-accuracy emotion models, enlarging generalized population in recruitment, and incorporating detailed sentiment analyses.

6.2 Future Work

Future research should replicate these findings with larger, demographically diverse samples in controlled lab settings. Extending the duration and richness of emotion induction—with dynamic or multi-stage protocols—would enable deeper engagement and more reliable measurement of affective responses. Technical robustness can be enhanced by integrating state-of-the-art facial-emotion models, adopting flexible camera setups that accommodate natural user behavior, and employing richer summarization methods (e.g., multi-sentence or temporal descriptors) that preserve the nuance of emotional trajectories. Crucially, empirical validation of the expressivity hypothesis will require comprehensive sentiment analysis of both text and facial-emotion streams to elucidate how individual differences shape the efficacy of multimodal cues. Finally, longitudinal studies and domain-specific investigations (such as mental health support for vulnerable populations) are needed to evaluate the sustained impact of empathetic chatbots on user well-being and to develop best practices for emotionally intelligent agents in diverse real-world contexts.

Ethical Impact Statement. This study adhered to ethical research protocols and was approved by the authors' institutional review board (IRB). Participants gave informed consent, were fully briefed on their rights (including the right to withdraw at any time), and were screened to exclude individuals with psychological vulnerabilities.

Privacy was a central concern: all identifiable data—including facial video used for emotion detection—was encrypted in transit and at rest. Facial videos were processed in real time to produce emotion summaries, and raw footage was not retained. All text logs, system outputs, and questionnaires were anonymized.

The emotion induction tasks were brief (30–60 s), mild in emotional intensity, and participants could skip or discontinue any task without penalty. Chatbot responses avoided manipulative or suggestive language, and participants were debriefed after the session.

This work contributes to the development of emotionally intelligent systems while upholding standards of transparency, privacy, and user dignity. However, we also acknowledge risks: emotion-aware systems could be misused for manipulation, surveillance, or profiling. Developers should incorporate safeguards against these risks, including transparency about emotion use, user control over input sharing, and ongoing interdisciplinary oversight. Emotion-aware AI has the potential to improve social well-being—but only when developed and deployed responsibly.

Acknowledgment. The work of Y. Li and M. Mancini was funded and is in line with the objectives of the Project PNRR PNC D3 4 Health - CUP B53C22006120001 (National Plan for Complementary Investments to the NRRP, mission 4, component 2, investment 3.5, spoke 3, PNCSALUTE-D3-4-HEALTH–SPOKE-3-DIAEE, Funded by the European Union - NextGenerationEU).

References

1. Abd-Alrazaq, A.A., Alajlani, M., Alalwan, A.A., Bewick, B.M., Gardner, P., Househ, M.: An overview of the features of chatbots in mental health: a scoping review. Int. J. Med. Inform. **132**, 103978 (2019)

2. Abdel-Khalek, A.M.: Measuring happiness with a single-item scale. Soc. Behav. Personal. Int. J. **34**(2), 139–150 (2006)

3. Adam, M., Wessel, M., Benlian, A.: AI-based chatbots in customer service and their effects on user compliance. Electron. Mark. **31**(2), 427–445 (2021)

4. Adamopoulou, E., Moussiades, L.: An overview of chatbot technology. In: Maglogiannis, I., Iliadis, L., Pimenidis, E. (eds.) AIAI 2020. IAICT, vol. 584, pp. 373–383. Springer, Cham (2020). https://doi.org/10.1007/978-3-030-49186-4_31

5. Ayers, J.W., et al.: Comparing physician and artificial intelligence chatbot responses to patient questions posted to a public social media forum. JAMA Intern. Med. **183**(6), 589–596 (2023)
6. Baron-Cohen, S., Wheelwright, S.: The empathy quotient: an investigation of adults with Asperger syndrome or high functioning autism, and normal sex differences. J. Autism Dev. Disord. **34**, 163–175 (2004)
7. Beadle, J.N., de la Vega, C.E.: Impact of aging on empathy: review of psychological and neural mechanisms. Front. Psych. **10**, 331 (2019)
8. Belkhir, A., Sadat, F.: Beyond information: is ChatGPT empathetic enough? In: Proceedings of the 14th International Conference on Recent Advances in Natural Language Processing, pp. 159–169 (2023)
9. Bilquise, G., Ibrahim, S., Shaalan, K.: Emotionally intelligent chatbots: a systematic literature review. Hum. Behav. Emerg. Technol. **2022**(1), 9601630 (2022)
10. Birnbaum, G.E., Mizrahi, M., Hoffman, G., Reis, H.T., Finkel, E.J., Sass, O.: What robots can teach us about intimacy: the reassuring effects of robot responsiveness to human disclosure. Comput. Hum. Behav. **63**, 416–423 (2016)
11. Cherakara, N., et al.: FurChat: an embodied conversational agent using LLMs, combining open and closed-domain dialogue with facial expressions. arXiv preprint arXiv:2308.15214 (2023)
12. Chu, Y., Liao, L., Zhou, Z., Ngo, C.W., Hong, R.: Towards multimodal emotional support conversation systems. arXiv preprint arXiv:2408.03650 (2024)
13. De Waal, F.B., Preston, S.D.: Mammalian empathy: behavioural manifestations and neural basis. Nat. Rev. Neurosci. **18**(8), 498–509 (2017)
14. Ehtesham-Ul-Haque, M., et al.: EmoBot: artificial emotion generation through an emotional chatbot during general-purpose conversations. Cogn. Syst. Res. **83**, 101168 (2024)
15. Ekman, P.: Emotional and conversational nonverbal signals. In: Larrazabal, J.M., Miranda, L.A.P. (eds.) Language, Knowledge, and Representation. Philosophical Studies Series, vol. 99, pp. 39–50. Springer, Dordrecht (2004). https://doi.org/10.1007/978-1-4020-2783-3_3
16. Elyoseph, Z., Hadar-Shoval, D., Asraf, K., Lvovsky, M.: ChatGPT outperforms humans in emotional awareness evaluations. Front. Psychol. **14**, 1199058 (2023)
17. Fatahi, S., Vassileva, J., Roy, C.K.: Comparing emotions in ChatGPT answers and human answers to the coding questions on stack overflow. Front. Artif. Intell. **7**, 1393903 (2024)
18. Goetz, J., Kiesler, S., Powers, A.: Matching robot appearance and behavior to tasks to improve human-robot cooperation. In: 2003 Proceedings of the 12th IEEE International Workshop on Robot and Human Interactive Communication, ROMAN 2003, pp. 55–60. IEEE (2003)
19. Hancock, J.T., Landrigan, C., Silver, C.: Expressing emotion in text-based communication. In: Proceedings of the SIGCHI Conference on Human Factors in Computing Systems, pp. 929–932 (2007)
20. Ioannidou, F., Konstantikaki, V.: Empathy and emotional intelligence: what is it really about? Int. J. Caring Sci. **1**(3), 118 (2008)
21. Jackson, P.L., Rainville, P., Decety, J.: To what extent do we share the pain of others? Insight from the neural bases of pain empathy. Pain **125**(1–2), 5–9 (2006)
22. Kim, C.Y., Lee, C.P., Mutlu, B.: Understanding large-language model (LLM)-powered human-robot interaction. In: Proceedings of the 2024 ACM/IEEE International Conference on Human-Robot Interaction, pp. 371–380 (2024)
23. Kim, W.B., Hur, H.J.: What makes people feel empathy for ai chatbots? Assessing the role of competence and warmth. Int. J. Hum. Comput. Interact. **40**(17), 4674–4687 (2024)
24. Kirkland, R.A., Peterson, E., Baker, C.A., Miller, S., Pulos, S.: Meta-analysis reveals adult female superiority in "reading the mind in the eyes test". North Am. J. Psychol. **15**(1) (2013)

25. Kring, A.M., Smith, D.A., Neale, J.M.: Individual differences in dispositional expressiveness: development and validation of the emotional expressivity scale. J. Pers. Soc. Psychol. **66**(5), 934 (1994)
26. Li, D., Cao, Y., Hui, B.P., Shum, D.H.: Are older adults more prosocial than younger adults? A systematic review and meta-analysis. Gerontologist **64**(9), gnae082 (2024)
27. Liu, Y.l., Hu, B., Yan, W., Lin, Z.: Can chatbots satisfy me? A mixed-method comparative study of satisfaction with task-oriented chatbots in mainland China and Hong Kong. Comput. Hum. Behav. **143**, 107716 (2023)
28. Liu-Thompkins, Y., Okazaki, S., Li, H.: Artificial empathy in marketing interactions: bridging the human-AI gap in affective and social customer experience. J. Acad. Mark. Sci. **50**(6), 1198–1218 (2022)
29. Ma, Y., Nguyen, K.L., Xing, F.Z., Cambria, E.: A survey on empathetic dialogue systems. Inf. Fus. **64**, 50–70 (2020)
30. Markovitch, D.G., Stough, R.A., Huang, D.: Consumer reactions to chatbot versus human service: an investigation in the role of outcome valence and perceived empathy. J. Retail. Consum. Serv. **79**, 103847 (2024)
31. Niewiadomski, R., Ochs, M., Pelachaud, C.: Expressions of empathy in ECAs. In: Prendinger, H., Lester, J., Ishizuka, M. (eds.) IVA 2008. LNCS (LNAI), vol. 5208, pp. 37–44. Springer, Heidelberg (2008). https://doi.org/10.1007/978-3-540-85483-8_4
32. Okabe-Miyamoto, K., Walsh, L.C., Ozer, D.J., Lyubomirsky, S.: Measuring the experience of social connection within specific social interactions: the connection during conversations scale (CDCS). PLoS ONE **19**(1), e0286408 (2024)
33. O'Brien, H.L., Cairns, P., Hall, M.: A practical approach to measuring user engagement with the refined user engagement scale (UES) and new UES short form. Int. J. Hum Comput Stud. **112**, 28–39 (2018)
34. Paiva, A., Leite, I., Boukricha, H., Wachsmuth, I.: Empathy in virtual agents and robots: a survey. ACM Trans. Interact. Intell. Syst. (TiiS) **7**(3), 1–40 (2017)
35. Pezenka, I., Aunimo, L., Janous, G., Dobrowsky, D.: Emotionality in task-oriented chatbots-the effect of emotion expression on chatbot perception. Commun. Stud. **75**(6), 825–843 (2024)
36. Powell, P.A., Roberts, J.: Situational determinants of cognitive, affective, and compassionate empathy in naturalistic digital interactions. Comput. Hum. Behav. **68**, 137–148 (2017)
37. Prkachin, K.M., Williams-Avery, R.M., Zwaal, C., Mills, D.E.: Cardiovascular changes during induced emotion: an application of Lang's theory of emotional imagery. J. Psychosom. Res. **47**(3), 255–267 (1999)
38. Rapp, A., Curti, L., Boldi, A.: The human side of human-chatbot interaction: a systematic literature review of ten years of research on text-based chatbots. Int. J. Hum Comput Stud. **151**, 102630 (2021)
39. Schmidmaier, M., Rupp, J., Cvetanova, D., Mayer, S.: Perceived empathy of technology scale (PETS): measuring empathy of systems toward the user. In: Proceedings of the 2024 CHI Conference on Human Factors in Computing Systems, pp. 1–18 (2024)
40. Siedlecka, E., Denson, T.F.: Experimental methods for inducing basic emotions: a qualitative review. Emot. Rev. **11**(1), 87–97 (2019)
41. Sorin, V., et al.: Large language models and empathy: systematic review. J. Med. Internet Res. **26**, e52597 (2024)
42. Stroessner, S.J., Benitez, J.: The social perception of humanoid and non-humanoid robots: effects of gendered and machinelike features. Int. J. Soc. Robot. **11**, 305–315 (2019)
43. Svikhnushina, E., Pu, P.: PEACE: a model of key social and emotional qualities of conversational chatbots. ACM Trans. Interact. Intell. Syst. **12**(4), 1–29 (2022)
44. Tak, A.N., Gratch, J.: Is GPT a computational model of emotion? In: 2023 11th International Conference on Affective Computing and Intelligent Interaction (ACII), pp. 1–8. IEEE (2023)

45. Welivita, A., Pu, P.: Is ChatGPT more empathetic than humans? arXiv preprint arXiv:2403.05572 (2024)
46. Xu, X., Wang, X., Li, Y., Haghighi, M.: Business intelligence in online customer textual reviews: understanding consumer perceptions and influential factors. Int. J. Inf. Manage. **37**(6), 673–683 (2017)
47. Yalçın, Ö.N.: Empathy framework for embodied conversational agents. Cogn. Syst. Res. **59**, 123–132 (2020)
48. Ze, O., Thoma, P., Suchan, B.: Cognitive and affective empathy in younger and older individuals. Aging Ment. Health **18**(7), 929–935 (2014)
49. Zhang, Y., Li, Q., Song, D., Zhang, P., Wang, P.: Quantum-inspired interactive networks for conversational sentiment analysis (2019)
50. Zhao, Y., Huang, Z., Seligman, M., Peng, K.: Risk and prosocial behavioural cues elicit human-like response patterns from AI chatbots. Sci. Rep. **14**(1), 7095 (2024)

Interactive Visualization of the Changing Light Environment in the Arctic Ocean

Esben Bay Sørensen[1](✉) ⓘ, Jakob Kusnick[1] ⓘ, Karl Attard[2] ⓘ,
and Stefan Jänicke[1] ⓘ

[1] Department of Mathematics and Computer Science, University of Southern Denmark, Campusvej 55, 5230 Odense, Denmark
`essoe@imada.sdu.dk`
[2] Department of Biology, University of Southern Denmark, Campusvej 55, 5230 Odense, Denmark

Abstract. The Arctic Ocean is experiencing rapid environmental change due to climate-induced warming, significantly altering underwater light conditions and the implications for benthic primary producers are uncertain. Through an iterative design process involving domain experts in Arctic marine science, we developed an interactive visualization tool that integrates large-scale remote sensing datasets to enable multi-scale exploration of temporal light dynamics. The tool features a geospatial map for regional and local analysis, a heatmap for visualizing monthly percentage changes across Arctic regions and fjords, and a line chart for examining and comparing temporal trends. Users can filter data based on minimum light requirements for four benthic primary producers and extract filtered subsets for further offline analysis. Qualitative evaluation with domain experts confirmed the tool's effectiveness in supporting research tasks and revealed insights about changing patterns of light availability in the Arctic Ocean, which has significant implications for understanding how this sensitive ecosystem responds to rapid climate change.

Keywords: Geospatial Visualization · User-Centered Design · Arctic Marine Research

1   Introduction

Human-driven climate change is challenging the entire globe, with increasing temperatures and extreme weather events that significantly affect human civilization, wildlife, and ecosystems [14]. The unique and fragile Arctic ecosystem has experienced even more drastic changes with temperatures increasing four times higher than the global average [2,3]. This rapid warming has led to a significant decline in sea ice extent, exposing the ocean surface to increased solar radiation and altering light dynamics in the water column [3–5]. Despite growing recognition of these changes, considerable uncertainty remains about

J. F. Krems et al. (Eds.): CHIRA 2025, CCIS 2836, pp. 318–329, 2026.
https://doi.org/10.1007/978-3-032-16454-4_18

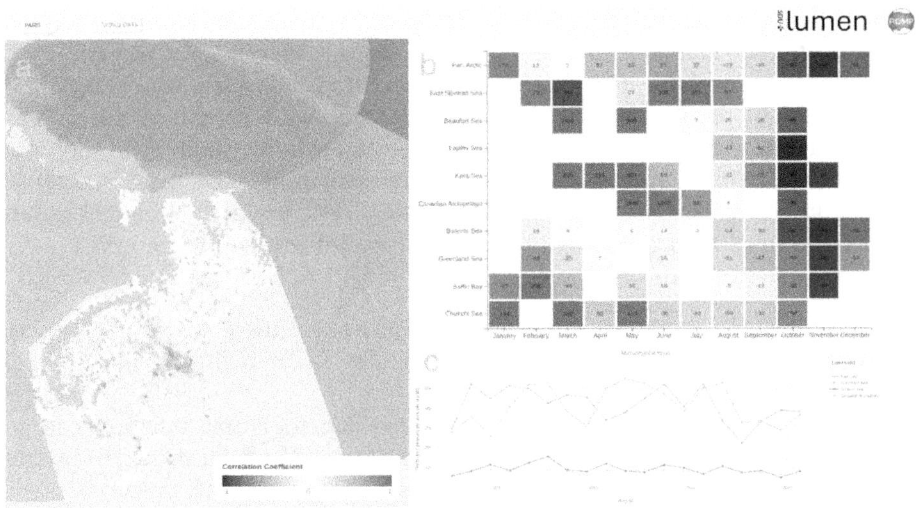

Fig. 1. Overview of the interactive visualization tool for exploring seasonal shifts in the light climate in the Arctic Ocean. The tool consists of three main elements **a**: geospatial interactive map, which supports visual exploration of the two large-scale remote sensing datasets, **b**: Heatmap representing each region or fjord and their percentage change for each month during the period, **c**: A line chart displaying the temporal change of multiple selected regions or hexagons for the chosen variable over time. A download button is available to the left of the line chart and will download a subset of the current present in the line chart. In the top left corner, one dropdown menu allows users to select different variables for analysis (e.g. species-specific and other variables), alongside a toggle button that switches between the two available datasets.

how the Arctic Ocean is adapting to shifting light regimes in the ocean, especially at the seafloor, and their implications for primary production [5]. Prior research discovered that the area of the seafloor exposed to light increased by $\sim 47{,}000 \text{ km}^2 \text{ y}^{-1}$ since 2003, yet no significant increase in benthic primary production was observed in the same period [5]. Understanding how these dynamics interplay is a central question for domain experts to grasp how the Arctic Ocean is adapting to the fast and rapid climate change.

At present, both in situ measurements, modeling, and large-scale remote sensing datasets are used to estimate temporal shifts in light availability and primary production in the Arctic Ocean [4,5,10,22]. However, the integration and interpretation of large-scale remote sensing data remain complex, and their use is limited to broad-scale analysis of annual temporal changes for the entire Arctic [5,22]. Although these datasets contain rich temporal and spatial information, their immense size and technical complexity have made it difficult for most researchers to utilize them for more detailed, seasonal-scale investigations of light dynamics in the Arctic Ocean. This, in turn, hampers efforts to effectively identify and prioritize new sampling locations for in situ research or for generating new hypotheses. Interactive visualization tools tailored to this context do not currently exist, limiting researchers' ability to intuitively explore and interpret the complex spatiotemporal changes in Arctic light availability.

In response, we have developed an interactive visualization tool through an iterative design process [16] in close collaboration with domain experts. This tool integrates two large-scale remote sensing datasets by Singh et al. [22] and Schlegel et al. [20] to explore patterns in light availability and benthic primary production across the Arctic Ocean, from Pan-Arctic scales (millions of square kilometers) down to regional and fjord level (several square kilometers). Our main contributions are:

- A participatory, iterative design process, incorporating feedback from Arctic marine scientists to adapt the tool's features for domain-specific research tasks.
- The development of an interactive visualization tool that integrates large-scale remote sensing datasets to enable multi-scale exploration of seasonal and long-term changes in light availability across the Arctic Ocean.

2   Related Work

Advances in satellite technologies and computational methods have led to a rapid growth in the volume and complexity of environmental data, including satellite-derived observations of the Arctic [8,9,19]. Numerous satellite-derived datasets, such as MODIS-Aqua [19], Sentinel-3 [8], and products from the Copernicus Marine Environment Monitoring Service (CMEMS) [9], have been widely used to assess light availability, sea surface temperature, and chlorophyll-a concentrations in Arctic waters. These datasets offer valuable insights at daily to monthly temporal resolutions and are often used in ecological and biogeochemical modeling. This high complexity of the data challenges visualizations due to visual overload, interpretation, and scalability [1,12]. Visualization platforms such as NASA's Worldview [18], the Copernicus MyOcean Viewer [7], and the Google Earth Engine [13] provide static or semi-interactive views of these data, yet they often lack customization, species-specific integration, or interactivity across spatial scales. As a result, researchers face challenges in exploring fine-scale dynamics, comparing spatiotemporal changes, and identifying regions of change for further study. Currently, multiple data and domain-specific visualization tools for large-scale datasets exist:

One of them is *pyParaOcean* by Jain et al. [15], which allows users to visualize and analyze large-scale oceanographic data using *ParaView*, supporting tasks such as eddy detection and water mass tracking. Although *pyParaOcean* provides useful tools for visualizing oceanographic models, it is primarily suited for large-scale physical processes and does not support multi-year time series data and temporal analysis, which can provide insights into long-term trends of the changing light regime in the Arctic Ocean.

More complex systems, such as *GeoSparkViz* [27], offer scalable geospatial visualization by integrating interactive, large-scale map rendering and visual analytics directly into the Apache Spark data processing pipeline. While it excels at producing high-resolution geospatial visualization and reducing data-to-visualization latency for billions of spatial points, its focus is primarily on generalized heatmap-style rendering and lacks domain-specific customization.

Despite the advancement in the above-mentioned visualization frameworks, they fall short in incorporating complex environmental datasets and domain-specific insights, which are essential for interpreting patterns in dynamic and rapidly changing ecosystems like the Arctic Ocean. Addressing this gap is crucial to enable fine-scale exploration, and identification of changing light regimes on a regional and sub-regional scale and how it impacts the primary production. We take a more simplistic approach compared to the complex visualization systems, where we utilize the domain-specific knowledge through an iterative design approach [16]. This approach allows us to prioritize interpretation, and usability for domain experts, ensuring that the resulting visualizations are tailored towards them.

3   User Tasks and Design Requirements

The tool has been developed in close collaboration with domain experts in Arctic marine science and their specific requirements have been incorporated in an iterative process guided by Tamara Munzner's *Nested Model* [16]. Further user tasks were proposed during the iterative process, which has directed the current design choices in the development of the tool:

- **T1: Explore Spatiotemporal Patterns of Light Availability:** Users need to interactively examine changes in light availability at both regional and local scales across the Arctic Ocean. This includes setting photosynthetic thresholds required to initiate growth for multiple benthic primary producers, to investigate potential expanding or contracting Arctic habitats.
- **T2: Investigate Species-Specific Light Requirements:** The tool must enable filtering and comparison based on minimum photosynthetic light requirement thresholds for different benthic primary producers. This supports analysis of possible species distributions under varying light conditions and potential shifts in species growth season and area.
- **T3: Extract Filtered Subsets for Further Analysis:** Users require the ability to export data that matches their selected filters and spatial constraints. This would enable them to focus on particular segments of the data filtered to their research requirements. Domain experts often collect their own data during field campaigns, and enabling offline comparison would allow them to validate and contextualize their observations against broader spatiotemporal patterns.
- **T4: Support Intuitive, User-Centered Interaction:** Given the varied backgrounds of potential users, the tool must offer simple designs, intuitive navigation, responsive filtering, and clear, interactive visualizations. Usability was prioritized throughout development to ensure accessibility for a wide range of domain experts.

4 Data

To support the analysis of temporal changes in light availability across the Arctic Ocean, we compiled and integrated two large-scale remote sensing datasets. Derived from remote sensing utilizing the Moderate Resolution Imaging Spectroradiometer(MODIS) from 2003 to 2020 for estimating photosynthetically available radiation at the seafloor (PARb) in the Arctic Ocean, Singh et al. presented a large-scale dataset in 2022 [22]. This provides a daily time series of integrated photosynthetically available radiation just below the water surface (PAR0), the light attenuation coefficient (KdPAR), and PARb, all at a spatial resolution of 1 km. To complement this pan-Arctic perspective, we incorporated the Fjord Light dataset by Schlegel et al. [20], which offers higher spatial and bathymetric resolution (50–200 m) for seven Arctic fjords, allowing for detailed regional analysis.

Abstraction for Domain Tasks: In close collaboration with domain experts, we defined the minimum light requirements for four key primary producer groups encompassing microscopic algae (microphytobenthos), coralline algae, seagrasses, and seaweeds [11] for incorporating species-specific layers. This can facilitate the study of benthic species distribution under varying light conditions and indicate the spatial areas where each species may occur.

Data Aggregation and Spatial Structuring: Large quantities of data can pose significant challenges for interactive visualizations due to computational limitations and scalability issues [1]. Multiple methods have been proposed to address these challenges in recent years, such as complex cloud-computing systems for data pre-processing, storage, and visualization [27]. In this study, we utilize a simpler approach, first proposed by Teanby et al. [23] and further developed by Wang et al. [26], to handle large datasets by aggregating and binning data into defined geographical regions. The minimum light requirements for the four benthic primary producers are applied as thresholds to subset the data prior to aggregation. This enables species-specific filtering in subsequent analyses, helping to identify spatial and temporal distribution patterns relevant to each species. We use 10 Arctic regions (MASIE) and the boundaries of 7 high Arctic fjords for binning and aggregating the two datasets [20,25]. To enable a more detailed spatial analysis, we further introduce a hexagonal grid of equal size (36.12km^2) within each region using the H3 library [24]. The choice of hexagons was informed by their favorable spatial properties, such as uniform adjacency and reduced edge effects, compared to square or triangular grids [6].

Temporal Aggregation and Statistical Analysis: To summarize temporal trends at different spatial scales, we performed regression analysis at the regional and fjord levels, calculating the percentage change over the time series for regions exhibiting significant trends (based on p-values and normalized residuals). At the hexagonal grid scale, we calculate Pearson's correlation coefficients to assess temporal trends, as the high variability in the data at this scale makes regression analysis less suitable. Although most hexagonal scale correlations were not statistically significant, they provide valuable indications of localized temporal patterns.

Computational Considerations: Throughout the design of our data abstraction and aggregation pipeline, we prioritized scalability and interactivity by reducing the sheer size of data and using preprocessed data. Rather than relying on complex cloud-based systems for pre-processing and visualization [27], we adopted a lightweight, locally executable workflow that supports rapid filtering and exploration for large-scale datasets.

Fig. 2. A closer look at the hexagon grid in the fjord of *Disko Bay* for August. The red areas indicate an increasing light availability, whereas blue areas indicate a decrease in light availability from 2003 to 2020.(Color figure online)

5 Visual Encoding and Interaction Design

Based on the principles of the *Information Seeking Mantra*, our tool offers an *overview, zoom levels*, species-specific *filtering options*, and visualizations to facilitate the comparison and analysis of temporal trends in *details on demand* [21]. We realized this by leveraging the scalability of visualizations, allowing to limit the amount of visual components while adapting to user input and the multiple levels of detail. Utilizing this flexibility, our primary focus has been to design an intuitive interface tailored to the needs of domain experts in Arctic marine science.

T1: Exploring Spatiotemporal Patterns: The main feature of the tool is a geospatial map that enables users to visually explore both datasets. Users can identify regional trends see Fig. 1a, zoom into specific fjords, and examine local variations using a fine hexagonal grid overlay see Fig. 2. Temporal changes in light availability are encoded using a diverging blue-to-red color scale for both regional polygons and hexagons of Arctic Ocean regions or specific fjords. Polygons for the regions reflect percentage change over time, ranging from -100% to 100%, while summarizing the underlying hexagonal, detailed data points. Thereby certain polygons may experience changes greater than ±100% but the diverging color scale is limited to this range to preserve comparative readability and avoid visual distortion caused by outliers. The hexagon colors represent the slope of the correlation coefficient ranging from -1 to 1, highlighting local increases or decreases of light availability at the seafloor. When selecting a certain region or fjord transitions are done by smooth zoom-animations into the selected region and switching from the large regional polygon to reveal the fine mesh of hexagons.

T2: Investigating Species-Specific Light Requirements: Species-specific filtering is available through a drop-down menu, allowing users to select among minimum light requirement thresholds for microscopic algae (microphytobenthos), coralline algae, seagrasses, and seaweeds, prepared in the data. This targeted filtering (**T2**) helps users analyze the potential distribution of each primary producer group under varying light conditions, enabling hypothesis verification or generation and the identification of ecologically significant areas for further field investigation. Accompanying the geospatial map, two y visualizations are displayed on the right. A line chart see Fig. 1c enables the user to compare the temporal changes for region, fjord, or hexagon area of the actual aggregated data (**T1**). The user can select and compare multiple areas to further analyze differences in light availability and compare the differences between species, in this case, the lines are getting further colors assigned to allow identification while avoiding confusion with the blue-red color scale.

T3: Extract Filtered Subsets: Facilitating the extraction of filtered data for offline analysis was identified as a high priority by domain experts. To address this need, the tool enables users to download structured *CSV* files reflecting their selected regions of interest, and species-specific thresholds. This functionality allows researchers to focus on particular segments of interest and integrate the data into their own workflows.

T4: Supporting Intuitive, User-Centered Interactions: To support various exploration tasks of the data, users can apply spatial, temporal, and species-based filters to focus on specific segments of the data. The heatmap see Fig. 1b and Fig. 3 presents an intuitive overview of the results from the regression analysis and can be used with click interactions to filter the other visualizations in the temporal dimension or zoom in on a selected region. The heatmap utilizes the same color scheme as the adjacent map, offering a consistent visual reference [17], whereby entirely white cells stand for non-significant regressions. This provides the users with an intuitive overview of the seasonal changes for each region or fjord and they can navigate to a certain month or region while maintaining a comprehensive overview. A toggle button is provided to enable seamless switching between the two available datasets mentioned above. This functionality ensures that users can compare and contrast the datasets as needed, while avoiding visual clutter or overlap when both datasets are presented concurrently.

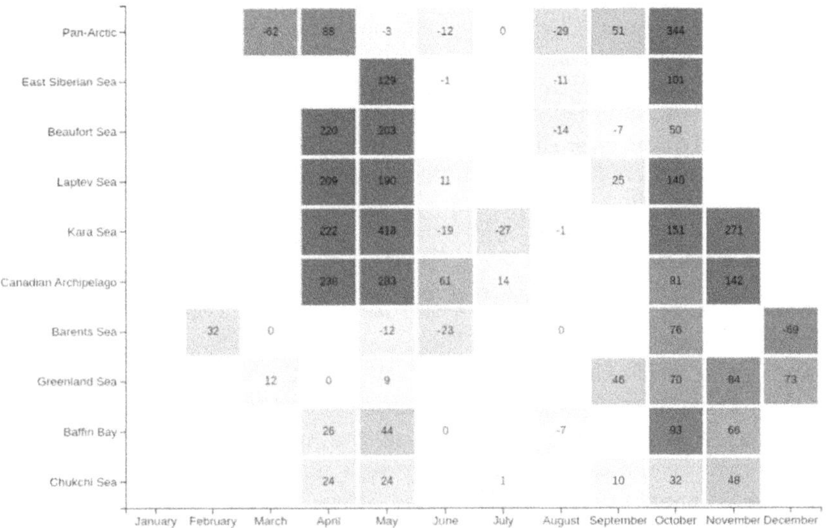

Fig. 3. Heatmap showing the monthly percentage change in turbidity in the water column (light attenuation coefficient (KdPAR)) for major Arctic regions. Each cell represents the percentage change for a given region and month, with red indicating an increase and blue indicating a decrease in water turbidity over the time series from 2003 to 2020. (Color figure online)

6   Discussion

To develop an effective interactive visualization tool for exploring the changing light environment in the Arctic Ocean, we engaged with domain experts throughout an iterative design process using the Nested Model [16]. By collaborating closely with marine biologists and oceanographers, we were able to ensure that the tool addressed both the practical challenges of handling large-scale remote sensing datasets and the specific analytical needs of Arctic researchers. In the following, we present qualitative insights from our user evaluation:

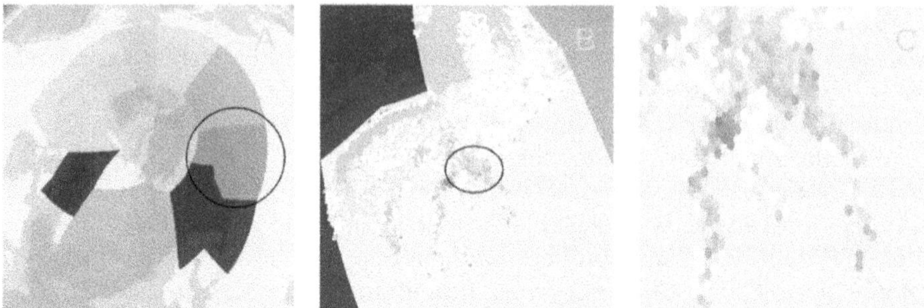

Fig. 4. Illustrating a typical analysis workflow with the tool. The user begins by exploring broad temporal trends in light availability across the Arctic using the overview map, heatmap as seen in Fig. 1. They identify a region and month showing significant change (**A**), then zoom into that area to examine finer details using the hexagonal grid (**B**). In this example, a drop in light levels near the outer bay may suggest increased water turbidity, possibly from river runoff, which could affect seafloor ecosystems (**C**). These insights help researchers form new hypotheses and guide future field studies.

6.1   User Evaluation

To evaluate the current iteration of the tool, we have conducted a small-scale qualitative evaluation with one of the co-authors and five external researchers from the Arctic marine science field. Given that the tool is still under development, the setting of the evaluation was informal and the session was kept simple. After a short walkthrough of the interface and main features, participants were invited to explore the tool freely. There were no predefined tasks or protocols; instead, participants clicked around, tried filters and views, and asked questions as they went. We observed their interactions, answered questions on the fly, and noted down comments and feedback for further implementations. The key points of feedback were as follows:

Intuitive User Experience: The domain experts found the tool intuitive to use, with clear navigation, consistent visual design, and responsive interactions. They were able to easily explore different spatial and temporal scales, apply filters, and interpret the visual encoding without requiring extensive instructions. The familiar map-based interface and coordinated linked views supported natural exploration, allowing users to efficiently focus on regions or months of interest and derive insights with minimal cognitive effort.

Species-Specific Light Requirements: Most domain experts found this feature to be highly insightful, as it helped them identify areas where light availability may limit or expand the distribution of certain benthic primary producers. However, some experts also emphasized that benthic primary producers are influenced by multiple environmental factors beyond light availability at the seafloor. Key factors such as nutrient supply, water depth, and substrate type also play a critical role in determining habitat suitability. Incorporating additional environmental parameters into the analysis could provide a more comprehensive understanding of the shifting habitats of benthic primary producers under the rapidly changing Arctic conditions.

Shape Selection and Aggregation: Some of the domain experts were missing the feature of selecting an area of hexagons (e.g. lasso selection) to get an aggregated view of the temporal changes in a specific area. This could furthermore help them in the process of filtering down areas of interest for extracting subsets of data.

6.2 Limitations and Future Work

While the tool successfully addresses key domain-specific tasks, we acknowledge the main limitations of our approach to data abstraction and user evaluation.

Data Abstraction: The use of pre-computed data in the visualization limits user flexibility in customizing temporal ranges, adjusting species-specific minimum light requirement thresholds, or modifying the size and shape of the hexagons used for spatial binning. These fixed parameters may constrain more exploratory or hypothesis-driven questions that require dynamic reconfiguration of the used data. Future work will focus on developing more flexible data workflows to support dynamically scalable hexagonal binning, enabling smoother transitions from broad overviews to fine-grained, detailed analysis.

User Evaluation: The present evaluation was intentionally small-scale and exploratory, providing early feedback but offering only limited generalizability as a result of the limited number of participants (n=6) and the absence of a structured evaluation protocol. We plan to expand the current evaluation by including more external experts from Arctic marine science and related fields, using a more formal setup with a structured evaluation protocol. Further quantitative user studies with a broader public audience could help assess the tool's usability, task performance, and overall effectiveness. Additionally, we aim to develop a visualization-based storytelling approach to communicate these complex processes more effectively to non-expert users through interactive narratives, thereby raising awareness of the rapidly changing Arctic Ocean.

7 Conclusion

In this work, we presented an interactive visualization tool designed to support Arctic marine scientists in exploring large-scale spatiotemporal changes in benthic light availability in the changing Arctic Ocean. The tool integrates two large-scale remote sensing datasets focused on light availability, each offering complementary spatial and temporal resolutions: one providing pan-Arctic coverage, and the other offering high-resolution insights into seven Arctic fjords. Developed through an iterative design process with domain experts, the tool addresses key research tasks, including spatial and temporal exploration and the assessment of potential habitat changes for benthic primary producers based on species-specific minimum light requirements. Guided by linked visualizations such as a geospatial map, heatmap, and line chart, users can investigate seasonal patterns, identify regions of interest, and compare areas with increasing or decreasing light availability over the time series. Our evaluation with domain experts demonstrated that the tool provides intuitive navigation and effective visual encoding allowing users to generate insights into changing habitat conditions. Further development is required to enhance the mapping of potential habitats for benthic primary producers by incorporating additional data on substrate type and nutrient availability. This would enable a more comprehensive understanding of the benthic primary production dynamics in a complex and fragile Arctic ecosystem.

Acknowledgments. This research was supported by the Independent Research Fund Denmark (♯2064-00021B).

References

1. Andrienko, G., et al.: Big data visualization and analytics: future research challenges and emerging applications (2021)
2. Arctic-Council: arctic climate change update 2021: key trends and impacts. summary for policy-makers. Arctic Monitoring and Assessment Programme (AMAP) (2021). https://www.amap.no/documents/download/6759/inline, tromsø, Norway. 16 pp
3. Ardyna, M., Arrigo, K.: Phytoplankton dynamics in a changing Arctic Ocean. Nature Clim. Change **10** (2020). https://doi.org/10.1038/s41558-020-0905-y
4. Arrigo, K.R., van Dijken, G., Pabi, S.: Impact of a shrinking Arctic ice cover on marine primary production. Geophys. Res. Lett. **35**(19) (2008). https://doi.org/10.1029/2008GL035028, https://agupubs.onlinelibrary.wiley.com/doi/abs/10.1029/2008GL035028
5. Attard, K., et al.: Seafloor primary production in a changing Arctic Ocean. PNAS **121**(11), e2303366121 (2024). https://doi.org/10.1073/pnas.2303366121
6. Birch, C.P., Oom, S.P., Beecham, J.A.: Rectangular and hexagonal grids used for observation, experiment and simulation in ecology. Ecol. Model. **206**(3), 347–359 (2007). https://doi.org/10.1016/j.ecolmodel.2007.03.041, https://www.sciencedirect.com/science/article/pii/S0304380007001949
7. Copernicus marine service: copernicus marine service data viewer. https://data.marine.copernicus.eu/viewer/expert, Accessed 24 Apr 2025
8. European space agency (ESA), copernicus: sentinel-3 mission. https://sentinels.copernicus.eu/web/sentinel/copernicus/sentinel-3, Accessed 24 Apr 2025
9. European union, copernicus: copernicus: europe's eyes on earth. https://www.copernicus.eu/en, Accessed 24 Apr 2025
10. Gattuso, J.P., Gentili, B., Antoine, D., Doxaran, D.: Global distribution of photosynthetically available radiation on the seafloor (2020). https://doi.org/10.5194/essd-12-1697-2020
11. Gattuso, J.P., B, G., Duarte, C., Kleypas, J., Middelburg, J., Antoine, D.: Light availability in the coastal ocean: impact on the distribution of benthic photosynthetic organisms and their contribution to primary production. Biogeosciences **3** (2006).https://doi.org/10.5194/bg-3-489-2006

12. Godfrey, P., Gryz, J., Lasek, P.: Interactive visualization of large data sets. IEEE Trans. Knowl. Data Eng. **28**(8), 2142–2157 (2016). https://doi.org/10.1109/TKDE.2016.2557324
13. Gorelick, N., et al.: Google earth engine: planetary-scale geospatial analysis for everyone. Remote Sens. Environ. (2017). https://doi.org/10.1016/j.rse.2017.06.031
14. Intergovernmental panel on climate change: climate change 2023: synthesis report. Contribution of Working Groups I, II and III to the Sixth Assessment Report of the Intergovernmental Panel on Climate Change (2023). https://www.ipcc.ch/report/ar6/syr/, core Writing Team
15. Jain, T., et al.: pyParaOcean: a system for visual analysis of ocean data (2023). https://doi.org/10.2312/ENVIRVIS.20231100, https://diglib.eg.org/handle/10.2312/envirvis20231100
16. Munzner, T.: A nested model for visualization design and validation. IEEE Trans. Visual Comput. Graphics **15**(6), 921–928 (2009). https://doi.org/10.1109/TVCG.2009.111
17. Munzner, T.: Visualization analysis and design. CRC Press, Boca Raton, FL (2014)
18. NASA EOSDIS worldview: NASA worldview. https://worldview.earthdata.nasa.gov/, Accessed 24 Apr 2025
19. NASA goddard space flight center, ocean ecology laboratory, ocean biology processing group: MODIS/Aqua level-2 ocean color data. https://oceancolor.gsfc.nasa.gov/data/10.5067/AQUA/MODIS/L2/OC/2022 (2022), Accessed 24 Apr 2025
20. Schlegel, R.W., et al.: Underwater light environment in arctic fjords. Earth Syst. Sci. Data **16**(6), 2773–2788 (2024). https://doi.org/10.5194/essd-16-2773-2024, https://essd.copernicus.org/articles/16/2773/2024/
21. Shneiderman, B.: The eyes have it: a task by data type taxonomy for information visualizations. In: Proceedings 1996 IEEE Symposium on Visual Languages, pp. 336–343 (1996). https://doi.org/10.1109/VL.1996.545307
22. Singh, R.K., et al.: Satellite-derived photosynthetically available radiation at the coastal arctic seafloor (2022). https://doi.org/10.3390/rs14205180, https://www.mdpi.com/2072-4292/14/20/5180
23. Teanby, N.: An icosahedron-based method for even binning of globally distributed remote sensing data (2006). https://doi.org/10.1016/j.cageo.2006.01.007
24. Uber technologies, Inc.: H3: A hexagonal hierarchical spatial index (2024). https://h3geo.org/, Accessed 22 Apr 2024
25. U.S. National Ice Center, national snow and ice data center: multisensor analyzed sea ice extent - northern hemisphere (MASIE-NH), version 1 (2010). https://doi.org/10.7265/N5GT5K3K, https://nsidc.org/data/G02186/versions/1
26. Wang, R., Ben, J., Zhou, J., Zheng, M.: Indexing mixed aperture icosahedral hexagonal discrete global grid systems. ISPRS Int. J. Geo-Inf. **9**(3) (2020). https://doi.org/10.3390/ijgi9030171, https://www.mdpi.com/2220-9964/9/3/171
27. Yu, J., Sarwat, M.: GeoSparkViz: a cluster computing system for visualizing massive-scale geospatial data. VLDB J. **30**(2), 237–258 (2021). https://doi.org/10.1007/s00778-020-00645-2

A Narrative Visualization Tool for Personalized Exploration of Long-Distance Hiking Trails

Anna Krogshave Dahlgren, Karen Sophie Skov Drewsen,
Julie Algren Rosenlund, Esben Bay Sørensen[✉], Jakob Kusnick,
and Stefan Jänicke

Department of Mathematics and Computer Science, University of Southern Denmark,
Campusvej 55, 5230 Odense, Denmark
`essoe@imada.sdu.dk`

Abstract. We introduce a visualization-based storytelling system designed to support the exploration and planning of long-distance hikes, exemplified through the Pacific Crest Trail. Designed to aid hikers and enthusiasts in understanding the trail's dynamics, our tool integrates trail-segment-based narratives with interactive geospatial maps, elevation profiles, and icon-based trail facilities and wildlife information. The system adapts to user-defined travel speed and rest patterns, generating customized narrative segments enriched with multimedia and trail-specific data, including weather, water sources, wildlife, campsites, and resupply points. To assess the tool's effectiveness and relevance, we conducted a preliminary evaluation with members of the hiking community, which highlighted the system's usability and potential to enhance trail familiarization. The resulting feedback informed iterative design improvements of how data storytelling can enrich both the practical and experiential dimensions of trail presentations, fostering more informed, engaging hiking experiences.

Keywords: User-Centered Design · Geospatial Storytelling · Trail Planning

1 Introduction

During the COVID-19 pandemic, we noticed changes in our daily lives, and researchers investigated the possible long-term changes in life that the pandemic could cause [27]. Reminding us of the lockdown periods we were not used to, it is not surprising that the outdoor leisure industry has already seen significant growth during the pandemic [21]. However, the trend continues unabated, and this article looks at the increasing popularity of one such activity: hiking [55].

© The Author(s), under exclusive license to Springer Nature Switzerland AG 2026
J. F. Krems et al. (Eds.): CHIRA 2025, CCIS 2836, pp. 330–347, 2026.
https://doi.org/10.1007/978-3-032-16454-4_19

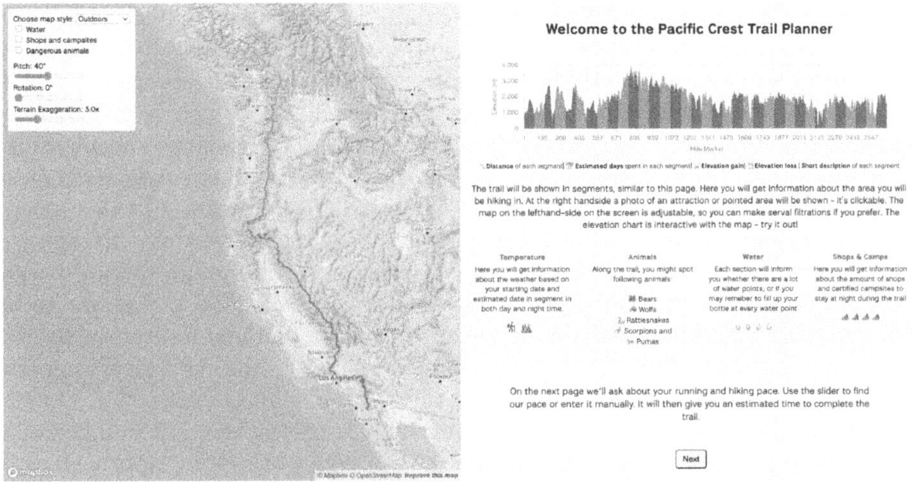

Fig. 1. Pacific Crest Trail: Landing page with its two column layout of geo-spatial map visualization (left) and multimedia narrative contents (right).

While short-distance hikes generally require limited preparation, long-distance hikes require precise equipment, possible training, and strategic planning. In the United States, the most popular trails for long-distance hiking are the Appalachian Trail, the Pacific Crest Trail, and the Continental Divide Trail, all of which are several thousand kilometers long. Normally, such a trail is covered in stages over time (section hiking). However, a further form of extreme hiking, known as thru-hiking, in which such a trail is hiked continuously within a single season, has gained popularity in the last decade [25]. Thru-hiking is physically demanding and logistically complex, but offers a profound experience of nature and the hiking community.

Despite the fact that reduced exposure to technology is one of the main motivations for hiking, technology has become an indispensable support for hikers to orient themselves, find trails, monitor changing weather conditions, etc. Most commonly used are wearables (e.g. GPS watches), which can be worn by the hiker on their wrist along the trail and guide them along the route with visual details on demand such as altitude, kilometers to the next waypoint or accessing real-time monitoring of physiological data (e.g. pulse and energy expenditure) [51]. In addition, there is a vast number of digital guides for the trails offered through specific websites and tailored smartphone apps (a comprehensive overview can be found in Sect. 2). However, no tool on the market can adapt to different walking speeds and at the same time provide structured information about the resulting individual route sections.

This paper aims to close this gap by investigating the utility of visualization-based storytelling for segmenting hiking trails and the corresponding information adaptively. The visualization community has for a long time primarily focused on developing sophisticated techniques for visual exploration [67]. However, the insights that can be gained from complex data through visual exploration must often be presented intuitively so that they are easily accessible to analysts or casual users who need not only factual but also understandable information [43]. In particular, news magazines showed us that visualizations can be neatly integrated and combined into exciting news stories [66]. Consequently, visualization-based storytelling can be seen as either a narration through a visualization or as including visualizations into a (written) narrative. We make use of this concept for guiding hikers across a long-distance trail. The overarching aim is to segment descriptive information relevant to hikers according to individual hiking paces. Training large language models to generate stories on demand [73] seems to be a clever solution to address this problem, but, next to their limitation to create compelling narratives [19], they also cannot satisfy the necessity to create trustworthy and accurate stories due to the risk of hallucinations [35]. On the other hand, creating curated information about trail sections is a cumbersome and not generalizable task. Our visualization-based storytelling approach only requires a set of rules to transform a comprehensive trail data collection into a narration capable of supporting hikers in planning their trip. We chose the Pacific Crest Trail as our guiding example to describe our concept. In summary, the contributions of this paper are:

- **Generic Trail Storytelling Concept:** We propose a novel method to dynamically segment data on a hiking trail into sections based on user preferences. For each section, visualizations are generated, and descriptive, textual, and visual information about a section is generated.
- **Detailed Pacific Crest Trail Scenario:** Our dataset includes a huge diversity of information about the Pacific Crest Trail–visualized in various story segments–including elevation, wildlife, weather, water sources, shops, and campsites.
- **Design Study for Visualization-Based Storytelling:** We describe the development of our solution–inspiring for relatable projects–based on Munzner's Nested model for visualization design [52], focusing on domain requirements, data, and task abstraction as well as visual encoding.

We conducted a preliminary user evaluation within the hiking community that confirmed the novelty and potential of our approach. Our solution is tailored to support hikes on the PCT, providing hikers with section-by-section information. Not only can this scenario be extended to other information, but our pipeline can also be adapted to other trail or route-based datasets with various supplementary information.

2   Related Work

Platforms like Komoot [7], AllTrails [1], FarOut [5], and The Trek [12] are widely used for local and long-distance hike planning. They offer trail maps, mile markers, elevation profiles, and practical info such as accommodations or resupply points. Many include social features like comments and tips [54], but they lack customization for user pace or ecological interests.

Trail-specific planners, such as those for the Pacific Crest Trail (PCT) [32], Camino de Santiago [4,59], or Continental Divide Trail [2], provide static maps and preparation guides. Craig's PCT Planner generates daily segments based on user inputs like pace and start date, offers height profiles and resupply points [3]. However, these tools lack interactivity and dynamic visualizations.

Interactive and interlinked visualizations are mostly explored in research. Some systems use 2D maps with contours and overlays to aid risk assessment [60,63,69], while others apply 3D or AR displays for more intuitive terrain understanding [29,48,65,71]. Both approaches have value depending on context, which is why our system supports both [63]. This is why we tried to find a trade-off by including both possibilities 2D and 3D.

Online geospatial tools also help with route planning and infrastructure insights [58], layering additional data such as water sources [54] or weather overlays [71]. Still, most focus on topography and logistics. Some also indicate dangers [69], POIs [29], or use slope-based coloring [13]. For novice hikers, clear visual cues on trail difficulty and hazards are especially important [22,70].

Digital storytelling is gaining traction in visualizations for its ability to simplify complex ideas, build engagement, and show change over time [28,43,49]. These developments throughout time can be depicted in data stories by users focused on timelines [41,42], whereas the geospatial trajectories are depicted on maps [18,40,64], often enhanced by multimedia and further statistical charts and visualizations [34,44,53]. There, the user is often taken on a narrative journey throughout time and space [23,45], building up tension, which gets released towards the end, and conveying a message [26]. Interactive scalability allows for both detailed and abstract exploration [17,39], though creating compelling stories still requires effort and skill [46], which needs to be addressed by new approaches in the future [47].

In hiking, storytelling is often personal and experiential [11,62]. Examples include GPS-triggered media guides [15], virtual rangers [30], and simulated hikes tied to real-world activity tracking [14]. Ecological storytelling remains rare, with only a few attempts to combine scientific, historical, and biodiversity data in accessible formats [16].

While storytelling aids comprehension and retention [50,66,68], studies show that classic formats like tables may communicate trail warnings more effectively than narrative formats [72]. Accordingly, we use easy-to-compare cards and tables for key data like weather, water, and facilities [20,36].

The Pacific Crest Trail Planner (ArcGIS-based) includes layered geospatial data like wildfires and ranger stations, but it lacks guided exploration or interactivity beyond a manual [31]. Ecological data, particularly on wildlife, is rarely integrated beyond static range maps [37].

Building on this work, our approach presents long-distance hikes—using the PCT as a case study—through interactive, personalized data stories. The narrative unfolds chronologically along the trail, with detours and landmarks available on demand. Each segment combines 2D/3D route views, elevation profiles, and multimedia annotations. Glyph-based summaries highlight essential comparisons (e.g., weather, water, wildlife, facilities), all dynamically adjusted to user preferences like pace and start date. The goal is to make planning more intuitive, informative, and personal, but also to attract more people to trails.

3   Domain Requirements and Data

The Pacific Crest Trail is attracting up to ca. 7000 thru-hikers each year [10] and the hiking stories are usually very personal also because they are from single persons or smaller groups so there have been many creative ways to capture and report on the trail experiences (e.g., [56]). In comparison, our visualization project aims to improve the experience of getting to know a trail for hikers and enthusiasts through a combination of interactive storytelling, practical tools, and visual design. To guide this design process, we refer to Tamara Munzner's nested model [52], a framework for visualization development that emphasizes structured decision-making across four levels (*Domain Characterization, Data & Task Abstraction, Visual Encoding & Interaction Design, Algorithm Implementation*). This model helps break down complex design challenges–from understanding user needs to choosing visual encodings–ensuring that each step supports the next.

3.1   Design Requirements and User Tasks

To support hikers and outdoor enthusiasts, it's essential to understand the specific information they need before and during a trip. Preparing for a trail involves more than just navigation—it includes:

- knowing the trail conditions (such as elevation and slope),
- planning for gear, food, and water (including access to shops and refill stations),
- identifying accommodation options like hostels, campsites, or shelters, and
- staying aware of weather conditions.

To get insights into how long a thru-hike would take, users also need to estimate their speed and plan trail segments accordingly, including certain days to rest and restock in between. Furthermore, recommendations for detours and highlights—such as scenic viewpoints or hidden landmarks—can also enrich the hiking experience and encourage exploration. Additionally, hikers need to be informed about potential risks along the way, including the presence of dangerous animals. These diverse needs shape the foundation of our visualization, helping us design a tool that addresses real concerns and supports practical decision-making for and on the trail.

Following **User Tasks** can be derived from this:

- **T1:** Visual geo-spatial exploration of the PCT route and its segments, infrastructure, highlights, and wildlife along the trail.

- **T2:** Personalization of the route segments and storytelling depending on hikers' experience, training, as well as start and recovery days.
- **T3:** Trail segment overview with elevation, narration, and facilities so that similarities and differences are perceivable through the story's progression.
- **T4:** Support intuitive and user-centered interaction, combining the different elements in a meaningful manner.

To offer a tool to support these user tasks, we combined the needed different data sources and designed visual encodings as well as a consistent interaction design to make them approachable for everyone.

3.2 Data

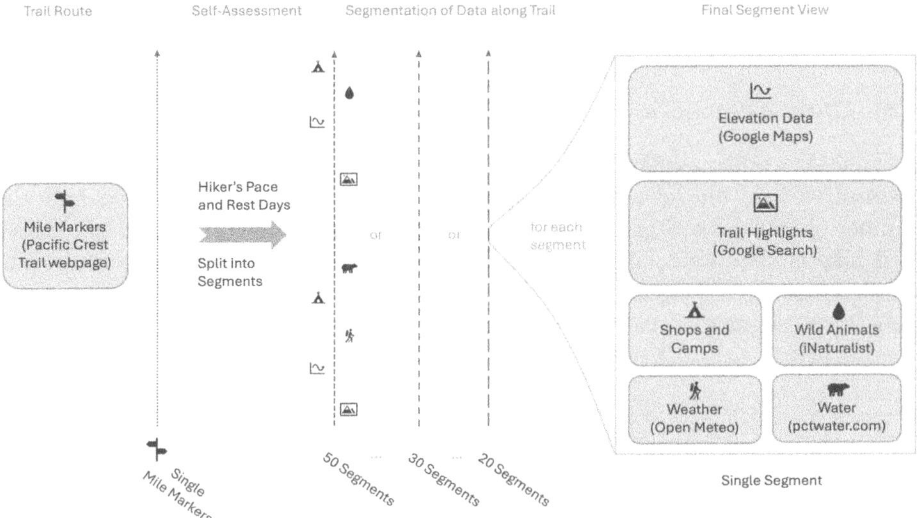

Fig. 2. Overview of the data and data resources used for the visualization tool, along with their processing. The users can personalize the segmentation (20 to 50 segments) of the whole trail according to their hiking pace. Along with the mile markers as an underlying coordinate system, various data sets contribute to the contextualization and narration of each of the segments.

The data used for our tool consists of different sources, which we merged into one GeoJSON file for ease of use and later visualization. We accessed the mile markers of the whole trail from the official PCT webpage [57]. To further add perception of the changing elevation through the trail, we used elevation data from Google Maps [33].

We further enriched the dataset with more location-specific information, useful for hikers: Water availability was informed by the community-driven and updated website according to the natural water availability in the area [61]. Furthermore, locations of shops were found on a PCT-related website called *Halfmile's PCT Maps*, where the shops are described in single PDF-files for each of the States [24]. To inform hikers about possible dangers from wild animals, we incorporated observational data from iNaturalist [38], filtering for records collected within a 10-meter radius of PCT mile markers. Only observations from the past two years with a minimum of 20 confirmed sightings per species were included. We further included weather data provided by an API from Open Meteo using historic data from 2023 [9]. Ultimately, we also added certain highlights along the route from various sources to our dataset to increase the immersive experience. The narrative description is based on the landmarks visible on the map by Mapbox [8] for each segment. The texts describing the segments and their landmarks are based on manual gathered information from Wikipedia and the PCT's official website. The images of landmarks are based for this test-phase based on Google searches. A schematic overview of the data and its processing can be seen in Fig. 2.

3.3 Data Abstraction

To facilitate personalization in the tool (**T2**), users will be prompted to place themselves into one of seven groups according to their hiking speed and the number of rest days. Starting the calculation from a chosen start date, the whole trail hike is then calculated. In this process, we split the full trail's route into smaller segments of equal distance according to their speed/skill group, ranging from 20–50 segments in steps of 5 segments. This approach tries to resemble the

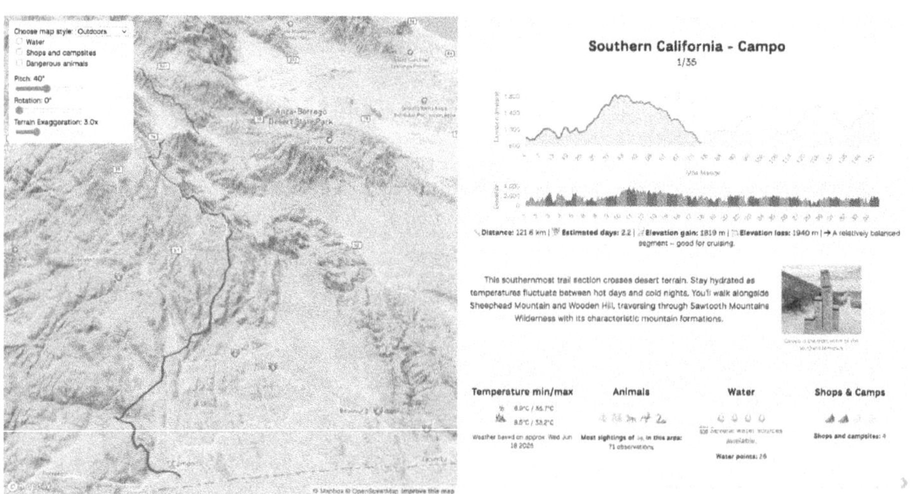

Fig. 3. Where the journey begins: The first segment of the Pacific Crest Trail starting from the Mexican border.

idea that slower hikers might need more and smaller segments to thru-hike than faster hikers.

The data foundation of our tool is built to handle similar trails or routes provided in a GeoJSON format, which makes it easily adjustable for utilizing it for other scenarios, such as Route 66 or the Appalachian Trail.

4   Visual Encoding

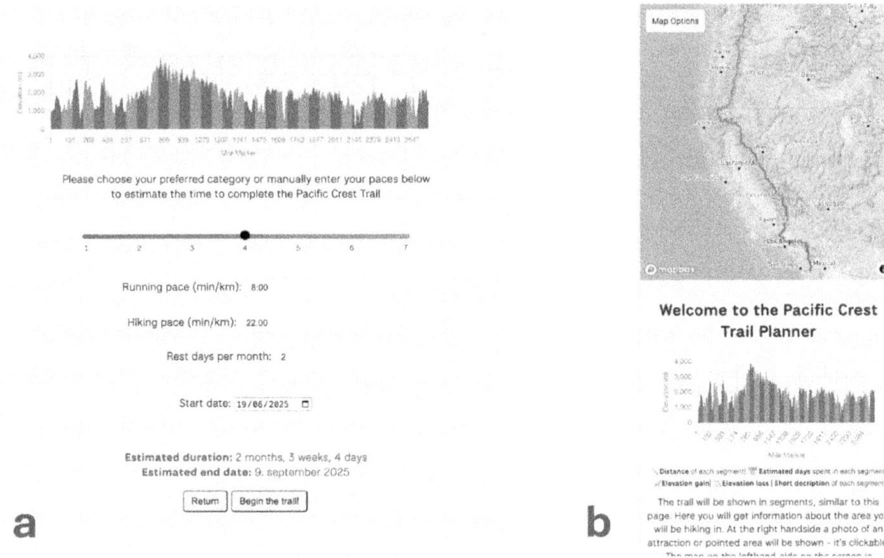

Fig. 4. Self-Assessment of hikers' experience level based on their speed (**a**) and the rearrangement of the elements in the responsive mobile version (**b**).

Landing Page: The visual interface of our tool is centered around a consistent two-column layout, which is already used at the tool's landing page with an overview trail map on the left and an introductory text on the right see Fig. 1. The introduction text presents the tool, its various elements, and options to the user. This allows the user to gain a certain understanding of the layout, functionalities, geo-spatial map, the overview of the elevation visualization, and glyph icons, which all will be used throughout the journey.

Self Assessment: The next button on the landing page directs the user to further choose a hiking pace group ranging from 1–7. This correlates with their speed of travel and the number of rest days along the 4,265 km route see Fig. 4, which also can be set manually via text input fields. As a result, users are informed about the estimated duration and date of completing the trail. After this self-assessment and introduction, the narrative of the trail can now begin...

Geo-Spatial Map: When entering the narrative initially, the map seamlessly zooms into the first segment of the trail. To ensure consistency for the user, the map is always located on the left side of the screen and is visible in all scenarios, positioning the user onto the trail. There, the trail is shown as a brown line on a by default green-shaded outdoor hiking map tileset [8], offering clear visibility of e.g. rivers, lakes, streams, but also the slope of hills and mountains through contour lines. To increase the immersion and perception of the changing elevation even more, we decided to exaggerate the terrain and angle the camera slightly by using Mapbox's functionalities, so that the two-dimensional map gets a third dimension. Along the trail, image annotations of scenic viewpoints and highlights invite to explore them, for example, Mount Jefferson as seen in Fig. 5. Additional icon-based glyphs representing water sources, campsites, shops, and wildlife along the route are accessible via an interactive control panel positioned in the top-left corner, as shown in Fig. 5.

Segment Stories: On the right of the screen, the segment story column is divided into four consistent rows with information about each segment of the trail in visualizations or multimedia.

Trail Elevation: The elevation chart presents a line chart of the elevation in the current segment on the route see Fig. 5a. The previous and upcoming segments are grayed out on each side for an intuitive comparison of the differences in elevation. The past, current, and future elevation challenges are thus clearly visible to the user to always contextualize the actual segment.

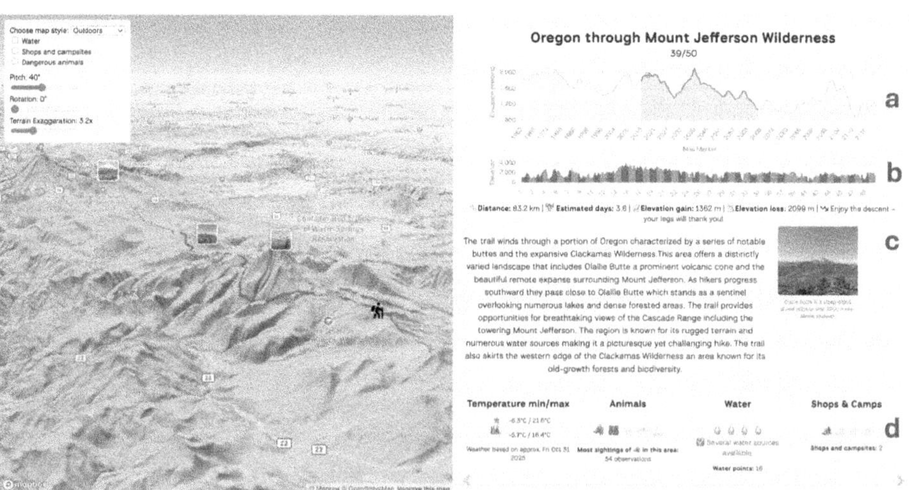

Fig. 5. The exaggeration of the terrain allows for conveying a three-dimensional feeling of the elevation along the trail and the placement of highlight photographs on top of the corresponding peaks. In the right column, the segment is narrated with Trail Elevation (**a**), Segment Overview (**b**), Narrative Text (**c**), and Icon Cards (**d**).

Segment Overview: To provide this context on a bigger scale, the segment overview gives an intuitive overview of what segment the users are currently in, and how far in the journey they are see Fig. 5b. The current segment is highlighted in green, and the chart presents a view of the entire elevation profile for the PCT and the planned segmentation. Just below, a combination of icons and text displays informs about basic summarizing values of the segment, such as the distance, duration, and elevation gain/loss.

Narrative Text: The narrative displays a brief overview of upcoming route conditions and the environment surrounding the trail for each segment in text form see Fig. 5c. The descriptions vary from highlighting the surrounding nature to small recommendations about hydration, e.g., Fig. 3. In addition to the other data-based information (e.g., elevation chart, trail on the map) and in combination with a selected highlight photograph, these story segments are supposed to convey a feeling of the current segment and outline what awaits the hikers through an overarching narrative.

Icon Cards: Finally, the row of icons at the bottom, grouped into four columns, provides a visual and textual overview of further interesting information for hikers, summarizing the segment's temperature, animal sightings, water sources, shops, and campsites within each segment see Fig. 5d. This glyph approach is meant to provide easy-to-read visual cues about potential risks, but also facilities for the particular segment.

Through the whole trail narrative, this layout stays the same while changing out its contents to allow consistent change and comparison of the current segment to the surrounding ones and to visualize the progression along the trail, analogous to the fly-to animation in the map.

5 Interaction Design

The two-column layout is interconnected through shared interactions between Geo-spatial Map, Elevation Chart, and Segment Overview. The trail location is shared between them via mouse-hover interactions, highlighting the corresponding position in each visualization depicted through circles in the charts and a hiker's silhouette icon on the map trail. This enhances spatial awareness and reinforces the interconnection of the various trail views.

Even though the overall visualization and narration setup is predestined for a *scrollytelling* approach where the main interaction is continuous scrolling, we decided against it in favor of the segmented methodology of the presented result with next and previous buttons for navigation. The scrolling through the segments is still possible, but not continuously mapped to further animation in visualizations. Since the given linearity of the PCT from south to north (or the opposite direction) calls for a linear narrative, our storytelling sticks to this chronological and linear story path, until now, only from south to north. Nevertheless, this segmentation also allows for the planning of section-hikes (in comparison to thru-hiking) and invites them, as well as showing the different segments, for example, in the elevation profile. The non-linear branching of the story flow could still be introduced through different focuses on the whole experience see Sect. 8.

6   Evaluation

We conducted a preliminary user study to assess the usability of the tool and gain valuable feedback for further development. Therefore we formalized a questionnaire (Google Forms) and were allowed to post it and the tool in the Nordic PCT group on Facebook. Participation was voluntary, and responses were anonymized except for optional email addresses submitted for a prize draw. The questionnaire was informal and we did not follow a specific protocol and no identifiable personal data was analyzed.

The questionnaire consisted of basic information such as age and gender, further details related to their hiking experience level and lastly a section for feedback on our tool. The qualitative feedback covered favorite features, ideas for improvement, or other tools they use, usually for their trail planning and hiking. The participants were asked to use at least 5 min to explore the tool before filling out the feedback part. The feedback, measured in a 7-level Likert scale (1-strongly-disagree to 7-strongly agree), asked for, among others, intuitiveness, learning effects, and clearness of the whole narrative experience but also the visualizations themselves. Since the experience with the narrated trail is linear and uni-directional the participants weren't tasked to fulfill concrete goals but to make themselves familiar with the trail, visualizations and narration.

Only seven participants answered with feedback throughout every question until now, which we will summarize in a short discussion in the following.

The survey participants were from various professional backgrounds, balanced in regards to gender (4 women, 3 men), and they were mainly between ages 20–39, and one above 59 see Fig. 6a. Since we posted the questionnaire

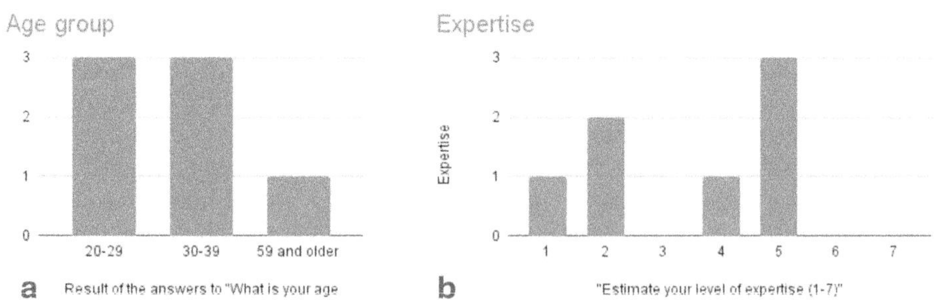

Fig. 6. Age group and self-assessment of hikers' experience level: (**a**) The answers to the question: "What is your age group?" – (**b**) The answers to the question "Estimate your level of expertise (1–7) in practices such as hiking, trail running, and trail or thru-hiking? (Never hiked - Beginner - Novice - Intermediate - Advanced - Expert - Professional)".

in a Facebook group specific for the PCT, we expected the participants to be interested in hiking, trail-running, or thru-hiking, or even to be familiar with the PCT already on an advanced level, which was confirmed by the numbers in Fig. 6b.

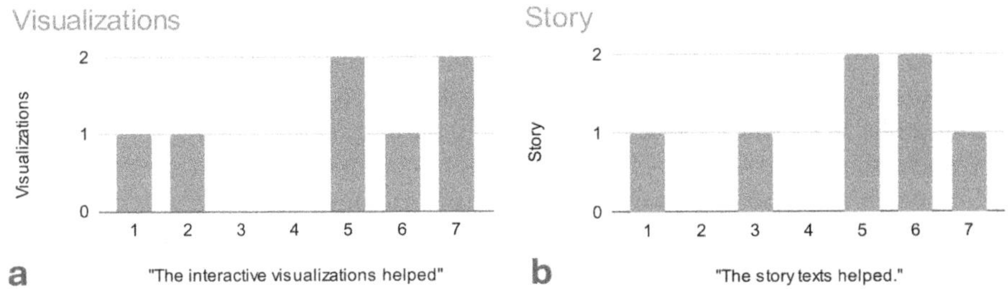

Fig. 7. Results of the quality of visualizations and the story texts. (**a**) "The interactive visualizations helped to understand, explore, and present the trail?" - (**b**) "The story texts helped to understand, explore, and present the trail?"

The answers of the 7 participants produced comparable data throughout the feedback questions. Most importantly, the visualizations as components themselves were perceived as intuitive and helped to convey data-driven insights of the trail throughout the experience contextualized by the textual narration (4 votes with ≥ 5, see Fig. 7a). The narrative and its implementation scored similarly see Fig. 7b.

Furthermore, the feedback gave insights into the concrete user experiences with the tool, which is also summarized in Table 1. We got the additional feedback from one participant that the story was not clear enough, but also that there should be room left for adventurous exploration of the trail and its surroundings. This might be due to our approach of using a loose narrative, offering only summarizing outlooks for the multi-day segments and avoiding strict storytelling, while still allowing space for virtual exploration with this desire in mind.

Table 1. The limitations and strengths of our PCT storytelling visualization tool.

Qualitative Feedback

— Mobile version is missing

— The narrative is not clear enough

+ Clear trail visualizations with trail highlights

+ Splitting the trail into smaller segments

+ Camps and facilities for the logistics on the trail

+ Animal icons adding entertainment and education

The most striking outlier in our data represents one participant who wished for a mobile version of the tool and was additionally completely satisfied with FarOut [5]. The responsive version of the tool was not in place at this point, and the tool was not interactive on a smaller screen. This resulted in one-point ratings (lowest category) in all of the questions. Rather meant as an engagement and planning tool for before the actual hike, we focused on the desktop browser compatibility, knowing that potentially more users would use a mobile device on the trail. Even though, based on the feedback, we adapted the website layout to be responsive, letting the two columns stack on top of each other, so that the elements like map and narration stay usable on mobile devices as well see Fig. 4.

Concerning the learning, most of the testers mentioned that they were happy finding out about the camps and facilities in combination with the trail and elevation profile. Participants mentioned that the tool helped them to understand, in comparison to their own experience, surprisingly steep inclines or even just to validate data and information from other resources they found, and vice versa. One of the participants answered: *"Animals are cute. I think the trail could use a good flora and fauna app."* This is stressing the point that our tool is the first one combining animal data with the rather commonly used topographical and facility data with fauna, and in the future, maybe flora.

7 Limitations

In addition to the collected feedback by the users we will discuss further shortcomings and derived future potential in the following.

Segmentation with Equal Distance Segments: Currently, our tool divides the route into equal-distance segments based on the user's selected pace group. This design decision was made based on the assumption, that equal-distance segmentation can provide a useful baseline for planning, yet many hikers prefer to adjust their daily distances based on how they feel rather than following a strictly prescribed schedule. However, it does not account for drastic changes in elevation, which could either increase or decrease the number of days required to complete each segment. Incorporating elevation into the calculation could provide users with more accurate estimates of time spent per segment and yield a more realistic overall travel time.

User Study: Our preliminary user study presented valuable feedback, even though the number of participants was limited. With only a few individuals contributing, each response carries significant weight in the overall interpretation. Therefore, a larger and more diverse sample will be necessary to gain a more nuanced and balanced understanding of how visual storytelling functions across different user groups and levels of hiking experience. By sourcing participants solely from a hiking community, the evaluation may have been influenced by assumed knowledge, making certain aspects of the visual storytelling clear to experienced hikers but less accessible to novices. Consequently, the needs of beginners may currently be underrepresented. Lastly, the lack of an on-site evaluation decreases the tools usability in real life scenarios. The tool has so far only been tested on a desktop, meaning its usability, performance, and data presentation have not been validated in contexts with limited connectivity, small-screen devices, or the physical constraints of an ongoing hike.

8   Conclusion and Future Work

This paper presents a new approach to visualize long-distance hiking trails through interactive, visualization-based storytelling. By combining a structured multimedia narrative with interactive maps, elevation profiles, and icon-based information, our tool offers hikers a data-rich and engaging way to explore the segments of the PCT visually. We introduce a new data-driven perspective to interactively inform hikers about their personalized segmentation of the whole trail, and the conditions, facilities, as well as possible animal encounters within these segments, by incorporating various data sets within an overarching narrative. Our preliminary evaluation showed promising results, and the feedback will be crucial in the further development of the tool. The evaluation highlighted how our tool integrates trail facilities and points of interest, with some users finding the trail segmentation particularly useful. However, feedback also indicated that the narrative could be made more clear for the users.

We could envision a future emphasis on expanding the animal sightings to include additional species and descriptions of edible and non-edible flora along the trail through the consideration of occurrence sightings (e.g., GBIF - Global Biodiversity Information Facility [6]). This could add further layers and personalization options to our current segment narratives. If possible, we aim to explore a user-guided narrative shaped by personal interests and experiences along the long journey the PCT presents. This could open up possibilities for branches of the narrative, depending on the user's preferences, focusing on, for example, the most spectacular panoramas or the exploration of stunning biodiversity and wildlife. This could be guided by machine learning models trained or fine-tuned on the related literature surrounding the trail to enhance the narrative's flexibility. Further work is needed to implement a realistic segment division that accounts for altitude changes, thereby allowing for a realistic travel time for each segment. Extending this framework of rule-based and then segmented storytelling to include other iconic trails such as the Appalachian Trail, Camino de Santiago, or other journey-guided scenarios such as road trips by car or bicycle, would demonstrate the versatility of the approach and broaden its applicability to a wider range of outdoor experiences and planning contexts.

References

1. AllTrails: trail guides and maps for hiking, camping, and running — alltrails.com. https://www.alltrails.com
2. Continental divide trail: the complete thru-hiking guide. https://www.greenbelly.co/pages/continental-divide-trail-map
3. Craig's PCT planner. https://pctplanner.com/

4. Digital camino de santiago. https://digitalcaminodesantiago.com/
5. FarOut: GPS maps for long-distance hiking, biking and paddling. https://faroutguides.com/
6. GBIF. https://www.gbif.org/
7. Komoot | find, plan and share your adventures. https://www.komoot.com
8. Mapbox outdoors: map style for hiking, running and biking. https://www.mapbox.com/maps/outdoors
9. Open-Meteo – free open-source weather API. https://open-meteo.com/
10. PCT visitor use statistics. https://www.pcta.org/our-work/trail-and-land-management/pct-visitor-use-statistics/
11. Reading the trail: exploring the literature and natural history of the California Crest - ProQuest. https://www.proquest.com/openview/a0e16da0842a6ff1455b30e77f5f10e0/1?pq-origsite=gscholar&cbl=18750&diss=y
12. The trek - appalachian trail, pacific crest trail, and all things thru-hiking. https://thetrek.co/
13. All the caminos in 3d | solvitur ambulando (2021). https://solviturambulando.es/en/el-camino-de-santiago/all-the-caminos-in-3d/
14. Pacific crest trail virtual challenge | the conqueror (2025). https://www.theconqueror.events/pacific/
15. Ahlers, D., Boll, S., Wichmann, D.: Virtual signposts for location-based storytelling
16. Antoniou, V., et al.: Creating a story map using geographic information systems to explore geomorphology and history of methana peninsula. ISPRS Int. J. Geo Inf. **7**(12), 484 (2018)
17. Arnold, T., Tilton, L.: Distant viewing: computational exploration of digital images. MIT Press (2023)
18. Ashkenas, J., Tse, A., Watkins, D., Yourish, K.: A rogue state along two rivers, published. https://www.nytimes.com/interactive/2014/07/03/world/middleeast/syria-iraq-isis-rogue-state-along-two-rivers.html
19. Beguš, N.: Experimental narratives: a comparison of human crowdsourced storytelling and ai storytelling. Human. Soc. Sci. Commun. **11**(1), 1–22 (2024)
20. Benner, C.: A test of endurance: beating the weather challenges on the pacific crest trail. weatherwise **68**(6), 36–43 (2015). https://doi.org/10.1080/00431672.2015.1086616, https://doi.org/10.1080/00431672.2015.1086616, publisher: Routledge _eprint
21. Bruton, M.: Outdoor recreation industry sees significant growth with changes in consumer behavior sparked by COVID-19 (2023). https://www.forbes.com/sites/michellebruton/2023/02/28/outdoor-recreation-industry-sees-significant-growth-with-changes-in-consumer-behavior-sparked-by-covid-19/, Accessed 27 Jun 2025
22. Calbimonte, J.P., Martin, S., Calvaresi, D., Cotting, A.: A platform for difficulty assessment and recommendation of hiking trails. In: Wörndl, W., Koo, C., Stienmetz, J.L. (eds.) Information and Communication Technologies in Tourism 2021, pp. 109–122. Springer International Publishing, Cham (2021). https://doi.org/10.1007/978-3-030-65785-7_9
23. Campbell, J.: The hero's journey: joseph campbell on his life and work, vol. 7. New World Library (2003)
24. Cooper, L.: Halfmile's pacific crest trail notes (2023). https://pctmap.net/trail-notes/ , Accessed 24 Jun 2025
25. Crowley, R.: Thru-hiking and why people do it (2018)
26. Dykes, B.: Effective data storytelling: how to drive change with data, narrative and visuals. John Wiley and Sons (2019)

27. Echegaray, F.: What post-COVID-19 lifestyles may look like? identifying scenarios and their implications for sustainability. Sustain. Produc. Consum. **27**, 567–574 (2021)
28. Figueiras, A.: How to tell stories using visualization. In: 2014 18th International Conference on Information Visualisation, pp. 18–18 (2014). https://doi.org/10.1109/IV.2014.78, https://ieeexplore.ieee.org/document/6902874, iSSN: 2375-0138
29. Fischer-Stabel, P., Mai, F., Schindler, S., Schneider, M.: Digital twins, augmented reality and explorer maps rising attractiveness of rural regions for outdoor tourism. In: Progress in IS, pp. 243–253. Springer International Publishing (2020). https://doi.org/10.1007/978-3-030-61969-5_17, iSSN: 2196-8705
30. Fluxguide: holoMuse - museum exhibition design and visitor system based on augmented reality enhanced wearables., published. https://youtu.be/XcKBAdEYMpY?si=9ve6wyjVDYCjUQV2&t=116
31. GIS, P.: Layer descriptions (2024). https://storymaps.arcgis.com/stories/1c7b0c3c34c84f0292a7c1dedebcedcd
32. Go, B.: Pacific crest trail data book: mileages, landmarks, facilities, resupply data, and essential trail information for the entire pacific crest trail, from mexico to canada. Wilderness Press (2013). google-Books-ID: JPkrDgAAQBAJ
33. Google: google maps platform. https://developers.google.com/maps
34. Halloran, N.: The fallen of world war II. http://www.fallen.io/ww2/, Accessed 04 Oct 2022
35. Halperin, B.A., Lukin, S.M.: Artificial dreams: surreal visual storytelling as inquiry into ai'hallucination. In: Proceedings of the 2024 ACM Designing Interactive Systems Conference, pp. 619–637 (2024)
36. Hine, R.: Water resources on the pacific crest trail: thru-hiker experiences and alternate water sources in 2019
37. https://www.Postholer.Com: John muir trail animals. https://Postholer.Com/trail-animals/John-Muir-Trail/4
38. iNaturalist: iNaturalist. https://www.inaturalist.org/
39. Jänicke, S., Franzini, G., Cheema, M.F., Scheuermann, G.: Visual text analysis in digital humanities. Comput. Graph. Forum **36**(6), 226–250 (2017)
40. Knight Lab: storymap - maps that tell stories. https://storymap.knightlab.com, accessed 17 Aug 2023
41. Knight lab: timeline - easy-to-make, beautiful timelines. https://timeline.knightlab.com, Accessed 17 Aug 2023
42. Knight Lab: timemapper - elegant timelines and maps created in seconds. http://timemapper.okfnlabs.org, Accessed 04 Sep 2021
43. Kosara, R., Mackinlay, J.: Storytelling: the next step for visualization. Computer **46**(5), 44–50 (2013)
44. Kusnick, J., Lichtenberg, S., Jänicke, S.: Visualization-based scrollytelling of coupled threats for biodiversity, species and music cultures. In: Workshop On Visualisation In Environmental Sciences. The Eurographics Association (2023)
45. Kusnick, J., et al.: Every thing can be a hero! narrative visualization of person, object, and other biographies. Informatics **11**(2), 26 (2024). https://doi.org/10.3390/informatics11020026
46. Lee, B., Riche, N.H., Isenberg, P., Carpendale, S.: More than telling a story: transforming data into visually shared stories. IEEE Comput. Graph. Appl. **35**(5), 84–90 (2015). https://doi.org/10.1109/MCG.2015.99
47. Li, H., Wang, Y., Liao, Q.V., Qu, H.: Why is AI not a panacea for data workers? an interview study on human-AI collaboration in data storytelling. IEEE Trans. Vis. Comput. Graph. (2025). publisher: IEEE

48. Li, N., Willett, W., Sharlin, E., Sousa, M.C.: Visibility perception and dynamic viewsheds for topographic maps and models. In: Proceedings of the 5th Symposium on Spatial User Interaction, pp. 39–47. SUI '17, Association for Computing Machinery, New York, NY, USA (2017). https://doi.org/10.1145/3131277.3132178, https://doi.org/10.1145/3131277.3132178
49. Ma, K.L., Liao, I., Frazier, J., Hauser, H., Kostis, H.N.: Scientific storytelling using visualization. IEEE Comput. Graph. Appl. **32**(1), 12–19 (2012). https://doi.org/10.1109/MCG.2012.24
50. Mar, R.A., Li, J., Nguyen, A.T., Ta, C.P.: Memory and comprehension of narrative versus expository texts: a meta-analysis. Psychon. Bull. Rev. **28**, 732–749 (2021), publisher: Springer
51. Market report analytics: comprehensive overview of outdoor sports smart watches trends: 2025-2033. https://www.marketreportanalytics.com/reports/outdoor-sports-smart-watches-33453, Accessed 22 Jun 2025
52. Munzner, T.: A nested model for visualization design and validation. IEEE Trans. Vis. Comput. Graph. **15**(6), 921–928 (2009), publisher: IEEE
53. Kristina, N., et al.: When napoleon ventured east. https://1812.tass.ru/en, Accessed 25 Jun 2023
54. Nevistić, Z., Špoljarić, D.: Web GIS in mountaineering in croatia. GeoScape **13**(2) (2019)
55. Obradović, S., Tešin, A.: Hiking in the COVID-19 era: motivation and post-outbreak intentions. J. Sport Tourism **26**(2), 147–164 (2022)
56. Odom, W., et al.: Capra: making use of multiple perspectives for capturing, noticing and revisiting hiking experiences over time. In: Proceedings of the CHI Conference on Human Factors in Computing Systems, pp. 1–27. ACM, Honolulu HI USA (2024). https://doi.org/10.1145/3613904.3642284, https://dl.acm.org/doi/10.1145/3613904.3642284
57. Pacific crest trail association:
58. PANDEY, R.K., Nétek, R.R., Klug, H.: Online visualisation of hiking activities. PhD Thesis, Palackỳ University Olomouc (2022)
59. Planner, C.J.: Interactive camino planner - plan your perfect pilgrimage. https://caminoplanner.org/
60. Popelka, S., Brychtova, A.: Eye-tracking study on different perception of 2D and 3D terrain visualisation. Cartogr. J. **50**(3), 240–246 (2013). https://doi.org/10.1179/1743277413Y.0000000058, publisher: Informa UK Limited
61. Report, P.C.T.W.: Pacific crest trail water report (2016). https://pctwater.com/
62. Ross, C.: Journey on the crest: walking 2600 miles from mexico to canada. mountaineers books (1987), google-Books-ID: YZMTCgAAQBAJ
63. Schobesberger, D., Patterson, T.: Evaluating the eïňĂectiveness of 2d vs. 3d trailhead maps
64. Scholars' Lab: neatline - Plot your course in space and time. https://neatline.org/, Accessed 17 Aug 2023
65. Sebastian, K., Joachim, P., M., H., P., G.: 3D panorama service on mobile device for hiking (2007)
66. Segel, E., Heer, J.: Narrative visualization: telling stories with data. IEEE Trans. Visual Comput. Graphics **16**(6), 1139–1148 (2010)
67. Shneiderman, B.: The eyes have it: a task by data type taxonomy for information visualizations. In: The Craft Of Information Visualization, pp. 364–371. Elsevier (2003)
68. Tong, C., et al.: storytelling and visualization: an extended survey. Information **9**(3), 65 (2018)

69. Tsen Lai, P., I Chen, C., Zheng, M.C.: The influence of hiking trail map representation on route selection. In: AHFE International. AHFE International (2023). https://doi.org/10.54941/ahfe1003694, iSSN: 2771-0718
70. Tîrlă, L., Matei, E., Cuculici, R., Vijulie, I., Manea, G.: Digital elevation profile: a complex tool for the spatial analysis of hiking trails. J. Environ. Tourism Anal. **2**, 48–66 (2014)
71. Wiehr, F., Daiber, F., Kosmalla, F., Kruger, A.: ARTopos. In: Proceedings of the 2017 ACM International Joint Conference on Pervasive and Ubiquitous Computing and Proceedings of the 2017 ACM International Symposium on Wearable Computers, pp. 1047–1050. ACM (2017). DOIurlhttps://doi.org/10.1145/3123024.3124446, http://dx.doi.org/10.1145/3123024.3124446
72. Wu, G., Jiang, A., Su, X., Chen, Z.: "Story Type" or "column Type": the differential impacts of different types of outdoor safety education on hikers' safety participation behaviors. J. Outdoor Recreat. Tour. **50**, 100898 (2025). https://doi.org/10.1016/j.jort.2025.100898, https://www.sciencedirect.com/science/article/pii/S2213078025000441
73. Xie, Z., Cohn, T., Lau, J.H.: the next chapter: a study of large language models in storytelling. In: Keet, C.M., Lee, H.Y., Zarrieß, S. (eds.) Proceedings of the 16th International Natural Language Generation Conference, pp. 323–351. Association for Computational Linguistics, Prague, Czechia (2023). https://doi.org/10.18653/v1/2023.inlg-main.23, https://aclanthology.org/2023.inlg-main.23/

Designing for (Digital) Nomad-AI Interaction

Daniel Schneider[1]([✉]), Marcos Antônio de Almeida[1], Mariangela Nascimento[1], António Correia[2], and Jano Moreira de Souza[1]

[1] Federal University of Rio de Janeiro, Rio de Janeiro, RJ, Brazil
`{schneider,malmeida,jano}@cos.ufrj.br`
[2] Faculty of Information Technology, University of Jyväskylä, Jyväskylä, Finland
`antonio.g.correia@jyu.fi`

Abstract. Digital nomadism, a lifestyle defined by location independence and the deep pursuit of autonomy, faces inherent challenges, including significant mobilization work and the continuous effort of adapting to diverse environments. This paper introduces an emergent Human-Computer Interaction (HCI) paradigm at the convergence of digital nomadism and Generative Artificial Intelligence (GAI). We argue that GAI moves beyond the role of a tool, emerging as a transformative agent that can redefine the nomad's experience by providing support across key domains—ranging from bureaucracy management, destination selection, and agenda planning to professional tools, community integration, and even occupational reinvention. This integration presents a critical paradox: while GAI can mitigate the cognitive load of mobility and support a more fluid and enriching nomadic journey, it also introduces new challenges like job market disruptions and threats to digital well-being. To guide the development of effective GAI technologies in this evolving landscape, we propose seven design principles aimed at fostering a symbiotic Nomad-AI partnership. The paper further discusses critical design implications, navigating dilemmas such as user autonomy versus AI automation, and exploring crucial opportunities to empower digital nomads. We outline future directions for HCI research that seek to establish a symbiotic relationship between nomads and AI, one that enriches the digital nomad experience while promoting holistic well-being.

Keywords: Digital Nomads · Digital Nomadism · Generative AI · Nomad-AI Interaction

1 Introduction

A significant shift in work dynamics has emerged recently, driven by widespread digital connectivity and a growing emphasis on professional autonomy and flexibility. In this context, the digital nomad (DN) has become a prominent figure: a professional who leverages technology to attain location independence, enabling them to conduct their work and lifestyle globally. As Hannonen [1] highlighted in her seminal work defining this phenomenon, digital nomadism goes beyond mere remote work: it's an intentional lifestyle, shaped by a complex interplay of personal, professional, and social motivations

J. F. Krems et al. (Eds.): CHIRA 2025, CCIS 2836, pp. 348–368, 2026.
https://doi.org/10.1007/978-3-032-16454-4_20

[2]. This mobile work arrangement, however, is not without its inherent complexities. Even in earlier explorations of nomadic work, researchers identified persistent challenges related to continuously managing resources, setting up functional work environments, and maintaining organizational integration while on the move [3]. These core insights underscore the enduring "mobilization work" that underpins the fluid nature of the nomadic lifestyle.

However, as digital nomadism matures, Generative Artificial Intelligence (GAI) emerges as a transformative force, poised to redefine the very nature of this lifestyle. Tools like Large Language Models (LLMs), image generators, and coding assistants aren't just incremental improvements; they represent a paradigm shift in HCI, fundamentally changing how work is done, how we learn, and how we interact with the digital world. This evolution exemplifies the broader concept of "hybrid intelligence", showcasing how the synergy of human and machine intelligences, often facilitated by sophisticated crowd-machine interaction mechanisms, can achieve capabilities beyond what either could alone [4].

This convergence of the DN's inherently mobile and adaptable nature with GAI's transformative capabilities creates a new and complex interaction paradigm. This emerging paradigm challenges existing notions of productivity, well-being, and the very meaning of work and mobility. While the impact of AI on DNs has been previously explored [5, 14], the rise of GAI demands a thorough re-evaluation of these interactions and, consequently, a redefinition of HCI design principles for this evolving domain. Crucially, this presents a paradox: GAI is primed to enhance the nomadic experience significantly, yet it also introduces new complexities such as job market disruptions and threats to digital well-being, potentially challenging the core principles of DN freedom and autonomy.

This paper aims to explore this critical intersection. We are particularly interested in developing a conceptual framework for thinking about and designing GAI-based systems that support digital nomadism, and we present some concepts and principles we consider helpful. The remainder of this paper is structured as follows. Section 2 deepens the understanding of the DN, their motivations, and the complexities of their mobile existence. Section 3 examines GAI as a transformative agent within the nomadic paradigm, detailing its benefits and risks. Section 4 discusses the essential role of physical space in the Nomad-AI interaction. Section 5 proposes a set of design principles to guide the creation of future GAI technologies for DNs. Section 6 explores the implications of these principles for HCI design, identifying challenges and potential solutions. Finally, Sect. 7 concludes the paper, summarizing the main findings and limitations, and pointing toward future HCI research directions.

2   Digital Nomads: Understanding Their Motivations and the Challenges of a Mobile Lifestyle

Understanding the essence of DNs goes beyond merely observing their capacity to work remotely. It's imperative to delve into the driving forces that propel these individuals and the challenges they face on their journey. The study by de Carvalho et al. [2] offers a comprehensive overview of these motivations, outlining the complex web of reasons that lead to the adoption and maintenance of this lifestyle. Such motivations are a complex web of "pull factors" like lifestyle, flexibility, autonomy, self-improvement, and adventure, and "push factors" such as rigid corporate structures or cost of living [2]. This duality highlights the intentionality behind nomadism. Interestingly, the Fear of Missing Out (FOMO) also acts as a significant "pull factor", stimulating DN adoption as individuals seek experiences seen elsewhere [6].

This freedom, however, involves substantial mobilisation work [7]—the continuous, often imperceptible, meta-work required to maintain productivity while constantly moving. This includes managing logistics like accommodations, visas, connectivity, and resource access, all vital for overcoming resource deprivation in dynamic, uncertain contexts [7]. Su and Mark [3] pioneered this view, identifying three crucial areas where nomadic workers face continuous challenges: assembling mobile offices, seeking resources (human and technological), and integrating with organizations [3]. These concerns remain central, though evolving with technology. While AI-driven automation promises to alleviate such mundane tasks, enhancing efficiency [17], it also introduces new considerations for work-life integration and skill relevance. Beyond operations, DNs manage complex "personal knowledge ecologies" (PKEs), synthesizing vast information from diverse sources—cultures, services, clients, and digital tools. This PKE management is complicated by digital platform asymmetries like unequal access or power imbalances, impacting autonomy and efficiency [8].

The rise of the DN is not a static phenomenon but a constantly evolving practice, whose nuances have been further accentuated by recent global events such as the COVID-19 pandemic. While imposing mobility restrictions, the crisis paradoxically catalyzed nomadism's proliferation and validation, compelling remote work adoption and offering aspirants a chance to test this lifestyle [16]. This period underscored location-independent work's viability, accelerating the acceptance of nomadism as a resilient work model [16]. Yet, for established DNs, the pandemic exposed vulnerabilities like navigating excessive online channels and changing travel regulations, emphasizing the need for robust support technologies [16]. This highlights DNs' adaptability and the importance of tools that mitigate cognitive load and meta-work in transit. Crisis narratives during COVID-19 further illustrate how unexpected events challenge DN practices [9]. Despite lockdowns, DNs showed remarkable resilience, reinventing their operations. However, this comes at a cost, particularly impacting work-life boundaries [9]. The constant negotiation of mobility freedom and work demands, often across time zones, requires tech support beyond productivity, encompassing well-being and boundary management.

The complexity of DN existence is intrinsically linked to space, as the physical environment profoundly shapes their work and well-being [10]. DNs utilize diverse spaces—domestic, "third places" like cafes, coworking spaces, transit hubs—each offering varying levels of productivity and social interaction [10]. This constant adaptation, infrastructure search, and ephemeral community management create challenges like social isolation, routine disruption, and the quest for a "sense of place" amidst fluidity.

Understanding the diversity within the DN population is essential. Beyond "full-time" and "part-time" DNs, "wannabes" (aspiring DNs) are crucial to the ecosystem, having distinct informational needs [11]. Cook [12] offers a contemporary taxonomy, categorizing DNs into five types (freelance, business owners, salaried, experimental, armchair) based on six variable themes (e.g., autonomy over mobility, work-life balance). This highlights that GAI support needs will vary significantly across profiles, from initial career transition planning for beginners to optimizing complex routines for experienced DNs, demanding tailored assistance, automation, and information access.

Ultimately, the conceptualization of the DN must acknowledge its constant evolution. While location independence ("work from anywhere" or WFA) defines it, nomadism has expanded "beyond working from (almost) anywhere" post-COVID-19 [13]. The pandemic popularized remote work, impacting the ecosystem by introducing new adherents and redefining expectations. This implies that designing for DNs must embrace new lifestyle facets—social, cultural, and well-being—transcending mere productivity. The DN's life is thus a relentless pursuit of flexibility and experience, sustained by complex mobilisation work and profoundly influenced by physical spaces. Understanding this intricate network is vital to recognizing how AI can transcend mere task efficiency to truly enhance the digital nomad experience and confront the structural frictions it entails.

3 Generative AI as a Transformative Agent in the Nomadic Paradigm

The emergence of GAI represents a key development in HCI, offering new possibilities for shaping the DN experience. As anticipated by [5], AI transcends being a mere tool, establishing itself as an active agent and a vector of rationalization and innovation in the nomad's mobile life. Research by [5] evidences a growing symbiosis between human capabilities and algorithmic affordances, redefining DNs' cognitive, organizational, and relational practices.

GAI primarily serves two key functions in this context. Firstly, its operational function focuses on task automation, content generation, and productivity support. Tools that generate optimized travel itineraries, suggest accommodations, or automate bureaucratic tasks free DNs from repetitive and cognitively demanding mobilization work [7]. This proactive automation mitigates "resource deprivation", allowing DNs to dedicate more energy to core tasks and cultural exploration. Furthermore, GAI acts as a powerful catalyst for amplifying productivity and creativity, serving as an unprecedented collaborative partner for knowledge workers [2]. LLMs can generate text drafts, assist in complex information retrieval, refine ideas, or create code snippets and visual designs. This capacity for co-creation and automation of early creative stages accelerates workflows and expands professional deliverables. Verma [14] corroborates these benefits, noting that automation, including advanced GAI, significantly increases efficiency, saves costs, and improves accuracy, freeing up valuable time.

Secondly, GAI performs a strategic function, intrinsically linked to knowledge management, professional planning, and occupational reinvention [5]. It acts as a cognitive partner contributing to medium- and long-term decisions. A central finding is GAI's role in enabling "pivoting" – a predominant adaptive strategy among DNs in response to labor market transformations, intensified by the COVID-19 pandemic and AI automation [5]. GAI is instrumental in fostering skill acquisition and facilitating the creation of new projects, products, or services. Its ability to access and synthesize vast quantities of on-demand knowledge makes continuous learning a fluid part of the nomadic lifestyle, fostering innovation and co-constructing pathways of human agency in the face of uncertainty. Moreover, GAI can play a crucial strategic role in navigating emerging digital economies like "tokenomics" and decentralized technologies. Given that DNs often have limited access and rely on community networks [15], GAI can act as an intelligent interface to demystify these new forms of work and remuneration, helping DNs identify, evaluate, and participate in decentralized projects, thereby expanding their work avenues.

Beyond work, GAI also holds the potential to enhance connectivity and social interactions, which are crucial for combating the isolation inherent in life on the move. While physical communities are vital [10], GAI can mediate global connections. Real-time translation tools eliminate language barriers, and AI assistants can suggest events and gatherings or help maintain ties with professional and personal networks regardless of distance.

The findings of [5] reinforce the need to revise theoretical frameworks for digital nomadism, proposing GAI's inclusion as a structural component of the "digital nomad toolkit". This conceptual repositioning recognizes AI not merely as infrastructure, but as an active element reconfiguring mobility, work, and subjectivity, aligning HCI studies with critical socio-technical approaches. However, the integration of GAI into nomadic practices is not without its risks. Verma [14] warns of potential job displacement or skill obsolescence for automatable tasks, technological dependence, and the unreliability of some tools. He also highlights that automation may fail to capture cultural nuances, compromising interaction accuracy and effectiveness.

In sum, GAI not only optimizes work but fundamentally alters the experience, alleviating burdens, expanding capabilities, and transforming the nature of the DN's interaction with technology and the world, including strategic career decisions. Indeed, digital nomadism is evolving to "go beyond working from (almost) anywhere" [13], implying that GAI must support this holistic lifestyle transformation. This transformation, however, also introduces new complexities and demands a careful approach to the design of its interfaces and functionalities—a topic we will explore in subsequent sections.

3.1 Moving Beyond WFA: Supporting a Holistic Nomadic Lifestyle

The evolution of digital nomadism beyond WFA [13] reflects a significant reconfiguration of the lifestyle. No longer reducible to the image of a laptop and a stable internet connection—a rhetorical shorthand for mobility—it is increasingly understood as a holistic mode of living that blends personal growth, cultural immersion, well-being, and community-building with professional engagement. As such, the role of GAI must move beyond task optimization to genuinely support this broader lifestyle transformation.

Emerging practices already point to this shift toward a more holistic nomadic lifestyle, with DNs organizing "coworkations", engaging in local projects, and demonstrating growing concerns for sustainability and community contribution. Such practices illustrate how coworkations foster not only productivity but also social interaction and shared values, blurring the boundaries between work and leisure [27]. This holistic orientation aligns with DNs' broader pursuit of freedom that integrates professional, personal, and experiential dimensions into a meaningful lifestyle [28]. Evidence from Chiang Mai, a well-known hub for DNs in northern Thailand, further shows how these practices extend beyond individual routines to shape the local visitor economy, as DNs engage with businesses and communities in ways that generate both economic vitality and social development [29].

GAI's utility for DNs thus encompasses their entire life experience. It fosters well-being and balance by assisting with work-life boundaries and mitigating social isolation, while also facilitating cultural adaptation and connection through support for navigating local customs and building genuine relationships. Furthermore, GAI can catalyze ongoing personal and professional development, enabling skill development and personalized learning paths. Beyond work logistics, GAI proactively streamlines broader lifestyle elements, from identifying suitable community-rich housing to pinpointing local activities. This ensures it supports not just the DN's productivity, but their complete life—their work, experiences, purpose, and vital social connections. Figure 1 visually outlines six key domains where GAI's utility extends beyond traditional WFA to support the multifaceted aspects of a holistic nomadic lifestyle.

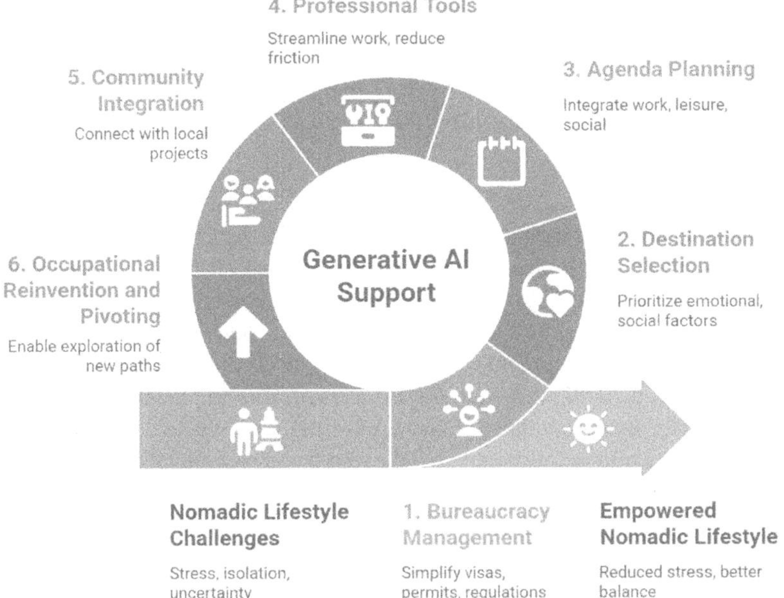

Fig. 1. GAI for moving beyond WFA. The six domains of GAI's transformative utility in the nomadic paradigm.

3.1.1 Bureaucracy Management

DNs often face complex logistical challenges, especially concerning visas, travel permits, and local regulations. This mobilization work and the fear of making bureaucratic mistakes can be a significant source of stress and anxiety, directly impacting the DN's emotional well-being. Research on the r/digitalnomad community found that this constant logistical burden is a key contributor to an emotional downward trend, with a rise in negative emotions like fear, loneliness, and anxiety [24]. GAI can act as an intelligent agent to simplify this burden. It can track visa requirements for a DN's target countries, send alerts for renewal deadlines, and generate personalized checklists for documentation. By automating these tasks, GAI minimizes the mental overhead and associated stress, allowing the DN to focus on their work and experiences, ultimately fostering a more stable emotional state.

3.1.2 Destination Selection

The choice of a new location is a critical decision for DNs, influenced by a myriad of factors. Recognizing that loneliness and social isolation are primary emotional challenges [24], GAI can directly support a DN's well-being by prioritizing emotional and social factors in destination selection. It can leverage a vast amount of data to suggest destinations tailored not just to infrastructure (e.g., coworking spaces, public transport), but also to the sentiment of the local community, social opportunities, and the presence of support networks for DNs. The system could recommend a city known for its vibrant arts scene and affordable housing or a town with a strong sense of community, providing detailed reports on each option. This moves beyond simple search results to a truly personalized recommendation engine that aligns with the DN's holistic lifestyle and social goals.

3.1.3 Agenda Planning

Amid constant change, maintaining a healthy work–life balance is a core challenge for DNs, and Xiao and Lutz [24] underscore the importance of lifestyle choices and emotional well-being. GAI can help by creating balanced agendas, integrating professional commitments with personal and leisure activities, and focusing on social connections. By understanding the DN's typical work hours and social preferences, GAI can propose schedules that include dedicated time for work, exploring the local area, self-care, and social events. It can also adapt these plans in real-time, for instance, by suggesting a later start to the workday after a late-night social event or rearranging tasks to accommodate a spontaneous day trip, ensuring a more sustainable and enjoyable lifestyle.

3.1.4 Professional Tools

While GAI is a powerful tool for work, its utility extends far beyond basic productivity. GAI can be a versatile professional partner for DNs, who often work across different industries and with global clients. This includes assisting with content creation, translating complex documents or presentations, and providing real-time language support for client meetings. By streamlining work and reducing professional friction, GAI can ease stress and frustration, supporting a sense of competence and control that is vital to DNs' emotional well-being [24]. This level of support enables DNs to be more agile and competitive in their professional endeavors, regardless of their location.

3.1.5 Community Integration

A key aspect of a holistic nomadic life is building meaningful connections. GAI can be designed to facilitate community integration by connecting DNs with local projects, events, and other individuals. Recognizing that DNs frequently experience loneliness and social isolation, and that community sentiment saw a notable emotional decline post-pandemic [24], GAI can be leveraged to help foster stronger community connections. For example, a GAI could identify local volunteer opportunities that match the DN's interests, suggest meet-ups for professionals in a similar field, or highlight cultural events to foster deeper immersion in the local community. By acting as a social connector, GAI helps to mitigate feelings of loneliness and isolation, empowering DNs to build a support network and a sense of belonging in each new place they inhabit.

3.1.6 Occupational Reinvention and Pivoting

The nomadic context, often defined by autonomy and exposure to new market realities, encourages adaptive strategies such as pivoting [5]. Pivoting, in this context, refers to the ability to rapidly adapt one's professional focus or business model in response to new opportunities or challenges, often involving a significant shift in skills or market niche. GAI systems should be designed not just to optimize existing work but to enable and facilitate occupational reinvention and the exploration of new career paths. This means AIs that can analyze market trends, identify skill gaps, suggest new competencies to acquire, and even co-create portfolios or proposals for new projects. AI should act as a strategic career partner, helping DNs navigate uncertainty and capitalize on opportunities agilely, transforming GAI into a vector of human agency in the face of structural changes in the job market. The role of wannabes who actively seek to plan and test the nomadic lifestyle [11] reinforces the importance of systems that ease this transition and the development of new skills, making career reinvention more accessible. Finally, in a scenario where digital nomadism is evolving to "go beyond working from (almost) anywhere" and impacting the traditional market [13], GAI can be crucial in helping DNs identify and prepare for these changes, ensuring their long-term relevance and success.

4 Rethinking the Role of Space in Nomad-AI Interaction

Despite location independence being a defining pillar of digital nomadism [1], physical space is far from irrelevant. It is, in fact, a central element that profoundly shapes DNs' work practices and well-being [10]. In this context, GAI holds the potential to redefine how DNs interact with these transient environments, optimizing them and mitigating their inherent challenges.

GAI can and should revolutionize space selection and optimization. DNs alternate among various environments, such as temporary apartments, cafes, libraries, coworking spaces, and even transit locations, each with its peculiarities regarding noise, privacy, connectivity, and resource access [10]. GAI tools can analyze a DN's preferences—such as productivity history in different scenarios, the type of task to be performed, and energy level—and, in real-time, suggest the most suitable space. For example, an AI could recommend a quiet zone in a coworking space for a high-focus task, or a bustling cafe for a creative brainstorming session, enhancing the effectiveness of the "space alternation" emphasized by Nash et al. [10].

Beyond mere recommendation, GAI can enhance the functionality and experience within these spaces. In temporary apartments, which often lack office infrastructure, an AI might suggest ideal lighting and sound configurations for video conferences, or even assist in the ergonomic arrangement of a limited space, adaptively personalizing the environment. Additionally, there is a viable path toward combating resource deprivation in unfamiliar environments and cultivating a digitally augmented sense of place. In a new city being explored by a DN, AI can provide contextual information about local services, regulations, and customs, acting as a proactive guide for adaptation. By collecting data on the DN's interactions with each environment, AI can build a digital record of their journey, connecting work experiences to specific locations. This digital memory can help foster a sense of continuity and belonging, even amidst constant transience, strengthening the "mobile sense of place" that DNs seek.

However, integrating AI with physical space also raises significant challenges. Privacy and surveillance issues in sensor-equipped environments require careful consideration to prevent loss of control or excessive monitoring. GAI design must prioritize cultural and social sensitivity, avoid biases, and promote respectful interactions. Ultimately, GAI should not only assist physical navigation but also optimize interaction with the physical environment, transforming generic spaces into personalized, responsive work ecosystems. This redefines the DN's relationship with location, demanding new design principles to ensure technology enhances, rather than diminishes, the rich experience of life on the move.

5   Design Principles for Nomad-AI Interaction

To begin, we need to clarify what we mean by Nomad-AI interaction: it refers to the *dynamic interplay between DNs and AI systems, particularly GAI, designed to support their unique work-life paradigm.* Moving beyond simple tool usage, AI is envisioned as an intelligent partner deeply integrated into the nomadic journey, assisting with logistical complexities, enabling continuous adaptation, and fostering well-being. This intentional design is crucial, as digital nomadism's inherent demands for constant flexibility and multifaceted support in diverse, unfamiliar contexts differ significantly from traditional work arrangements. Without a deliberate focus, AI risks becoming a task optimizer that reinforces—rather than alleviates—existing challenges such as work-life imbalance and social isolation.

This approach significantly benefits HCI researchers, providing a rich domain for studying human-AI interaction in highly fluid environments. It also directly aids technology developers in creating more effective, user-centric AI solutions, and ultimately, DNs themselves, by enriching their experiences and enabling sustainable lifestyles.

Drawing upon nomadic motivations [2], the nature of mobilization work [7], the intrinsic role of space [10], and the recent appropriation of GAI by DNs [5], we propose seven fundamental design principles. These principles, depicted in Fig. 2, aim to guide GAI development to positively impact the DN, enriching their experience by mitigating potential risks to their autonomy and fostering their holistic well-being. Applying these principles can elevate the Nomad-AI interaction from a passive utility to a symbiotic partnership, where the AI actively collaborates with the DN to achieve their goals, while also intentionally safeguarding their freedom, purpose, and overall quality of life on the move.

To achieve this, Nomad-AI systems must evolve across three key fronts. First, they require greater context and personal data awareness, moving beyond isolated functionality to integrate with the DN's calendar, health data, finances, and geolocation—enabling, for example, timely reminders of visa renewals or personalized suggestions like a local cooking class aligned with the user's interests. Second, they must rely on predictive and proactive models that anticipate needs rather than merely responding to them, such as recommending a lighter schedule or a relaxing activity when detecting signs of sleep deprivation. Finally, they should cultivate sensitivity and emotional attunement, offering support beyond productivity, like proposing a museum visit on a rainy day to alleviate boredom, or identifying early signs of burnout and encouraging restorative breaks.

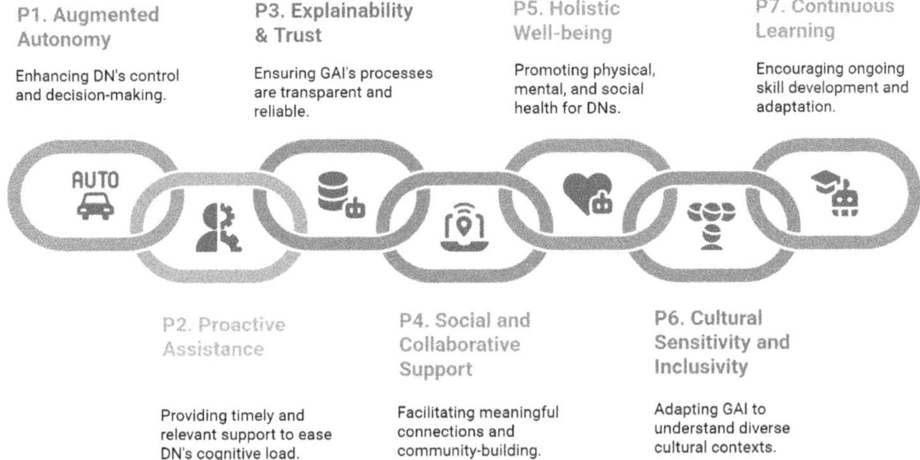

Fig. 2. Design Principles for Nomad–AI Interaction. The seven principles form a chain of interconnected links, representing an integrated ecosystem.

The seven design principles proposed are not independent directives but form an integrated ecosystem. This interdependence can be understood through the metaphor of a chain of interconnected links; they are mutually reinforcing, and if one link fails, the entire interaction may be compromised. This synergistic relationship is critical to understand for designers aiming to create sustainable GAI solutions for the nomadic lifestyle.

In fact, the failure of one principle can trigger a negative chain reaction. The absence of "Augmented Autonomy" can turn the AI into a "black box", eroding "Explainability And Trust". This loss of control and transparency directly harms the DN's "Holistic Well-Being" and compromises the effectiveness of "Proactive Assistance", as the GAI's suggestions may be viewed with suspicion or as an invasion. Similarly, a GAI that prioritizes only productivity and neglects "Holistic Well-Being" can lead to burnout, hindering "Continuous Learning" and causing "Proactive Assistance" to be perceived as an unwanted intrusion. Poorly implemented assistance, with untimely interruptions, increases cognitive load instead of alleviating it, undermining trust and making social and well-being support (*Principles P4 and P5*) ineffective.

Finally, a lack of support for "Continuous Learning" can stagnate the DN's skills, making them dependent on the AI and less able to adapt to new cultural contexts. A GAI that lacks "Cultural Sensitivity and Inclusivity" can generate offensive or irrelevant recommendations, eroding trust, harming "Social and Collaborative Support", and isolating the DN, which in turn negatively affects "Holistic Well-Being". The failure to facilitate meaningful connections (*Principle P4*) compromises well-being (*Principle P5*) and weakens continuous learning (*Principle P7*). We will now describe the seven proposed principles in detail.

- **Principle P1: Design for Augmented Autonomy**

The core motivation of the DN lies in the pursuit of flexibility and autonomy [2]. GAI systems should be designed to significantly expand this autonomy, transforming the very nature of nomadic freedom. This means offering meaningful choices and ensuring the DN retains ultimate control over decisions, even as GAI streamlines complex tasks. Instead of full automation, AI should act as an intelligent partner, providing sophisticated information, nuanced suggestions, and optimized pathways, but always leaving the final decision to the DN. The design must avoid "black box" approaches and algorithmic imposition, prioritizing transparency and user comprehension. DNs can customize AI intervention and understand its recommendations, which builds trust and strengthens their agency. This is particularly crucial for managing their work and life on the move, helping them navigate the informational and control asymmetries within the digital platforms that form their personal knowledge ecologies [8].

- **Principle P2: Design for Proactive Assistance**

The nomadic lifestyle inherently involves significant mobilization work [7] and a high cognitive load associated with constantly adapting to new environments and managing diverse responsibilities. GAI systems must be designed as essential partners, intelligently offering proactive assistance to streamline both operational tasks and mental burdens. This involves comprehending and continuously adapting to the DN's diverse and changing contexts—including time zones, local languages, network infrastructure, regulations, and subtle cultural nuances. By processing vast amounts of contextual data, GAI can proactively anticipate needs, offer precise recommendations, and automate repetitive or complex logistical tasks.

Building on insights into visualizing proximity [18], AI-based systems should seamlessly provide essential spatial information like reliable internet sources, optimal workspaces, or local services, mitigating common infrastructure and access challenges [3]. GAI is uniquely suited for these nuanced and proactive forms of contextual adaptation, enabling it to generate creative solutions and insights highly relevant to nomadic life's dynamic and qualitative aspects. This includes leveraging factors that increase a place's attractiveness for DN residential mobility [21] to offer personalized location recommendations.

Furthermore, GAI can specifically assist in navigating and optimizing coworking spaces and other work infrastructures, addressing the disruptions and repairs of place experienced by DNs [22]. On the other hand, GAI can significantly reduce cognitive load by acting as a sophisticated "meta-work" manager, automating administrative, research, and organizational tasks that consume valuable time and mental energy. By intelligently curating a digital memory of the DN's interactions with each temporary environment, connecting work experiences and personal discoveries to specific locations, GAI fosters continuity and strengthens their elusive mobile sense of place amidst constant transience, thus helping to mitigate the inherent impermanence of "liquid modernity" [24] and fostering a crucial sense of place-belongingness [26]. In essence, this proactive assistance principle ensures GAI enhances the DN's efficiency, frees up mental resources, and cultivates a more profound, less burdensome connection with their dynamic lifestyle.

- **Principle P3: Design for Explainability and Trust**

GAI systems for DNs must be transparent and understandable, fostering user trust and enabling informed decision-making. This principle emphasizes that DNs should not only receive AI-generated outputs but also comprehend how those outputs were derived. In this context, explainability involves clearly articulating the GAI's reasoning, highlighting the data used, and making its underlying logic accessible. This is crucial for nomadic work where decisions often have real-world, high-stakes consequences (e.g., travel logistics, legal compliance, financial management). Trust is built when DNs perceive the AI as reliable, unbiased, and aligned with their goals. Given the prevalent digital platform asymmetries—where users often lack full control over their data or understanding of platform mechanisms [8]—GAI systems must actively work to bridge these gaps. By offering transparent and explainable processes, GAI can empower DNs to manage their personal knowledge ecologies better, mitigating informational and power imbalances and ensuring that AI operates as an extension of user agency rather than a black box.

- **Principle P4: Social and Collaborative Support**

Despite the pursuit of independence, DNs benefit immensely from connection, and community-building is a crucial aspect of their holistic lifestyle (as emphasized in Sect. 3.1). GAI systems should be designed to provide robust social and collaborative support, enabling meaningful interactions integral to their holistic lifestyle. This includes supporting seamless virtual team collaboration across time zones, suggesting local networking events or coworking communities, and even fostering serendipitous encounters with other DNs or locals. This is underscored by research that reveals DNs frequently experience loneliness, depression, and social isolation, with community sentiment showing a notable emotional decline, particularly in the post-COVID phase [24]. Recognizing that location independence and connecting with locals are crucial for successfully integrating digital nomadism into local contexts, and that loneliness can be a significant challenge for DNs [25], GAI can serve as a vital bridge for establishing transient yet impactful social networks. By identifying shared interests or professional needs among geographically dispersed individuals, GAI can promote the formation of supportive communities and reinforce the collective intelligence of the nomadic ecosystem.

Furthermore, GAI can play a vital role in connecting DNs with local projects and initiatives, fostering their contribution to sustainability efforts and deeper cultural immersion, aligning with their evolving desire for a more integrated and purposeful nomadic life (as discussed in Sect. 3.1). This comprehensive support for social integration is essential for enhancing the DN's overall well-being and sense of place-belongingness amidst constant movement, a concept explored in detail by [26].

- **Principle P5: Design for Holistic Well-being**

Nomadic life, despite its freedoms and attractions, can lead to challenges such as isolation, mental health issues, and difficulty maintaining well-being routines. GAI systems should be designed to act as catalysts for the DN's well-being in its physical, cognitive, and social dimensions. This includes functionalities that monitor burnout, suggest active breaks, promote healthy habits adapted to the local context, and, crucially, facilitate connection with both local and digital communities [10], reinforcing the goal of *Principle P4*. GAI shouldn't replace human interaction, but rather enrich it, acting as a "connecting agent" that facilitates integration with their organization and local communities—a persistent challenge for the nomadic worker [3]. Analysis of DN narratives during the pandemic [9] underscores the critical importance of supporting the management of work-life boundaries, a fundamental aspect of well-being that GAI can help balance, preventing flexibility from becoming overload. Indeed, AI-driven automation significantly improved DNs' work-life balance and ability to meet deadlines by streamlining tasks [17]. However, research also highlights a key dilemma: while efficiency increases, automation can inadvertently blur the lines between work and leisure, potentially increasing self-imposed pressure and making it harder for DNs to disconnect. This challenge underscores the perspective of recent studies, such as Nascimento et al. [23], which call for an essential balance between connecting and disconnecting to navigate the many facets of digital well-being.

Research corroborates these challenges, with studies on the r/digitalnomad community revealing that emotional well-being is a key concern. For example, Xiao and Lutz [24] found that DNs frequently experience loneliness, depression, and social isolation, identifying emotional needs as the second most discussed topic within the community. Their analysis of community sentiment further revealed a notable increase in negative emotions such as fear, loneliness, and anger in the post-COVID phase, while happiness decreased, highlighting a general emotional downward trend. In response to these pressing issues, GAI-powered applications could directly support emotional and mental well-being. Wellness chatbots, for instance, could offer a private space for DNs to express their feelings, analyze sentiment patterns over time, and provide proactive, context-aware suggestions like mindfulness techniques or recommendations for local wellness activities, thereby mitigating feelings of loneliness and depression. Additionally, understanding concepts like "work-life blending" [31], which describes the intentional integration of work and personal life, is crucial here, as GAI can either facilitate harmonious blending or exacerbate boundarylessness. GAI design must thus explicitly incorporate features that enable DNs to set and enforce clear boundaries, facilitating intentional disengagement from work and promoting time for rest, social activities, and exploration.

Finally, FOMO, driven by different facets such as the desire to explore everything (wanderlust FOMO), experience local culture (experience FOMO), and maintain social connections (social FOMO), significantly detracts from well-being [6]. By automating repetitive tasks and optimizing mobilisation work, GAI frees up time, allowing DNs to engage in self-care and socialization. GAI can also identify FOMO signs and suggest real-world actions (e.g., attending a local event, meeting DNs, disconnecting) to mitigate these feelings and transform triggers into concrete well-being opportunities [6]. This proactive, contextually relevant support, as emphasized in *Principle P2*, is vital for mitigating social isolation and mental exhaustion from constant adaptation and ephemeral communities [10].

- **Principle P6: Design for Cultural Sensitivity and Inclusivity**

GAI for DNs must recognize and respect the diverse cultural contexts in which they operate. This means going beyond linguistic translation to understand and adapt to local norms, social cues, and legal frameworks. Studies on DN culture and local social practices, such as [20], underscore the profound influence of local customs on daily life and interaction. Inclusivity requires ensuring GAI benefits are accessible to DNs with diverse abilities, backgrounds, and technological literacy. AI should avoid imposing a monolithic view of productivity or lifestyle, instead offering culturally appropriate suggestions for activities, communication styles, and work-life integration. This principle is crucial for fostering positive interactions between DNs, locals, and global teams, promoting mutual understanding and preventing algorithmic bias from inadvertently creating cultural friction or misunderstanding.

- **Principle P7: Design for Continuous Learning**

Digital nomadism is a journey of constant learning and adaptation. GAI systems should be designed not only to support but actively promote the DN's continuous learning, whether it's about new professional skills, local cultures, or lifestyle optimization. This learning must be dynamic and evolutionary, with AI adapting to changes in location, projects, and the DN's life stage to offer highly personalized resources and real-time feedback. AI can act as a mentor, content curator, or brainstorming partner, tailoring its support to individual learning needs. Research on wannabes, as highlighted by [11], underscores that design should address the needs of different stages of the journey, from initial planning and acquiring new competencies for transition to the continuous upskilling of experienced DNs. Furthermore, in the context of new digital economies and emerging productive arrangements like tokenomics, where information access and navigation are complex and reliant on human networks [15], GAI can personalize learning pathways and simplify comprehension, making the acquisition of new skills and adaptation to these scenarios more accessible.

6 Design Implications: Addressing Challenges and Building Solutions

The transition to a Nomad-AI paradigm, guided by the design principles presented in the preceding section, engenders significant implications for HCI designers and developers. This is not merely a matter of integrating AI into existing tools, but of fundamentally rethinking interactions for an inherently mobile user driven by autonomy. The delineated principles point to significant challenges, but equally reveal vast avenues for exploration.

6.1 Fundamental Design Dilemmas in Nomad-AI Interaction

The emergence of GAI in the DN context poses several critical dilemmas that designers must navigate. One central dilemma is the balance between nomadic autonomy and AI automation. While GAI can optimize tasks and reduce mobilization work, there's an inherent risk that excessive automation could erode the very motivation for flexibility and control that drives DNs [2]. This concern is corroborated by [14], who warns of the potential for job displacement or skill obsolescence for DNs, particularly in routine, easily automatable tasks. There's empirical evidence that while GAI significantly improves deadline adherence and work-life balance, it also raises considerable concerns among DNs about job displacement and the need for new skill development due to automation [17]. Designers must thus conceive systems that function as intelligent co-pilots, not autopilots, offering meaningful choices, allowing the DN to retain ultimate control over decisions, and facilitating occupational reinvention to mitigate the risk of displacement. Further emphasizing this tension, Dalisaymo & Patalay [17] highlight that automation, despite its efficiency benefits, can inadvertently lead to a state of constant connectivity, making it harder for DNs to disconnect and maintain clear boundaries between their professional and personal lives. This underscores the critical need for GAI design to intentionally support boundary management, rather than solely focusing on productivity gains.

A second design challenge lies in balancing AI-driven efficiency with the DN's holistic well-being. GAI's ability to optimize routines and workflows can, paradoxically, lead to an "always-on, always-productive" culture, exacerbating the risk of burnout and social isolation—challenges already prevalent in digital nomadism [10]. De Almeida et al. [9] highlight the impact on work-life boundaries, reinforcing the urgency of design that supports this balance. Furthermore, as mentioned before, FOMO (wanderlust, experience, and social FOMO) is a significant detractor of well-being [6]. Verma [14] emphasizes that DNs must find a balance between embracing automation and retaining personal touch and human connection for success in the future of work. Design must go beyond mere productivity, incorporating functionalities that promote breaks, suggest well-being activities adapted to the spatial context, and facilitate authentic social connections, combating the temptation to make AI the DN's sole "companion".

Another pressing dilemma revolves around ethical considerations and potential biases in GAI systems. As GAI influences decisions related to travel, work opportunities, and local interactions, any inherent biases in its training data or algorithms could inadvertently lead to discriminatory outcomes or reinforce existing inequalities. [14] warns that GAI might fail to capture cultural nuances, leading to inappropriate suggestions or interactions. Designers must actively work to identify and mitigate these biases, ensuring fairness and equitable access to the benefits of GAI for all DNs, regardless of their background or location. This challenge may be exacerbated by existing digital platform asymmetries, where GAI, if poorly designed, could amplify informational and power imbalances, making it harder for DNs to manage their personal knowledge ecologies effectively [8] or to contest algorithmic decisions. The goal should be to design GAI as a tool for empowerment, not control.

Finally, the trustworthiness and explainability of AI become even more critical in a nomadic context. DNs heavily rely on technology for navigation, security, and financial management in unfamiliar environments. The "black box" nature of GAI algorithms can undermine trust when AI decisions affect critical aspects like travel logistics or project delivery. Verma [14] raises pertinent concerns about technological dependence and the potential unreliability of some automated tools, which can lead to frustration and productivity loss. Furthermore, he highlights that automation may fail to capture cultural nuances or differences, impacting the accuracy and effectiveness of its responses, especially in interaction tools. Designers must innovate interfaces that make AI operations transparent and its recommendations explainable. This ensures the DN understands why a suggestion was made and can trust it, particularly in high-pressure or risky situations in a new country. It is vital that AI be culturally sensitive and that its limitations are communicated. This aligns with recent research by Schneider et al. [30], who argue that online platforms must prioritize a human-centered design approach that supports AI-mediated collaboration and algorithmic contestability, allowing users to interactively question, challenge, and provide feedback on algorithmic behavior.

6.2 Opportunities for Designers

Despite these challenges, the Nomad-AI interaction opens vast opportunities for HCI breakthroughs. The design principles proposed in the previous section pave the way for developing solutions that should be:

- **Contextually Adaptive:** Presents the opportunity to create AIs that detect context (time zone, language, infrastructure) and proactively adapt to it with minimal or no user intervention. This can include dynamically changing interfaces, AI assistants that adjust their tone and vocabulary to the local culture, or tools that optimize performance based on connection quality. This addresses Verma's [14] concern about automation's failure to capture cultural nuances.
- **Proactively Facilitating Meta-Work:** GAI can be the catalyst for transforming mobilisation work from a heavy burden into an almost imperceptible process. Designers can focus on creating intelligent "mobilisation agents" that anticipate needs, automate cross-border bureaucracies, and provide contextual support even before the DN perceives the need. This also includes minimizing "AI mobilization work"—the effort to manage the AI itself—through fluid and self-learning interfaces.
- **Enabling Community and Authentic Connection:** GAI offers the chance to overcome communication and location barriers to strengthen DNs' social networks. Designers can conceive platforms that use AI to suggest meet-ups with other DNs who share similar interests, translate conversations in real-time in multicultural environments, or even help create digital "rituals" that foster a sense of belonging amidst constant change, reinforcing the balance [14] points to between automation and human connection. GAI can also be designed to identify and mitigate the different facets of FOMO by proactively suggesting real-world activities and connections, transforming the anxiety of missing out into a stimulus for enriching experiences [6].

- **Simplifying Interaction with New Digital Economies:** With the emergence of complex productive arrangements like tokenomics and decentralized ecosystems (Web3), there's an opportunity for GAI to act as an abstraction layer. Designers can create AIs that simplify the interface and understanding of these new economies, helping DNs identify opportunities, manage digital assets, and navigate complex platforms. This would reduce the barrier to entry and the meta-work associated with exploring these new markets. DNs rely heavily on human networks to access these opportunities [15], suggesting that GAI can bridge this gap, democratizing access to new forms of compensation.
- **Promoting Equity and Inclusion in Nomad-AI Interaction:** Designers have a significant opportunity to ensure that GAI solutions serve the plurality of experiences and contexts of DNs. This implies designing AIs sensitive to different cultural backgrounds, levels of technological access, skill needs, and professional goals, as stated by *Principle P6*. Designers can develop tools that detect and mitigate algorithmic biases, offer personalization options that respect diversity, and ensure that AI access and benefits do not deepen inequalities but rather empower a broader range of individuals to thrive in digital nomadism [5].

6.3 Nomad-AI Interaction in Practice: From Principles to Tools

The seven proposed design principles serve as a strategic guide, assisting developers and researchers in creating GAI solutions that empower DNs beyond mere task optimization. The principles thus provide HCI researchers with a robust framework for both shaping research agendas and evaluating existing AI tools for their efficacy in nomadic contexts. A key question arises here: will we see the broad appropriation of general-purpose GAI tools by DNs, or the emergence of dedicated GAI solutions tailored specifically for this community? Both scenarios will likely unfold, and this duality is critical to understanding the future of Nomad-AI interaction.

On the one hand, the creative appropriation of existing GAI platforms is already a reality. DNs are actively using tools like *ChatGPT* and *Gemini* to streamline tasks, generate content, and manage logistics [5]. However, these tools, while powerful, are not explicitly designed to address the specific nuances of the nomadic lifestyle, such as managing work-life balance, combating social isolation, or navigating constant shifts in context and infrastructure, as highlighted by *Principles P2, P4* and *P5*. This often requires significant effort to prompt and adapt the tools for their unique needs, and the "symbiotic partnership" remains elusive.

On the other hand, the design principles outlined in this paper provide a roadmap for the intentional development of GAI tools built from the ground up for the nomadic community. Implementing these principles will yield a range of appropriate solutions for DNs, explicitly designed to offer proactive assistance and contextual awareness. A dedicated GAI assistant for DNs emerges as a promising central solution, leveraging its natural language understanding, contextual reasoning, and knowledge synthesis to offer personalized recommendations for logistics, work-life management, and career development. Beyond a singular LLM, multi-agent systems based on LLMs hold significant potential. In this configuration, the DN would interact with multiple AI partners, each with a specialized role and specific goals (e.g., logistics, well-being, career, productivity). By enabling collaboration among these agents, this framework can provide more refined, robust, and collaborative Nomad-AI support, mirroring human team dynamics and ensuring the agents' actions align to serve the DN's holistic aspirations better. Crucially, in both monolithic and multi-agent configurations, GAI must be designed to preserve the DN's agency by supporting decision-making, not dictating critical choices.

6.4 GAI's Double-Edged Sword for Digital Nomads: Emerging Challenges and AI-Driven Mitigations

Digital nomadism faces new challenges from the GAI revolution, which is redefining nomadic work and well-being. Paradoxically, while contributing to these shifts, GAI also offers key mitigation strategies.

One significant hurdle is GAI's disruptive impact on job markets. As GAI automates cognitive tasks, many DN roles may see reduced demand, necessitating a relentless pursuit of "future-proof" skills and continuous occupational reinvention. This can heighten career precarity. However, GAI can provide personalized learning pathways and real-time market insights (as stated by *Principle P7*), helping DNs identify new niches and acquire competencies efficiently. For instance, a dedicated GAI assistant could analyze a DN's skills against global trends to suggest bespoke training or practice scenarios.

Another critical challenge stems from threats to digital well-being and blurred work-life boundaries. In contrast, GAI can streamline mobilization work (*Principle P2*), its pervasive nature risks fostering an "always-on" culture, leading to digital fatigue and exacerbated FOMO [6]. Paradoxically, GAI can be designed as a proactive well-being agent: intelligently enforcing digital boundaries, recognizing burnout, and generating personalized prompts for breaks or social engagement to foster intentional disconnection.

Furthermore, GAI's proliferation introduces new complexities in information management and cognitive load. The sheer volume of AI-generated information and the need to verify its accuracy create new cognitive overhead for DNs managing complex personal knowledge ecologies [8]. This demands enhanced AI literacy and critical thinking. GAI can paradoxically act as a sophisticated "meta-work" manager, intelligently filtering information, summarizing datasets, and providing explainability (as proposed by *Principle P3*), transforming overload into actionable intelligence.

Finally, GAI's increasing reliance raises significant ethical and fairness concerns for a globally diverse nomadic population. Biases in GAI models can lead to inequitable recommendations or misinterpret cultural nuances (addressed by *Principle P6*). For DNs, a biased GAI could inadvertently create social friction. The paradox lies in GAI's capacity for ethical design and training on diverse datasets, acting as a "cultural bridge" that promotes understanding. Moreover, transparent GAI (addressed by *Principle P3*) empowers DNs to verify outputs, ensuring the technology genuinely empowers rather than disadvantages.

In essence, while the GAI revolution introduces new complexities for DNs, the intentional design of Nomad-AI interaction can transform these challenges into opportunities, establishing GAI as an indispensable ally in their evolving journey.

7   Conclusions, Limitations and Future Work

Driven by intrinsic motivations for flexibility and autonomy and the omnipresence of mobilisation work in their constantly transitioning existence, the rise of the DN establishes an intriguing scenario for HCI. As we have explored, the advent of GAI has the potential to redefine this landscape, transforming technology from a passive tool into an active partner. GAI not only could optimize tasks and facilitate adaptation to new spaces but also holds the potential to amplify the DN's productivity, creativity, and well-being, while fostering stronger social connections and enriching their overall nomadic experience. This paper argues that this convergence gives rise to a new Nomad-AI interaction paradigm, demanding specific design principles to empower DNs and preserve their autonomy, thereby safeguarding the core essence of the nomadic ideal. The proposed principles serve as a roadmap for designers seeking to build GAI systems that resonate with the complexities and aspirations of nomadic life.

The implications for design are multifaceted. Designers must carefully navigate between AI's promise of efficiency and the risk of eroding autonomy, striving for a balance that preserves the essence of nomadism. This involves creating interfaces that promote explainability and control, minimize AI mobilization work, and prioritize the DN's holistic well-being.

While providing a conceptual framework for Nomad-AI interaction, the present study is subject to a few limitations. Firstly, its theoretical and conceptual nature means the proposed design principles are based on literature synthesis rather than direct empirical validation (e.g., through user studies or prototyping). The insights derived from existing case studies (particularly analyses of online communities on Reddit) offer valuable perspectives but may not capture the full diversity of individual nomadic experiences, necessitating more granular research. Secondly, the rapidly evolving nature of GAI and the very nature of digital nomadism present a significant constraint. The design principles proposed here reflect the current state-of-the-art but are susceptible to becoming partially outdated as GAI advances and the dynamic DN lifestyle shifts due to global factors. Finally, the generalizability of the principles and research claims may be limited across all DN contexts. Distinct nomadic niches (e.g., varying professions or geographical preferences) possess unique needs and priorities, suggesting that these principles could be further nuanced or elaborated for specific subgroups.

The Nomad-AI paradigm presents diverse and fruitful avenues for HCI research, necessitating empirical studies—similar to those in [5, 6, 9, 11, 13, 15]—to investigate how DNs adopt and adapt GAI tools in their daily lives, and the long-term impacts on their productivity, mental health, social relationships, and sense of community. Online social networks like Reddit are well-suited for this investigation, as they enable the social and collaborative creation and sharing of narratives through social curation [19].

Finally, the collaboration between humans and AI in the nomadic context represents one of the most exciting frontiers of HCI. However, navigating this future isn't without its complexities. The rise of GAI introduces significant challenges like job market disruptions, heightened cognitive load, and threats to digital well-being. This creates a fundamental paradox: the very GAI designed to empower DNs could inadvertently undermine the freedom and well-being central to their lifestyle. The implications of this paradox call for a proactive and ethically informed approach to Nomad-AI interaction, lest these challenges compromise the core essence of the nomadic ideal. In the struggle to overcome this critical dilemma, what's at stake is the very future of digital nomadism.

References

1. Hannonen, M.A.: In search of a digital nomad: defining the phenomenon. Inf. Technol. Tourism **22**, 335–353 (2020)
2. de Carvalho, A.F.P., Ciolfi, L., Gray, B.: Detailing a spectrum of motivational forces shaping nomadic practices. In: Proceedings of the ACM on Human-Computer Interaction, vol. 4, no. CSCW1, Article 34 (2020)
3. Su, N.M., Mark, G.: Designing for nomadic work. In: Proceedings of the 7th ACM Conference on Designing Interactive Systems, pp. 305–314 (2008)
4. Correia, A., et al.: Designing for hybrid intelligence: a taxonomy and survey of crowd-machine interaction. Appl. Sci. **13**(4), 2198 (2023)
5. de Almeida, M.A., Correia, A., Barbosa, C.E., de Souza, J.M., Schneider, D.: AI and digital nomads: glimpsing the future human-computer interaction. In: International Conference on Computer-Human Interaction Research and Applications, pp. 198–211. Springer, Cham (2024)
6. de Almeida, M.A., et al.: FOMO as a trigger to embrace the digital nomad lifestyle. In: 2025 IEEE 28th International Conference on Computer Supported Cooperative Work in Design (CSCWD). IEEE (2025)
7. Perry, M.: Enabling nomadic work: developing the concept of 'Mobilisation Work'. In: ECSCW 2007 workshop: Beyond mobility: Studying nomadic work, Limerick, Ireland (2007)
8. De Almeida, M.A., De Souza, J.M., Correia, A., Schneider, D.: Exploring personal knowledge ecologies: dealing with digital platform asymmetries. In: 2024 27th International Conference on Computer Supported Cooperative Work in Design (CSCWD), pp. 1417–1423. IEEE (2024)
9. De Almeida, M.A., Correia, A., De Souza, J.M., Schneider, D.: Digital nomads during the COVID-19 pandemic: evidence from narratives on Reddit discussions. In: 2022 IEEE 25th International Conference on Computer Supported Cooperative Work in Design (CSCWD), pp. 1510–1516. IEEE (2022)
10. Nash, C., Jarrahi, M.H., Sutherland, W.: Nomadic work and location independence: the role of space in shaping the work of digital nomads. Hum. Behav. Emerg. Technol. **3**(2), 271–282 (2021)
11. De Almeida, M.A., De Souza, J.M., Correia, A., Schneider, D.: The role of wannabes in the digital nomad ecosystem in times of pandemic. In: 2022 IEEE International Conference on Systems, Man, and Cybernetics (SMC), pp. 3354–3359 (2022)
12. Cook, D.: What is a digital nomad? Definition and taxonomy in the era of mainstream remote work. World Leisure J. **65**(2), 256–275 (2023)
13. De Almeida, M.A., De Souza, J.M., Correia, A., Schneider, D.: Post-Covid-19 digital nomadism: Beyond work from (almost) anywhere. In: 2023 IEEE International Conference on Systems, Man, and Cybernetics (SMC), pp. 4605–4611. IEEE (2023)
14. Verma, A.: The future of work for digital nomads: the benefits and risks of automation. Int. J. Res. Bus. Soc. Sci. (IJRBS) **12**(4), 162–167 (2023)
15. de Almeida, M.A., Correia, A., de Souza, J.M., Schneider, D.: Mapping tokenomics arrangements to expand the digital nomad ecosystem. In: 2023 26th International Conference on Computer Supported Cooperative Work in Design (CSCWD), pp. 167–174. IEEE (2023)
16. de Almeida, M.A., Correia, A., Schneider, D., de Souza, J.M.: COVID-19 as opportunity to test digital nomad lifestyle. In: 2021 IEEE 24th International Conference on Computer Supported Cooperative Work in Design (CSCWD), pp. 1209–1214 (2021)

17. Dalisaymo, L.M., Patalay, M.M.: Artificial intelligence impact on digital nomad work life balance: the role of automation. In: 2024 2nd International Conference on Computing and Data Analytics (ICCDA), pp. 1–6. IEEE (2024)
18. Marinos, C.: Visualising proximity using generative artificial intelligence: the case of digital nomads in Bali, Indonesia. HAL (2025)
19. Schneider, D., de Souza, J.: Engaging citizens with news stories through social curation: a design research project. In: Proceedings of the 14th Brazilian Symposium on Human Factors in Computing Systems, pp. 1–10 (2015)
20. Sun, Y., Zhou, C.: A study of digital nomad culture and local social practices–based on fieldwork research in a certain area of southwest China. In: China National Conference on Big Data and Social Computing, pp. 301–308. Springer, Singapore (2024)
21. Ilyina, I.A., Teor, T.R., Kulibanova, V.V.: Factors increasing place attractiveness for residential mobility of digital nomads. In: 2025 Communication Strategies in Digital Society Seminar (ComSDS), pp. 114–118. IEEE (2025)
22. Methorst, J.J., Johnston, L., Collins, F.L.: Digital nomads and coworking spaces' infrastructures: disruptions and repairs of place, bodies and labour during pandemic times. Appl. Mobilities 1–22 (2025)
23. Nascimento, M., Motta, C., Correia, A., Schneider, D.: Switching off to switch on: an ontological inquiry into the many facets of digital well-being. In: International Conference on Human-Computer Interaction, pp. 153–162. Springer, Cham (2024)
24. Xiao, Y., Lutz, C.: Wayfarers in cyberspace: a temporal investigation of digital nomads based on liquid modernity theory. J. Travel Res. **64**(4), 966–984 (2025)
25. Orel, M.: Wanderlust workforce: a journey into understanding digital nomadism. World Leisure J. **65**(2), 143–149 (2023)
26. Mohseni, H., de Almeida, M.A., Schneider, D., Correia, A.: 'Do I Belong Here, There, or Elsewhere?': the materiality and intangible benefits of technology in digital nomads' place-belongingness. In: 2024 8th International Symposium on Multidisciplinary Studies and Innovative Technologies (ISMSIT), pp. 1–4. IEEE (2024)
27. Chevtaeva, E., Denizci-Guillet, B.: Digital nomads' lifestyles and coworkation. J. Destin. Mark. Manag. **21**, 100633 (2021)
28. Reichenberger, I.: Digital nomads–a quest for holistic freedom in work and leisure. Ann. Leisure Res. **21**(3), 364–380 (2018)
29. Jiwasiddi, A., Schlagwein, D., Cahalane, M., Cecez-Kecmanovic, D., Leong, C., Ractham, P.: Digital nomadism as a new part of the visitor economy: the case of the "digital nomad capital" Chiang Mai, Thailand. Inf. Syst. J. **34**(5), 1493–1535 (2024)
30. Schneider, D., Chaves, R., Pimentel, A.P., de Almeida, M.A., De Souza, J.M., Correia, A.: AI-mediated collaborative crowdsourcing for social news curation: the case of acropolis. In: Proceedings of the 2025 ACM International Conference on Interactive Media Experiences, pp. 395–401. ACM (2025)
31. Marx, J., Fischer-Preßler, D., Schlagwein, D.: Work-Life Blending with Data Analytics: Evidence from a Study of Digital Nomads (2025)

An Architecture for Predictive Path Planning on Simulated Robotics

Lucio Agostinho Rocha$^{(\boxtimes)}$ Ⓜ

Federal University of Technology, Campus Apucarana, Apucarana, Brazil
`luciorocha@utfpr.edu.br`

Abstract. This paper proposes an architecture for predictive path planning applied to transportation problems for simulated robotics. The aim is to evaluate scenarios where Machine Learning (ML) strategies contribute to optimizing the path planning in environments modeled as multi-layered flat networks and formulated as Linear Programming (LP) problems. This proposal reduces the computational time to obtain large logical trajectories in navigation maps queried by mobile robots to reach targets at minimum cost. In the proposed architecture a dataset with feasible solutions is produced to represent the optimization of link costs, and the ML strategies use this dataset to discover alternative paths on demand in reduced time. In mobile robotics, multi-layer networks for path planning have importance for complex dynamic systems, and the modeling is generally done with neural networks and deep reinforcement learning. In this paper, the focus is on the evaluation of ML algorithms for the discovery of routes for simulated robotics with the extraction of features from logical links. The statistical results reveal a gain in performance in predicting the optimum solution for a large supervised dataset.

Keywords: Multi-agent System · Machine Learning · Operating Research

1 Introduction

In this paper, the problem that has been addressed is an evaluation of Machine Learning (ML) algorithms for predictive path planning. This evaluation is done through an architecture for predictive path planning applied to transportation problems for simulated robotics. The aim is to evaluate scenarios where ML strategies contribute to optimizing the path planning in environments modeled as multi-layered flat networks and formulated as Linear Programming (LP) problems. In this proposal, the modeling represents paths that robots query to navigate at minimum cost. This navigation involves the discovery of many alternative paths to reach the target destination. But the computational cost to solve large transportation models is highly dependent of the number of alternative paths. So, the supervised learning with structured data becomes useful to reduce the computational time to discover on-demand paths when compared with other similar approaches.

In mobile robotics, multi-layer networks for path planning are important for modeling complex dynamic systems, and this modeling is generally done with neural networks [4–7]. Wu et al. [11] consider a multi-layer approach with deep reinforcement

J. F. Krems et al. (Eds.): CHIRA 2025, CCIS 2836, pp. 369–384, 2026.
https://doi.org/10.1007/978-3-032-16454-4_21

learning for the discovery of routes in vehicular networks. A similar approach is covered by Liu et al. [8] for autonomous vehicles with the extraction of trajectory features and reinforcement learning-based control with multi-layer dense networks. In all these proposals, an NP-hard problem is found when the number of paths is high and there are no patterns in the network links, difficulting to compute a large network on demand. So, heuristics and auxiliary divide-and-conquer optimization techniques (e.g., click in graphs, nearest neighbors, job-shop scheduling, and others) are considered. Until recently, few works dealt with multi-layered networks for path planning prediction with ML algorithms. The multi-layered modeling also has important applications in network computing [1,2].

Multi-layered networks are also useful for the discovery of routes in geolocalization. For example, the OpenStreetMap project offers an open global map with geographical data supported by volunteers. However, the computing of routes is done by other external tools. One of the well-known solutions is the Open Source Routing Machine (OSRM) project [9]. OSRM is a C++ routing engine to run over OpenStreetMap data. It offers mainly an HTTP server and an API to request routes over the Internet. A typical deployment involves the setup of a frontend to visualize the discovery routes, and a backend to calculate the routes. The computation of routes is done with the geographical data from OpenStreetMap maps. OSRM uses the Multi-Level Dijkstra (MLD) algorithm to compute many alternative routes. But it is not practical to evaluate environments in reduced scale where routes may change on demand, especially when mobile robots navigate in indoor environments.

In this sense, the new knowledge contributed by this work is a methodology to formulate multi-layered flat networks for path planning prediction, and also a systematic evaluation of ML algorithms through a set of interrelated metrics. The statistical results reveal a gain in performance in predicting the optimum solution for a large supervised dataset.

The remains of this paper is organized as follows. Section 2 relates the methodology; Sect. 3 describes the evaluation, analysis and results; Sect. 4 does the discussion of the results; finally, Sect. 5 cover the final considerations.

2   Methodology

The path planning is done by the mobile robots when it begins its navigation in a supply node and queries the minimum cost link to reach a destination node in a layer, as shown in the Fig. 1.

In order to standardize this path planning, the methodology is directed to automatically generate and solve transportation problems modeled as multi-layered flat networks. The motivation is to obtain a set of random feasible solutions for ML algorithms to train and to predict the optimum solution of new models submitted to the system. These models are formulated in CPLEX LP format to be solved with GNU Linear Programming Kit. A model contains the objective function that minimizes the link capacities, the link restrictions of each layer, and its variables. The solution found is translated into an array to compose one row of the dataset, as shown in the Fig. 2.

So, each array represents the solution of the LP model with the values of the minimization of the link capacities between the sources and their destinations in a specific

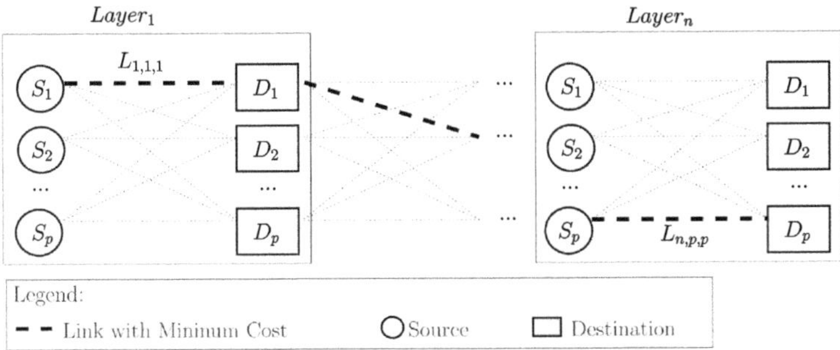

Fig. 1. Overview of the Multi-Layered Flat Network.

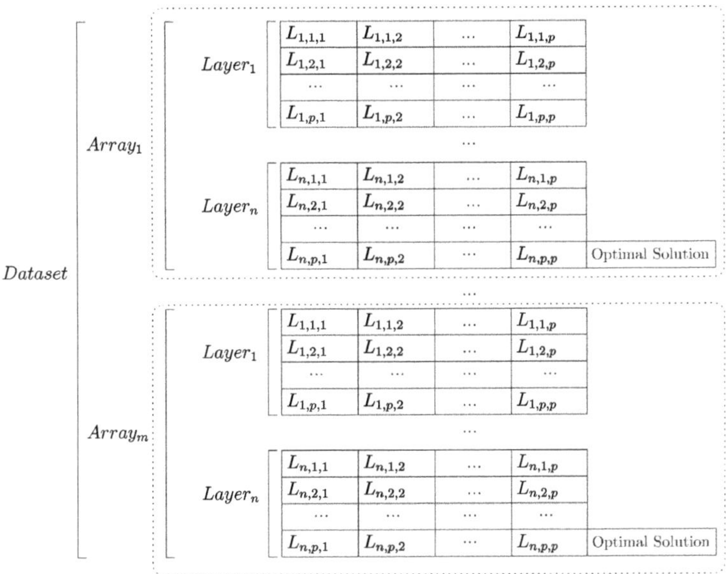

Fig. 2. Arrays in the Dataset.

layer, and the last cell is the value of the objective function found. The dataset of arrays is used to train and predict the optimum solution of new LP models with ML algorithms.

The architecture to accomplish this methodology has two main components, as shown in the Fig. 3: a) Hard Computing Component (HCC): solves LP models and produces the dataset; b) Soft Computing Component (SCC): responsible for predicting the optimum solution of new LP models submitted to the system. The description of them is as follows.

2.1 Hard Computing Component (HCC)

The HCC produces a set of feasible transportation models with a random distribution of link costs. The motivation is to produce a large data set of feasible solutions to train

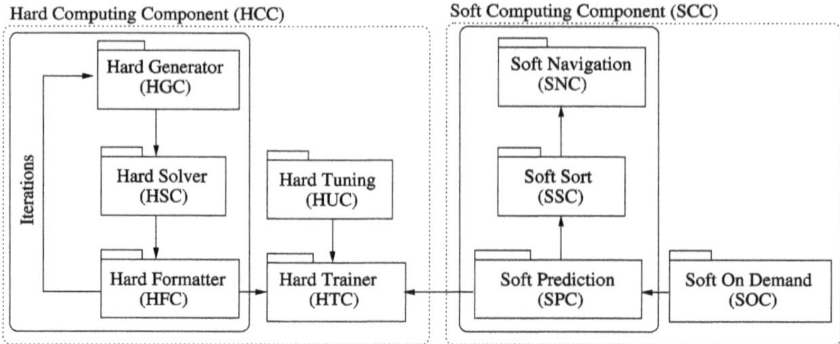

Fig. 3. UML Architecture for Predictive Transportation.

ML algorithms and to predict the optimum solution of new LP transportation models. This task is time consuming because it generates and solves, in each iteration, an LP model with a large set of variables. This component is composed of the following:

1. Hard Generator Component (HGC): on each iteration, one LP model is produced with random link capacities. The formulation presented in the next section guarantees that all LP models produced are feasible.
2. Hard Solver Component (HSC): this component solves the LP model produced by the latter component.
3. Hard Formatter Component (HFC): in this component, the minimum link costs and the result of the objective function are translated and appended in the dataset, as shown in the Fig. 2. Each line of the dataset represents a feasible solution of a transportation model.
4. Hard Tuning Component (HUC): this component performs ML tuning to adjust parameters according to the given dataset.
5. Hard Trainer Component (HTC): each ML algorithm trains the same dataset using the link costs as multiple features. After this training, the ML algorithm is ready to predict the objective function value of new LP models.

2.2 Soft Computing Component (SCC)

The SCC runs multiple times and reduces the computing time to predict the objective function value. This component is composed of the following:

1. Soft On Demand Component (SOC): it is common that the navigation maps change the trajectories according to the characteristics of the environment. So, this model produces new LP models that represent these random changes in the link costs. However, the solution of the objective function is predicted by the ML algorithm in the next step.
2. Soft Prediction Component (SPC): this component receives the LP model from the previous step and does the prediction of the objective function value using the trained dataset. The motivation is to reduce the computing time to predict the objective function value of new LP models.

3. Soft Sort Component (SSC): this component sorts the solutions according to the prediction of objective function values from the latter step.
4. Soft Navigation Component (SNC): this step receives the best prediction from the latter step and translates the array data to navigation data for the mobile robot.

2.3 Formulation of the Multi-Layered Transportation Model

The modeling defines a dataset composed of m arrays. Each array has the same number of n layers, as presented in the Fig. 2. The array is generated after the transportation model be solved by the LP solver. This array represents a feasible solution of a transportation model, and it is composed of the amount of resources to transport in each link (e.g., link capacities), and the optimum solution found for the respective model.

Each layer has the same number p of supply nodes and p of demand nodes. The p sources of supply $S_1, S_2, ..., S_p$ have MS units of supply to be transported to p destinations $D_1, D_2, ..., D_p$ that have MD units of demand. The links have unitary costs to exchange data, and differ by their capacities. The motivation is to potentially explore solutions that could reduce the energy consumption by choosing low-capacity links with minimum cost for a mobile robot to navigate over the layers.

The indexes in links define the layer, the source, and the destination, respectively. For example, $L_{a,b,c}$ is the number of resources to transport in the $Layer_a$ between the source S_b to the destination D_c. So, the transportation problem minimizes the objective function, as shown in Eq. 1.

$$\text{Minimize } Z = \sum_{a=1}^{n} \sum_{b=1}^{p} \sum_{c=1}^{p} L_{a,b,c} \tag{1}$$

This objective function is subject to the supply constraints of the Eq. 2, and the demand constraints of the Eq. 3. Also, $L_{a,b,c} \geq 0$ for all sources b and destinations c, respectively.

$$\sum_{b=1}^{p} L_{a,b,c} = MS, \ c = 1, 2, ..., p \tag{2}$$

$$\sum_{c=1}^{p} L_{a,b,c} = MD, \ b = 1, 2, ..., p \tag{3}$$

The Eq. 4 guarantees feasible solutions for a model with n layers. The interpretation is that the same amount of supply provided by sources is consumed by demand nodes in each layer.

$$\sum_{a=1}^{n} Layer_a \times \left(\sum_{b=1}^{p} MS - \sum_{c=1}^{p} MD \right) = 0 \tag{4}$$

The computation of supply and demand on each layer produces feasible solutions that are stored in the arrays of the dataset. This step of the research focused on evaluating how accurate the chosen ML algorithms are in predicting these same values using the same dataset. The motivation is to evaluate how multi-layered modeling influences the mechanisms of prediction of the chosen ML algorithms.

A common ML algorithm considers a set of samples and tries to perform predictions on unknown data. These samples bring features from the problem. In supervised learning, the data are labelled and presented in columns of a dataset. If the desired output has continuous values, then the supervised learning is called regression. A regression makes predictions from the data features of the problem. ML algorithms use properties from a dataset and test these properties against other datasets. These data are split into two datasets: a training set to learn from its properties, and a testing set to test the learned properties.

However, it is not feasible to predict the optimum solution with a single link capacity. Then, the prediction with ML algorithms uses all link capacities in the array as features, and the optimum solution (i.e., the fitness) is the target for the prediction. Firstly, it is defined x_i as the ith feature for fitness prediction given by the ith array, as presented in the Eq. 5.

$$x_i = \sum_{a=1}^{n} \sum_{b=1}^{p} \sum_{c=1}^{p} L_{a,b,c} + fitness_i \tag{5}$$

Then, it is performed a multiple linear regression [3] formally defined in the Eq. 6. In this equation, y is the predicted fitness, the term α and the coefficient β are parameters learned by the ML algorithm, and x_i is known as explanatory variable. In our case, x_i are the features given by the link capacities in the arrays of the dataset.

$$y = \alpha + \sum_{i=1}^{n} \beta_i x_i \tag{6}$$

3   Evaluation and Results

In this proposal, the implementation of the architecture is done in Java language using the GNU Linear Programming Kit. The training and prediction are implemented in the Python language using ML algorithms of the Scikit-learn libraries. These programs run on a host Intel(R) Core(TM) i7-8550U CPU @ 1.80 GHz.

The evaluations were obtained with 100 (one hundred) samples of LP models, and each LP model is automatically generated with 2k (two thousands), 8k, and 18k variables, respectively. These number of variables are obtained by increasing the number of supply nodes and demand nodes on each layer. The LP model with 2k variables has 100 links and 20 layers; the LP model with 8k variables has 400 links and 20 layers; and the LP model with 18k variables has 900 links and 20 layers. The number of layers is arbitrarily defined to give a non-trivial complexity to the solver. An evaluation with a different number of layers (fewer and greater) is a source for future work.

The Table 1 shows the list of ML algorithms chosen. These algorithms were selected because have reduced running time to perform predictions, and this feature is useful for evaluations of models on-demand. The samples were split in the proportion of 80% for training and 20% for test. The fitness prediction of these algorithms is compared with the optimum solution given by the GNU LP Solver (GLP). The Table 2 present the tuning settings for each ML algorithm.

Table 1. List of Acronymous.

Acronymous	Meaning
ANN	Artificial Neural Network
DTR	Decision Tree Regressor
GBR	Gradient Boosting Regressor
GLP	GNU LP Solver
GPR	Gaussian Process Regressor
KRR	Kernel Ridge Regressor
NNC	Nearest Neighbors Centroid
LIR	Linear Regressor
LOR	Logistic Regressor
GNB	Gaussian Naive Bayes
PLS	Partial Least Square
RFR	Random Forest Regressor
SGD	Stochastic Gradient Descent
SVM	Stochastic Vector Machine

3.1 Average Time Prediction

The Average Time Prediction (ATP) is a measure of time-consuming to obtain the fitness prediction. The Fig. 4 shows the ATP obtained for each ML algorithm chosen.

Table 2. ML Algorithms Settings.

ML Algorithm	Classifier	Parameters
ANN	MLPClassifier	solver = 'lbfgs', alpha = 1e−5, random_state = 1
DTR	DecisionTreeRegressor	random_state = 42
GBR	GradientBoostingRegressor	default
GPR	GaussianProcessRegressor	kernel = 1.0 * ExpSineSquared(1.0, 5.0, periodicity_bounds = (1e−2, 1e1)) + WhiteKernel(1e−1), alpha = 10.0
KRR	KernelRidge	alpha = 1.0
NNC	NearestCentroid	default
LIR	LinearRegression	default
LOR	LogisticRegression	default
GNB	GaussianNB	default
PLS	PLSRegression	default
RFR	RandomForestRegressor	random_state = 42
SGD	SGDClassifier	default
SVM	SVM	default

When compared to GLP, the results indicate a considerable gain in performance in obtaining the fitness prediction for almost all ML algorithms. When compared with GLP, the algorithms LOR, and SGD have the lowest ATP results for LP models with 18k variables. As a conclusion for this evaluation, ATP metrics indicate that for most of the ML algorithms chosen, the gain in performance is considerable when the dataset is previously trained.

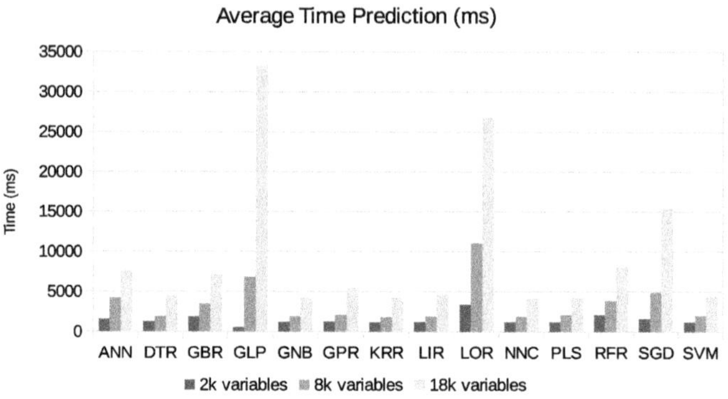

Fig. 4. Average Time Prediction (ms).

3.2 Average RMSE

The RMSE is a metric to measure the differences between the output expected and the output predicted, as shown in Eq. 7. In this equation, x_e is the expected value and x_o is the expected output.

$$RMSE = \sqrt{(x_e - x_o)^2} \tag{7}$$

The Fig. 5 shows the average RMSE obtained with 100 samples for each ML algorithm. The samples were generated with 2k, 8k, and 18k variables in each LP Model. The best results were obtained with LIR and KRR, probably due these algorithms have a prediction mechanism similar at the GLP solver. As a conclusion for this evaluation, for all algorithms, the increasing of the number of variables increases the average RMSE.

3.3 Precision

The precision metric verifies how often the classifier predicts the positive results, as shown in the Eq. 8.

$$Precision = \frac{TP}{TP + FP} \tag{8}$$

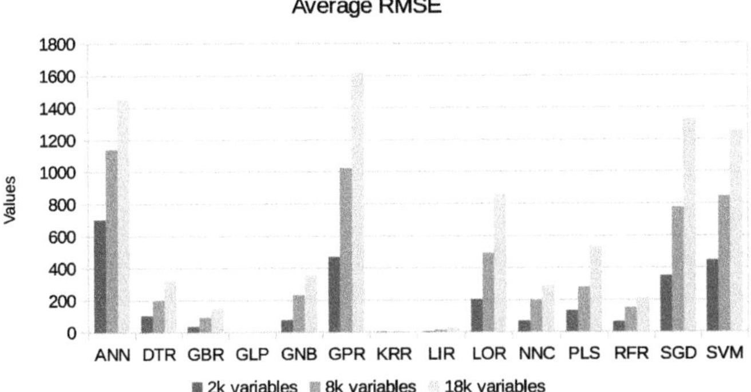

Fig. 5. Average RMSE.

Table 3. Restrictions to Measure Precision and Recall.

Restrictions	R_1	R_2	R_3	R_4
RMSE	$<\delta_1$	$[\delta_1, \delta_2)$	$[\delta_2, \delta_3)$	$\geq\delta_3$

$$TP = \begin{cases} 1, & \text{if } R_1 \\ 0, & \text{otherwise} \end{cases} \tag{9}$$

$$FP = \begin{cases} 1, & \text{if } R_2 \\ 0, & \text{otherwise} \end{cases} \tag{10}$$

$$FN = \begin{cases} 1, & \text{if } R_3 \\ 0, & \text{otherwise} \end{cases} \tag{11}$$

$$TN = \begin{cases} 1, & \text{if } R_4 \\ 0, & \text{otherwise} \end{cases} \tag{12}$$

In this classification, each sample is a predicted optimum value obtained by an ML algorithm. So, the samples are classified in True Positive (TP), False Positive (FP), False Negative (FN) and True Negative (TN), according to the Eqs. 9, 10, 11 and 12, respectively. This classification also respects the rules of the Table 3. In this table, δ_1, δ_2 and δ_3 are constants to classify the samples in ranges of their $RMSE$. These latter are normalized to obtain values between 0 and 1 for all samples. In the classification, the constants were defined in $\delta_1 = 0.1, \delta_2 = 0.25$, and $\delta_3 = 0.5$. These samples are classified in only one of four mutually exclusive labels, as follows:

1. True Positive (TP): a sample is classified as TP if R_1 is satisfied, i.e., if the $RMSE$ obtained in regression is lower than δ_1. Then, TP is set to 1, and 0 otherwise;
2. False Positive (FP): a sample is classified as FP if R_2 is satisfied, i.e., if the $RMSE$ is between δ_1 and δ_2. Then, FP is set to 1, and 0 otherwise;

3. False Negative (FN): a sample is classified as FN if R_3 is satisfied, i.e., if the $RMSE$ obtained in regression is between δ_2 and δ_3. Then, FN is set to 1, and 0 otherwise;
4. True Negative (TN): a sample is classified as TN if R_4 is satisfied, i.e., if the $RMSE$ obtained in regression is greater than or equal δ_3. Then, TN is set to 1, and 0 otherwise.

The results of precision indicate that ANN, GNB, GPR, LOR, SGD, and SVM obtained the lowest precision, with values below 0.5 units in this normalized scale. As a conclusion for this metric, and considering a higher precision above of 0.8 units in this normalized scale, the most of ML algorithms fail, i.e., the ATP is not followed by the precision metrics. On the other hand, these results indicate that the precision increases almost linearly for all algorithms when the number of variables increases. This is an indication that the number of features influences the precision metrics (Fig. 6).

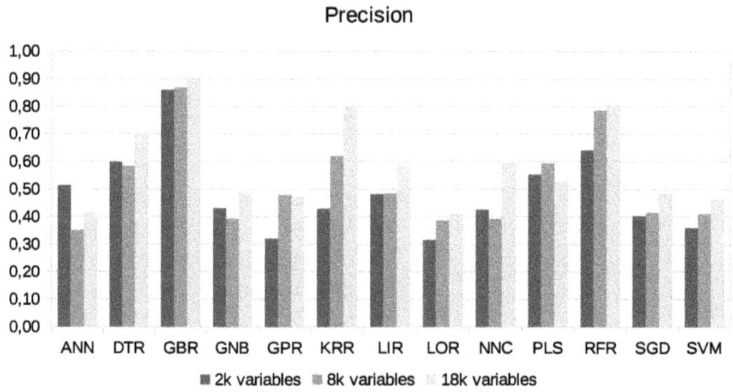

Fig. 6. Precision.

3.4 Recall

The recall metric is a sensitivity analysis that evaluates of rate of TP, as shown in the Eq. 13. The result of this metric indicates the rate of relevant samples.

$$Recall = \frac{TP}{TP + FN} \tag{13}$$

The Fig. 7 reveals that ANN, GNB, GPR, LOR, SGD, and SVM have the lowest recall results for samples of LP models with 2k, 8k, and 18k variables. As a conclusion, and considering a higher recall above of 0.8 units in this normalized scale, the most of ML algorithms fail, similarly at the previous result with precision metrics. But these results indicate that the recall increases almost linearly for all algorithms when the number of variables in the samples increases. This is an indication that the number of features influences the recall metrics.

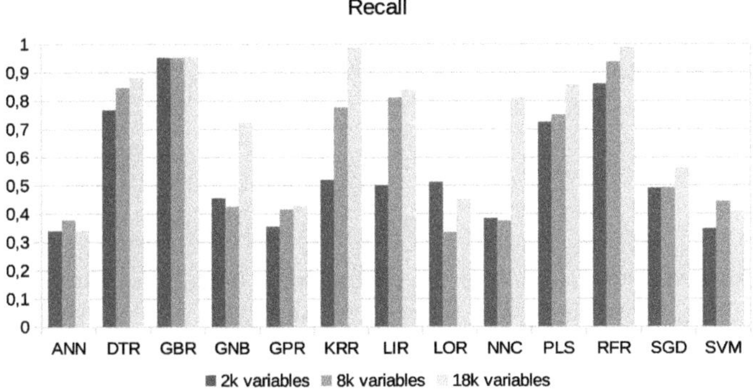

Fig. 7. Recall.

3.5 F-Score

The F-Score metric is a test of accuracy that uses the weighted harmonic mean of the precision and recall metrics. The Eq. 14 shows how this metric is obtained.

$$\text{F-Score} = 2 \times \frac{(Precision \times Recall)}{(Precision + Recall)} \tag{14}$$

The Fig. 8 shows that ANN, GNB, GPR, LOR, SGD, and SVM have the lowest F-Score results for samples of LP models with 2k, 8k, and 18k variables. As a conclusion for this metric, and considering a higher F-score above of 0.8 units in this normalized scale, the most of ML algorithms fail, similarly at the previous result with precision metrics. But these results indicate that the F-score increases almost linearly for all algorithms when the number of variables in the samples increases. This is an indication that the number of features influences the F-score metrics.

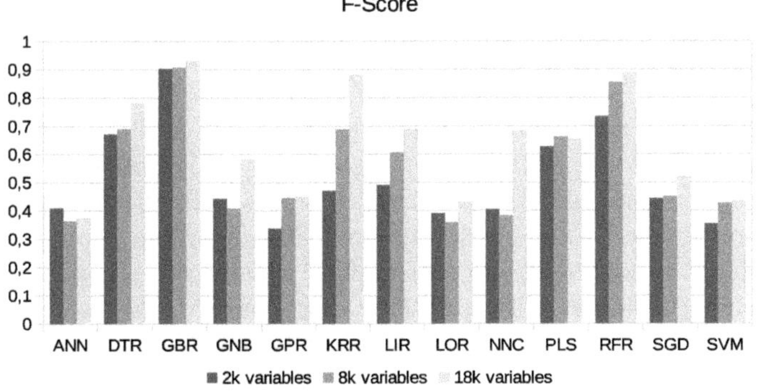

Fig. 8. F-Score.

3.6 Accuracy

The accuracy is a metric that identifies the best algorithms considering as correct predictions the predictions with TP and TN in the samples. The Eq. 15 shows how this metric is calculated.

$$Accuracy = \frac{TP + TN}{TP + FP + TN + FN} \tag{15}$$

The Fig. 9 shows the accuracy of the chosen ML algorithms. The results show that ANN, GNB, GPR, LOR, SGD, and SVM have the lowest results. As a conclusion for this metric, and considering a higher accuracy above of 0.8 units in this normalized scale, the most of ML algorithms fail, similarly at the previous results. But these results indicate that the accuracy increases almost linearly for all algorithms when the number of variables in the samples increases. This is an indication that the number of features influences the accuracy metrics.

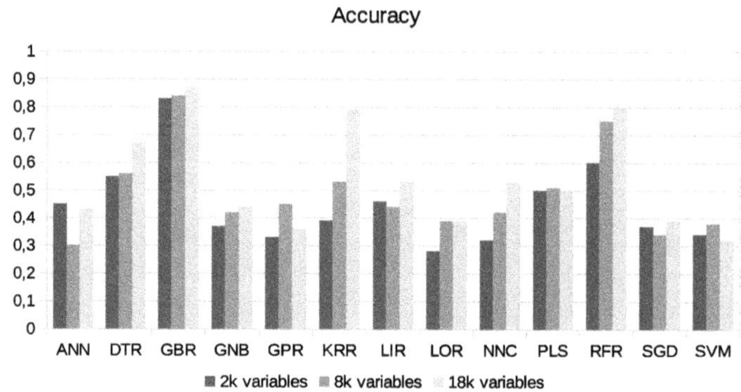

Fig. 9. Accuracy.

4 Discussion of the Results

The results indicate that utilizing a good base dataset with feasible solutions is important for better predictions. Additionally, the strategy of pre-train the ML algorithms before receiving on demand LP models reduces significantly the ATP. However, it is a difficult task obtain the best results for a specific ML algorithm in all the chosen metrics. Due to this, it is not possible to declare that a specific ML algorithm is better than others, considering only an individual metric. For a further analysis, it is necessary to consider the group of metrics. Also, the results can vary with adjustments for better tuning of the many parameters of each ML algorithm, and this latter is a source for future works. In the following, it is done a discussion of the worst case and the best case for predict the fitness for LP models with 18k variables. In this analysis, the metrics of precision, recall, and f-score are considered as intermediary metrics, and the accuracy is the target metric to perform the most accurate predictions in the considered scenarios.

1. Worst case: the ATP metric indicates that when the ANN, GNB, GPR, and SVM are compared with GLP, the gain of performance is higher than 70% when the number of variables in the LP model reaches 18k variables. However, the average RMSE is around 1k units, and this latter indicates imprecision in obtaining the fitness. Indeed, this information is confirmed in the metrics of precision, recall, and f-score, with values around 40% in the normalized scale for the same 18k variables. As a consequence, the accuracy results are also around 40% approximately.

Table 4. Prediction Evaluations of ML algorithms (Note: GLP is given for comparison).

Algorithm	Metrics	2k variables	8k variables	18k variables
ANN	ATP	1583.80	4232.73	7621.56
	Average RMSE	701.60	1139.60	1447.40
	Precision	0.51	0.35	0.41
	Recall	0.33	0.37	0.34
	F-score	0.40	0.36	0.37
	Accuracy	0.45	0.30	0.43
DTR	ATP	1260.93	1940.17	4509.83
	Average RMSE	101.6	200.00	323.20
	Precision	0.60	0.58	0.70
	Recall	0.76	0.84	0.88
	F-score	0.67	0.69	0.78
	Accuracy	0.55	0.56	0.67
GBR	ATP	1858.79	3461.97	7118.44
	Average RMSE	33.93	92.07	150.54
	Precision	0.86	0.86	0.91
	Recall	0.95	0.95	0.96
	F-score	0.90	0.90	0.93
	Accuracy	0.83	0.84	0.87
GLP	ATP	564.27	6799.68	33312.35
	Average RMSE	0.00	0.00	0.00
	Precision	1.00	1.00	1.00
	Recall	1.00	1.00	1.00
	F-score	1.00	1.00	1.00
	Accuracy	1.00	1.00	1.00
GNB	ATP	1233.26	1913.81	4183.8
	Average RMSE	73.4	231.6	351.00
	Precision	0.43	0.39	0.49
	Recall	0.45	0.42	0.72
	F-score	0.44	0.40	0.58
	Accuracy	0.37	0.42	0.44

Table 5. Prediction Evaluations of ML algorithms.

Algorithm	Metrics	2k variables	8k variables	18k variables
GPR	ATP	1247.28	2118.38	5447.23
	Average RMSE	469.46	1021.72	1613.33
	Precision	0.32	0.47	0.47
	Recall	0.35	0.41	0.43
	F-score	0.33	0.44	0.45
	Accuracy	0.33	0.45	0.36
KRR	ATP	1180.08	1857.25	4238.91
	Average RMSE	0.24	0.52	0.69
	Precision	0.43	0.47	0.47
	Recall	0.51	0.77	0.99
	F-score	0.46	0.68	0.88
	Accuracy	0.39	0.53	0.79
LIR	ATP	1222.95	1937.03	4680.09
	Average RMSE	2.92	10.98	22.74
	Precision	0.48	0.48	0.58
	Recall	0.50	0.81	0.84
	F-score	0.49	0.60	0.69
	Accuracy	0.46	0.44	0.53
LOR	ATP	3370.45	11074.41	26784.62
	Average RMSE	204.6	490.4	855.20
	Precision	0.32	0.47	0.47
	Recall	0.51	0.33	0.45
	F-score	0.38	0.35	0.43
	Accuracy	0.28	0.39	0.39
NNC	ATP	1221.70	1935.16	4136.41
	Average RMSE	69.60	199.00	287.00
	Precision	0.43	0.39	0.59
	Recall	0.38	0.37	0.81
	F-score	0.40	0.38	0.68
	Accuracy	0.32	0.42	0.53
PLS	ATP	1221.43	2110.00	4222.89
	Average RMSE	133.41	279.56	529.49
	Precision	0.55	0.59	0.53
	Recall	0.72	0.75	0.85
	F-score	0.62	0.66	0.65
	Accuracy	0.50	0.51	0.50
RFR	ATP	2110.81	3876.04	8058.56
	Average RMSE	63.70	151.90	210.95
	Precision	0.64	0.78	0.81
	Recall	0.85	0.93	0.99
	F-score	0.73	0.85	0.89
	Accuracy	0.60	0.75	0.80

Table 6. Prediction Evaluations of ML algorithms.

Algorithm	Metrics	2k variables	8k variables	18k variables
SGD	ATP	1635.44	4903.74	15315.08
	Average RMSE	350.40	774.60	1324.00
	Precision	0.40	0.41	0.49
	Recall	0.49	0.49	0.56
	F-score	0.44	0.45	0.52
	Accuracy	0.37	0.34	0.39
SVM	ATP	1217.38	2006.27	4443.55
	Average RMSE	444.66	843.91	1249.37
	Precision	0.36	0.41	0.46
	Recall	0.34	0.44	0.41
	F-score	0.35	0.42	0.43
	Accuracy	0.34	0.38	0.32

2. Better case: in this scenario, the ATP metric indicates that when the KRR, RFR, and GBR are compared with GLP, the gain of performance is higher than 70% when the number of variables in the LP model reaches 18k variables. Also, the average RMSE is below 1k units, and this latter indicates a good precision in obtaining the fitness. This information is confirmed in the metrics of precision, recall, and f-score, with values around 90% in the normalized scale for the same 18k variables. As a consequence, the accuracy metric also reveals results around 90% approximately. Similarly, KRR and RFR have low ATP and high accuracy around 80%.

The Tables 4, 5 and 6 summarize the obtained results.

5   Conclusion

In this paper is proposed an architecture for predictive path planning applied to transportation problems for simulated robotics. The methodology uses supervised strategies with ML algorithms to predict the minimum cost links. The research proposes an architecture with structured data to reduce the computational time to discover on-demand paths. The results indicate a gain in performance for most of the ML algorithms chosen. This proposal has applications in simulated robotics, and may potentially optimize the energy consumption for data warehouse transportation. This research also may be potentially useful for autonomous control of assistive mobile robots to optimize the navigation in indoor environments [10]. Future works include the evaluation of this architecture with open-source routing technologies in geographical maps.

References

1. The multi-layered network design problem: Eur. J. Oper. Res. **183**(1), 87–99 (2007). https://doi.org/10.1016/j.ejor.2006.07.046
2. Measuring similarity for clarifying layer difference in multiplex Ad Hoc duplex information networks. J. Inform. **14**(1), 100987 (2020). https://doi.org/10.1016/j.joi.2019.100987
3. Gavin, H.: Mastering Machine Learning with Scikit-learn (2014)
4. Hu, F., Kong, X., Song, Y., Zhao, Y., Chen, J.: DynMLP-GNN: a dynamic sampling graph neural network with multi-layer perceptron for knowledge graph reasoning. In: 2024 4th International Conference on Artificial Intelligence, Robotics, and Communication (ICAIRC), pp. 1016–1020 (2024). https://doi.org/10.1109/ICAIRC64177.2024.10900080
5. Hua, X., Liu, W.: Spatial-temporal network data-driven multi-layer traffic knowledge graph reconstruction for dynamic prediction. In: 2022 4th International Conference on Robotics and Computer Vision (ICRCV), pp. 20–24 (2022). https://doi.org/10.1109/ICRCV55858.2022.9953231
6. Kang, C.H., Kim, S.Y.: HNN-transformer integrated network for estimating robot position. in: 2023 23rd International Conference on Control, Automation and Systems (ICCAS), pp. 1278–1281 (2023). https://doi.org/10.23919/ICCAS59377.2023.10316909
7. Li, Z., Gao, Y., Wang, S., Liu, J.: Localizability of laser SLAM robot based on deep learning. In: 2019 IEEE International Conference on Robotics and Biomimetics (ROBIO), pp. 364–369 (2019). https://doi.org/10.1109/ROBIO49542.2019.8961679
8. Liu, J., et al.: Reinforcement learning-based high-speed path following control for autonomous vehicles. IEEE Trans. Veh. Technol. **73**(6), 7603–7615 (2024). https://doi.org/10.1109/TVT.2024.3352543
9. Luxen, D., Vetter, C.: Real-time routing with OpenStreetMap data. Association for Computing Machinery, New York (2011). https://doi.org/10.1145/2093973.2094062
10. Olivi, L.R., Neto, W.A., Costa, E.B., Dos Santos, M.F., Mercorelli, P., Cardozo, E.: Vector fields autonomous control for assistive mobile robots. In: 2024 25th International Carpathian Control Conference (ICCC), pp. 01–06 (2024). https://doi.org/10.1109/ICCC62069.2024.10569539
11. Wu, J., Ye, Z., He, L., Wang, T., Gao, L.: A multi-layer deep reinforcement learning approach for joint task offloading and scheduling in vehicular edge networks. In: IEEE International Conference on Communications, ICC 2023, pp. 3872–3877 (2023). https://doi.org/10.1109/ICC45041.2023.10279516

Leveraging Augmented Reality for Enhanced Smart and Connected Product Design: An Experimental Approach

Pedro Chacon Acuna[1]([✉]), Khansaa Alzein[1], Jean Camille[2], and Ruding Lou[1]

[1] Arts et Métiers Institute of Technology, Lispen, 71100 Chalon-Sur-Saône, France
`pedro_rafael.chacon_acuna@ensam.eu`
[2] Arts et Métiers Institute of Technology, LCPI, 75013 Paris, France

Abstract. The Internet of Things (IoT) is transforming all sectors by enabling traditional products to become smart and connected, capable of collecting, analyzing, and exchanging data. In parallel, Augmented Reality (AR) has emerged as a promising technology to support product design by offering immersive and interactive ways to visualize and iterate ideas. This paper presents an AR-based application developed to assist designers during the early ideation phase of IoT product conception. The system enables visualization of virtual objects and interaction with 14 sensor capability cards and 12 user experience elements. An experimental study involving 14 undergraduate engineering students was conducted to compare the proposed AR tool with a traditional 2D paper-based method, using two design cases: a connected bicycle and a smart window. Quantitative results from NASA-TLX and SUS questionnaires indicate that the AR method maintained or reduced perceived workload, particularly in terms of complexity and time pressure, while achieving usability scores comparable to or better than the traditional approach. These findings demonstrate the potential of AR as an effective and cognitively sustainable tool for enhancing creativity in early-stage product design.

Keywords: Smart and Connected Product design · Augmented Reality · Sensors · User experience

1 Introduction

The rapid advancement of the Internet of Things (IoT) has ushered in a new era where traditional products are being transformed into smart and connected products. These devices communicate with other devices, collect and analyze data, and provide enhanced functionalities, significantly improving user experiences across various sectors. The integration of IoT into everyday objects, from household appliances to industrial machinery, is revolutionizing how we interact with technology, making our lives more efficient, convenient, and informed.

In parallel, Augmented Reality (AR) has emerged as a revolutionary technology in product design. AR overlays digital content onto the physical world, providing designers with innovative ways to visualize, iterate, and collaborate on their projects [13]. By

J. F. Krems et al. (Eds.): CHIRA 2025, CCIS 2836, pp. 385–402, 2026.
https://doi.org/10.1007/978-3-032-16454-4_22

enabling real-time visualization and interaction with virtual prototypes, AR facilitates a more dynamic and flexible interactive design process. This is particularly valuable in the early stages of product development, where creativity and rapid iteration are crucial.

This paper explores the integration of AR in the creativity phase of smart and connected product design, proposing an innovative application to support designers in upgrading traditional products. By leveraging AR, designers can bypass the limitations of physical prototypes, allowing for more efficient and collaborative brainstorming and ideation.

This article is structured as follows: Sect. 2 provides a background on smart and connected product design, along with an overview of related work in AR applications. Section 3 details the proposed AR application, including its technical specifications and functionalities. Section 4 presents the developed prototype of the AR application. Section 5 describes the experimental setup, methodology, and results of testing the AR application prototype with participants. Finally, Sect. 6 discusses the findings, implications, and future directions for research and development in this area.

2   Background

2.1   Smart and Connected Product Design

Smart and connected products are typically equipped with sensors, actuators, and connectivity technologies. These components allow the products to collect data from their environment or from the product itself. Common sensors measure parameters such as temperature, motion, light, humidity, and pressure. The data collected by these sensors is transmitted to computers or mobile devices via Wi-Fi, Bluetooth, or cellular networks (e.g., 4G, 5G). This data is then processed and analyzed to provide valuable insights or to trigger actuators to perform specific actions, thereby enhancing the functionality and user experience of the product.

Applications of smart and connected products span several domains [19]. In smart homes, these products enhance convenience, security, and energy efficiency. In the health and fitness sectors, fitness trackers and smartwatches monitor health metrics and provide actionable insights. In industry, smart and connected products enable predictive maintenance, automation, and process optimization, increasing efficiency and reducing downtime. In smart cities, they support traffic, waste, and energy management, contributing to urban sustainability. These diverse applications demonstrate the transformative potential of smart and connected products in enhancing both product functionality and user experience across multiple sectors.

However, designing smart and connected products entails significant challenges across methodological, financial, environmental, and ethical dimensions [21, 22]. Through a literature review, a workshop with academics and a campaign of industrial interviews, Briard et al. (2023) [20] confirm this point and emphasize the lack of a structured methodological framework for designing such products, which hinders designers from fully harnessing the potential of the involved technologies.

2.2 Sensor Capabilities Creativity Tool

Within the process design domain, the exploration and integration of data and sensor potential represents a promising area of research, as it opens significant opportunities for innovation in product design. The literature presents various methods proposing frameworks or tools for sensor selection and choice, including sensor kits [24], card games [25], analytical approaches, financial and technical evaluations [26], as well as technical abacuses [27]. Despite these methods, it is essential to recognize that sensor selection and choice are frequently conducted empirically by designers [28]. Moreover, the frameworks discussed for sensor selection do not adopt a holistic perspective for value creation based on captured data. They tend to focus on solutions addressing technical problems or user needs. Similarly, the selection approaches primarily consider sensor characteristics (performance, costs, integration into the product, etc.) without evaluating their roles within the entire system.

In response, we proposed previously an innovative method for identifying potential value creation through the integration of captured data into the creative phases of design [23]. They introduced a sensors capabilities creativity tool that represents the main data that can be collected by embedded sensors. This identification was accomplished by examining the technical specifications of sensors from five major companies in the sector: Bosch Sensortec, Infineon Technologies, NXP Semiconductors, STMicroelectronics, and Murata Manufacturing. By representing the detection capabilities of embedded sensors rather than the sensors themselves, the tool bypasses the technical aspects of the sensors. This ensures that expertise is not a limiting factor, allowing all designers to engage in creative discussions about potential value creations related to captured data for the product. While the list of detection capabilities is not exhaustive, its systematic construction is expected to represent most capabilities (Fig. 1). In real life practice these sensors take the form of physical cards (Fig. 2a) that can be used to show the place of the sensor on the product and share the idea (Fig. 2b). Each card represents physical phenomena and quantities that can be measured using sensors.

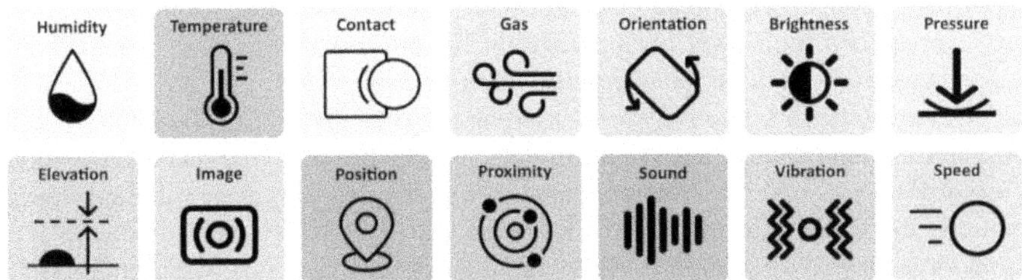

Fig. 1. The 14 detection capabilities in the form of cards [23].

To use this tool, Briard et al. (2024) [23] propose a method that considers each phase of the product life cycle individually to initiate creative reflections on how detection capabilities can contribute to potential value creation. In their case study, they focus on user experience value creation by utilizing a list of 12 keywords to describe the user experience, based on the findings of Law et al. (2014) [29]. These selected keywords represent measurable experiential qualities (Fig. 2).

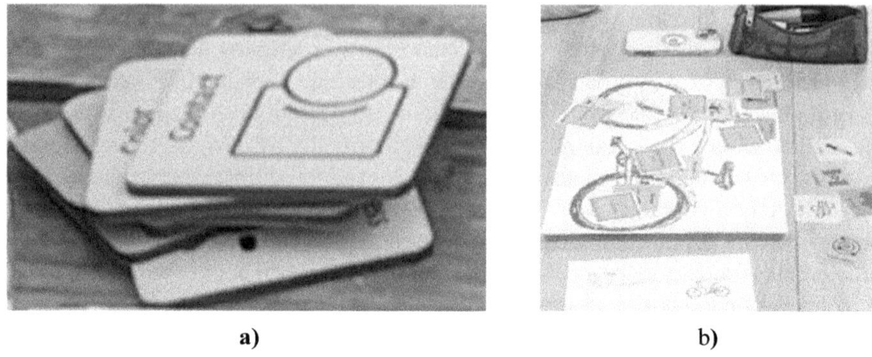

a)   b)

Fig. 2. Physical cards and cubes manufactured in reality [23].

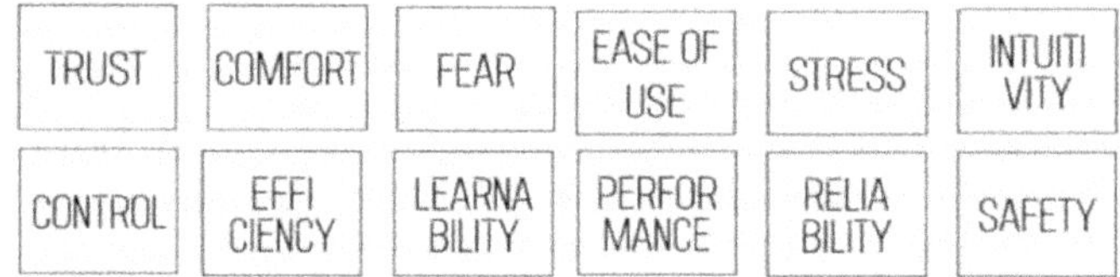

Fig. 3. The 12 keywords of the user experience [Briard'24].

This approach was tested in a case study with a shared bicycle company. The experimental results indicate that the tool significantly enhances the generation of novel and higher-quality concepts compared to traditional ideation methods. Additionally, participants expressed a high level of appreciation for the tool, noting that it significantly enhanced creative exploration and collaboration (Fig. 3).

However, while this creativity tool based on physical cards [1, 2] facilitates tangible interaction, it also presents important limitations. For instance, the physical manipulation of cards may slow down ideation, reduce the possibility of remote collaboration, and complicate the systematic recording of ideas generated during sessions. In contrast, digital and virtual tools—particularly Augmented Reality—can accelerate iteration cycles, support distributed teams, and ensure automatic saving of ideas for future reuse. This motivates the exploration of AR as a medium to extend the benefits of the physical tool while addressing its limitations.

2.3 Leveraging Augmented Reality (AR) to Enhance the Sensor Capabilities Creativity Tool

Augmented Reality (AR) is revolutionizing design practices across various industries by offering new ways to visualize, interact with, and test designs in real-time and within real-world contexts. There is a growing demand for AR applications to support various stages of the design process, as noted by Giunta [3]. Beyond product design, AR technologies are extensively utilized throughout different phases of product development, from initial concept ideas to final manufacturing stages [4].

The integration of AR into design processes has opened new possibilities for creativity, collaboration, and efficiency. Especially there are needs of AR applications to support various stages of the design process [3]. Besides product design, AR technologies are also largely used in various stages of product development, from initial design ideas to final product manufacturing [4]. For the sake of considering the end-user experience in early product design stages AR technologies can facilitate involvement of end-user in the design creativity workshops. Thanks to the AR application end-users can manipulate and modify virtual prototypes of designed products in real-time. This helps users to express their ideas and feedback in the early design stage. The participation of users in the design process can efficiently reach optimal product design solution that meets user requirements accurately [5]. The comparison between classical design activities in real environment and the one in virtual environment has been made for novice designers' education. Designers' creativity and idea generation are largely stimulated by the virtual condition thanks to AR technologies [6].

AR aided 3D sketching interface is devised to designed digitalized the traditional sketching tools and mediums. Mobile devices serve as sketching platforms and use AR techniques to support on-site 3D virtual shapes authoring and visualization directly within a physical environment. In addition, these systems propose interactive and intuitive manipulation of the virtual geometric models to enhance the designer's creativity and ability to express ideas in the mixed world with virtual and physical elements [7–10].

AR can also enhance collaborative and real-time product design process by facilitating collaboration among team members and improving collaborative interaction with 3D virtual models and simultaneous design modifications [11]. In the education domain, collaborative product design within a learning factory environment uses cloud-based AR technologies to improve learning experience and facilitate understanding and engagement of learners by allowing users to see how design solutions in a physical space and improving spatial awareness and design accuracy [12]. In the specific Additive Manufacturing (AM) area, AR can help designers to better explore all the opportunities of AM during early design stage [13]. In addition, a farmwork combining AR, AM and Digital Twin (DT) technologies can share and visualize in real-time the manufacturing data for various product innovation stakeholders and support them in decision-making [14]. Virtual reality (VR) technology emerged early then AR and is also used in collaborative product design for enabling multi-disciplines product visualization. Completely immerged in the virtual environment where the product is used, the users can see and interact with the virtual product representations according to their interest/discipline [15, 16].

Despite the research there's few works directly address the ideation phase of product design, where creativity and rapid exploration are most critical. This gap emphasizes the need for AR-based tools explicitly designed to support early-stage brainstorming and concept generation, rather than only focusing on later prototyping or manufacturing stages. Our work addresses precisely this missing link.

Based on the current state of the art, our literature review did not identify any research that integrates Augmented Reality (AR) for the exploration and integration of data and sensors to support IoT product design activities. This gap in the literature highlights an unexplored intersection of AR technology and creative design tools aimed at enhancing design processes. Consequently, the objective of this study is to introduce an AR application designed to leverage AR to enhance creativity for sensor capabilities integration and to evaluate its impact on creativity and collaboration within design teams. By doing so, this study seeks to provide empirical evidence on the effectiveness of AR-enhanced creativity tools in the product design process.

3 Proposed Approach

After having reviewed the current physical support for IoT product design and the virtual technologies used in design creativity, this paper aims to propose an innovative augmented reality (AR) application paradigm for assisting IoT product design activities. The main objective is to provide designers with a digital tool in which they can visualize the 3D virtual mockup of the product in the real world and express their design ideas (sensors capabilities and user experience) directly on the virtual product.

Users can penetrate the virtual representation of a product to gain a comprehensive understanding of its internal structure. This immersive capability allows for a detailed examination of each component and their interactions within the product. Real-time 3D rendering will enable users to visualize fluently the 3D mockup of the product embedded in any real environment and illusion of interacting with real product in the environment. The virtual prototyping function will allow users to quickly generate ideas. Designers can add and interact with virtual sensors capabilities onto the products offering a detailed perspective on how these sensors would be positioned spatially on the product. In addition, designers can also attach user experience value creation. Once all the design ideas have been expressed the application saves the work that means the added sensors capabilities with user experiences. So that for a new creativity session designers can load the previously saved design solutions. It is possible to save several design solutions that the designers can compare to find an optimal one.

This AR app will facilitate creative brainstorming for generating design ideas. Figure 4 illustrates the workflow of using an AR aided IoT design activities.

This paradigm will meet following requirements that are defined to answers the first needs:

- Visualization and interaction with virtual mock-up of the product that is embedded naturally in the real environment.
- Interactive animation of the virtual mock-up for helping designers to better understand how the product works and what are internal components through exploded view.

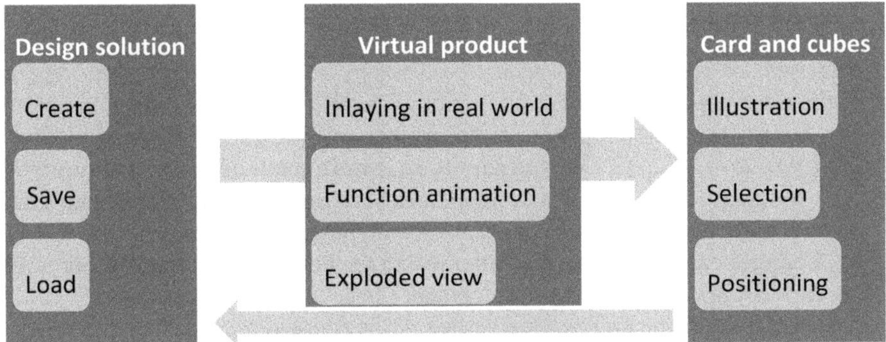

Fig. 4. General approach for AR aided IoT Design.

- Presentation, explanation and examples illustration for the various cards of detection capabilities in IoT technologies. Possibility of adding and positioning them onto the virtual product.
- Presentation, explanation and examples illustration for the various cubes for keywords of user experience. Possibility of adding and positioning them onto the virtual product.
- Creation, saving and opening a design project that contains all the design ideas. Each idea correspond to a card, a cube and a comment as well as their spatial position. When opening an existing design solution all the cards, cubes and comments will appear and positioned relative to the virtual product.
- Online team work sessions through network connection to allow a collaborative design creativity workshop where each designer can express their ideas through his/her device.
- Demonstration of new functional features of the upgraded product with new detection capabilities. For example when a position detection capacity is added to bike, its trajectory can be visualized on a smartphone.

In this study, the 3D mock-ups used within the AR application were derived from existing product models, either adapted from CAD files or openly available 3D assets (e.g., bicycles, windows). This approach allowed us to focus on the integration of sensors and user experience elements into recognizable product shapes. For the design of completely new products, future work could integrate AR-based sketching or rapid 3D modeling techniques, enabling designers to generate initial product geometries before applying sensor capability and user experience elements but today's proposal relies on the addition of well-designed 3D models or the use of the ones available in the application.

4 Prototyped AR Application

According to the ambitions declared in the previous chapter, preliminary proof of concept (POC) has been developed and proposed in this paper. This POC corresponds to an AR application that allows designers to generate IoT ideas directly on the virtual product visualized in the real environment. The essential functions have been prototyped so that experimentation has been conducted with participants (Sect. 5).

4.1 Technical Specifications

The proposed AR application has been prototyped by using the game engine Unity. It is one of the most popular and powerful platforms for 3D development due to numerous benefits. Unity allows developers to build applications for a wide range of platforms, including Windows, macOS, Linux, Android, etc. from a single codebase. Unity provides an intuitive graphic interface so that developers can add and configure 3D mockups easily. Its powerful computation core enables rapid prototyping, allowing developers real-time editing. Changes can be made in real-time within the editor during run time, providing immediate feedback and reducing development time.

In terms of AR the technology markerless AR is adopted because it does not rely on predefined visual markers. Instead, it uses the environment's natural features to determine the position and orientation of virtual objects in the real world. Unity's AR Foundation provides a unified framework to develop markerless AR applications that work across different AR platforms like ARCore (Android) and ARKit (iOS). Therefore, the developed AR application can analyze real environment to detect planes, estimate light source position so that the virtual mockup can have correct illumination and plausible position relative to the real environment.

4.2 Functions for Designers

The home page of the prototyped AR application is illustrated in Fig. 5a. It allows designers to select 3D models of products to upgrade, insert sensor capability, user experience and add comments for each design idea. Other buttons on the top correspond to "go back", "options" and "quit". A quick overview of the main steps involved in using the application is illustrated in Figs. 5a–d: importing and positioning the virtual model in the real environment, inserting sensor capabilities and user experiences attached to the various product components, and adding comments to finalize the design idea.

When the designer clicks on the button "Models" (Fig. 5a) a scrollable list of available product models will appear on the right side of the screen (Fig. 5e). Once a model is selected, the 3D mockup will appear in the real environment, eg. a bike on the table (Fig. 5b) and the position, orientation and size of the 3D mockup can be adjusted with designers' fingers. Then designers can approve to fix the model. It is possible to click on the model to enable its adjustment.

When clicking on the model, there is a function available that allows the user to watch an exploded view of the product. A slider appears to adjust the distance for separating components (Fig. 6). Depending on the model to evaluate, in this case a bike, this can be seen as a major advantage compared to complex real objects and certainly 2D pictures printed on paper.

Also, once the virtual product (eg. bike) is inserted and fixed somewhere in the real environment, the designer can click on the cards button (Fig. 5a) a scrollable vertical list of 14 sensor capabilities appears on the right of the screen (Fig. 5f). It is also possible to add a user experience cube by clicking on the cubes button (Fig. 5a) a scrollable horizontal list of 12 experiences appears on the top of the screen (Fig. 5g). The chosen sensors capability or user experience is a 3D object embedded in the real environment (Fig. 5c) and its position, orientation and size can be adjusted by designers. It is also

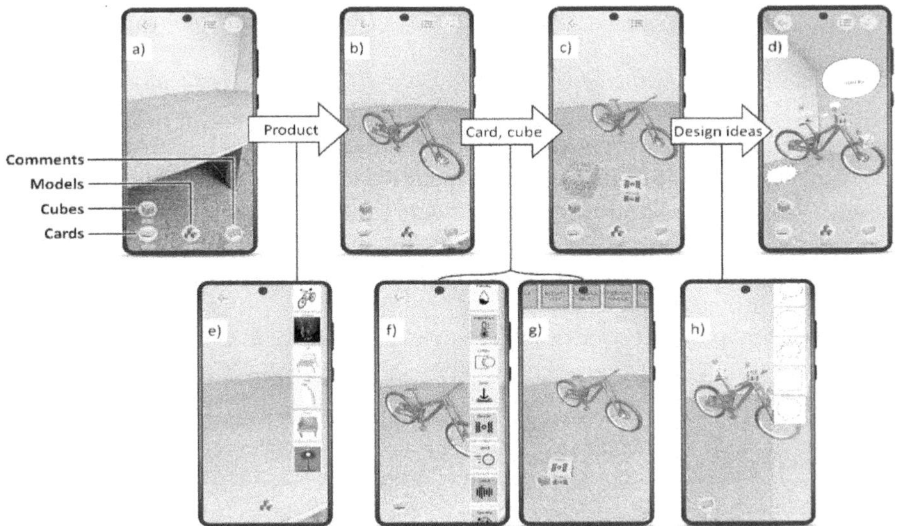

Fig. 5. AR application function: insertion of a 3D mock-up.

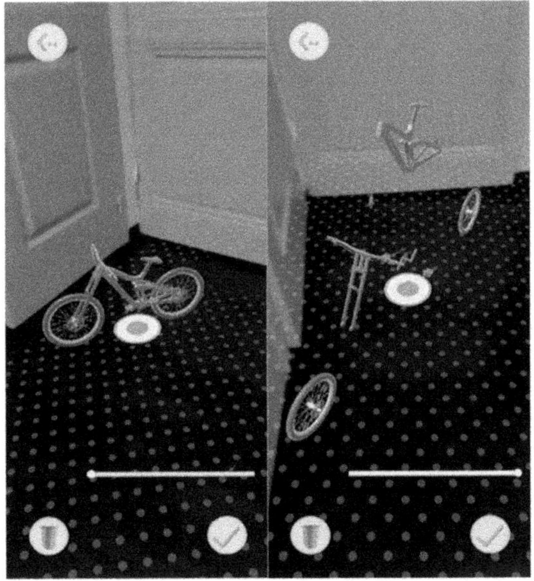

Fig. 6. AR application function: Exploded view of a 3D mock-up.

possible to attach the couples (card + cube) onto the 3D product (Fig. 5d). Designers can also add various comments (Fig. 5h) on to the designed product (Fig. 5d).

5 Experimentation

For the sake of compare the proposed AR aided IoT Design application and a traditional method frequently used, an experimental study was conducted with **14** Bachelor **students** (12 male, 2 female) major in **Mechanical Engineering and product** Design. Participants were divided into two groups and worked on two predefined IoT-related design study cases: a smart **bicycle** and a smart **window**. The main idea was to face a Traditional Method (TM) design based on picture of product printed on paper and the Augmented Reality (AR) aided design tool allowing visualization and exploded views of the objects in augmented reality.

For each group the session lasted approximately **two hours** and organized as two distinct phases:

- **Phase 1:** Participants performed brainstorming based idea generation using the **TM** tool for one design study case.
- **Phase 2:** Participants focused on another design study case and used the **AR** tool for ideation task.

The participants were asked to express their design concepts using both methods (TM & AR), onto **individual idea sheets** describing context, sensor, and user experience component choice (Fig. 7).

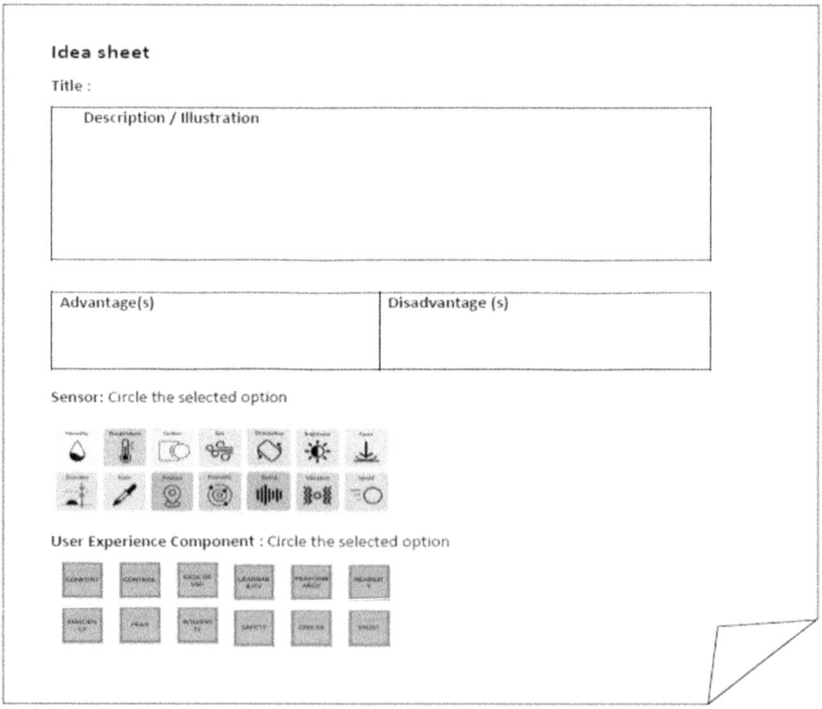

Fig. 7. Ideas sheets.

5.1 Evaluation Tools

To assess the usability and cognitive load of each method, two standard questionnaires in the literature were used:

- **System Usability Scale (SUS)** [17]: A 10-item questionnaire evaluating perceived ease of use, learnability, integration, and user confidence.
- **NASA-TLX** [18]: A 6-item workload assessment covering mental and physical demand, time pressure, perceived complexity, stress, and distraction.

  Participants answered both questionnaires at the end of each phase.

Fig. 8. Briefing with participants.

5.2 Experimental Procedure

- **Briefing** (10 min): presentation of the Internet of Things (IoT) concept, product design followed by an explanation of design aim and tasks using 14 sensors and 12 user experiences. (Fig. 8)
- **First Design** creativity sessions using **TM** tool (35 min): Presentation of a different use cases for each team and providing an A2 paper printed with the product to use as a support for placing sensors and user experiences as shown in Fig. 9.
- User experience **feedback** for **TM** (5 min): Experiment feedback through questionnaires based on SUS and NASA TLX.
- Explanation and training of the AR app's interface and functionalities to the participants.
- **Second Design** creativity session using **AR** tool (35 min): Exchanges of use cases between groups to now generate ideas by using AR application as support for the design process (Fig. 10).
- User experience **feedback** for **AR** (5 min): Experiment feedback through questionnaires based on SUS and NASA TLX.

Fig. 9. Phase Traditional Method.   **Fig. 10.** Phase AR Method.

5.3 Results Analysis

The first measurable and significant aspect of the experiment lies in the number of ideas generated by each method, to define the level of production. It is necessary to mention that there are certain factors that influence this data, and the analysis must take them into account, as well as improve the quality of the data collected in future sessions.

The two working groups were very close to each other, as shown in Fig. 9. They were on opposite sides of the same table, which allowed them to communicate with each other and share information about their use cases to be evaluated, and the ideas generated during the first session (TM). This first session generated a total of 15 idea cards between the two groups, bearing in mind that each group had a different topic.

At the beginning of the second session, both groups were predisposed to the "new" use case due to their prior knowledge of it, which led to some ideas being repeated or prevented other participants from expressing their ideas because "the previous group had already done so". Fatigue due to the long duration of the session was also noticeable, generating disinterest among the students. In the end, the AR method generated 10 idea cards, 5 fewer than those generated in the first session by TM. That is why it is important to know the students' opinion regarding the usability and workload of the methods, which will be our main source of data for making the corresponding comparisons.

To evaluate the cognitive workload and perceived usability of the two design supports—paper-based traditional method (TM) and Augmented Reality (AR) tool—we analyzed the participants' responses to the NASA-TLX and SUS questionnaires. The data were collected from 14 participants who completed both evaluations after using each method.

Cognitive Workload – NASA TLX

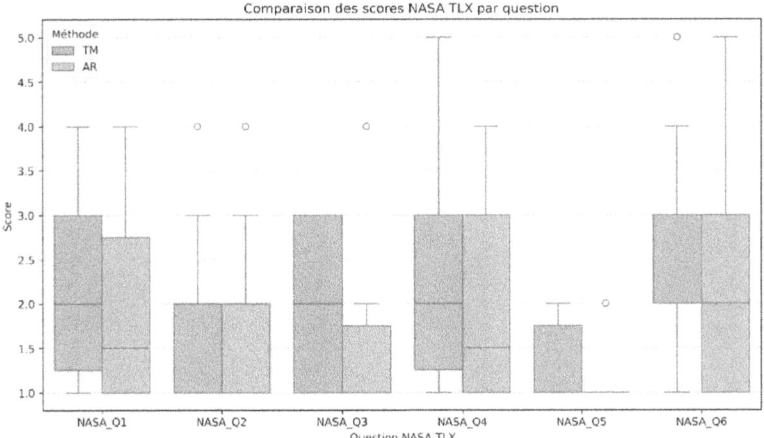

Fig. 11. NASA TLX comparison (lower is better).

Figure 10 illustrates the comparison of average scores for each NASA TLX dimension across the two methods. Overall, the AR method did not increase the cognitive load compared to the traditional approach. In particular:

- **Mental Demand (Q1)** and **Perceived Complexity (Q4)** show slightly lower median values for AR, suggesting that participants experienced the AR method as more cognitively manageable.
- **Time Pressure (Q3)** was also perceived as slightly less demanding with AR, potentially due to the dynamic visualization aiding quicker decision-making.
- **Physical Demand (Q2)** remained low and nearly identical for both methods, as expected in a product design ideation task.
- **Stress/Anxiety (Q5)** and **Distraction (Q6)** scores were similar across both methods, with a slightly larger variance observed in the TM method.

These findings suggest that the AR-based tool maintained a comparable or reduced level of mental and temporal demand, while not introducing additional stress or distraction. This supports its feasibility as an ergonomic alternative in the ideation phase of IoT design.

Usability – System Usability Scale (SUS)

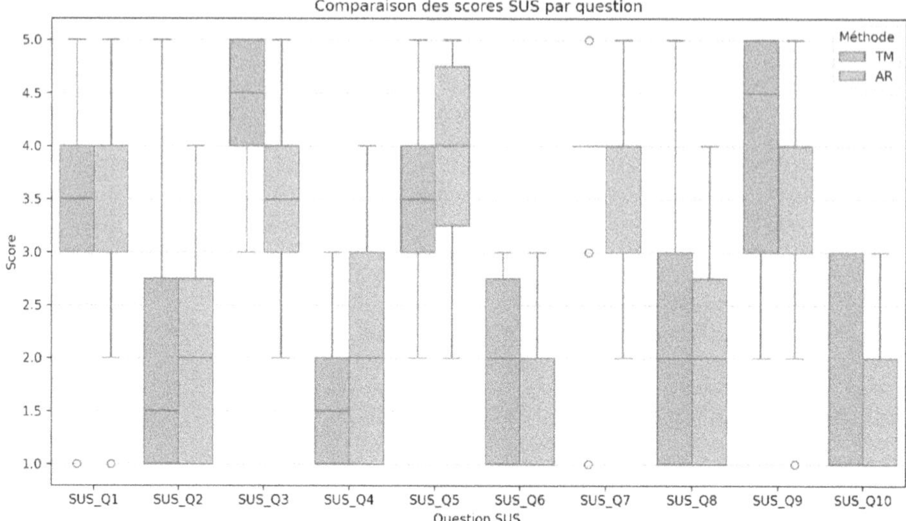

Fig. 12. SUS comparison (higher is better).

The usability assessment results are depicted in Fig. 11. Both methods received relatively positive scores, with a few distinguishing trends (Fig. 12):

- Participants reported comparable levels of **perceived ease of use** (Q3), **integration of functionalities** (Q5), and **learnability** (Q7) for both methods.
- The AR method scored **higher** in **perceived efficiency** (Q8), with participants indicating it was less cumbersome than the traditional method.
- However, TM had a slight advantage in **initial confidence** (Q1) and **lack of need for technical support** (Q4), likely due to its simplicity and familiarity.
- **Q10 (need to learn many things)** indicated a slightly higher learning curve for AR, although the variance was not substantial.

Despite a minor increase in perceived learning effort, the AR system was well accepted by participants and scored similarly—or higher—than the traditional method (TM) in most aspects of usability. The results suggest that the AR tool provides a user-friendly and engaging platform that does not compromise efficiency or clarity.

5.4 Discussion

The results of this study provide meaningful insights into the comparative effectiveness of Augmented Reality (AR) as a support tool during the ideation phase of IoT design. Although traditional methods (TM) remain widely used due to their simplicity and familiarity, the findings suggest that AR-based tools can offer added value without increasing cognitive load or compromising usability.

In terms of workload, participants did not report greater mental effort, stress, or distraction when using AR. On the contrary, AR was perceived as slightly less complex and more time-efficient, likely due to the interactive and immersive nature of the interface.

These observations align with prior work highlighting the potential of AR to reduce cognitive overload in early design tasks by making abstract systems more tangible.

From a usability perspective, the AR tool achieved levels of user satisfaction comparable to the traditional paper-based method. It was particularly well rated in terms of ease of interaction, integration of features, and overall user engagement. Despite a slightly higher initial learning curve, users quickly adapted to the system, suggesting strong learnability and low technical resistance.

Interestingly, the positive reception of the AR tool did not depend on prior experience with similar systems. This observation reinforces the idea that properly designed AR applications can be intuitive and accessible even for novice users, opening new avenues for integration into educational and creative contexts.

It should be noted that the experimental protocol always followed the same sequence (TM first, AR second). This fixed order may have introduced learning bias or fatigue effects that could partly influence the results, that's the main reason why we can observe a better performance in TM session, we were able to see it in the amount of ideas generated and, as well, in the details exposed in the idea cards, the latest registered in the AR session were barely described compared to the first ones in the TM session.

Future studies should counterbalance the order of conditions to better isolate the impact of the tool.

Another observed limitation was that the study did not assess the quality of the ideas generated, but only their number and the participants' perceptions of usability and workload. Evaluating idea quality, for instance, in terms of novelty, feasibility, or relevance, would provide a more complete picture of the contribution of AR in early-stage product design.

Finally, while questionnaires provided structured feedback, complementary qualitative insights from interviews or observational notes could enrich the interpretation of user experience with the AR tool. In any case, even without a qualitative survey, we did observed some interesting behaviors like, students taking the bicycle's size to a real scale to "get on it" and also to take a better look of all the pieces in the exploded view; during the phase of onboarding to the application, they were interested in understanding every functionality in the application, sharing some good opinions about the activity the were doing.

6 Conclusion and Perspectives

In this paper, an innovative AR aided design tool has been proposed and prototyped. This can overcome the absence of the physical product during IoT product design creativity workshop, and designers can interact intuitively with 3D virtual product using AR tool whereas it is not possible when using 2D picture. An experiment with 14 participants has been conducted to compare 2D and 3D methods.

This experimental study aimed to assess the feasibility and benefits of an AR-based application for supporting creativity and ideation in the context of IoT product design. By comparing it with a traditional method in a controlled setting involving undergraduate students, the study highlights several advantages of AR:

- Comparable or lower cognitive workload, especially in terms of complexity and time pressure.
- Almost equal usability perceptions, including ease of use, feature integration, and engagement.
- Rapid user adaptation, even in the presence of a slightly steeper learning curve.

These findings support the integration of Augmented Reality tools in early-stage product design processes, particularly within Design Thinking frameworks where ideation, creativity, and user experience are central.

Future work consists of technical development of the AR tool as well as scientific issues. Technically the aspect of networking can be a game changer allowing to creativity, design, and team work to get to the next level with coop sessions in which everybody can look, participate and shared his ideas with the other no matter where they are. Another interesting feature could be saving and loading projects that will allow the users to recover the last point of work easily and keep track of different versions and gain time in between.

In terms of scientifical issue it would focus on scaling the experiment with a larger and more diverse participant base, as well as on longitudinal studies to evaluate the impact of AR on idea quality and design outcomes. The latest experiences also showed a guideline to follow to avoid the influence of external agents within the design process.

References

1. Chang, Y.S., Kao, J.Y., Wang, Y.Y.: Influences of virtual reality on design creativity and design thinking. Thinking Skills Creativity **46**, Article 101127 (2022). https://doi.org/10.1016/j.tsc.2022.101127
2. Lyu, Q., Watanabe, K., Umemura, H., Murai, A.: Design-thinking skill enhancement in virtual reality: a literature study. Front. Virtual Real (2023)
3. Giunta, L., O'Hare, J., Gopsill, J., Dekoninck, E.: A review of augmented reality research for design practice: looking to the future. In: Paper Presented at the DS 91 NordDesign 2018, (Linköping) (2018)
4. Schumann, M., Fuchs, C., Kollatsch, C., Klimant, P.: Evaluation of augmented reality supported approaches for product design and production processes. Procedia CIRP **97**, 160–165 (2021)
5. Maurya, S., Arai, K., Moriya, K., et al.: A mixed reality tool for end-users participation in early creative design tasks. Int. J. Interact. Des. Manuf. **13**, 163–182 (2019)
6. Cindioglu, H.C., Gursel Dino, I., Surer, E.: Proposing a novel mixed-reality framework for basic design and its hybrid evaluation using linkography and interviews. Int. J. Technol. Des. Educ. **32**, 2775–2800 (2022)
7. Xin, M., Sharlin, E., Sousa, M.C.: Napkin sketch: handheld mixed reality 3D sketching. In: Proceedings of the 2008 ACM Symposium on Virtual Reality Software and Technology (VRST 2008), pp. 223–226. Association for Computing Machinery, New York (2008)
8. Yee, B., Ning, Y., Lipson, H.: Augmented reality in-situ 3D sketching of physical objects. In: IUI Sketch Recognition Workshop (2009)
9. Langlotz, T., Mooslechner, S., Zollmann, S., et al.: Sketching up the world: in situ authoring for mobile Augmented Reality. Pers. Ubiquit. Comput. **16**, 623–630 (2012). https://doi.org/10.1007/s00779-011-0430-0

10. Hagbi, N., Grasset, R., Bergig, O., Billinghurst, M., El-Sana, J.: In-place sketching for augmented reality games. Comput. Entertain. **12**, 1–18 (2015)
11. Smparounis, K., Mavrikios, D., Pappas, M., Xanthakis, V., Viganò, G.P., Pentenrieder, K.: A virtual and augmented reality approach to collaborative product design and demonstration. In: 2008 IEEE International Technology Management Conference (ICE), Lisbon, Portugal, pp. 1–8 (2008)
12. Mourtzis, D., Siatras, V., Angelopoulos, J., Panopoulos, N.: An augmented reality collaborative product design cloud-based platform in the context of learning factory. Procedia Manuf. 546–551 (2020)
13. Cui, J., Lou, R., Mantelet, F., et al.: Integration of additive manufacturing and augmented reality in early design phases: a way to foster remote creativity. Int. J. Interact. Des. Manuf. **18**, 609–625 (2024)
14. Xu, S., Lu, Y., Yu, C.: Augmented reality-assisted cloud additive manufacturing with digital twin technology for multi-stakeholder value co-creation in product innovation. Heliyon. **10**(4), e25722 (2024)
15. Li, B., Lou, R., Posselt, J., Segonds, F., Merienne, F.: Multi-view VR system for co-located multidisciplinary collaboration and its application in ergonomic design. In: VRST, Gothenburg, Sweden. 8–10 November 2017
16. Li, B., Segonds, F., Mateev, C., Lou, R., Merienne, F.: Design in context of use: an experiment with a multi-view and multi-representation system for collaborative design. Comput. Ind. **103**, 28–37 (2018)
17. Brooke, J.: SUS: a quick and dirty usability scale. Usability Eval. Ind. **189** (1995)
18. Hart, S.G., Staveland, L.E.: Development of NASA-TLX (task load index): results of empirical and theoretical research. Adv. Psychol. **52**, 139–183 (1988)
19. Porter, M.E., Heppelmann, J.E.: How smart, connected products are transforming companies. Harv. Bus. Rev. **93**(10), 97–114 (2015)
20. Briard, T., Jean, C., Aoussat, A., Véron, P.: Challenges for data-driven design in early physical product design: a scientific and industrial perspective. Comput. Ind. **145**, 103814 (2023). https://doi.org/10.1016/j.compind.2022.103814
21. Cantamessa, M., Montagna, F., Altavilla, S., Casagrande-Seretti, A.: Data-driven design: the new challenges of digitalization on product design and development. Des. Sci. **6**, e27 (2020). https://doi.org/10.1017/dsj.2020.25
22. Chiarello, F., Belingheri, P., Fantoni, G.: Data science for engineering design: state of the art and future directions. Comput. Ind. **129**, 103447 (2021). https://doi.org/10.1016/j.compind.2021.103447
23. Briard, T., Jean, C., Aoussat, A., Véron, P.: Sensors capabilities as a creativity tool for engineering product design. J. Eng. Des. (2024). https://doi.org/10.1080/09544828.2024.2333195
24. Ambe, A.H., Brereton, M., Soro, A., Chai, M.Z., Buys, L., Roe, P.: Older people inventing their personal internet of things with the IoT un-kit experience. In: Proceedings of the 2019 CHI Conference on Human Factors in Computing Systems, pp. 1–15 (2019). https://doi.org/10.1145/3290605.3300552
25. Angelini, L., Mugellini, E., Couture, N., Khaled, O.A.: Designing the Interaction with the Internet of Tangible Things: A Card Set Proceedings of the Twelfth International (2018)
26. Jones, P.M., et al.: A straightforward route to sensor selection for IoT systems. Res.-Technol. Manage. **61**, 41–50 (2018). https://doi.org/10.1080/08956308.2018.1495965. Conference on Tangible, Embedded, and Embodied Interaction, Stockholm, Sweden. https://doi.org/10.1145/3173225.3173288
27. Shieh, J., Huber, J.E., Fleck, N.A., Ashby, M.F.: The selection of sensors. Prog. Mater. Sci. **46**, 461–504 (2001). https://doi.org/10.1016/S0079-6425(00)00011-6

28. Kirchner, E., Martin, G., Vogel, S.: Sensor integrating machine elements—key to in-situ measurements in mechanical engineering. In: Schützer, K. (ed.) Proceedings of the 23rd International Seminar on High Technology (2018)
29. Law, E.L.-C., van Schaik, P., Roto, V.: Attitudes towards user experience (UX) measurement. Int. J. Hum. Comput. Stud. **72**, 526–541 (2014). https://doi.org/10.1016/j.ijhcs.2013.09.006

In-Situ Audio Experiences: Leveraging RAG and TTS for Accessible, Hyperlocal Heritage Engagement

Marcus Winter[✉]

University of Brighton, Brighton, UK
`marcus.winter@brighton.ac.uk`

Abstract. This position paper presents an application concept adapting Retrieval Augmented Generation (RAG) for geographic contexts, and combining it with Text-to-Speech (TTS) technology to automate the creation of audio narrations for locative media experiences. By minimizing the costs for research and media production, it addresses a critical barrier for archives to remediating their content and catering for audiences who are not able to, or not inclined to, read written materials. The application concept is contextualized in efforts to create alternative media representations that convey content in-situ to increase its relevance. It is illustrated with a prototype application aiming to engage people with their local history through audio narrations fictionalizing archive materials related to their location. A discussion of technical and user interface aspects offer insights into design considerations informing the prototype development.

Keywords: Retrieval Augmented Generation (RAG) · Text-to-Speech (TTS) · Location-Based Interaction · Hyperlocal Media · Cultural Heritage · Accessibility

1 Introduction

Location-based applications leverage GPS, Wi-Fi, Bluetooth beacons, and other positioning technologies to deliver context-aware services tailored to a user's physical location. These applications span a wide range of uses, from practical wayfinding and local discovery to educational and leisure-oriented locative media. One well-established category of locative media experiences are walking tours providing audio narratives triggered by users' geographic location to create immersive storytelling experiences. Walking tours and similar locative media have been shown to deepen engagement with historical or cultural sites [7, 9, 28], however, developing such experiences involves substantial effort associated with curating content and creating related media resources. Research to identify relevant materials, script writing to create narratives, and the production of voice recordings can be costly and time-consuming, posing economic barriers especially for smaller heritage organizations operating on small budgets.

This position paper presents an application concept addressing this problem with Large Language Models (LLM) and Text-to-Speech (TTS) models to automate content

© The Author(s), under exclusive license to Springer Nature Switzerland AG 2026
J. F. Krems et al. (Eds.): CHIRA 2025, CCIS 2836, pp. 403–413, 2026.
https://doi.org/10.1007/978-3-032-16454-4_23

curation and media production based on existing archive materials. In order to increase content relevancy and accuracy, it adapts an approach known as Retrieval Augmented Generation (RAG) [26] for location-based content generation. RAG systems are typically designed for question answering scenarios: they carry out a semantic search over a content database to find materials most closely related to a user's question, and then include both the question and the retrieved materials in a prompt for the LLM to generate an informed answer. We adapt this process by using a user's location instead of a question as the original input, carrying out a proximity search instead of semantic search, and then constructing a prompt asking the LLM to generate a story based on the archive materials retrieved for that location (Fig. 1). The generated story text is then converted into an audio narration by a TTS model, using voices that are plausible for the target area and content.

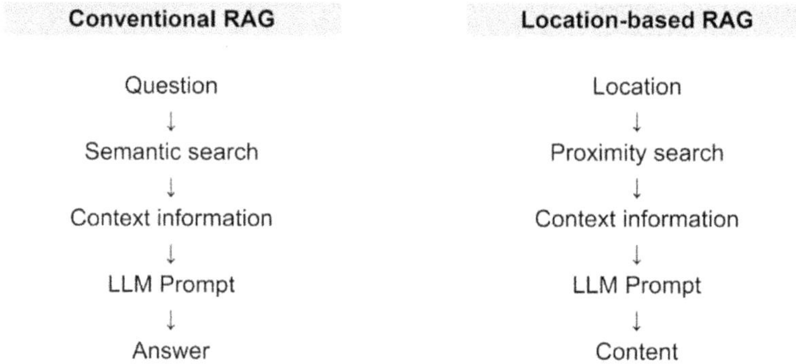

Fig. 1. Conventional and location-based Retrieval Augmented Generation (RAG).

The main contributions of this position paper are:

- The conceptualization of location-based RAG as a mechanism to generate relevant content for a geographic location
- The operationalization of this mechanism in a prototype application that draws on archive materials to engage people with their local history.

This work is significant because it provides a pathway for archives and other content providers towards remediating their written materials as locative media, without incurring the substantial costs related to content curation and media production. This enables even small archives with specialist and local knowledge to create locative media experiences and reach new audiences.

The following sections contextualize this work in the literature, describe the application concept and present its implementation in a prototype locative media application, drawing on the archive of a small community publisher. The paper discusses considerations informing the technical and user interface design of the prototype, before setting out future work aiming to empirically evaluate the prototype with target audiences and support the uptake of the application concept by other archives.

2 Background

Locative media encompass a wide range of technologies, media types, engagement practices and theoretical perspectives [51], but is most commonly understood as digital content tied to specific geographic locations, requiring users to move through space to access it [45]. They create embodied, often narrative-driven, experiences that are increasingly leveraged in tourism, place-making and cultural heritage.

In a tourism context, they enhance traditional activities by embedding information within physical spaces to support flexible planning and discovery [3, 6, 25]. In a place-making context, they can influence how a space is perceived and valued in order to foster a sense of attachment and meaning associated with it [9, 16]. In a cultural heritage context, they make historical interpretations more accessible and engaging, by providing information in-situ and experimenting with different narrative formats [28, 34, 42].

Challenges in locative media experiences range from practical concerns, such as battery drain and GPS drift [5] to ethical aspects such as privacy concerns about location tracking [2, 24] and digital exclusion due to limited digital literacy or lack of access to high-end mobile devices [19, 31]. A key challenge in *developing* locative media experiences are the high costs of curating content and creating media resources. While there is a rich ecosystem of platforms for location-based delivery [e.g., 11, 22, 41, 43, 48], the related content and media production, including archival research, script writing, voice acting and audio recording, can involve substantial effort and costs. This poses a barrier especially for smaller archives, who often hold content that can enrich the understanding of local histories by contributing marginalized and lesser known perspectives [33, 49], but cannot afford to create locative media experiences based on their collections as they operate on small budgets.

One early attempt to automate content creation for locative media walks is WikEar [38], which leverages Wikimedia's Geosearch API [50] to generate location-based audio stories for walks between two places in a city. Rather than using GPS to locate users, this application uses image recognition technologies described in [37] enabling users to point their mobile phone camera at a public city map and then select a spatial feature (e.g., building, landmark) as a destination. This automatically generates a narrative walking tour between the location of the city map and the destination using Minotour [17], a system designed for tourism-based education that "frees the content of Wikipedia from existing physical and organizational restrictions by generating appealing narratives relevant to a user's current activity space" [18]. The generated narrative is then turned into audio using TTS technology.

More recently, LLMs have transformed visitor engagement in cultural heritage by enabling people to chat with institutions, virtual curators and even specific objects [4, 36, 46], showing impressive capabilities in remediating existing knowledge in the form of interactive conversations without requiring additional research, script writing or editing. Some of these systems combine Automatic Speech Recognition (ASR) and TTS technologies to enable spoken language interaction [21, 44], and involve avatars of historic figures to add further realism to the experience [8]. While such systems are typically object-centered rather than location-based, some projects integrate them with locative experiences. For example, the Vocal Museum [39] combines proximity sensing technologies with LLMs, ASR and TTS to locate visitors inside the gallery space and enable them to communicate with relevant exhibits via text or voice. Exhibot [44] offers similar functionality for outdoor environments, using Bluetooth beacons and a mobile application to detect visitors approaching statues, and then enabling them to converse with the statue in spoken language.

Of critical importance in this context is that the generated content is accurate and relevant for an object or location. LLMs are known to present false or misleading information as fact when prompted on aspects underrepresented in their training data, a phenomenon commonly referred to as hallucinations. The basic idea of RAG is to increase response relevance and minimize hallucinations by providing LLMs with additional information as part of the prompt. Several projects exploring LLMs in heritage environments use RAG to increase the relevance and quality of responses [e.g., 21, 23, 27, 35], however, to the best of our knowledge there has been no work on adapting RAG for location-based retrieval and content generation.

In summary, locative media and walking tours offer engaging ways to experience content in-situ with demonstrated benefits across tourism, place-making and heritage. The costs and effort associated with producing locative media poses economic barriers for smaller organizations to leverage their benefits, however, technologies such as LLMs, RAG and TTS hold great potential to automate content production. An application concept combining these technologies to produce locative media from archive content is presented in the following section.

3 Application Concept

The proposed application concept is based on a series of sequential steps carried out in a loop for continuous media production and presentation during a walk:

```
1   while (true)
2       pick up user's current location
3       retrieve materials relevant for location
4       generate story text based on materials
5       generate audio narration from story text
6       play audio narration
```

- Line 1: Main application loop; user interface controls enable users to start, pause and resume storytelling, and to interrupt the currently narrated story to generate a new one; closing the application exits the loop and releases related resources.
- Line 2: Retrieve user's current location; try to access precise location (GPS), fall back to coarse location (cell tower).
- Line 3: Search the archive for materials relevant to user's current location.
- Line 4: Prompt the LLM with content creation instructions (story length, tone, etc.) and the retrieved archive materials; read the generated story text.
- Line 5: Split the story into sentences; generate audio narration for each sentence.
- Line 6: Play audio narration for each sentence in sequence.

Unlike conventional locative media experiences, which revolve around fixed points of interest (POIs) triggering media playback when users approach them, this application concept provides continuous coverage for an area, with media being dynamically generated for a user's geographic location based on relevant archive materials. Relevance is determined by proximity: the N archive entries closest to a given location. Users can therefore access relevant stories at any location in the area covered by the archive, and stories are not *triggered* by the user's location but *informed* by it. Whenever a story ends, the user's current location at that point in time informs the generation of the next story.

A key aspect of this approach is that different users walking in the same area, or even the same user walking repeatedly in the same area, will hear different stories, depending on their specific location at the time of story generation, which determines the selection of archive materials, and the non-deterministic output of the LLM, which might generate different stories from the same source materials. This makes the experience serendipitous, rewards repeat visits with new stories exploring different facets of the same area, creates potential for co-visitors to discuss and supplement the different stories they listened to, and accepts that generated stories fictionalize archive materials in ways that might not always be historically accurate. As such it is fundamentally different from more conventional approaches, which might use LLMs to pre-generate a finite set of stories that can be filtered by a curator for accuracy and adherence to application themes and policies before being served. While that would be a safer approach and ensure historical accuracy, it would also limit story variety, make the experience predictable, and involve costs for research and review.

The application concept readily integrates with a wide range of archives and repositories offering Application Programming Interfaces (APIs) to search their contents by location. Some directly support geospatial querying by latitude/longitude [e.g., 10, 12, 13, 20, 50], while others support search by place names [e.g., 29, 30], requiring an intermediate step to resolve geographic coordinates to place names [e.g., 14, 15]. In addition to archives and repositories already offering APIs to search by location, agentic LLM workflows promise to automate the process of geo-indexing archives not currently offering that functionality. By automatically extracting place-, street- and landmark names from archive materials, and querying suitable location APIs to resolve them to geospatial coordinates [e.g., 14, 15], such workflows can drastically reduce the costs of preparing legacy archives for geographic location search.

4 Prototype

In order to demonstrate the viability of location-based RAG and the proposed application concept to automatically generate locative media, a prototype was developed in the cultural heritage domain. QueenSpark Books, a registered charity and community publisher in Brighton, United Kingdom, have a back catalogue of over 120 books and keep a unique archive of materials about the city's 20th century history, told by the people who live(d) there. This archive is currently not readily accessible to people who are not able to, or inclined to, research and read written texts available on the archive website. Key audiences in this context include the visually impaired and younger people. The prototype aims to make the archive more accessible to these groups and engage people with their local history by remediating its materials for delivery by a hyperlocal walking companion that generates and narrates short stories relevant to a user's location as they walk through the city.

4.1 Archive Materials

As a proof-of-concept, the prototype covers a limited pilot area of approximately 200 × 200 m between Carlton Hill and Albion Hill in Brighton, a residential area rich in local history. Four members of QueenSpark Books' volunteer community geo-referenced a small subset of archive materials for this area, selecting 95 text passages from a total of nine books and relating them to geographic locations. The text passages and location information were then stored in a relational database and made available to client applications via a Representational State Transfer (REST) API supporting geospatial search of archive materials by latitude/longitude.

Considering its hyperlocal context, the location search is implemented using simple Euclidean distance on a flat surface rather than Haversine distance on a sphere or Vincenty distance on an ellipsoid. This is sufficiently accurate for small distances in a local context and improves retrieval performance as it only involves basic numeric operations, which can be implemented directly in Structured Query Language (SQL) to query the database and sort results by proximity.

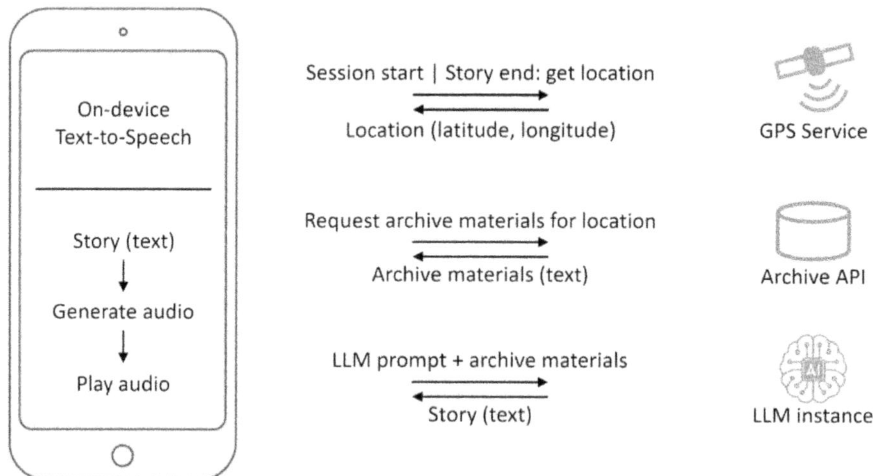

Fig. 2. Application prototype involving a location service, an archive API supporting geospatial querying, an LLM instance to generate stories based on archive materials, and on-device TTS to generate and play an audio narration based on the story text.

4.2 Large Language Model

The prototype (Fig. 2) uses a small, open-weight model from the Llama 2 family, with 7 billion parameters quantized to 8-bit integers to improve inference performance on CPUs [52], running on server-less infrastructure. The choice of model is based on the following considerations:

- The application primarily leverages the model's language capabilities and does not require any "reasoning" capabilities provided by more recent model generations.
- Smaller, quantized models offer better inference performance, require less energy, and can run on more economical hardware, resulting in lower costs.

The LLM prompt informs the model about its role and purpose, provides guidance on language use, story length and tone, and instructs it to generate a narrative based on the provided archive materials.

4.3 Text-to-Speech Model

Considering the purpose of the application to generate hyperlocal stories that engage people with the local history of the targeted pilot area in Brighton, the prototype uses UK English voices to improve the authenticity and relatability of audio narrations. The voices are trained on the open source Voice Cloning Toolkit (VCTK) corpus of speech data uttered by 110 English speakers with various accents [47, 53].

The prototype uses client-side TTS to minimize server load and data transfer. This reduces server-side compute requirements and keeps costs low for the heritage organization. It also makes the application more accessible for people on restricted mobile data plans, as only location information (latitude, longitude) and story text are being exchanged between the client device and the archive API (Fig. 2).

Client-side TTS in the prototype uses the open source Sherpa ONNX Text-to-Speech toolkit [40], which runs voice models on the hardware-accelerated Open Neural Network Exchange (ONNX) runtime [32]. The toolkit supports a range of hardware platforms, operating systems and voice model formats, offering scope for future extension and internationalization of the application.

4.4 User Interface

The user interface (Fig. 3) is designed to not distract from the listening experience by limiting required screen interactions while also providing fallback functionality to read the story text when required.

Information is provided during start-up with notifications about acquiring location data and loading the TTS model, and during operation by showing the story text on screen and high-lighting the currently spoken sentence. This enables users to verify content when they are unsure about the narrator's pronunciation or when the narration is unintelligible due to ambient noise.

Buttons at the bottom of the screen enable users to start/pause/resume story generation and narration, to interrupt a story and generate a new one, and to activate the Settings and About screens. The Settings screen enables users to select a specific narrator voice or shuffle between voices, which is the default setting. The About screen provides users with information about the context and purpose of the application. Following guidance on the design of AI-enhanced applications [1], this screen also explains that narratives - while based on archive materials - are AI-generated and raises awareness about potential limitations to their factual correctness.

In anticipation of a planned empirical evaluation of the prototype, the About screen also informs users about their anonymous participant ID and provides functionality to share anonymous walk data with the research team. Anonymous walk data includes time-stamped location traces, generated stories, story narration start and end times, and technical logs. The data is stored locally on the mobile device and requires users' explicit interaction to share it with the research team, addressing concerns around transparency and data collection in location-based applications [2, 24].

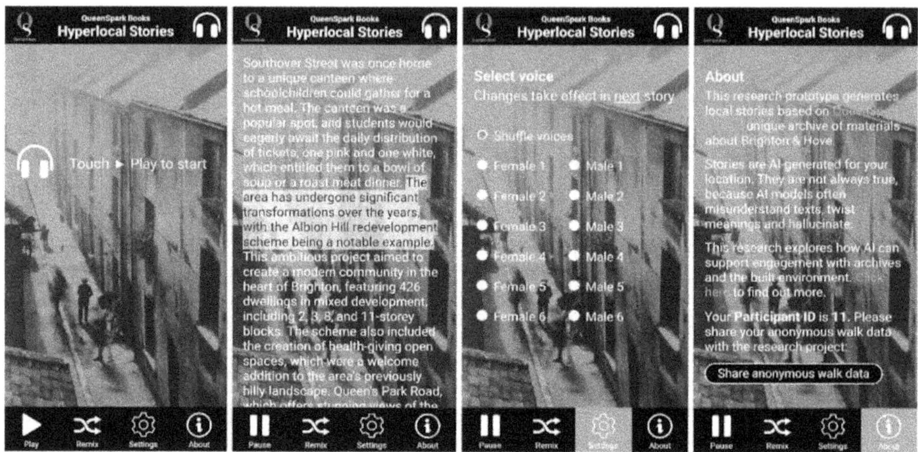

Fig. 3. User interface from left to right: (a) start screen after location access has been obtained and the TTS model is loaded; (b) play screen highlighting current sentence, enabling users to look up the spoken text; (c) settings screen enabling users to select the narrator's voice; and (d) about screen informing users about the purpose and context of the prototype, explaining that stories are AI generated and not always factually correct, and enabling users to share anonymous walk data with the research team.

5 Conclusions

This paper introduces location-based RAG and a related application concept automating the generation and presentation of locative media content. Instead of retrieving information through semantic search based on a user question to generate an answer, as in conventional RAG, it retrieves information through proximity search based on a user location to dynamically generate content for locative media experiences.

The significance of this new approach lies in its scalability and ready integration with a wide range of archives and content repositories supporting location search. It minimizes production costs for locative media and lowers economic barriers for archives and repositories - who often operate on small budgets - to remediate their content for location-based experiences in order to reach new audiences.

To illustrate this concept and demonstrate its viability, we present a prototype application engaging people with the archive of a community publisher holding historic materials about the city of Brighton in the United Kingdom. The prototype generates short audio narratives as users walk in a pilot area, based on archive materials relating to their current location. A discussion of technical and user interface aspects offer insights into design considerations informing the prototype development.

Future work will focus on the empirical evaluation of the prototype with target users to better understand performance and usability aspects; evaluate how audiences relate to and engage with automatically generated locative media; and assess whether the application helps people to engage with their local history. A second strand of work will focus on agentic LLM workflows to automate the process of geo-indexing archives in order to support wider uptake of the presented application concept.

References

1. Amershi, S., et al.: Guidelines for human-AI interaction. In: Proceedings of 2019 CHI Conference on Human Factors in Computing Systems, pp. 1–13. ACM (2019)
2. Andrejevic, M.B.: Surveillance and alienation in the online economy. Surveill. Soc. **8**(3), 278–287 (2011)
3. Berger, S., Lehmann, H., Lehner, F.: Location-based services in the tourist industry. Inf. Technol. Tourism **5**(4), 243–256 (2002)
4. Boiano, S., Borda, A., Gaia, G., Rossi, S., Cuomo, P.: Chatbots and new audience opportunities for museums and heritage organisations. In: Electronic Visualisation and the Arts. BCS Learning & Development (2018)
5. Brown, B., Chalmers, M.: Tourism and mobile technology. In: Proceedings of Eighth European Conference on Computer Supported Cooperative Work, pp. 335–354. Springer (2003)
6. Butler, T.: A walk of art: the potential of the sound walk as practice in cultural geography. Soc. Cult. Geogr. **7**(6), 889–908 (2006)
7. Butler, T.: Memoryscape: how audio walks can deepen our sense of place by integrating art, oral history and cultural geography. Geogr. Compass **1**(3), 360–372 (2007)
8. Constantinides, N., Constantinides, A., Koukopoulos, D., Fidas, C., Belk, M.: Culturai: exploring mixed reality art exhibitions with large language models for personalized immersive experiences. In: Adj. Proc. 32nd ACM Conference on User Modeling, Adaptation and Personalization, pp. 102–105 (2024)
9. Cornelio, G.S., Ardévol, E.: Practices of place-making through locative media artworks. Communications **36**, 313–333 (2011)
10. Digital Public Library of America. API Codex. https://pro.dp.la/developers/api-codex/. Accessed 21 July 2025
11. Echoes. Geolocated audio tours. https://echoes.xyz/. Accessed 22 July 2025
12. Europeana Search API. https://pro.europeana.eu/page/apis. Accessed 21 July 2025
13. FourSquare Places API. https://foursquare.com/products/places/. Accessed 21 July 2025
14. GeoNames. https://www.geonames.org/export/web-services.html. Accessed 21 July 2025
15. Google Places Library. https://developers.google.com/maps/documentation/places/web-service/op-overviewx. Accessed 21 July 2025
16. Gordon, E., de Souza e Silva, A.: Net locality: Why location matters in a networked world. Wiley (2011)
17. Hecht, B., Dara-Abrams, D., Starosielski, N., Goldsberry, K., Dillemuth, J., Roberts, Clarke, K.: Minotour: a location-aware mobile tour application that weaves a spatial tale from Wikipedia. In: Proceedings of 2007 Meeting of the AAG (2007)
18. Hecht, B., Rohs, M., Schöning, J., Krüger, A.: Wikeye - using magic lenses to explore geo-referenced Wikipedia content. In: Proceedings of 3rd International Workshop on Pervasive Mobile Interaction Devices (2007)

19. Helsper, E.J.: A corresponding fields model for the links between social and digital exclusion. Commun. Theory **22**(4), 403–426 (2012)

20. Historic England Open Data Search API. https://opendata-historicengland.hub.arcgis.com/api/search/definition/. Accessed 21 July 2025

21. Ho, H.P., Ramesh, V., Zaloudek, I., Rikhtehgar, D.J., Wang, S.: Enhancing visitor engagement in interactive art exhibitions with visual-enhanced conversational agents. In: Proceedings of 30th International Conference on Intelligent User Interfaces, pp. 660–671 (2025)

22. izi.TRAVEL. Storytelling platform. https://izi.travel/en. Accessed 22 July 2025

23. Kelly, P., Schild, J., Jafari, A.: FolkRAG: a retrieval-augmented generation system for cultural heritage materials. Neural Comput. Appl. **2025**, 1–17 (2025)

24. Leaver, T., Lloyd, C.: Seeking transparency in locative media. In: Locative Media, pp. 162–174. Routledge (2014)

25. Lee, S.J.: A review of audio guides in the era of smart tourism. Inf. Syst. Front. **19**(4), 705–715 (2017)

26. Lewis, P., et al.: Retrieval-augmented generation for knowledge-intensive NLP tasks. Adv. Neural. Inf. Process. Syst. **33**, 9459–9474 (2020)

27. Loffredo, R., De Santo, M.: Using ontologies for LLM applications in cultural heritage. In: 3rd Workshop on Artificial Intelligence for Cultural Heritage (2024). https://ceur-ws.org/Vol-3865/06_paper.pdf. Accessed 15 July 2025

28. Millard, D.E., Packer, H., Howard, Y., Hargood, C.: The balance of attention: the challenges of creating locative cultural storytelling experiences. J. Comput. Cult. Heritage (JOCCH) **13**(4), 1–24 (2020)

29. National Archives (UK). Discovery API. https://www.api.gov.uk/tna/discovery/. Accessed 21 July 2025

30. National Archives (US). API. https://www.archives.gov/research/catalog/help/api. Accessed 21 July 2025

31. Ofcom (Office of Communications): Digital exclusion: A review of Ofcom's research on digital exclusion among adults in the UK. https://www.ofcom.org.uk/siteassets/resources/ documents/research-and-data/media-literacy-research/adults/adults-media-use-and-attitudes-2022/digital-exclusion-review-2022.pdf. Accessed 15 July 2025

32. ONNX Runtime. https://onnxruntime.ai/. Accessed 17 July 2025

33. Papachristou, D.: Locative media walks: geo-locative media as a means of subverting hegemonic historiography. SOBRE **8**, 31–40 (2022)

34. Rosenthal, D.: Revisioning the city: public history and locative digital media. In: Hidden Cities, pp. 21–38. Routledge (2022)

35. Sánchez-Berriel, I., Pérez-Nava, F., Pérez-Rosario, L.: Natural interaction in virtual heritage: enhancing user experience with large language models. Electronics **14**(12), 2478 (2025)

36. Schaffer, S., Ruß, A., Sasse, M.L., Schubotz, L., Gustke, O.: Questions and answers: Important steps to let AI chatbots answer questions in the museum. In: Proceedings of International Conference on ArtsIT, Interactivity and Game Creation, pp. 346–358. Springer (2021)

37. Schöning, J., Krüger, A., Müller, H. J.: Interaction of mobile devices with physical maps. In: Adj. Proceedings of 4th International Conference on Pervasive Computing, pp. 121–124 (2006)

38. Schöning, J., Hecht, B., Rohs, M., Starosielski, N.: WikEar - automatically generated location-based audio stories between public city maps. In: Adj. Proceedings of 9th International Conference on Ubiquitous Computing, pp. 128–131 (2007)

39. Sernani, P., Vagni, S., Falcionelli, N., Mekuria, D.N., Tomassini, S., Dragoni, A.F.: Voice interaction with artworks via indoor localization: a vocal museum. In: Proceedings of International Conference on Augmented Reality, Virtual Reality and Computer Graphics, pp. 66–78. Springer (2020)

40. Sherpa ONNX. https://github.com/k2-fsa/sherpa-onnx. Accessed 17 July 2025
41. SmartGuide. https://www.smartguide.app/. Accessed 22 July 2025
42. Speed, C.: Walking through time: use of locative media to explore historical maps. In: Mapping Cultures: Place, Practice, Performance, pp. 160–180. Palgrave Macmillan (2012)
43. Tourient. Tour Builder. https://tourient.app/. Accessed 22 July 2025
44. Tsepapadakis, M., Gavalas, D.: Are you talking to me? An audio augmented reality conversational guide for cultural heritage. Pervasive Mob. Comput. **92**, 101797 (2023)
45. Tuters, M., Varnelis, K.: Beyond locative media: giving shape to the internet of things. Leonardo **39**(4), 357–363 (2006)
46. Vasic, I., Fill, H.G., Quattrini, R., Pierdicca, R.: LLM-aided museum guide: personalized tours based on user preferences. In: Proceedings of International Conference on Extended Reality, pp. 249–262 (2024)
47. Veaux, C., Yamagishi, J., King, S.: The voice bank corpus: design, collection and data analysis of a large regional accent speech database. In: Proceedings of International Conference on Oriental COCOSDA, pp. 1–4. IEEE (2013)
48. VoiceMap. https://voicemap.me/. Accessed 22 July 2025
49. Wagner, S., Fernández-Ardèvol, M.: Decolonizing mobile media: mobile internet appropriation in a Guaraní community. Mob. Media Commun. **8**(1), 83–103 (2020)
50. Wikimedia Commons Geosearch API. https://www.mediawiki.org/wiki/API:Geosearch. Accessed 21 July 2025
51. Wilken, R., Goggin, G.: Locative media. Routledge (2015)
52. Wu, H., Judd, P. Zhang, X., Isaev, M., Micikevicius. P.: Integer quantization for deep learning inference: principles and empirical evaluation. arXiv:2004.09602 (2020)
53. Yamagishi, J., Veaux, C., MacDonald, K.: VCTK Corpus: English Multi-speaker Corpus for CSTR Voice Cloning Toolkit. University of Edinburgh (2019)

Human-Centred LLMs in Personalized Healthcare: A Survey

Giordano de Pinho Souza[1]([✉])(iD), Glaucia Melo[2](iD), and Daniel Schneider[1](iD)

[1] Federal University of Rio de Janeiro, Rio de Janeiro, RJ 21941-853, Brazil
giordano@ufrj.br, schneider@nce.ufrj.br
[2] Toronto Metropolitan University, Toronto, ON M5B-2K3, Canada
glaucia@torontomu.ca

Abstract. The integration of Large Language Models (LLMs) into personalized, patient-centric healthcare represents an emerging paradigm and transformative frontier in digital medicine. This new paradigm is reshaping how patients interact with digital systems, introducing new possibilities for patient-centred experiences. However, this growing field remains fragmented across technical, clinical, and interactional dimensions, making it difficult to synthesize common patterns and design principles. In this survey, we address this gap by presenting a comprehensive taxonomy that organizes current research across four human-centric pillars: Application Domains, Interaction Architectures, Data Integration for Patient Modelling, and Evaluation Methodologies. We emphasize how LLMs are being embedded into tools that support patient engagement, emotional support, and decision-making, raising essential questions about explainability, trust, safety, and the evolving role of clinicians in human-in-the-loop systems. Through this lens, our analysis reveals a critical tension at the heart of the field: while architectural innovation in areas such as Retrieval-Augmented Generation and multimodal systems is accelerating, progress is fundamentally hindered by persistent challenges in clinical reliability, data privacy, and justified skepticism from healthcare professionals. By bridging the perspectives of HCI, AI, and Health Informatics, we lay the groundwork for building more usable, equitable, and trustworthy systems for personalized care.

Keywords: Large Language Models · Patient-Centered Design · Personalized Health Informatics · Recommendations · Human-AI Interaction · Explainable AI

1 Introduction

Modern medicine has long aimed to deliver deeply personalized healthcare [4,15,18, 20,27,33,39,47]. This vision transcends static treatment protocols, aiming for a model of care that is continuously adaptive to an individual's unique biology, behavioral patterns, and personal context [14,28]. Achieving this requires systems that can understand and respond to the nuances of each patient's journey.

While the progressive digitization of healthcare has created vast data repositories from Electronic Health Records (EHRs) and wearables [4,15,20,40,44], these systems

J. F. Krems et al. (Eds.): CHIRA 2025, CCIS 2836, pp. 414–431, 2026.
https://doi.org/10.1007/978-3-032-16454-4_24

largely function as passive containers, lacking the reasoning capabilities to activate this latent information for dynamic, individualized patient interactions [6,40]. Large Language Models (LLMs) [9,29] represent a critical technological inflection point. Specifically, their ability to interpret and synthesize unstructured and multimodal data streams, such as clinical notes, conversational histories, and biometric signals [50], is catalyzing a new generation of systems engineered for personalized health interventions, empathetic support, and tailored interaction recommendations [1,9,11,20,30,39].

As this field matures, distinct architectural patterns are emerging to address inherent challenges such as knowledge grounding, factual consistency (hallucination) [17], and task complexity [32]. Foundational approaches, such as prompt engineering [26,46] and fine-tuning [8], are being augmented by more sophisticated frameworks. These include Retrieval-Augmented Generation (RAG) to ground responses in curated and contextual medical knowledge, and Multi-Agent Systems [25] to orchestrate complex clinical workflows by assigning specialized roles to different AI components [30]. These diverse technical strategies share a common objective: to create adaptive interaction systems that move beyond static, one-size-fits-all care.

Our work is built upon a systematic literature search across four major scientific databases: ACM Digital Library, IEEE Xplore, Scopus, and Nature. The search focused on peer-reviewed literature published between 2020 and 2025, specifically targeting studies that design, implement, or evaluate LLM-powered systems for personalized healthcare interactions. Our inclusion criteria prioritized works demonstrating clear personalization components, such as context-aware prompting, fine-tuning on patient data, or the use of RAG, within explicit healthcare settings.

This survey provides a structured synthesis of this emerging field, moving beyond a simple literature summary to deliver a critical analysis. Our primary contribution is a novel taxonomy that deconstructs the research landscape into four key dimensions: Application Domains, Architectural Patterns, Data Integration, and Evaluation Methodologies. Through this lens, we reveal a critical tension: while architectural sophistication is rapidly advancing with techniques like Retrieval-Augmented Generation (RAG) and multi-agent systems, their clinical applicability is consistently undermined by issues of factual inaccuracy and a profound lack of robust, real-world evaluation.

The remainder of this survey is structured as follows (see Fig. 1 for an overview): Sect. 2 provides the necessary background on the core concepts of LLMs, Telehealth, and personalization. Section 3 introduces our proposed taxonomy of the field and presents a detailed analysis of current research in this area. Section 4 identifies critical gaps and challenges in the current study and application of LLMs for personalized healthcare. Section 5 discusses broader design implications for LLM systems in healthcare, targeting key stakeholders, and Sect. 6 concludes with a summary of our contributions and a vision for future work.

2 Background

2.1 LLMs for Personalization

The recent emergence of Large Language Models (LLMs), exemplified by architectures like the Transformer and models such as GPT-3.5/4 and BERT, has revolutionized Natural Language Processing with unprecedented capabilities in understanding, generation,

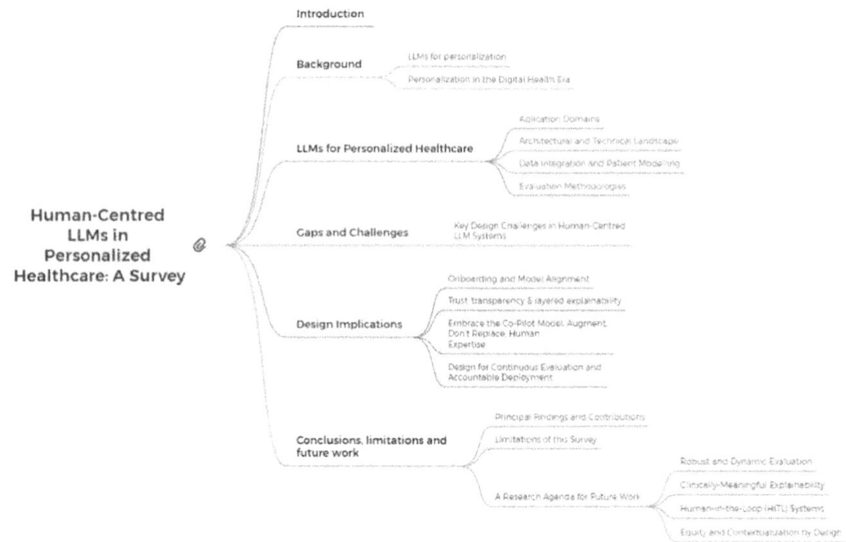

Fig. 1. Breakdown of Survey Structure.

and complex reasoning in zero-shot or few-shot settings [8,45]. While their general proficiency is well-established, applying LLMs in specialized, high-stakes domains like healthcare necessitates deep personalization to address unique challenges. LLMs are uniquely positioned to meet this demand due to their advanced natural language understanding and generation capabilities, which enable them to process complex medical information and interact with users in a highly empathetic and context-aware manner. Personalization in LLMs involves adapting model outputs to individual or group preferences, needs, and characteristics through user-specific data, historical interactions, and contextual information. This shift transforms personalization from a passive information filtering function (e.g., traditional recommendation systems) to an active, engaging approach that proactively explores user needs and delivers natural, interactive, and explainable responses [12,36].

Traditionally, personalization has been conceptualized across granularities: user-level (optimizing for unique individuals), persona-level (grouping users by shared traits), and global preference (adhering to broad norms). LLMs significantly advance this paradigm by enabling a far more nuanced and dynamic application of these levels within healthcare. This capability supports real-time adaptation changing contexts, not merely filtering information but proactively exploring user needs and dynamically adjusting interaction styles, content, and tone. LLMs can facilitate personalized health education, treatment adherence support, mental health interventions, and even symptom assessment by processing individual health records, lifestyle data, and preferences, thereby moving beyond generic advice to provide tailored, actionable insights and support. [51].

2.2 Personalization in the Digital Health Era

Remote care, electronic health records and wearables now generate vast, multimodal patient data [6,40,44]. Spanning from structured clinical records to unstructured conversational data from telemedicine and real-time biometric streams from wearable devices, it provides the raw material for a new frontier in medicine: "deeply personalized healthcare". This paradigm moves beyond generalized, population-based guidelines toward a model of care tailored to an individual's unique biological, behavioral, and contextual characteristics. [7,42].

However, leveraging Electronic Health Records (EHRs) for large-scale analytics and personalization is significantly constrained by several inherent challenges. A substantial portion of EHR data exists as high-volume, unstructured text, such as clinical notes, lab reports, and imaging descriptions. Extracting or summarizing information from this data is a complex task [40,43]. The process must preserve the clinical accuracy and integrity of the source while condensing vast amounts of information into a concise, intelligible format, a task that renders manual annotation and interpretation infeasible at scale.

Overlaying these technical issues is the critical imperative of patient privacy. Health data possess inherently sensitive characteristics, and deficiencies in management processes can result in significant privacy breaches and inappropriate utilization of clinical information. The increasing dependence of artificial intelligence systems on extensive patient datasets intensifies concerns regarding data security and risks of unauthorized exploitation. Therefore, there is a critical need to implement rigorous protocols for the collection, storage, and processing of health data to preserve patient confidentiality and ensure informational integrity [3,48].

Achieving dynamic adaptation requires a comprehensive user model, a computational representation of an individual's traits, goals, preferences, and current health state. In modern healthcare, this is increasingly enabled by digital phenotyping [28], which infers health and behavior from data collected via smartphones and wearables. LLMs can process unstructured, longitudinal data, from conversations to sensor streams, supporting richer, more nuanced patient models than traditional structured-data approaches, and enabling adaptive, context-aware interventions [43].

3 LLMs for Personalized Healthcare

3.1 A Taxonomy of LLMs in Personalized Healthcare

The application of LLMs in personalized healthcare is a rapidly expanding yet multi-faceted field. To provide a structured understanding of the current landscape, we propose a taxonomy that categorizes existing research along five fundamental dimensions: (1) Application Domains, defining what is being built; (2) Architectural Landscape, describing how it is built; (3) Data Integration and Patient Modeling, detailing the data that fuels these systems; (4) Evaluation Methodologies, assessing how their performance and impact are measured; and crucially, (5) Security and Privacy Measures, addressing the critical safeguards for sensitive health data. This taxonomy, illustrated in Fig. 2, serves as a framework for our analysis, enabling a systematic examination of the state-of-the-art, key trends, and prevailing practices.

To complement this conceptual framework, we conducted a quantitative synthesis of the literature. Table 1 presents a consolidated overview, detailing the prevalence of articles addressing each category across these five taxonomic dimensions. The analysis reveals a research landscape primarily driven by clinical applications like 'Personalized Treatment and Diagnosis' (43.8%) and traditional data sources such as 'EHR, Clinical notes' (37.5%), often evaluated through 'Accuracy-based metrics' (56.3%) and 'Human expert evaluation' (31.3%). While architectural sophistication is emerging with 'Multimodal LLMs' (31.3%), there remains a significant underutilization of real-time data from 'Sensors, Wearables' (18.8%) and critical gaps in explicit 'Security and Privacy Measures' (e.g., 'Self-Hosted LLMs' at 12.5%), highlighting a disparity between technological potential and practical, trustworthy deployment in healthcare.

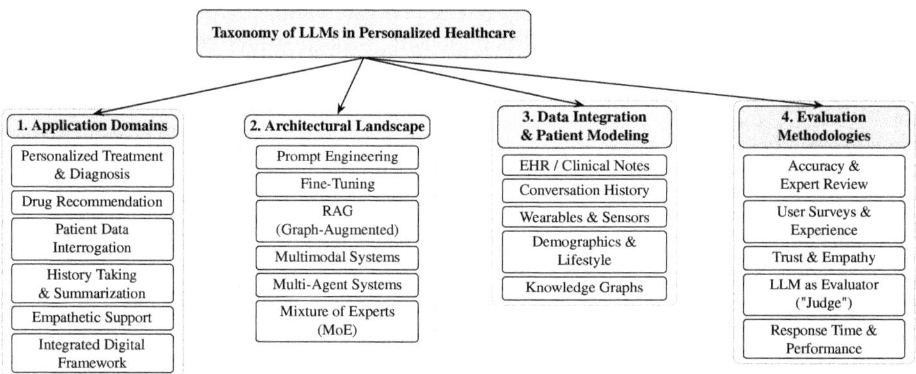

Fig. 2. Taxonomy of LLMs in personalized healthcare organized in four dimension.

3.2   Application Domains

The primary goals driving the adoption of LLMs in healthcare manifest in several distinct application domains. Our analysis identifies two major axes of development: systems focused on direct clinical treatment and decision support, and those designed to provide personalized empathetic support.

The most prominent domain is Personalized Clinical Treatment. These systems leverage the analytical capabilities of LLMs to move beyond generalized guidelines and engineer bespoke medical recommendation systems. Key applications include:

- **Personalized Treatment Plans and Diagnosis:** Assisting clinicians in formulating care pathways and refining diagnostic accuracy [11,16,18,21,24,35].
- **Drug Recommendation:** Tailoring prescriptions based on individual profiles, genetic predispositions, and treatment history [4].
- **Patient Data Interrogation:** Developing intelligent LLM-chatbots that allow patients to query their health records and receive understandable, personalized insights [15,16,30,39].

Table 1. Quantitative Synthesis of Key Taxonomic Dimensions.

Dimension	Category	Prevalence (%)
1. Application	Personalized Treatment	43.8%
	Patient Data Interrogation	25.0%
	History Taking	25.0%
	Empathetic Support	18.8%
	System Evaluation	18.8%
	Drug Recommendation	6.3%
	Integrated Digital Framework	6.3%
2. Architecture	Prompt Engineering	37.5%
	Fine-tuning	37.5%
	Multimodal LLMs	31.3%
	RAG	25.0%
	Multi-agent Systems	12.5%
	Mixture of Experts	6.3%
	Not Specified	6.3%
3. Data Integration	EHR/Clinical notes	37.5%
	Conversation history	37.5%
	Demographics	31.3%
	Sensors/Wearables	18.8%
	Lifestyle/Dietary Prefs.	12.5%
	Knowledge-graph	6.3%
	None/Not Specified	12.5%
4. Evaluation	Accuracy-based metrics	56.3%
	Human expert evaluation	31.3%
	LLM/Automated Evaluator	18.8%
	Response time/Performance	18.8%
	Reliability/Trustworthiness	18.8%
	User-centered Likert/Surveys	18.8%
	Generation Quality	12.5%
	Emotion/Empathy	12.5%
	Relevance/Comprehensiveness	12.5%
5. Security	De-identified Data/Public	31.3%
	Self-Hosted LLMs	12.5%
	Secured API	6.3%

– **History Taking and Summarization:** Automating the collection of patient histories and generating concise summaries of complex medical narratives [19,21,24].

For instance, LLMs can engage in nuanced dialogues to maintain diagnostic quality under time constraints [19] or analyze records to suggest appropriate drugs [4].

A second emerging domain focuses on Personalized Empathetic Support [18, 20, 38]. This area explores a more humanistic application, building conversational interfaces with capabilities for emotional recognition and empathetic response to address issues like loneliness in elderly care [38] or provide mental health support [20].

Finally, a nascent but critical area involves creating Integrated Digital-Hospital Frameworks [33]. This domain transcends single-task applications by aiming to embed personalized AI agents across the entire clinical data stack, a concept exemplified by emerging 'virtual hospital' frameworks. The architectural complexity in such systems is immense, requiring a sophisticated orchestration layer capable of integrating and synthesizing vast, heterogeneous, and multimodal data streams, from handwritten clinical notes and EHRs to real-time IoT sensor data [41], medical imaging, and even genomic sequences. This often involves an ensemble of diverse models (LLMs, VLMs) and techniques like federated learning [23] to address data privacy and locality within different hospital departments, all while leveraging Retrieval-Augmented Generation (RAG) to ensure responses are grounded in the full, longitudinal patient record.

3.3   Architectural and Technical Landscape

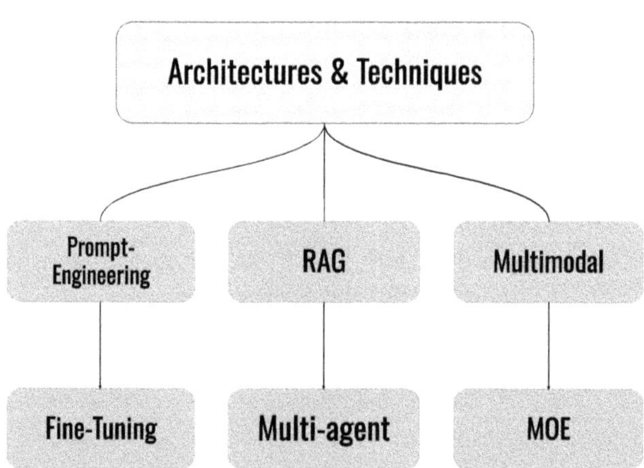

Fig. 3. Key LLM Architectures in Personalized Healthcare.

The implementation of these applications is supported by an evolving set of architectural patterns and techniques, which can be organized by increasing complexity. The prevalence of these techniques is summarized in Fig. 3.

The foundation for specializing LLMs relies on Prompt Engineering and Fine-tuning. Prompt engineering has matured from simple queries to a collaborative design tool for shaping model behavior [19], with performance being highly sensitive to the chosen prompting strategy (e.g., zero-shot, few-shot, or chain-of-thought [8,22,46]). Complementarily, fine-tuning adapts model parameters to domain-specific datasets and interaction styles [4,37].

To address inherent limitations, such as hallucinations, a core architectural pattern is Retrieval-Augmented Generation (RAG) [17]. RAG grounds model responses in reliable, curated sources, a safety feature for healthcare applications [16,30]. This paradigm is itself evolving towards more advanced forms, such as graph-augmented RAG, which enhances retrieval by using knowledge graphs to handle structured health data more effectively [39].

More sophisticated applications are increasingly built upon Multimodal Systems, which integrate data beyond text, such as speech [38], physiological streams from wearables [15], and medical imagery [11]. This approach often leads to ensembles of diverse models (LLMs, SLMs, VLMs) orchestrated under a unified framework. Sometimes overlapping with Mixture of Experts (MoE) architectures, this configuration enables the system to dynamically adapt to multimodal data integration by selectively activating specialized sub-models for different data types or tasks [11,33,50]. Additionally, Multi-agent systems can be architected to generate clear and understandable explanations for their decisions. ArgMedAgents serves as a direct example, representing a multi-agent framework developed for explainable clinical decision reasoning [25,51].

3.4   Data Integration and Patient Modelling

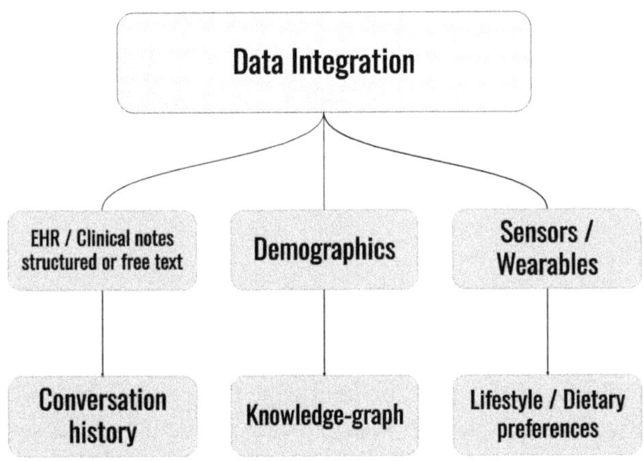

Fig. 4. Data Integration Strategies for LLMs in Personalized Healthcare.

The efficacy of personalized systems depends critically on the richness and diversity of data used to model patient state. Current literature demonstrates a clear trend toward integrating multiple data streams for comprehensive patient profiling, as illustrated by the prevalence of these approaches in Fig. 4.

The most prevalent data sources are formal clinical records, such as EHRs and unstructured clinical notes. This grounds the LLM in the patient's documented medical history, providing a stable foundation for personalization [4,24,30,40]. This is often complemented by rich conversational history, a dynamic source of personalization that captures real-time patient input, preferences, and even sentiment through mechanisms like personalized memory [38] and sentiment analysis [20].

A significant forward-looking trend is the integration of dynamic data from sensors and wearables. This approach grounds personalization in continuous physiological and behavioral monitoring, equipping the LLM with a quantitative, real-time understanding of a user's health (e.g., sleep quality, physical activity, heart rate) and making complex trends intelligible [15]. In some cases, this is further enhanced by structured, semantically rich context from integrated knowledge graphs, moving beyond raw data to pre-processed relational information to improve model reasoning.

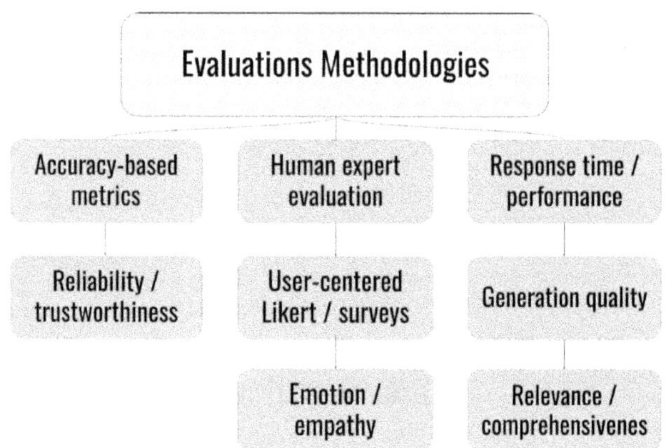

Fig. 5. Key Evaluation Strategies for LLM in Personalized Healthcare.

3.5   Evaluation Methodologies

Assessing the performance of LLM-based systems in high-stakes domains like healthcare requires a multi-layered evaluation landscape that extends beyond traditional NLP metrics. Our analysis reveals three primary themes in evaluation, as shown in Table 5.

First, the cornerstone remains Clinical Correctness and Safety. This is predominantly measured using accuracy-based metrics that align LLM outputs with established medical facts or ground truth [19,24,35]. Crucially, this quantitative assessment is frequently complemented by human expert evaluation, where clinicians appraise clinical nuance, safety, and real-world applicability, representing a best practice for validating model performance [47].

Second, recognizing that personalization extends beyond clinical accuracy, a significant body of work focuses on the User-Centric and Qualitative Dimensions. This is typically measured via user-centred Likert scales and surveys to assess the impact on user understanding, motivation, and overall experience [1, 15, 21]. This is further refined with more granular metrics assessing the relevance, comprehensiveness, and actionability of advice [39], and emerging factors like empathy and trustworthiness [19, 20].

Third, to address the significant scalability challenges of manual expert evaluation, an emerging paradigm is the use of an LLM as an Automated Evaluator (also known as the "LLM-as-a-judge" approach) [15, 19, 39]. This hybrid, human-validated framework leverages a powerful model (e.g., GPT-4) to systematically rate another LLM's output. It offers a scalable alternative for assessing both correctness and nuanced qualitative criteria, as exemplified by frameworks like CRAFT-MD [19].

4   Gaps and Challenges

Addressing the identified tensions requires a research agenda that is dynamically adaptive to the rapid evolution of LLM technology. Because the capabilities of LLMs evolve rapidly, evaluation frameworks must evolve beyond static benchmarks. The field requires methodological infrastructure that is flexible, modular, and continuously updated, capable of testing new models across evolving metrics such as factuality, empathy, bias, and safety. Rather than fixed leaderboards, this calls for iterative pipelines with reproducibility, versioning, and clinician-in-the-loop refinement.

A significant gap remains between experimental validation and clinical utility. Most studies rely on retrospective, de-identified datasets, testing LLMs on static data [19, 21, 47], which overlook the complexities of longitudinal, real-world deployment. Efforts should prioritize piloting these systems in live workflows, assessing not only diagnostic accuracy but also outcomes such as consultation time, clinician workload, patient satisfaction, and patient safety.

4.1   Key Design Challenges in Human-Centred LLM Systems

The analysis presented in this survey reveals that the path from technical prototypes to effective clinical tools is fraught with significant design challenges. These are not merely algorithmic hurdles but complex sociotechnical problems that lie at the intersection of AI, Human-Computer Interaction, and clinical practice [13, 31, 34, 45].

A primary challenge for designers is overcoming the inherent friction between novel AI systems and established clinical workflows. The fast-paced, high-stakes nature of healthcare leaves little room for tools that are hard to navigate. Designers must therefore grapple with how to embed LLM-powered features directly into existing interfaces, like the EHR, without introducing odd context-switching or increasing cognitive load. A key difficulty is presenting complex, AI-generated information in concise, scannable formats that clinicians can rapidly comprehend and act upon, moving beyond the default of dense, unstructured text [34].

A second, and perhaps more profound, challenge is building and maintaining user trust in the face of a technology prone to factual errors. Designers must find ways to provide verifiable transparency, for instance, through source-linked citations or layered explanations, without overwhelming users with excessive detail. The challenge lies in creating interfaces that help clinicians and patients accurately calibrate their trust, clearly signaling the uncertainty of probabilistic inferences versus the certainty of retrieved facts [12,31,51].

Designers are also confronted with the ethical challenge of ensuring that these systems promote health equity rather than amplifying existing disparities. Because LLMs learn from vast datasets that reflect historical and societal biases, there is a significant risk of creating tools that provide less accurate or inappropriate recommendations for marginalized populations. The challenge is to move beyond reactive "debiasing" techniques and to proactively embed equity into the design process itself, through inclusive data practices, accessibility features like plain-language and multilingual support, and co-design with diverse patient communities [12,14,31,52].

Furthermore, designers face the intricate task of defining and supporting a true human-AI collaboration model. The goal of a "co-pilot" system is easy to state but difficult to achieve. The challenge is to design interactions that augment, rather than override, human expertise. This involves creating systems that not only uphold the clinician's agency to question, edit, and approve outputs but also gracefully handle the ambiguity of clinical language. Designers must build mechanisms for users to correct the model's misinterpretations, fostering a dialogue that refines the AI's understanding over time [31,45,48].

5   Design Implications

5.1   Design Implications for Human-Centred LLM Systems in Healthcare

The preceding taxonomy and gap analysis demonstrate that technical excellence alone is insufficient for the safe, effective, and equitable adoption of LLMs in personalized healthcare. The challenges identified are not merely technical hurdles but fundamental issues at the intersection of technology, human cognition, and clinical practice. Addressing them requires a human-centred design approach [5,10,19,34,47]. Based on our analysis, we distill four key design implications to guide the development of future LLMs for Personalized Healthcare.

These implications are rooted in several core tensions that define the current landscape. To address these complexities and underscore actionable areas for design and future research, Table 2 summarizes these fundamental tensions and proposes corresponding solutions or design principles.

5.2   Onboarding and Model Alignment

Clinicians do not treat AI systems as infallible oracles; instead, they calibrate their trust as they would with a human colleague, seeking to understand the system's scope, strengths, and blind spots [5]. The initial interaction is, therefore, critical for establishing an accurate mental model. To facilitate this, systems must move beyond "black box" deployments and provide proactive transparency from the first use.

- **Provide a "Model Card" at First Use:** A concise, standardized summary should clearly state the model's intended use, its training data provenance, validated performance ceilings, and known limitations or contraindications. Frameworks like those proposed by the Coalition for Health AI (CHAI) offer a strong starting point [10,34].

Table 2. Key Tensions in Human-Centred LLMs for Personalized Healthcare and Corresponding Design Principles.

Key Tension	Proposed Solutions/Design Principles
Factual Correctness vs. AI Reliability	RAG; Expert evaluation
Human Trust vs. AI Opacity	Layered explainability; Differentiate Fact/Inference; Meaningful Explainability; Model Cards
AI Integration vs. Clinical Workflows	Seamless EHR integration; Minimize context-switching; Human-in-the-Loop
AI Scalability vs. Robust Evaluation	Continuous evaluation; In-situ feedback; Dynamic Evaluation
AI Generalization/Bias vs. Health Equity	Accessibility; Co-design; Live monitoring for equity

- **Enable Safe Simulation:** Allow users to test the model on prototypical or edge-case scenarios. This helps them build an intuitive understanding of how the model "thinks" and where it might fail, accelerating trust calibration [10,34].

5.3   Trust, Transparency and Layered Explainability

While transparency is crucial, information overload can undermine comprehension as much as opacity can. The solution lies in designing explanations that are layered and interactive, a principle known as "progressive disclosure" [2]. This approach provides a simple answer by default but allows the user to "drill down" for deeper context.

- **Default to Simplicity, Offer Depth:** Present answers in plain language. A "show rationale" option should then reveal granular details, such as confidence scores or, for RAG systems, links to the specific evidence snippets used for the response, a feature seen in several reviewed works [30,39].
- **Differentiate Fact from Inference:** The user interface must clearly distinguish between factual information retrieved from a knowledge base and probabilistic inferences generated by the LLM. This semantic distinction is a critical principle for building intelligible systems [2].

5.4   Embrace the Co-Pilot Model: Augment, Don't Replace, Human Expertise

Our analysis reveals a consensus that LLMs in healthcare should be designed as co-pilots that augment clinician capabilities, not as autonomous decision-makers. This is reflected in studies developing "doctor assistance tools" [24] or tools for "supporting healthcare professionals" [21]. This philosophy of human-in-the-loop (HITL) collaboration is essential for safety and accountability [19,49].

- **Ensure Human Oversight and Agency:** The interface must always allow the clinician to question, override, or approve LLM outputs. The final decision must remain with the human expert [49].

– **Integrate Seamlessly into Clinical Workflow:** To be an asset rather than a burden, LLM-powered suggestions should be embedded directly into existing tools, such as the EHR. Minimizing context-switching is key to addressing the real-world needs of practitioners [10].

5.5   Design for Continuous Evaluation and Accountable Deployment

Our analysis revealed that static, offline metrics (e.g., BLEU, ROUGE, accuracy) are insufficient for the high-stakes context of healthcare. They fail to capture critical real-world factors such as clinician workload, patient comprehension, or longitudinal safety [5]. Therefore, evaluation must be treated as a continuous, integrated process, not a one-time validation. This requires designing systems that are inherently transparent, monitorable, and accountable throughout their entire lifecycle.

– **Instrument for In-Situ Feedback:** To move beyond accuracy, systems should embed lightweight, periodic feedback mechanisms directly into the user interface. This includes instrumenting validated usability probes (e.g., NASA-TLX), trust scales, or simple post-interaction questions to measure patient comprehension and satisfaction in a real-world context [2]. Several studies in our analysis used user-centred surveys, but designing for continuous feedback streamlines this process [15,21].
– **Implement Live Monitoring for Performance and Equity:** LLM performance can drift over time as input data patterns or clinical guidelines change. Systems must be built with an integrated monitoring layer that provides a real-time view of their performance. This includes dashboards that compare predicted outcomes with actual clinical results and flag significant deviations. This monitoring must extend beyond accuracy to track key sociotechnical dimensions such as **fairness, bias, and toxicity**. This involves continuously assessing whether the model's outputs or performance vary systematically across different demographic groups, ensuring that the system does not perpetuate or amplify existing health disparities.

6   Conclusions, Limitations and Future Work

6.1   Principal Findings and Contributions

This survey reveals that Large Language Models are catalyzing a paradigm shift toward precision-driven healthcare, which we have deconstructed through a four-dimensional taxonomy: Personalized Clinical Treatment, Empathetic Patient Support, Integrated Digital Frameworks, and Specialized Evaluation Methodologies. The dominance of applications for clinical treatment underscores the field's ambition to redefine individualized care. Simultaneously, the emergence of empathetic support systems and dedicated evaluation methodologies signals a growing maturation, recognizing that effective healthcare transcends clinical accuracy to encompass psychosocial dimensions and that traditional computational metrics are insufficient for these high-stakes applications.

However, our central finding is a critical tension between rapid technological advancement and persistent clinical fragility. While architectural sophistication accelerates with techniques like RAG and multi-agent systems, the path from technical innovation to safe, equitable, and clinically meaningful implementation remains obstructed by fundamental challenges in model reliability, data privacy, and real-world integration. This gap fosters a justified skepticism among clinicians, creating a formidable barrier to adoption that technology alone cannot overcome.

6.2 Limitations of This Survey

This survey has several limitations. First, the field of LLMs in healthcare is evolving at an extraordinary pace; this work represents a snapshot in time, and it is likely that new architectures and findings will have emerged even by the time of publication. Second, our analysis is based on a limited number of studies; while representative, this scope may not capture insights from the grey literature, such as industry white papers, or very recent preprints. Finally, like any review, our findings may be subject to publication bias, where studies reporting successful outcomes are more likely to be published than those highlighting failures, potentially painting an overly optimistic picture of the field's current maturity.

6.3 A Research Agenda for Future Work

Addressing the tensions identified in this survey requires a concerted, interdisciplinary research agenda that shifts the focus from demonstrating capability ("can we build it?") to ensuring reliability and trustworthiness ("how do we deploy it responsibly?"). We propose a research agenda centred on four key pillars:

- **Robust and Dynamic Evaluation:** The field must move beyond static benchmarks. Future work should focus on developing dynamic evaluation frameworks that can keep pace with evolving LLMs, incorporating metrics for safety, fairness, and clinical nuance.
- **Clinically-Meaningful Explainability (XAI):** To bridge the trust deficit, research must prioritize explainability methods that are meaningful to clinicians. This includes exploring chain-of-thought rationales, counterfactual explanations, and attribution maps that clarify *why* an LLM made a specific recommendation.
- **Human-in-the-Loop (HITL) Systems:**Future research should focus on designing and validating "co-pilot" systems where LLMs assist human experts. This necessitates a parallel stream on workforce preparedness, including simulation-based training to equip clinicians with the competencies needed to effectively supervise and collaborate with AI.
- **Equity and Contextualization by Design:** A critical direction is to explore how LLMs can reason over Social Determinants of Health (SDOH) and geographical data to provide recommendations that are not only clinically sound but also practical and accessible, especially in low-resource settings.

6.4 Concluding Remarks

LLMs are significantly transforming healthcare, enabling deeply personalized care through the interpretation and synthesis of vast, multimodal patient data for tailored interventions and empathetic support. However, their primary dilemma lies in the critical tension between rapid architectural innovation and persistent clinical fragility. This manifests in challenges such as ensuring clinical reliability, safeguarding data privacy, overcoming inherent biases, and addressing professional skepticism. Tackling these issues requires a strategic shift from merely demonstrating technological capability to proactively ensuring reliability and trustworthiness in deployment. This involves a sustained, interdisciplinary research agenda focused on robust and dynamic evaluation, clinically meaningful explainability, human-in-the-loop systems that augment human expertise, and the proactive integration of equity by design. In the struggle to overcome this critical dilemma, what's at stake is the very future of healthcare systems.

Disclosure of Interests. The authors have no competing interests to declare that are relevant to the content of this article.

References

1. Abbasian, M., et al.: Foundation metrics for evaluating effectiveness of healthcare conversations powered by generative AI. NPJ Digit. Med. **7**(1), 82 (2024). https://doi.org/10.1038/s41746-024-01074-z
2. Abdul, A., Vermeulen, J., Wang, D., Lim, B.Y., Kankanhalli, M.: Trends and trajectories for explainable, accountable and intelligible systems: an HCI research agenda. In: Proceedings of the 2018 CHI Conference on Human Factors in Computing Systems, Montreal, QC, Canada, pp. 1–18. ACM (2018). https://doi.org/10.1145/3173574.3174156
3. Abouelmehdi, K., Beni-Hessane, A., Khaloufi, H.: Big healthcare data: preserving security and privacy. J. Big Data **5**(1), 1–18 (2018). https://doi.org/10.1186/s40537-017-0110-7
4. Balakrishna, C., Yadav, A., Singh, J., Saba, M., Shashikant, Shrivastava, V.: Smart drug delivery systems using large language models for real-time treatment personalization. In: 2024 2nd World Conference on Communication and Computing (WCONF), Raipur, India, pp. 1–6. IEEE (2024). https://doi.org/10.1109/WCONF61366.2024.10692060
5. Bedi, S., Liu, Y., Orr-Ewing, et al.: Testing and evaluation of health care applications of large language models: a systematic review. JAMA J. Am. Med. Assoc. **333**(4), 319–328 (2025). https://doi.org/10.1001/jama.2024.21700. https://jamanetwork.com/journals/jama/fullarticle/2825147
6. Berisha, V., et al.: Digital medicine and the curse of dimensionality. NPJ Digit. Med. **4**(1) (2021). https://doi.org/10.1038/s41746-021-00521-5
7. Blasiak, A., et al.: Omnichannel communication to boost patient engagement and behavioral change with digital health interventions. J. Med. Internet Res. **24**(11), e41463 (2022). https://doi.org/10.2196/41463
8. Brown, T.B., Mann, D., et al.: Language Models are Few-Shot Learners (2020). https://doi.org/10.48550/ARXIV.2005.14165, version Number: 4
9. Bubeck, S., Chandrasekaran, Y., et al.: Sparks of Artificial General Intelligence: Early experiments with GPT-4 (2023). https://doi.org/10.48550/ARXIV.2303.12712, version Number: 5
10. Cai, C.J., Winter, S., Steiner, D., Wilcox, L., Terry, M.: "Hello AI": uncovering the onboarding needs of medical practitioners for human-AI collaborative decision-making. Proc. ACM Hum.-Comput. Interact. **3**(CSCW), 1–24 (2019)

11. Cai, H.: Multimodal hybrid healthcare recommendation system based on ERT-MOE and large language model enhancement. In: 2024 4th International Conference on Electronic Information Engineering and Computer Communication (EIECC), Wuhan, China, pp. 1222–1226. IEEE (2024). https://doi.org/10.1109/EIECC64539.2024.10929467

12. Chen, J., Liu, Z., Huang, E., et al.: When large language models meet personalization: perspectives of challenges and opportunities. World Wide Web **27**(4) (2024). https://doi.org/10.1007/s11280-024-01276-1

13. Choudhury, A., Chaudhry, Z.: Large Language Models and User Trust: Consequence of Self-Referential Learning Loop and the Deskilling of Health Care Professionals (Preprint) (2024). https://doi.org/10.2196/preprints.56764

14. Chunara, R., et al.: Social determinants of health: the need for data science methods and capacity. Lancet Digit. Health **6**(4), e235–e237 (2024). https://doi.org/10.1016/s2589-7500(24)00022-0

15. Fang, C.M., et al.: PhysioLLM: supporting personalized health insights with wearables and large language models. In: 2024 IEEE EMBS International Conference on Biomedical and Health Informatics (BHI), Houston, TX, USA, pp. 1–8. IEEE (2024). https://doi.org/10.1109/BHI62660.2024.10913781

16. Garima, S., Swapnil, M., Shashank, S.: Harnessing the power of language models for intelligent digital health services. In: 2024 ITU Kaleidoscope: Innovation and Digital Transformation for a Sustainable World (ITU K), New Delhi, India, pp. 1–8. IEEE (2024). https://doi.org/10.23919/ITUK62727.2024.10772761

17. Huang, L., et al.: A survey on hallucination in large language models: principles, taxonomy, challenges, and open questions. ACM Trans. Inf. Syst. **43**(2), 1–55 (2025). https://doi.org/10.1145/3703155

18. Jaiswal, S., et al.: Building personality-adaptive conversational AI for mental health therapy. In: Proceedings of the 15th ACM International Conference on Bioinformatics, Computational Biology and Health Informatics, Shenzhen, China, p. 1. ACM (2024). https://doi.org/10.1145/3698587.3701489

19. Johri, S., et al.: An evaluation framework for clinical use of large language models in patient interaction tasks. Nat. Med. **31**(1), 77–86 (2025). https://doi.org/10.1038/s41591-024-03328-5

20. Kambare, S.M., Jain, K., Kale, I., Kumbhare, V., Lohote, S., Lonare, S.: Design and evaluation of an AI-powered conversational agent for personalized mental health support and intervention (MindBot). In: 2024 International Conference on Sustainable Communication Networks and Application (ICSCNA), Theni, India, pp. 1394–1402. IEEE (2024). https://doi.org/10.1109/ICSCNA63714.2024.10863855

21. Kim, J., et al.: Artificial intelligence tools in supporting healthcare professionals for tailored patient care. NPJ Digit. Med. **8**(1), 210 (2025). https://doi.org/10.1038/s41746-025-01604-3

22. Kojima, T., Gu, S.S., Reid, M., Matsuo, Y., Iwasawa, Y.: Large language models are zero-shot reasoners. https://doi.org/10.48550/ARXIV.2205.11916, version Number: 4

23. Kuang, W., et al.: Federatedscope-LLM: a comprehensive package for fine-tuning large language models in federated learning. In: Proceedings of the 30th ACM SIGKDD Conference on Knowledge Discovery and Data Mining, KDD 2024, pp. 5260–5271. Association for Computing Machinery, New York (2024). https://doi.org/10.1145/3637528.3671573

24. Kumar, G.: A doctor assistance tool: personalized healthcare treatment recommendations journey from deep reinforcement learning to generative AI. In: 2024 3rd Edition of IEEE Delhi Section Flagship Conference (DELCON), New Delhi, India, pp. 1–9. IEEE (2024). https://doi.org/10.1109/DELCON64804.2024.10866814

25. Li, X., Wang, S., Zeng, S., Wu, Y., Yang, Y.: A survey on LLM-based multi-agent systems: workflow, infrastructure, and challenges. Vicinagearth **1**(1), 9 (2024). https://doi.org/10.1007/s44336-024-00009-2

26. Liu, P., Yuan, W., Fu, J., Jiang, Z., Hayashi, H., Neubig, G.: Pre-train, prompt, and predict: a systematic survey of prompting methods in natural language processing. ACM Comput. Surv. **55**(9), 1–35 (2023). https://doi.org/10.1145/3560815

27. Louca, S.: Personalized medicine - a tailored health care system: challenges and opportunities. Croatian Med. J. **53**(3), 211–213 (2012). https://doi.org/10.3325/cmj.2012.53.211

28. Onnela, J.P.: Opportunities and challenges in the collection and analysis of digital phenotyping data. Neuropsychopharmacology **46**(1), 45–54 (2021). https://doi.org/10.1038/s41386-020-0771-3

29. OpenAI, Achiam, W.: GPT-4 Technical Report (2023). https://doi.org/10.48550/ARXIV.2303.08774, version Number: 6

30. Pap, I.A., Oniga, S.: eHealth assistant AI chatbot using a large language model to provide personalized answers through secure decentralized communication. Sensors **24**(18), 6140 (2024). https://doi.org/10.3390/s24186140

31. Park, Y.J., et al.: Assessing the research landscape and clinical utility of large language models: a scoping review. BMC Med. Inform. Decis. Making **24**(1) (2024). https://doi.org/10.1186/s12911-024-02459-6

32. Radford, A., Wu, J., Child, R., Luan, D., Amodei, D., Sutskever, I.: Language Models are Unsupervised Multitask Learners

33. Rahman, M.A., Al-Hazzaa, S.: Next-generation virtual hospital: integrating discriminative and large multi-modal generative AI for personalized healthcare. In: GLOBECOM 2024 - 2024 IEEE Global Communications Conference, Cape Town, South Africa, pp. 3509–3514. IEEE (2024). https://doi.org/10.1109/GLOBECOM52923.2024.10901624

34. Rajashekar, Shung, D., et al.: Human-algorithmic interaction using a large language model-augmented artificial intelligence clinical decision support system. In: Proceedings of the CHI Conference on Human Factors in Computing Systems, Honolulu, HI, USA, pp. 1–20. ACM (2024). https://doi.org/10.1145/3613904.3642024

35. Akilesh, S., Abinaya, R., Dhanushkodi, S.: A novel AI-based chatbot application for personalized medical diagnosis and review using large language models. In: 2023 International Conference on Research Methodologies in Knowledge Management, Artificial Intelligence and Telecommunication Engineering (RMKMATE), Chennai, India, pp. 1–5. IEEE (2023). https://doi.org/10.1109/RMKMATE59243.2023.10368616

36. Shi, R., Huang, H., Zhou, W., Yin, K., Zhao, K., Zhao, Y.: From General to Specific: Tailoring Large Language Models for Personalized Healthcare (2024). https://doi.org/10.48550/arXiv.2412.15957, [cs]

37. Singhal, K., Tu, T., Gottweis, V., et al.: Toward expert-level medical question answering with large language models. Nat. Med. **31**(3), 943–950 (2025). https://doi.org/10.1038/s41591-024-03423-7

38. So, K., et al.: A conversational interaction framework using large language models for personalized elderly care. In: 2025 IEEE International Conference on Consumer Electronics (ICCE), Las Vegas, NV, USA, pp. 1–2. IEEE (2025). https://doi.org/10.1109/ICCE63647.2025.10930020

39. Subramanian, A., Yang, Z., Azimi, I., Rahmani, A.M.: Graph-augmented LLMs for personalized health insights: a case study in sleep analysis. In: 2024 IEEE 20th International Conference on Body Sensor Networks (BSN), Chicago, IL, USA, pp. 1–4. IEEE (2024). https://doi.org/10.1109/BSN63547.2024.10780466

40. Tang, A.S., Woldemariam, S.R., Miramontes, S., Norgeot, B., Oskotsky, T.T., Sirota, M.: Harnessing EHR data for health research. Nat. Med. **30**(7), 1847–1855 (2024). https://doi.org/10.1038/s41591-024-03074-8

41. Uslu, B.Ç., Okay, E., Dursun, E.: Analysis of factors affecting IoT-based smart hospital design 9(1), 67. https://doi.org/10.1186/s13677-020-00215-5. https://journalofcloudcomputing.springeropen.com/articles/10.1186/s13677-020-00215-5

42. Van Kessel, R., Ranganathan, S., Anderson, M., McMillan, B., Mossialos, E.: Exploring potential drivers of patient engagement with their health data through digital platforms: a scoping review. Int. J. Med. Inform. 189, 105513 (2024). https://doi.org/10.1016/j.ijmedinf.2024.105513

43. Vest, J.R., Grannis, S.J., Haut, D.P., Halverson, P.K., Menachemi, N.: Using structured and unstructured data to identify patients' need for services that address the social determinants of health. Int. J. Med. Inform. 107, 101–106 (2017). https://doi.org/10.1016/j.ijmedinf.2017.09.008

44. Waller, M., Stotler, C.: Telemedicine: a primer. Curr. Allergy Asthma Rep. 18(10), 1–9 (2018). https://doi.org/10.1007/s11882-018-0808-4

45. Wang, Y., Zhao, Y., Petzold, L.: Are Large Language Models Ready for Healthcare? A Comparative Study on Clinical Language Understanding (2023). https://doi.org/10.48550/arXiv.2304.05368, [cs]

46. Wei, J., et al.: Chain-of-Thought Prompting Elicits Reasoning in Large Language Models (2022). https://doi.org/10.48550/ARXIV.2201.11903, version Number: 6

47. Williams, C.Y.K., Miao, B.Y., Kornblith, A.E., Butte, A.J.: Evaluating the use of large language models to provide clinical recommendations in the Emergency Department. Nat. Commun. 15(1), 8236 (2024). https://doi.org/10.1038/s41467-024-52415-1

48. Williamson, S.M., Prybutok, V.: Balancing privacy and progress: a review of privacy challenges, systemic oversight, and patient perceptions in AI-driven healthcare. Appl. Sci. 14(2), 675 (2024). https://doi.org/10.3390/app14020675

49. Wilson, B., et al.: Dimensions of human-machine combination: prompting the development of deployable intelligent decision systems for situated clinical contexts. In: Computer Supported Cooperative Work (CSCW) (2025). https://doi.org/10.1007/s10606-025-09514-4

50. Yin, S., et al.: A survey on multimodal large language models. Natl. Sci. Rev. 11(12) (2024). https://doi.org/10.1093/nsr/nwae403

51. Zhang, Z., et al.: Personalization of Large Language Models: A Survey (2025). https://doi.org/10.48550/arXiv.2411.00027, [cs]

52. Zhang, Z., Rossi, R.A., Wang, Y., et al.: Personalization of large language models: a survey (2025). https://arxiv.org/abs/2411.00027

Author Index